Communications
in Computer and Information Science 83

Marjan Gusev Pece Mitrevski (Eds.)

ICT Innovations 2010

Second International Conference
ICT Innovations 2010
Ohrid, Macedonia, September 12-15, 2010
Revised Selected Papers

Springer

Volume Editors

Marjan Gusev
University Sts. Cyril and Methodius
Faculty of Natural Sciences and Mathematics
Institute of Informatics
Skopje, Macedonia
E-mail: marjangusev@gmail.com

Pece Mitrevski
University of St. Clement Ohridski
Faculty of Technical Sciences
Department of Computer Science and Engineering
Bitola, Macedonia
E-mail: pece.mitrevski@uklo.edu.mk

ISSN 1865-0929 ISSN 1865-0937 (eBook)
ISBN 978-3-642-19324-8 ISBN 978-3-642-19325-5 (eBook)
DOI 10.1007/978-3-642-19325-5
Springer Heidelberg Dordrecht London New York

Library of Congress Control Number: 2011921595

CR Subject Classification (1998): C.2, F.1, I.2, H.3, J.1, F.2

Typesetting: Camera-ready by author, data conversion by Scientific Publishing Services, Chennai, India

Printed on acid-free paper

Springer is part of Springer Science+Business Media (www.springer.com)

Preface

The primary scientific action of the Macedonian Society on Information and Communication Technologies (ICT-ACT), the ICT Innovations conference, celebrated its second year of providing a platform for academics, professionals and practitioners to interact and share their research findings related to innovative fundamental and applied research in ICT.

Credit for the quality of the conference proceedings goes first and foremost to the authors. In all, 155 authors from 13 countries contributed a great deal of determination and inspiration to produce this work, and we are very thankful that they chose ICT Innovations as the place to present it. Undoubtedly, they are all responsible for keeping the program vital. Only 33 papers were selected for this edition via an extensive reviewing process. Seventy-three Program Committee members, 28 of whom from the Republic of Macedonia, were chosen for their leadership in the field, their reputation for decency and good decree, and their aptitude to relish and appreciate other people's work. Reviewers also deserve a lot of credit, with nothing in return except the contentment of serving the ICT community.

ICT Innovations 2010 was held in Ohrid, Macedonia, during September 12–15, 2010. The conference focused on a variety of ICT fields:

- Internet applications and services
- Artificial intelligence and bioinformatics
- Internet, mobile and wireless technologies
- Multimedia information systems
- Computer networks and systems
- Computer security systems

Ivo Ivanovski, Minister of Information Society, and Velimir Stojkovski, Rector of the Ss. Cyril and Methodius University in Skopje, addressed the participants at the opening session. Our work was made much easier by following the procedures developed and passed along by the ICT Innovations 2009 Conference and Program Chair, Danco Davcev. The editors would like to express their sincere gratitude to those that sponsored the publication of the present book, and personally to Anastas Misev and Vlado Trajkovik for their unreserved support given during the preparation and publication of the book. We pride ourselves on having the opportunity to serve this vibrant, enthusiastic and forward-thinking community.

September 2010

Marjan Gusev
Pece Mitrevski

Organization

ICT Innovations 2010 was organized by the the Macedonian Society on Information and Communication Technologies (ICT-ACT).

Conference and Program Chair

Marjan Gusev	University Ss Cyril and Methodius, Macedonia

Program Committee

Ackovska Nevena	University Ss Cyril and Methodius, Macedonia
Amata Garito Maria	Uninetuno - International Telematic University, Italy
Andova Suzana	Technical University Eindhoven, The Netherlands
Andonovic Ivan	University of Strathclyde, UK
Antovski Ljupco	University Ss Cyril and Methodius, Macedonia
Atanassov Emanouil	IPP BAS, Bulgaria
Bakeva Verica	University Ss Cyril and Methodius, Macedonia
Bosnacki Dragan	Technical University Eindhoven, The Netherlands
Cakmakov Dusan	University Ss Cyril and Methodius, Macedonia
Celakovski Sasko	ITgma, Macedonia
Chitkuchev Lubomir	Boston University, USA
Davcev Danco	University Ss Cyril and Methodius, Macedonia
Dika Zamir	South East Europe University, Macedonia
Dimitrova Nevenka	Philips Research, USA
Dimov Zoran	Microsoft - Vancouver, Canada
Eleftherakis George	University of Sheffield, City College, UK
Fullana Pere	ESCI - Barcelona, Spain
Furht Borko	Florida Atlantic University, USA
Gavrilovska Liljana	University Ss Cyril and Methodius, Macedonia
Gievska-Krliu Sonja	George Washington University, USA
Gjorgjevikj Dejan	University Ss Cyril and Methodius, Macedonia
Gligoroski Danilo	University of Trondheim, Norway
Grunwald Norbert	Hochschule Wismar, Germany
Haak Liane	University Oldenburg, Germany
Hadzi-Velkov Zoran	University Ss Cyril and Methodius, Macedonia
Ivanovic Mirjana	Univeristy of Novi Sad, Serbia
Jonoska Natasha	University of South Florida, USA
Josimovski Saso	University Ss Cyril and Methodius, Macedonia
Junker Horst	IMBC, Germany
Jurca Ioan	UTT, Romania

Kalajdziski Slobodan	University Ss Cyril and Methodius, Macedonia
Kalpic Damir	University of Zagreb, FER, Croatia
Kimovski Goran	SAP, Canada
Kocarev Ljupco	University Ss Cyril and Methodius, Macedonia
Kon-Popovska Margita	University Ss Cyril and Methodius, Macedonia
Kulakov Andrea	University Ss Cyril and Methodius, Macedonia
Kut Alp	9 Eylul University Izmir, Turkey
Lazarova-Molnar Sanja	UAE University, UAE
Loskovska Suzana	University Ss Cyril and Methodius, Macedonia
Lukovic Ivan	University of Novi Sad, Serbia
Madevska Ana	University Ss Cyril and Methodius, Macedonia
Markovski Smile	University Ss Cyril and Methodius, Macedonia
Marovic Branko	University of Belgrade, Serbia
Marx Gomez Jorge	Oldenburg University, Germany
Milentijevic Ivan	University of Nis, Serbia
Milosavljevic Milan	Singidunum University Belgrade, Serbia
Misev Anastas	University Ss Cyril and Methodius, Macedonia
Mitreski Kosta	University Ss Cyril and Methodius, Macedonia
Mitrevski Pece	University St Clement Ohridski, Macedonia
Mustafa Blerim	Macedonian Telekom, Macedonia
Manolopoulos Yannis	Aristotle University, Greece
Nanevski Aleksandar	IMDEA, Spain
Olariu Stephan	ODU, USA
Paris Francois	University of Houston, USA
Parychek Peter	University of Donau, Austria
Patel Dilip	London South Bank University, UK
Patel Shushma	London South Bank University, UK
Profumo Francesco	Politecnico di Torino, Italy
Pudlowski Zenon J.	WIETE, Melbourne, Australia
Radevski Vladimir	South Eastern Europe University, Macedonia
Sjursen Harold	New York University, USA
Stojanov Georgi	American University of Paris, France
Stojcev Mile	University of Nis, Serbia
Tasic Jurij	University of Ljubljana, Slovenia
Tochtermann Klaus	University of Graz, Austria
Trajanov Dimitar	University Ss Cyril and Methodius, Macedonia
Trajkovic Ljiljana	SFU, Canada
Trajkovik Vladimir	University Ss Cyril and Methodius, Macedonia
Trajkovski Igor	University Ss Cyril and Methodius, Macedonia
Trichet Francky	Nantes University, France
Vasileska Dragica	ASU, USA
Velinov Goran	University Ss Cyril and Methodius, Macedonia
Zdravkova Katerina	University Ss Cyril and Methodius, Macedonia

Sponsoring Institutions

UKIM University Ss Cyril and Methodius
UKIM Faculty of Natural Sciences and Mathematics - Institute of Informatics
UKIM Faculty of Electrical Engineering and Information Technologies
Asseco South Eastern Europe
Duna computers
Lancom Computers
Netcetera
Neocom

Table of Contents

Invited Keynote Papers

Proceeding Papers

Finite State Automata by DNA Self-assembly

Nataša Jonoska[1] and Nadrian C. Seeman[2]

[1] Department of Mathematics,
University of South Florida,
Tampa, Fl 33620, USA
[2] Chemistry Department,
New York University, New York, NY 10003, USA

Abstract. Several models of finite state automata in biomolecular computing are already in literature and some of these models have been also implemented in vitro showing their possible feasibility. On the other side, DNA self assembly of two-dimensional arrays have been achieved by variety of DNA-like tiles, moreover, algorithmic self assembly simulations of the Sierpinski triangle and binary counters have also been recorded. With this talk we describe an implementation of couple of models by DNA and we concentrate on the recent implementation of a finite state transducer (finite state automaton with output) by Wang like DNA tiles simulated with triple cross-over DNA molecules.

Keywords: transducers, finite state automata with output, picture languages, DNA tiles, robotic arms, DNA arrays.

Synthetic DNA has been designed and shown to assemble into complex species that entail the lateral fusion of DNA double helices, such as DNA double crossover (DX) molecules [9], triple crossover (TX) molecules [18] or paranemic crossover (PX) molecules. Double and triple crossover molecules have been used as tiles and building blocks for large nanoscale arrays [27,26], including the Sierinski triangle assembly by DX molecules [25]. Theoretically, it is shown that two-dimensional arrays made of DX or TX DNA can simulate the dynamics of a bounded one-dimensional cellular automaton and so are capable of potentially performing computations as a Universal Turing machine [27]. The essential part in these observations is the natural representation of a Wang tile with a DX or a TX molecule.

Wang tiles have been extensively used in the study of two-dimensional languages and there is a natural correspondence between the sets of blocks assembled with Wang tiles and local two-dimensional languages. The physical representation of Wang tiles with double crossover DNA molecules demonstrated in [26,27] provides another motivation for studying sets of rectangular blocks of symbols namely two-dimensional languages. It is well known that by iteration of generalized sequential machines (finite state machines mapping symbols into strings) all computable functions can be simulated (see for ex. [22,24]). The full computational power depends on the possibility that finite sequential machines can be iterated. Moreover, there is a natural simulation of transducers as well

M. Gusev and P. Mitrevski (Eds.): ICT Innovations 2010, CCIS 83, pp. 1–4, 2011.

as their iterations with Wang tiles, hence generating all recursive (computable) functions with Wang tiles is possible [27,12]. This idea has been developed further in [5] where a successful experimental simulation of a programmable transducer (finite state machine mapping symbols into symbols) with TX DNA molecules having iteration capabilities is reported. This experimental development provides means for generating patterns and variety of two-dimensional arrays at the nano level. Motivated by this recent experimental development we can define a class of two-dimensional languages generated by iteration of transducers, called transducer generated languages. Furthermore, we can show how physical realization of arrays corresponding to such a language can be used as platforms for arranging robotic nano-arms. A description of transducer generated languages appears in [8], their potential implementation and complexity of the arrays have been studied in [7].

Although there are fairly well developed classifications and theories to study one-dimensional languages, in particular regular languages, the case of two-dimensional languages remains elusive. The class REC defined by A. Restivo and D. Giammarresi [10,11] was introduced as a natural extension of regular languages in one-dimensional case. They showed that the emptiness problem for these languages is undecidable which implies that many other questions that are easily solved in one-dimensional case become undecidable in two-dimensional case. Recent work by several authors attempts to better understand REC through various approaches such as: design of variants of finite state automata that recognize these languages [1,2,16,17], characterization of determinism of two-dimensional recognizable languages [3,4], or study of the factor languages of two-dimensional shift spaces [13,14]. Therefore, the transducer generated languages introduced in [8,7] define another sub-class of REC languages whose analysis may provide a way to understand some properties of the whole class of REC.

Transducer generated languages with rectangular arrays can be naturally described with rectangular blocks obtained by assembling Wang tiles. Although Wang tiles are usually associated with tilings of the plane, the Wang tiles corresponding to a given transducer contain boundary colors such that the rectangular arrays surrounded with these boundary colors cannot be extended further. Each Wang tile can be implemented with a triple crossover (TX) DNA molecule. We present a possible implementation of transducer generated arrays with TX DNA molecules in [7]. Such arrays can serve as platforms for arranging robotic nano-arms. A PX-JX_2 device introduced in [28], has two distinct positions and each is obtained by addition of a pair of DNA strands that hybridizes with the device such that the molecule is in either PX or in JX_2 position. This device has been assembled sequentially [20] and in an array [6]. The sequential device assembly is used to implement the input of the transducer [5]. In the two-dimensional device arrays it has been shown that a molecular robotic arm can be attached to each device in the array and the movement of all of the arms can be controlled simultaneously. The successful molecular implementation of a transducer [5] and the two-dimensional device arrays [6] form a basis for assembling transducer generated arrays incorporating molecular robotic arms to be moved in preprogrammed directions simultaneously.

Acknowledgement. This work has been supported in part by the NSF grants CCF-0726396 and DMS-0900671 to N.J. and by grants GM-29554 from NIGMS, grants DMI-0210844, EIA-0086015, CCF-0432009, CCF-0726396 and CTS-0548774, CTS-0608889 from the NSF, 48681-EL and W911NF-07-1-0439 from ARO, N000140910181 from the office of Naval Research and a grant from the W.M. Keck Foundation, to N.C.S.

References

1. Anselmo, M., Giammarresi, D., Madonia, M.: Tiling automaton: A computational model for recognizable two-dimensional languages. In: Holub, J., Žďárek, J. (eds.) CIAA 2007. LNCS, vol. 4783, pp. 290–302. Springer, Heidelberg (2007)
2. Anselmo, M., Giammarresi, D., Madonia, M.: From determinism to non-determinism in recognizable two-dimensional languages. In: Harju, T., Karhumäki, J., Lepistö, A. (eds.) DLT 2007. LNCS, vol. 4588, pp. 36–47. Springer, Heidelberg (2007)
3. Anselmo, M., Giammarresi, D., Madonia, M., Restivo, A.: Unambiguous recognizable two-dimensional languages. RAIRO - Inf. Theor. Appl. 40, 277–293 (2006)
4. Anselmo, M., Jonoska, N., Madonia, M.: Framed versus unframed two-dimensional languages. In: Nielsen, M., Kučera, A., Miltersen, P.B., Palamidessi, C., Tůma, P., Valencia, F. (eds.) SOFSEM 2009. LNCS, vol. 5404, pp. 79–92. Springer, Heidelberg (2009)
5. Chakraborty, B., Jonoska, N., Seeman, N.C.: Programmable transducer by DNA self-assembly (in preparation)
6. Ding, B., Seeman, N.C.: Operation of a DNA robot arm inserted into a 2d DNA crystalline substrate. Science 314, 1583–1585 (2006)
7. Dolzhenko, E., Jonoska, N., Seeman, N.C.: Transducer generated arrays of robotic nano-arms. Natural Computing 9(2), 437–455 (2010), doi:10.1007/s11047-009-9157-5
8. Dolzhenko, E., Jonoska, N.: On complexity of two-dimensional languages generated by transducers. In: Ibarra, O.H., Ravikumar, B. (eds.) CIAA 2008. LNCS, vol. 5148, pp. 181–190. Springer, Heidelberg (2008)
9. Fu, T.J., Seeman, N.C.: DNA double crossover structures. Biochemistry 32, 3211–3220 (1993)
10. Giammarresi, D., Restivo, A.: Recognizable picture languages. In: Nivat, M., Saoudi, A., Wang, P.S.P. (eds.) Proc. 1st Internat. Colloq. on Parallel Image Processing (1992); Internat. J. Pattern Recognition Artif. Intell. 6, 231–256
11. Giammarresi, D., Restivo, A.: Two-dimensional languages. In: Handbook of Formal Languages, vol. 3, pp. 215–267. Springer, Berlin (1997)
12. Jonoska, N., Liao, S., Seeman, N.C.: Transducers with programmable input by DNA self-assembly. In: Jonoska, N., Păun, G., Rozenberg, G. (eds.) Aspects of Molecular Computing. LNCS, vol. 2950, pp. 219–240. Springer, Heidelberg (2003)
13. Jonoska, N., Pirnot, J.B.: Transitivity in two-dimensional local languages defined by dot systems. International Journal of Foundations of Computer Science 17, 435–464 (2006)

14. Jonoska, N., Pirnot, J.B.: Finite state automata representing two-dimensional subshifts. In: Holub, J., Žďárek, J. (eds.) CIAA 2007. LNCS, vol. 4783, pp. 277–289. Springer, Heidelberg (2007)
15. Kari, J.: A small aperiodic set of Wang tiles. Discrete Math. 160, 259–264 (1996)
16. Kari, J., Moore, C.: Rectangles and squares recognized by two-dimensional automata, http://www.santafe.edu/~moore/pubs/picture.html
17. Kari, J., Moore, C.: New results on alternating and non-deterministic two-dimensional finite-state automata. In: Ferreira, A., Reichel, H. (eds.) STACS 2001. LNCS, vol. 2010, pp. 396–406. Springer, Heidelberg (2001)
18. LaBean, T.H., Yan, H., Kopatsch, J., Liu, F., Winfree, E., Reif, J.H., Seeman, N.C.: The construction, analysis, ligation and self-assembly of DNA triple crossover complexes. J. Am. Chem. Soc. 122, 1848–1860 (2000)
19. Latteux, M., Simplot, D., Terlutte, A.: Iterated length-preserving rational transductions. In: Brim, L., Gruska, J., Zlatuška, J. (eds.) MFCS 1998. LNCS, vol. 1450, pp. 286–295. Springer, Heidelberg (1998)
20. Liao, S., Seeman, N.C.: Translation of DNA signals into polymer assembly instructions. Science 306, 2072–2074 (2004)
21. Lind, D., Marcus, B.: An introduction to symbolic dynamics and coding. Cambridge University Press, Cambridge (1995)
22. Manca, V., Martin-Vide, C., Păun, G.: New computing paradigms suggested by DNA computing: computing by carving. BioSystems 52, 47–54 (1999)
23. Mao, C., LaBean, T.H., Reif, J.H., Seeman, N.C.: Logical computation using algorithmic self-assembly of DNA triple-crossover molecules. Nature 407, 493–496 (2000)
24. Păun, G.: On the iteration of gsm mappings. Rev. Roum. Math. Pures Appl. 23(4), 921–937 (1978)
25. Rothemund, P., Papadakis, N., Winfree, E.: Algorithmic self-assembly of DNA Sierpinski triangles. PLoS Biology 2(12), e424 (2004), http://biology.plosjournals.org/perlserv/?request=get-document&doi=10.1371/journal.pbio.0020424&ct=1
26. Winfree, E., Liu, F., Wenzler, L.A., Seeman, N.C.: Design and self-assembly of two-dimensional DNA crystals. Nature 394, 539–544 (1998)
27. Winfree, E.: Algorithmic self-assembly of DNA: theoretical motivations and 2D assembly experiments. Journal of Biomolecular Structure and Dynamics 11(S2), 263–270 (2000)
28. Yan, H., Zhang, X., Shen, Z., Seeman, N.C.: A robust DNA mechanical device controlled by hybridization topology. Nature 415, 62–65 (2002)
29. Zheng, J., Constantinou, P.E., Micheel, C., Alivisatos, A.P., Kiehl, R.A., Seeman, N.C.: 2D Nanoparticle arrays show the organizational power of robust DNA motifs. NanoLetters 6, 1502–1504 (2006)

Length Extension Attack on Narrow-Pipe SHA-3 Candidates

Danilo Gligoroski

Department of Telematics, Norwegian University of Science and Technology,
O.S.Bragstads plass 2B, N-7491 Trondheim, Norway
danilo.gligoroski@item.ntnu.no

Abstract. In this paper we show that narrow-pipe SHA-3 candidates BLAKE-32, BLAKE-64, Hamsi, SHAvite-3-256, SHAvite-3-512, Skein-256-256 and Skein-512-512 do not provide n bits of security where n is the hash output size. The actual security against length extension attack that these functions provide is $n-k$ bits of security, where k is an arbitrary value chosen by the attacker who wants to perform one-time pre-computation of 2^{k+1} compression functions. The attack can be in two variants: 1. The attacker is not collecting the hash values given by the user or 2. The attacker is collecting the hash values given by the user. In any case, the attacker does not know the content of the hashed messages. The optimal value for this attack from the perspective of minimizing the number calls to the compression function and increasing the probability of the successful attack is achieved when k has a value $k = \frac{n}{2}$, thus reducing the security against the length-extension attack from n to $\frac{n}{2}$ bits.

1 Introduction

The usefulness of the concept of the cryptographic hash functions have been confirmed in practice with the fact that they have became the fundamental building part of the modern cryptography and information security and their presence is evident in numerous protocols and schemes such as: digital signatures, commitment schemes, password protection schemes, in algorithms for checking the data integrity, key derivation functions and cryptographic random number generators, authentication schemes and many others.

The most used family of hash functions is the family called "SHA", as a worldwide accepted industry standard for cryptographic hash functions. They have been designed by the National Security Agency (NSA) and published by the National Institute of Standards and Technology (NIST) as a U.S. Federal Information Processing Standard [1,2]. The acronym SHA stands for Secure Hash Algorithm. There are two types of SHA algorithms: SHA-1, and SHA-2, and although they have some similarities, they have also significant differences. SHA-1 is the most used member of the SHA hash family, employed in countless different applications and protocols. However, in 2005, a very significant theoretical development in detecting some security flaws in SHA-1 has been made by Wang et.al [3].

M. Gusev and P. Mitrevski (Eds.): ICT Innovations 2010, CCIS 83, pp. 5–10, 2011.

SHA-2 is actually a family of its own, consisting of four algorithms that differ from each other by different digest size, different initial values and different word size. The digest sizes are: 224, 256, 384 and 512 bits. Although no attacks have yet been reported on the SHA-2 variants, they are algorithmically similar to SHA-1, and NIST have felt the need for and made efforts to develop an improved new family of hash functions [4]. The new hash standard SHA-3, is currently under development - the function will be selected via an open competition running between 2008 and 2012. In the First Round there were 51 proposals [5] and in July 2009 NIST has chosen 14 Second Round candidates [6].

In their call for the SHA-3 competition [4], NIST has defined several security requirements such as collision resistance of $\frac{n}{2}$ bits, preimage resistance of n bits, resistance against second preimages of 2^{n-k} bits for messages long 2^k bits and resistance against length-extension attack. However, in the SHA-3 call there is no clear statement how many bits of security should SHA-3 candidates provide against length extension attack.

On my request for clarification submitted to the SHA-3 hash forum list on 12 December 2008, I got the following answer by the NIST representative submitted to the hash forum list on 14 January 2009:

> "We expect the winning n-bit hash function to be able to provide n bits of security against length extension attacks. That is, given $H(M)$, with M wholly or partially unknown to the attacker: the cost of finding (Z, x) so that $x = H(M||Z)$ should be greater than or equal to either the cost of guessing M or 2^n times the cost of computing a typical hash compression function."

In this paper we will show that four SHA-3 candidates that are narrow-pipe designs do not provide n bits of security. Those narrow-pipe designs are: BLAKE-32 and BLAKE-64 [8], Hamsi [9], SHAvite-3-256 and SHAvite-3-512 [10], and narrow-pipe Skein versions (Skein-256-256 and the primary submission variant of Skein, Skein-512-512) [11].

2 A Generic Modeling of the Narrow-Pipe Iterative Finalization

In order to launch a length-extension attack to the narrow-pipe designs we will need to model the finalization of the iterative process that narrow-pipe designs do when they are processing messages. Moreover, we will assume that the length of the digested messages is such that the final processed block does not have any bits from the message but is a constant $PADDING$ that consist only from the bits defined by the padding rule of that hash function.

In that case, the modeling of the narrow-pipe hash designs can be expressed by the following expression:

$$H = f(parameters, \mathbf{compress}(H_{chain}, parameters, PADDING)) \quad (1)$$

and is graphically described in Figure 1.

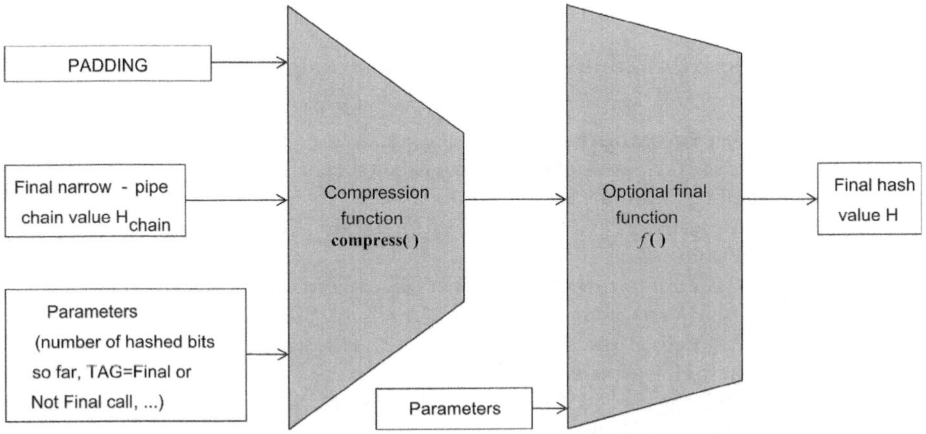

Fig. 1. A graphic representation of narrow-pipe hash designs finalization of the iterative process of message digestion

Note that in the narrow-pipe designs where the final function $f()$ is missing, we can treat it as the identity function in the expression (1) and that although the parts *parameters* are different for all four designs, it will not change our analysis and our attack.

How narrow-pipe designs are protected from the length-extension attack?

Since the designers of narrow-pipe hash functions are designing the compression function as one-way pseudo-random function, the value H_{chain}, which is the internal state of the hash function, is hidden from the attacker. That means that by just knowing the final hash value H it is infeasible for the attacker to find the preimage H_{chain} that has produced that value H. Consequently, the attacker will have a difficulty to produce a message Z such that only by knowing the value H (where $H = Hash(M)$ and the message M is unknown to the attacker), he/she can produce a valid hash value $x = Hash(M||Z)$.

In what follows our goal will be to show that the attacker can recover that internal state H_{chain} with much less complexity than 2^n calls to the compression function - the complexity that NIST requires in order to claim that the design is offering n bits of security against the length-extension attack.

3 Generic Length Extension Attack on Narrow-Pipe SHA-3 Candidates

Our attack is based on the old Merkle's observation [7] that when an adversary is given 2^k distinct target hashes, (second) preimages can be found after hashing about 2^{n-k} messages, instead of expected 2^n different messages. In our attack we use the Merkle's observation not on the whole hash function, but on the two final invocations of the compression function. In order our attack to work, we

Table 1. A generic length-extension attack on narrow-pipe hash functions

A generic length-extension attack on narrow-pipe hash functions

1. **One time pre-computation phase**
   Step 0. Fix the length of the messages such that the $PADDING$ block does not posses any message bits.
   Step 1. Produce 2^k pairs (h_{chain}, h) for random values h_{chain} with the expression:
   $h = f(parameters, \mathbf{compress}(h_{chain}, parameters, PADDING))$.
   This phase has a complexity of 2^k calls to the compression function (or 2^{k+1} calls if the design has a final transformation $f()$).
2. **Query (attack) phase**
   Step 2. Ask the user to produce a hash value $H(M)$ where M is unknown (but its length is fixed in **Step 0**).
   Step 3. If there exists a pre-computed pair (h'_{chain}, h') such that $H(M) = H = h'$, put $H_{chain} = h'_{chain}$, put whatever message block Z and produce a valid $x = H(M||Z)$.

will assume that the length of the messages is such that after the padding, the final padded block is without any message bits (which is usual situation when the length of the message is a multiple of 256, 512 or 1024 bits).

A generic description of the length-extension attack on narrow-pipe hash functions is given in Table 1.

Proposition 1. *The probability that the condition in* **Step 3** *is true is* $\frac{1}{2^{n-k}}$.

Proof. The proof is a trivial application of the ratio between the volume of the pre-computed pairs (h_{chain}, h) which has a value 2^k and the volume of all possible hash values of n bits which is 2^n. □

Proposition 2. *For the conditional probability that the corresponding h'_{chain} is the actual chaining value H_{chain} the following relation holds:*

$$P(H_{chain} = h'_{chain} \mid H(M) = h') \geq 0.58 \times 2^{k-n} \approx 2^{k-n-0.780961}. \qquad (2)$$

Proof. (Sketch) It is sufficient to notice that for an ideal random function $g : \{0,1\}^n \rightarrow \{0,1\}^n$ that maps n bits to n bits, the probability that an n-bit value has m preimages for the first 8 values of m is approximately given in the Table 2 (the precise analytical expressions for the given probabilities can be a nice exercise in the Elementary Probability courses).

The relation (2) follows directly from Proposition 1 and from Table 2. □

Corollary 1. *After approximately $2^{n-k+0.780961}$ queries the attacker should expect one successful length extension.* □

Table 2. The probabilities an n bit value to have m preimages for an ideal random function $g : \{0,1\}^n \rightarrow \{0,1\}^n$

Number of preimages m	Probability P
0	0.36787
1	0.36787
2	0.18394
3	0.06131
4	0.01533
5	0.00307
6	0.00051
7	0.00007

Corollary 2. *The security of narrow-pipe hash designs is upper bounded by the following values:*

$$\max(2^{\frac{n}{2}}, 2^{n-k+0.780961}), \tag{3}$$

where $k \leq n$.

Proof. The minimal number of calls to the compression function of the narrow-pipe for which the attack can be successful is achieved approximately for $\frac{n}{2}$. □

The interpretation of the Corollary 2 is that narrow-pipe hash designs do not offer n bits of security against length-extension attack but just $\frac{n}{2}$ bits of security.

4 Why Wide-Pipe Designs Are Resistant to Our Attack?

A natural question is raising about the security of wide-pipe hash designs and their resistance against the described attack in this paper. The reason of the success of our attack is the narrow size of just n bits of the hidden value H_{chain} that our attack is managing to recover with a generic collision search technique.

Since in the wide-pipe hash designs that internal state of the hash function has at least $2n$ bits, the search for the internal collisions would need at least 2^n calls to the compression function which is actually the value that NIST needs for the resistance against the length-extension attack.

5 Conclusions

When it comes to the properties of the hash functions designed by humans, that are trying to mimic the expected properties of ideal random functions (i.e mimicking the random oracle model [12]) the narrow-pipe designs are showing pretty big number of abberations from that model. In this paper we have showed that they are not giving n bits of security against the length-extension attack, that NIST is demanding from SHA-3 candidates. Narrow-pipe designs are offering just $\frac{n}{2}$ bits of security, while in the same time, wide-pipe (double-pipe) hash designs are offering the requested security of n bits against the length-extension attack.

Acknowledgement

I would like to thank Vlastimil Klima, Rune Jensen, Svein Johan Knapskog and Rune Ødegård for their useful comments and suggestions to improve the clarity of text.

References

1. FIPS 180-1: Secure Hash Standard, Federal Information Processing Standards Publication 180-1, U.S. Department of Commerce/NIST, National Technical Information Service, Springfield, Virginia (April 1995)
2. FIPS 180-2: Secure Hash Standard, Federal Information Processing Standards Publication 180-2, U.S. Department of Commerce/NIST, National Technical Information Service, Springfield, Virginia (August 2002)
3. Wang, X., Yin, Y.L., Yu, H.: Collision Search Attacks on SHA-1. In: Shoup, V. (ed.) CRYPTO 2005. LNCS, vol. 3621, pp. 17–36. Springer, Heidelberg (2005)
4. National Institute of Standards and Technology: Announcing Request for Candidate Algorithm Nominations for a New Cryptographic Hash Algorithm (SHA-3) Family. Federal Register 27(212), 62212–62220 (November 2007), `http://csrc.nist.gov/groups/ST/hash/documents/FR_Notice_Nov07.pdf` (2009/04/10)
5. NIST: SHA-3 First Round Candidates, `http://csrc.nist.gov/groups/ST/hash/sha-3/Round1/submissions_rnd1.html`
6. NIST: SHA-3 Second Round Candidates, `http://csrc.nist.gov/groups/ST/hash/sha-3/Round2/submissions_rnd2.html`
7. Merkle, R.C.: Secrecy, authentication, and public key systems, Ph.D. thesis, Stanford University, pp. 12–13 (1979), `http://www.merkle.com/papers/Thesis1979.pdf` (2010/08/08)
8. Aumasson, J.-P., Henzen, L., Meier, W., Phan, R.C.-W.: SHA-3 proposal BLAKE, Submission to NIST (Round 2), `http://csrc.nist.gov/groups/ST/hash/sha-3/Round2/documents/BLAKE_Round2.zip` (2010/05/03)
9. Kücük, Ö.: The Hash Function Hamsi, Submission to NIST (Round 2), available `http://csrc.nist.gov/groups/ST/hash/sha-3/Round2/documents/Hamsi_Round2.zip` (2010/05/03)
10. Biham, E., Dunkelman, O.: The SHAvite-3 Hash Function, Submission to NIST (Round 2), `http://csrc.nist.gov/groups/ST/hash/sha-3/Round2/documents/SHAvite-3_Round2.zip` (2010/05/03)
11. Ferguson, N., Lucks, S., Schneier, B., Whiting, D., Bellare, M., Kohno, T., Callas, J., Walker, J.: The Skein Hash Function Family, Submission to NIST (Round 2), `http://csrc.nist.gov/groups/ST/hash/sha-3/Round2/documents/Skein_Round2.zip` (2010/05/03)
12. Bellare, M., Rogaway, P.: Random oracles are practical: A paradigm for designing efficient protocols. In: CCS 1993: Proceedings of the 1st ACM Conference on Computer and Communications Security, pp. 62–73 (1993)

Review of Knowledge Sharing: Conceptual Foundations for Micro-level Knowledge Sharing and Readiness-for Change Related Behaviours

Dilip Patel, Khalid Samara, and Shushma Patel

Centre for Information Systems and Management (CISM)
The Faculty of Business, Department of Informatics,
London South Bank University, London SE1 OAA
{dilip,samarakb,shushma}@lsbu.ac.uk

Abstract. In the organisational change and knowledge sharing literature, recognition of high failures of change efforts is said to be associated to the organisations lack of understanding of how to manage readiness for change. In this paper, the case for change readiness is invoked by a need for further explanation of micro level foundations. A survey of 105 scholarly academic journals in the area of knowledge sharing research from 1994 to 2009 with keywords salient to knowledge sharing studies was conducted to explore current thinking about organisational change issues. The findings reveal that there is yet no well-established method or clear conceptual definition to exploring the phenomena of change for knowledge sharing on both individual and organisational levels. Based on the literature survey a model is proposed to integrate the relevant themes that influence knowledge readiness. A discussion is presented, demonstrating future directions towards knowledge sharing for micro-level knowledge sharing and readiness for change related behaviours.

Keywords: Knowledge-sharing, readiness for change, organisational-change, knowledge- management, micro-foundations.

1 Introduction

Interest in knowledge management has increased rapidly as reflected in the expansion in the literature surrounding the concept since the mid-1990s. It is claimed that the only resource that provides an organisation with sustainable competitive advantages is knowledge [1] [2]. To date, proponents argue that the importance and factors that acts as a barrier to successful knowledge management is the sharing of knowledge [3]. The ability of an organisation to share and apply knowledge is however hard to do without the change of culture to support a new attitude. Irrespective of the growing awareness of the benefits of knowledge sharing, there has been relatively little understanding of the change factors, and how it can nurture a knowledge sharing culture [4].

In the organisational change and knowledge sharing literature, recognition of high failures of change efforts is said to be associated with the organisations lack of understanding of how to manage readiness for change [5] [6] [7] [8]. Not surprisingly,

M. Gusev and P. Mitrevski (Eds.): ICT Innovations 2010, CCIS 83, pp. 11–26, 2011.

many studies who show organisations introducing information technology as a means to encourage knowledge sharing, also note that this is not straightforward because assessed readiness for change is low [9] [10]. The notion of change readiness is described as the initial part of the natural cycle of change. It insists on clear micro foundations, in that it requires people to focus their attention in a state of action readiness for change [7].

While the notion of readiness for change has been explored in the change literature, it is however a concept that has not yet been fully explored or understood in the knowledge literature. More generally, the relationship between knowledge research and change remains under-represented, theoretically as well as empirically. To date, few studies that have explored the combined contributions of organisational change and knowledge sharing have been much devoted to informal constructs as facilitators of organisational change [11] [12]. For example, these types of studies relied heavily on organisational level knowledge sharing, that of networks of individual influences as the focal unit of analysis to solve the organisation knowledge problem [13]. We argue that these studies do not account for any well-articulated theories of change or explicitly compare the connections between the individual's level readiness and organisations change to promote knowledge sharing. In other words, change and the inability to change are often viewed as macro-level phenomena and what constitutes as a change facilitator is perceived in terms of the role of informal factors in shaping the appropriate change effort [7].

Although the understanding of informal factors is of prime importance, such macro-level explanations of knowledge have ignored the central role of individual level factors, which can serve to maintain organisational level knowledge issues [14]. The paper validates recent theoretical calls for a stronger focus on micro level explanations [13] [14] [7]. To accomplish this aim, an extensive review merging both knowledge, and change literature is warranted, to advance and direct future research in organisational knowledge sharing practices. The paper surveys 105 scholarly academic journals in the area of knowledge sharing research to provide a better understanding of the phenomena of change. The review includes search for journals that conceptually define and explore organisational change, including any that consider readiness for change.

The paper contributes to the knowledge literature by introducing the notion that readiness for change is an organisational mechanism that can provoke a transition to existing knowledge related initiatives between the individual knowledge workers, where knowledge resides, and the level of the organisation where knowledge and change can be obtained. More specifically, we ask the following two research questions: What are the various change developments on knowledge sharing initiatives that have been investigated in the knowledge literature? What readiness for change methods have been used within the area so far?

The paper is structured as follows: Section 2 covers current and early theoretical foundations in the knowledge and change literature as well as the theoretical justifications proposed for developing readiness for change. Section 3 presents the method used for surveying the literature, followed by Section 4, which presents the results of the literature survey. Section 5 presents the knowledge readiness model drawn on literature from fields such as change and knowledge related research. The paper concludes in section 6 and 7 with some discussions and research questions to guide future work.

2 The Current Trends in Knowledge Sharing Research

2.1 Knowledge and Sharing Knowledge in Organisations

Knowledge management as an interdisciplinary field covers a broad spectrum of activities, which has come to describe a continuum of organisational practice and academic theory. All of these initiatives involve processes comprised of various methods, concepts, and propositions, designed to support individuals, groups and organisations, as prime movers to make use of organisations collective expertise [15]. The prevailing view of the characteristics of these firms or of particular characteristic of work within a firm as knowledge intensive implies a more significant role for knowledge [16]. Indeed, the extent that knowledge is scarce and tacit has become increasingly important to find ways of transferring its economic value [17]. [19] argues that the nature of this knowledge develops in organisational culture and a direct result of human action, rather than human design. The cost of maintaining such knowledge is also not small and the costs are strongly constrained by: 'imitability and replicability consideration' [15] [16]. These values are deeply embedded, tacit assumptions and are difficult to talk about and even harder to change. Thus, implicit in this, is that much of organisational knowledge is constrained at the level of individuals [19].

A constant theme in most definitions of knowledge management is the sharing of knowledge. Research on knowledge sharing refers to a broad line of studies that draws upon different concepts, and definitions based on various established frameworks. For example, [51] maintains that different perceptions of knowledge sharing occur when the "different objectives of knowledge sharing are appreciated". More importantly, knowledge sharing directly involves the individual and organisational level, in which knowledge creation can take place [19] [2]. It is still an emerging area of inquiry, insisting on further identification, observation and definition [13].

The most regularly cited, as one of the concerns for improving knowledge sharing initiatives is the organisational culture seeking to understand how the organisational characters determine the success of knowledge sharing [12]. Some scholars argue that [21] [8] [20], while organisational cultures are an ever present and dominant force in shaping behaviours they are generally too complex to change directly. Indeed, the nature of knowledge and knowledge sharing that develops in organisational culture and a direct result of human actions usually makes change readiness to improve knowledge sharing initiatives difficult to establish.

While culture has been an overriding theme in the knowledge literature, often in connection with other central themes (e.g., knowledge work in an intra-organisational network) for theorising different knowledge processes, several writings question how such explanations of knowledge can capture vital explanatory mechanisms on the micro level [14] [22] [23]. This view is echoed by [14] who argues that considerable attention should be paid to explanatory mechanisms that are located at the micro-level foundations and that can serve to maintain macro-level behaviours. For example, [14] forcefully argues that while there is a direct connection between organisational collective culture and organisational performance, intervention would have very limited effect on culture change without assessing the level of individual level actions and interactions. They suggest that what are missing in the extant literature are clear micro-foundations.

Consistent with this emphasis of the individual's level approach was that of [2], who expressed dissatisfaction with the notion of organisational level knowledge. [2] argues that, "viewing the organisation as the entity which creates, stores and deploys knowledge, the organisational processes through which individuals engage in these activities maybe obscured". More recent studies suggest that knowledge management studies would benefit more from commencing from low level concepts and methodologically develop theory upwards to identify how macro knowledge related results emerge from micro-level antecedents [22] [23]. The following section based on current and early studies, establishes the role of knowledge sharing in the knowledge and change literature.

2.2 Theories of Change and Organisational Knowledge Sharing

Although there is much research about why managing knowledge is important to organisations, there is noticeably less on how organisations can enact change in individuals. Theories typically placed in the organisational camp, specify that change is a process of continually refining the organisations structure and capacity to serve the ever-changing needs of external and internal customers. Subsequent research has found that change initiatives can equally affect the use of knowledge in the organisation and weaken the effectiveness of established knowledge sharing relations [24] [11] [15]. As prior studies show, even under the best of circumstances, knowledge sharing is formative, and socially constructed, akin to high-level of 'autonomy, complexity, and uncertainty', which may channel knowledge work, time and energy in different ways [26] [25]. Pressures stemming from these human factors can both facilitate or inhibit the performance of change in organisation.

Several studies have yielded support for these perspectives. [27] asserts that the quality of relationships among individuals can play an important role in shaping interpretations of change. They argue that in the course of complex change, while individuals need for information increases, both the quantity and quality of available information often decline. Indeed, individuals are likely to rely on other individuals to share knowledge, typically through reliance on informal sources to make sense of what is happing, leading to more complex understandings of any change effort [27].

Research conducted by [28] for example, offers a framework that facilitates an examination of the potential role of knowledge sharing for improving knowledge work processes. He found that employees increased reliance on informal sharing and receiving of knowledge demands greater change effort. As [26] found that management involvement may have limited influence, affecting change to sharers in the course of their everyday-work. They showed that sharers who engage in complex decision sharing on their own demonstrate a high-level of autonomy and self-management. Also, [29] pointed out that such networks or communities of practice are not amenable to change through formal intervention. [30] found that learning is more difficult in new situations, and more generally, an individual's 'know-how in what he or she knows well', will only change in incremental fashion. Also [31] maintains that, "new ideas and practices are adapted not just adopted".

Alternatively, the seminal work of [32], 'Improving Knowledge Work Processes', showed that organisations who design a change program to knowledge creation improvements, should propose a change that is more conducive to autonomous social behaviours. Moreover, evidence suggests that a social approach appears to be more pertinent to organisations that share knowledge and learn through informal processes [33] [11] [29] [35]. [35], perceptively noted, that informal approach allows greater learning and sharing of knowledge, because of the flexibility and decentralised nature of this coordination. On the other hand, evidence suggests that such studies focus heavily on the use of informal channels as the focal unit of analysis [22] [23] and do not go far enough with respect to accounting for individual interests, knowledge and beliefs [13]. According to [7] in their examination of individuals change processes found that even at the collective-level that takes place in the organisation are the results of some incorporation of the activities of individual level members.

2.3 Importance of Readiness for Change in Knowledge Research

Research on readiness for change and knowledge management models converge on similar dimensions of organisational change affecting issues of how organisations can enact change in individuals. These studies aside, very little empirical research has focused on the individual's perceived readiness 'that of more micro-level explanations', because they largely centre on the role of top level management to create readiness [36]. At the same time, it is argued that the inabilities to change are often viewed as macro-level phenomena [7]. Thus, researchers have come to view inability to change as mainly stemming from the organisational level issues, while neglecting parts of the individual level [7]. Such dissatisfaction is manifest in the knowledge literature. For example, [37] puts it, that knowledge management undergoes a similar problem as many other management and organisational change labels, in that organisations treat knowledge as an object and amenable to being' managed'- by a subject (a manager). [38], explains that there is a practical and theoretical disregard to confuse individual change with modification in organisational level variables.

Theory and research on readiness for change focuses on the initial change preparation, capturing the knowledge, that resides within individuals and beginning the moving process. The key essence of change readiness therefore is the interplay between the behaviours and actions of an individual and the cultural and organisational influences on that individual. It is particularly seen as a response to traditional change theory, whose models are perceived as more conducive to organisational-level issues [39] and which has dominated much of the organisational change literature [41] [5] [40]. Readiness for change models, which correspond to the notion of unfreezing behaviour, [5] have been applied extensively to numerous behavioural factors combining organisational [5] and individual models [40].

There maybe many ways to define readiness for change. Authors such as [40], describe readiness as an initial preparation for individuals to begin the moving process. They consider readiness as the cognitive basis to "minimise resistance to, or support for, a change effort". [36], describes readiness as a reflection of an organisational member's beliefs, intentions and attitudes regarding the extent to which an individual is disposed to adopt and accept a plan to purposefully alter the status quo. This definition of readiness suggests that individuals have preconceived notions regarding the degree to which the organisation is ready for change [42]. The notion of readiness for change was expanded by [39] who postulated that readiness is an essential part of underlying the initiation of a change intervention that can change or alter an individual's readiness. For instance, [8], reinforced this point of view, and argue that it is important to create a sense of urgency so that individuals are ready to change. With no sense of urgency, [8] insist that change will not occur.

The role of readiness in change related outcomes could be further explained using Armenakis and colleagues [40] change readiness model. Specifically, their conceptual principle of the theory proposes that readiness compromises five message components to create readiness for change: discrepancy (or sense of urgency) principle support, (the belief that leaders must support the change effort) efficacy (increasing confidence of individual ability to successfully implement the change), appropriateness (is the action taken a correct one), and personal valence (employees ask, what is in it for me and what the positive and negative outcomes are). The model proposed by [40] as depicted in Figure 1, suggests that each component overlaps, and each influence or determines the others and determines organisational members' readiness for change.

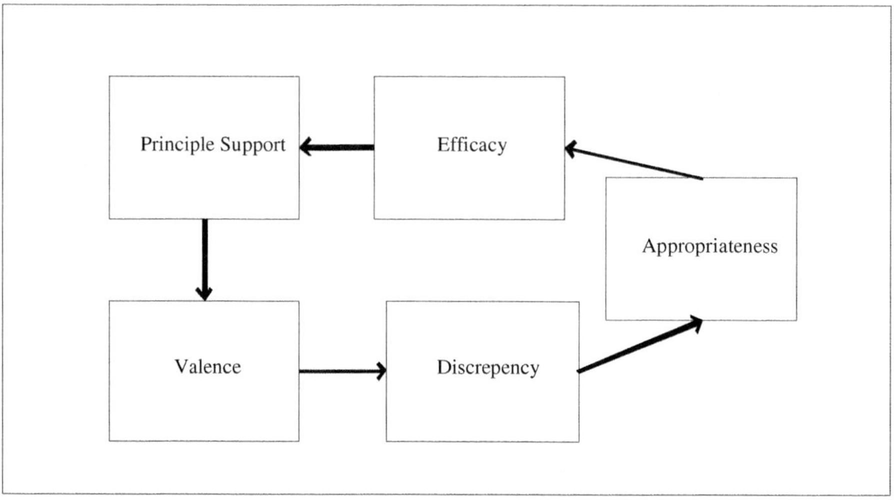

Fig. 1. Readiness for Change Model adapted from Armenakis and colleagues [40]

The overall theoretical perspective proposed by the readiness for change model in Figure 1, contributes to the notion that change resides within individual levels. This focus of readiness is central to understanding change in organisations, and change in the way in which knowledge initiatives are implemented and which often stems from the efforts of people. The human centred approach to intervention is also fundamental to what [13] demonstrates in a recent review of the knowledge sharing literature. As [13] maintains, that literatures are often preoccupied with examining informal mechanisms at the cost of formal ones. They postulate that an integrated view is needed, in which both formal and informal factors have more potential to develop efficient organisation for knowledge sharing.For example, informal factors such as culture that is harder to change could be guided by formal arrangements (i.e. coordination mechanisms) that could establish what fosters readiness for change within knowledge sharing cultures.

Other examples are [4] of a study concerning the definition and measurement for addressing change readiness on organisational knowledge management efforts. According to [4] found that what is often required for knowledge management efforts are significant organisational change. They forecasted three different stages toward change. Firstly, readiness would occur when the individual's attitudes are such that they are open to an upcoming knowledge management initiative. Secondly, adoption occurs when individuals adjust their attitudes and behaviours to agree to the expectations of the knowledge management effort. Finally, institutionalisation occurs when knowledge management becomes a permanent part of employees' behaviour and fabric of the organisation. In the following section, we elaborate on the methods adopted and the results from the literature survey.

3 Method

The review method of identifying change theories in the knowledge sharing literature is an adaptation of the approach proposed by [43] which proceeds in the following stages: (*a*) Firstly, key contributions are likely to be in leading journals including conference papers with a reputation for its quality (*b*) Secondly, identifying other relevant research should include search for citations or reference from the existing journals considered (*c*) In the final stage, the relevant journals should be determined.

A range of knowledge management perspectives has been reported on the concept of knowledge sharing in organisations. This research study carried out a literature survey and targeted only scholarly published journals primarily through online electronic databases. The journals selected were from the field of computer science, organisational, managerial and social sciences. The search was limited to the knowledge research field. Table 1 presents the names and number of journals found. These journals where published between 1994 and 2009 with key words salient to knowledge sharing studies, including knowledge- sharing, knowledge-transfer and knowledge-exchange.

After filtering the various topics, the search resulted in 105 journals. The initial review of the literature began with an analysis of publications that discussed the concept of organisational change and how change activities are used in developing knowledge initiatives. The review process was then narrowed down to publications that referred exclusively to the change readiness or any early change activities within organisations for knowledge sharing practices.

Table 1. Selection and Number of Journals

Journals	No. of Journals
Academy of Management Journal	6
Academy of Management Executives	2
Organisation Science	10
Administrative Science	3
Academy of Management Review	1
Management Science	2
Strategic Management journal	7
MIS Quarterly	4
Organisational Studies	2
Journal of Management IS	3
Organisational Dynamics	2
International Journal of IM	2
Decision Support Systems	5
Journal of Human Resource Management	2
International Journal of the Economics of Business	1
Journal of the Association for IS	1
Organisational Behaviour & Human Decision Processes	7
International Journal of Electronic Collaboration	1
Journal of Information Technology	2
Journal of Strategic Information Systems	3
Information Systems Journal	1
British Journal of Management	1
Management Learning	1
Knowledge and Process Management	1
Experts Systems with Applications	1
International Business Review	1
International Journal of Project Management	2
California Management (US) Review	1
Journal of Knowledge management	5
Sloan Management Review	3
Journal of Management Studies	2
Information Resources Management Journal	2
Journal of the American Society for Information Science& Technology	1
Harvard Business Review	1
Information Strategy, the Executives Journal	1
Long Range Planning	3
European Management Journal	1
British Journal of Educational Psychology	1
ICIS: International Conference on Information Systems	1
Journal of Information Science	1
International Journal of Human Computer Studies	1
Information & Management	1
Journal of Management	1
American Journal of Sociology	1
Journal of International Business Studies	1
Knowledge Management Research & Practice	1
International Journal of Human Resource Management	2

4 Results

The literatures reveal that very few knowledge management theories exhibited the concept of change. The review identified that out of the 105 journals surveyed, 54 (or *51.4%)* appeared to be addressing knowledge sharing primarily from a network perspective (e.g., knowledge work in an intra-organisational network). This category includes all journals that described groups, cross-functional teams, networks and community issues to knowledge sharing activities. In 47 journals *(44.8%),* the literature appeared to outline two other central themes, namely organisational level constructs and the characteristics of knowledge. The former includes literature that reasons directly from the organisational structures, capabilities, competitive advantage, and information technology perspectives, while the latter focuses on taxonomies of knowledge and the different dimensions of knowledge (tacit versus explicit knowledge).

By comparison, in three of the journals (*2.9%*) change was linked to cultural barriers to sharing knowledge, the support of organisational informal networks for a change strategy, and the affect of organisational change on knowledge management strategies. For example, [44] study of organisational knowledge initiatives, change involve mixes of knowledge (tacit and explicit), and was more concerned with the status of technology and how they can best be utilised during a change strategy. At the same time, our review revealed that one journal (*0.9%*) [4] focused on readiness, emphasising on the appropriate readiness for change measures for organisations undergoing a knowledge management initiative.

At an overall level, despite of the term used to denote organisational change, the journals offered no conceptual definition of organisational change. Instead, it was observed that the literature often use the term change 'loosely', and relied on readers commonsense to rationalise the terms that they use, such as 'behavioural change,' [45], 'inability to change people,' [46], and 'knowledge change', [47]. Some authors described change, as a behavioural and cognitive approach in terms of the individual intentions, beliefs or ability to adopt certain behaviours e.g. [48] [49], while some use the term to describe firm-level capabilities as indicators of managing the organisations resources e.g. [28].

There were no significant journals found that drew upon existing change models e.g. [7] [5] [39] [8] and little on the broader aspects of the nature of organisational change. In general, the vast majority of the findings revealed that change readiness constructs could not be determined. Finally, our literature search demonstrate that knowledge sharing literatures have been too preoccupied with informal constructs, namely through 'networks of individual influences as the focal unit of analysis'.

5 Integrating Themes That Influence Knowledge Readiness

In recognition of the challenges of change efforts identified in the knowledge literature this section presents a model that will be used to further analyse the potential role of knowledge sharing and change readiness factors in organisations. To this end, the paper builds on the readiness for change model proposed by [40] five message domains (discrepancy, appropriateness, principle-support, efficacy, and valence). The model as shown in Figure 2 demonstrates the interplay among the [40] readiness constructs to consider the relationships between knowledge sharing and readiness for change related behaviours.

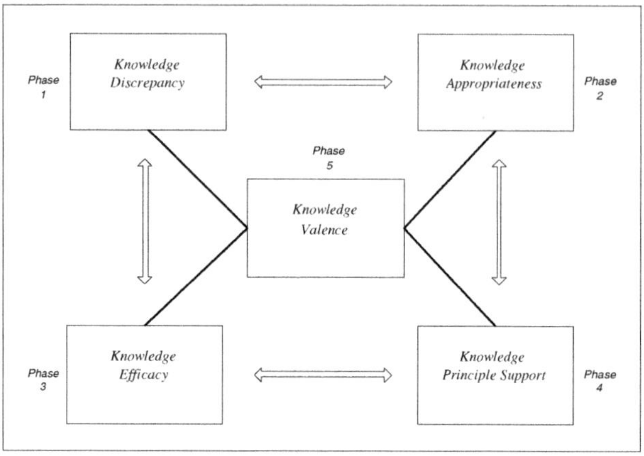

Fig. 2. Model of Knowledge Readiness adapted from Armenakis and colleagues [40]

For the purpose of demonstrating the significance of each readiness construct, Table 2 illustrates the different dimensions and relationship of each construct. Academic and practitioner interpretations of knowledge sharing are captured against the themes identified in Armenakis model to consider whether these theories can be enhanced once they are incorporated.

The model (Figure 2) serves to illuminate micro-level factors and how they influence other factors that support or impede organisational knowledge related change (macro-level). The model illustrated is cyclical, however, for explanatory purposes; it is beneficial to start at *Phase 1*, (*Knowledge Discrepancy*) where change readiness stems from how an organisation conveys a change message. Researchers have observed that people's initial interpretation of change can influence their understanding of it [27] [8]. These interpretations can exert a mediating effect on other individual's readiness. More important, the reactions and relations between organisational culture, subculture and their commitment to change can reflect the circumstance of individual level readiness [20]. However, a change message maybe more effective by determining the work of existing knowledge sharing cultures, hence, 'adapting a knowledge initiative to an existing culture,' as opposed to starting from the beginning[33].

The next phase (*Knowledge Appropriateness*) of the model conveys that socialising change on individuals can be used to communicate the appropriateness of the suggested change. For that reason, at this stage it maybe useful to consider the conditions and environments that facilitate a process of socialising the appropriateness of change readiness in order to engage in dialogue and to form a common language, which can diminish the barriers [50] among multiple individuals with different backgrounds. Furthermore, in the organisational change literature, it is observed that 'short-term results' can help people to understand the appropriateness of a change message more clearly [8].

Table 2. Knowledge and Readiness for Change related themes

Discrepancy (Definition)	Appropriateness (Definition)	Principle Support (Definition	Efficacy (Definition)	Valence (Definition)
Discrepancy is the term used to describe a departure from a current state of the organisation to some desired end state [40]	Appropriateness conveys that the proposed change solution or the end-state intended, should be the appropriate one.	Principle Support conveys that change efforts can fail due to lack of support from key people to support a change initiative.	Efficacy focuses on increasing confidence of individual ability to successfully implement the change	Personal Valence refers to the perceived benefit one may expect as a result of an organisational change [40]
A change process could be guided by establishing the work of existing knowledge sharing cultures as opposed to start from the beginning [33]	Short-term results' have been observed to help people to understand a change message more clearly [8]	[52] argues that when change occurs, there will be instability, in which differences of opinion must be reconciled	Individuals may choose not to participate in a knowledge sharing initiative because individuals are more willing to participate if they believe their contributions will be valuable to others [48] [49]	Individual members must be informed about the benefits of knowledge sharing and given the opportunities to experience the advantages themselves [41] [20] [33]
Change researchers have commonly used this approach in describing the creation of beliefs that a change is necessary [7] [41]	Knowledge sharing initiatives are complex and change is a long-term process, short-term impact will enable employees with understanding of how change is occurring [10] [11]	Change initiatives should relate to the motivation for knowledge sharing [3] [23] [51]	You have to create trust [3] from people if a change process is to succeed.	Employees may not share what they know with other co-members due to insufficient knowledge of the benefits of doing so or because they cannot handle [45]

In *Phase 3 (Knowledge Efficacy)* the model illustrates how individuals are more willing to adopt a change initiative if they consider their personal contributions will be valuable to others [48] [49]. It reveals the key role that individuals play in the change process and the sources of resistance, such as outcome expectancy, self-efficacy and inertia can often delay the cycle of change [7]. The notion of trust and organisational incentives can however motivate readiness and may lead to organisational members to support a change [3].

In the course of change, 'key people' (such as organisational managers, leaders) may not be inclined to participate in a change initiative. This issue is highlighted in *Phase 4*, (*Knowledge Principle Support*) which illustrate how key people to a certain degree can dictate the actions, behaviours and attitudes of other organisational member's decision to participate in a change initiative and hence, influence their own/others readiness.

The final aspect of the model illuminates the perceived benefits of change (*Knowledge Valence*). Individuals assess the potential impact of the change, in terms of how it will benefit them. For example, despite the large investments in knowledge management systems, such change may not be adequate on their own, because individuals may not be ready to take part or share what they know with other co-members due to insufficient knowledge of the perceived benefits of doing so [49]. It is often argued that the benefits of such change initiatives should be internalised through action and practice, to become a part of the individual's tacit knowledge base, in the form of 'technical know-how' [50]. Change experts argue that individual members must be informed about the benefits of change and provided the opportunities to experience the advantages themselves, if not this can delay the implementation of the change initiative [8] [39] [5].

6 Discussion and Future Research Directions

This paper is based on a literature survey of 105 scholarly academic journals in the area of knowledge sharing research from 1994 to 2009 with keywords salient to knowledge sharing studies to explore current thinking about organisational change issues. The review includes search for journals that conceptually define and explore organisational change, including any that consider readiness for change. The analysis in this paper confirms that while a continuum of research in knowledge sharing address the role of motivational and informal-level factors (particularly research on intra-knowledge sharing networks) there exists little conceptual definition of both individual and organisational level change. The findings of the literature survey also reported that there is a lack of direct evidence or theory to exploring the phenomena and relationship between organisational knowledge initiatives and organisational readiness for change. It was observed that the literature often use the term change loosely, or change was used in general terms, and relied on readers commonsense to rationalise the terms that they use.

Given the significant challenges to effective knowledge initiatives in organisations the paper validates recent theoretical calls for a stronger focus on micro-level foundations [13] [14] [53] Following these similar models, we have attempted to extend our knowledge towards understanding individual perceptions of readiness for change and its effects on knowledge related initiatives in organisations. The paper further contributes to the knowledge literature by introducing the notion that readiness for change is an organisational mechanism that can provoke a transition to existing knowledge related initiatives between the individual level knowledge workers, where knowledge resides, and the organisational level, where both knowledge and change can be obtained. Therefore, the central assumption we make in this paper is that since knowledge sharing (creation, and use of knowledge) is a phenomenon inspired and executed through individual and group level processes, research needs to consider commencing from micro-level explanations in order to achieve a clear understanding of individual readiness for change.

Our proposed model serves to illuminate micro-level factors and how they influence other factors that support or impede knowledge related change-factors. Five-novel knowledge factors were constructed using the Armenakis [40] five-message domains. The model may provide valuable guidance in identifying a set of essential readiness for change actions necessary to an organisation and individual's knowledge initiative.

This paper contends that further conceptual and theoretical issues for reconciling knowledge related and organisational change initiatives are in need of future research. Some possible future research questions include: (1) How do organisational environments influence readiness for change on existing knowledge work? (2) What readiness for change mechanisms can influence the 'role of individual's motivations' to share knowledge? (3) How do individual's perceptions of readiness affect the 'adoption phase' of a knowledge related initiative? (4) How do managers and leaders create a state of organisational readiness for change to knowledge sharing initiatives? More work is needed to explore these benefits of organisational change mechanisms on knowledge work in order to determine individual-level characteristics for change readiness. The work presented in this paper, may provide a further step towards this direction.

7 Conclusion and Limitations

In the organisational change and knowledge sharing literature recognition of high failure of change efforts is said to be associated to the organisations lack of understanding of how to manage readiness for change. Typically, the inability to change people's beliefs, attitudes, and intentions restrains all other aspects to managing change. We argued that change and the inability to change, in the knowledge literature are often viewed as macro-level phenomena and what constitutes as a change facilitator is perceived in terms of the role of informal factors in shaping the appropriate change effort. However, the paper reinforces the argument that while the understanding of informal and organisational level factors holds an important place in the knowledge management domain, such macro-level explanations maybe enriched by consideration of the individual level change. Knowledge management research in general has yet to fully engage the notion of readiness for change on the role of knowledge sharing initiatives in organisational work processes.

It should be noted that the study is subject to limitations. The first, in particular, is the limitation in the number or volume of the literatures obtained. Future research might provide larger volume and variation of journals to explore the area. However, we trust the volume of the literature obtained in this study is of sufficient number, and that it should not deter the fact that the notions of organisational change, and above all change readiness has not been fully explored in knowledge research. Next, since this study is limited to the investigation of knowledge sharing, future research, may establish the relationship between other knowledge activities, such as knowledge-creation, and knowledge-work behaviours or virtual-knowledge teamwork, based on the role of organisational change readiness contributions. Finally, findings from this study may encourage fruitful opportunities to increase the limited store of empirical investigations on readiness for change to organisational knowledge sharing initiatives.

References

1. Martensson, M.A.: Critical Review of Knowledge Management as a Management Tool. Journal of Knowledge Management 4, 204–216 (2000)
2. Grant, R.M.: Toward a Knowledge-Based Theory of the Firm. Strategic Management Journal 17, 109–122 (1996)

3. Staples, S.S., Webster, J.: Exploring the effects of Trust, task Interdependence and Virtualness on Knowledge Sharing in Teams. Information Systems Journal 18, 617–640 (2008)
4. Holt, D.T., Bartczak, S.E., Clark, S.W., Trent, M.R.: The Development of an Instrument to Measure Readiness for Knowledge Management. Knowledge Management Research and Practice 5, 75–92 (2007)
5. Armenakis, A.A., Harris, S.G., Mossholder, K.W.: Creating Readiness for Organisational Change. Human Relations 46, 681–703 (1993)
6. Judge, T.A., Thoresen, C.J.: Managerial Coping with Organisational Change: A Dispositional Perspective. Journal of Applied Psychology 84, 107–122 (1999)
7. George, J.M., Jones, G.R.: Towards a Process Model of Individual Change in Organisations. Human Relations 54, 419–444 (2001)
8. Kotter, J.: Leading Change: Why Transformation Efforts Fail. Harvard Business Review (March/April 1995)
9. Backer, T.: Assessing and enhancing readiness for change: Implications for Technology Transfer. In: Backer, T., David, S., Soucy, D. (eds.) Reviewing the Behavioural Science Knowledge Base on Technology Transfer, pp. 21–41 (1995)
10. Hislop, D.: Mission Impossible? Communicating and Sharing Knowledge via Information Technology. Journal of Information Technology 17, 165–177 (2002)
11. Cross, R., Borgatti, S.P., Parker, A.: Making Invisible Work Visible: Using Social Network Analysis to Support Strategic Collaboration. California Management Review 44 (2002)
12. McDermott, R.: How Information Technology Inspired, but Cannot Deliver Knowledge Management. California Management Review 41, 103–117 (1999)
13. Foss, N., Husted, K., Michailova, S.: Governing Knowledge Sharing in Organisations: Level of Analysis, Governance Mechanisms, and Research Directions. Journal of Management Studies 47, 455–482 (2009)
14. Abell, P., Felin, T., Foss, N.: Building Microfoundations for the Routines, Capabilities and Performance Link. Managerial and Decision Economics 29, 489–502 (2008)
15. Quintas, P.: Managing Knowledge in a New Century. In: Little, S., Quintas, P., Ray, T. (eds.) Managing Knowledge: An Essential Reader. Sage Publications, London (2002)
16. Teece, D.J.: Capturing Value from Knowledge Assets. California Management Review 40, 55–76 (1998)
17. Kogut, B., Zander, U.: Knowledge of the Firm, Combinative Capabilities and the Replication of Technology. Organisation Science 3, 383–397 (1992)
18. Carlisle, Y.: Strategic Thinking and Knowledge Management. In: Little, S., Quintas, P., Ray, T. (eds.) Managing Knowledge, The Open University, Sage Publications, First Published (2002)
19. Nonaka, I., Takeuchi, H.: The Knowledge Creating Company: How Japanese Companies Create The Dynamics of Innovation. Oxford University Press, New York (1995)
20. De Long, D., Fahey, L.: Diagnosing Cultural Barriers to Knowledge Management. Academy of Management Executive 14 (2000)
21. Fullan, M.: Leading in a Culture of Change. Jossey-Bass, San Francisco (2001)
22. Felin, T., Spender, J.C.: An Exchange of Ideas about Knowledge Governance: Seeking First Principles and Microfoundations. In: Foss, N., Snejina, M. (eds.) Knowledge Governance: A Multi- Disciplinary Perspective, pp. 247–271. Oxford University Press, Oxford (2008)
23. Osterloh, M., Frost, J., Frey, B.S.: The Dynamics of Motivation in New Organisational Forms. International Journal of The Economics of Business 9, 61–77 (2002)

24. Kelloway, K., Barling, J.: Knowledge Work as Organizational Behaviour. International Journal of Management Reviews 2, 287–304 (2000)
25. Hansen, M.T., Mors, M.L., Lovas, B.: Knowledge Sharing in Organisations: Multiple Networks, Multiple Phases. Academy of Management Journal 48, 776–793 (2005)
26. Lichtenstein, S., Hunter, A.: Receiver Influences on Knowledge Sharing. Paper presented at the 13th European Conference on Information Systems. Regensburg, Germany (2005)
27. Rousseau, D.M., Tojoriwala, S.A.: What's a Good Reason to Change? Motivated Reasoning and Social Accounts in Promoting Organisational Change. Journal of Applied Psychology 84, 514–528 (1999)
28. Zack, M.: Managing Codified Knowledge. Sloan Management Review 40, 45–58 (1999)
29. Bate, P., Robert, G.: Knowledge management and communities of practice in the private sector: lessons for modernizing the NHS in England and Wales. Public Administration 80, 643–663 (2002)
30. Cohen, W., Levinthal, D.: Absorptive Capacity: A New Perspective on Learning and Innovation. Administrative Science Quarterly 35, 128–152 (1990)
31. Rogers, E.M., Medina, U.E., Rivera, M.A., Wiley, J.C.: Complex Adaptive Systems and the Diffusion of Innovations, The Innovation Journal. The Public Sector Innovation Journal 10, article 29 (2005)
32. Davenport, T., Jarvenpaa, S., Beers, M.: Improving Knowledge Work Processes. Sloan Management Review 37, 53–65 (1996)
33. McDermott, R., O'Dell, C.: Overcoming Cultural Barriers to Sharing Knowledge. Journal of Knowledge Management 5, 76–85 (2001)
34. Reagans, R., McEvily, B.: Network structure and knowledge transfer: The effects of cohesion and range. Administrative Science Quarterly 48, 240–267 (2003)
35. Tsai, W.: Social Structure of Coopetition within a Multiunit Organisation: Coordination, Competition, and intra-organisational Knowledge Sharing. Organisation Science 13, 179–190 (2002)
36. Armenakis, A.A., Bedeian, A.G.: Organisational Change: A Review of Theory and Research in the 1990s. Journal of Management 25, 293–315 (1999)
37. Quintas, P., Lefrere, P., Jones, G.: Knowledge management: a Strategic Agenda. Long Range Planning 30, 385–399 (1997)
38. Worren, N., Ruddle, K., Moore, K.: From Organisational Development to Change Management: The Emergence of a New Profession. Journal of Applied Behavioural Science 35, 273–286 (1999)
39. Prochaska, J.M., Prochaska, J.O., Levesque, D.A.: A Transtheoretical Approach to Change Organisations. Administration and Policy in Mental Health 28 (2001)
40. Armenakis, A.A., Harris, S.G.: Crafting a Change Message to Create Transformational Readiness. Journal of Organisational Change Management 15, 169–183 (2002)
41. Lehman, W.E.K., Greener, J.M., Simpson, D.D.: Assessing Organisational Readiness for Change. Journal of Substance Abuse Treatment 22, 197–209 (2002)
42. Eby, L.T., Adams, D.M., Russell, E.A., Gaby, S.H.: Perceptions of Organisational Readiness for Change: Factors Related to Employees Reactions to Implementation of Team Based Selling. Human Relations 53, 419–442 (2000)
43. Webster, J., Watson, R.T.: Analysing the Past to Prepare for the Future: Writing a Literature Review. MIS Quarterly 26, xiii–xxiii(2002)
44. Bloodgood, J.M., Salisbury, W.D.: Understanding the Influence of Organisational Change Strategies on Information Technology and Knowledge Management Strategies. Decision Support Systems 31, 55–69 (2001)

45. Scarbrough, H., Swan, J.: Explaining the diffusion of knowledge management: the role of fashion British. Journal of Management 12, 3–12 (2001)
46. Leidner, D., Alavi, M., Kayworth, T.: The role of Culture in Knowledge management: A case study of two Global Firms. The International Journal of Electronic Collaboration 2, 17–40 (2006)
47. Argote, L., Ingram, P., Levine, J.M., Moreland, R.L.: Knowledge Transfer in Organisations: Learning from the Experience of Others. Organisational, Behaviour and Human Decision Processes 82, 1–8 (2000)
48. Bock, G.W., Zmud, R.W., Kim, Y.G., Lee, J.N.: Behavioral Intention Formation in Knowledge Sharing: Examining the roles of Extrinsic Motivators, Social Psychological Forces and Organisational Climate. MIS Quarterly 29, 87–111 (2005)
49. Cabrera, A., Cabrera, E.: Knowledge Sharing Dilemmas. Organisation Studies 23, 687–710 (2002)
50. Nonaka, I., Toyama, R., Konno, N.: SECI, Ba and Leadership: a Unified Model of Dynamic Knowledge Creation. Long Range Planning 33, 5–34 (2000)
51. Hendriks, P.: Why Share Knowledge? The Influence of ICT on the Motivation for Knowledge Sharing. Knowledge and Process Management 6, 91–100 (1999)
52. Fullan, M.: The Change Leader. Educational Leadership 59, 16–20 (2002)
53. Foss, N.: Alternative Research Strategies in the Knowledge Movement: from Macro Bias to Micro-Foundations and Multi-level Explanation. European Management Review 6, 16–28 (2009)

Inferring Causal Interpretations of Change-Readiness Using Causal-Models: A Knowledge-Based Perspective

Shushma Patel, Khalid Samara, and Dilip Patel

Centre for Information Systems and Management (CISM)
The Faculty of Business, Department of Informatics,
London South Bank University, London SE1 OAA
{shushma,samarakb,dilip}@lsbu.ac.uk

Abstract. The ability to understand the conditions in which humans make causal judgements continues to arouse debate from cognitive science, philosophy, and even the domain of computer science. While for most organisations, change is a necessary impetus to sustainability, it is difficult to directly infer cause and affect relationships on human readiness without understanding how humans arrive causal inferences during a complex change situation. To explore the causal interpretations of human readiness-for change the research applies the systems thinking approach, utilising causal models to analyse the cause and effect of human readiness. The research contributes to a knowledge-based perspective examining the various factors effecting readiness-feedback, and how readiness-for change knowledge is received, and processed. The paper demonstrates the application of causal models to interpret the role of human readiness through a case study on the infectious outbreak of Clostridium Difficile (C. *difficile*). Then we propose a theory of readiness-for change through the lenses of Systems Thinking into a Knowledge Based Reasoning Framework.

Keywords: Readiness-for change, causal inferences, systems thinking, causal-loop diagrams, organisational change.

1 Introduction

The ability to understand the conditions in which humans make causal judgements continues to arouse debate from cognitive science, philosophy, and even the domain of computer science. It forms the bases for researchers to comprehend how humans develop inferences from their own environment and observations that can inform the consequences of human actions. Inferences are a cognitive process in which the 'human-sensory' will deduce from connecting causal relations determined by a set of cause and effect occurrences in a given situation [1]. Scholars especially in the field of social cognition have shown that human judgements are often inferred from various social cognitive factors [2]. For example, the ways in which humans make inferences maybe influenced by past-interpretations of similar change events. In addition, there is a growing body of theory, who claim that the accessibility of past interpretations has causal effects on human readiness and openness for change [3].

In the present research, the interest is on how one can draw causal inferences of human change readiness. The notion of change readiness is described as the initial

M. Gusev and P. Mitrevski (Eds.): ICT Innovations 2010, CCIS 83, pp. 27–39, 2011.

part of the natural cycle of change [4]. Readiness is a cognitive-state and a necessary antecedent to behaviours of either resistance or support for a change effort [5]. It insists on clear micro-foundations, in that it requires people to focus their attention in a state of action readiness for change [3].

While for most organisations change is a necessary impetus to sustainability, it is difficult to directly infer cause and affect relationships on human readiness without understanding how humans arrive causal inferences during a complex change situation. To interpret the causal structure of human readiness-for change, the research applies the systems thinking approach, utilising causal models to analyse the cause and effect of human readiness. The paper contributes to a knowledge-based perspective and establishes through the various causal models how readiness-for change and individuals knowledge behaviour, converge on similar dimensions affecting issues of how organisation can enact readiness in individuals. It amplifies the various factors effecting readiness feedback, and how the readiness-for change knowledge is received, and processed.

The paper unfolds as follows: Section 2 begins with a discussion on the various theoretical perspectives on readiness for change. Section 3 presents a discussion on the implication of the cause and effect relationships on human readiness for change. Section 4 demonstrates the role of readiness through utilising Causal Loop Diagrams on a real-life case study. Section 5 examines the various systems conditions that enable organisation and human readiness-for change. Next, as a means of accomplishing the purpose of the paper, we propose a framework that serves to clarify and interpret micro-macro level factors and the cause and effect influences related to readiness for change. We conclude by discussing the contributions of this paper and directions for future research.

2 Definition of Readiness for Change

Change usually develops a fuzzy, unknown and dynamic situation. In fact, the most notable characteristics recognised in the organisation today, is the fact that they are moving at a pace faster than the frameworks that govern them and, also they are amplified by non-linear cause-effect relationships, and time delays [6] which are governed by feedback among various macro and micro level agents [7]. These factors can lead to issues of how to manage human readiness-for change.

Theory and research on readiness-for change focuses on the initial change preparation, capturing the knowledge, which resides within individuals, and beginning the moving process [8] [9] [10] [11]. Behavioural change researchers have generally employed this method in describing the creation of attitudes that change is needed [4]. [12], defines readiness as a reflection of an organisational member's beliefs, intentions and attitudes regarding the extent to which an individual is disposed to adopt and accept a plan to purposefully alter the status quo. Readiness relies when the human aspect of change is known and handled effectively [13]. Indeed, the fundamental nature of readiness is the interplay between the behaviours and actions of an individual and the organisational influences on that individual. It relies largely on the motivation, and the characteristics of groups of individuals in the form of cultures, who play a key role in the factors which lead to change.

Readiness can be considered as a cognitive process that comes into play as an indication of willingness or openness to engage in a particular behaviour [14]. [5], describes readiness as an initial preparation for individuals to begin the moving process. [4], described readiness as a significant part of underlying initiation of a change intervention that can alter an individual's readiness. [11] reinforced this point of view, and argues that it is important to create a sense of urgency so that individuals are ready to change. With no sense of urgency, [11] insist that change will not occur.

The literature also indicates that readiness for change maybe explored by additional change factors, namely, (a) context (b) individual-attributes, (c) process, and (d) content. Researchers have placed considerable emphasis on the role of context, for providing essential explanations of cause and effect relationships [8]. They maintain that the connection between the causal factors and their effects is not predetermined, but relies on the context within which the different causal factors operate [9] [10]. The focus of individual-attributes is on micro level individuals. Such micro level explanations are considered too complex in determining because causality among the relationships between humans or micro social processes is harder to establish [5] [9]. Furthermore, researchers argue that when a change process takes place the individual level behaviours often determine the outcome of the change process and the stability of the content being changed [9]. Writers in the readiness for change field, such as [12], claim that these four factors can serve as essential mediators for human readiness.

3 Causal Interpretations of Change-Readiness

The definitions of readiness and the consequences of change are likely to reveal a much more complex image of human judgements, needs and attitudes. Research has largely accepted that change efforts and human readiness are in fact causally connected [3]. In addition, a readiness perspective of change can help clarify what is often problematic on the perceived complexity of human causal reasoning during a change situation. Indeed, the absence of knowledge on human causal reasoning can give rise to a fundamental restraint on the existing change process. The feedback process implied by this problem is summarised in figure 1, as a positive causal link (and *R* in the middle indicates that the loop is reinforcing) in which the two nodes move in the same direction. Accordingly, an increase in pressure to deal with organisational change can exert pressure on human readiness-for change.

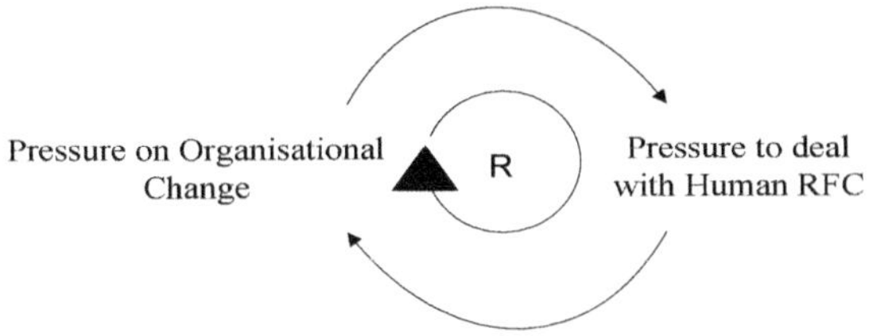

Fig. 1. Reinforcing Loop Pressure on Organisational Change

The concept of human readiness is generally an important source of knowledge, that is, it attempts to expose individual's commitment and receptiveness to change. At the same time, different forms of social patterns and the many levels of cognition can make the precise causal behaviours difficult to observe and structure. This is a phenomenon especially relevant, because very often behaviour differs from excepted behaviours [7]. Further, the cause of change can have a multidimensional effect on human readiness. For instance, it is recognised that people use pre-existing schemas to perceive, interpret and make sense of organisational environments [3]. Change researchers contend that individuals may have preconceived notions regarding the degree to which the organisation is ready for change [13] [3]. Such preconceived notions of readiness are also transmittable to other members in the change phenomena [15]. This means that new information may have little or no effect on their existing schemas because a negative experience maybe shaped by previous perceptions of change. For example, pre-existing schemas can be associated to numerous behavioural components by which a range of negative or positive emotions, such as trust, inertia, and dissatisfaction can ultimately determine the readiness process [5].

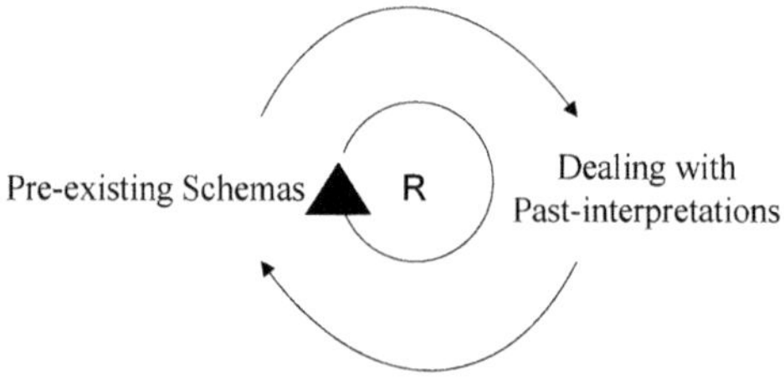

Fig. 2. Reinforcing Loop on Pre-existing Schemas

The different possible reactions to readiness-for change that can occur from previous experience of change is illustrated in figure 2.The implication of this for the issue of human readiness raises the question of how humans arrive causal inferences during a change situation, and how do we exploit this knowledge in a more meaningful way while taking account of the different system levels toward exploring the intricate nature of human-readiness. The present research considers causal inference from a Systems Thinking point of view. Systems' thinking is an interdisciplinary approach to describing and understanding the existence and the importance of systems [6]. For this purpose, the study proposes a systems thinking perspective of readiness-for change, one that can interpret the causal and multifaceted role of human readiness. Without an awareness of systems can lead to an incomplete representation between the different system levels, such as the interactions between people's apprehensions and the organisation plan for change readiness.

3.1 Knowledge Based Perspective

As well as adopting a systems thinking view of readiness-for change, in this study we also incorporate with it a knowledge-based perspective. While the notion of readiness for change has continued to take place in the change literature, it is however a concept that has not yet been fully explored or understood in the knowledge literature. A knowledge-based perspective converges on issues, such as how readiness for change knowledge is acquired, interpreted, and culminated by individuals. Indeed, the way in which readiness knowledge is received and processed can have a causal influence on the individual's readiness-for change.

Prior studies show that during a change effort organisations are often inundated with knowledge, some which are harder to pin-down than others [16]. What is often implicit in these arguments is that much of organisation knowledge is constrained at the level of individuals [17]. In fact, several studies have expressed that even under the best of circumstances, knowledge is formative, and socially constructed, akin to high level of 'autonomy, complexity, and uncertainty', which may channel knowledge work, time and energy in different ways [18] [19].

At the same time, it is argued that in the course of complex change, while individuals need for information increases, both the quantity and quality of existing information often declines [15]. Indeed, individuals are likely to infer from other individuals to share information, typically through reliance on informal practice to make sense of what is happing, leading to more complex understandings of any change effort [15]. This view is important because it accentuates the causality between how knowledge is actually executed from peoples 'collective knowledge' and the way in which information of readiness is planned and instituted.

4 Case Study

The case study herein describes the infectious outbreak of Clostridium Difficile (C. *difficile*) at the Maidston and Tunbridge Wells NHS Trust [23]. The case study will be used to analyse and to demonstrate how causal models and systems thinking can be used to explore and interpret the *causal role* of human readiness for change.

4.1 Infectious Outbreak of Clostridium Difficile

In the period between April 2004 and September 2006 there were approximately 90 deaths reported at the Maidstone and Tunbridge Wells NHS Trust [20]. The main cause of these deaths was a result of an infectious outbreak of Clostridium Difficile (C. *difficile*). The sources of the outbreak at the hospital include a myriad of factors from a combination of management, teams-work and leadership factors on infections to a decline in clinical monitoring of patient care [20]. For example, reports from the Healthcare Commission identified that there was insufficient knowledge of the procedures and processes of C. *difficile* [21]. This accounted for high level of disregard of patient care, which in turn reflected on the quality of decision-making and a lack of clarity about the individual roles and responsibilities [20].

A further report from, [20] [21] describes that many of the factors associated to the outbreak was prompted by a lack of change management procedures. It could also be speculated that poor change procedures manifest behaviour of clinician's readiness for change within the trust. For example, [20] reported that while change was frequently carried out there was an absence of communication and active involvement with consultants in decision-making. Based on the aforementioned discussions the following sections propose the use of Causal Loop Diagrams (CLD) as a tool for readiness for change investigation.

4.1.1 Causal Loop Diagrams of Human Readiness for Change

Causal Loop Diagrams (CLD) is used to build mental models of a real world and to examine how it constructs dynamic behaviour over time [6]. These tools allow to explore change (and human readiness), which is more complex to observe in the real world. They are widely employed and are effective at revealing the reasons behind an actual phenomenon. It has certain advantages, as [6] puts it, "by linking the past to the present by depicting how present environments take place, and projecting the present into alternative futures under a variety of conditions".

For example, figure 3 depicts the causal relationship of C. *difficile* outbreak and the interrelated readiness for change factors. The arrows indicate the causal relationships. The signs (*S* or *O*) at the arrowheads indicate that the effect is related to the cause. First the inadequate knowledge of C. *difficile* outbreaks is affected by change to improve knowledge of disease-infected outbreaks. Further, pressure to communicate readiness for change, which can effect decisions to manage people's attitudes and behaviours. Meanwhile, as inadequate knowledge of C. *difficile* increases so does low morale, putting pressure on human readiness and, simultaneously, increasing risk on clinical errors. Further, as inadequate knowledge of C. *difficile* increases, so does the pressure on clinical management and poor reviews of patients, at the same time, diminishing the quality of decision-making.

The need to increase the readiness knowledge of disease-infected outbreaks is a key factor to enhance the readiness of individual change beliefs and attitudes. Figure 4 shows the causal relationships and the pressure to increase the readiness knowledge of disease-infected outbreaks. Such a knowledge base will demand readiness to increase awareness of C. *difficile* outbreak. Any change initiative may however involve time and delay because of the multiple emotional reactions involved during change. As demand to improve readiness knowledge of outbreaks increases, workers inadequate knowledge of C. *difficile* outbreak diminishes having a positive influence on managing attitudes of readiness. Also the knowledge gap between clinical workers is eventually reduced. The knowledge gap reduction can also have a positive effect on clinical workers discrepancy and inconsistency beliefs of change, which drives the process of individual change [3]. The quality of the clinical decisions made also has a positive influence on the quality of patient care. Past interpretations of change (pre-existing schemas) could also have a positive effect on the quality of patient care. These constrains play a causal role on the individuals work performance, at the same time exerting pressure on the quality of decision-making and the perceived benefits of change.

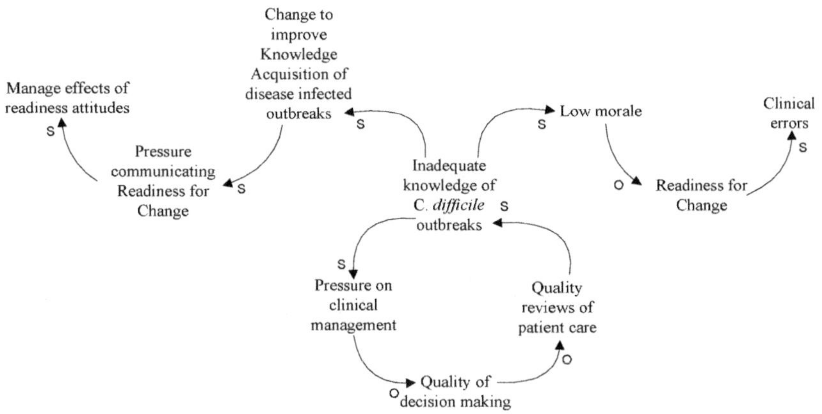

Fig. 3. The Causal Relationship of C. *difficile* outbreak

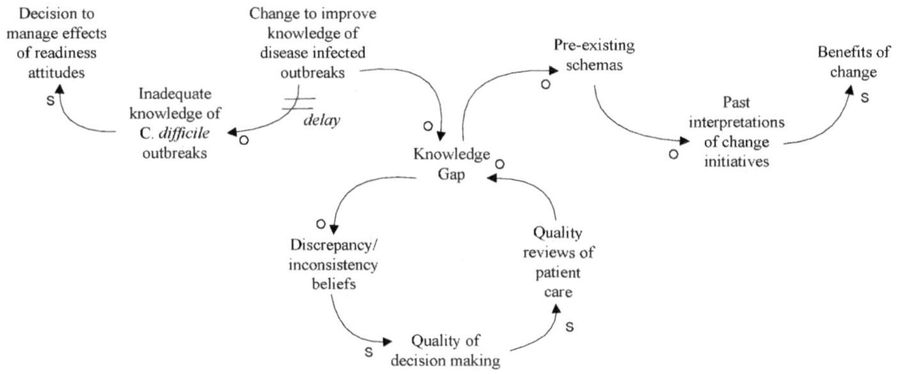

Fig. 4. The Causal Relationship of C. *difficile* outbreak

5 A Systems Thinking Perspective of Readiness for Change

In this section, we examine the various system conditions that enable organisation and human readiness for change using [7] Mental Data Base Model. Knowledge and readiness for change perspectives can be perceived as congregates of organisational change that is, affecting issues of how to enact readiness on individuals toward a change initiative. One way of illustrating the causal role of human readiness to bring together a knowledge and readiness perspective can be described through [7] as shown in figure 5, who propose a theoretical framework of three overlapping categories to articulate and unify knowledge of different systems. According to [22] argue that management and social sciences have in past excessively limited themselves to measured data and have neglected the "far richer and more informative body of information that exists in the knowledge and experience of those in the active, working world". The unshaded sections of the model represents knowledge of systems into three dimensions to exhibit the strengths and limitations of mental models.

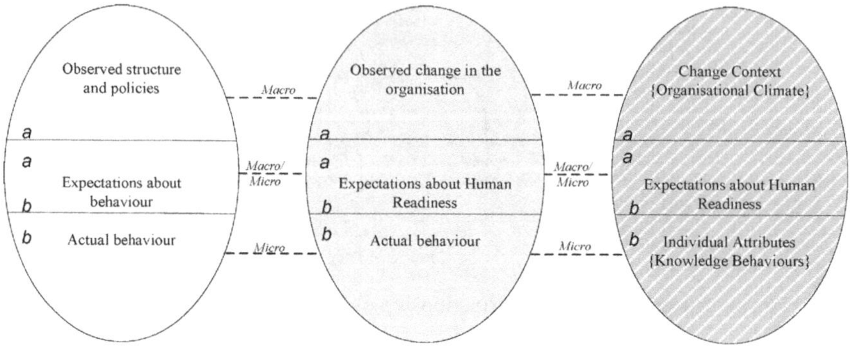

Fig. 5. Mental Data Base adapted from Forrester [7]

Each dimension however, is more than just making mental models explicit but rather how to understand the deeper multiple causes of systems and systems readiness. The observed structures and policies in the first top unshaded area of the model, describes the fundamental parts of the system. It identifies the way in which policies govern and structure the flow of knowledge, the key influences upon it, and the extent to which they control decisions. Such decisions about who controls the system can also be compared at the macro-level. The policies and structures associated with macro-level practices are heavily embedded in the organisation context and cultural environment that can determine the ideas for change. The expectation about behaviours in the middle area of the model is based on the influences of the observed structures and policies. This means that policies in the top section can change to accomplish expected behaviours that are associated in the middle section of the model.

The middle section are also examples of both macro and micro level constraints, because expectations of how behaviours should be changed in the system will require varying degrees of change in the top section to achieve the behaviour observed at the micro-level. That is, the impact on expectations of a change at the macro level also requires a great deal of human readiness, or micro-level considerations determined by different attributes of individuals. [7] puts it, that actual systems behaviour differs from expected behaviours in which discrepancies exist within a causal boundary *b-b*/*a-a*. Indeed, this is a phenomenon not new from scholars both in the knowledge and organisational change field were linkages between actual behaviours, and the required change initiative should match preferred human and organisational readiness.

As [7], persist that most initiatives like policies and structures, lead not to the expected behaviours, but to the actual behaviours. That is, discrepancies often exist not within the boundaries of *a-a*, at the macro level, but within the boundaries of *b-b*, were micro level behaviours are often fuzzy and unpredictable [7]. For instance, in the case study example of the C. *difficile* outbreak, while there may have been clinical protocols in place, associated with disease-infected outbreaks, the lack of transparency about the dynamics of actual behaviours in the trust may have influenced patient safety. Further a key factor that is manifest is the performance outcomes of the organisation and the attributes of individuals that influenced the outbreak. Therefore, the evaluation of readiness and stages of change, not only includes the process of change to deliver the content into the boundaries of the organisation. It also includes determining the actual behaviours within the boundaries, embedded in the interpretations and attributes of change. Based on this discussion, the next section proposes a framework for assessing human causal inferences of readiness for change.

6 A Causal Knowledge Based Reasoning Framework

The causal-readiness theory that is supported in this study embodies fundamental assumptions about human causal inferences of readiness for change, in that: (a) people are able to make predictive inferences from a cause to a probable effect, thus people may have strong interpretation of change, and a causal link is related to their interpretations, which in turn can influence their understanding of it; and (b) while certain cultures are often referred to as the power base of the organisation, such social interdependence and knowledge-bases on readiness (who believe in the same cause and effect relationship), can often show a degree of influence over other peoples interpretations concerning change; and (c) also such strong causal influences, can impact on whether a new change has the characteristics to yield more value over currently available alternatives. In addition, these types of inferences have important, context, content, process, and individual level differences. Four of these components were identified by [12]. The interplay of these components defines the readiness for change constraints that may emerge during an organisation change [12]. For the purpose of demonstrating the value of each of these, we have integrated them into a Framework through the lenses of Systems Thinking [7]. We now consider each of these readiness components individually.

6.1 Individual Attributes to Readiness

Individual-attributes are defined as micro level characteristics of those people, who are required to undergo change. However, systems are not linear chains of cause and effect. Rather, there are different degrees of complexity in which different individual-attributes can lead to difficulty in the system, where cause and effect is often distant in time and in space [7]. Indeed, within a causal domain, micro level effects can cause delay, or distant behaviours are maybe different, or unknown. It is further asserted that within these complex systems different individual-attributes or networks placed in the same environment tend to behave in a similar way. For instance, group information processing of individual-readiness is said to be shaped by the readiness of others [5]. Furthermore, much of the organisation knowledge is proscribed at the level of individuals [17] [26]. This implies that as individual characteristics and personality from previous knowledge becomes well developed, they become more complex, in that they exert further attributes, and more difficult to change [3] [26].

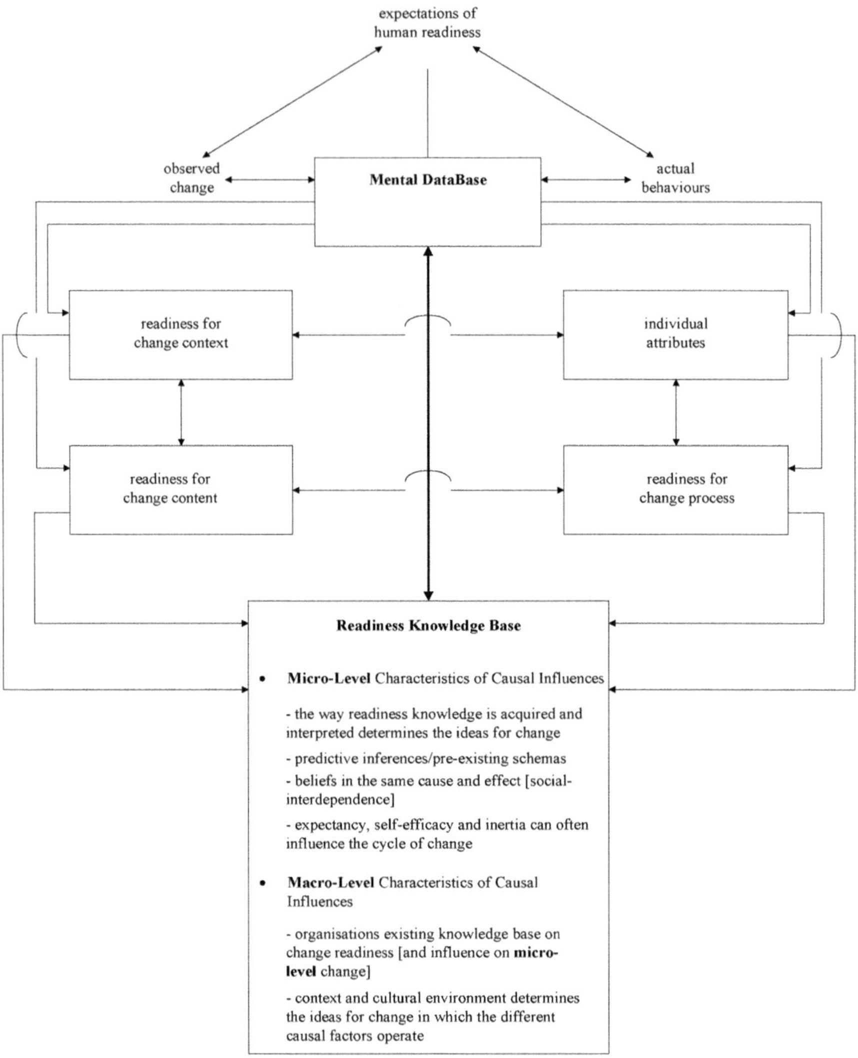

Fig. 6. Causal Knowledge Based Reasoning Framework

6.2 Readiness-for Change Content

The contents of change are defined as the proposed ideas or the attributes being changed (i.e. what is being changed). The change content that is advocated here is the change in people's interpretations and perceptions toward the change content. Such factors can determine the speed and pace in which the change content will take its final form. People's interpretation of change and the causal influences related to their interpretations can also influence their adoption behaviours. According to [23] views the process of adoption as a type of behavioural change. That is, the process of adopting change is mainly linked to individual beliefs, associated with the perceived benefits of the new practice, and whether a new practice has the characteristics to yield more value over currently available alternatives. In fact, some scholars have identified that factors that drives an individual to engage in a behaviour can be based on the number of individuals in the social system already engaged in the behaviour [24]. This is consistent with [25], who describes the diffusion process as a lengthened process, in which a few members of a social system at first adopts an innovation, eventually more individuals adopt until eventually the remaining individuals adopt the new idea.

6.3 Readiness-for Change Process

A readiness for change process specifies the steps followed during a change initiative. It is defined as the means by which individuals are engaged in the process of initiating a change. The process involved during a change initiative has a strong influence over whether individuals decide to or not to take part in this process. This can stem from the perceived benefits [26] of the change process, or key people who can dictate the actions, behaviours and attitudes of other organisational member's decision, so that certain predictive interpretations are minimised [8] [9] [10].

7 Conclusions

The ability to understand the conditions in which humans make causal judgements is a fundamental part of individual's readiness for change. In the present study, the interest is on how one can draw causal inferences on human change readiness. The study proposed a systems thinking perspective of change, one that can interpret the causal and complex role of human readiness. Without an awareness of systems can lead to a lack of representation between the different system levels, such as the interactions between people's apprehensions and the organisation preparation for change. The paper also contributes to a knowledge-based perspective. Indeed, the way in which knowledge of readiness is acquired and processed in the organisation can equally affect issues, such as people's interpretation of change which can influence their readiness behaviour. However, knowledge research in general has yet to fully engage the notion of readiness for change in organisational work processes.

We argued that readiness for change might be enriched by consideration of micro level change. In fact, organisation knowledge is often constrained at the micro level which in essence is akin to high level of social 'autonomy, complexity, and uncertainty'. These factors can constrain a readiness for change process, because of strong causal influences, related to deeper social inter-dependences which in turn can exert a mediating effect on other individual's readiness. We proposed a readiness framework that serves to clarify and interpret both micro-macro level factors and the cause and effect influences related to readiness for change. The framework presented demonstrated several important components for guiding readiness, namely readiness for change context, individual attributes, readiness for change content and readiness for change process.

The paper shows how one could draw such inferences to explore and interpret both the role of human and organisation readiness through utilising Causal Loop Diagrams, which we applied on a real-life case study. Findings from this study may encourage researchers to explore the limited store of empirical investigations on readiness for change through a knowledge based and systems thinking perspective for different types of organisational change.

References

1. Pearl, J.: Reasoning with Cause and Effect. Artificial Intelligence Magazine 23, 95–112 (2002)
2. Bandura, A.: Social Cognitive Theory: An Agentic Perspective. Annual Review Psychology 52, 1–26 (2001)
3. George, J.M., Jones, G.R.: Towards a Process Model of Individual Change in Organisations. Human Relations 54, 419–444 (2001)
4. Prochaska, J.M., Prochaska, J.O., Levesque, D.A.: A Transtheoretical Approach to Change Organisations. Administration and Policy in Mental Health and Mental Health Research 28, 247–261 (2001)
5. Lehman, W.E.K., Greener, J.M., Simpson, D.D.: Assessing Organisational Readiness for Change. Journal of Substance Abuse Treatment 22, 197–209 (2002)
6. Forrester, J.W.: Systems Dynamics, Systems Thinking, and Soft OR. Systems Dynamics Review 10, 245–256 (2006)
7. Forrester, J.W.: Lessons from Systems Modeling. In: The 1986 International Conference of the System Dynamic Society, Sevilla (1986)
8. Armenakis, A.A., Harris, S.G.: Crafting a Change Message to Create Transformational Readiness. Journal of Organisational Change Management 15, 169–183 (2002)
9. Armenakis, A.A., Harris, S.G., Mossholder, K.W.: Creating Readiness for Organisational Change. Human Relations 46, 681–703 (1993)
10. Armenakis, A.A., Bedeian, A.G.: Organisational Change: A Review of Theory and Research in the 1990s. Journal of Management 25, 293–315 (1999)
11. Kotter, J.: Leading Change: Why Transformation Efforts Fail. Harvard Business Review (March/April 1995)
12. Holt, D.T., Armenakis, A.A., Field, H., Harris, G.S.: Readiness for Organisational Change: The Systematic Development of a Scale. Journal of Applied Behavioural Science 43, 232–255 (2007)
13. Eby, L.T., Adams, D.M., Russell, E.A., Gaby, S.H.: Perceptions of Organisational Readiness for Change: Factors Related to Employees' Reactions to Implementation of Team Based Selling. Human Relations 53, 419–442 (2000)
14. DiClemente, C.C., Schlundt, D., Gemmell, L.: Readiness and Stages of Change in Addiction Treatment. The American Journal on Additions 13, 103–119 (2004)
15. Rousseau, D.M., Tojoriwala, S.A.: What's a Good Reason to Change? Motivated Reasoning and Social Accounts in Promoting Organisational Change. Journal of Applied Psychology 84, 514–528 (1999)
16. Nonaka, I., Takeuchi, H.: The Knowledge Creating Company: How Japanese Companies Create The Dynamics of Innovation. Oxford University Press, New York (1995)
17. Foss, N.: Alternative Research Strategies in the Knowledge Movement: from Macro Bias to Micro-Foundations and Multi-level Explanation. European Management Review 6, 16–28 (2009)
18. Hansen, M., Mors, M.L., Lovas, B.: Knowledge Sharing in Organisations: Multiple Networks, Multiple Phases. Academy of Management Journal 48, 776–793 (2005)

19. Lichtenstein, S., Hunter, A.: Receiver Influences on Knowledge Sharing. Paper presented at the 13th European Conference on Information Systems. Regensburg, Germany (2005)
20. Investigation into outbreaks of Clostridium difficile at Maidstone and Tunbridge Wells NHS Trust. Healthcare Commission (October 2007)
21. Waterson, P.: Infection Outbreaks in Acute Hospitals: A Systems Approach. Journal of Infection Prevention 11, 19–23 (2010)
22. Forrester, J.: System Dynamics and the Lessons of 35 Years (1991), `http://sysdyn.mit.edu/people/jay-forrester.html`
23. Straub, E.T.: Understanding technology adoption: Theory and future directions for informal learning. Review of Educational Research 79, 625–649 (2009)
24. Nabeth, T., Roda, C., Angehrn, A.A., Mittal, P.K.: Using Artificial Agents to Stimulate Participation in Virtual Communities; IADIS. In: International Conference CELDA (Cognition and Exploratory Learning in Digital Age) (2005)
25. Valente, T.W.: Social Network Thresholds in the Diffusion of Innovations. Soc. Networks 18, 69–89 (1996)
26. Cabrera, A., Cabrera, E.: Knowledge Sharing Dilemmas. Organisation Studies 23, 687–710 (2002)

E-Business, Emerging Trends in the European Union

Peter Sonntagbauer

Lecturer, University of Applied Science, Vienna, Austria
Peter.Sonntagbauer@technikum-wien.at

Abstract. E-Business is often linked with business to consumer (B2C) processes, but a larger and still to a large extent not exploited potential exists in business-to-business (B2B) and government-to-business (G2B) processes. The European Commission encourages businesses and governments to increase the uptake in order to promote European competitive performance. Various initiatives have been launched, which have shown some impact, but the great large scale breakthrough across Europe is still ahead. There are big differences between countries and economic sectors in approaching E-Business. Critical success factors can be extracted from those, which have successfully implemented B2B and G2B initiatives on a broad scale.

Keywords: e-business, e-ordering, e-invoicing, e-procurement.

1 Introduction

E-Business is often linked with business to consumer (B2C) processes, but a larger and still to a large extent not exploited potential exists in business-to-business (B2B) and government-to-business (G2B) processes.

B2C processes refer to all processes between consumers (individual customers) and businesses. They are initiated through a website or an online shop of the company. A typical example of B2C applications are online shops of retail chains.

B2B processes refer to all transaction between businesses such as electronic tender, electronic ordering of goods, electronic invoicing or electronic transmission of whole catalogues. Transactions go beyond B2C transaction since they involve supply chain management processes, which consist of several sequences of transactions. G2B refers to all government to business transactions and is similar to B2B. It has however some peculiarities caused by the public procurement laws. Governments are probably the least developed sector of the E-Business landscape despite recent advances in electronic procurement.

2 E-Business in the European Union

2.1 Current Strategies

The EU-Commission is strongly supporting efforts to standardize E-Business in order to reduce obstacles for companies in the internal market and to enhance the competiveness of European companies. In several strategies e-Business activities are mentioned as a priority:

M. Gusev and P. Mitrevski (Eds.): ICT Innovations 2010, CCIS 83, pp. 40–50, 2011.

1. eEurope Action Plans of 2002 and 2005:
A goal was to promote "take-up of e-business with the aim of increasing the competitiveness of European enterprises"
2. i2010 Strategic Framework:
The strategy anticipates "a new era of e-business solutions", based on integrated ICT systems and tools, which will lead to an increased business use of ICT.

2.2 Europe 2020

The report of the i2010 achievements states however that consolidating the online single market has yet to be achieved, despite solid progress during the past years. Europe still faces legal fragmentation, with payment systems, security, privacy and other obstacles that discourage businesses and consumers to go digital [1].

It is obvious that the overwhelming volume of transactions takes place on a domestic basis despite the size of cross border trade in the EU. Trading partners located in different countries experience challenges in understanding legal requirements as well as technical and organizational problems to exchange data. There are only a few real pan-European initiatives such as the PEPPOL project (Pan-European Public Procurement Online), service provider initiatives (HubAlliance) and initiatives from the financial service industry initiated by the Euro Banking Association (EBA).

It can be expected that more initiatives in the Europe 2020 strategy [2] will be launched to further push the E-Business agenda.

3 Benefits

3.1 Structured Information Required

The *full benefits* of E-Business in a B2B or G2B environment can be reaped only if the information exchanged is structured in a way that a software package can read and interpret the content easily. The major benefit is that the information can be processed automatically and need not be reentered. Files in a graphical format (TIFF, JPEG..), DOC or PDF do not fulfill this condition. They have to be printed on the other end and reentered. An OCR program can be used to speed up the process of reentering, but it will again require manual intervention to correct mistakes and check the output.

3.2 Process Integration Beneficial

Another important factor is the *integration of processes*. The more processes of the procurement process are electronically integrated the better. Purchase-to-Pay systems automate *all* purchase to payment processes and integrate all data to minimize double entries.

The electronic process chain consists of:

1. eSourcing: preparatory activities to collect information for the preparation of a call
2. eNoticing: notifications of calls for tenders in electronic format

3. eAccess: electronic access to tender documents and specifications
4. eSubmission: submission of offers in electronic format to the contracting authority/entity,
5. eAwarding: opening and evaluation of the tenders received
6. eContract: conclusion and monitoring of a contract through electronic means
7. eOrders: preparation and issuing of an electronic order by the customer
8. eInvoicing: preparation and delivery of an electronic invoice
9. ePayment: electronic payment

3.3 Cycle Time and Process Costs

In case the documents are processed automatically the cycle time and the process costs will be lower. The cycle time (means the duration to process business documents) can be drastically reduced, because there is no delay caused by data entry in processing the business document. Likewise the process costs will be lower, because there is no manual data entry workload. At the same time the number of data entry errors will be zero and there is no additional workload to correct mistakes.

For example in case of E-invoicing it permits more optimal payables management. In view of the shorter time taken to approve e-invoices, a buyer becomes able to take advantage of prompt payment discounts or so called _dynamic discounts', which it is often unable to do with long drawn out paper invoice processes. If liquid, a buyer may choose to use its own cash resources to promptly pay suppliers and take advantage of discounts (perhaps a better risk-free return on the cash than money market deposits) [12].

3.4 Archiving and Retrieval

Electronic business documents can be easily retrieved and the cost of storing (archiving space) are much lower than paper documents.

3.5 Transmission Costs

The costs of electronic transmission are much lower than producing and sending the documents with ordinary mail.

3.6 Estimation of Benefits

The estimates of process costs and potential benefits differ to a large extent for the following reasons:

1. The organizational structure of the underlying study sample is different. It makes a difference, if the sample consists of SME´s with a few employees, one location and simple procurement processes or it consists of large corporations with procurement processes stretching across different locations and departments.
2. The methodology of the estimation as well as the degree of detail vary
3. There are regional differences in costs, salaries and the legal situation. It has certainly an impact on the costs savings in absolute figures whether those are based on salaries in a high or low income country.

UBS AG estimates that the costs of processing an invoice are 150 CHF and 50 % of process steps can be saved with electronic invoicing [10]. Research into the potential cost savings of electronic invoicing in SME's, shows savings on inbound side ranging from € 10 to € 25 compared to a manual process, depending on the level of automation. [11] On the outbound side, cost savings are estimated between € 7 and € 10, depending on the level of automation [12]. SAP estimates the typical paper invoicing cost on biller and customer side in the range between 10-30 € [14].

4 Standards – A Critical Success Factor

4.1 Interoperability Layers and Standards

Interoperability means the capability of ICT systems and of the business processes they support to exchange data on all levels. Consequently interoperability is defined as a set of standards and guidelines that describes the way in which organizations have agreed to interact with each other.

The exchange of business documents between two organizations requires interoperability on several layers as shown in the diagram below, which takes the order-invoicing business process in a B2B and G2B relation in the EBIZ4ALL project [3] as an example:

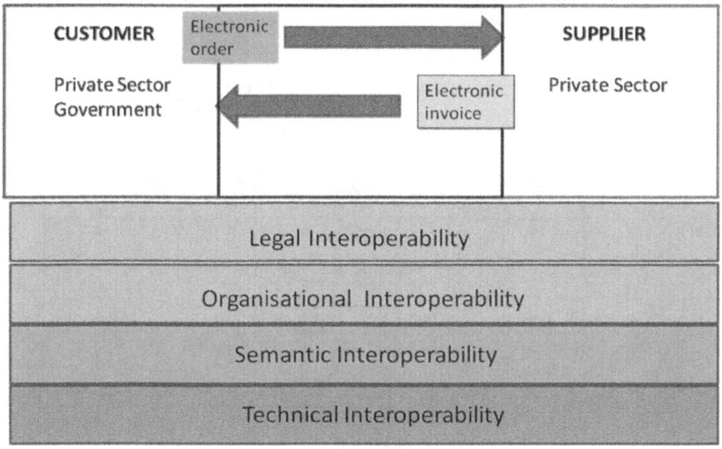

Fig. 1. Interoperability layers

As can be seen the standard is not limited to the electronic message only, it comprises all aspects of business process. Missing standardization or different standards are recognized as an important obstacle and often prevents governments and companies from introducing E-Business on a large scale.

4.2 Legal Interoperability

The different laws in nations, where buyer / supplier are located does have an impact on the overall business interoperability. This is especially true for a number of issues in cross border electronic invoicing. For example it matters if an electronic signature is a legal requirement for an invoice in one country and in the other country it is not.

4.3 Organizational Interoperability

This aspect of interoperability is concerned with modeling business processes and defining the collaboration of buyers and suppliers that wish to exchange information and may have different internal structures and processes. It is unrealistic to believe that buyers / suppliers are harmonizing their internal business processes because of data exchange requirements. The key to organizational interoperability is therefore to identify and document those "business interoperability interfaces" (BII) through which they are able to interoperate.

That is why recent approaches like those contained in the CEN/BII workshop agreement define the relationships and the sequence in a so called "business profile".

The choreography of business collaborations defines the sequence of interactions when the profile is run within its context. Each sequence of interactions can be understood as a run-time scenario.

An example is provided below.

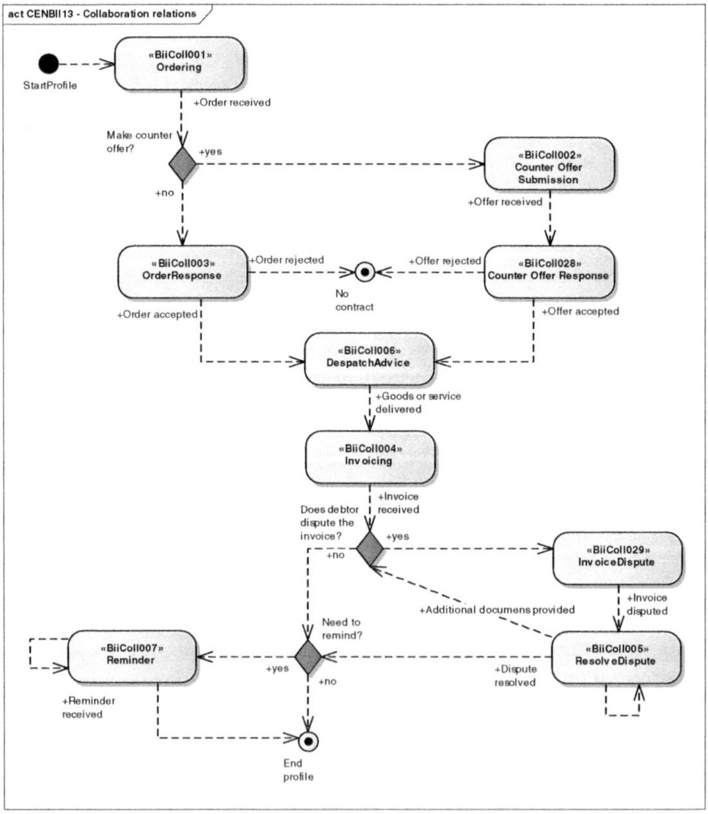

Fig. 2. Example CEN/BII Advanced Procurement with Dispatch [18]

4.4 Semantic Interoperability

Alignment of processes and information interchange between buyer and supplier is based on well defined standards. To move from simply presenting information to where computer software can exchange it and further process it in a meaningful manner, requires agreement on a broad range of issues that relate to the *context* within which the information is created and used. This is the subject of *semantic interoperability*.

For example it includes agreement on ways to discover, represent and give a context to information. *(e.g. in XML)* It allows *automated software packages* to process information, even when they have been designed independently.

4.5 Technical Interoperability

This aspect of interoperability covers the technical issues of linking computer systems and services. It includes key aspects such as interconnection services, data integration and middleware, data presentation and exchange, accessibility and security services. (e.g. Internet, transport protocol,....).

4.6 A Single European Standard?

It is obvious that there are a number of standards on the market.

A few accepted standards are provided below:

EDIFACT: United Nations/Electronic Data Interchange For Administration, Commerce and Transport (UN/EDIFACT) is an international EDI standard developed under the umbrella of the United Nations Centre for Trade Facilitation and Electronic Business (UN/CEFACT) under the UN Economic Commission for Europe. It is a long time on the market. [4]

UBL: Universal Business Language (UBL) was developed by an OASIS Technical Committee. It is based on XML and aims at facilitating E-Businessfor small and medium-sized businesses. [5]

ebXML: ebXML (Electronic Business using eXtensible Markup Language)is as a joint initiative of the United Nations Centre for Trade facilitation and Electronic Business (UN/CEFACT) and Organization for the Advancement of Structured Information Standards (OASIS). It is a modular suite of specifications that enables enterprises of any size and in any geographical location to conduct business over the Internet. ebXML is aiming at a standard method to exchange business messages, conduct trading relationships, communicate data in common terms and define and register business processes. [6]

ROSETTANET: RosettaNet is a subsidiary of GS1 US aiming at B2B standards in the *electronic industry* (computer and consumer electronics, semiconductor..) These standards form a common e-business language, which is based on XML. [7]

IATA – XML Standard: The Aviation Invoice Standard aims at the standardization of charges and billing data exchange between the *airlines* and their main suppliers.
IATA leads an Airport Invoice Task Force (AITF), comprised of Airlines and Airports, and an Air Navigation Task Force (ANSITF), comprised of Airlines and Air

Navigation Service Providers, to develop and maintain the invoice data standards and commonly associated terms, definitions and codes. [8]

ODETTE: Odette International is an organization, formed by the automotive industry for the *automotive industry.* It sets the standards for e-business communications, engineering data exchange and logistics management, which link the 4000 plus businesses in the European motor industry and their global trading partners. [9]

ELEMICA: Elemica was formed through the partnership of many chemical industry leaders and is focused on the chemical industry. [13]

It is not realistic to believe that all those will be replaced by a single European or worldwide standard. *There* is *no "single" European standard emerging*, however it is advisable to take existing standards into consideration, when starting an E-Business / E-Businessproject.

"Country or company specific" standards, which are incompatible to accepted standards and guidelines have *no future*, because *they cannot be used in cross-border transactions* and they are not supported by *international software companies.* (ERP-vendors). They will support a standard, if it has a broad coverage and there is a sufficient large demand from their customers.

Large corporation may even adopt more than one standard as can be seen from the case study of UBS AG, a large Swiss bank. Suppliers can deliver invoicing data as xCBL, UN/EDIFACT, IDOC or as a flat file [10].

5 Consolidators Approach

5.1 Single Consolidator Approach

Adopting several standards and maintaining the required IT infrastructure to link customers and suppliers is costly and feasible for large corporations only. It is not realistic for small and medium sized companies, which do not have the IT-resources to do that.

As a consequence most E-Business initiatives have used consolidators or value added network service providers (VANs). They maintain the IT infrastructure and provide other services such as conversion of different message standards to ensure technical interoperability. This approach eliminates also some of the barriers regarding e.g. authenticity of origin, integrity of content, readability and storage.

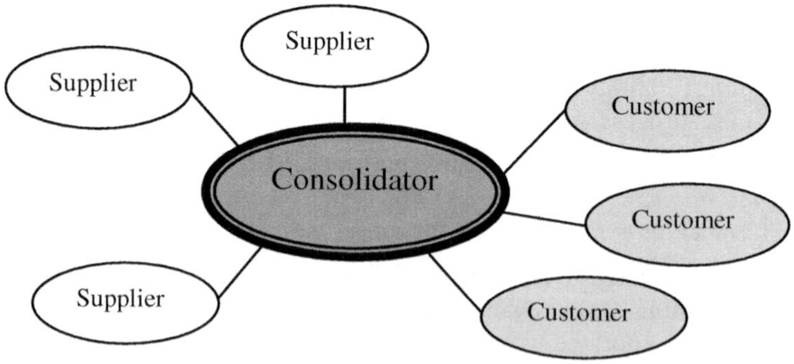

Fig. 3. Single consolidator approach

However the single consolidator approach has the disadvantage that it can only link suppliers and customers on the *same network.*

5.2 The GSM of E-Business – Linking Consolidators

However the single consolidator approach has the disadvantage that it can only link suppliers and customers on the *same network.* It is therefore useful to connect existing consolidator networks and allow roaming of e-Business transactions between consolidators. The connection of different consolidators is the most likely future E-Business scenario, even though a number of issues need to addressed, before it can happen.

The main issues are:

1. Addressing and routing
2. Roaming agreements
3. Roaming charges
4. Certification of participating consolidators
5. Internetwork message standards

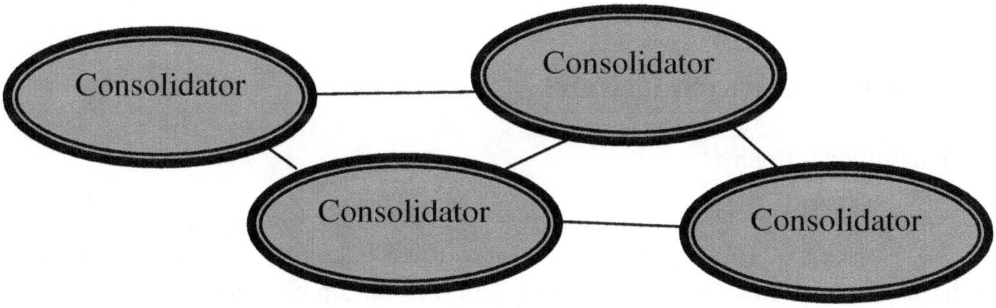

Fig. 4. Connecting consolidators

The PEPPOL project (co-financed by the CIP program of the EC) proposes to link the various VAN infrastructures through a common network. A VAN would be the access -point to this common infrastructure. An Access Point handles possible protocol and payload conversion between national e-business frameworks and the common infrastructure. The Access Points authenticates the business entities (private companies or public sector institutions) behind the business transactions. Envelopes used to send business documents between Access Points are signed by the Access Points.

The model proposes also the setting-up of a central European E-Business registry with subordinated 2nd level registries to locate a specific company.

The central registry contains the link to the subordinated registry in which further information about the company can be found. The subordinated registry contains the endpoint address of a company as well as other communication and e-business specific parameters (e.g. the EDI format used etc.)

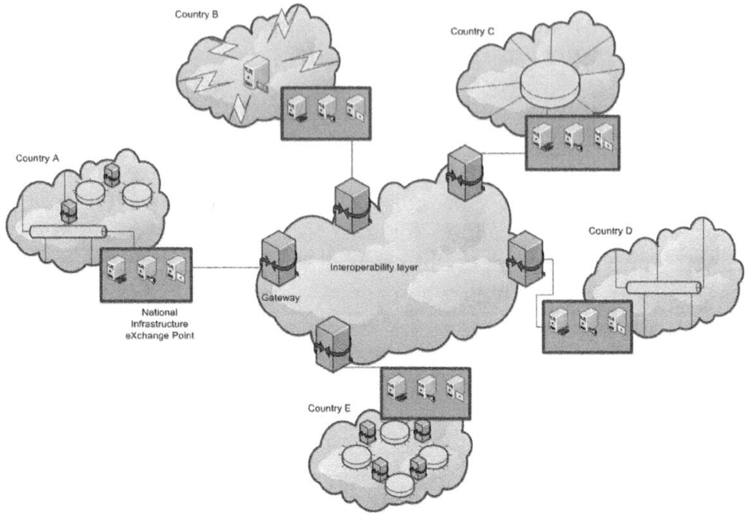

Fig. 5. Proposed PEPPOL infrastructure [17]

6 Strategies to Reach Critical Mass

6.1 Customer – Push

In a number of sectors large customers were pushing their suppliers to connect to their systems. Sometimes it is even a precondition to be a supplier. Typical examples are the large retail chains in the food sector or the automotive industry. It is always working quite well, if there are a few large dominant corporation with a relative large number of small suppliers.

6.2 Legislation

Legislation-based strategies refer to laws demanding from suppliers to shift from paper-based to electronic formats. This approach is open to governments only. It has been quite successful to obtain a critical mass of users in a short time. A successful example is the public sector in Denmark.

Denmark was an early adopter of electronic invoicing in Europe. As of 1 February 2005, all public institutions in Denmark were required only to accept invoices from suppliers in electronic format. Thus, all public-sector entities have been required to convert all systems and administrative processes from physical to digital handling of invoices, credit notes and other transactions. This reform affected approximately 15 million invoices a year and applied to the *entire public sector*. Electronic invoicing requires a transportation system – which in the Danish case is based on an existing VANS network (Value Added Network Services) [15].

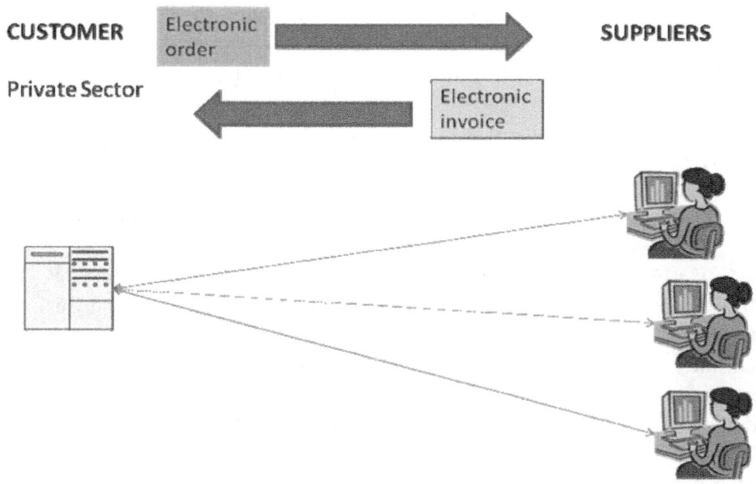

Fig. 6. Large customer – small suppliers

Other governments in Europe have already followed and started similar initiatives. The Swedish government decided that all government agencies shall handle invoices electronically by July 1 2008. The Swedish National Financial Management Authority (ESV) is leading and coordinating the introduction of e-invoicing in the central government. The German government has introduced legal steps to make electronic tender submission increasingly mandatory.

7 Conclusion

The European Commission is strongly supporting efforts to standardize E-Business in order to reduce obstacles for companies in the internal market and efforts to push standardization and the adoption rate will continue.

Best practice shows that companies or governments introducing E-Business should try to cover the whole process chain and exchange structured data, which can be processed by software packages.

The exchange of structured information is intrinsically linked to standards. There are numerous standards on the market and it is unlikely that a single standard will emerge. This underlines the importance of consolidators, which link suppliers and customers and take care of message conversion. It can be expected that consolidators will link and a network structure between consolidators will be created.

The push to modernize the E-Business infrastructure of companies is often imposed by large customers, likewise the strategy of mandatory electronic processes imposed by law has been successful.

References

1. European Commission: Europe's Digital Competitiveness Report, Main achievements of the i2010 strategy 2005-2009, Brussels, p. 10 (2009)
2. European Commission: Europe 2020, a strategy for smart, sustainable and inclusive growth, Brussels (2010)

3. Gusev, M., Stefanovic, N., Schmölzer, W., Sonntagbauer, P., Tomic-Roth, S.: EBIZ4ALL Requirements Analysis, Vol. I, Vienna (2010)
4. UNCEFACT, http://www.unece.org/trade/untdid/welcome.htm
5. OASIS, http://www.oasis-open.org/committees/tc_home.php?wg_abbrev=ubl
6. EBXML, http://www.ebxml.org/geninfo.htm
7. ROSETTANET, http://www.rosettanet.org/
8. IATA: XML Standard For Electronic Aviation Invoices, V1.0.0 (October 2007)
9. ODETTE, http://www.odette.org/
10. Tanner, C.: Fallstudie "UBS AG". In: Schubert, P., Wölfle, R., Dettling, W. (Hrsg.) (eds.) E-Business mit betriebswirtschaftlicher Standardsoftware - Einsatz von Business Software in der Praxis, pp. 169–180. Hanser Verlag, München (2004)
11. Electronic Invoicing Initiatives in Finland, Helsinki School of Economics (2008)
12. Lichter, G., Liezenberg, C., Nienhuis, J., Bryant, J. -C.: E-Invoicing 2010, European market guide, p. 50, Euro Banking Association (EBA) and Innopay (2010)
13. ELEMICA, http://www.elemica.com/about/fact-sheet.html
14. Hornburg, M.: SAP Biller Consolidator E-Document Exchange Platform, p. 3, presentation to UNECE (2005)
15. Cimander, R., and Hippe Brun, M.: National IT and Telecom Agency, Denmark, Good Practice Case, eInvoicing in Denmark (2007)
16. Gusev, M., Stefanovic, N., Schmölzer, W., Sonntagbauer, P., Tomic-Roth, S.: EBIZ4ALL Requirements Analysis, Vol. I, Vienna, p. 7 (2010)
17. PEPPOL, http://www.peppol.eu
18. CEN/BII Profile Advanced Procurement with Dispatch, CEN/ISSS WA, Bruxelles, p.11 (2010)

On Some Cryptographic Properties of the Polynomial Quasigroups

Simona Samardjiska

Department of Telematics, Faculty of Information Technology, Mathematics and Electrical Engineering, NTNU, Trondheim, Norway
simonas@item.ntnu.no

Abstract. A polynomial quasigroup is said to be a quasigroup that can be defined by a polynomial over a ring. The possibility for use of these quasigroups in cryptography mainly relies on their simple properties, easy construction and huge number. The quasigroup string transformations that are usually used in cryptographic primitives make use of the quasigroup operation as well as one of the parastrophic operations. That is why one of the most important questions posed about the polynomial quasigroups is the one concerning the nature of their parastrophic operations. In this paper we investigate the parastrophes of the polynomial quasigroups of order 2^w and propose effective algorithm for finding them.

Keywords: Polynomial quasigroup, n-ary quasigroup, parastrophic operation.

1 Introduction

Recently, quasigroups have found their way as building parts of new cryptographic algorithms. Several new primitives have been proposed in the last few years, like the hash functions Edon-R [4],[5] and Nasha [13], the stream cipher Edon-80 [6], and the public key cryptosystem MQQ [8]. They all use binary quasigroups of different orders, small or huge, and usually make use of quasigroup string transformations [10], [12]. These transformations are based on the identities that hold true for the quasigroups and their parastrophes. It is very convenient if the quasigruop operation and the parastrophic operation can be easily evaluated. That is why it is very important to find types of quasigroups that have this property.

In this paper we investigate the so called polynomial quasigroups that can be defined by polynomials over a ring. We prove that the quasigroups defined by parastrophic operations, are also polynomial, and propose an algorithm for finding them. This opens an opportunity for these quasigroups to be used in various cryptographic applications.

First we need some basic definitions.

An n-ary quasigroup is a pair (Q, f) of a nonempty set Q and an n-ary operation f with the property that for any given n elements $a_1, \ldots, a_{i-1}, a_{i+1}, \ldots \ldots, a_{n+1} \in Q$ and any $i = 1, 2, \ldots, n$, there is a uniquely determined element

M. Gusev and P. Mitrevski (Eds.): ICT Innovations 2010, CCIS 83, pp. 51–60, 2011.

$a_i \in Q$ such that $f(a_1, a_2, \ldots, a_n) = a_{n+1}$. Equivalently, (Q, f) is an n-ary quasigroup if the unary operations

$$f_{a_1,\ldots,a_{i-1},a_{i+1},\ldots,a_n}(x) = f(a_1, \ldots, a_{i-1}, x, a_{i+1}, \ldots, a_n)$$

are permutations on Q.

For an arbitrary permutation σ over $\{1, \ldots, n+1\}$, i.e. $\sigma \in \mathcal{S}_{n+1}$, and an n-ary quasigroup (Q, f), an operation ${}^{\sigma}f$ can defined by

$${}^{\sigma}f(x_{\sigma(1)}, \ldots, x_{\sigma(n)}) = x_{\sigma(n+1)} \quad \Leftrightarrow \quad f(x_1, \ldots, x_n) = x_{n+1},$$

called σ- parastrophe of the quasigroup (Q, f), or just a parastrophe.

A polynomial $P(x) = a_0 + a_1 x + \cdots + a_d x^d$ in a finite ring R is said to be a *permutation polynomial* if P permutes the elements of R.

We say that an n-ary quasigroup (Q, f) is a *polynomial n-ary quasigroup* if there is a ring $(Q, +, \cdot)$ and a polynomial $P(x_1, x_2, \ldots, x_n) \in Q[x_1, x_2, \ldots, x_n]$ such that $f(x_1, x_2, \ldots, x_n) = P(x_1, x_2, \ldots, x_n)$ for every $x_1, x_2, \ldots, x_n \in Q$. Note that for $n = 1$ we have a set Q endowed with a permutation f, and for $n = 2$ we have a usual binary quasigroup.

In the sequel we consider only the case when the ring is $R = \mathbb{Z}_{2^w}$, where w is a positive integer. In [14], Rivest gives the next, rather simple criteria for permutation polynomials and binary polynomial quasigroups.

Theorem 1. (a) *Let $P(x) = a_0 + a_1 x + \cdots + a_d x^d$ be a polynomial with integral coefficients. Then $P(x)$ is a permutation polynomial modulo 2^w, $w \geq 2$, if and only if a_1 is odd, $(a_2 + a_4 + a_6 + \ldots)$ is even, and $(a_3 + a_5 + a_7 + \ldots)$ is even.*

(b) *A bivariate polynomial $P(x, y) = \sum_{i,j} a_{i,j} x^i y^j$, represents a quasigroup operation in $\mathbb{Z}_{2^w}$, $w \geq 2$, if and only if the four univariate polynomials $P(x, 0)$, $P(x, 1)$, $P(0, y)$ and $P(1, y)$, are all permutation polynomials in $\mathbb{Z}_{2^w}$.*

We note that in [11], the same result was infered through a rather different construction, by considering permutation polynomials on tne units of $\mathbb{Z}_{2^w}$.

This result was extended for general n-ary quasigroup in [15].

Theorem 2. *Let $P(x_1, x_2, \ldots, x_n)$ be a polynomial over the ring $(\mathbb{Z}_{2^w}, +, \cdot)$. $P(x_1, x_2, \ldots, x_n)$ is a polynomial that defines an n-ary quasigroup, $n \geq 2$, if and only if for every $(a_1, \ldots, a_{n-1}) \in \{0, 1\}^{n-1}$ each of the polynomials*

$$\begin{aligned} P_1(x_1) &= P(x_1, a_1, \ldots, a_{n-1}), \\ P_2(x_2) &= P(a_1, x_2, \ldots, a_{n-1}), \\ &\vdots \\ P_n(x_n) &= P(a_1, \ldots, a_{n-1}, x_n). \end{aligned} \tag{1}$$

is a permutation polynomial.

Of course, there are infinitely many polynomials in n variables over the ring $(\mathbb{Z}_{2^w}, +, \cdot)$ that satisfy the conditions (1), but still the number of different polynomial functions that are induced by these polynomials is finite. Each polynomial quasigroup is defined by a single polynomial function, that has a unique representation of the form

$$P(\boldsymbol{x}) \equiv \sum_{\substack{\boldsymbol{k} \in \mathbb{N}_0^n \\ \nu_2(\boldsymbol{k}!) < w}} \alpha_{\boldsymbol{k}} \boldsymbol{x}^{\boldsymbol{k}},$$

where $\boldsymbol{x} = (x_1, x_2, \ldots, x_n)$, $\nu_2(\boldsymbol{k}!) = max\{x \in \mathbb{N}_0 : 2^x \mid \boldsymbol{k}!\}$, $\boldsymbol{x}^{\boldsymbol{k}} = \prod_{i=1}^n x_i^{k_i}$, $\boldsymbol{k}! = \prod_{i=1}^n k_i!$ and $\alpha_{\boldsymbol{k}} \in \{0, 1, \ldots, 2^{w-\nu_2(\boldsymbol{k}!)} - 1\}$. (For details, see for example [9], [16].)

2 The Nature of the Parastrophes of a Polynomial Quasigroup

Let $(\mathbb{Z}_{2^w}, f)$ be a polynomial quasigroup, and let $P(x_1, x_2, \ldots, x_n)$ be its polynomial representation over the ring $(\mathbb{Z}_{2^w}, +, \cdot)$. Let $(\mathbb{Z}_{2^w}, {}^\sigma f)$ be the quasigroup defined by some parastrophic operation ${}^\sigma f$ of f.

We are interested whether there is a polynomial $P_\sigma(x_1, \ldots, x_n)$ over the ring $(\mathbb{Z}_{2^w}, +, \cdot)$ that is a representation of $(\mathbb{Z}_{2^w}, {}^\sigma f)$, i.e. a polynomial that satisfies

$$P_\sigma(x_1, x_2, \ldots, x_n) = x_{n+1} \Leftrightarrow {}^\sigma f(x_1, x_2, \ldots, x_n) = x_{n+1}.$$

In the sequel, without loss of generality, we focus on the parastrophic operation ${}^\backslash f$, defined by the permutation (x_n, x_{n+1}) i.e.,

$${}^\backslash f(x_1, x_2, \ldots, x_{n-1}, x_{n+1}) = x_n \Leftrightarrow f(x_1, x_2, \ldots, x_{n-1}, x_n) = x_{n+1}.$$

For the binary case, we will denote this parastrophe by the usual notation $\backslash$. Clearly, the following proposition is true.

Proposition 1. *Let $(\mathbb{Z}_{2^w}, f)$ be a polynomial quasigroup, and let $P(x_1, \ldots, x_n)$ be its polynomial representation over the ring $(\mathbb{Z}_{2^w}, +, \cdot)$. If $P_\backslash$ is a polynomial satisfying the conditions $P_\backslash(x_1, x_2, \ldots, x_{n-1}, P(x_1, x_2, \ldots, x_n)) = x_n$ and $P(x_1, x_2, \ldots, x_{n-1}, P_\backslash(x_1, \ldots, x_n)) = x_n$, than it defines the quasigroup $(\mathbb{Z}_{2^w}, {}^\backslash f)$.*

We will show that for a given polynomial quasigroup, the polynomial $P_\backslash$ always exists. For that we need to make the following construction.

Let S_d be the set of all mappings $f : \mathbb{Z}_m^d \to \mathbb{Z}_m$ such that the projection $f_{\boldsymbol{a}}(x) = f(a_1, \ldots, a_{d-1}, x)$ is permutation for every element $\boldsymbol{a} = (a_1, \ldots, a_{d-1}) \in \mathbb{Z}_m^{d-1}$. Let $\boldsymbol{x} = (x_1, \ldots, x_{d-1}) \in \mathbb{Z}_m^{d-1}$. We define an operation "$\bullet$" on S_d by:

$$f \bullet g(\boldsymbol{x}, x_d) = f(\boldsymbol{x}, g(\boldsymbol{x}, x_d)).$$

Theorem 3. *$(S_d, \bullet)$ is a group.*

Proof. Let $f, g \in S_d$ and let $(\boldsymbol{x}, x_d) \in \mathbb{Z}_m^d$. Then $(f \bullet g)_{\boldsymbol{x}}(x_d) = f \bullet g(\boldsymbol{x}, x_d) = f(\boldsymbol{x}, g(\boldsymbol{x}, x_d)) = f_{\boldsymbol{x}}(g(\boldsymbol{x}, x_d)) = f_{\boldsymbol{x}}(g_{\boldsymbol{x}}(x_d)) = f_{\boldsymbol{x}} \circ g_{\boldsymbol{x}}(x_d)$. The later is a composition of permutations, thus a permutation, which means that $f \bullet g \in S_d$, i.e. the set S_d is closed under the operation "$\bullet$".

The equality $f \bullet (g \bullet h)(\boldsymbol{x}, x_d) = f(\boldsymbol{x}, g \bullet h(\boldsymbol{x}, x_d)) = f(\boldsymbol{x}, g(\boldsymbol{x}, h(\boldsymbol{x}, x_d))) = f \bullet g(\boldsymbol{x}, h(\boldsymbol{x}, x_d)) = (f \bullet g) \bullet h(\boldsymbol{x}, x_d)$, confirms the associative law, so $(S_d, \bullet)$ is a semigroup.

The mapping $e(\boldsymbol{x}, x_d) = x_d$, clearly belongs to S_d, and it is the identity element in S_d since $f \bullet e(\boldsymbol{x}, x_d) = f(\boldsymbol{x}, e(\boldsymbol{x}, x_d)) = f(\boldsymbol{x}, x_d)$, and $e \bullet f(\boldsymbol{x}, x_d) = e(\boldsymbol{x}, f(\boldsymbol{x}, x_d)) = f(\boldsymbol{x}, x_d)$, for every mapping $f \in S_d$.

Let $f \in S_d$. We define a mapping $f' : \mathbb{Z}_m^d \to \mathbb{Z}_m$ by $f'(\boldsymbol{x}, x_d) = z \Leftrightarrow f(\boldsymbol{x}, z) = x_d$, and show that $f' = f^{-1}$. Since $f'_{\boldsymbol{x}}(x_d) = f'(\boldsymbol{x}, x_d) = z \Leftrightarrow f(\boldsymbol{x}, z) = x_d \Leftrightarrow f_{\boldsymbol{x}}(z) = x_d$, it follows that $f'_{\boldsymbol{x}} = f_{\boldsymbol{x}}^{-1}$, which means that $f'_{\boldsymbol{x}}$ is a permutation, i.e. $f' \in S_d$. Furthermore, since $z = f' \bullet f(\boldsymbol{x}, x_d) = f'(\boldsymbol{x}, f(\boldsymbol{x}, x_d)) \Leftrightarrow f(\boldsymbol{x}, z) = f(\boldsymbol{x}, x_d) \Leftrightarrow f_{\boldsymbol{x}}(z) = f_{\boldsymbol{x}}(x_d) \Leftrightarrow z = x_d$, we get that $f' \bullet f(\boldsymbol{x}, x_d) = x_d = e(\boldsymbol{x}, x_d)$. Similarly, from $w = f \bullet f'(\boldsymbol{x}, x_d)$ we get that $w = x_d$, i.e., that $f \bullet f'(\boldsymbol{x}, x_d) = x_d = e(\boldsymbol{x}, x_d)$. Hence, $f \bullet f' = f' \bullet f = e$, i.e. f' is the inverse element of f.

The set S_d, due to its nature, can be considered as a sort of an extension of the notion of permutation. That is best confirmed by the next important theorem.

Theorem 4. *Let $\mathcal{S}_m$ be the group of permutations of the set $\mathbb{Z}_m$. Then $S_d \cong {\mathcal{S}_m}^{m^{d-1}}$, where ${\mathcal{S}_m}^{m^{d-1}}$ is a direct product of $\mathcal{S}_m$.*

Proof. We define a mapping $\varphi : S_d \to {\mathcal{S}_m}^{m^{d-1}}$ by $\varphi(f) = (f_{\boldsymbol{i}_0}, f_{\boldsymbol{i}_1}, \ldots, f_{\boldsymbol{i}_{m^{d-1}-1}})$, where, the multi-indexes $\boldsymbol{i}_0, \boldsymbol{i}_1, \ldots, \boldsymbol{i}_{m^{d-1}-1}$ are all the elements of the set $\mathbb{Z}_m^{d-1}$ in a lexicographic order.

The mapping is well defined.

Indeed, let $(f_{\boldsymbol{i}_0}, f_{\boldsymbol{i}_1}, \ldots, f_{\boldsymbol{i}_{m^{d-1}-1}})$ and $(f'_{\boldsymbol{i}_0}, f'_{\boldsymbol{i}_1}, \ldots, f'_{\boldsymbol{i}_{m^{d-1}-1}})$ be two distinct elements of the set ${\mathcal{S}_m}^{m^{d-1}}$. This means that there is a multi-index $\boldsymbol{i}_j \in \mathbb{Z}_m^{d-1}$, such that $f_{\boldsymbol{i}_j} \neq f'_{\boldsymbol{i}_j}$. So, there exists $x \in \mathbb{Z}_m$ such that $f_{\boldsymbol{i}_j}(x) \neq f'_{\boldsymbol{i}_j}(x)$. In other words, $f((i_j)_1, \ldots, (i_j)_{d-1}, x) \neq f'((i_j)_1, \ldots, (i_j)_{d-1}, x)$, i.e, $f \neq f'$.

We show that the mapping φ is a bijection.

Let $f', f'' \in S_d$ and let $\varphi(f') = \varphi(f'')$. Then, $f'_{\boldsymbol{i}} = f''_{\boldsymbol{i}}$, for every $\boldsymbol{i} \in \mathbb{Z}_m^{d-1}$, i.e, $f'(\boldsymbol{i}, x_d) = f''(\boldsymbol{i}, x_d)$, for every $\boldsymbol{i} \in \mathbb{Z}_m^{d-1}$, and every $x_d \in \mathbb{Z}_m$. Thus, $f' = f''$, and φ is an injection.

For every $(\alpha_{\boldsymbol{i}_0}, \alpha_{\boldsymbol{i}_1}, \ldots, \alpha_{\boldsymbol{i}_{m^{d-1}-1}}) \in {\mathcal{S}_m}^{m^{d-1}}$, we define a mapping $f \in S_d$ by $f_{\boldsymbol{i}_j}(x_d) = \alpha_{\boldsymbol{i}_j}(x_d)$. Then, $\varphi(f) = (\alpha_{\boldsymbol{i}_0}, \alpha_{\boldsymbol{i}_1}, \ldots, \alpha_{\boldsymbol{i}_{n^{d-1}-1}})$, so φ is a surjection.

Next, let $x \in \mathbb{Z}_m$.

$$\begin{aligned}
\varphi(f \bullet g)(x) &= ((f \bullet g)_{\boldsymbol{i}_0}, (f \bullet g)_{\boldsymbol{i}_1}, \ldots, (f \bullet g)_{\boldsymbol{i}_{m^{d-1}-1}})(x) = \\
&= ((f \bullet g)_{\boldsymbol{i}_0}(x), (f \bullet g)_{\boldsymbol{i}_1}(x), \ldots, (f \bullet g)_{\boldsymbol{i}_{m^{d-1}-1}}(x)) = \\
&= ((f \bullet g)(\boldsymbol{i}_0, x), (f \bullet g)(\boldsymbol{i}_1, x), \ldots, (f \bullet g)(\boldsymbol{i}_{m^{d-1}-1}, x)) = \\
&= (f(\boldsymbol{i}_0, g(\boldsymbol{i}_0, x)), f(\boldsymbol{i}_1, g(\boldsymbol{i}_1, x)), \ldots, f(\boldsymbol{i}_{m^{d-1}-1}, g(\boldsymbol{i}_{m^{d-1}-1}, x))) = \\
&= (f(\boldsymbol{i}_0, g_{\boldsymbol{i}_0}(x)), f(\boldsymbol{i}_1, g_{\boldsymbol{i}_1}(x)), \ldots, f(\boldsymbol{i}_{m^{d-1}-1}, g_{\boldsymbol{i}_{m^{d-1}-1}}(x))) = \\
&= (f_{\boldsymbol{i}_0}(g_{\boldsymbol{i}_0}(x)), f_{\boldsymbol{i}_1}(g_{\boldsymbol{i}_1}(x)), \ldots, f_{\boldsymbol{i}_{m^{d-1}-1}}(g_{\boldsymbol{i}_{m^{d-1}-1}}(x))) = \\
&= (f_{\boldsymbol{i}_0} \circ g_{\boldsymbol{i}_0}(x), f_{\boldsymbol{i}_1} \circ g_{\boldsymbol{i}_1}(x), \ldots, f_{\boldsymbol{i}_{m^{d-1}-1}} \circ g_{\boldsymbol{i}_{m^{d-1}-1}}(x)) = \\
&= (f_{\boldsymbol{i}_0}, \ldots, f_{\boldsymbol{i}_{m^{d-1}-1}}) \circ (g_{\boldsymbol{i}_0}, \ldots, g_{\boldsymbol{i}_{m^{d-1}-1}})(x) = \varphi(f) \circ \varphi(f)(x).
\end{aligned}$$

Therefore φ is a homomorphism.

Note that this isomorphism gives the cardinal number of the set S_d.

Corollary 1. $|S_d| = (m!)^{m^{d-1}}$.

The next corollary follows immediately from the definition of a quasigroup.

Corollary 2. *Let* $(\mathbb{Z}_m, f)$ *be a* n*-ary quasigroup. Then* f *belongs to the set* S_n*.*

The next theorem, which is a consequence of Theorem 3, characterizes the nature of the polynomial quasigroups.

Theorem 5. *Every polynomial* n*-ary quasigroup* $(\mathbb{Z}_m, f)$*, defined by a polynomial over the ring* $(\mathbb{Z}_m, +, \cdot)$*, has a polynomial parastrophe* $(\mathbb{Z}_m, {}^{\setminus}f)$*.*

Proof. Let $(\mathbb{Z}_m, f)$ be a polynomial n-ary quasigroup defined by the polynomial P. Clearly, $P \in S_n$. Since S_n is a finite group, every element has a finite order, so there exists $r \in \mathbb{N}$, $r \leq |S_n|$, such that $P^r = e$. Thus, P^{r-1} is the inverse element of P.

Of course, $P^{r-1}(x_1, \ldots, x_n) = P(x_1, \ldots, P(x_1, \ldots, P(x_1, \ldots, x_n) \ldots))$ is a polynomial.

All that is left to prove is that P^{r-1} defines the quasigroup $(\mathbb{Z}_m, {}^{\setminus}f)$. But that follows directly from Proposition 1 and the fact that

$$P(x_1, P^{r-1}(x_1, \ldots, x_n)) = e(x_1, \ldots, x_n) = x_n = P^{r-1}(x_1, P(x_1, \ldots, x_n)).$$

Note that a similar construction as the one made above, can be made for any parastrophic operation of f. Hence the next is true.

Theorem 6. *All parastrophic operations of a polynomial* n*-ary quasigroup* $(\mathbb{Z}_m, f)$*, have polynomial representations over the ring* $(\mathbb{Z}_m, +, \cdot)$*.*

The later two results open the question for creating an algorithm that finds the parastrophes of a given polynomial quasigroup. For an arbitrary quasigroup, this problem is of enormous time and memory complexity, and practically insolvable.

In the next section, we construct algorithms for finding the polynomial representation of the parastrophe $(\mathbb{Z}_{2^w}, \setminus)$, for a given polynomial binary quasigroup $(\mathbb{Z}_{2^w}, *)$ and analyze their complexity. The case for ternary and in general for n-ary quasigroups is a natural generalization of the procedure, but is very complex and inefficient. Nevertheless, at the moment the focus is on binary quasigroups, since there exist quasigroup transformations using binary quasigroups whose properties are well studied.

3 Algorithms for Finding the Polynomial Representation of a Parastrophe of a Polynomial Binary Quasigroup

Let P be a polynomial in a canonical form over $\mathbb{Z}_{2^w}$ that defines the binary quasigroup $(\mathbb{Z}_{2^w}, *)$. In this section, we use the usual notation for the order of the quasigroup $n = 2^w$.

In [16] it was proven that the maximal degree in one of the variables, that this polynomial can have is $s = max\,\{m \,|\, \nu_2(m!\,0!) < w\}$.

Denote by $reduce(P)$, the algorithm for reduction of a polynomial to its canonical form. One implementation of such algorithm was made in [17], and it was proven that it has a complexity $O(s^2)$.

The correctness of the next algorithm for finding the parastrophe $(\mathbb{Z}_{2^w}, \backslash)$, follows directly from Theorem 5.

Algorithm $Parastrophe(P)$:
Input $\rightarrow$ polynomial P over $\mathbb{Z}_{2^w}$ that defines a quasigroup
Output $\leftarrow$ polynomial P_{pom} over $\mathbb{Z}_{2^w}$ that defines the parastrophic quasigroup

$P_{pom} \leftarrow P$
for $i = 2$ **to** $\frac{(2^w)!^{2^w}}{2}$ **do**
  $P'_{pom} \leftarrow P_{pom} \bullet P$
  $reduce(P'_{pom})$
  if $P'_{pom} = e$ **then**
    return P_{pom}
  else
    $P_{pom} \leftarrow P'_{pom}$
  end if
end for

Note that the complexity of this algorithm is $O((n)!^n)$ regardless the complexity of the algorithm $reduce(P)$ and the algorithm for performing the operation "$\bullet$" (their complexity is far smaller). Obviously, this complexity is enormous, making this procedure for finding the polynomial representation of the parastrophe extremely inefficient.

That is why we will create a different algorithm that reduces the problem to solving a system of Diophantine equations modulo 2^w.

The polynomial $P(x, y)$ can be written in the form

$$P(x,y) = \sum_{i=0}^{s}\sum_{j=0}^{s-i} \alpha_{ij} x^i y^j + \sum_{i=0}^{\frac{s-1}{2}} \alpha_{(2i+1)(s-2i)} x^{2i+1} y^{s-2i}.$$

The same can be done for the polynomial $P_\backslash(x, y)$.

$$P_\backslash(x,y) = \sum_{i=0}^{s}\sum_{j=0}^{s-i} \beta_{ij} x^i y^j + \sum_{i=0}^{\frac{s-1}{2}} \beta_{(2i+1)(s-2i)} x^{2i+1} y^{s-2i}.$$

Since we already established that this polynomial exists, this algorithm actually finds the coefficients β_{ij}.

From the condition $P_\backslash(x, P(x, y)) = y$, that defines this parastrophe, for every $x, y \in \mathbb{Z}_{2^w}$, we have

$$\sum_{i=0}^{s}\sum_{j=0}^{s-i} \beta_{ij} x^i P(x,y)^j + \sum_{i=0}^{\frac{s-1}{2}} \beta_{(2i+1)(s-2i)} x^{2i+1} P(x,y)^{s-2i} = y, \quad \forall x,y \in \mathbb{Z}_{2^w}. \quad (2)$$

(2) is a system of 2^{2w} equations with $\frac{(s+1)(s+3)}{2}$ unknowns β_{ij} over the ring $\mathbb{Z}_{2^w}$, and it can be rewritten as

$$\begin{cases} \sum_{i=0}^{s}\sum_{j=0}^{s-i} \beta_{ij} 0^i P(0,0)^j + \sum_{i=0}^{\frac{s-1}{2}} \beta_{(2i+1)(s-2i)} 0^{2i+1} P(0,0)^{s-2i} = 0 \\ \sum_{i=0}^{s}\sum_{j=0}^{s-i} \beta_{ij} 0^i P(0,1)^j + \sum_{i=0}^{\frac{s-1}{2}} \beta_{(2i+1)(s-2i)} 0^{2i+1} P(0,1)^{s-2i} = 1 \\ \vdots \\ \sum_{i=0}^{s}\sum_{j=0}^{s-i} \beta_{ij} (2^w-1)^i P(2^w-1, 2^w-1)^j + \\ \qquad + \sum_{i=0}^{\frac{s-1}{2}} \beta_{(2i+1)(s-2i)} (2^w-1)^{2i+1} P(2^w-1, 2^w-1)^{s-2i} = 2^w - 1 \end{cases} \tag{3}$$

Our task, thus, is reduced to solving this system. Rewritten in matrix form, the system is the following.

$$\begin{pmatrix} 1 & P(0,0)^1 & P(0,0)^2 & \dots & 0^s P(0,0) \\ 1 & P(0,1)^1 & P(0,1)^2 & \dots & 0^s P(0,1) \\ \vdots & & & & \\ 1(2^w-1)^0 P(2^w-1, 2^w-1)^1 & (2^w-1)^0 P(2^w-1, 2^w-1)^2 & . & . & (2^w-1)^s P(2^w-1, 2^w-1) \end{pmatrix} \cdot$$

$$\cdot \begin{pmatrix} \beta_{00} \\ \beta_{01} \\ \vdots \\ \beta_{2^w-1, 2^w-1} \end{pmatrix} = \begin{pmatrix} 0 \\ 1 \\ \vdots \\ 2^w - 1 \end{pmatrix}$$

For better readability, we denote the matrix of the system by A.

A standard method for solving this system over the ring $\mathbb{Z}_{2^w}$, is by reducing the matrix A to some of the normal forms of matrices, like the Smith or the Hermite normal form. This reduction process is a variant of the Gauss elimination, that allows only elementary unimodular row and column transformations, i.e. permutations, multiplication by units of $\mathbb{Z}_{2^w}$, and addition of one row, or column multiplied by a unit, to another. These transformations bring the system to an equivalent one, that is easy to be solved. The Hermite and Smith normal form always exist and are unique. The Hermite matrix is upper triangular, while the Smith matrix, diagonal. Taking into account their wide use, there is a great number of algorithms for their computing.

In the implementation of the algorithm for finding the parastrophe of a quasigroup, the given system is solved by reduction to a Hermite normal form. The algorithm used for reduction is created by *Storjohann* and *Labahn* [18]. This algorithm computes the Hermite normal form H of a matrix $A \in \mathbb{Z}^{n \times m}$ of rank m, together with an unimodular matrix U, such that $UA = H$. The complexity of the algorithm is $O^{\sim}(m^{\theta-1} n \mathbf{M}(m log \|A\|))$ bit operations for computing both matrices H and U. $\|A\| = max_{ij} |A_{ij}|$, $\mathbf{M}(t)$ bit operations are required for multiplication of two $\lceil t \rceil$ bit integer numbers, and θ denotes the exponent for matrix multiplication over a ring: two $m \times m$ matrices over the ring R can be multiplied in $O(m^\theta)$ ring operations from R. Using standard multiplication, $\theta = 3$, while the best known algorithm of *Coppersmith* and *Winograd* [2] allows $\theta = 2.38$. The "soft-oh" notation $O^\sim$ denotes: for any $f, g : \mathbb{R}^n \to \mathbb{R}$, $f = O^\sim(g)$ if and only if $f = O(g \cdot log^c g)$ for some constant $c > 0$.

Note that there are algorithms with similar complexity (*Hafner*, *McCurley* [7]), but they don't find the matrix U, which is essential for our needs, i.e. for solving a system of linear Diophantine equations.

The rank of the matrix A is $\frac{(s+1)(s+3)}{2}$ so the complexity in this case is $O^\sim((\frac{(s+1)(s+3)}{2})^{\theta-1} 2^{2w} \mathbf{M}(\frac{(s+1)(s+3)}{2} log(2^w - 1)))$. Hence, we can take that the complexity is less than $O^\sim(s^4 n^2 \mathbf{M}(s^2 log\, n))$.

Note that, before applying the algorithm for solving the system (2), the polynomial $P(x, y)$ has to be evaluated for all $x, y \in \mathbb{Z}_{2^w}$. Using the Horner schema it can be done in $2^w(s+1)(s+2)\mathbf{M}(w) = n(s+1)(s+2)\mathbf{M}(log\, n)$ bit operations.

What is left in the end, is solving a system of simple linear equations over the ring, which can be done, for example, using the method of Hensel lifting.

Example 1. Let $P(x, y) = 3 + 5x + 7y + 2xy^2 + 4x^3y^3$ be a polynomial over the ring $\mathbb{Z}_{2^3}$. After the reduction, this polynomial is transformed to its canonical form $P(x, y) = 3 + 5x + 7y + 4xy + 2xy^2$.

The polynomial that defines the parastrophic operation is $P_\backslash(x, y) = 3 + 3x + 2x^3 + 3y + 2x^3y^2 + 4y^3 + 2xy^3 + 2x^3y^3$ with canonical form $P_\backslash(x, y) = 3 + 3x + 2x^3 + 7y + 4xy + 2xy^2$. Both quasigroups are given in Table 1.

Table 1. The quasigroup $(\mathbb{Z}_{2^3}, *)$ and its left parastrophe $(\mathbb{Z}_{2^3}, \backslash)$

*	0	1	2	3	4	5	6	7
0	3	2	1	0	7	6	5	4
1	0	5	6	3	4	1	2	7
2	5	0	3	6	1	4	7	2
3	2	3	0	1	6	7	4	5
4	7	6	5	4	3	2	1	0
5	4	1	2	7	0	5	6	3
6	1	4	7	2	5	0	3	6
7	6	7	4	5	2	3	0	1

\	0	1	2	3	4	5	6	7
0	3	2	1	0	7	6	5	4
1	0	5	6	3	4	1	2	7
2	1	4	7	2	5	0	3	6
3	2	3	0	1	6	7	4	5
4	7	6	5	4	3	2	1	0
5	4	1	2	7	0	5	6	3
6	5	0	3	6	1	4	7	2
7	6	7	4	5	2	3	0	1

4 Application of Polynomial Quasigroups in Cryptography

In the previous sections we proved that the parastrophes of the polynomial quasigroups are polynomial as well, and that their canonical form can be found in polynomial time. This means that quasigroup transformations can be used for these quasigroups as well. In this case they are transformations that are in fact performed using operations over the ring $\mathbb{Z}_{2^w}$.

Let denote by $\mathbb{Z}_{2^w}^+$ the set of all nonempty words formed by the elements of $\mathbb{Z}_{2^w}$. Let $P_i, i = 1, \ldots, k$ be the polynomial representations of k polynomial quasigroup operations, not necessarily different, on the set $\mathbb{Z}_{2^w}$. Now the quasigroup string transformations $e_{l;P_1,\dots P_k}, d_{l;P_1,\dots P_k} : \mathbb{Z}_{2^w}^+ \rightarrow \mathbb{Z}_{2^w}^+$, known also as e–transformation and d–transformation, have the following form.

Let $a_i \in \mathbb{Z}_{2^w}$, $M = a_1a_2\dots a_k$. Then

$$e_{l;P_1,\dots,P_k}(M) = b_1\dots b_k \leftrightarrow b_1 = P_1(l,a_1),\ b_2 = P_2(b_1,a_2),\dots,b_k = P_k(b_{k-1},a_k),$$

$$d_{l;P_1,\dots,P_k}(M) = c_1\dots c_k \leftrightarrow c_1 = P_1(l,a_1),\ c_2 = P_2(a_1,a_2),\dots,c_k = P_k(a_{k-1},a_k).$$

The transformations $e_{l;P_1,\dots,P_k}$, $d_{l;P_1\backslash,\dots,P_k\backslash}$ are mutually inverse permutations, and thus can be used to perform encryption and decryption.

We must note a few important things about using polynomial quasigroups for cryptographic primitives.

First, it is advisable to use different polynomials P_i in the quasigroup transformation. This is because these quasigroups are very structured. Their structure comes from the identities

$$P_i(x, y + l2^m) \equiv P(x,y) \pmod{2^m},$$
$$P_i(x + l2^m, y) \equiv P(x,y) \pmod{2^m}.$$

for every $m < w$, $l < 2^w$ $(m, l \in \mathbb{N}_0)$, and can be observed in the example above. The same is true for the parastrophes.

Second, since efficiency and speed is very important when creating crypto-primitives, only polynomials of small degree should be used. We also experimentally determined that the parastrophes of these quasigroups have different degree, and when using a random polynomial quasigroup, if the parastrophe has a very big degree, it might not be efficient to use it this way.

Another important issue is that usually, quasigroups in cryptographic primitives are in the form of a vector valued boolean functions, and the quasigroup transformations are performed over the field $GF(2)$. Now, it becomes possible to define crypto-systems over the ring $\mathbb{Z}_{2^w}$, or define hybrid systems, that exploit the good properties of the field $GF(2)$ and the ring $\mathbb{Z}_{2^w}$. This hybridization may also mean resistance to known attacks that usually work either on $GF(2)$ or on $\mathbb{Z}_{2^w}$, but not on both. This is one of the most promising directions for implementation of these quasigroups in an actual cryptosystem.

At the end, let just note that the pool of the polynomial binary quasigroups defined by polynomials over $\mathbb{Z}_{2^w}$ is an enormous one. Their number was found in [16]. Here we give the number for the first few values of w.

Table 2. Number of polynomial functions over $\mathbb{Z}_{2^w}$ that define quasigroups

$\mathbb{Z}_{2^w}$	$\mathbb{Z}_2$	$\mathbb{Z}_{2^2}$	$\mathbb{Z}_{2^3}$	$\mathbb{Z}_{2^4}$	$\mathbb{Z}_{2^5}$	$\mathbb{Z}_{2^6}$	$\mathbb{Z}_{2^7}$	$\mathbb{Z}_{2^8}$
$\lvert PQ(\mathbb{Z}_{2^w})\rvert$	2	2^5	2^{21}	2^{45}	2^{84}	2^{132}	2^{185}	2^{252}
$\mathbb{Z}_{2^w}$	$\mathbb{Z}_{2^9}$	$\mathbb{Z}_{2^{10}}$	$\mathbb{Z}_{2^{11}}$	$\mathbb{Z}_{2^{12}}$	$\mathbb{Z}_{2^{13}}$	$\mathbb{Z}_{2^{14}}$	$\mathbb{Z}_{2^{15}}$	...
$\lvert PQ(\mathbb{Z}_{2^w})\rvert$	2^{341}	2^{437}	2^{549}	2^{692}	2^{852}	2^{1020}	2^{1209}	...

References

1. Belousov, V.D.: n-ary Quasigroups, Shtiintsa, Kishinev (1972)
2. Coppersmith, D., Winograd, S.: Matrix multiplication via arithmetic progressions. Journal of Symbolic Computation 9, 251–280 (1990)
3. Dénes, J., Keedwell, A.D.: Latin Squares and their Applications. English Univer. Press Ltd. (1974)
4. Gligoroski, D., Markovski, S., Kocarev, L.: Edon-R, An Infinite Family of Cryptographic Hash Functions. International Journal of Network Security 8(3), 293–300 (2009)
5. Gligoroski, D., Knapskog, S.J.: Edon-R(256,384,512) an efficient implementation of Edon-R family of cryptographic hash functions. Journal: Commentationes Mathematicae Universitatis Carolinae 49(2), 219–239 (2008)
6. Gligoroski, D., Markovski, S., Knapskog, S.J.: The Stream Cipher Edon80. In: Robshaw, M.J.B., Billet, O. (eds.) New Stream Cipher Designs. LNCS, vol. 4986, pp. 152–169. Springer, Heidelberg (2008)
7. Hafner, J.L., McCurley, K.S.: Asymptotically fast triangularization of matrices over rings. SIAM Journal of Computing 20(6), 1068–1083 (1991)
8. Gligoroski, D., Markovski, S., Knapskog, S.J.: Multivariate quadratic trapdoor functions based on multivariate quadratic quasigroups. In: American Conference on Applied Mathematics, Harvard, USA (March 2008)
9. Hungerbuhler, N., Specker, E.: A generalization of the Smarandache function to several variables. INTEGERS: Electronic Journal of Combinatorial Number Theory 6, A23 (2006)
10. Markovski, S.: Quasigroup string processing and applications in cryptography. In: Proc. 1st Inter. Conf. Mathematics and Informatics for industry MII, Thessaloniki, pp. 278–290 (2003)
11. Markovski, S., Shunic, Z., Gligoroski, D.: Polynomial functions on the units of $\mathbb{Z}_{2^n}$. Quasigroups and related systems 18, 59–82 (2010)
12. Markovski, S., Gligoroski, D., Bakeva, V.: Quasigroup String Processing: Part 1. Maced. Acad. of Sci. and Arts, Sc. Math. Tech. Scien. XX 1-2, 13–28 (1999)
13. Markovski, S.,Mileva, A.: NaSHA cryptographic hash function, contributors - Samardziska, S., Jakimovski, B., (programmers) SHA-3 Submission and Round-1 candidate, `http://csrc.nist.gov/groups/ST/hash/sha-3/Round1/documents/NaSHA.zip`, `http://en.wikipedia.org/wiki/NaSHA`
14. Rivest, R.L.: Permutation polynomials modulo 2^w. Finite Fields and Their Applications 7, 287–292 (2001)
15. Samardziska, S., Markovski, S.: Polynomial n-ary quasigroups. Mathematica Macedonica 5, 77–81 (2007)
16. Samardziska, S., Markovski, S.: On the number of polynomial quasigroups of order 2^{w}. In: Proceedings of the IV Congress of the Mathematicians of R. Macedonia (2008) (in print)
17. Shekhar, N., Kalla, P., Enescu, F., Gopalakrishnan, S.: Equivalence verification of polynomial datapaths with fixed-size bit-vectors using finite ring algebra. In: Proceedings of the 2005 IEEE/ACM International Conference on Computer-Aided Design, San Jose, CA, pp. 291–296 (2005)
18. Storjohann, A., Labahn, G.: Asymptotically Fast Computation of Hermite Normal Forms of Integer Matrices. In: Proceedings of the 1996 International Symposium on Symbolic and Algebraic Computation, pp. 259–266 (1996)

Some Probabilistic Properties of Quasigroup Processed Strings Useful for Cryptanalysis

Verica Bakeva and Vesna Dimitrova

Faculty of the Natural Sciences and Mathematics,
Institute of Informatics, P.O.Box 162
Skopje, Republic of Macedonia
{verica,vesnap}@ii.edu.mk

Abstract. Quasigroup string transformations are already used for designing of several cryptographic primitives. The application of quasigroup transformations as encryption algorithm is based on the previously proved result: the distribution of m-tuples in arbitrary string processed by application of quasigroup $E^{(n)}$-transformation is uniformly distributed for $m \leq n$. In this paper, we give some probabilistic properties of quasigroup processed strings that can be used in cryptanalysis. Namely, we find the distribution of m-tuples in an arbitrary string processed by application of quasigroup $E^{(n)}$-transformation ($m > n$). Since this distribution is not uniform, it can be used for statistical attack in order to discover the original message and we give an algorithm for this kind of attack. Suitable experimental results are presented as well.

Keywords: Quasigroup, quasigroup string transformations, distribution of m-tuples, uniform distribution.

1 Preliminaries

The quasigroup string transformations E, and their properties, were considered in several papers ([1], [2], [3], [4] and [5]). Here we investigate the distributions of m-tuples in quasigroup processed strings (QPS) obtained after n applications of quasigroup transformations E on input messages (string) when $m > n$.

Recall that a quasigroup $(Q, *)$ is a groupoid satisfying the law:

$$(\forall u, v \in Q)(\exists! x, y \in Q) \ \ (x * u = v \ \& \ u * y = v) \tag{1}$$

In fact, (1) says that a groupoid $(Q, *)$ is a quasigroup if and only if the equations $x * u = v$ and $u * y = v$ have unique solutions x and y for each given $u, v \in Q$. Given a quasigroup $(Q, *)$, a new operation "$\backslash$", called a parastrophe, can be derived from the operation $*$ as follows:

$$x * y = z \qquad \Leftrightarrow \qquad y = x \setminus z. \tag{2}$$

Let $A = \{1, \ldots, s\}$ be an alphabet ($s \geq 2$) and denote by $A^+ = \{x_1 \ldots x_k | \ x_i \in A, \ k \geq 1\}$ the set of all finite strings over A. Note that $A^+ = \bigcup_{k \geq 1} A^k$, where

M. Gusev and P. Mitrevski (Eds.): ICT Innovations 2010, CCIS 83, pp. 61–70, 2011.

$A^k = \{x_1 \dots x_k | \; x_i \in A\}$. Assuming that $(A, *)$ is a given quasigroup, for a fixed letter $l \in A$ (called leader) we define transformation $E = E_l^{(1)} : A^+ \to A^+$ by

$$E(x_1 \dots x_k) = y_1 \dots y_k \Leftrightarrow \begin{cases} y_1 = l * x_1, \\ y_i = y_{i-1} * x_i, \quad i = 2, \dots, k \end{cases} \tag{3}$$

where $x_i, y_i \in A$. Then, for given quasigroup operations $*_1, *_2, \dots, *_n$ on the set A, we can define mappings $E_1, E_2, \dots, E_n$, in the same manner as previous by choosing fixed elements $l_1, l_2, \dots, l_n \in A$ (such that E_i is corresponding to $*_i$ and l_i). Let

$$E^{(n)} = E^{(n)}_{l_n, \dots, l_1} = E_n \circ E_{n-1} \circ \dots \circ E_1,$$

where $\circ$ is the usual composition of mappings ($n \geq 1$). It is easy to check that the mappings E is a bijection.

In the paper [1], Markovski et al. proposed a transformation $E^{(n)}$ as an encryption function and proved the following theorem.

Theorem 1. *Let $\alpha \in A^+$ be an arbitrary string and $\beta = E^{(n)}(\alpha)$. Then m-tuples in β are uniformly distributed for $m \leq n$.*

In the same paper, the authors remarked that generally, the distribution of the substrings of length m is not uniform for $m > n$, but these distributions are not found there.

Here, we find these distributions theoretically and we give suitable experimental results. Without loss of generality, we take all operations $*_1$, $*_2, \dots$, $*_n$ to be the same (denoted by $*$). The same results will be obtained for arbitrary $*_1$, $*_2, \dots$, $*_n$.

In Section 2 we give distribution of $(n+1)$-tuples after application of $E^{(n)}$-transformation. The distribution of m-tuples ($m > n$) after application of $E^{(n)}$-transformation is given in Section 3. In Section 4 we present some experiments in order to visualize our theoretical results. We give an algorithm for statistical attack presented in Section 5. Some conclusions are given in Section 6.

2 Distribution of $(n+1)$-tuples After Application of $E^{(n)}$-transformation

Let the alphabet A be as above. A randomly chosen element of the set A^k can be considered as a random vector $(X_1, X_2, \dots, X_k)$, where A is the range of X_i, $i = 1, \dots, k$. We consider these vectors as input messages. Let $(Y_1^{(n)}, Y_2^{(n)}, \dots, Y_k^{(n)})$ be defined as follows.

$$(Y_1^{(n)}, Y_2^{(n)}, \dots, Y_k^{(n)}) = E^{(n)}(X_1, X_2, \dots, X_k).$$

According to (3), for each $i = 1, 2, \dots, k$, we have

$$Y_i^{(r)} = Y_{i-1}^{(r)} * Y_i^{(r-1)} \tag{4}$$

for $r = 1, 2 \dots, n$, where $Y_i^{(0)} = X_i$. Note that $Y_0^{(r)} = l_r$ is leader, $r = 1, 2 \dots, n$.

Let the distribution of each letter from the input message $(X_1, \ldots, X_k)$ be given by $P\{X_i = j\} = p_j$, $j = 1, 2, \ldots, s$, where $\sum_{j=1}^{s} p_j = 1$, for $i = 1, 2, \ldots, k$ and let the letters in input message occur independently. These means that $X_1, X_2, \ldots, X_k$ are independent and identically distributed random variables.

Theorem 2. *Let $(p_1, p_2, \ldots, p_s)$ be the distribution of letters in an input string and let $p_1, p_2, \ldots, p_s$ be distinct probabilities, i.e., $p_i \neq p_j$ for $i \neq j$. The probabilities of $(n+1)$-tuples in $(Y_1^{(n)}, Y_2^{(n)}, \ldots, Y_k^{(n)})$ are divided in s classes. Each class contains s^n elements with the same probabilities and the probability of each $(n+1)$-tuple in i-th class is $\frac{1}{s^n} p_i$, for $i = 1, 2, \ldots, s$.*

Proof. Let $n = 1$. By total probability theorem, we obtain:

$$\begin{aligned} &P\{Y_i^{(1)} = y_i, Y_{i+1}^{(1)} = y_{i+1}\} \\ &\quad = \sum_{y_{i-1}=1}^{s} P\{Y_{i-1}^{(1)} = y_{i-1}\} P\{Y_i^{(1)} = y_i, Y_{i+1}^{(1)} = y_{i+1} | Y_{i-1}^{(1)} = y_{i-1}\} \end{aligned}$$

According to Theorem 1, the distribution of $Y_{i-1}^{(1)}$ is uniform on the set A, so $P\{Y_{i-1}^{(1)} = y_{i-1}\} = \frac{1}{s}$. Using (4) and applying (2), we obtain

$$\begin{aligned} &P\{Y_i^{(1)} = y_i, Y_{i+1}^{(1)} = y_{i+1}\} = \\ &\quad = \frac{1}{s} \sum_{y_{i-1}=1}^{s} P\{Y_{i-1}^{(1)} * X_i = y_i, \quad Y_i^{(1)} * X_{i+1} = y_{i+1} | Y_{i-1}^{(1)} = y_{i-1}\} \\ &\quad = \frac{1}{s} \sum_{y_{i-1}=1}^{s} P\{y_{i-1} * X_i = y_i, \quad y_i * X_{i+1} = y_{i+1}\} \\ &\quad = \frac{1}{s} \sum_{y_{i-1}=1}^{s} P\{X_i = y_{i-1} \setminus y_i, X_{i+1} = y_i \setminus y_{i+1}\}. \end{aligned}$$

Note that if y_{i-1} runs over all values of A then for fixed y_i, the expression $y_{i-1} \setminus y_i = x$ runs over all values of A, too. Applying the total probability theorem, we get

$$\begin{aligned} P\{Y_i^{(1)} = y_i, Y_{i+1}^{(1)} = y_{i+1}\} &= \frac{1}{s} \sum_{x=1}^{s} P\{X_i = x, X_{i+1} = y_i \setminus y_{i+1}\} \\ = \frac{1}{s} P\{X_{i+1} = y_i \setminus y_{i+1}\} &= \frac{1}{s} P\{X_{i+1} = r\} = \frac{1}{s} p_r, \end{aligned}$$

where $r = y_i \setminus y_{i+1}$.

Let the inductive hypothesis be the following: The probabilities of n-tuples in $(Y_1^{(n-1)}, Y_2^{(n-1)}, \ldots, Y_k^{(n-1)})$ are divided in s classes. Each class contains s^{n-1} elements with the same probabilities and the probability of each n-tuple in i-th class is $\frac{1}{s^{n-1}} p_i$ for $i = 1, 2, \ldots, s$.

In the next inductive step, using the total probability theorem, the equality (4) and the equivalence (2), for probability of an arbitrary $(n+1)$-tuple after application of $E^{(n)}$-transformation, we obtain the following.

$$\begin{aligned}
&P\{Y_i^{(n)} = y_i, Y_{i+1}^{(n)} = y_{i+1}, \ldots, Y_{i+n}^{(n)} = y_{i+n}\} \\
&= \sum_{y_{i-1}=1}^{s} P\{Y_{i-1}^{(n)} = y_{i-1}\} P\{Y_i^{(n)} = y_i, Y_{i+1}^{(n)} = y_{i+1}, \ldots, Y_{i+n}^{(n)} = y_{i+n} | Y_{i-1}^{(n)} = y_{i-1}\} \\
&= \frac{1}{s} \sum_{y_{i-1}=1}^{s} P\{Y_i^{(n-1)} = y_{i-1} \setminus y_i, Y_{i+1}^{(n-1)} = y_i \setminus y_{i+1}, \ldots, Y_{i+n}^{(n-1)} = y_{i+n-1} \setminus y_{i+n}\} \\
&= \frac{1}{s} P\{Y_{i+1}^{(n-1)} = y_i \setminus y_{i+1}, \ldots, Y_{i+n}^{(n-1)} = y_{i+n-1} \setminus y_{i+n}\}
\end{aligned}$$

Now, from the inductive hypotheses if n-tuple $(y_i \setminus y_{i+1}, \ldots, y_{i+n-1} \setminus y_{i+n})$ belongs to the r-th class, then we obtain

$$P\{Y_i^{(n)} = y_i, Y_{i+1}^{(n)} = y_{i+1}, \ldots, Y_{i+n}^{(n)} = y_{i+n}\} = \frac{1}{s} \frac{1}{s^{n-1}} p_r = \frac{1}{s^n} p_r.$$

Previously, we obtained that

$$\begin{aligned}
P\{Y_i^{(n)} &= y_i, Y_{i+1}^{(n)} = y_{i+1}, \ldots, Y_{i+n}^{(n)} = y_{i+n}\} \\
&= \frac{1}{s} P\{Y_{i+1}^{(n-1)} = y_i \setminus y_{i+1}, \ldots, Y_{i+n}^{(n-1)} = y_{i+n-1} \setminus y_{i+n}\}.
\end{aligned}$$

If each of y_i, y_{i+1}, ..., y_{i+n} runs over all values of A then

$$(y_i \setminus y_{i+1},\ y_{i+1} \setminus y_{i+2},\ \ldots,\ y_{i+n-1} \setminus y_{i+n})$$

runs over all values of A^n. This implies that each class contains s^n elements.

Corollary 1. If $p_{i_1} = p_{i_2} = \ldots = p_{i_\nu}$ for some $1 \le i_1 < \ldots < i_\nu \le s$ in Theorem 2, then the classes with probabilities $\frac{1}{s^n} p_{i_1}, \frac{1}{s^n} p_{i_2}, \ldots, \frac{1}{s^n} p_{i_\nu}$ will be merged in one class with νs^n elements.

3 Distribution of m-tuples $(m > n)$ After Application of $E^{(n)}$-transformation

In this section we give a generalization of result obtained in the previous one. Namely, we give the distribution of m-tuples after application of $E^{(n)}$-transformation, where m is an arbitrary integer greater than n.

Theorem 3. *Let $(p_1, p_2, \ldots, p_s)$ be the distribution of the letters in an input string and let K be the number of all distinct products $p_{i_1} \cdots p_{i_{m-n}}$ for $i_1, i_2, \ldots, i_{m-n} \in A$. Then the probabilities of m-tuples $(m > n)$ in $(Y_1^{(n)}, Y_2^{(n)}, \ldots, Y_k^{(n)})$ are divided in K classes. The m-tuples in a class have the same probabilities.*

Proof. According to Theorem 1, if $r \leq n$, we have that $P\{Y_i^{(r)} = y_i\} = \frac{1}{s}$, for each $y_i \in A$ and each $i = 1, 2, \ldots, k$. Using the same procedure as in the proof of Theorem 2, we find the distribution of m-tuples in $(Y_1^{(n)}, Y_2^{(n)}, \ldots, Y_k^{(n)})$ for $m > n$. In the first step, we obtain

$$
\begin{aligned}
&P\{Y_i^{(n)} = y_i^{(n)}, Y_{i+1}^{(n)} = y_{i+1}^{(n)}, Y_{i+2}^{(n)} = y_{i+2}^{(n)}, \ldots, Y_{i+m-1}^{(n)} = y_{i+m-1}^{(n)}\} \\
&= \sum_{k_1=1}^{s} P\{Y_{i-1}^{(n)} = k_1\} P\{Y_i^{(n)} = y_i^{(n)}, Y_{i+1}^{(n)} = y_{i+1}^{(n)}, Y_{i+2}^{(n)} = y_{i+2}^{(n)}, \ldots, \\
&\qquad\qquad \ldots, Y_{i+m-1}^{(n)} = y_{i+m-1}^{(n)} | Y_{i-1}^{(n)} = k_1\} \\
&= \frac{1}{s} \sum_{k_1=1}^{s} P\{Y_i^{(n-1)} = k_1 \setminus y_i^{(n)}, Y_{i+1}^{(n-1)} = y_i^{(n)} \setminus y_{i+1}^{(n)}, Y_{i+2}^{(n-1)} = y_{i+1}^{(n)} \setminus y_{i+2}^{(n)}, \\
&\qquad\qquad \ldots, Y_{i+m-1}^{(n-1)} = y_{i+m-2}^{(n)} \setminus y_{i+m-1}^{(n)}\} \\
&= \frac{1}{s} P\{Y_{i+1}^{(n-1)} = y_i^{(n)} \setminus y_{i+1}^{(n)}, Y_{i+2}^{(n-1)} = y_{i+1}^{(n)} \setminus y_{i+2}^{(n)}, \ldots Y_{i+m-1}^{(n-1)} = y_{i+m-2}^{(n)} \setminus y_{i+m-1}^{(n)}\} \\
&= \frac{1}{s} P\{Y_{i+1}^{(n-1)} = y_{i+1}^{(n-1)}, Y_{i+2}^{(n-1)} = y_{i+2}^{(n-1)}, \ldots, Y_{i+m-1}^{(n-1)} = y_{i+m-1}^{(n-1)}\}
\end{aligned}
$$

where $y_t^{(n-1)} = y_{t-1}^{(n)} \setminus y_t^{(n)}$ for $t = i+1, i+2, \ldots, i+m-1$.

In the second step, we obtain the following.

$$
\begin{aligned}
&P\{Y_i^{(n)} = y_i^{(n)}, Y_{i+1}^{(n)} = y_{i+1}^{(n)}, Y_{i+2}^{(n)} = y_{i+2}^{(n)}, \ldots, Y_{i+m-1}^{(n)} = y_{i+m-1}^{(n)}\} \\
&= \frac{1}{s} \sum_{k_2=1}^{s} P\{Y_i^{(n-1)} = k_2\} P\{Y_{i+1}^{(n-1)} = y_{i+1}^{(n-1)}, Y_{i+2}^{(n-1)} = y_{i+2}^{(n-1)}, \ldots, \\
&\qquad\qquad \ldots, Y_{i+m-1}^{(n-1)} = y_{i+m-1}^{(n-1)} | Y_i^{(n-1)} = k_2\} \\
&= \frac{1}{s^2} \sum_{k_2=1}^{s} P\{Y_{i+1}^{(n-2)} = k_2 \setminus y_{i+1}^{(n-1)}, Y_{i+2}^{(n-2)} = y_{i+1}^{(n-1)} \setminus y_{i+2}^{(n-1)}, \ldots, \\
&\qquad\qquad \ldots, Y_{i+m-1}^{(n-2)} = y_{i+m-2}^{(n-1)} \setminus y_{i+m-1}^{(n-1)}\} \\
&= \frac{1}{s^2} P\{Y_{i+2}^{(n-2)} = y_{i+1}^{(n-1)} \setminus y_{i+2}^{(n-1)}, \ldots, Y_{i+m-1}^{(n-2)} = y_{i+m-2}^{(n-1)} \setminus y_{i+m-1}^{(n-1)}\} \\
&= \frac{1}{s^2} P\{Y_{i+2}^{(n-2)} = y_{i+2}^{(n-2)}, \ldots, Y_{i+m-1}^{(n-2)} = y_{i+m-1}^{(n-2)}\}
\end{aligned}
$$

where $y_t^{(n-2)} = y_{t-1}^{(n-1)} \setminus y_t^{(n-1)}$ for $t = i+2, \ldots, i+m-1$. If we continue on this way, in the n-th step, we have the following.

$$
\begin{aligned}
&P\{Y_i^{(n)} = y_i^{(n)}, Y_{i+1}^{(n)} = y_{i+1}^{(n)}, Y_{i+2}^{(n)} = y_{i+2}^{(n)}, \ldots, Y_{i+m-1}^{(n)} = y_{i+m-1}^{(n)}\} \\
&= \frac{1}{s^n} P\{Y_{i+n}^{(0)} = y_{i+n}^{(0)}, \ldots, Y_{i+m-1}^{(0)} = y_{i+m-1}^{(0)}\} \\
&= \frac{1}{s^n} P\{X_{i+n} = y_{i+n}^{(0)}, \ldots, X_{i+m-1} = y_{i+m-1}^{(0)}\}.
\end{aligned}
$$

Since $X_{i+n}, \ldots X_{i+m-1}$ are independent random variables, we obtain the distribution of m-tuples given below.

$$P\{Y_i^{(n)} = y_i^{(n)}, Y_{i+1}^{(n)} = y_{i+1}^{(n)}, Y_{i+2}^{(n)} = y_{i+2}^{(n)}, \ldots, Y_{i+m-1}^{(n)} = y_{i+m-1}^{(n)}\}$$
$$= \frac{1}{s^n} P\{X_{i+n} = y_{i+n}^{(0)}\} \cdots P\{X_{i+m-1} = y_{i+m-1}^{(0)}\} = \frac{1}{s^n} p_{y_{i+n}^{(0)}} \cdots p_{y_{i+m-1}^{(0)}},$$

where p_i are initial probabilities of letters in A, $i = 1, \ldots, s$.

Now, if K is the number of all distinct values of the previous product, it is clear that the probabilities of m-tuples in $(Y_1^{(n)}, Y_2^{(n)}, \ldots, Y_k^{(n)})$ are divided in K classes.

Corollary 2. Let r be a number of different probabilities $p_1, p_2, \ldots, p_s$ of letters in the alphabet A. If all products $p_{i_1} \ldots p_{i_{m-n}}$ are distinct then their number is $\overline{C}_r^{m-n}$, where $\overline{C}_r^k$ is the total number of k-combinations with repetitions of r-element set.

The proof of Corollary 2 follows directly from Theorem 3.

From the proof of the previous theorem we can notice that the probability of m-tuples is

$$P\{Y_i^{(n)} = y_i^{(n)}, Y_{i+1}^{(n)} = y_{i+1}^{(n)}, \ldots, Y_{i+m-1}^{(n)} = y_{i+m-1}^{(n)}\} = \frac{1}{s^n} p_{y_{i+n}^{(0)}} \cdots p_{y_{i+m-1}^{(0)}},$$

and it can be presented in a form $\frac{1}{s^n} p_1^{n_1} p_2^{n_2} \ldots p_r^{n_r}$ where $n_1+n_2+\ldots+n_r = m-n$.

Let the sequence $n_1, n_2, \ldots, n_r$ contain a distinct values $n_{i_1}, n_{i_2}, \ldots, n_{i_a}$. We denote by f_j the frequency of n_{i_j} in the sequence $n_1, n_2, \ldots, n_r$, $j = 1, \ldots, a$. Therefore $f_1 + f_2 + \ldots + f_a = r$.

Let $P_n(i_1, i_2, \ldots, i_k)$ be the number of permutations with repetitions of n elements, where $i_1 + i_2 + \ldots + i_k = n$. The following theorem gives the number of classes with the probability $\frac{1}{s^n} p_1^{n_1} p_2^{n_2} \ldots p_r^{n_r}$ and the number of elements in each class.

Theorem 4. *Let $(p_1, p_2, \ldots, p_s)$ be the distribution of letters in an input string, where $p_1, p_2, \ldots, p_s$ are distinct probabilities and all products $p_1^{n_1} p_2^{n_2} \ldots p_s^{n_s}$ are distinct for $n_1+n_2+\ldots+n_s = m-n$. Let m-tuples be divided in classes with the same probabilities as in Theorem 3. Then the following statements are satisfied.*

i) If the probability of m-tuples in a class is $\frac{1}{s^n} p_1^{n_1} p_2^{n_2} \ldots p_s^{n_s}$ then this class contains $s^n P_{m-n}(n_1, n_2, \ldots, n_s)$ elements.
ii) The number of classes with $s^n P_{m-n}(n_1, n_2, \ldots, n_s)$ elements is $P_s(f_1, f_2, \ldots, f_a)$ where a is the number of distinct values in the sequence $n_1, n_2, \ldots, n_s$, and $f_1, f_2, \ldots, f_a$ are the corresponding frequencies.

Proof. *i)* For fixed $l \in A$, if we apply the $E_l^{(1)}$-transformation on a fixed $(m-n)$-tuple $(y_{i+n}^{(0)}, \ldots, y_{i+m-1}^{(0)})$ we obtain the $(m-n+1)$-tuple $(l, y_{i+n}^{(1)}, \ldots, y_{i+m-1}^{(1)})$.

For each $l = 1, 2, \ldots, s$, we obtain a different $(m - n + 1)$-tuple. This means that after applying of $E_l^{(1)}$-transformation for $l = 1, 2, \ldots, s$, we have totaly s different $(m - n + 1)$-tuples.

In this way, after application of $E^{(n)}_{l_n,\ldots,l_1}$ on the $(y^{(0)}_{i+n}, \ldots, y^{(0)}_{i+m-1})$ for $(l_1, l_2, \ldots, l_n) \in A^n$, we obtain s^n different $(m - n + n)$-tuples, i.e. s^n different m-tuples.

On the other side, we have $P_{m-n}(n_1, n_2, \ldots, n_s)$ different $(m-n)$-tuples with the same probability $\frac{1}{s^n} p_1^{n_1} p_2^{n_2} \ldots p_s^{n_s}$. Namely, these are all $(m-n)$-tuples, where 1 appears n_1 times, 2 appears n_2 times, and so on.

We have proved that the number of $(m - n)$-tuples with the probability $\frac{1}{s^n} p_1^{n_1} p_2^{n_2} \ldots p_s^{n_s}$ is $P_{m-n}(n_1, n_2, \ldots, n_s)$. Each $(m - n)$-tuple produces s^n different m-tuples after application of $E^{(n)}$- transformation with different choice of n leaders. Therefore, the number of elements in the class with probability $\frac{1}{s^n} p_1^{n_1} p_2^{n_2} \ldots p_s^{n_s}$ is $s^n P_{m-n}(n_1, n_2, \ldots, n_s)$.

ii) Let $(\sigma(1), \sigma(2), \ldots, \sigma(s))$ be a permutation of $(n_1, n_2, \ldots, n_s)$. The classes with the probabilities $\frac{1}{s^n} p_1^{n_1} p_2^{n_2} \ldots p_s^{n_s}$ and $\frac{1}{s^n} p_1^{\sigma(1)} p_2^{\sigma(2)} \ldots p_s^{\sigma(s)}$ have the same number of elements since $P_{m-n}(n_1, n_2, \ldots, n_s) = P_{m-n}(\sigma(1), \sigma(2), \ldots, \sigma(s))$. This implies that the number of classes with $s^n P_{m-n}(n_1, n_2, \ldots, n_s)$ elements is equal to the total number of permutations of $(n_1, n_2, \ldots, n_s)$, i.e. $P_s(f_1, \ldots, f_a)$.

Corollary 3. If the probability $p_1^{n_1} p_2^{n_2} \ldots p_s^{n_s}$ in Theorem 3, can be obtained in two (or more) ways with different choices of $n_1, n_2, \ldots, n_s$ $(n_1 + n_2 + \ldots + n_s = m - n)$ then two (or more) classes will have a same probability and these classes will be merged in one class.

Theorem 4 gives the results when probabilities $p_1, p_2, \ldots, p_s$ are distinct and all products $p_1^{n_1} p_2^{n_2} \ldots p_s^{n_s}$ are distinct, too. In the next theorem we give the similar results when some of these probabilities are equal.

Theorem 5. *Let m-tuples be divided in classes with the same probabilities as in Theorem 3. Let $p_1, p_2, \ldots, p_s$ be distinct probabilities except b of them (without loss of generality, let $p_1 = p_2 = \ldots = p_b$) and all products $\frac{1}{s^n} p_1^{n_1} p_{b+1}^{n_{b+1}} \ldots p_s^{n_s}$ be distinct for $n_1 + n_{b+1} + \ldots + n_s = m - n$.*

i) *If the probability of m-tuples in a class is $\frac{1}{s^n} p_1^{n_1} p_{b+1}^{n_{b+1}} \ldots p_s^{n_s}$ then the number of element in this class is*

$$s^n \sum_{\substack{i_1, \ldots, i_b \\ i_1 + \ldots + i_b = n_1}} P_{m-n}(i_1, i_2, \ldots, i_b, n_{b+1}, \ldots, n_s) \tag{5}$$

ii) *The number of classes which contain (5) elements (m-tuples) is $P_{s-b}(f_1, f_2, \ldots, f_a)$ where a is the number of distinct values in the sequence $n_{b+1}, \ldots, n_s$ and f_j are the corresponding frequencies.*

The proof of this theorem follows directly from Theorem 4 since $p_1^{n_1}$ is the probability of all n_1-tuples, where 1 appears i_1 times, 2 appears i_2 times,..., b appears i_b times and $i_1 + i_2 + \ldots + i_b = n_1$.

Let note that Corollary 3 holds for Theorem 5 when some of the products $\frac{1}{s^n} p_1^{n_1} p_{b+1}^{n_{b+1}} \ldots p_s^{n_s}$ are not distinct.

4 Experimental Results

We made several experiments in order to illustrate some of the previous theoretical results. At first, we have randomly chosen a message with 1,000,000 letters of the alphabet $A = \{1, 2, 3, 4\}$ with the following distribution of the letters:

$$p_1 = 0.45, \quad p_2 = 0.3, \quad p_3 = 0.2, \quad p_4 = 0.05. \tag{6}$$

For our experiments we use the following quasigroup: 2143||4321||3214||1432.

The distributions of 4-tuples after applying $E^{(4)}$, $E^{(3)}$ and $E^{(2)}$-transformations are presented in Figure 1 a), b) and c), correspondingly. In this figure, experimental probabilities are presented by points, and theoretical probabilities are presented by lines.

From the Figure 1 a), we can see that 4-tuples after applying of $E^{(4)}$ are almost uniformly distributed according to Theorem 1. In Figure 1 b), probabilities of 4-tuples, after applying of $E^{(3)}$, are divided in 4 classes and each class contains 64 elements. This result corresponds to theoretical statements in Theorem 2. From Figure 1 c), we can see that 4-tuples after applying of $E^{(2)}$ are divided in 9 classes. Namely, if all products $p_{i_1} p_{i_2}$ are distinct then the number of classes will be $\overline{C}_4^{4-2} = 10$. Since $p_1 p_3 = p_2^2$, the classes with same probability $\frac{1}{4^2} p_1 p_3 = \frac{1}{4^2} p_2^2 = \frac{9}{1600}$ are merged in one class with $32 + 16 = 48$ elements. Therefore, we obtain 9 instead 10 classes. Obtained number of elements in a class corresponds to number given by Theorem 3, Theorem 4 and Corollary 3.

In order to illustrate the results from Theorem 5 we made an experiment where we apply $E^{(2)}$ on an input message with length 1,000,000, where distribution of letters is given by $p_1 = 0.4, p_2 = 0.3, p_3 = p_4 = 0.15$. The probabilities of 4-tuples are divided in 6 classes according to Theorem 5 (see Figure 1 d)).

5 Cryptanalysis with Statistical Attack

We will show how these theoretical results can be used for statistical attack for discovering the original message. Therefore, we give an algorithm which present how this attack can be done.

Let the sender write a message M, encrypt it using encryption algorithm based on $E^{(n)}$-quasigroup transformation for fixed n and send the obtained message $C = E^{(n)}(M)$. Let an intruder catch the encrypted message C and try to find the original message M. Suppose that the intruder knows that encryption algorithm

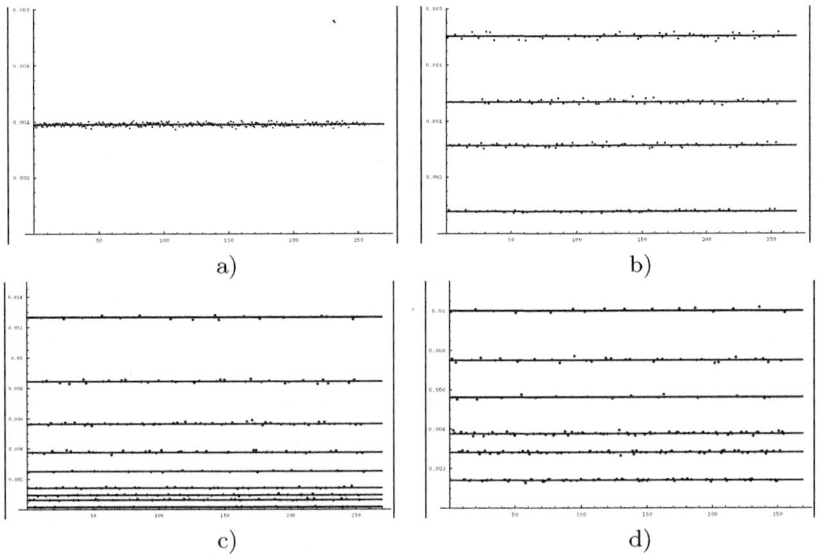

Fig. 1. The distributions of 4-tuples after application of $E^{(n)}$ transformation

based on $E^{(n)}$-quasigroup transformation is used. Also, let suppose that the distribution of the letters $(p_1, p_2, \ldots, p_s)$ in language used in original message is known. The intruder can do a statistical attack using the algorithm given in Table 1.

Table 1.

Algorithm of statistical attack

Input: An encrypt message C and the distribution $(p_1, p_2, \ldots, p_s)$ of the letters in language.

Output: The original message M.

Step 1. Find the relative frequencies (statistical probabilities) of letters, pairs, 3-tuples and so on, until you obtain distribution which is not uniform. Let say that n is the smallest number such that $(n+1)$-tuples are not uniformly distributed.

Step 2. Process whole message C in the following way.
Take the first $(n+1)$-tuple and find its relative frequency f.

2.1. Find i such that $|f - \frac{1}{s^n} p_i| = \min_{1 \leq j \leq s} |f - \frac{1}{s^n} p_j|$.

2.2. Decrypt this $(n+1)$-tuple with the letter i.

2.3. Take the next $(n+1)$-tuple and find its relative frequency f and go to step 2.1.

Note that the first two letters from the original message M can not be find in this way. They can be easy find by questing if it is important for message.

A most important thing for application of this algorithm is the length of the message C. Namely, it must be enough long in order to obtain relative frequencies of $(n+1)$-tuples as soon as closer to their probabilities in the language. If C is a short message then we cannot do a real statistical analysis of the text and the decrypted message M_1 will not correspond to the original message M.

We made several experiments taking randomly chosen messages with different lengths of the alphabet $A = \{1, 2, 3, 4\}$ with the distribution of the letters (6). We encrypted each message M using the $E^{(2)}$-transformation with the quasigroups given before. We found the relative frequencies of 3-tuples and applied the previous algorithm. The obtained results are the following ones. If a message length is 12 000 letters, then the whole message is correctly decrypted. If a message length is 11 000 letters, then 0,1% of letters are incorrectly decrypted. For for message length 10 000 - 1,8% and for message length 5 000 - 5%, and so on. It is clear that shorter message length gives the larger number of incorrectly decrypted letters.

We obtained the similar results when $E^{(3)}$-transformation is applied for encryption on the longer messages.

6 Conclusion

In this paper, we find the distributions of m-tuples in arbitrary string processed by application of quasigroup $E^{(n)}$-transformation for $m > n$. We show how the obtained results can be used in cryptanalysis.

If $E^{(n)}$-transformation is used as an encryption algorithm then according to our results we can find the distributions of $(n + 1)$-tuples. If n is not enough large number, then we can find the empirical distribution of $(n + 1)$-tuples and use them for statistical attack in order to discover the original message.

Note that if an intruder catches and concatenates a lot of short messages encrypted by the same $E^{(n)}$-transformation, it will obtain a long message and it can apply a statistical attack. It will be impossible if different quasigroups are used in encryption $E^{(n)}$-transformation.

The previous implies that n must be enough large number to be impossible for intruder to find statistical probabilities of $(n+1)$-tuples if it catches enough large message (or makes it by concatenation of short messages) and to provide an encryption algorithm resistant on statistical kind of attacks. Also, most frequently changing of quasigroups used in $E^{(n)}$-transformation is recommended.

References

1. Markovski, S., Gligoroski, D., Bakeva, V.: Quasigrouop string processing: Part 1. Contributions. Sec. Math. Tech. Sci., MANU XX 1-2, 13–28 (1999)
2. Markovski, S., Kusakatov, V.: Quasigroup String Processing: Part 2. Contributions, Sec. Math. Tech.Sci., MANU XXI, 1-2, 15–32 (2000)
3. Markovski, S., Kusakatov, V.: Quasigroup String Processing: Part 3. Contributions, Sec. Math. Tech.Sci., MANU XXIII-XXIV, 1-2, 7–27 (2002-2003)
4. Markovski, S., Bakeva, V.: Quasigrouop string processing: Part 4. Contributions, Sec.Math.Tech.Sci., MANU XXVII-XXVIII, 1-2, 41–53 (2006-2007)
5. Markovski, S.: Quasigroup string processing and applications in cryptography. In: First Intern. Conf. Mathematics and Informatics for Industry, Thessaloniki, Greece, pp. 278–289 (2003)

A Compositional Method for Deciding Program Termination

Aleksandar Dimovski

FON University, Faculty of Information and Communication Technologies, Skopje, Macedonia
aleksandar.dimovski@fon.edu.mk

Abstract. One of the major challenges in computer science is to put programming on a firmer mathematical basis, in order to improve the correctness of programs. This paper describes a concrete implementation of a semantic-based approach for verifying termination of open nondeterministic programs with finite data types. The presentation is focused on Erratic Idealized Algol, which represents a nondeterministic programming language that embodies many of the core ingredients of imperative and higher-order functional languages. The fully abstract game semantics of the language is used to obtain a compositional, incremental way of generating accurate models of programs. The CSP process algebra is used as a concrete formalism for representation of game models and their efficient verification. Termination of programs is decided by checking divergence-freedom of CSP processes using the FDR tool. The effectiveness of this method is presented by several examples.

Keywords: Software verification, Game semantics, CSP process algebra.

1 Introduction

Software verification addresses the problem of checking that programs satisfy certain properties. There are two main classes of program properties of interest: *safety* and *liveness*. The safety properties demand that the program never performs an undesirable operation. For example, it never divides by zero. The liveness properties demand that the program eventually performs desirable operations. For example, it eventually terminates. In general, both problems are undecidable but, in the past decades, significant advances have been made by developing methods which show that verification problems are becoming increasingly feasible. Model checking [4] has proved to be one of the most effective methods of automatic software verification. In model checking, the program to be verified is represented by a model, which consists of a description of all possible program executions (behaviors) in a mathematical structure like a finite state automaton. The property to be established is a formula in a logic that is interpreted over such structures (e.g. temporal logic). Program correctness is then shown by computing that the formula is satisfied by the model. This check is performed by exhaustively exploring the entire state space of the model

M. Gusev and P. Mitrevski (Eds.): ICT Innovations 2010, CCIS 83, pp. 71–80, 2011.

to ensure that all possible behaviors generated indeed satisfy the property. The traditional approach to building models of software is based on operational semantics. The notion of a *program state* is central to this approach. The state captures the values of the program variables at a certain moment in the execution of the program. The models are then obtained by representing the state and the way it changes in the course of execution. By applying predicate abstraction [11] on the state, i.e. by using truth assignments for a set of chosen predicates to abstractly represent the set of states where the truth assignments are satisfied, the models become finite and can be model checked. This modeling technique has been applied successfully to verifying realistic industrial software. Some of the best-known tools that adopt this approach are SLAM [2] and BLAST [13] for verifying safety properties and Terminator [5] for verifying liveness properties of programs.

Game semantics is a particular kind of denotational semantics which constructs models of programs by looking at the ways in which a program can observably *interact* with its context (environment). This modeling technique has been shown to provide useful algorithms for software model checking [1]. In this framework, computation is seen as a game between two players, the environment and the program, and the model of a program is given as a *strategy* for the second player. Strategies can be then given concrete representations using various automata or process theoretic formalisms, thus providing direct support for model checking. Game semantics is compositional, i.e. defined recursively on the syntax, which is essential for the modular analysis of larger programs. Namely, the model of a program is constructed out of the models of its subprograms, which facilitates breaking down the verification of a larger program into verifications of its subprograms.

In this work we show how for second-order recursion-free Erratic Idealized Algol (EIA for short) with finite data types game semantic models can be represented as CSP processes, i.e. any program is compositionally modeled as a CSP process whose traces and divergences sets are exactly all the plays of the strategy for the program. This enables a range of safety and liveness properties, such as termination and divergence, of programs to be decided by checking traces refinement and divergence-freedom of CSP processes by using the FDR tool.

CSP [16] is a particularly convenient formalism for encoding game semantic models. The FDR model checker [9] can be used to automatically check refinements between two processes and a variety of properties of a process, and to debug interactively when a refinement or a property does not hold. FDR has direct support for three different forms of refinement: traces, failures, and failures-divergences; and for the following properties: deadlock-freedom, divergence-freedom, and determinism. Then, composition of strategies, which is used in game semantics to obtain the strategy for a program from strategies for its subprograms, is represented in CSP by renaming, parallel composition and hiding operators, and FDR is highly optimized for verification of such networks of processes. Finally, FDR builds the models gradually, at each stage compressing the submodels to produce an equivalent process with many fewer states. A number of hierarchical compression algorithms are available in FDR, which can be applied during either model generation or refinement checking.

The paper is organized in the following way. Section 2 introduces the language considered in this paper. The game semantic model of the language, its CSP representation, and decidability of program termination are shown in Section 3. The effectiveness of this approach is evaluated in Section 4. In the end, we conclude and present some ideas for future work.

2 The Programming Language

Erractic Idealized Algol [12] is a nondeterministic imperative-functional language which combines the fundamental imperative features, locally-scoped variables, and full higher-order function mechanism based on a typed call-by-name λ-calculus.

The *data types* `D` are a finite subset of the integers (from 0 to n-1, where n>0) and the Booleans (`D ::=` $\texttt{int}_n$ `| bool`). The phrase types consists of base types: expressions, commands, variables (`B ::= expD | com | varD`), and 2nd-order function types (`T ::= B | B → T`). *Terms* are formed by the following grammar:

```
M ::= x | v | skip | diverge | M op M | M;M | if M then
M else M | while M do M | M := M | !M | newvarD x:=v in
M | mkvar MM | M or M | λx.M | MM | YM
```

where `v` ranges over constants of type `D`. The language contains integer and Boolean constants and arithmetic-logic operations `op`. The other constants are a "do nothing" command `skip` which always terminates successfully, and for each base type there is a constant `diverge` which causes a program to enter an unresponsive state similar to that caused by an infinite loop. The usual imperative constructs are employed: sequential composition, conditional, iteration, assignment, and de-referencing. Block-allocated local variables are introduced by a new construct: `newvarD x:=v in M`, which initializes the variable `x` to `v` and makes it local to the given block `M`. There are constructs for nondeterminism, recursion, function creation and application.

Well-typed terms are given by typing judgments of the form `Γ |- M : T`. Here `Γ` is a type context consisting of a finite number of typed free identifiers, i.e. of the form $x_1:T_1, \ldots, x_k:T_k$, where all identifiers x_i are distinct. The typing rules of the language can be found in [12], extended with a rule for the diverge constant: `Γ |- diverge : B`.

The operational semantics of our language is given in terms of *states*. We begin by defining a notion of state. Given a type context $\Gamma = x_1:\mathrm{varD}_1, \ldots, x_k:\mathrm{varD}_k$ where all identifiers are variables, which is called var-context, we define a `Γ`-state `s` as a (partial) function assigning data values to the variables $x_1, \ldots, x_k$. The canonical forms are defined by `V ::= x | v | λx.M | skip | mkvarMN`. The operational semantics is defined by a big-step reduction relation:

```
Γ |- M, s => V, s'
```

where `Γ |- M : T` is a term, `Γ` is a var-context, `s, s'` are `Γ`-states, and `V` is a canonical form. Reduction rules are those of EIA (see [12] for details), plus a rule for the `diverge` constant which is not reducible.

Since the language is nondeterministic, it is possible that a term may reduce to more than one value. Given a term `Γ |- M: com` where `Γ` is a var-context, we say that `M` *may terminate* in state `s`, if there exists a reduction `Γ |- M, s => skip, s'` for some state `s'`. We say that `M` *must terminate* in a state `s`, if all reductions at start state `s` end with the term `skip`. Next, we define a context `C[-]:com` with hole to be a term with (possibly several occurrences of) a hole in it, such that if `Γ |- M : T` is a term of the same type as the hole then `C[M]` is a well-typed closed term of type com, i.e. `|- C[M] : com`. Then, we say that a term `Γ |- M : T` is a *may&must-approximate* of a term `Γ |- N : T`, if and only if for all program contexts `C[-]:com`, if `C[M]` may terminate then `C[N]` also may terminate, and if `C[M]` must terminate then `C[N]` also must terminate. If two terms approximate each other they are considered observationally *may&must-equivalent.*

3 The Game Model

In game semantics, a kind of game is played by two participants. The first, Player, represents the term (open program) under consideration, while the second, Opponent, represents the environment in which the term is used. The two take turns to make moves, each of which is either a question (a demand for information) or an answer (a supply of information). Opponent always plays first. What these moves are, and when they can be played, are determined by the rules of each particular game. For example, in the game for integer expressions `expint`, Opponent has a single move, the question "What is the number?", and Player can then respond by playing a number.

The game involved in modeling a function of type `expint → expint` is formed from "two copies of the game for `expint`", one for input, and one for output. In the output copy, Opponent can demand output and Player can provide it. In the input copy, the situation is reversed, Player demands input and Opponent provides it. A *play* in this game when Player is playing the predecessor function might look like this:

Opponent	"What is the output?"
Player	"What is the input?"
Opponent	"The input is 5"
Player	"The output is 4"

So, the predecessor function becomes a strategy for Player: "When Opponent asks for output, Player responds by asking for input; when Opponent provides input *n (n>0)*, Player supplies *n-1* as output; when Opponent provides input 0, Player can not respond". This is the key idea in game semantics. Types are interpreted as *games*, and open programs are interpreted as *strategies* for Player to respond to the moves Opponent can make. If Player can not respond at some point of a play then this is reflected by an appropriate divergence sequence in the strategy. For example, the strategy for the predecessor function is $[[\texttt{pred} : \texttt{expint}_0 \rightarrow \texttt{expint}_1]] = (T_{[[pred]]}, D_{[[pred]]})$, where the *traces* set is $T_{[[pred]]}=\{\varepsilon, q_1\, q_0, q_1\, q_0\, n_0\, n\text{-}1_1 \mid n>0\}$ and the *divergences* set is $D_{[[pred]]}=\{q_1\, q_0\, 0_0\}$. Here, ε denotes an empty sequence. For simplicity, every move is tagged with the index of type component where it occurs. The trace set is a non-empty prefix-closed set of even-length sequences, and the divergences set contains only odd-length sequences.

A term $\Gamma \vdash M : T$, where $\Gamma = x_1:T_1, \ldots, x_k:T_k$, is interpreted by a strategy $[[\Gamma \vdash M : T]]$ for the game $[[\Gamma \vdash T]] = [[T_1]] \times \ldots \times [[T_k]] \to [[T]]$. Language constants and constructs are interpreted by strategies and compound terms are modeled by composition of the strategies that interpret their constituents. For example, some of the strategies are [12]: $[[n:expint]]=(\{\varepsilon, q\ n\}, \emptyset)$, $[[skip:com]]=(\{\varepsilon, run\ done\}, \emptyset)$, $[[diverge:com]]=(\{\varepsilon\}, \{run\})$, $[[op : expD_0 \times expD_1 \to expD_2]]=(\{\varepsilon, q_2\,q_0, q_2\,q_0\,n_0\,q_1, q_2\,q_0\,n_0\,q_1\,m_1\,(n\ op\ m)_2 \mid n,m \in D\}, \emptyset)$, $[[or : expD_0 \times expD_1 \to expD_2]]=(\{\varepsilon, q_2\,q_0, q_2\,q_1, q_2\,q_0\,n_0\,n_2, q_2\,q_1\,n_1\,n_2 \mid n \in D\}, \emptyset)$, free identifiers are interpreted by identity strategies, etc. Using standard game-semantic techniques, it has been shown in [12] that this model is fully abstract (i.e. sound and complete). In particular, we are interested in the following result.

Proposition 1. Let $\Gamma \vdash M : com$. M must terminate if and only if $D_{[[\Gamma \vdash M]]} = \emptyset$.

3.1 CSP Interpretation

We now show how the game semantics models of second-order recursion-free EIA can be represented using the CSP process algebra. This translation is an extension of the one presented in [6, 8], where the considered language is IA and the model takes account of only safety properties. CSP (Communicating Sequential Processes) [16] is a language for modeling interacting components. Each component is specified through its behavior which is given as a process. CSP processes are defined in terms of the events that they can perform.

With each type T, we associate a set of possible events: an alphabet $Al_{[[T]]}$. It contains events $q \in Q_{[[T]]}$, called questions, which are appended to a channel with name Q, and for each question q, there is a set of events $a \in A_{[[T]]}$ called answers, which are appended to a channel with name A.

$$Al_{[[intn]]} = \{0, \ldots, n-1\} \qquad Al_{[[bool]]} = \{tt, ff\}$$
$$Q_{[[expD]]} = \{q\} \qquad A^{q}_{[[expD]]} = Al_{[[D]]}$$
$$Q_{[[com]]} = \{run\} \qquad A^{run}_{[[com]]} = \{done\}$$
$$Q_{[[varD]]} = \{read, write(v) \mid v \in Al_{[[D]]}\}$$
$$A^{read}_{[[varD]]} = Al_{[[D]]} \qquad A^{write(v)}_{[[varD]]} = \{ok\}$$
$$Al_{[[T]]} = Q.Q_{[[T]]} \cup A.\cup_{q \in Q[[T]]} A^{q}_{[[T]]}$$

We shall define, for any term $\Gamma \vdash M : T$, a CSP process $[[\Gamma \vdash M : T]]$ which represents its game semantics. Processes for language constants are the following:

$$[[\Gamma \vdash v : expD]] = Q.q \to A.v \to SKIP,\ v \in Al_{[[D]]}$$
$$[[\Gamma \vdash skip : com]] = Q.run \to A.done \to SKIP$$

$$[[\Gamma \vdash diverge : B]] = Q?q : Q_{[[B]]} \to div$$

The process for diverge performs the div process after communicating the initial question event. The div process represents a special divergent process in CSP which does nothing but diverge. It is equivalent to the recursive process $\mu p.p$. For each language construct `c', a process P_c which corresponds to its strategy is defined. For example, some of the processes are:

$P_{op} = Q.q \rightarrow Q_1.q \rightarrow A_1?a_1{:}A^q_{[[expD]]} \rightarrow Q_2.q \rightarrow A_2?a_2{:}A^q_{[[expD]]} \rightarrow A.(a_1 op a_2) \rightarrow SKIP$
$P_{or} = Q.q \rightarrow (Q_1.q \rightarrow A_1?a_1{:}A^q_{[[expD]]} \rightarrow A.a_1 \rightarrow SKIP)\ []\ (Q_2.q \rightarrow A_2?a_2{:}A^q_{[[expD]]} \rightarrow$
$A.a_2 \rightarrow SKIP)$
$P_{;} = Q?q{:}\ Q_{[[B]]} \rightarrow Q_1.run \rightarrow A_1.done \rightarrow Q_2.q \rightarrow A_2?a{:}A^q_{[[B]]} \rightarrow A.a \rightarrow SKIP$
$P_{if} = Q.q{:}\ Q_{[[B]]} \rightarrow Q_0.q{:}\ Q_{[[B]]} \rightarrow A_0?a_0{:}A^q_{[[expbool]]} \rightarrow if\ (a_0)\ then\ (Q_1.q \rightarrow$
$A_1?a_1{:}\ A^q_{[[B]]} \rightarrow A.a_1 \rightarrow SKIP)\ else\ (Q_2.q \rightarrow A_2?a_2{:}\ A^q_{[[B]]} \rightarrow A.a_2 \rightarrow SKIP)$
$P_{while} = Q.run \rightarrow \mu\ p\ .\ Q_1.q \rightarrow A_1?a_1{:}\ A^q_{[[expbool]]} \rightarrow if\ (a_1)\ then\ (Q_2.run \rightarrow A_2.done \rightarrow$
$p)\ else\ (\ A.done \rightarrow SKIP)$

P_{or} nondeterministically runs either its first or its second argument. Events of the first (resp., second) argument of `or` occur on channels tagged with index 1 (resp., 2). Then, for each composite term c(`M`$_1$`, ..., M`$_n$) consisting of a language construct `c' and subterms `M`$_1$`, ..., M`$_n$, we define [[c(`M`$_1$`, ..., M`$_n$)]] from the process $P_c$ and processes [[`M`$_i$]] and [[`M`$_i$]]* using only the CSP operators of renaming, parallel composition and hiding. P* is a process which performs the process P arbitrary many times. For example, the process for `or` is defined as:

$$
\begin{aligned}
&[[\Gamma \vdash \mathtt{M1\ or\ M2} : \mathtt{expD}]] = \\
&\quad ([[\Gamma \vdash \mathtt{M1} : \mathtt{expD}]]\ [Q_1/Q, A_1/A]\ []\ SKIP) \parallel_{\{|Q1,\ A1|\}} \\
&\quad (([[\Gamma \vdash \mathtt{M2} : \mathtt{expD}]]\ [Q_2/Q, A_2/A]\ []\ SKIP) \parallel_{\{|Q2,\ A2|\}} \\
&\quad P_{or} \backslash \{|Q_2, A_2|\}) \backslash \{|Q_1, A_1|\}
\end{aligned}
$$

After renaming the channels Q, A to Q_1, A_1 in the process for `M1`, and to Q_2, A_2 in the process for `M2` respectively, the processes for `M1` and `M2` are composed with P_{or}. The composition is performed by synchronizing the component processes on events occurring on channels Q_1, A_1, Q_2, A_2, which are then hidden. Since one of the processes for `M1` and `M2` will not be run in the composition, SKIP is used to enable such empty termination.

Example 1. Consider the term below, which uses a local variable *x*, and a non-local function `f`:

```
f : com → com → com |- newint₂ x := 0 in
                        f (x:=1, if (x = 1) then diverge) : com
```

The procedure-call mechanism is by-name, so every call to the first argument of `f` increments `x`, and any call to the second argument of `f` uses the new value of `x`.

The labeled transition system (LTS) of the CSP process representing this term is shown in Fig. 1. It illustrates only the possible behaviors of this term: if the non-local procedure `f` calls its first argument, two or more times, and afterwards its second argument then the term diverges, i.e. it can perform an infinite sequence of consecutive internal events called τ; otherwise the term terminates successfully, i.e. there is an edge with label √ that leads to a special final state Ω. The model does not assume that `f` uses its arguments, or how many times or in what order. Notice that no references to the variable `x` appear in the model because it is locally defined and so not visible from the outside of the term.

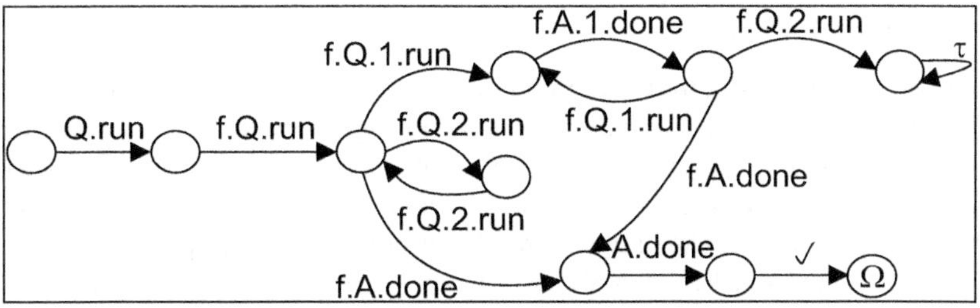

Fig. 1. A strategy as a labelled transition system

3.2 Formal Properties

We show that for any term from second-order recursion-free EIA, the sets of all even-length traces and minimal divergences of its CSP interpretation is isomorphic to its fully abstract game semantic model. Given a term `Γ |- M : T`, we denote by `[[Γ |- M : T]]`^{GS} its game semantic model as described in Section 3, and we denote by `[[Γ |- M : T]]`^{CSP} its CSP model as described in Section 4.

Theorem 2. For any term `Γ |- M : T`, we have:

$$\text{traces}^{ev}([[\Gamma \ |\text{-}\ M : T]]^{CSP}) \equiv^{\phi} T_{[[\Gamma|\text{-}M:T]]GS}$$

$$\text{min}(\text{divergences}([[\Gamma \ |\text{-}\ M : T]]^{CSP})) \equiv^{\phi} D_{[[\Gamma|\text{-}M:T]]GS}$$

where traces^{ev}(P) is the set of all even-length traces of process P, min(divergences(P)) is the minimal set of all divergences of P, and ϕ is an isomorphism between the moves in both, CSP and game semantics, representations.

By using Proposition 1 and Theorem 2, we can verify whether a term `Γ |- M : T` *terminates* by checking one divergence-freedom test:

`[[Γ |- M : T]]`^{CSP} is divergence-free

If the test does not hold, then the term diverges and one or more counter-examples reported by the FDR tool can be used to explore the reasons why. Otherwise, the term does not diverge, i.e. it *terminates*.

The checks performed by FDR terminate only for finite-state processes, i.e. those whose labelled transition systems are finite. We have shown in [6, 8] that this is the case for the processes interpreting the IA terms. The process for 'or' is also finite-state. As a corollary, we have that termination is decidable using FDR.

Example 2. By testing the process for the term `|- while (true) do skip : com` for divergence-freedom, we can verify that the term diverges. The counter-example is: Q.run.

In the same manner, we can verify that the term from Example 1:

```
newint₂ x := 0 in  f (x:=1, if (x = 1) then diverge)
```

diverges. The obtained counter-example represents a function f evaluating its first and then its second argument: Q.run f.Q.run f.Q.1.run f.A.1.done f.Q.2.run.

4 Applications

We have implemented a tool, which automatically converts a term into a CSP process which represents its game semantics. The resulting CSP process is defined by a script in machine readable CSP which the tool outputs. In the input syntax, we use simple type annotations to indicate what finite sets of integers will be used to model integer free identifiers and local variables. An integer constant n is implicitly defined of type $\mathtt{int}_{n+1}$. An operation between values of types $\mathtt{int}_n$ and $\mathtt{int}_m$ produces a value of type $\mathtt{int}_{\max\{n,m\}}$. The operation is performed modulo max{n,m}.

We now analyse an implementation of the linear search algorithm:

```
x[k] varint2, y expint2 |-
 newint2 a[k] := 0 in
 newintk+1 i := 0 in
 while (i < k) do { a[i] := x[i] ; i := i + 1 ;}
 newint2 z := y in
 newbool present:=false in
 while (not present) do {
    if (i < k) then if (a[i] = z) then present := true;
    i := i + 1; }: com
```

The code includes a meta variable k>0, representing array size, which will be replaced by several different values. The data stored in the arrays and the expression y is of type $\mathtt{int}_2$, i.e. two distinct values 0 and 1 can be stored, and the type of index i is $\mathtt{int}_{k+1}$, i.e. one more than the size of the array. The program first copies the input array x into a local array a, and the input expression y into a local variable z. Then, the local array is searched for an occurrence of the value y. The array being effectively searched, a[], and the variable z, are not visible from the outside of the term because they are locally defined, so only reads from the non-local identifiers x and y are seen in the model of this term.

A labelled transition system of the CSP process for the term with k=2 is shown in Fig. 2. It illustrates the possible behaviours of this term: if the value read from y has occurred in x[] then the term terminates successfully; otherwise the term diverges. If we test its process for divergence-freedom, we obtain the following counter-example:

Q.run x[0].Q.read x[0].A.1 x[1].Q.read x[1].A.1 y.Q.q y.A.0

So the linear search term diverges when the value read from y does not occur in the array x[] making the while loop forever.

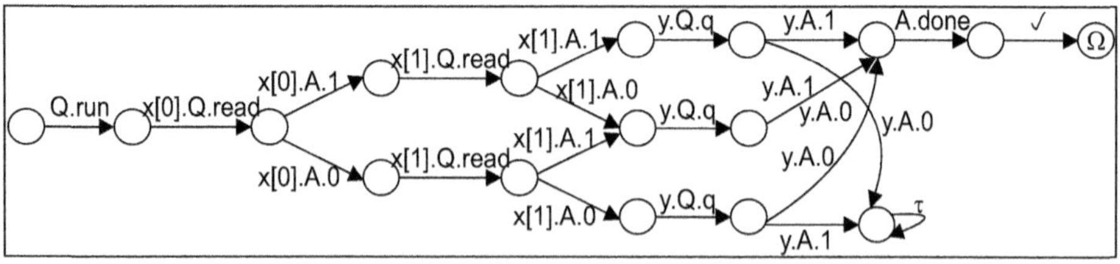

Fig. 2. Model for linear search with k=2

Table 1 shows some experimental results for checking divergence-freedom. The experiment consisted of running the tool on the linear search term with different values of `k`, and then letting FDR generate its model and test its divergence-freedom. For different values of `k`, we list the execution time in seconds, and the size of the final model. We ran FDR on a Machine AMD Sempron Processor 3500+ with 2GB RAM.

Table 1. Model generation of linear search

Array size	Time (sec)	Model states
5	2	35
10	5	65
20	39	125
30	145	185

5 Conclusion

We presented a compositional approach for verifying termination of open nondeterministic sequential programs with finite data types. In [15] it has been described algorithms for deciding a range of verification problems for nondeterministic programs, such as: may-equivalence, must-equivalence, may&must-equivalence, termination and other properties. In this paper we have described a concrete implementation of the procedure for deciding termination of nondeterministic programs by using the FDR model checker. We have also extended the CSP representation of game semantic models given in [6, 8] by interpreting the '`or`' construct. So, here we take account of EIA (IA+`or`) and liveness properties of programs, while in [6, 8] we consider IA and only safety properties of programs. This can be considered as the main contribution of the presented work, as well as giving tutorial introduction trough examples to game semantics.

We have used off-the-shelf model checker FDR, which does not exploit the features of our semantics perfectly. So, building a new model checker from scratch, which will support composition and suit more naturally to our semantic models, is a possible direction for research. Also an interesting direction for extension is to consider infinite integers with all the usual operators. Counter-example guided abstraction refinement procedures [7] for verifying safety properties can be adapted to the specific setting for verifying liveness properties. It is also important to extend the proposed approach to programs with concurrency [10], probabilistic constructs [14], and other features.

References

1. Abramsky, S., Ghica, D.R., Murawski, A.S., Ong, C.H.L.: Applying game semantics to compositional software modeling and verification. In: Jensen, K., Podelski, A. (eds.) TACAS 2004. LNCS, vol. 2988, pp. 421–435. Springer, Heidelberg (2004)

2. Ball, T., Rajamani, S.K.: Automatically validating temporal safety properties of interfaces. In: Dwyer, M.B. (ed.) SPIN 2001. LNCS, vol. 2057, pp. 103–122. Springer, Heidelberg (2001)
3. Clarke, E.M., Grumberg, O., Jha, S., Lu, Y., Veith, H.: Counterexample-guided abstraction refinement. In: Emerson, E.A., Sistla, A.P. (eds.) CAV 2000. LNCS, vol. 1855, pp. 154–169. Springer, Heidelberg (2000)
4. Clarke, E.M., Grumberg, O., Peled, D.: Model Checking. MIT Press, Cambridge (2000)
5. Cook, B., Podelski, A., Rybalchenko, A.: Abstraction refinement for termination. In: Hankin, C., Siveroni, I. (eds.) SAS 2005. LNCS, vol. 3672, pp. 86–101. Springer, Heidelberg (2005)
6. Dimovski, A.: Software Verification Based on Game Semantics and Process Algebra. VDM Verlag (2009)
7. Dimovski, A., Ghica, D.R., Lazić, R.S.: Data-abstraction refinement: A game semantic approach. In: Hankin, C., Siveroni, I. (eds.) SAS 2005. LNCS, vol. 3672, pp. 102–117. Springer, Heidelberg (2005)
8. Dimovski, A., Lazic, R.: Compositional software verification based on game semantics and process algebras. International Journal on Software Tools for Technology Transfer (STTT) 9(1), 37–51 (2007)
9. Formal Systems (Europe) Ltd. Failures-Divergence Refinement: FDR2 Manual (2000), `http://www.fsel.com`
10. Ghica, D.R., Murawski, A.S.: Angelic semantics of fine-grained concurrency. In: Walukiewicz, I. (ed.) FOSSACS 2004. LNCS, vol. 2987, pp. 211–225. Springer, Heidelberg (2004)
11. Graf, S., Saidi, H.: Construction of abstract state graphs with pvs. In: Grumberg, O. (ed.) CAV 1997. LNCS, vol. 1254, pp. 72–83. Springer, Heidelberg (1997)
12. Harmer, R.: Games and Full Abstraction for Nondeterministic Languages. Ph.D. Thesis. University of London, Imperial College (1999)
13. Henzinger, T.A., Jhala, R., Majumdar, R., Sutre, G.: Software verification with BLAST. In: Ball, T., Rajamani, S.K. (eds.) SPIN 2003. LNCS, vol. 2648, pp. 235–239. Springer, Heidelberg (2003)
14. Legay, A., Murawski, A.S., Ouaknine, J., Worrell, J.B.: On automated verification of probabilistic programs. In: Ramakrishnan, C.R., Rehof, J. (eds.) TACAS 2008. LNCS, vol. 4963, pp. 173–187. Springer, Heidelberg (2008)
15. Murawski, A.: Reachability Games and Game Semantics: Comparing Nondeterministic Programs. In: Proceedings of LICS, pp. 173–183. IEEE, Los Alamitos (2008)
16. Roscoe, A.W.: Theory and Practice of Concurrency. Prentice-Hall, Englewood Cliffs (1998)

Practical Consequences of the Aberration of Narrow-Pipe Hash Designs from Ideal Random Functions

Danilo Gligoroski[1] and Vlastimil Klima[2]

[1] Faculty of Information Technology, Mathematics and Electrical Engineering Department of Telematics, Norwegian University of Science and Technology, Trondheim, Norway
Danilo.Gligoroski@item.ntnu.no

[2] Independent Cryptologist - Consultant, Prague, Czech Republic
v.klima@volny.cz

Abstract. In a recent note to the NIST hash-forum list, the following observation was presented: narrow-pipe hash functions differ significantly from ideal random functions $H : \{0,1\}^N \rightarrow \{0,1\}^n$ that map bit strings from a big domain where $N = n + m$, $m \geq n$ ($n = 256$ or $n = 512$). Namely, for an ideal random function with a big domain space $\{0,1\}^N$ and a finite co-domain space $Y = \{0,1\}^n$, for every element $y \in Y$, the probability $Pr\{H^{-1}(y) = \varnothing\} \approx e^{-2^m} \approx 0$ where $H^{-1}(y) \subseteq \{0,1\}^N$ and $H^{-1}(y) = \{x \mid H(x) = y\}$ (in words - the probability that elements of Y are "unreachable" is negligible). However, for the narrow-pipe hash functions, for certain values of N (the values that are causing the last padded block that is processed by the compression function of these functions to have no message bits), there exists a huge non-empty subset $Y_\varnothing \subseteq Y$ with a volume $|Y_\varnothing| \approx e^{-1}|Y| \approx 0.36|Y|$ for which it is true that for every $y \in Y_\varnothing$, $H^{-1}(y) = \varnothing$.

In this paper we extend the same finding to SHA-2 and show consequences of this abberation when narrow-pipe hash functions are employed in HMAC and in two widely used protocols: 1. The pseudo-random function defined in SSL/TLS 1.2 and 2. The Password-based Key Derivation Function No.1, i.e, PBKDF1.

1 Introduction

The importance of cryptographic functions with arbitrary input-length have been confirmed and re-confirmed numerous times in hundreds of scenarios in information security. The most important properties that these functions have to have are collision-resistance, preimage-resistance and second-preimage resistance. However, several additional properties such as multi-collision resistance, being pseudo-random function, or being a secure MAC, are also considered important.

All practical cryptographic hash function constructions have iterative design and they use a supposed (or conjectured to be close to) ideal finite-input random

M. Gusev and P. Mitrevski (Eds.): ICT Innovations 2010, CCIS 83, pp. 81–93, 2011.

function (called compression function) $C : \{0,1\}^m \to \{0,1\}^l$ where $m > l$, and then the domain of the function C is extended to the domain $\{0,1\}^*$ in some predefined iterative chaining manner.

The way how the domain extension is defined reflects directly to the properties that the whole cryptographic function has. For example domain extension done by the well known Merkle-Damgård construction transfers the collision-resistance of the compression function to the extended function. However, as it was shown in recent years, some other properties of this design clearly show non-random behavior (such as length-extension vulnerability, vulnerability on multi-collisions e.t.c.).

The random oracle model has been proposed to be used in cryptography in 1993 by Bellare and Rogaway [1]. Although it has been shown that there exist some bogus and impractical (but mathematically correct) protocols that are provably secure under the random oracle model, but are completely insecure when the ideal random function is instantiated by any concretely designed hash function [2], in the cryptographic practice the random oracle model gained a lot of popularity. It has gained that popularity during all these years, by the simple fact that protocols proved secure in the random oracle model when instantiated by concrete "good" cryptographic hash functions, are sound and secure and broadly employed in practice.

In a recent note to the NIST hash-forum list [3] it was shown that four of the SHA-3 [4] second round candidates: BLAKE [5], Hamsi [6], SHAvite-3 [7] and Skein [8] act pretty differently than an ideal random function $H : \mathcal{D} \to \{0,1\}^n$ where $\mathcal{D} = \bigcup_{i=0}^{\text{maxbitlength}} \{0,1\}^i$ and "maxbitlength" is the maximal bit length specified for the concrete functions i.e, $2^{64} - 1$ bits for BLAKE-32, Hamsi, and SHAvite-3-256, $2^{128} - 1$ bits for BLAKE-64 and SHAvite-3-512 and $2^{99} - 8$ bits for Skein.

In this paper we extend that finding also to the current cryptographic hash standard SHA-2 [9] and we show what are the security consequences if those hash functions would be used in HMAC and in two widely used protocols: 1. The pseudo-random function defined in SSL/TLS 1.2 [10] and 2. The Password-based Key Derivation Function No.1, i.e, PBKDF1 as defined in PKCS#5 v1 [11].

2 Some Basic Mathematical Facts for Ideal Random Functions

We will discuss the properties of ideal random functions over finite and infinite domains.[1] More concretely we will pay our attention for:

Finite narrow domain: Ideal random functions $C : X \to Y$ mapping the domain of n-bit strings $X = \{0,1\}^n$ to itself i.e, to the domain $Y = \{0,1\}^n$, where $n > 1$ is a natural number;

[1] The infinite domain $\{0,1\}^*$ in all practical implementations of cryptographic hash functions such as SHA-1 or SHA-2 or the next SHA-3 is replaced by some huge practically defined finite domain such as the domain $\mathcal{D} = \bigcup_{i=0}^{\text{maxbitlength}} \{0,1\}^i$, where maxbitlength $= 2^{64} - 1$ or maxbitlength $= 2^{128} - 1$.

Finite wide domain: Ideal random functions $W : X \rightarrow Y$ mapping the domain of $n+m$-bit strings $X = \{0,1\}^{n+m}$ to the domain $Y = \{0,1\}^n$, where $m \geq n$;

Proposition 1. *([3]) Let $\mathcal{F}_C$ be the family of all functions $C : X \rightarrow Y$ (where X and Y are two sets with equal cardinality) and let for every $y \in Y$, $C^{-1}(y) \subseteq X$ be the set of preimages of y i.e, $C^{-1}(y) = \{x \in X \mid C(x) = y\}$. For a function $C \in \mathcal{F}_C$ chosen uniformly at random and for every $y \in Y$ the probability that the set $C^{-1}(y)$ is empty is approximately e^{-1} i.e,*

$$Pr\{C^{-1}(y) = \varnothing\} \approx e^{-1}. \tag{1}$$

□

Corollary 1. *([3]) If the function $C \in \mathcal{F}_C$ is chosen uniformly at random, then there exists a set $Y_{\varnothing}^C \subseteq Y$ such that for every $y \in Y_{\varnothing}^C$, $C^{-1}(y) = \varnothing$ and*

$$|Y_{\varnothing}^C| \approx e^{-1}|Y| \approx 0.36|Y|.$$

□

Proposition 2. *([3]) Let $\mathcal{F}_W$ be the family of all functions $W : X \rightarrow Y$ where $X = \{0,1\}^{n+m}$ and $Y = \{0,1\}^n$. Let for every $y \in Y$, $W^{-1}(y) \subseteq X$ be the set of preimages of y i.e, $W^{-1}(y) = \{x \in X \mid W(x) = y\}$. For a function $W \in \mathcal{F}_W$ chosen uniformly at random and for every $y \in Y$ the probability that the set $W^{-1}(y)$ is empty is approximately e^{-2^m} i.e,*

$$Pr\{C^{-1}(y) = \varnothing\} \approx e^{-2^m}. \tag{2}$$

□

In what follows for the sake of clarity we will work on bit-strings of length which is multiple of n. Namely we will be interested on strings $M = M_1||\ldots||M_i$ where every $|M_j| = n, j = 1,\ldots,i$. Further, we will be interested in practical constructions of cryptographic hash functions that achieve a domain extension from a narrow-domain to the full infinite domain. We will need the following Lemma:

Lemma 1. *([3]) Let $\mathcal{F}_{C_\nu}$ be a countable family of functions $C_\nu : X \rightarrow Y$, $\nu \in \mathbb{N}$ and let $C : X \rightarrow Y$ be one particular function, where C_ν and C are chosen uniformly at random. Let us have a function $Rule : \mathbb{N} \times Y \rightarrow \mathcal{F}_{C_\nu}$ that chooses some particular random function from the family $\mathcal{F}_{C_\nu}$ according to a given index and a value from Y. If we define a function $H : (\{0,1\}^n)^i \rightarrow Y$ that maps the finite strings $M = M_1||\ldots||M_i$ to the set of n-bit strings $Y = \{0,1\}^n$ as a cascade of functions:*

$$\begin{aligned} H(M) = H(M_1||\ldots||M_i) = & C_{Rule(1,IV)}(M_1) \circ C_{Rule(2,C_{Rule(1,IV)}(M_1))}(M_2) \circ \\ & \circ \cdots \circ \\ & \circ C_{Rule(i,C_{Rule(i-1,\cdot)}(M_{i-1}))}(M_i) \circ \\ & \circ C \end{aligned} \tag{3}$$

then for every $y \in Y$ the probability that the set $H^{-1}(y)$ is empty is approximately e^{-1}. □

Proposition 3. *Let $C_1 : X \to Y$, $C_2 : X \to Y$ are two particular functions, chosen uniformly at random (where $X = Y = \{0,1\}^n$). If we define a function $C : X \to Y$ as a composition:*

$$C = C_1 \circ C_2 \tag{4}$$

then for every $y \in Y$ the probability P_2 that the set $C^{-1}(y)$ is empty is $P_2 = e^{-1+e^{-1}}$.

Proof. We can use the same technique used in the proof of Proposition 1 in [3] but extended to two domains (i.e, one intermediate domain Z) since we have a composition of two functions. Thus let us put the following notation:

$$C \equiv C_1 \circ C_2 : X \xrightarrow{C_1} Z \xrightarrow{C_2} Y$$

From Proposition 1 it follows that for every $z \in Z$ the probability that the set $C_1^{-1}(z)$ is empty is approximately e^{-1} i.e, the probability that z has a preimage is $(1 - Pr\{C_1^{-1}(z) = \varnothing\}) = (1 - e^{-1})$.

Now, for the probability that the set $C^{-1}(y)$ is empty (for every $y \in Y$) we have:

$$Pr\{C^{-1}(y) = \varnothing\} = \left(1 - \frac{1}{2^n}\right)^{2^n(1-Pr\{C_1^{-1}(y)=\varnothing\})} \approx e^{-1+e^{-1}}.$$

Lemma 2. *$C_1, C_2, \ldots C_k : X \to Y$ are k particular (not necessary different) functions, chosen uniformly at random (where $X = Y = \{0,1\}^n$). If we define a function $C : X \to Y$ as a composition:*

$$C = C_1 \circ C_2 \circ \ldots \circ C_k \tag{5}$$

then for every $y \in Y$ the probability P_k that the set $C^{-1}(y)$ is empty is approximately $P_k = e^{-1+P_{k-1}}$, where $P_1 = e^{-1}$.

Proof. The lemma can be proved by using mathematical induction for the value of k and the Proposition 3.

The Lemma 2 models the probability of some element in Y to have a preimage if we apply consecutively different random functions defined over the same narrow domain $\{0,1\}^n$. Is the sequence P_k convergent? If yes, what is the limit value and what is the speed of the convergence?

In this paper we will give answers on these questions, but we have to stress that the mathematical proofs for some of those answers will be given elsewhere.[2,3]

---

[2] In the initial version of this paper the Lemma 3 was given as a Conjecture, but in the mean time Zoran Šunić from the Department of Mathematics, Texas A&M University, USA has proven it for which we express him an acknowledgement.

[3] After reading our first version of the paper submited to the eprint archive, we got an email from Ernst Schulte-Geers from the German BSI for which we express him an acknowledgement, pointing out that in fact Lemma 3 was known long time ago from the paper of Flajolet and Odlyzko [13].

Lemma 3. *Let* $P_1 = e^{-1}$ *and* $P_k = e^{-1+P_{k-1}}$. *Then the following limit holds:*

$$\lim_{i \to \infty} (\log_2(1 - P_{2^i}) + i - 1) = 0 \tag{6}$$

As a direct consequence of Lemma 3 is the following Corollary:

Corollary 2. *The entropy* $E(C(X))$ *of the set* $C(X) = \{C(x) \mid x \in X\}$, *where the function* C *is a composition of* 2^i *functions mapping the domain* $\{0,1\}^n$ *to itself, as defined in (5) is:*

$$E(C(X)) = n + \log_2(1 - P_{2^i}) \tag{7}$$

□

The last corollary can be interpreted in the following way: With every consecutive mapping of a narrow domain $\{0,1\}^n$ to itself by any random function defined on that domain, the volume of the resulting image is shrinking. The speed of the shrinking is exponentially slow i.e, for shrinking the original volume 2^n of $X = \{0,1\}^n$ to an image set with a volume of 2^{n-i+1} elements, we will need to define a composition of 2^i functions i.e,

$$C = C_1 \circ C_2 \circ \ldots \circ C_{2^i}.$$

3 The Narrow-Pipe Nature of SHA-2 and Four SHA-3 Candidates

3.1 The Case of SHA-2

Let us analyze the iterated procedure defined in SHA-256 (and the case for SHA-512 is similar)[9]. First, a message M is properly padded:

$$M \leftarrow M || 1000 \ldots 000 \langle l_{64} \rangle$$

where the 64-bit variable $\langle l_{64} \rangle$ is defined as the length of the original message M in bits. Then the padded message is parsed into N, 512-bit chunks:

$$M \equiv m^0, \ldots, m^{N-1}.$$

The iterative procedure for hashing the message M then is defined as:

$h^0 = \text{IV}$
for $i = 0, \ldots, N-1$
    $h^{i+1} =$ **CompressSHA256**(h^i, m^i)
return h^N

where **CompressSHA256**() is the compression function for SHA-256.

Now, let us hash messages that are extracted from some pool of randomness with a size of 1024 bits. The padding procedure will make the final block that would be compressed by the **CompressSHA256**() to be always the same i.e, to be the following block of 512 bits:

$$\underbrace{1000\ldots00010000000000}_{512\ bits}$$

If we suppose that the compression function **CompressSHA256**() is ideal, from the Proposition 1 and Lemma 1 we get that there is a huge set $Y_{\varnothing} \subseteq \{0,1\}^{256}$, with a volume $|Y_{\varnothing}| \approx 0.36 \times 2^{256}$ i.e,

$$Pr\{SHA\text{-}256^{-1}(M) = \varnothing\} = e^{-1}.$$

On the other hand, for an ideal random function $W : \{0,1\}^{1024} \rightarrow \{0,1\}^{256}$ from Proposition 2 we have that

$$Pr\{W^{-1}(M) = \varnothing\} = e^{-2^{768}} \approx 0.$$

3.2 The Case of the Second Round SHA-3 Candidates BLAKE, Hamsi, SHAvite-3 and Skein

In [3] it was shown that the second round candidates BLAKE, Hamsi, SHAvite-3 and Skein all manifest abberations from ideal random functions defined over wider domains. The basic method how this was shown was the fact that for certain lengths of the messages that are hashed, the final padding block does not contain any bits from the message, and thus acts as an independent random function defined over a narrow domain $X = \{0,1\}^n$ that is mapped to itself.

4 Practical Consequences of the Observed Abberations of the Narrow-Pipe Designs

We point out several concrete protocols that are widely used and where the observed abberations of narrow-pipe hash designs from the ideal random function will be amplified due to the iterative use of hash functions in those protocols.

4.1 Reduced Entropy Outputs from Narrow-Pipe Hash Functions

The first practical consequence is by direct application of the Lemma 2.

Let us consider the following scenario: We are using some hash function that gives us 256 bits of output, and we have a pool of randomness of a size of 2^{20} blocks (where the block size is the size of message blocks used in the compression function of that hash function). The pool is constantly updated by actions from the user and from the running operating system. We need random numbers obtained from that pool that will have preferably close to 256 bits of entropy.

If we use narrow-pipe hash design, then depending on the nature of the distribution of the entropy in the randomness pool, we can obtain outputs that can have outputs with entropy as low as 237 bits or outputs with entropy close to 256 bits.

More concretely, if the distribution of the entropy in the pool is somehow concentrated in the first block (or in the first few blocks), then from the Lemma 2 we have that the entropy of the output will not be 256 bits but "just" slightly more than 237 bits. We say "just" because having 237 bits of entropy is really high enough value for any practical use, but it is much smaller than the requested value of 256 bits of entropy. In a case of more uniform distribution of the entropy in the whole pool of randomness, the narrow-pipe hash design will give us outputs with entropies close to 256 bits. The cases where due to different reasons (users habits, user laziness, regularity of actions in the operating system, to name some), the pool is feeded with randomness that is concentrated more on some specific blocks, the outputs will have entropy between 237 and 256 bits.

On the other hand, we want to emphasize, if in all this scenarios we use wide-pipe hash design, the outputs will always have close to 256 bits of entropy, regardless where the distribution of the entropy in the pool will be.

From this perspective, we can say that although the consequences can be just of theoretical interest, there are real and practical scenarios where the abberation of narrow-pipe hash design from ideal random functions can be amplified to some more significant and theoretically visible level.

4.2 Reduced Entropy Outputs from HMACs Produced by Narrow-Pipe Hash Functions

HMAC [12] is one very popular scheme for computing MAC - Message Authentication Codes when a shared secret is used by the parties in the communication. We are interested in a possible loss of entropy in the HMAC construction if we use narrow-pipe hash constructions.

Proposition 4. *Let a message M be of a size of 256 bits and has a full entropy of 256 and let "secret" be shared secret of 256 bits. If in HMAC construction we use a narrow-pipe hash function that parses the hashed messages in 512 blocks, then $mac = HMAC(secret, M)$ has an entropy of 254.58 bits.*

Proof. Let we use the hash function SHA256 that has the compression function **CompressSHA256**(). From the definition of HMAC we have that

$$mac = HMAC(secret, M) = hash((secret \oplus opad)||hash((secret \oplus ipad)||M))$$

where $\oplus$ is the operation of bitwise xoring and $||$ is the operation of string concatenation.

Computing of mac will use four calls of the compression function **CompressSHA256**() in the following sequence:

1. $h_1 = \textbf{CompressSHA256}(iv_{256}, (secret \oplus ipad)) \equiv C_1(iv_{256})$
2. $h_2 = \textbf{CompressSHA256}(h_1, M||CONST256) \equiv C_2(h_1)$, where

$$CONST256 = \underbrace{1000\ldots000100000000}_{256\ bits}.$$

3. $h_3 =$ **CompressSHA256**$(iv_{256}, (secret \oplus opad)) \equiv C_3(iv_{256})$
4. $mac = h_4 =$ **CompressSHA256**$(h_3, h_2||CONST256) \equiv C_4(h_3)$

For a fixed secret key "*secret*" the value h_1 will be always the same and will be obtained with $C_1(iv_{256})$. The function C_2 depends from the message M that has a full entropy of 256 bits, thus C_2 is not one function but it represent a whole class of 2^{256} random functions mapping 256 bits to 256 bits. Thus, we can consider that any call of the function C_2 decreases the entropy of h_2 to $256 + \log_2(1 - P_1)$.

For the value h_3 we have a similar situation as for h_1. Similarly as $C_2()$, the function $C_4()$ is a class of random functions that depends of the value h_2. Since we have already determined that the entropy of h_2 is $256+\log_2(1-P_1)$, it follows that for computing the entropy of mac we can apply the Corollary 2 obtaining that entropy $E(mac)$ is

$$E(mac) = 256 + \log_2(1 - P_2),$$

where $P_1 = \frac{1}{e}$, and $P_2 = e^{-1+\frac{1}{e}}$ which gives us the value $E(mac) = 254.58$. □

What is the difference if we use a double-pipe hash function instead of narrow-pipe in Proposition 4? The first difference is off course the fact that the initialization variable in the compression function as well as the intermediate variables h_1, h_2, h_3 and h_4 are 512 bits long, and we will need final chopping. Then, under the assumption that the compression function acts as ideal random function mapping 512 bits to 512 bits, and having the entropy of the message M to be 256, we have that the entropy of h_2 is also 256 (not $256 + \log_2(1 - P_1)$). The same applies for the entropy of h_4 which will give us that the entropy of mac after the chopping will be 256 bits.

Proposition 5. *Let a message M be of a size of 512 bits and has a full entropy of 512 and let "secret" be shared secret of 256 bits. If in HMAC construction we use a narrow-pipe hash function that parses the hashed messages in 512 blocks, then $mac = HMAC(secret, M)$ has an entropy of 254.58 bits.*

Proof. Let we use the hash function SHA256 that has the compression function **CompressSHA256**(). From the definition of HMAC we have that

$$mac = HMAC(secret, M) = hash((secret \oplus opad)||hash((secret \oplus ipad)||M))$$

where $\oplus$ is the operation of bitwise xoring and $||$ is the operation of string concatenation.

Computing of mac will use five calls of the compression function **Compress SHA256**() in the following sequence:

1. $h_1 =$ **CompressSHA256**$(iv_{256}, (secret \oplus ipad)) \equiv C_1(iv_{256})$
2. $h_2 =$ **CompressSHA256**$(h_1, M) \equiv C_2(h_1)$

3. $h_3 = \textbf{CompressSHA256}(h_2, CONST512) \equiv C_3(h_2)$, where

$$CONST512 = \underbrace{1000\ldots0001000000000}_{512\ bits}.$$

4. $h_4 = \textbf{CompressSHA256}(iv_{256}, (secret \oplus opad)) \equiv C_4(iv_{256})$
5. $mac = h_5 = \textbf{CompressSHA256}(h_4, h_3||CONST256) \equiv C_5(h_4)$, where

$$CONST256 = \underbrace{1000\ldots000100000000}_{256\ bits}.$$

Above, we consider the call of the function $\textbf{CompressSHA256}(iv_{256}, (secret \oplus ipad))$ as a call to an ideal random function $C_1 : \{0,1\}^{256} \rightarrow \{0,1\}^{256}$ that will map the 256-bit value iv_{256} to the 256-bit value h_1. The function C_2 is a specific one. Actually, since it depends from the message M that has a full entropy of 512 bits, C_2 is not one function but it represent a whole class of 2^{512} random functions mapping 256 bits to 256 bits. Thus, we can consider that there is no entropy loss for h_2 i.e, it has a full entropy of 256 bits.

For the value h_3 we start to consider the entropy loss again from the value 256. The call to the function C_3 will decrease the entropy of h_3 to $256 + \log_2(1 - P_1)$. For a fixed secret key "*secret*" the value h_4 will be always the same and will be mapped with $C_5(h_4)$ to the final value mac. Similarly as $C_2()$, the function $C_5()$ is a class of random functions that depends of the value h_3. Since we have already determined that the entropy of h_3 is $256 + \log_2(1 - P_1)$, it follows that for computing the entropy of mac we can apply the Corollary 2 obtaining that entropy $E(mac)$ is

$$E(mac) = 256 + \log_2(1 - P_2),$$

where $P_1 = \frac{1}{e}$, and $P_2 = e^{-1+\frac{1}{e}}$ which gives us the value $E(mac) = 254.58$.

□

Again, if we are interested to know what will happen if we use a double-pipe hash function in the Proposition 5, we can say that the entropy of the 512-bit variable h_3 will start to decrease from the value 512 and will be $512 + \log_2(1 - P_1)$, and the entropy of h_5 will be $512 + \log_2(1 - P_2)$, that after the final chopping will give us a mac with full entropy of 256.

4.3 Loss of Entropy in the Pseudo-random Function of SSL/TLS 1.2

SSL/TLS 1.2 is one very popular suit of cryptographic algorithms, tools and protocols defined in [10]. Its pseudo-random function PRF which is producing pseudo-random values based on a shared secret value "*secret*", a seed value "*seed*" (and by an optional variable called "*label*") is defined as follows:

$$PRF(secret, label, seed) = P_{<hash>}(secret, label \mid\mid seed), \qquad (8)$$

where the function $P_{<hash>}(secret, seed)$ is defined as:

$$\begin{aligned} P_{<hash>}(secret, seed) = & HMAC_{<hash>}(secret, A(1) \mid\mid seed) \mid\mid \\ & HMAC_{<hash>}(secret, A(2) \mid\mid seed) \mid\mid \\ & HMAC_{<hash>}(secret, A(3) \mid\mid seed) \mid\mid \\ & \dots \end{aligned} \tag{9}$$

and where $A(i)$ are defined as:

$$\begin{aligned} A(0) &= seed \\ A(i) &= HMAC_{<hash>}(secret, A(i-1)). \end{aligned} \tag{10}$$

Proposition 6. *Let "secret" be shared secret of 256 bits. The entropy $E(A(i))$ of the i-th value $A(i)$ as defined in the equation (10) for the hash function SHA-256 can be computed with the following expression:*

$$E(A(i)) = 256 + \log_2(1 - P_{2i}) \tag{11}$$

where the values P_{2i} are defined recursively in the Lemma 2.

Proof. We can use the same technique described in the previous subsection and in the proof of Proposition 4. Since we have two volume compressive calls of the compression function, and since the computation of $A(i)$ depends on the value of the previous value $A(i-1)$ in the computation of $A(i)$ we have $2i$ times shrinking of the entropy. □

As a direct consequence of the previous Proposition we have the following:

Corollary 3. *Let the size of "$A(i) \mid\mid seed$" be 512 bits, and let "secret" be shared secret of 256 bits. For the i-th part $PRF_i = HMAC_{SHA-256}(secret, A(i) \mid\mid seed)$ as defined in the equation (9) the entropy $E(PRF_i)$ can be computed with the following expression:*

$$E(PRF_i) = E(PRF_i) = 256 + \log_2(1 - P_{2i+3}) \tag{12}$$

Proof. Computing of PRF_i will use five calls of the compression function **CompressSHA256**() in the following sequence:

1. $h_1 =$ **CompressSHA256**$(iv_{256}, (secret \oplus ipad)) \equiv C_1(iv_{256})$
2. $h_2 =$ **CompressSHA256**$(h_1, A(i) \mid\mid seed) \equiv C_2(h_1)$
3. $h_3 =$ **CompressSHA256**$(h_2, CONST1024) \equiv C_3(h_2)$, where

$$CONST1024 = \underbrace{1000\ldots0010000000000}_{512\ bits}.$$

4. $h_4 =$ **CompressSHA256**$(iv_{256}, (secret \oplus opad)) \equiv C_4(iv_{256})$
5. $PRF_i = h_5 =$ **CompressSHA256**$(h_4, h_3 \mid\mid CONST256) \equiv C_5(h_4)$, where

$$CONST256 = \underbrace{1000\ldots000100000000}_{256\ bits}.$$

Similarly as in Proposition 5 we can see that the function C_2 is a specific one since it depends from $A(i) \mid\mid seed$. For a given and fixed *seed*, the entropy of "$A(i) \mid\mid seed$" is the entropy of $A(i)$ and from Proposition 6, it is $E(A(i)) = 256 + \log_2(1 - P_{2i})$ bits. From here it follows that the entropy of h_2 is $E(h_2) = 256 + \log_2(1 - P_{2i+1})$.

For the value h_3 we further have $E(h_2) = 256 + \log_2(1 - P_{2i+2})$. For a fixed secret key "*secret*" the value h_4 will be always the same and will be mapped with $C_5(h_4)$ to the final value PRF_i, with an entropy

$$E(PRF_i) = 256 + \log_2(1 - P_{2i+3}). \qquad \square$$

For illustration we can say that the entropy of $E(PRF_1) = 253.463$, but the entropy of $E(PRF_{60}) = 250.00$.

On the other hand, having in mind the discussions about the different attitude of double-pipe hash function in used HMACs, it is clear that with double-pipe hash designs we will not face this kind of entropy loss.

4.4 Loss of Entropy in the PBKDF1

The Password-Based Key Derivation Function number 1 is defined in PKCS#5 v1 [11] and is frequently used in many software products that are generating keys (further used for different cryptographic operations) from passwords.

In its definition the following iterative process is used:

$T_1 = \text{Hash}(P \mid\mid S)$
for $i = 2$ to $Count$
    $T_{i+1} = \text{Hash}(T_i)$
return T_{Count}

where P is the password value and S is an 8 byte salt.

As a direct consequence of Lemma 2 and the Corollary 2 we have the following corollary:

Corollary 4. *If the hash function used in PBKDF1 is a hash function with a compression function that is mapping n-bits to n-bits, then the entropy $E(T_{Count})$ of the value T_{Count} can be computed with the following expression:*

$$E(T_{Count}) = n + \log_2(1 - P_{Count}) \qquad (13)$$

where the values P_{Count} are defined recursively in the Lemma 2. $\square$

What is interesting, is that in different standards and programmers manuals the recommended values of $Count$ are in the range from 2^{10} to 2^{24}. That means that the loss of entropy in the final value T_{Count} will be from 10 to 24 bits if we use narrow-pipe hash designs, and there will be no entropy loss if we use wide-pipe hash design.

4.5 SHA-2 and Narrow-Pipe SHA-3 Candidates Would Suffer from the Same Successful Attack Exploiting the Narrow-Pipe Abberation

There is one more inconvenience with narrow-pipe hash designs that directly breaks one of the NIST requirements for SHA-3 hash competition [4]. Namely, one of the NIST requirement is: *"NIST also desires that the SHA-3 hash functions will be designed so that a possibly successful attack on the SHA-2 hash functions is unlikely to be applicable to SHA-3."*

Now, from all previously stated in this paper it is clear that if an attack is launched exploiting narrow-pipe weakness of SHA-2 hash functions, then that attack can be directly used also against narrow-pipe SHA-3 candidates.

5 Conclusions and Future Cryptanalysis Directions

We have shown that SHA-2 and the narrow-pipe SHA-3 candidates differ significantly from ideal random functions defined over huge domains. The first consequence from this is that they can not be used as an instantiation in security proofs based on random oracle model.

Further, as an interesting research direction we point to investigations of the stability of the limit in the equation (6). Namely, for the ideal random functions the Corollary 2 says that we need 2^i applications of the functions in order to decrease the entropy of the final image for $i-1$ bits. However, our initial experiments show that if we work with some concrete compression function, then the exact value of the number $e \approx 2.7182818...$ has to be replaced by some other concrete value $e \pm \epsilon$. And then, the speed of the entropy loss can increase dramatically faster than with the case of an ideal random function.

We have shown also several other consequences of using these functions as PRFs or KDFs or MACs (or HMACs). Namely, the outputs from those functions differ significantly from outputs of ideal random functions and have less entropy than it would be expected.

Acknowledgement

We would like to thank Jean-Philippe Aumasson (from the team of BLAKE hash function), and Orr Dunkelman (from the team of SHAvite-3 hash function) for their great comments, and precise remarks that have improved the text significantly. We would like also to thank Zoran Šunić from the Department of Mathematics, Texas A&M University, USA, for his proof of Lemma 3, as well as Ernst Schulte-Geers from the German BSI, pointing out that in fact Lemma 3 was known long time ago from the paper of Flajolet and Odlyzko [13].

References

1. Bellare, M., Rogaway, P.: Random oracles are practical: A paradigm for designing efficient protocols. In: CCS 1993: Proceedings of the 1st ACM conference on Computer and Communications Security, pp. 62–73 (1993)

2. Canetti, R., Goldreich, O., Halevi, S.: The random oracle methodology, revisited. In: 30th STOC, pp. 209–218 (1998)
3. Gligoroski, D.: Narrow-pipe SHA-3 candidates differ significantly from ideal random functions defined over big domains. NIST hash-forum mailing list (May 7, 2010)
4. National Institute of Standards and Technology: Announcing Request for Candidate Algorithm Nominations for a New Cryptographic Hash Algorithm (SHA-3) Family. Federal Register 27(212), 62212–62220 (November 2007), http://csrc.nist.gov/groups/ST/hash/documents/FR_Notice_Nov07.pdf (2009/04/10)
5. Aumasson, J.-P., Henzen, L., Meier, W., Phan, R. C.-W.: SHA-3 proposal BLAKE, Submission to NIST (Round 2), http://csrc.nist.gov/groups/ST/hash/sha-3/Round2/documents/BLAKE_Round2.zip (2010/05/03)
6. Kücük, Ö.: The Hash Function Hamsi, Submission to NIST (Round 2), http://csrc.nist.gov/groups/ST/hash/sha-3/Round2/documents/Hamsi_Round2.zip (2010/05/03)
7. Biham, E., and Dunkelman, O.: The SHAvite-3 Hash Function, Submission to NIST (Round 2), http://csrc.nist.gov/groups/ST/hash/sha-3/Round2/documents/SHAvite-3_Round2.zip (2010/05/03)
8. Ferguson, N., Lucks, S., Schneier, B., Whiting, D., Bellare, M., Kohno, T., Callas, J., and Walker, J.: The Skein Hash Function Family, Submission to NIST (Round 2), http://csrc.nist.gov/groups/ST/hash/sha-3/Round2/documents/Skein_Round2.zip (2010/05/03)
9. NIST FIPS PUB 180-2: Secure Hash Standard, National Institute of Standards and Technology, U.S. Department of Commerce (August 2002)
10. Dierks, T., Rescorla, E.: The Transport Layer Security (TLS) Protocol Version 1.2. RFC 5246 (August 2008)
11. RSA Laboratories. PKCS #5 v2.1: Password-Based Cryptography Standard (October 5, 2006)
12. Krawczyk, H., Bellare, M., Canetti, R.: HMAC: Keyed-Hashing for Message Authentication. RFC 2104 (February 1997)
13. Flajolet, P., Odlyzko, A.M.: Random mapping statistics. In: Quisquater, J.-J., Vandewalle, J. (eds.) EUROCRYPT 1989. LNCS, vol. 434, pp. 329–354. Springer, Heidelberg (1990)

Unique and Minimum Distance Decoding of Linear Codes with Reduced Complexity

Dejan Spasov and Marjan Gusev

University Ss. Cyrill and Methodious, Faculty of Natural Sciences and Mathematics, Institute of Informatics, Skopje, Macedonia
dejan@ii.edu.mk, marjangusev@gmail.com

Abstract. Given a linear $[n, Rn, \delta n]$ code, we show that for $R \geq \delta/2$ the time complexity of unique decoding is $O\left(n^2 q^{nRH(\delta/2/R)}\right)$ and the time complexity of minimum distance decoding is $O\left(n^2 q^{nRH(\delta/R)}\right)$. The proposed algorithms inspect all error patterns in the information set of the received message of weight less than $\delta n/2$ or δn, respectively.

Keywords: nearest neighbor decoding, unique decoding, bounded distance decoding, minimum distance decoding, syndrome decoding.

1 Introduction

Let F_q be finite field of q elements and let F_q^n be n-dimensional vector space over F_q. Then a code C is any subset of F_q^n of M elements. Elements of the code $c \in C$ are called codewords.

Let $d(x, y)$ denote the Hamming distance, i.e. the number of coordinates in which two vectors x and y differ, and let $wt(x)$ denote the (Hamming) weight, i.e. the number of nonzero coordinates of x. We say that the code C has (minimum) distance d if

$$d = \min_{\substack{c_i, c_j \in C \\ i \neq j}} \{d(c_i, c_j)\}. \tag{1}$$

The code C is linear if its codewords form k- dimensional linear subspace in F_q^n. We will write $[n,k,d]_q$ to emphasize that the code C is linear. For linear codes there exist k basis vectors that are kept as rows in a matrix G called the generator matrix. Each linear code has a generator matrix of type $G = [I \quad A]$, known as the standard form of the generator matrix. It is well-known that for linear codes there exist additional matrix, known as the parity check matrix H, such that $\forall c_i \in C \;\; Hc_i^T = 0$. Let $G = [I \quad A]$ is the generator matrix, then $H = \left[-A^T \quad I\right]$ is the parity check

M. Gusev and P. Mitrevski (Eds.): ICT Innovations 2010, CCIS 83, pp. 94–101, 2011.

matrix of the code C. Two additional parameters that are frequently used to describe a code are the code rate $R = k/n$ and the relative distance $\delta = d/n$.

The *covering radius* ρ of a code is the largest possible distance between the code C and a vector from F_q^n, i.e.

$$\rho = \max_{x \in F_q^n} \min_{\forall c \in C} d(x,c). \tag{2}$$

In this paper, we are mainly interested in decoding of *maximal codes* [2], i.e. codes with $\rho \leq d-1$. It is well known that these codes meet the asymptotical Gilbert-Varshamov bound

$$R \geq 1 - H(\delta). \tag{3}$$

where $H(\delta)$ is the entropy function.

A *Hamming ball* $Ball(x,d)$ with radius d and center in x is the set of points

$$Ball(x,d) = \{ y \in F_q^n \mid d(x,y) \leq d \}. \tag{4}$$

The *volume* (cardinality) $V(n,d)$ of the Hamming ball is equal to

$$V(n,d) = \sum_{i=0}^{d} (q-1)^i \binom{n}{i}. \tag{5}$$

In estimating the complexity of an algorithm we will use the asymptotical relation between the entropy $H(\delta)$ the volume of a ball $V(n,\delta n)$

$$\lim_{n \to \infty} \left\{ \frac{\log(V(n,\delta n))}{n} \right\} \to \begin{cases} H(\delta) & \text{for } \delta \leq \frac{1}{2} \\ 1 & \text{for } \delta > \frac{1}{2} \end{cases}. \tag{6}$$

We adopt Random Access Machine (RAM) as a computational model and, hence, the time complexity is measured as the number of basic (sequential) steps needed for instance of the algorithm to end. It is considered that RAM has unlimited memory with instant access. Thus the space complexity is simply the number of registers used by an instance of the algorithm. We will use the standard Big-O asymptotic notation to describe the space and time complexity. Given $f, g : \mathrm{N} \to \mathrm{N}$ we will write $f = O(g)$ if there exist a constant $c > 0$ such that $f(n) \leq c \cdot g(n)$ holds true for each $n \in \mathrm{N}$. If $f(n) = c \cdot g(n)$ then we will write $f = \Theta(g)$.

2 Combinatorial Decoding Strategies

Let C be a linear code with parameters $[n,k,d]$ and parity check matrix H. Let assume that the sender has sent the codeword c_x and the receiver has received the message y, such that $y \neq c_x$. The decoder's job is, in acceptable time, to make a proper decision on which codeword has been sent, based on the observations of the received vector y. The decoding process is in general NP-hard problem [1,2].

The received message y can be considered as an array of real numbers $y=(y_1,\ldots,y_n), y_i \in \mathrm{R}$. Let $p(y/c)$ denotes the conditional probability that the message y is received, given that the codeword c has been sent. Given y the goal of the *Maximum Likelihood (ML) Decoding* is to find the codeword c such that $p(y/c)$ is maximal, i.e.

$$\hat{c} = \arg\max_{c \in C} p(y/c). \tag{7}$$

If we assume $q-$ary symmetric channel, then ML decoding is simplified and known as *Nearest Neighbor Decoding* or *Minimum Distance (MD) Decoding*. In MD decoding, the received message y is considered as array of field elements of $GF(q)$, $y=(y_1,\ldots,y_n), y_i \in GF(q)$. The decoder's job is to find the codeword c such that $d(y,c)$ is minimal, i.e.

$$\hat{c} = \arg\min_{c \in C} d(y,c). \tag{8}$$

The time complexity of MD decoding is $O(nq^{Rn})$ [2]. Let assume that the $[n,k,d]$ code C is maximal. Then as MD decoding is considered the following approach: subtract from the received vector $y=(y_1,\ldots,y_n), y_i \in GF(q)$, all possible error patterns e of weight $\leq d$ and output all vectors $y-e$ such that $y-e \in C$. The time complexity of this approach is $O(n^2 q^{H(\delta)n})$. Thus, combining these two MD decoding strategies, we obtain the time complexity of MD decoding

$$O\left(n^2 q^{\min(R,H(\delta))n}\right). \tag{9}$$

It is well known that Hamming balls $Ball(c,t)$ with radius $t=\lfloor (d-1)/2 \rfloor$ around the codewords $c \in C$ are disjoint. Let y is the received message. Then the *Unique Decoding* strategy is to find the codeword $c_y \in C$, such that $y \in Ball(c_y,t)$, or return incomplete decoding, i.e. $y \notin Ball(c,t) \forall c \in C$. Trivial way to do this is to inspect all q^k codewords and return the first c_y such that $d(y,c_y) \leq t$. The time complexity of this approach is $O(nq^{Rn})$. Another alternative, with time complexity $O(nq^{H(\delta/2)n})$, is to inspect all $V(n,t)$ error patterns e and find the pattern such that $y-e \in C$. Combining these two decoding strategies, we obtain the time complexity of the unique decoding

$$O\left(n^2 q^{\min\left(R, H\left(\delta/2\right)\right)n}\right). \tag{10}$$

Each linear code C defines partitioning of the space F_q^n in q^{n-k} disjoint sets known as *cosets*. Each coset has q^k vectors. Two vectors x and y belong to same coset iff $x - y \in C$. Each coset K can be spanned by a vector x from the coset, namely

$$K \in \{x + c \mid c \in C\}. \tag{11}$$

Each coset has two special vectors: a unique *syndrome* $s \in F_q^{n-k}$ and *coset leader* $e(s) \in K$. Coset leader $e(s)$ is one of the minimum weight vectors in the coset K. The syndrome is obtained from the multiplication $s = H \cdot x^T$, where H is the parity check matrix of the code and x is arbitrary coset member. For the needs of *syndrome decoding* all pairs $(s, e(s))$ are stored in array known as *the standard array*. In syndrome decoding the error vector e that corrupted the message is considered to be the coset leader $e(s)$ of the coset to which the received message y belongs. Given the received message y, first the syndrome is computed $s_y = H \cdot y^T$, then using the array $(s, e(s))$ the leader $e(s_y)$ is found and the codeword $y - e(s_y)$ is outputted. Syndrome decoding has space complexity of exponential size $O\left(nq^{(1-R)n}\right)$.

In [3] it is given a variation of syndrome decoding with space complexity $O\left(\log(n) q^{(1-R)n}\right)$ and time complexity $O(n)$. In this approach, pairs $(s, w(s))$ are kept in memory, where $w(s)$ is the Hamming weight of the coset leader $e(s)$. In the decoding process all error vectors of weight 1 are subtracted from the received message y. Let $w(s_y)$ be the weight of the coset with syndrome $s_y = H \cdot y^T$. Then the error vector e that corrupted the sent message is sum of all error vectors e_1 of weight 1 such that $w\left(H \cdot (y - e_1)^T\right) < w(s_y)$.

3 New Algorithms for Unique and Minimum Distance Decoding of Linear Codes

We will use $\langle a|b \rangle$ to denote concatenation of two vectors, such that a belongs to the information set and b belongs to the check set of a codeword. Let the message x be encoded in the codeword $c_x = \langle x|r \rangle$ and sent over a noisy channel. Random error pattern is denoted with $e = \langle v|u \rangle$ and the received word is denoted with $y = \langle y_x | y_r \rangle$.

Let assume systematic $[n,k,d]$ code and let $t=\lfloor (d-1)/2 \rfloor$. The unique decoding algorithm, below, inspects all error patterns in the information set $e=\langle v|0\rangle$ with weight $wt(e)\le t$ and outputs the message $\langle x|u\rangle$ if y belongs to some $Ball(c,t)$:

```
Unique_Decoding(y)
   t ← ⌊(d−1)/2⌋
   s_y ← Hy^T
   if wt(s_y) ≤ t return y
   foreach v ∈ F_q^k
        if wt(v) ≤ t
             e ← ⟨v|0⟩
             s_e ← He^T
             if wt(e)+wt(s_y − s_e) ≤ t return y−e
   return -1 // incomplete decoding
```

Proposition 1. The `Unique_Decoding(y)` algorithm removes any error pattern of weight $\le \left\lfloor \frac{d-1}{2} \right\rfloor$ from the received message y.

Proof: Let $e_v=\langle v|0\rangle$, $wt(e_v)\le t$, is the coset leader and $s_v=He_v^T$ is the syndrome of a coset. Let assume that the pairs (s_v,e_v) are explicitly known; for example, they are stored in a look-up table.

We will consider the error pattern $e=\langle v|u\rangle$ as a linear combination of two vectors

$$e=\langle v|0\rangle+\langle 0|u\rangle=e_v+e_u . \tag{12}$$

Since $wt(e_u)\le t$ and $s_u=He_u^T=u$, we can say that e_u is the leader and u is the syndrome of the same coset. Hence, the syndrome s of the received message y is

$$s=Hy^T=H(c_x+e_v+e_u)^T=s_v+u . \tag{13}$$

From (13), we can formulate the decoding strategy: for each e_v in the table (s_v,e_v) denote with $x=y-e_v$ and compute the syndrome $s_x=Hx^T$. If $wt(e_v)+wt(s_x)\le t$ then the error pattern that corrupted the message is $e=\langle e_v|s_x\rangle$. ∎

Theorem 1. The time complexity of the `Unique_Decoding` algorithm is upper-bounded by

$$\begin{cases} O\left(n^2 q^{R\cdot H\left(\frac{\delta}{2R}\right)n}\right) & \text{for } R \geq \frac{\delta}{2} \\ O\left(n^2 q^{R\cdot n}\right) & \text{for } R \leq \frac{\delta}{2} \end{cases}. \tag{14}$$

Proof: Given a systematic $[n,k,d]$ code, the `Unique_Decoding` algorithm checks all error patterns of weight $\leq \left\lfloor \frac{d-1}{2} \right\rfloor$ in the information set of k bits. There are

$$V\left(k,\frac{d}{2}\right) = V\left(Rn,\frac{\delta}{2}n\right) \approx q^{n\frac{\log\left(V\left(Rn,\frac{\delta}{2}n\right)\right)}{n}}$$

possible error patterns that can occur in the information set. Thus using (6) we obtain (14). ■

If we use the fact that for long random linear codes the covering radius is equal to d, where d is the largest integer solution of the Gilbert-Varshamov inequality [4]

$$V(n,d-1) \leq q^{n-k} \tag{15}$$

Then we can formulate Minimum Distance Decoding algorithm that inspects all error patterns of weight less than d in the information set:

```
MD_Decoding(y)
 error ← 0
 error_wt ← n
 s_y ← H y^T
 if wt(s_y) ≤ t return y
 foreach v ∈ F_q^k
     if wt(v) ≤ d
     e ← (v | 0)
     s_e ← H e^T
     if wt(e) + wt(s_y − s_e) ≤ error_wt
         error ← e
         error_wt ← wt(e) + wt(s_y − s_e)
 return y − error
```

The proof of correctness of the above algorithm is similar to the proof of Proposition 1. Using (6) we obtain the time complexity of MDD decoding

$$\begin{cases} O\left(n^2 q^{R\cdot H\left(\frac{\delta}{R}\right)n}\right) & \text{for } R \geq \frac{\delta}{2} \\ O\left(n^2 q^{R\cdot n}\right) & \text{for } R \leq \frac{\delta}{2} \end{cases}. \tag{16}$$

This result improves the previously known bounds on MD decoding found in [5]. Figure 1 plots the functions in the exponents of the complexity bounds (9) and (15), i.e. $\min\left(R, H\left(\delta\right)\right)$ and $RH\left(\frac{\delta}{R}\right)$ for maximal codes. These codes meet the asymptotical Gilbert-Varshamov bound

$$R \geq 1 - H\left(\delta\right). \tag{17}$$

Using (17) we can remove the dependency on the code rate R in the functions $\min\left(R, H\left(\delta\right)\right)$ and $RH\left(\frac{\delta}{R}\right)$. From figure 1 we can observe the improvement of the new complexity expression (15) over the well-known complexity expression (9).

The space complexity of `Unique_Decoding(y)` and `MD_Decoding(y)` is proportional with the dimension of the generator matrix, i.e. $O\left(n^2\right)$.

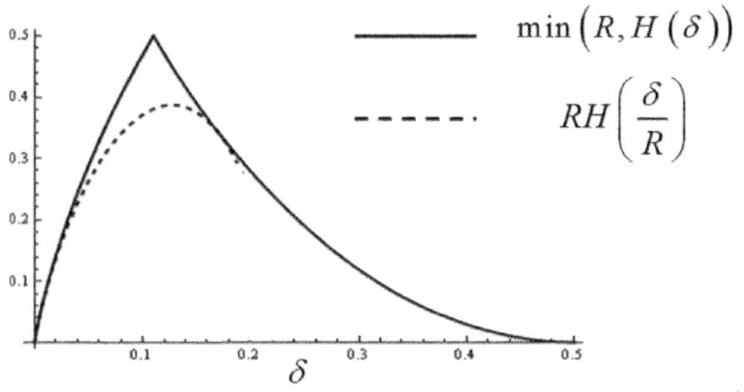

Fig. 1. Plot of the functions $\min\left(R, H\left(\delta\right)\right)$ and $RH\left(\frac{\delta}{R}\right)$

4 Conclusion

The main importance of *`Unique_Decoding(y)`* and *`MD_Decoding(y)`* algorithms is that they can be used to decode any linear code. Hence, they improve previously known complexity bounds on linear-code decoding. In [6] Evseev published a decoding algorithm with complexity $O\left(q^{R(1-R)n}\right)$ that pertains only to binary codes. Our decoding algorithms can decode linear codes over any alphabet.

Possible application of the `Unique_Decoding(y)` and `MD_Decoding(y)` may be found in *concatenated codes*. Concatenated codes were first introduced in [7] as a method for obtaining asymptotically good codes and they were used in deep space communications in the '70s and '80s [8]. Concatenated codes are obtained by combining two codes called *inner code* and *outer code*. The outer code is usually Reed-Solomon code, while the inner code can be a code meeting the Gilbert-Varshamov bound. Examples of such codes are the greedy codes. From figure 1 we can see that these codes can be decoded with reduced complexity with the new decoding algorithms.

References

1. Berlekamp, E.R., McEliece, R.J., van Tilborg, H.C.A.: On the Inherent Intractability of Certain Codiig Problems. IEEE Transactions on Information Theory 24(3), 384–386 (1978)
2. Barg, A.: Complexity Issues in Coding Theory. In: Brualdi, R.A., Huffman, W.C., Pless, V. (eds.) Handbook of Coding Theory. Elsevier, Amsterdam (1998)
3. Peterson, W.W., Weldon Jr., E.J.: Error-Correcting Codes, 2nd edn. The Massachusetts Institute of Technology (1996)
4. Barg, A., Krouk, E., van Tilborg, H.: On the complexity of Minimum Distance Decoding of Long Linear Codes. IEEE Transactions on Information Theory 45(5), 1392–1405 (1999)
5. Dumer, I.: Suboptimal decoding of linear codes: Partition technique. IEEE Trans. Inform. Theory 42(6), 1971–1986 (1996)
6. Evseev, G.S.: Complexity of decoding for linear codes. Probl. Inform. Transm. 19(1), 3–8 (in Russian); 1–6 (English translation) (1983)
7. Forney, G.D.: Concatenated Codes. PhD Thesis, Massachusetts Institute of Technology, Cambridge, MA (1965)
8. Concatenated codes, `http://en.wikipedia.org/wiki/Concatenated_error_correction_code`

Comparison of the Power Consumption of the 2nd Round SHA-3 Candidates

Benedikt Westermann[1], Danilo Gligoroski[2], and Svein Knapskog[1]

[1] NTNU/Q2S*, 7491 Trondheim, Norway
[2] NTNU/ITEM, 7491 Trondheim, Norway

Abstract. In the paper we show that the second round candidates of the NIST hash competition differ up to 22 % in their power consumption. We perform a detailed analysis of the candidates with respect to different performance parameters. Finally, we discuss the *time*, the *power consumption*, and the *energy per byte* as criteria to distinguish the candidates with respect to the performance.

1 Introduction

In the last decades the energy consumption of hardware and software have become a serious research topic. While various researchers focus on embedded systems and its energy constraints, other researchers for example analyze the economical challenges of the energy consumption of ICT systems.

In the area of embedded systems one challenge is to implement algorithms in hardware devices as efficient as possible such that the algorithms can run with the actually available power, which may be limited. For example, RFID tags only provide $30 - 50\mu W$[1] to the circuits and therefore this amount of power represents the upper limit for the power available for a computation.

On the global scale the energy consumption is also a serious challenge. In [2] the authors estimate that server farms consume roughly 180 billion kWh each year with a doubling every 4 - 5 years. Thus, the increasing energy consumption is not only a challenge for the electricity industry, but also an economical challenge. An example of Lucas Arts shows that there is a tremendous potential to save costs. The company managed to reduce their energy costs by $ 343,000 a year by selecting hard- and software that consume less energy [3].

With respect to the current NIST hash competition[4] the global influence is rather of minor importance due to the nature of the hash algorithms. However, the power consumption is a meaningful criterion with respect to embedded systems. Nowadays embedded systems have to fulfill more and more security requirements and thus also cryptographic primitives gain more importance and thus also their power consumption. This fact is our motivation to research the energy consumption of the candidates and to evaluate whether it is a well suited

* "Center for Quantifiable Quality of Service in Communication Systems, Center of Excellence" appointed by The Research Council of Norway, funded by the Research Council, NTNU and UNINETT. `http://www.q2s.ntnu.no`

M. Gusev and P. Mitrevski (Eds.): ICT Innovations 2010, CCIS 83, pp. 102–113, 2011.

criterion for the selection process. Due to the number of second round candidates we chose to evaluate the energy consumption with respect to conventional computers. This has the advantage that we can evaluate all candidates with reasonable costs. The comparison of the power consumption represents the main contribution of the paper. Moreover, we discuss the measured parameters as possible criteria for the selection process of the SHA-3 candidate.

The paper is structured as followed. In Section 2 we explain our methodology and describe the setup of our experiment. The results are presented in Section 3 followed by the related works in Section 4. In Section 5 we discuss our results. The paper concludes with Section 6.

2 Methodology

We have performed our measurements for all candidates of the second round[1] of the NIST Hash competition[4], and measured the power consumption of the 256 bit versions as well as the 512 bit versions. In the following part we describe how we generated the binaries of the candidates. In the last part of this section, we explain how we measured the power consumption of the different candidates.

2.1 Creating the Binary with Supercop

For our measurement we utilized the sources of the second round candidates that are available due to the Supercop project[5]. We used the version 20100818 of *Supercop*. Supercop is a toolkit to measure the performance of cryptographic algorithms amongst others cryptographic hash functions. It tries to find the best suited compiler together with the best suited parameters for the compiler for every algorithm that is included in Supercop. Therefore, Supercop represents for several reasons a well suited tool to compile and create binaries for our measurements. One reason is that the selection process is more objective than just determine some more or less random compiler options for the candidates. The latter could introduce a distortion of the results by selecting a parameter that is non-optimal for one candidate, but optimal for another one.

We used in our measurements the sources of the second round candidates that are included in the Supercop package. This has two advantages. Firstly, the versions of the candidates are mostly more optimized than the versions that are available on the official hash competitions website. Secondly, only small modifications on Supercop are necessary to adopt it to our needs. Thereby, we minimize the risk of introducing bugs which may interfere with the measurements.

The mentioned modifications are necessary, since the binary that is produced by Supercop does not accept any parameters. Thus, it is not possible to determine the amount of data the binary hashes. To this end, we had to modify some files in Supercop to fit the produced binaries to our needs. We modified the `measure.c` in the `crypto_hash` directory to suppress the output and to hash more data in

[1] `http://csrc.nist.gov/groups/ST/hash/sha-3/Round2/index.html`

a single run of the binary. In a single run we hashed 16 MB 1024 times. Thus, in total we hashed 16 GB of data with every execution of a binary and thus with each candidate. Thereby, 16 GB represent a trade-off between the time the measurement takes and the number of samples of the power consumption that could be collected. To avoid unnecessary delay during the measurement, we also fixed the hashed message to a constant value. For both, the 256 bit versions and the 512 bit versions we used the same `measure.c`.

In addition to the modifications of the `measure.c`, we also modified the `do` script of Supercop in order to extract the best performing binary of a candidate. The extracted version was optimized with respect to used CPU cycles and therewith not necessarily optimized to minimize the power consumption.

During the search of the best parameters we have disabled the dynamic frequency selection of the CPU. The CPU was set to a frequency of 2.27 GHz.

On our system there were two different compilers installed that are compatible with Supercop. Supercop used these two compilers and picked the best compiler together with its best suited parameters for each candidate. A `gcc` in version 4.3 was the first compiler which is shipped with the used Ubuntu 9.04 operating system. The second compiler was the `icc` compiler of Intel. We used the version 11.1 20100414 for the `icc` compiler. The extracted binaries were used to measure the consumed power of the candidates.

2.2 Power Measurement

In order to perform the measurement of the power consumption, we utilized the ACPI functions of our test machine, a Dell Studio 1537 notebook. Various parameters are given in the file `/proc/acpi/battery/BAT0/state` on our Ubuntu system. The content of the file is depicted in Figure 1. Some required values, e.g., *present rate* are only available when the machine runs on battery. Thus, we ran all tests on battery and had to recharge the battery after every round of the measurements. We sampled the values of the file every other second. This sample rate roughly corresponds to the refresh rate of the parameters in the file.

The parameter *present rate* provides either the current or the consumed energy that is drained from the battery each second. The displayed value depends on the system. Note that the unit of power is energy per second ($\frac{J}{s} = W$).

```
present:                 yes
capacity state:          ok
charging state:          discharging
present rate:            1620 mW
remaining capacity:      2299 mWh
present voltage:         11391 mV
```

Fig. 1. Content of the file /proc/acpi/battery/BAT0/state

Due to a bug in the system, the unit for the current is not correctly displayed. Instead of the correct unit mA the unit is stated as mW. However, this is at least for our used system not correct. In order to compute the consumed power P we need to multiply the voltage U (*present voltage*) with the current I (*present rate*). Thus, the power is calculated by $P = U \cdot I$ and represents the power consumption of the whole system.

For our measurements we are not interested in the power consumption of the whole system, but in the power consumption of the hash algorithms. In order to retrieve the power consumption the hashing of data requires, we first recorded the consumed power in the idle mode. After that, we recorded the power consumption when the system was hashing data. The difference of both values is, in the optimal case, the power consumed by the hash algorithm.

We measured the idle power prior to each run of a candidate. To this end, we sampled the current and the voltage for one minute. In total, we collected 30 samples prior to each run. The samples were stored in a SQLite3 database. By measuring the power consumption prior to every run, we avoid that a slight increase of the power consumption have a significant influence on the long run e.g., if we consider that the accuracy of measurement depends on the remaining energy in the battery.

After we have collected the 30 samples we started the compiled binary of a candidate and measured the time it took to execute the binary and thereby to hash 16 GB of data. Additionally, four seconds after the binary was started, we started to measure the power consumption. We sampled again the current and the voltage. With help of the values we calculated the power consumption of the system. We chose the delay of four seconds to avoid that values from the idle mode are counted for the hashing mode and therefore distort the measurement.

During the measurement every unnecessary service was stopped. Thereby, we limit the power consumptions of other processes and reduce possible side effects and sources of interference.

As soon as the binary had been terminated, we stopped the power measurement. The power consumption of a SHA-3 candidate was computed by the difference of the two collected median values of the power consumption. We chose the median to lower the impact of short distortions, for example short irregular spikes caused by other processes. The difference of both values represents the power the systems requires to hash the data. Naturally, this includes also the additional power that is necessary to cool the system.

We repeated this measurement 10 times for every candidate and every version. With each run we randomized the order of the candidates to avoid positioning effects. Additionally, we waited 15 seconds between two measurements.

For the different versions we measured the time and the power needed by every candidate to hash the data.

3 Results

In this section we present our measurement results. In 3.1 we show the measurement results of the 256 bit versions. Afterwards, we introduce the measurement results with respect to the 512 bit versions.

For all measurements we used a Dell Studio 1537 notebook equipped with a P8400 Core 2 Duo CPU from Intel. 4 GB of RAM were installed at the notebook. The operating system was a 64-bit version of Ubuntu 9.04. The installed kernel had the identifier `2.6.28-18-generic` and was the kernel shipped the in kernel package of the distribution.

During the whole measurement the CPU was set to a frequency of 2.27 GHz.

3.1 Results of the 256 Bit Versions

In addition to the official round 2 candidates, the Supercop versions of MD5, SHA-1 and SHA-256 were included in the measurements of the 256 bit versions. As some candidates in Supercop produce only a single executable for 256 bit and 512 bit, we used the same version for both measurements. To this end, we used the same binary for 256 bit and 512 bit versions for each of Hamsi, CubeHash, Keccak, Fugue, and Shabal.

The results of the time measurements of the 256 bit versions are depicted in Figure 2(a). The figure shows a clear difference among the candidates regarding the time that is needed to hash the 16 GB of data. The solid horizontal line represents the time SHA-256 needs to hash the data. While Blake, and Blue Midnight Wish are even faster than SHA-1, the candidates Echo, Fugue, Groestl, Hamsi, JH and Shavite are slower than SHA-1 and also slower than SHA-256.

Figure 2(b) depicts the power required by each candidate to hash data. Please note, that the x-axis starts at 10 W. Even though the differences are not as significant as the time differences, there are clear differences among the candidates. MD5 is the hash function with the lowest power consumption. The SHA-3 candidate with the lowest power consumption is most probably Skein, at least regarding our system and the 256 bit versions. It is interesting that the used power does not correlate with the used time. In fact the rank correlation coefficient of time and power is 0.37. A value near to -1 means that a higher power consumption correlates with a shorter runtime of the binary, while a correlation of 1 means that the power consumption comes hand in hand with a longer time to hash the data. However, in our case the value indicates that there is no linear correlation between the power consumption and the execution time.

With the help of the power and the time used to hash 16 GB of data, we can compute the energy that is necessary to hash a single byte. The value can be computed by:

$$energy\ per\ byte[J/Byte] = \frac{power\ [J/s] \cdot time\ [s]}{data\ volume\ [Byte]}$$

The resulting energy for hashing a single byte (*energy per byte*) is depicted in Figure 2(c). Due to the calculation of the values and the huge differences in time compared to the power consumption, there is a strong similarity to the time plot shown in Figure 2(a).

However, it is worth to note that the power consumption of the different candidates is not totally negligible. For example, while Cubehash is on rank eight regarding time, it is on the 16th rank with respect to the power consumption. At least if we only consider the expected values of the candidates (see Table 1). This indicates that also the power consumption of a candidate is a meaningful criterion regarding the performance of the hash algorithms, especially if the

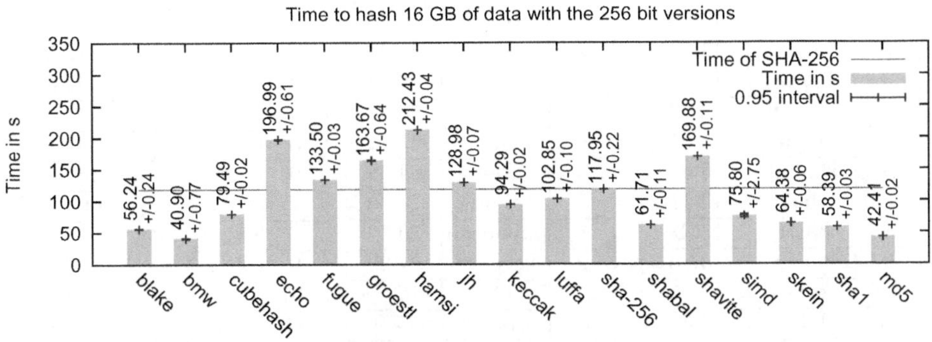

(a) Time in s to hash 16 GB of data

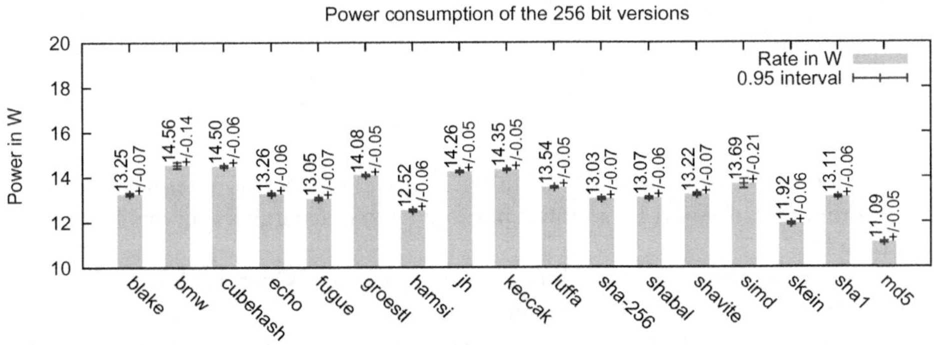

(b) Consumed power in W while hashing data

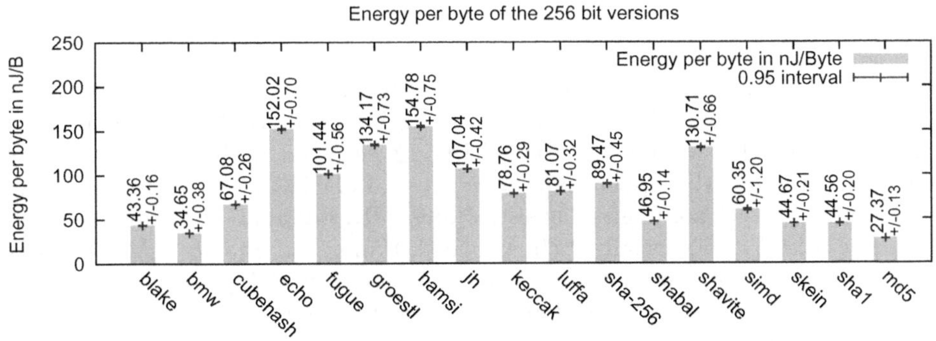

(c) Energy per Byte in nJ/B

Fig. 2. The results of the measurements of the 256 bit versions

Table 1. The measured parameters of the 256 bit candidates

Power

Rank	Name	Rate [W]
1	md5	11.09
2	skein	11.92
3	hamsi	12.52
4	sha256	13.03
5	fugue	13.05
6	shabal	13.07
7	sha1	13.11
8	shavite	13.22
9	blake	13.25
10	echo	13.26
11	luffa	13.54
12	simd	13.69
13	groestl	14.08
14	jh	14.26
15	keccakc	14.35
16	cubehash	14.50
17	bmw	14.56

Time

Rank	Name	Time [s]
1	bmw	40.90
2	md5	42.41
3	blake	56.24
4	sha1	58.39
5	shabal	61.71
6	skein	64.38
7	simd	75.80
8	cubehash	79.49
9	keccakc	94.29
10	luffa	102.85
11	sha256	117.95
12	jh	128.98
13	fugue	133.50
14	groestl	163.67
15	shavite	169.88
16	echo	196.99
17	hamsi	212.43

Energy

Rank	Name	Energy [nJ/B]
1	md5	27.37
2	bmw	34.65
3	blake	43.36
4	sha1	44.56
5	skein	44.67
6	shabal	46.95
7	simd	60.35
8	cubehash	67.08
9	keccakc	78.76
10	luffa	81.07
11	sha256	89.47
12	fugue	101.44
13	jh	107.04
14	shavite	130.71
15	groestl	134.17
16	echo	152.02
17	hamsi	154.78

needed time to hash the data is similar. Since the criterion *energy per byte* depends on both, it could be a suited parameter to distinguish among the different candidates.

By splitting the candidates into two groups, those which perform better than SHA-256 and those which perform worse than SHA-256, we end up with the same groups, regardless if we split with respect to the time or to the energy per byte.

3.2 Results of the 512 Bit Versions

In this part we present the results of the 512 bit versions. Figure 3(a) shows the time that is needed by each candidate to hash 16 GB of data. As in Figure 2(a) the solid line marks the time SHA-512 needs to hash the same amount of data. We used the upper confidence interval of SHA-512 as reference value. The candidates Echo, Fugue, Groestl, Hamsi, JH, Luffa, and Shavite need more time as SHA-512. Especially, Echo, Groestl, Hamsi and Shavite take a lot more time than all other candidates in the compiled version of Supercop. For example, Shavite needs around 10 times longer to hash the same amount of data than the fastest 512 bit candidate. It's also worth to mentioned that the 512 bit version of Blue Midnight Wish is more than twice as fast as Shabal which is the third fastest candidate regarding the 512 bit candidates. Even with respect to Skein, the second fastest candidate in this measurement, it is more than a factor of 1.8.

Figure 3(b) presents the power consumption of the different 512 bit candidates. Blue Midnight Wish is the candidates with the highest power consumption, but it is the fastest regarding the time. It requires $1.04W$ (7%) more power for its computation than the average candidate. This might be an indicator that Blue Midnight Wish is already highly optimized.

However, in general there is no linear correlation between the power consumption and the time a candidate needs to hash the data, as the rank correlation coefficient is only 0.14 in the case of the 512 bit versions.

Figure 3(c) shows the energy that is necessary to hash a single byte for the 512 bit candidates. The differences between the different candidates are significant, mostly due to the significant differences in the time that is needed to hash the data. Most notable is the fact that the 512 bit version of Blue Midnight Wish is likely to consume less energy to hash a byte than MD5. While MD5 requires $27.37 \pm 0.13 \frac{nJ}{B}$, Blue Midnight Wish in the 512 bit version needs $24.31 \pm 0.12 \frac{nJ}{B}$.

Table 2. The measured parameters of the 512 bit candidates

Power

Rank	Name	Rate [W]
1	hamsi	12.51
2	shavite	12.93
3	fugue	13.06
4	shabal	13.06
5	skein	13.55
6	echo	13.61
7	blake	13.90
8	luffa	13.93
9	sha512	14.08
10	jh	14.25
11	keccakc	14.33
12	groestl	14.35
13	simd	14.38
14	cubehash	14.47
15	bmw	14.86

Time

Rank	Name	Time [s]
1	bmw	28.10
2	skein	50.00
3	shabal	61.77
4	blake	76.95
5	cubehash	79.48
6	simd	80.61
7	keccakc	94.30
8	sha512	96.73
9	jh	128.63
10	fugue	133.45
11	luffa	151.16
12	hamsi	212.37
13	groestl	229.84
14	echo	261.12
15	shavite	278.71

Energy

Rank	Name	Energy [nJ/B]
1	bmw	24.31
2	skein	39.43
3	shabal	46.96
4	blake	62.27
5	cubehash	66.96
6	simd	67.46
7	keccakc	78.64
8	sha512	79.29
9	fugue	101.44
10	jh	106.68
11	luffa	122.55
12	hamsi	154.65
13	groestl	192.03
14	echo	206.88
15	shavite	209.63

3.3 Comparison between the 256 Bit and the 512 Bit Versions

In the Figure 4 we compare the 256 bit versions with their 512 bit pendants. As mentioned above, we used for some candidates the same version for both measurements, namely CubeHash, Fugue, Hamsi, Keccak and Shabal.

In the comparison we can see that all these five candidates have almost the same expected energy consumption: there is no significant difference according to a two-sided t-test with a 0.95 confidence interval. This provides some evidence that our methodology result in reproducible and valid results. The candidate JH does not differ in the expected value either, even though different binaries were used. All other candidates ended up in different expected values according to a t-test.

4 Related Works

There are only a few publications that have reported the energy consumption of hash algorithms. In [6] the authors analyzed among others the energy consumption of MD2-MD4,SHA, and SHA-1, and determined the energy that is consumed to hash a single byte. Contrary to our measurements, they used a PDA with an ARM processor as test system. The energy per byte in their setup resulted in $760nJ/B$ for SHA-1 and $590nJ/B$ for MD5. Thus, their results differ by a factor of roughly 17 with respect to SHA-1 and a factor 21 with respect to MD5. The reasons for the huge difference are probably the CPU architecture as well as the size of the circuits of the used CPU.

In [1] the authors present a ultra-low power SHA-1 hardware design. The analysis of their implementation showed that their design consumes $1.49nJ/B$ for SHA-1. This is a factor of 30 lower than our results for SHA-1. Obviously, a specific hardware design could be much more energy efficient than the versions we measured.

5 Discussion

There are some caveats to be aware of when interpreting the results. The most important restriction is that the results are only valid with respect to the used CPU. A test with different CPUs, especially with a complete different architecture are likely to result in significantly different values as it is shown in Section 4. While the energy per byte on the ARM processor used in [6] for SHA-1 is 17 times higher as on our system, the hardware implementation in [1] consumes 30 times less energy per byte than our used SHA-1 version.

With respect to our measurements, a source of interference might be the sensor that was used to measure the current and the voltage of our system. The sensor is integrated in the system and therefore somehow dependent on the system state. This could influence the accuracy of the chip itself. During our measurements we could observe a slight increase of the power consumption over time: the lower the battery energy the higher was the power consumption of the system. With respect to the overall consumption the decrease is negligible, especially since we determined the idle power consumption prior to each run of a candidate. Additionally, we tried to minimize the effect by the randomizing the order of the candidates. Another problem might be that the sensor is not very precise and thus provides a constantly to high or to low value.

As mentioned above, the power consumption includes the power the fan of the notebook consumes during the measurements. Naturally, the fan was more frequently used during the hashing operations. Therefore, the measured results are most likely a upper bound for our test system.

6 Conclusion

In this paper we provided an evaluation of the power consumption for the SHA-3 candidates, and we have shown that the different hash candidates differ not only with respect to the needed time to hash data, but also with respect to the power consumption. Both, the power consumption and the time are therefore important criteria for the performance of the candidates. *Energy per byte* considers both criteria. Up to now, the time differences among the candidates dominate the overall picture. With respect to the criterion energy per byte, BMW256 clearly outperforms all other SHA-3 candidates in the 256-bit arena. Most notable, BMW256 and Blake-32 are even more energy efficient than the SHA-1 function which is the current standard. Only MD5, a broken 128-bit hash function, is more energy efficient than BMW256 and thus more efficient than all other candidates. Also in the 512-bit arena, BMW512 outperforms all other candidates concerning the energy-per-byte criterion by a significant margin. However, the candidates Skein512, Shabal, Blake-64, CubeHash, SIMD, and Keccak outperform the current standard SHA-2.

Due to future optimization and the selection process it is likely that the time differences between the candidates become less and therefore the criterion *energy per byte* may become an important parameter for the selection process.

References

1. Kaps, J.P., Sunar, B.: Energy comparison of aes and sha-1 for ubiquitous computing. In: Zhou, X., Sokolsky, O., Yan, L., Jung, E.-S., Shao, Z., Mu, Y., Lee, D.C., Kim, D.Y., Jeong, Y.-S., Xu, C.-Z. (eds.) EUC Workshops 2006. LNCS, vol. 4097, pp. 372–381. Springer, Heidelberg (2006)
2. Fettweis, G., Zimmermann, E.: Ict energy consumption - trends and challenges. In: Proceedings of the 11th International Symposium on Wireless Personal Multimedia Communications (2008)
3. Ruth, S.: Green it more than a three percent solution? IEEE Internet Computing 13(4), 74–78 (2009)
4. National Institute of Standards and Technology: Cryptographic hash algorithm competition, `http://csrc.nist.gov/groups/ST/hash/sha-3/index.html` (visited 09.05.2010)
5. VAMPIRE lab: Supercop: System for unified performance evaluation related to cryptographic operations and primitives, `http://bench.cr.yp.to/supercop.html` (visited 09.05.2010)
6. Potlapally, N.R., Ravi, S., Raghunathan, A., Jha, N.K.: Analyzing the energy consumption of security protocols. In: ISLPED 2003: Proceedings of the 2003 International Symposium on Low Power Electronics and Design, pp. 30–35. ACM, New York (2003)

A Appendix: Additional Diagrams and Tables

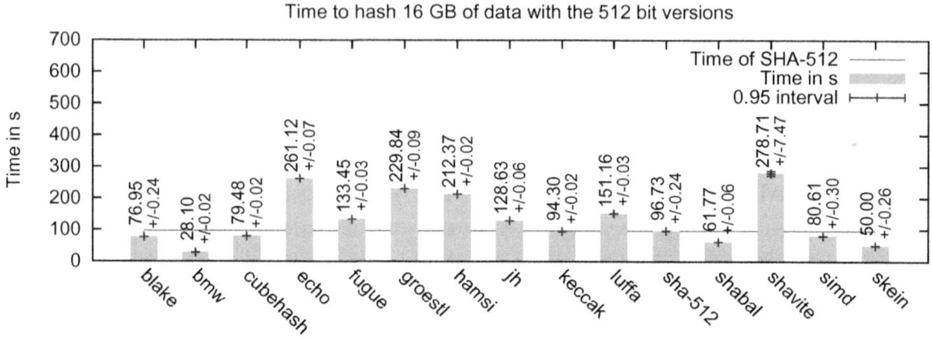

(a) Time in s to hash 16 GB of data

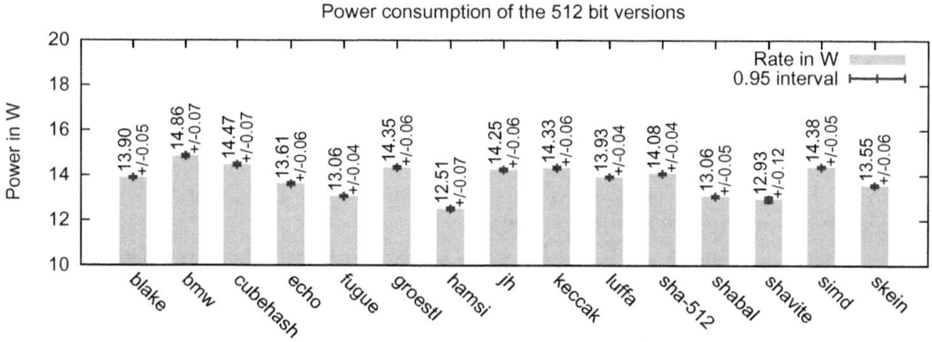

(b) Consumed power in W while hashing data

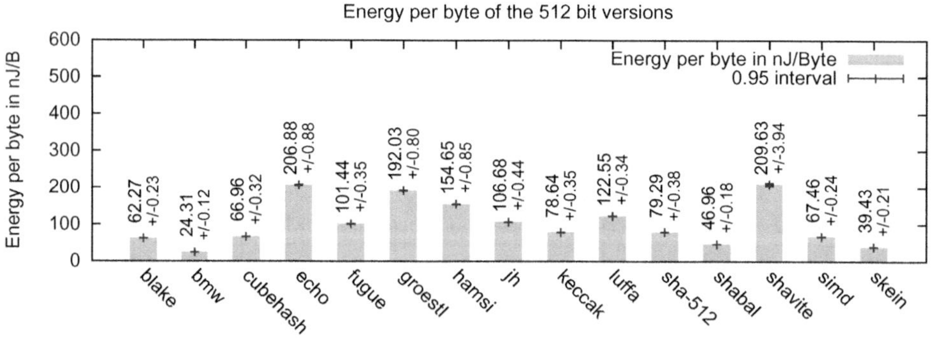

(c) Energy per Byte in nJ/B

Fig. 3. The results of the measurements of the 512 bit versions

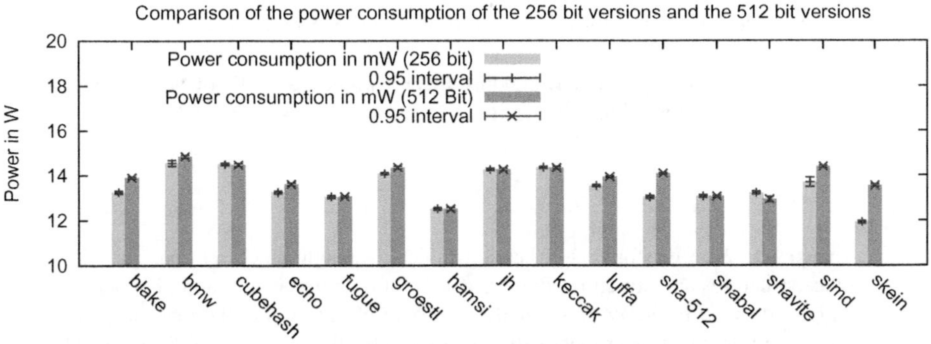

(a) Comparison of the power consumption.

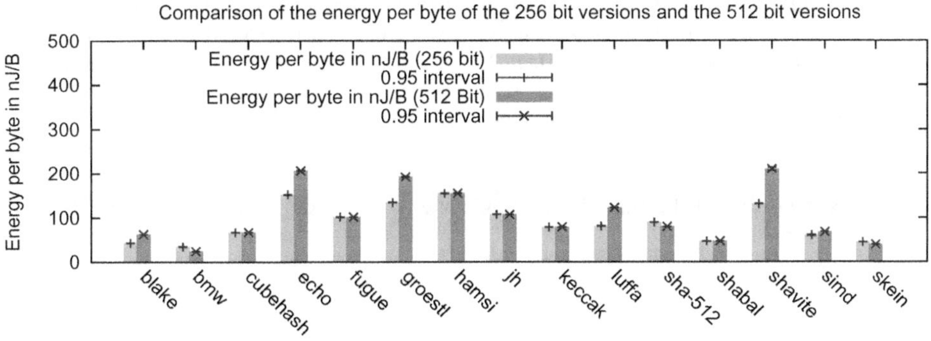

(b) A comparison of the energy per byte.

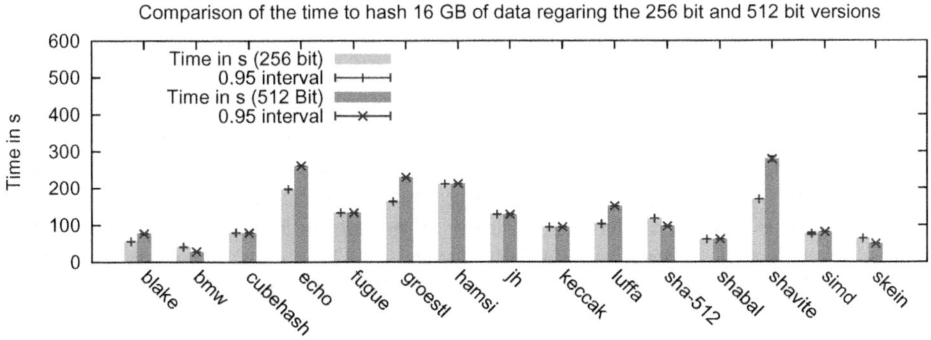

(c) A comparison of the time to hash 16 GB of data

Fig. 4. Comparison of the 256 bit versions and the 512 bit version

Self-Heating Effects in High Performance Devices

Katerina Raleva[1], Dragica Vasileska[2], and Stephen M. Goodnick[2]

[1] University Sts Cyril and Methodius, FEIT, Skopje, Republic of Macedonia
[2] Arizona State University, Tempe, AZ 85287-5706, USA

Abstract. We investigate self-heating effects in single-gate and dual-gate device structures and structures that have AlN (aluminum nitride) and diamond as a buried oxide layer. We also investigate both electrical and thermal enhancement and degradation respectively, due to self-heating effects in fully-depleted SOI devices that have arbitrary transport and crystallographic direction. Our simulation analysis suggests that in all these alternative device technologies self-heating is dramatically reduced in short channel devices due to the pronounced velocity overshoot effect. Moreover, the use of AlN and diamond as a buried oxide layer further reduces the current degradation due to self heating to insignificant values because of the drastic reduction of the thermal resistance of the buried oxide layer.

Keywords: self-heating effects, single and dual-gate devices, arbitrary crystallographic directions.

1 Introduction

Device scaling of conventional MOSFETs will eventually reach its limits due to two factors: (1) limitations of the lithography process and (2) fluctuations in device characteristics due to random dopants, line edge roughness, etc. Therefore, alternative transistor designs are being sought that minimize or completely eliminate these effects. One avenue is to use alternative materials such as strained Si, SiGe, even GaAs integrated in the silicon process. Another avenue that is being pursued, and is already replacing the conventional MOSFET at the 20 nm technology node, is to use alternative device designs. These include fully-depleted (FD) silicon on insulator (SOI) devices, dual-gate (DG) device structures, tri-gate FETs or FinFETs, and multiple-gate structures (MugFET). Thus, immediate need arises to investigate these alternative device designs as they contain the buried oxide layer (BOX) that is not good thermal conductor. Also, the active silicon film in these device structures is very thin and phonon boundary scattering significantly reduces the thermal conductivity of the thin Si film when compared to bulk Si.

The purpose of this research work is to investigate transport in single-gate, dual-gate, devices with AlN and diamond buried oxide (BOX) layer and single-gate fully-depleted (FD) devices having arbitrary crystallographic directions. To get meaningful

M. Gusev and P. Mitrevski (Eds.): ICT Innovations 2010, CCIS 83, pp. 114–122, 2011.

results, we employ our 2D electro-thermal device simulator which self-consistently solves the Boltzmann transport equation (BTE) for the electrons with the energy balance (EB) equations for acoustic and optical phonons. A flow-chart of the simulator is shown in Fig. 1. Details of the theoretical model implemented can be found in Refs. [1-3].

The paper is organized as follows. In Section 2 we compare the self-heating effects in single-gate and dual-gate devices. The role of the BOX on the amount of self-heating and the use of AlN and diamond as BOX materials is described in Section 3. In Section 4 we describe self-heating effects in FD SOI devices with several different transport directions. We finish this paper with conclusive comments from the work performed that are given in Section 5.

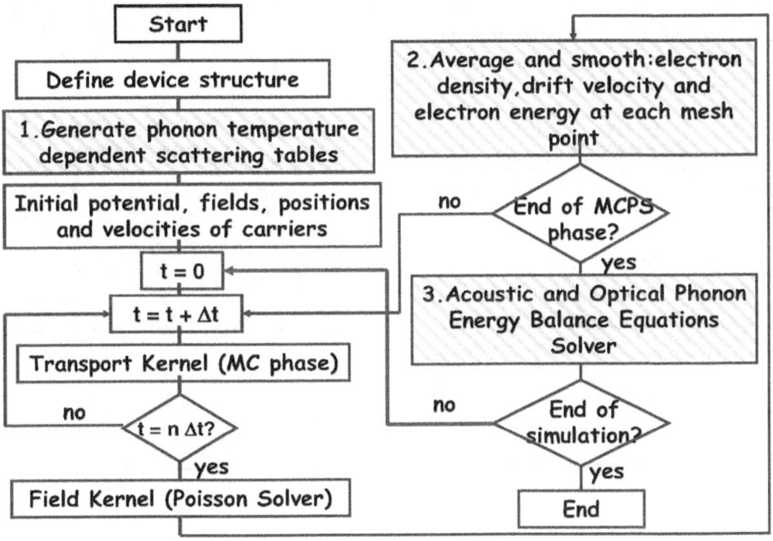

Fig. 1. Flow-chart of the electro-thermal device simulator

2 Single-Gate vs. Dual-Gate FD SOI Devices

As already noted in the Introduction section of this paper, to get better device performance and eliminate threshold voltage fluctuations due to random dopant fluctuations [4], line edge roughness [5] and other imperfections that arise during the fabrication of nanoscale devices, researchers in the last 10 years have focused on alternative device designs such as dual-gate devices, tri-gate (FinFET) devices and multi-gate devices. The first proposal for dual-gate devices was vertical structures (see Fig. 2) [6], whereas later proposals involve in-plane devices that are easily integrated in the CMOS process. Since at the time when this research work was performed we only had 2D electro-thermal particle-based device simulator, we focus on the comparison of performance degradation due to self-heating effects in single-gate and vertical dual-gate devices (both the electrical and heat flow occur in a plane).

The on-current degradation for different boundary conditions on the gate electrode in single-gate FD SOI device (Fig. 2 – left panel) and the corresponding current degradation for dual gate device (Fig. 2 – right panel) and different boundary conditions on the temperature of both the top and the bottom gates is shown in Table 1. We find that the dual gate device has almost the same current degradation as a single-gate device, but carries about 1.5-1.8 times more current. However, the lattice temperature in the hot-spot region is higher for dual-gate device and there exists larger bottleneck between acoustic and optical phonons in this device structure when compared to the single-gate FD SOI device structure (see Fig. 3). This is easily explainable with the fact that there are more carriers in the DG structure and the optical to acoustic phonon decay is not fast enough so that heating has more influence on the carrier drift velocity and, therefore, on-state current in dual-gate devices. In fact, we do observe degradation in the average carrier velocity in the dual-gate devices when compared to single-gate FD SOI device structure (Fig. 4).

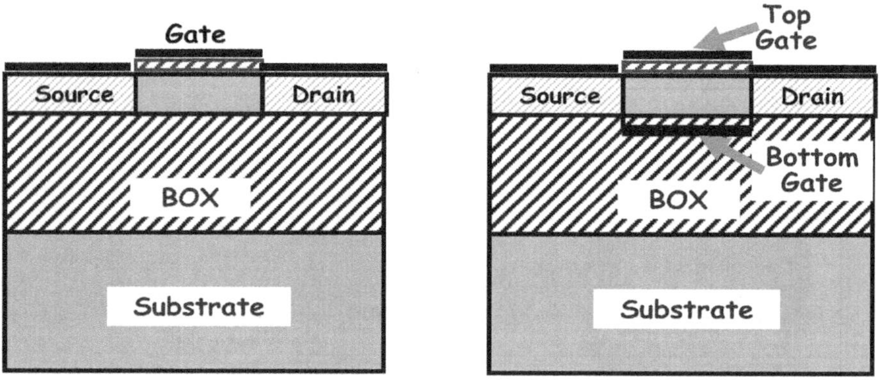

Fig. 2. Schematic of the single-gate (left panel) FET and the dual-gate (right panel) FET structure being modelled. The doping/geometrical dimensions of these two structures are: $N_D=1\times10^{19}cm^{-3}$ (source and drain region), $N_A=1\times10^{17}cm^{-3}$ (channel region), $L_{gate}=25nm$ (channel length), $t_{ox}=2nm$ (gate-oxide thickness), $t_{si}=12nm$ (Si-layer thickness) and $t_{BOX}=50nm$ (BOX thickness).

Table 1. Current degradation due to a self-heating for single-gate (SG) and dual-gate (DG) structures given in Fig. 2, for $V_{GS}=1.2$ V and $V_{DS}=1.2V$. Temperature boundary conditions on the DG device gate electrodes are set to 300K.

Type of simulation	25nm SG FD-SOI		25nm GD FD-SOI	
	Current (mA/um)	Current Decrease	Current (mA/um)	Current Decrease
isothermal	1.9423	\	3.0682	\
thermal	1.764	9.18%	2.788	9.13%
thermal	1.664	14.35%	2.627	14.37%
thermal	1.4995	22.82%	2.3153	24.54%

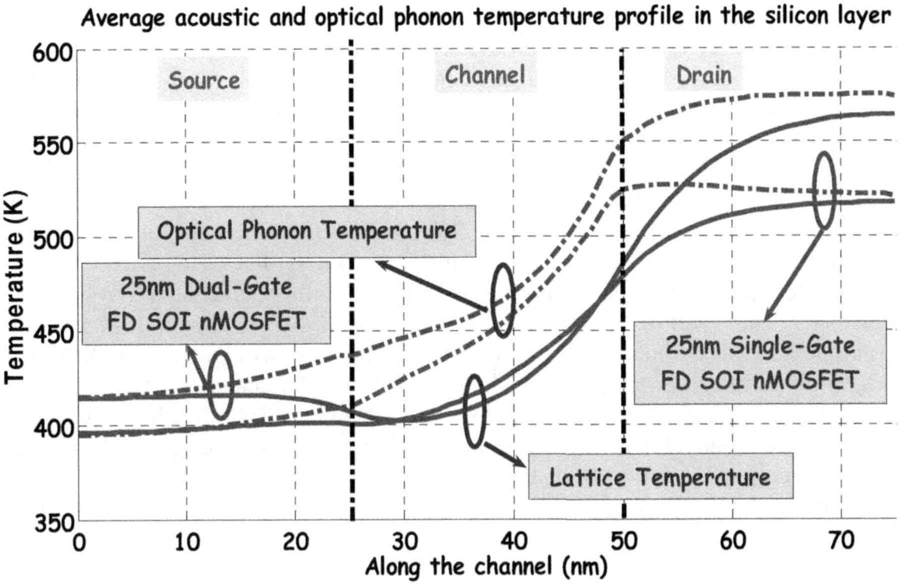

Fig. 3. Phonon bottleneck in single-gate and dual-gate FD SOI device structure

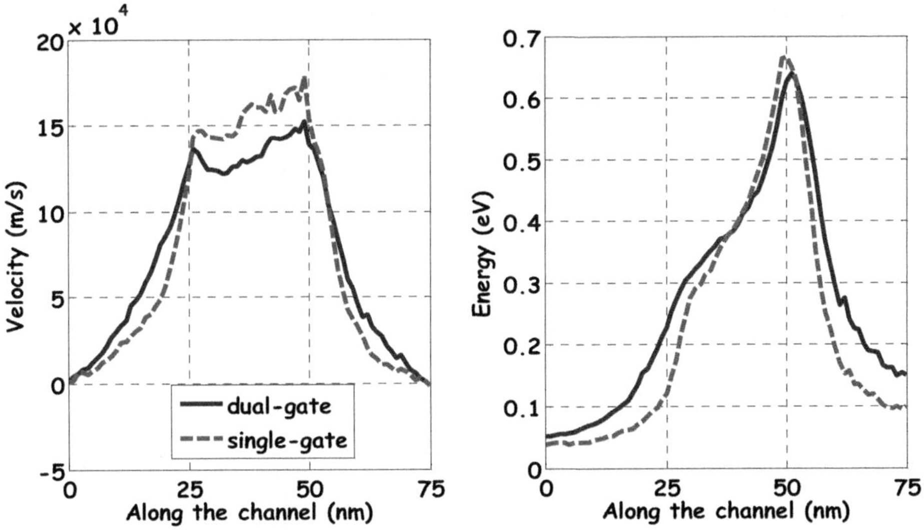

Fig. 4. Average electron velocity (left panel) and average electron energy (right panel) in 25nm channel-length single-gate and dual-gate SOI devices

3 FD-SOI Devices with Diamond and AlN BOX

One way of improving device performance from an electrical and thermal perspective is to use multi-gate device structures. An alternative approach is to reduce the thermal resistance of the BOX. Suitable materials that can serve as BOX layers are diamond, AlN, SiC, etc. Silicon on diamond (SOD) is a substrate engineered to address the major challenges of silicon-based Ultra Large Scale Integrated (ULSI) technology, in particular, to provide for enhanced thermal management and charge confinement. The SOD concept is achieved by joining a thin, single crystalline Si device layer to a highly oriented diamond (HOD) layer that serves as an electrical insulator, heat spreader and supporting substrate. Therefore, SOD represents an alternative Si on insulator (SOI) concept, where the thermally insulating SiO_2 has been replaced by highly thermally conductive diamond. The advantage of this approach is that diamond combines its inherent electrical insulating properties with the best thermal conductivity found in nature [7]. The room-temperature thermal conductivity of diamond, both single crystalline and thick film polycrystalline, can reach values as high as 2400 W/mK [8]. Thus, the operating temperature of devices and ICs fabricated on SOD wafers is expected to be significantly lower than that of standard SOI or silicon technology (provided that identical heat sinking measures are used), since the active electronics is intimately coupled to the best heat spreading material found in nature. As a consequence, the SOD concept allows higher power consumption per device in the IC, or a higher integrated power density at similar power losses.

An alternative to Diamond is to replace the buried silicon dioxide by another insulator that has higher thermal conductivity. As already mentioned, one of the interesting candidates for such novel buried insulators is aluminum nitride (AlN), which has thermal conductivity that is about 100 times higher than that of SiO_2 (136 W/m-K versus 1.4 W/m-K) and roughly equal to that of bulk silicon itself (145 W/m-K). Furthermore, AlN has excellent thermal stability, high electrical resistance, and a coefficient of thermal expansion close to that of silicon. Thus, the use of AlN as the buried

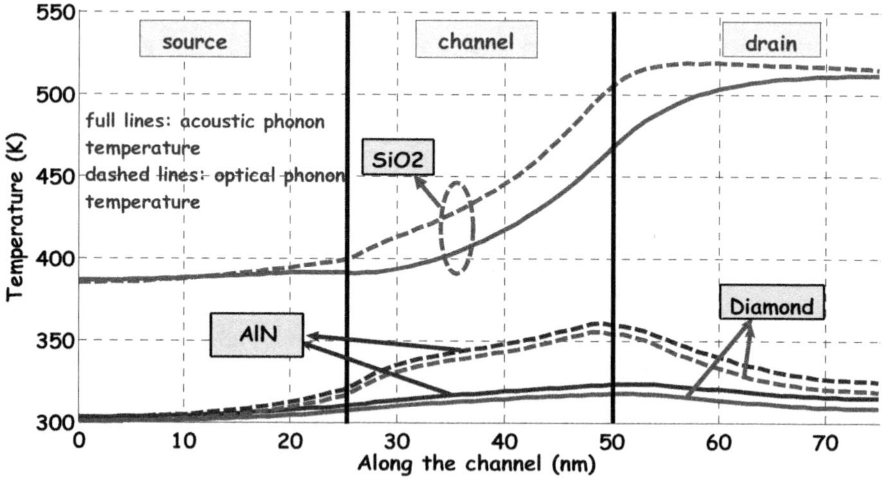

Fig. 5. Average acoustic and optical phonon temperature profile in the active silicon layer for 25nm channel-length fully-depleted SOI, SOD and SOAlN devices. Note that the phonon energy bottleneck is higher when SiO_2 is used as a BOX material.

insulator in silicon-on-aluminum nitride (SOAlN) as an alternative to SOD may mitigate the self-heating penalty of the SOI materials enabling more general and high-temperature applications.

Simulation results for 25nm channel-length FD-SOD(SOAlN) devices show: (1) lattice heating plays minor role in the current degradation, and (2) the spread of the temperature across the bottom side of the wafer is more uniform (which means that hot-spots are less-likely to occur in these two technologies if adopted). There is slightly better heat spread in the SOD than in the SOAlN devices (see Fig. 5), which is in agreement with the results from Ref. [9].

4 Inclusion of Arbitrary Crystallographic Orientations

Yet another way that researchers from major Labs have explored in recent years is use of alternative transport directions which were expected to improve device electrical performance by about 30% and move ahead one technology node. In here, we explore both the electrical and the thermal behavior of devices fabricated along different major crystallographic directions. To take into account the wafer orientation into the theoretical model, we use the standard effective mass approach which describes the band edge electronic properties in an approximate manner. Silicon Δ-valley effective masses and subband degeneracy for (100), (111) and (110) wafer orientations are given in Table 2, where m_l and m_t are the longitudinal and the transverse effective masses, respectively. The expressions for the effective mass are derived according to [10] (see Fig. 6).

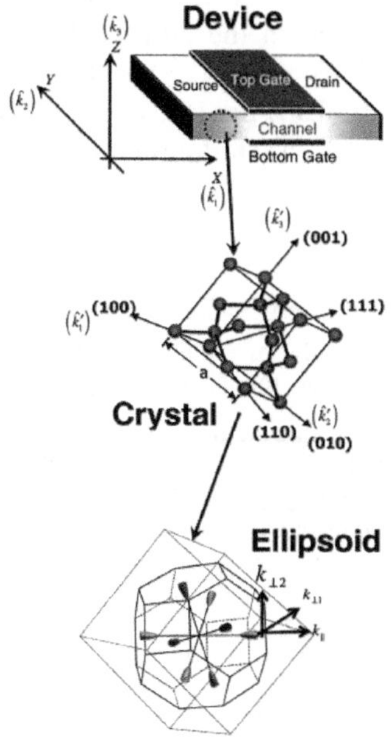

Fig. 6. Three orthogonal coordinate systems: Device coordinate system (DCS), Crystal coordinate system (CCS), and Ellipse coordinate system (ECS) used in the calculation of the effective-mass tensor [10] for arbitrary crystallographic orientation

Table 2. Silicon Δ-valley effective masses and subband degeneracy for (100), (111) and (110) wafer orientations. (m_l=0.91, m_t=0.19)

Wafer	m_x (transport eff. mass)	m_y (confinement eff. mass)	m_z (width eff. mass)	Deg.
(100)	m_t	m_l	m_t	2
	m_l	m_t	m_t	2
	m_t	m_t	m_l	2
(111)	$3m_lm_t/(2m_l+m_t)$	$(2m_l+m_t)/3$	m_t	2
	$(2m_l+m_t)/6$	$3m_t(m_l+m_t)/(2m_l+m_t)$	$2m_lm_t/(m_l+m_t)$	4
(110)	m_t	$2m_lm_t/(m_l+m_t)$	$(m_l+m_t)/2$	4
	m_l	m_t	m_t	2

The simulation results for different wafer orientations ((100) and (110)) obtained using different thermal conductivity models are summarized in Table 3 and Figs. 7 and 8. As model 1 we use our anisotropic (temperature and position dependent) model for the thermal conductivity [11]. Model 2 is the thermal conductivity tensor model provided by Aksamija and co-workers [12].This model does not account for thickness dependence of the thermal conductivity. From the current degradation and lattice temperature profiles one can conclude that the device with (110) crystallographic orientation is better from both electrical and thermal point of view. For the device with (100) crystallographic orientation, thermal conductivity model 2 gives 1% smaller current degradation (Table 3). For the (110) device, there is no change in the current degradation due to a self-heating with both thermal conductivity models, but the on-current is slightly higher compared to the value of the (100) device. Also, from Figs. 7 and 8 one can observe that the device with (110) crystallographic direction has the lower temperature in the hot-spot region.

Table 3. Current degradation for 25 nm channel-length FD SOI devices with (100) and (110) crystallographic orientations. Two types of thermal conductivity (κ_{th}) model are used: 1- temperature and position dependent κ_{th} model; 2 – temperature dependent κ_{th} tensor model.

Wafer orientation	Type of simulation	k_{th} model	Current (mA/um)	Current Degradation (%)
(100)	isothermal	/	1.828	\
(100)	thermal	1	1.757	3.88
(100)	thermal	2	1.768	2.28
(110)	isothermal	/	1.825	\
(110)	thermal	1	1.785	2.19
(110)	thermal	2	1.785	2.19

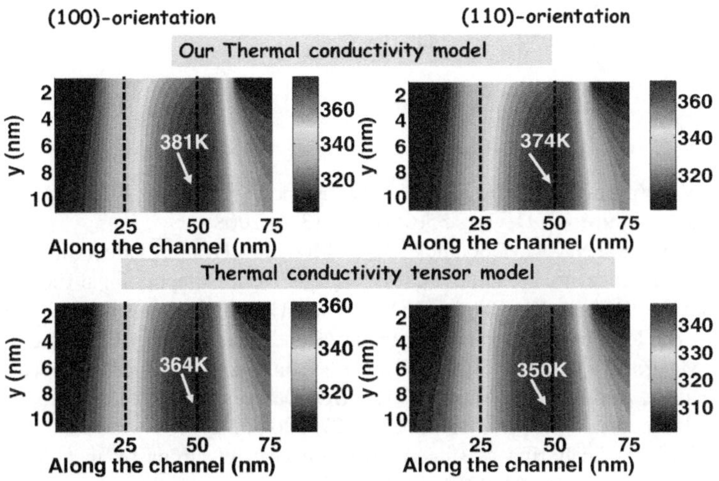

Fig. 7. Lattice temperature profiles in the active silicon-layer for 25 nm channel-length FD SOI devices with (100) and (110) crystallographic orientations

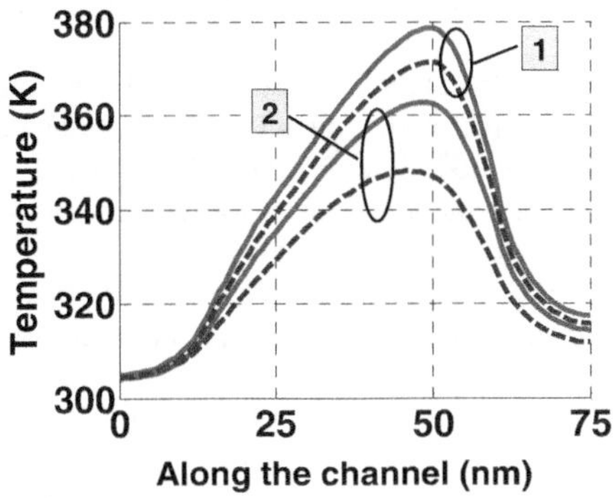

Fig. 8. Average lattice temperature profile in the active Si-layer (1-our thermal conductivity model; 2-thermal conductivity tensor). Solid lines – (100) crystallographic orientations; dashed lines – (110) crystallographic orientations.

5 Conclusions

In summary, we have presented simulation results for structures that are potentially going to replace conventional silicon due to the fact that there is either electrical or thermal benefit of using these structures or both. For example, dual gate devices for the same current degradation due to self-heating effects provide 1.5-1.8 times more current. On the other hand SOD and SOAlN structures have almost zero degradation due to practically almost zero thermal resistance of the BOX layer. Finally we find that devices in which transport occurs along [110] direction are better than structures with different transport direction both from an electrical and thermal perspective. Thus, the future holds to planar dual-gate devices with either diamond or AlN BOX fabricated along [110] direction. Nanowire transistors also fall in this category.

Acknowledgments. This work was supported in part by a Grant from National Science Foundation NSF ECCS 0901251.

References

1. Raleva, K., Vasileska, D., Goodnick, S.M.: Modeling Thermal Effects in Nanodevices. IEEE Trans. on Electron Devices 55(6), 1306–1316 (2008)
2. Vasileska, D., Raleva, K., Goodnick, S.M.: Modeling Heating Effects in Nanoscale Devices: The Presence and the Future, a review paper for J. Computational Electronics (2008)
3. Vasileska, D., Raleva, K., Goodnick, S.M.: Self-Heating Effects in Nano-Scale FD SOI Devices: The Role of the Substrate, Boundary Conditions at Various Interfaces and the Dielectric Material Type for the BOX. IEEE Trans. on Electron Devices 68 (December 2009)
4. Vasileska, D., Ahmed, S.S.: Narrow-Width SOI Devices: The Role of Quantum Mechanical Size. IEEE Trans. Electron Devices 52, 227–236 (2005)
5. Li, J., Ma, T.P.: Scattering of silicon inversion layer electrons by metal/oxide interface roughness. J. Appl. Phys. 62, 4212–4215 (1987)
6. Hisamoto, D., Kaga, T., Kawamoto, Y., Takeda, E.: A fully depleted lean-channel transistor (DELTA)—A novel vertical ultra thin SOI MOSFET. IEDM Tech. Dig., 833 (1989)
7. Field, J.E.: Strength, fracture and erosion properties of CVD diamond. In: Field, J.E. (ed.) The Properties of Natural and Synthetic Diamond, pp. 473–513. Academic Press Ltd., London (1992)
8. Graebner, J.E., Jin, S., Kammlott, G.W., Wong, Y.-H., Herb, J.A., Gardinier, C.F.: Thermal conductivity and the microstructure of state-of-the-art chemical-vapordeposited (CVD) diamond. Diamond Related Mater 2, 1059–1063 (1993)
9. Chu, P.K.: Novel silicon-on-insulator structures for reduced self-heating effects. IEEE Circuits and Systems Magazine 5(4), 18–29 (2005)
10. Rahman, A., Lundstrom, M.S., Ghosh, A.W.: Generalized effective-mass approach for n-type metal-oxide-semiconductor field-effect transistors on arbitrarily orientated wafers. J. Appl. Phys. 97, 53702–53713 (2005)
11. Vasileska, D., Raleva, K., Goodnick, S.M.: Electrothermal Studies of FD SOI Devices That Utilize a New Theoretical Model for the Temperature and Thickness Dependence of the Thermal Conductivity. IEEE Transactions on Electron Devices 57(3), 726–728 (2010)
12. Martin, P., Aksamija, Z., Pop, E., Ravaioli, U.: Impact of phonon-surface roughness scattering on thermal conductivity of thin si nanowires. Phys. Rev. Lett. 102(12), 125503 (2009)

Performance Analysis of Dual-Hop MIMO Systems

Jovan Stosic[1] and Zoran Hadzi-Velkov[2]

[1] Makedonski Telekom, Orce Nikolov bb, 1000 Skopje, Macedonia
jovan.stosic@telekom.mk
[2] Ss. Cyril and Methodius University, Faculty of Electrical Engineering and Information Technologies, Karpos 2 bb, 1000 Skopje, Macedonia
zoranhv@feit.ukim.edu.mk

Abstract. In this paper we study the end-to-end bit error and outage probability (OP) performance of dual-hop multiple input multiple output (MIMO) systems with Alamouti's coding using modified amplify and forward (MAF) relaying under flat Rayleigh fading channels. The bit error performances of dual-hop MIMO systems with variable gain relays is compared with dual-hop single antenna systems and regenerative i.e. decode and forward (DF) dual-hop MIMO system. We show that MAF MIMO systems achieve significantly lower bit error probability then dual-hop single-antenna systems and comparable performance with DF systems. The performance gap increases with usage of dual antenna in relay and the receiver. The OP performances of these systems are compared with single-antenna dual-hop and dual-antenna single-hop systems. We show significant improvement of OP performance compared to single-antenna dual-hop and comparable performance with dual-antenna single-hop systems.

Keywords: Cooperative wireless communications, MIMO, Alamouti space time block coding, dual-hop relay systems, bit error probability, outage probability, Rayleigh fading.

1 Introduction

The new hot topic in the contemporary wireless communications is user and infrastructure-based cooperation, which has already occupied an entire new area of research in the wireless communications, called cooperative communications. Cooperative terminals exploit the properties of the multipath transmission of the radio signal in order to increase the efficiency and robustness of their communication. That means that the neighboring wireless stations, which are in the area of one transmitter-receiver pair, are "assisting" the communication between them in their "leisure time" by performing the function of relay. Beside cooperation of the user terminals i.e. user cooperation, another cooperative scenario is cooperation of base stations i.e. infrastructure-based cooperation. In this paper the proposed multiple antennas systems are intended for such scenario, mostly due to the space and cost limitations of the mobile stations. Namely, in order to provide transmit or receive diversity and sufficient decorrelation of the transmitted signals, antennas in the mobile station should be separated about three wavelengths. The sufficient separation of antennas in

M. Gusev and P. Mitrevski (Eds.): ICT Innovations 2010, CCIS 83, pp. 123–132, 2011.

the base station is about ten wavelengths but there is no space limitation. Additionally, taking in account that each base station serves many mobile stations it is more cost efficient to add on complexity in the base station.

In wireless communications systems the bit error probability (BEP) and outage probability (OP) are most important performance measure of the cooperative relaying system. Therefore, we investigated the end-to-end BEP and OP performance of the dual-hop relay systems using multiple antennas with Alamouti's space time block coding (STBC), operating over independent Rayleigh fading channels. We analyzed modified amplify and forward (MAF) dual-hop dual-antenna systems with variable gains, and compared their BER performance to regenerative DF systems as well as with dual-hop single antenna systems. The MAF scheme compared to pure non-regenerative amplify and forward (AF) scheme requires implementation of Alamouti decoder in the relay. Moreover we analyzed OP performance of these systems and compared it with single-antenna dual-hop and dual-antenna single-hop systems. We used variable gain relays [1] which require knowledge of the instantaneous channel state information (CSI) of each hop. The fixed gain relays which require knowledge of the average fading signal-to-noise ratio (SNR) of the previous hop were not considered due to the fact that for decoding of Alamouti's space time block code knowledge of CSI is required.

The remainder of this paper is organized as follows. Next Section presents the system and channel model. In Section 3 we derive expressions for end-to-end SNR needed for successful analysis of outage probability of the systems. Results are presented in Section 4, and Section 5 concludes the article.

2 System and Channel Models

In this paper we analyzed MIMO relay systems utilizing Alamouti scheme in three different configurations: 2x1x1 MIMO system where only the source is equipped with two antennas, 2x2x1 MIMO system where source and relay are equipped with two antennas, and 2x2x2 MIMO where source, relay and destination are equipped with two antennas. Fig. 1 presents the studied dual-hop MIMO communication system, which consists of the source *S*, the destination *D* and MAF relay *R*. It is assumed that each hop is subjected to the independent but non-identical Rayleigh fading, for which the per-hop SNR γ is distributed according to the probability distribution function (PDF) given by [4]:

$$p(\gamma) = \frac{1}{\bar{\gamma}} e^{-\frac{\gamma}{\bar{\gamma}}}, \quad \gamma \geq 0 . \tag{1}$$

where $\bar{\gamma}$ is the average per-hop SNR. We assumed that average per-hop SNR is equal for each hop i.e. $\bar{\gamma} = \bar{\bar{\gamma}}$. It is also assumed that the amplitudes of fading from each transmit antenna to each receive antenna are mutually uncorrelated, Rayleigh distributed and that the average signal powers at each receive antenna from each transmit antenna are the same. Further, we assumed that the relay and the receiver have perfect knowledge of the channel.

In case of MAF system, the relay amplifies and forwards the received signal, while in case of decode and forward (DF) the relay fully decodes the received signal and then forwards it to the next hop. The variable gain relaying is modeled according to concepts presented in [1], and the dual-antenna systems with transmit diversity are designed by using of Alamouti's scheme given in [2].

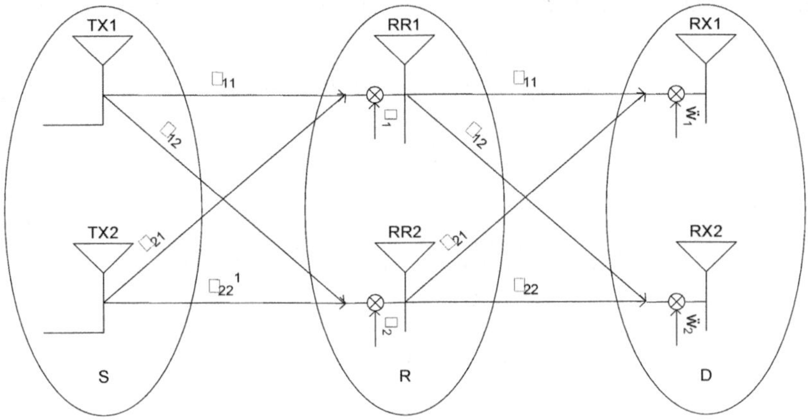

Fig. 1. Dual-hop MIMO system model

In following sections of the paper we will use notation given in the Fig. 1. Namely all variables related to the first hop will be notated with dot above the symbol and all variables related to the second hop will be notated with double dot above the symbol. The first index in the subscript of channel coefficients identifies the transmitting antenna and the second index identifies the receiving antenna.

2.1 Dual-Hop 2x1x1 MIMO System

For analysis of 2x1x1 system we assume that only the first antennas of the relay and the destination depicted on Fig.1 are active. The transmitted signal at the source S is given in following form:

$$x = [x_1, x_2, x_3, \dots, x_N] . \tag{2}$$

The received signals in first antenna of the relay R in the first and second time slots are given with:

$$\dot{y}_1 = \sqrt{E}\left(\dot{h}_{11} \cdot x_1 + \dot{h}_{21} \cdot x_2\right) + \dot{n}_{11} , \tag{3}$$

$$\dot{y}_2 = \sqrt{E}\left(-\dot{h}_{11} \cdot x_2^* + \dot{h}_{21} \cdot x_1^*\right) + \dot{n}_{21} , \tag{4}$$

where x_1 and x_2 are the transmitted symbols, h_{ij} are the channel coefficients, n_{i1} are noise components in the first and second time slot in the first relay antenna, and E is radiating power of one source antenna. It is assumed that radiating power of any antenna at the source and the relay are equal to E. The noise in the first hop and first antenna of the relay can be presented in following form:

$$\dot{w}_1 = [\dot{n}_{11}, \dot{n}_{21}, \dot{n}_{31}, \dots \dot{n}_{N1}] . \tag{5}$$

In the relay we used reduced complexity receiver with Alamouti decoder and without detector. Such implementation of the relay reduces the complexity (especially for more advanced modulation schemes) and versatility of the system. The decoded signal is:

$$\hat{y}_1 = \dot{h}_{11}^* y_1 + \dot{h}_{21} \dot{y}_2^* = \sqrt{E}\, \dot{\Delta}_1 x_1 + \dot{\xi}_1 , \tag{6}$$

$$\hat{y}_2 = \dot{h}_{21}^* y_1 - \dot{h}_{11} \dot{y}_2^* = \sqrt{E}\, \dot{\Delta}_1 x_2 + \dot{\xi}_2 , \tag{7}$$

where:

$$\dot{\Delta}_1 = |\dot{h}_{11}|^2 + |\dot{h}_{21}|^2 , \qquad \dot{\xi}_1 = \dot{h}_{11}^* \dot{n}_1 + \dot{h}_{21} \dot{n}_2^*, \qquad \dot{\xi}_2 = \dot{h}_{21}^* \dot{n}_1 - \dot{h}_{11} \dot{n}_2^* . \tag{8}$$

Decoded signal can be presented in following form:

$$\dot{r}_1 = [\hat{y}_1, \hat{y}_2, \hat{y}_3 \dots \hat{y}_N] . \tag{9}$$

where N represents total number of transmitted symbols. The decoded signal is amplified and forwarded towards the destination. Since we assume that in the destination only the first antenna is active ($\ddot{h}_{12} = \ddot{h}_{22} = 0$), the received signal is given with:

$$\ddot{r}_1 = G_1 \ddot{h}_{11}\, \hat{y}_1(t) + \ddot{w}_1(t). \tag{10}$$

Where G_I is the gain of the relay and $\ddot{w}_1(t)$ is an additive white Gaussian noise in the second hop of the system and the first destination antenna with average power N_0. It is helpful to stress that subscript index for G_i, r_i, w_i and Δ_i is related to the type of Alamouti's code used in the given hop i.e. to the number of the receiving antennas. If the code is with two transmit antenna and one receive antenna $i = 1$, and if code is with two transmit antenna and two receive antenna $i = 2$.

Taking in consideration that the CSI for the first hop are required in order to implement the Alamouti decoder, we have chosen variable gain in the relay in order to cancel the effect of the channel in the first hop. If we change (6) or (7) in (10) and following the definition of G for variable gain relays in (4) from [1] the equation for the gain of 2x1x1 system can be expressed in following form:

$$G_1 = \sqrt{\frac{\ddot{E}}{\dot{E}\, \dot{\Delta}_1^2 + \dot{\Delta}_1\, N_0}} , \tag{11}$$

where $\dot{E}$ and $\ddot{E}$ are the radiating powers of single antenna at the source S and relay R. However, it is assumed: $\dot{E} = \ddot{E} = E$. In the destination D the $\ddot{r}_1$ signal is equalized and detected with maximum likelihood detector.

2.2 Dual-Hop 2x2x1 and 2x2x2 MIMO Systems

If we consider 2x2x1 system the received signals in first relay antenna in the first and second time slots are given with:

$$\dot{y}_{11} = \sqrt{E}\,\dot{h}_{11} \cdot x_1 + \sqrt{E}\,\dot{h}_{21} \cdot x_2 + \dot{n}_{11}, \tag{12}$$

$$\dot{y}_{21} = -\sqrt{E}\,\dot{h}_{11} \cdot x_2^* + \sqrt{E}\,\dot{h}_{21} \cdot x_1^* + \dot{n}_{21}. \tag{13}$$

The signals in second antenna of the relay in the first and second time slots are:

$$\dot{y}_{12} = \sqrt{\dot{E}}\,h_{12} \cdot x_1 + \sqrt{E}\,\dot{h}_{22} \cdot x_2 + \dot{n}_{12}, \tag{14}$$

$$\dot{y}_{22} = -\sqrt{E}\,\dot{h}_{12} \cdot x_2^* + \sqrt{E}\,\dot{h}_{22} \cdot x_1^* + \dot{n}_{22}, \tag{15}$$

where n_{ij} are noise components in the first and second time slot in the first and second antenna. The noise in the first hop and the first antenna of the relay is presented with equation (5) and the noise in the first hop and the second antenna of the relay can be presented in following form:

$$\dot{w}_2 = [\dot{n}_{12,}\dot{n}_{22}, \dot{n}_{32}, \dots\ \dot{n}_{N2}]. \tag{16}$$

The outputs of each antenna combiner are added to each other in order to get the decoded signals in first and second timeslot:

$$\hat{\dot{z}}_1 = \dot{h}_{11}^*\dot{y}_{11} + \dot{h}_{21}\dot{y}_{21}^* + \ \dot{h}_{12}^*\dot{y}_{12} + \dot{h}_{22}y_{22}^* = \sqrt{E}\,\dot{\Delta}_2 x_1 + \dot{\eta}_1\,, \tag{17}$$

$$\hat{\dot{z}}_2 = \dot{h}_{21}^*\dot{y}_{11} - \dot{h}_{11}\dot{y}_{21}^* + \ \dot{h}_{22}^*\dot{y}_{12} - \dot{h}_{12}\dot{y}_{22}^* = \sqrt{E}\,\dot{\Delta}_2 x_2 + \dot{\eta}_2\,, \tag{18}$$

where:

$$\dot{\Delta}_2 = |\dot{h}_{11}|^2 + |\dot{h}_{12}|^2 + |\dot{h}_{21}|^2 + |\dot{h}_{22}|^2\,, \tag{19}$$

$$\dot{\eta}_1 = \dot{h}_{11}^*\dot{n}_{11} + \dot{h}_{21}\dot{n}_{21}^* + \dot{h}_{12}^*\dot{n}_{12} + \dot{h}_{22}\dot{n}_{22}^*\,, \tag{20}$$

$$\dot{\eta}_2 = \ \dot{h}_{21}^*\dot{n}_{11} - \dot{h}_{11}\dot{n}_{21}^* + \dot{h}_{22}^*\dot{n}_{12} - \dot{h}_{12}\dot{n}_{22}^*\,. \tag{21}$$

The decoded signal at the output of the combiner is:

$$\dot{r}_2 = [\hat{\dot{z}}_1, \hat{\dot{z}}_2, \hat{\dot{z}}_3 \dots\ \hat{\dot{z}}_N]\,. \tag{22}$$

This signal is amplified and forward towards the destination. The received signal at the destination is:

$$\ddot{r}_2 = G_2\ddot{h}_{11}\,\hat{\dot{z}}_1(t) + \ddot{w}_1(t). \tag{23}$$

The signal $\dot{r}_2$ is transmitted in same manner as the signal x in the source. We have chosen variable gain of the relay in order to reverse the effect of the channel in the first hop. Taking in consideration equations (17), (18) and (4) in [1] the selected gain in the relay is:

$$G_2 = \sqrt{\frac{E}{E \cdot \dot{\Delta}_2^2 + \dot{\Delta}_2 N_0}} \tag{24}$$

In case of single antenna at the destination, similarly to the 2x1x1 MIMO system the signal is equalized and detected with maximum likelihood detector. In case of 2x2x2 MIMO system where two antennas are used at the destination the signal is decoded in same manner as in the relay i.e. by using equations (17) and (18). The output of the combiner i.e. the decoded signal is fed to the maximum likelihood detector.

3 Outage Probability of Dual-Hop Dual-Antenna Systems

The outage probability is defined as the probability that the instantaneous SNR falls below a predetermined threshold ratio γ_{th}

$$P_{out} = P(\gamma_{eq} < \gamma_{th}) \tag{25}$$

where γ_{eq} represent equivalent i.e. end-to-end instantaneous SNR of the dual-hop system. In order to successfully find outage probability we derived the equivalent (end-to-end) SNR for 2x1x1, 2x2x1, and 2x2x2 dual-hop system.

For 2x1x1 MIMO system the first step is to derive the instantaneous SNR ($\dot{\gamma}_1$) of the first hop i.e. the goal is to find instantaneous SNR for system with two transmit and one receive antenna with Alamouti STBC. From equations (6) and (7) it is easy to derive that the instantaneous SNR in the first hop is:

$$\dot{\gamma}_1 = \frac{E}{N_0} \cdot \dot{\Delta}_1 \,. \tag{26}$$

The received signal at the destination in the first time slot can be presented in following form:

$$\ddot{r}_1 = G_1\, \ddot{h}_{11}\, \hat{y}_1 + \ddot{w}_1(t) = G_1\, \ddot{h}_{11} \sqrt{E} \cdot \dot{\Delta}_1 \cdot x_1 + \; G_1 \ddot{h}_{11} \dot{\xi}_1 \; + \ddot{w}_1(t) \,. \tag{27}$$

Since in the second hop we deal with 1x1 system (1 transmit and 1 receive antenna) in order to depict the system from Fig.1 we assumed that all channel parameters of the second hop are set to 0 except $\ddot{h}_{11}$. Taking in consideration equation (27) it is easy to show that end-to-end SNR for 2x1x1 dual-hop system is given with:

$$\gamma_{eq1} = \frac{E}{N_0} \cdot \frac{G_1^2 \left|\ddot{h}_{11}\right|^2 \dot{\Delta}_1^2}{G_1^2 \left|\ddot{h}_{11}\right|^2 \dot{\Delta}_1 + 1} \tag{28}$$

For 2x2x1 dual-hop system the first step is to derive the instantaneous SNR ($\dot{\gamma}_2$) of the first hop i.e. we should find instantaneous SNR for system with 2 transmit and 2 receive antennas with Alamouti STBC. From equations (17) and (18) it is easy to derive that the instantaneous SNR in the first hop is:

$$\dot{\gamma}_2 = \frac{E}{N_0} \cdot \dot{\Delta}_2 \,. \tag{29}$$

Decoded signal in first time slot of first antenna of the destination (second antenna is not active) can be present in similar manner to equation (6):

$$\hat{\hat{y}}_1 = G_2\, \ddot{\Delta}_1 \hat{z}_1 + \ddot{\xi}_1 \tag{30}$$

where analogous to (8) $\ddot{\xi}_1$ is given with:

$$\ddot{\xi}_1 = \ddot{h}_{11}^* \ddot{n}_1 + \ddot{h}_{21} \ddot{n}_2^* \tag{31}$$

If we replace (17) in (30) we will get:

$$\hat{\hat{y}}_1 = G_2\, \ddot{\Delta}_1 \hat{z}_1 + \ddot{\xi}_1 = G_2\, \ddot{\Delta}_1\, \dot{\Delta}_2 \sqrt{E}\, x_1 + G_2\, \ddot{\Delta}_1\, \dot{\eta}_1 + \ddot{\xi}_1 \tag{32}$$

Taking in account (32) it is straightforward to show that the end-to-end SNR is:

$$\gamma_{eq2} = \frac{E}{N_0} \cdot \frac{G_2^2\, \ddot{\Delta}_1 \dot{\Delta}_2^2}{G_2^2\, \ddot{\Delta}_1 \dot{\Delta}_2 + 1} \,. \tag{33}$$

Where analogous to (8) $\ddot{\Delta}_1$ is given with

$$\ddot{\Delta}_1 = \left|\ddot{h}_{11}\right|^2 + \left|\ddot{h}_{21}\right|^2 . \tag{34}$$

For 2x2x2 dual-hop system the decoded signal in first time slot is:

$$\hat{\hat{y}}_1 = G_2\, \ddot{\Delta}_2 \hat{z}_1 + \ddot{\eta}_1 = G_2\, \ddot{\Delta}_2\, \dot{\Delta}_2 \sqrt{E}\, x_1 + G_2\, \ddot{\Delta}_2\, \dot{\eta}_1 + \ddot{\eta}_1, \tag{35}$$

where:

$$\ddot{\Delta}_2 = \left|\ddot{h}_{11}\right|^2 + \left|\ddot{h}_{12}\right|^2 + \left|\ddot{h}_{21}\right|^2 + \left|\ddot{h}_{22}\right|^2 , \tag{36}$$

$$\ddot{\eta}_1 = \ddot{h}_{11}^* \ddot{n}_{11} + \ddot{h}_{21} \ddot{n}_{21}^* + \ddot{h}_{12}^* \ddot{n}_{12} + \ddot{h}_{22} \ddot{n}_{22}^* . \tag{37}$$

Therefore, that end-to-end SNR for 2x2x2 system is:

$$\gamma_{eq3} = \frac{E}{N_0} \cdot \frac{G_2^2\, \ddot{\Delta}_2 \dot{\Delta}_2^2}{G_2^2\, \ddot{\Delta}_2 \dot{\Delta}_2 + 1} \,. \tag{38}$$

4 Numerical Results

Usually, in real world applications the system radiation power is limited, therefore in the simulations we kept the total radiating power constant. In order to have the same total radiated power from two transmit antennas with the power of the single transmit antenna, the energy allocated to each symbol was halved. For the simulations we have chosen BPSK modulation scheme. In order to have good reference for analyzing the results we have chosen result for dual-hop variable gain system as upper bound and the result for single-hop receive diversity system with 4 antennas and maximum ratio combiner as lower bound. The results were expected to be located between these two BER (Bit Error Rate) curves. Obtained bit error probabilities for the 2x1x1, 2x2x1, and 2x2x2 dual-hop dual-antenna systems are given on Fig. 2.

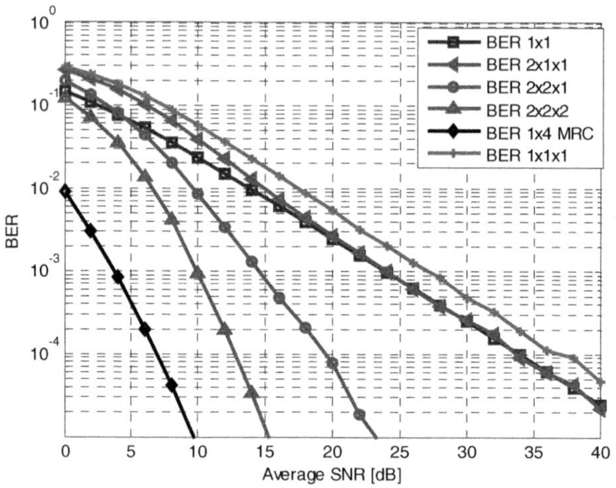

Fig. 2. BER for dual-hop dual-antenna MAF systems

From the Fig. 2 it is obvious that in 2x2x1MIMO scheme we obtain diversity gain of 15dB at BER at 10^{-4} and for 2x2x2 MIMO scheme we obtain diversity gain of 25dB at BER of 10^{-4} which are similar to diversity gains for single-hop MIMO systems given in [2]. Furthermore, on Fig.3 we present comparison of the BER for non-regenerative MAF system with the BER performance of regenerative DF system. DF system slightly outperforms MAF system. The performance gap increases as number of used antenna at the relay and the destination increases.

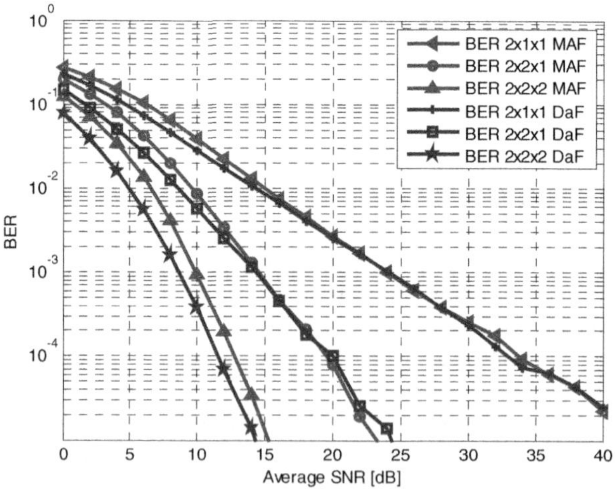

Fig. 3. BER for dual-hop and dual-antenna MAF and DF systems

On Fig.4 we present results of simulation of the outage probability (OP) of the analyzed dual-hop dual-antenna systems. For the sake of simple comparison on the same picture we presented results for single-hop single-antenna system, dual-hop single-antenna system, single-hop 2x1 antenna system, and single-hop 2x2 antenna system. It is obvious that 2x1x1 system has similar OP performance as dual-hop single-antenna system. If we remove the constraint of same total radiated power the OP performance of 2x1x1 system would improve around 3 dB. The OP performance for 2x2x1 and 2x2x2 systems are better than dual-hop single-antenna system for 16dB and 25dB at OP of 10^{-3}. Moreover, these two systems are lagging the OP performance of single-hop 2x1 and 2x2 system from 0dB to 4dB.

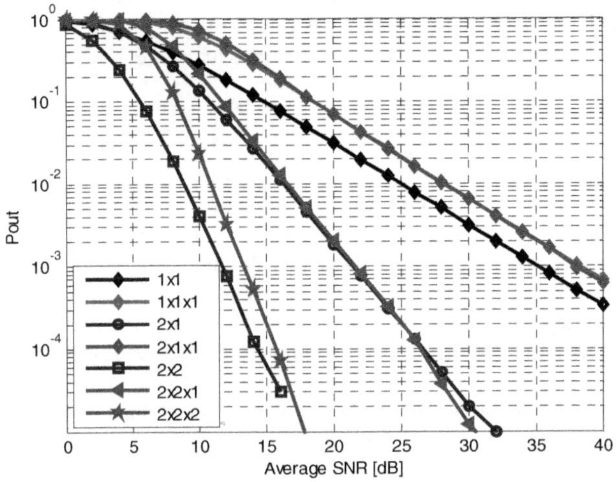

Fig. 4. Outage probability of 2x1x1, 2x2x1 and 2x2x2 MAF system (γ_{th}=5dB)

The overall performance of 2x1x1 system is not worth the cost of implementation. However, the usage of 2x2x1 system gives substantial improvement in performance compared to the single-antenna dual-hop systems. We believe this is the most-feasible configuration to be met in the reality. One possible 2x2x1 configuration is where originating base station has two antennas, the cooperating base station acting as relay has two antennas, and the mobile station has single antenna. The 2x2x2 system gives best BER and OP performance, however its usage in future wireless communications seams less probable.

5 Conclusion

In this paper, the bit error probability and outage probability performance of three dual-hop MIMO configurations (2x1x1, 2x2x1 and 2x2x2) with modified AF variable gain relays in Rayleigh fading have been studied. The BER performances of the systems were compared with dual-hop single antenna system with variable gain relay and with corresponding configurations of dual-hop dual antenna non-regenerative DF systems. The diversity gain of dual-hop MIMO MAF system compared to single-antenna AF system is ranging from 15 to 25 dB at BER of 10^{-4} depending of the number of antennas employed in the destination. However, there is only 3dB gain at BER of 10^{-4} for 2x1x1 MIMO system. The BER performances of dual-antenna MAF systems are slightly worse than dual-antenna DF systems (0-2dB). The performance gap increases with increase of the number of antennas in the relay and the destination. The OP performances of the systems were compared with single-antenna dual-hop systems, and dual-antenna single-hop systems. While the benefit of usage of 2x1x1 system is marginal, the OP performances for 2x2x1 and 2x2x2 systems are better than dual-hop single-antenna systems for 16dB and 25dB at OP of 10^{-3}.

Taking in account the superior performance compared to dual-hop single antenna systems, their lower complexity and slightly inferior performance compared to dual-antenna DF, we have shown that usage of dual-antenna could be very beneficial in future wireless communications systems with infrastructure-based cooperation.

References

1. Hasna, M.O., Alouini, M.S.: A Performance Study of Dual-Hop Transmissions With Fixed Gain Relays. IEEE Transactions on Wireless Communications 3(6) (November 2004)
2. Alamouti, S.M.: A Simple Transmit Diversity Technique for Wireless Communications. IEEE Journal on Select Areas in Communications 16(8) (October 1998)
3. Proakis, J.: Digital Communications, 4th edn. McGraw-Hill, New York (August 2000)
4. Simon, M.K., Alouini, M.S.: Digital Communication over Fading Channels, 2nd edn. Wiley, New York (2005)
5. Sklar, B.: Digital Communications: Fundamentals and Applications, 2nd edn. Prentice-Hall, Englewood Cliffs (January 2001)
6. Sendonaris, A., Erkip, E., Aazhang, B.: User Cooper¬ation Diversity Part I and Part II. IEEE Trans. Commun. 51(11), 1927–1948 (2003)
7. Nosratinia, A., Hunter, T.E., Hedayat, A.: Cooperative Communication in Wireless Networks. IEEE Communications Magazine (October 2004)
8. Liu, P., Tao, Z., Lin, Z., Erkip, E., Panwar, S.: Cooperative wireless communications: A cross-layer approach. IEEE Wireless Communications (August 2006)
9. Laneman, J.N., Wornell, G.W.: Exploiting Distributed Spatial Diversity in Wireless Networks. In: Proc. 40th Allerton Conf. Communication, Control, Computing, Allerton Park, IL, pp. 775–785 (September 2000)
10. Oyman, Ö., Laneman, J.N., Sandhu, S.: Multihop relaying for broadband wireless mesh networks: From theory to practice. IEEE Communications Magazine 45(11), 116–122 (2007)
11. Spencer, Q.H., Peel, C.B., Swindlehurst, A.L., Haardt, M.: An introduction to the multi-user MIMO downlink. IEEE Communications Magazine 42(10) (October 2004)

Parallel Machine Translation for gLite Based Grid Infrastructures

Miloš Stolić and Anastas Mišev

University Ss Cyril and Methodius, Faculty of Natural Sciences and Mathematics, Institute of Informatics, Arhimedova b.b. Skopje, Macedonia
{milos,anastas}@ii.edu.mk

Abstract. Statistical machine translation is often criticized for slow decoding time. We address this issue by presenting a new tool for enabling Moses, a state of the art machine translation system, to be run on gLite based Grid infrastructures. It implements a workflow model for equally distributing the decoding task among several worker nodes in a cluster. We report experimental results for possible speed-ups and envision how natural language processing scientists can benefit from existing Grid infrastructures for solving processing, storage and collaboration issues.

Keywords: Statistical machine translation, Grid, Data parallelism.

1 Introduction

Statistical machine translation has vastly improved in recent years and has emerged as one of the most widely used machine translation techniques. One of its major drawbacks compared to other non data-driven methods is time and processing requirements for training such systems, as well as slow translation time. Optimization techniques like minimum error rate training or validation of systems using methods as ten-fold cross validation involves translation of large amounts of texts. Improving translation (decoding) time would enable faster research.

The gLite distribution [9] is a Grid middleware developed and used in the Enabling Grids for E-science (EGEE) project [11]. It is deployed in more than 250 computing centers around the world and supports various scientific disciplines, among which is the LHC Computing Grid (LHC) project [12].

This paper describes modifications to the Moses decoder [1], which enable it to be run in parallel on gLite based Grid infrastructures such as SEE-GRID [2] and EGI [7]. It is based on the existing `moses-parallel` tool, but improved and adapted for gLite based Grids. It implements a simple yet efficient workflow model to equally distribute the decoding process among several machines in a cluster, thus improving translation time. Further, we envision how other Natural Language Processing applications can use Grid infrastructures to enable easier processing, storing and sharing data and applications between researches.

The paper is organized as follows: in the next section we give an overview of the existing efforts for parallelizing the decoding task in Moses, while in the third section

M. Gusev and P. Mitrevski (Eds.): ICT Innovations 2010, CCIS 83, pp. 133–141, 2011.

we describe our new tool for parallelizing decoding with Moses in a gLite Grid cluster. In the forth section we present experimental results of possible speed-ups when decoding with Moses on a Grid cluster using variable number of processes, and in fifth section we present a new framework for enabling Natural Language Processing applications for Grid platforms. Finally, in the last section we offer some conclusions and suggestions for future development.

2 Related Work

Significant effort has been placed in improvement in translation (i.e. decoding) speed for Moses. In fact, Moses comes with a tool named `moses-parallel` for distributing the decoding process between several machines in a cluster running Oracle Grid Engine [18], formerly known as Sun Grid Engine. `Moses-parallel` is intended to be run on the master (head) node, where it splits the input text for translation into several equal segments. Each of these segments is passed for decoding to a different execution host. When all tasks finish, the head node collects all translations and concatenates them, thus producing the final output.

The advantage of this approach is that the speedup is proportional to the number of execution hosts used. Using additional hosts should further improve performance. On the other hand, all hosts need to have access to the same data, which implies heavy network load and overhead for copying translation tables, language models etc.

Another approach is to use multiple threads within a single Moses process [3]. The advantage of this implementation is that all threads share the same memory, so translation models need to be loaded only once. Since everything is run on one node, threads can be coupled to work more closely, which makes balancing the decoding load between threads easier. The downside is that the machine where the translation takes place must be a significantly more powerful than the execution hosts used in clusters in order to provide performance compared to cluster parallelism. This approach is useful for implementation of real-time translation system like on-line translation service.

3 Moses on Grid Infrastructure

Adapting software to be able to run on a Grid platform is a non-trivial task. Moses relies on several other tools for word alignment, language modeling etc, which also have to be configured, so the entire installation process is not simple to be fully automated.

The gLite middleware is significantly different to the Sun Grid Engine, mostly due to the fact that SGE is actually an extended cluster platform. The `moses-parallel` tool relies on job control commands `qsub, qrun, qdel` etc, which are not available to end users in gLite middleware. Instead, users submit formalized job descriptions written in the Job Description Language [10], which specify which files are needed to run the job, which files should be returned to the end user, where they should be stored, where the job should be executed and other options. Job submission and control is performed through command line tools like `glite-wms-job-submit`, `glite-wms-job-status`, `glite-wms-job-output` etc.

We have deployed Moses along with all its supporting tools on one cluster part of the SEE-GRID network, consisted of 30 worker nodes. Each worker node contains the Moses executables, and can perform decoding individually. Parallelism is controlled from the User Interface, where the end user runs the new `moses-parallel-glite` tool.

3.1 Algorithm

The described tool operates as illustrated in Figure 1. When `moses-parallel-glite` is run, it uploads all translation tables, reordering models and language models to a storage element. Then, the tool splits the input text into N equal parts, depending on the number of jobs that the user has specified. For each part, a job description file and an execution script is generated. All jobs are added to a job submission queue.

1. Upload large files to a storage element
2. Split input sample into N equal parts
3. For each part, create a job description file (*jdl*) and execution script
4. Add all jdl's to job submission queue *Q*
5. Submit jobs in *Q* to the Workload Management System
6. Check if any job has finished and retrieve its output
7. If a job has been aborted, cancelled or its translation is incomplete, add it to *Q*
8. Repeat steps 5-7 until all jobs have been cleared successfully

Fig. 1. Execution of `moses-parallel-glite`

Next, the tool submits all queued jobs to the Workload Management System and follows their execution through their job identifier URI. When a job finishes, it retrieves its output and checks if the according translation is complete. If a job is cancelled, aborted or the retrieved translation is incomplete, it is resubmitted to the WMS. After all jobs have been finished, the partial translations are concatenated into the final output.

The execution script on each worker node first copies all translation tables, reordering models, language models from the storage element to the local hard drive. Then Moses decodes the input text, and the output is returned through the output sandbox. It is important that the local copies are not network mounted (i.e. NFS share) since tables and models used by Moses are large in size and require frequent access, especially when using on-disk mode.

We have decided against using Direct Acyclic Graph (DAG) workflow because jobs may finish prematurely, producing incomplete translation. DAG jobs cannot implement such checks for job resubmission, so if only one translation part fails, the entire job has to be resubmitted.

3.2 Usage

Like all support tools for Moses, `moses-parallel-glite` is controlled through several command line arguments. To preserve compatibility with other tools relying on the existing `moses-parallel`, it responds to exactly the same arguments and adds six of its own. The switch `--large-files` is used to specify which files should be copied from/to the storage element. On the other hand, `--upload-large-files` is used to limit copying files only from the storage element to worker nodes, i.e. should be used when all translation, reordering and language models are already placed on a storage element. Switches `--storage-element` and `--storage-prefix` specify to which storage element and in which subfolder the files should be copied to. Finally, `--computing-element` is used to identify on which cluster the jobs should be executed, and `--root-path` signals where Moses is installed on local worker nodes.

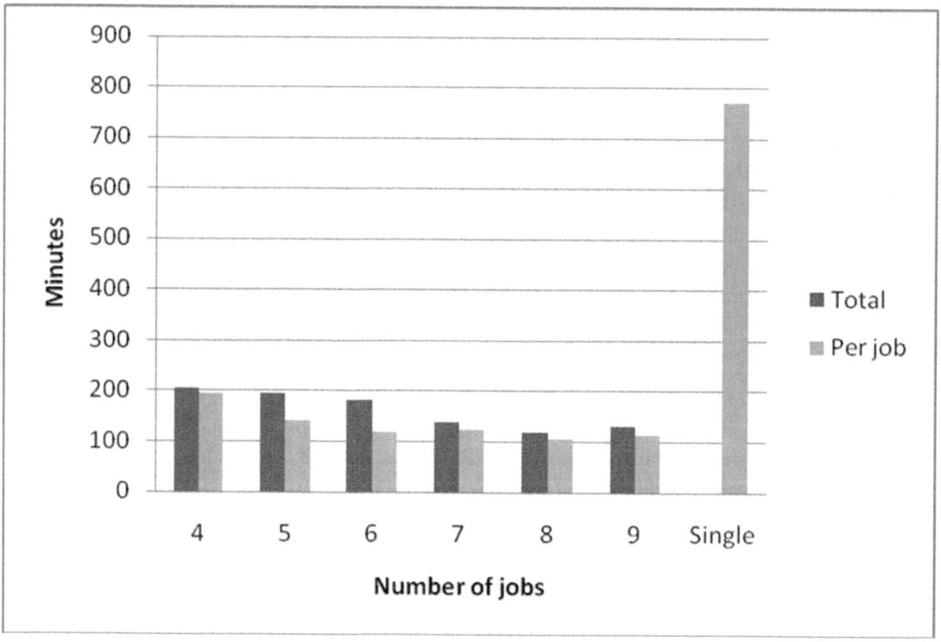

Fig. 2. Average translation time for 15.000 sentences. Total is the time needed for a job to complete, including scheduling time, waiting in a queue, job transfer etc. Per job is the average execution time of the decoding process only.

4 Experiments

The performance of the `moses-parallel-glite` tool was tested on a cluster part of SEE-GRID, consisted of 30 identical machines with 2.66GHz Intel Core 2 Duo processor and 512 MB RAM. Moses was manually pre-installed on all worker nodes. Decoding times were measured for English to Macedonian translation. The translation and reordering models were trained on the parallel data from the Southeast European Times corpus [4] [5], while a trigram language model was trained using IRSTLM [6] only on the Macedonian side of this data. Because of the small available RAM memory, all models were used in binarised format with on-demand loading.

The experiments consisted of decoding a sample text from English to Macedonian language using one job (a single machine) and using several jobs, varying from 4 to 9. For each job, two times were being measured. The first is the total time needed for a job to be completed, including scheduling time, queue time, job transfer, reported by ULMon [8]. The second time was the actual processing time for the job. Each translation process was repeated 3 times, and the mean times were recorded. It should be noted that no jobs failed during all runs. The first set of experiments was done with a 15.000 sentence sample text, and the according decoding times are shown in Fig. 2.

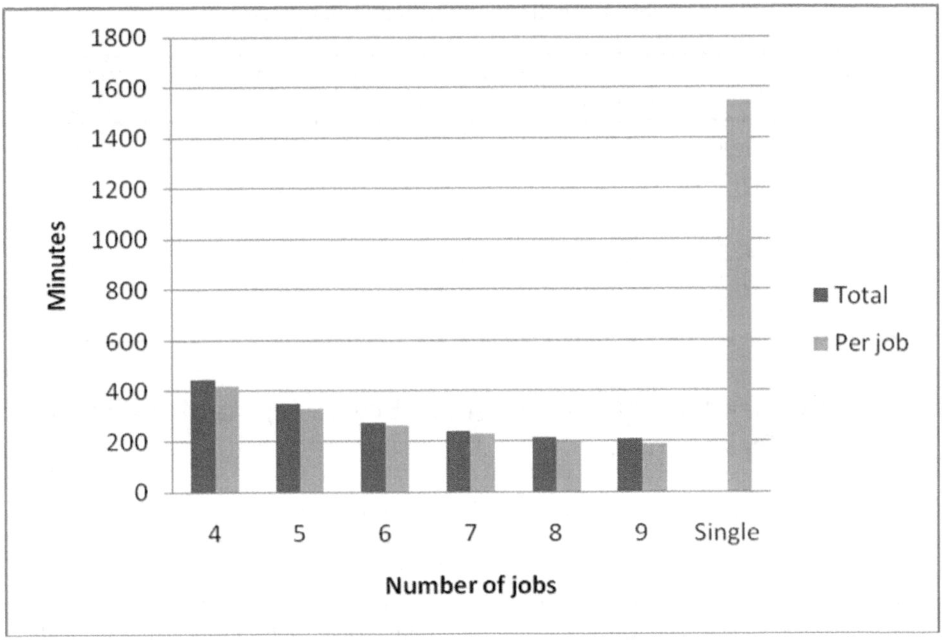

Fig. 3. Average translation time for 30.000 sentences

It can be observed that the speed-up varies between 3.75 when 4 jobs are used, to the maximum of 6.5, when 8 jobs are used. A significant difference between average machine processing time and total job execution time can be noticed in some runs, like when using 5 jobs. One of the reasons for this behavior is that submitted jobs have to wait to get scheduled, and since the cluster is shared between users, queuing times can even be longer compared to processing times. Another anomaly is evident when observing translation using nine jobs. It provided slower translation compared to using eight jobs, because during the testing process for that sample, the cluster was heavily used by other processes as well, degrading performance mainly during copying files from the storage element.

The second set of experiments were done using a sample of 30.000 sentences, twice as much as in the first set. Average decoding times are shown in Figure 3. The speedup is more obvious, ranging from 3.75 times when 4 jobs are used, to 8.2 times using 9 jobs. In this run, the average processing time for each job is relatively large, so the overhead from the Grid job scheduling and queuing system can be marginalized.

Summary of both test runs are shown in Table 1. Both set of experiments indicate that while speed-up increases when using more jobs, it is not linear and tends to saturate. For instance, moving from eight to nine jobs when translating 30.000 sentences yield increase in speedup of only 0.3 times, which can actually result in degraded results if the cluster has no more free nodes where the job can be run and it is forced to wait.

Table 1. Sublimed results from both test runs

Number of jobs	*15.000 sentences*		*30.000 sentences*	
	Total time	Speed-up	Total time	Speed-up
1	772	1.00	1550	1.00
4	206	3.75	445	3.71
5	194	3.98	349	4.68
6	182	4.24	272	5.94
7	139	5.55	240	6.80
8	119	6.49	215	7.79
9	131	5.89	206	8.20

5 Framework for Natural Language Processing Applications on Grid Infrastructure

Decoding is just a small piece of the entire machine translation process. Data-driven machine translation relies on large amounts of data which may need to be processed, annotated, aligned, segmented etc. Many of these phases are constantly repeated by different researches on the same data, mostly because of lack of means of collaboration. The Grid infrastructure can help solve both processing as well as storage problems in natural language processing applications.

We propose a framework illustrated in Figure 4 for utilizing Grid resources and infrastructure. Researches can store data (raw text or speech corpora, annotated corpora, alignments etc) on multiple storage elements, but all information about their location is recorded in a central metadata repository such as AMGA [13]. Entries in the repository are stored in a directory structure, sorted by category, language, annotation level, purpose or any other information, as pictured in Figure 5.

Through the User Interface machine, scientist can select which tasks should be performed over some data, creating dependencies between them. For instance, one would choose to Part of Speech tag the raw English text from the SETimes corpus using the SVMTool tagger [14], trained on the annotated EuroParl corpus [15]. Next, the raw Macedonian text from SETimes should be tagged using SVMTool trained on the "1984" [16] corpus. Both annotated corpuses are then used to train a factored model using Moses, and validated against a sample from EuroParl.

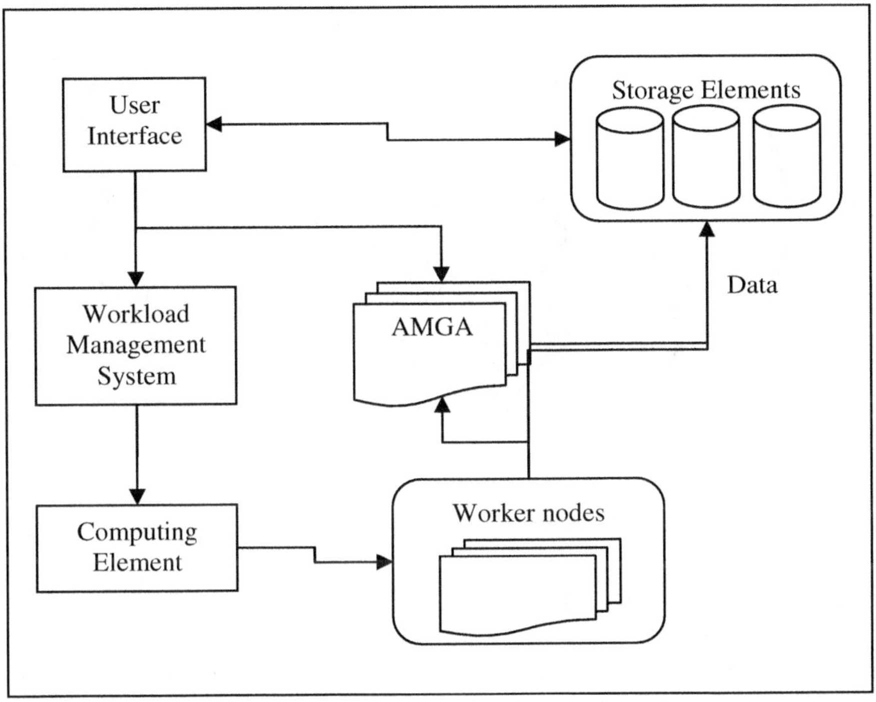

Fig. 4. Framework for Natural Language Processing Applications on Grid Infrastructure

For tasks like the mentioned one, the User Interface creates a workflow consisted of several jobs, which are run on multiple worker nodes from many clusters. Each job is responsible for retrieving appropriate applications and data from the central repository as specified by the user, processing that data and then forward results to both the central repository and other queued jobs.

In cases where multiple instances for the same category exists, like many English-to-Macedonian translation tables, a simple voting system can be used to select which entry should be used. Alternatively, automatic metrics can also be implemented, as BLEU [17] score for machine translation systems or precision and recall for alignments, part of speech tagging etc. Tests on all samples can be run at regular intervals (daily), and scores for each entry are added to the repository. Such information can be used when deploying production services, which should serve end users. For example, if an online English-to-Macedonian translation service is provided, the algorithm for translation (statistical, rule based, example based, trained on different data etc) can be dynamically selected depending on the latest test results.

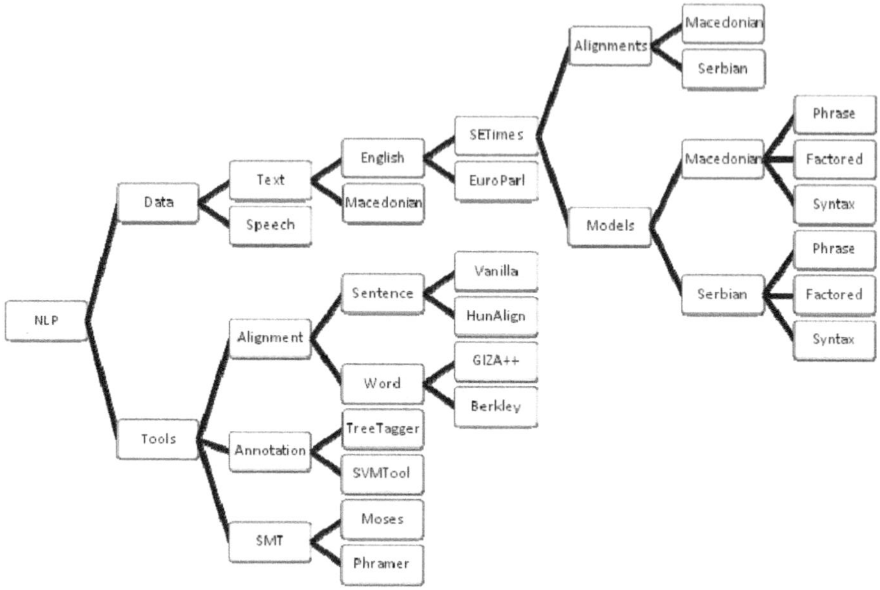

Fig. 5. Directory structure for storing Natural Language Processing Applications and Data

6 Conclusions and Further Work

In this paper we introduced `moses-parallel-glite`, a tool for running Moses on gLite based Grid infrastructure. It uses a workflow model to equally distribute the decoding task between several machines in cluster, fully automating job submission and monitoring, copying files from and to storage elements and collecting results. Initial results show speed-up up to 8.2 times when using 9 machines for decoding a sample text of 30.000 sentences. The tool in its current form can be easily implemented in non-real time translation service for large texts like books, manuals etc. Further investigation is needed to verify that other tools in the Moses platform relying on `moses-parallel` can also use the new tool without modifications.

Decrease in performance can occur when one of the submitted jobs fails and needs to be re-submitted. One way to minimize the effect of cancelled jobs would be to split the input into overlapping segments. This way even if a job fails, the according translation can be recovered from jobs responsible for translating neighboring segments. The downside of this approach is that it introduces additional overhead which in optimal cases where no jobs have failed, causes unnecessary usage of additional worker nodes.

With the introduction of the described tool, we hope to encourage researches in natural language processing to use Grid infrastructures for their data and applications. We believe that the platform is stable and mature enough to be relied on for storage and processing requirements. The presented framework shows how data and resources can be organized to provide easier usage and management. In the near future we anticipate the foundation of a specialized natural language processing virtual organization.

References

1. Koehn, P., Hoang, H., Birch, A., Callison-Burch, C., Federico, M., Bertoldi, N., Cowan, B., Shen, W., Moran, C., Zens, R., Dyer, C., Bojar, O., Constantin, A., Herbst, E.: Moses: Open Source Toolkit for Statistical Machine Translation. In: Annual Meeting of the Association for Computational Linguistics (ACL), demonstration session, Prague, Czech Republic (2007)
2. SEE-GRID eInfrastructure for regional eScience, `http://www.see-grid-sci.eu/`
3. Haddow, B.: Adding Multi-Threaded Decoding to Moses. In: The Prague Bulletin of Mathematical Linguistics, Prague, Czech Republic, pp. 57–66 (2010)
4. Stolić, M., Zdravkova, K.: Resources for machine translation of the Macedonian language. In: 1st International Conference ICT Innovations, Ohrid, Macedonia (2009)
5. Tyers, F., Alperen, M.: South-East European Times: A parallel corpus of the Balkan languages. In: Proceedings of the Workshop on Exploitation of multilingual resources and tools for Central and (South) Eastern European Languages LREC (2010)
6. Federico, M., Bertoldi, N., Cettolo, M.: IRSTLM: an Open Source Toolkit for Handling Large Scale Language Models. In: Proceedings of the Interspeech, Brisbane, Australia (2008)
7. EGI European Grid Initiative, `http://www.egi.eu/`
8. Misev, A., Atanassov, E.: ULMon - Grid Monitoring from User Point of View. In: Proceeding of the 31st International Conference on Information Technology Interfaces ITI 2009, Cavtat/Dubrovnik, Croatia, pp. 621–626 (2009)
9. Laure, E., Hemmer, F., Prelz, F., Beco, S., Fisher, S., Livny, M., Guy, L., Barroso, M., Buncic, P., Kunszt, P.: Middleware for the next generation grid infrastructure. In: Proceedings of CHEP, Interlaken, Switzerland (2004)
10. Pacini, F.: JDL attributes specification. Technical report, EGEE Document EGEE-JRA1-TEC-590869-JDL-Attributes-v0-9 (2007)
11. EGEE: Enabling grids for E-sciencE, `http://www.eu-egee.org/`
12. LHC Computing Grid, `http://lcg.web.cern.ch/LCG/`
13. Santos, N., Koblitz, B.: Metadata services on the grid. In: Proceedings of Advanced Computing and Analysis Techniques ACAT, Berlin, Germany (2005)
14. Giménez, J., Màrquez, L.: SVMTool: A general POS tagger generator based on Support Vector Machines. In: Proceedings of the Fourth International Conference on Language Resources and Evaluation, Lisbon, Portugal (2004)
15. Koehn, P.: Europarl: A Parallel Corpus for Statistical Machine Translation. In: Machine Translation Summit X, Phuket, Thailand, pp. 79–86 (2005)
16. Erjavec, T.: MULTEXT-East Version 4: Multilingual Morphosyntactic Specifications, Lexicons and Corpora. In: The Seventh International Conference on Language Resources and Evaluation, LREC 2010, Malta (2010)
17. Papineni, K., Roukos, S., Ward, T., Zhu, W.J.: BLEU: A method for automatic evaluation of machine translation. In: 40th Annual Meeting of the Association for Computational Linguistics, Philadelphia, USA, pp. 311–318 (2002)
18. Oracle Grid Engine, `http://www.oracle.com/us/products/tools/oracle-grid-engine-075549.html`

e-Consumer Online Behavior: A Basis for Obtaining e-Commerce Performance Metrics

Pece Mitrevski[1] and Ilija Hristoski[2]

[1] University of St. Kliment Ohridski, Faculty of Technical Sciences, Ivo Lola Ribar bb, 7000 Bitola, Macedonia
[2] University of St. Kliment Ohridski, Faculty of Economics, Gjorce Petrov bb, 7500 Prilep, Macedonia
{Pece.Mitrevski,Ilija.Hristoski}@uklo.edu.mk

Abstract. Nowadays the e-Commerce and e-Business paradigm have prevailed all over the world, definitely changing the way of running businesses and shaping the new business environment. The Web-based business solutions have produced a novel type of a consumer, the e-Consumer, and a specific way of doing business on the Net, based upon the human – computer – Web interaction. The online behavior of the e-Consumer has proven to be a key not only to a successfulness of a given e-Commerce site, but also a key to obtain a significant knowledge about customer's habits, needs, expectations, etc. Nonetheless, the e-Consumer online behavior can also be used as a basis for obtaining the basic Web performance metrics, necessary for assuring a relevant level of Quality of Service (QoS) through capacity planning. The paper aims to highlight some of the most important aspects of modeling e-Consumer online behavior regarding Web performance. We propose a novel approach to modeling online behavior, based on usage of Deterministic and Stochastic Petri Nets (DSPNs).

Keywords: e-Consumer, online behavior, performance analysis, modeling, Petri Nets.

1 Introduction

There has been quite a lot of time elapsed from 1943 when Thomas J. Watson, Sr. (IBM) remarked "I think there is a world market for maybe five computers", until 1999 when Andrew Grove (Intel) stated that "Within five years of time, all companies will be Internet companies or they won't be any companies at all". The contemporary running of businesses means extensive usage of Web-based technologies and e-Business solutions built upon the e-Commerce paradigm. This global phenomenon includes all modalities of Web-based trading and shopping, where all activities between the two parties involved are carried out online via Internet.

As a direct consequence, a new type of consumer has emerged. Holding the characteristics of the traditional customer, the e-Customer explicitly uses Internet and a whole new set of novel abilities focused towards online shopping of products and services. This phenomenon relies on existence of two basic premises:

M. Gusev and P. Mitrevski (Eds.): ICT Innovations 2010, CCIS 83, pp. 142–151, 2011.

- Web-based services, including e-Commerce, that rely on complex, large-scale systems consisting of thousands of computers, heterogeneous networks, and software components;
- Users, i.e. electronic consumers or e-Customers, who interact with the previously mentioned Web services unpredictably and stochastically.

As in the case of traditional, “brick-and-mortar” model of doing business, the highest priority task and a fundamental premise for the successfulness of the novel, “click-and-mortar” business model remains assuring e-Customers' satisfaction. It is not a trivial task, because it is based on analysis of a complex mixture of various quantitative and qualitative factors and variables. Such multidisciplinary approach undoubtedly relies on a usage of a plethora of relevant models, mechanisms, techniques, software and hardware solutions and tools, etc.

A starting point for satisfying e-Consumers' expectations and needs is their online behavior analysis, which aims to highlight the interaction and interface between e-Consumers and e-Commerce systems. In addition, it also aims to explain the different online behavior modalities during e-Commerce sessions, as well as to clarify the impact of the e-Commerce system design (both software and hardware) upon e-Consumer's perception, attitude, behavior, intentions and satisfaction.

The analysis of the e-Consumer online behavior can lead to:

- significant increase of the enterprise revenues, a goal which can be achieved through employing Web analytics techniques such as Web logs data mining techniques (e.g. Principal Component Analysis, clustering, decision tree models, regression models), Web tracking of click streams, etc. in order to perform e-Customer segmentation; the objective is to promote specific products or services to those e-Customers (both to individuals and to specific groups) who are most likely to buy them, and to determine or predict which products or services a specific e-Customer is most likely to purchase online in the future; all of these aspects are in the focus of Customer Relation Management (CRM) analysis, business intelligence, customer intelligence and marketing; from this point of view, the analysis of the e-Consumer online behavior is crucial to attract more visitors, retain or attract new customers for goods or services, or to increase the money volume each customer spends online;
- significant improvement of the “look and feel” of the e-Commerce Web site, its design and functionality, ease of use, as well as the intuitiveness of its user interface; all of these aspects, which are mainly focused on the software implementation, also have a great influence on the potential e-Consumer, and can attract or reject one, thus directly influencing the successfulness of an online business;
- assuring appropriate QoS levels through proper capacity planning of the underlying hardware resources, based on performance and reliability analysis of the relevant predictive models of the e-Business system; in this case the analysis of such a model, based on e-Consumer's online behavior, can lead towards obtaining relevant Web performance indicators;

The aim of this paper is to emphasize some of the most important aspects of modeling the e-Consumer online behavior as a foundation for estimating performance measures of a system (response time, throughput, network utilization, etc.).

2 The Problem of Capacity Planning

Capacity planning is a crucial part of the e-Commerce Web site deployment. It is a systematic approach to assuring appropriate QoS levels in terms of maintaining desired levels of performance characteristics, based on development of performance and availability predictive models. Such approach is completely different from the one relying on usage of QoS management technologies, especially dedicated networking QoS protocols. Both of these strategies have a common objective – assuring e-Customer's satisfaction. However, albeit both of these concepts are not mutually excluded, there is a substantial difference between them. According to Menascé & Almeida [1], "... capacity planning is the process of predicting when the future load levels will saturate the system and determining the most cost-effective way of delaying system saturation as much as possible", based on natural evolution of the existing workload, the deployment of new applications and services, as well as the unpredictable and stochastic changes in e-Consumer behavior. In other words, its main goal is to allow performance monitoring, i.e. tracking the intensity of the workload, detect system bottlenecks, predict future capacity shortcomings, and determine the most cost-effective way to upgrade Web-based systems to overcome performance problems and cope with increasing workload demands [1]. On the other hand, QoS is a broad term used to describe the overall experience a user or application will receive over a network. QoS management involves a wide-ranging set of technologies, architectures, and protocols to ensure end-to-end consistency of traffic flows.

Capacity planning requires appliance of predictive models, in order to perform performance prediction of the system's performance parameters or measures, such as: server-side and client-side response times, throughput, network utilization, or resource queue length. All of these measures have to be estimated for a given set of known (input) parameters: system parameters (e.g. network protocols used), resource parameters (e.g. hard disk seek time, network bandwidth, router latency), and workload parameters (e.g. number of sessions per day, number of database transactions per unit time, total transmission time). The necessity for capacity planning comes out from the practical needs to apply a scientific approach instead of intuitive ad hoc procedures or rules of thumb when estimating the optimal hardware resources' characteristics in order to meet desired QoS user demands and service levels. On a contrary, the lack of proactive and continuous capacity planning may lead to unexpected unavailability and performance problems caused by any system hardware component, which can be financially devastating to a company. Capacity planning decisions affect a significant portion of future company revenues, because it implies considerable costs control and risk reduction.

3 e-Consumer Online Behavior Modeling

Models are essential tools to simplifying the representation of complex systems and, at the same time, to capturing their most relevant characteristics. A plethora of models portraying e-Consumer online behavior have been developed so far, including:

- *Flowchart (logical) model*; it is presented by a flowchart diagram, depicting the logical sequence of activities, i.e. the general logical flow of e-Consumer's actions from his/her entrance in the virtual shop until his/her leaving. Each of the activities can be further decomposed into more detailed flowcharts, depending on the level of details needed. Albeit the logical model can be useful for identifying the main activities and their sequence ordering, it is not useful for prediction making;
- *Entity-Relationship (E-R) model*; such a model can be used not only for description of the underlying e-Commerce site database conceptual structure, but also for building up a database system for capturing temporal dynamics of e-Consumers' interactions in terms of storing date/time stamps of his/her activities while invoking specific e-Commerce functions (browse, search, add to cart, ...). Later on, such Web logs can be analyzed with corresponding data mining tools in order to discover certain patterns of e-Consumer's online behavior;
- *UML model*; Combining best techniques from data modeling (entity relationship diagrams), business modeling (workflows), object modeling, and component modeling, UML can be also used to specify, visualize, modify, construct and document the artifacts related to e-Consumer's online behavior. Such model incorporates both static (domain model, class diagram) and dynamic (use case model, robustness diagram, and sequence diagram) aspects of the complex e-Commerce framework.

Hereby we present three well-known models of e-Consumer online behavior described in the literature, leading to building up predictive models.

3.1 State Diagram

Markellou et al. [2] have analyzed the overall process of how online consumer interacts with an e-shop. They have divided the whole e-shopping lifecycle into 13 states, belonging to three main phases: the phase from the purchase stimulus to entering an e-shop (states 1-2), the phase of the shopping process from entering to leaving the e-shop (states 3-9) and, finally, the phase of product receipt, customer support, and overall assessment (states 10-13). Fig. 1 shows the state diagram of the second phase. State diagrams require that the system described is composed of a finite number of states. They are used to give an abstract description of the behavior of a system. This behavior is analyzed and represented in series of events that could occur in one or more possible states. By identifying particular states and events, this kind of model is a step closer towards building a predictive model.

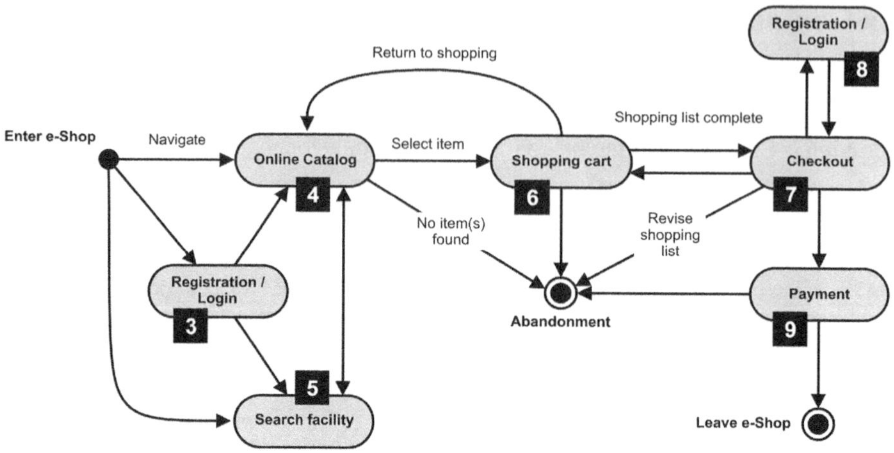

Source: Markellou et al. [2]

Fig. 1. State diagram of the e-shopping process

3.2 CBMG Diagram

One of the models useful to make an insight into the way e-Customers interact with an e-Commerce site is the Customer Behavior Model Graph (CBMG), a graph-based model that characterizes Web sessions. It was initially proposed by Menascé & Almeida [5], who were the first to introduce first-order Markov chain to model e-Consumer online sessions. As a result, a dominant fraction of existing Web workload models, as well as workload generators of Web server performance benchmarks (e.g. TPC-W) use first- or higher-order Markov chains. CBMG is a state-transition diagram, used to capture navigational pattern of a user through a site, based on a matrix of transition probabilities, which captures how an e-Customer moves from one state to the next. In CBMG, states denote results (Web pages) of service requests, and transitions denote possible service invocations.

In order to build a CBMG, one needs to determine the set of functions provided to the users of the system (e.g. login, register, browse, search, select, add to cart, pay, etc.) and then to refine the set of functions according to resource consumption.

The final step is to determine the possible transitions between states (this can be done by analyzing the layout of the user interface offered to e-Customers and the functions available when invoking them). Basically, a CBMG model can be built given a transition probability matrix. In CBMG, a state is represented using an oval with the name of the state and a number. A transition is represented by an arrow with the probability as label. The CBMG consisting of 7 states, along with correspondent transition probabilities, is presented on Fig. 2.

In the CBMG model, state transitions are governed by transition probabilities p_{ij} of moving from state '*i*' to '*j*'. Equation 1 shows that, for each state '*i*', the sum of probabilities corresponding to its all outcome transitions is equal to 1.

$$(\forall i)\ \sum_{j=1}^{N-1} p_{ij} = 1 \tag{1}$$

where:

N: Number of states in the CBMG;
i, j: States;
p_{ij}: Probability of a transition from state 'i' to state 'j'.

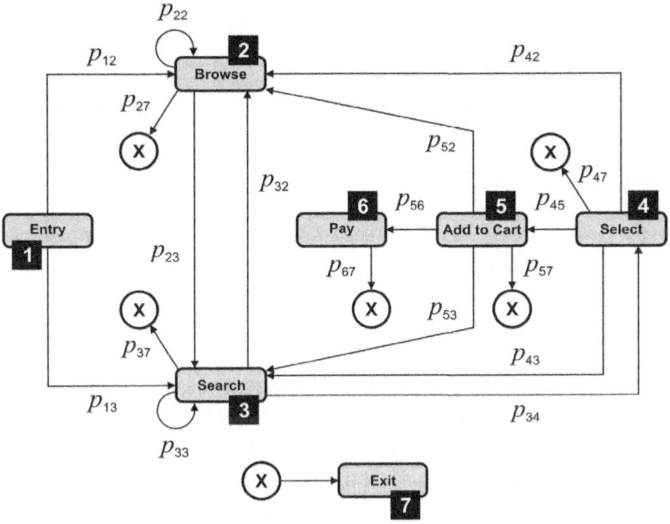

Source: Adapted from Menascé & Almeida [1]

Fig. 2. CBMG of the e-shopping process

The values of V_j, the average number of visits to state 'j' can be obtained by solving the system of linear equations given by Equation 2.

$$\begin{cases} V_1 = 1 \\ V_j = \sum_{k=1}^{N-1} V_k \cdot p_{kj} \end{cases} \quad \text{for all } j = 2, 3, \ldots, N-1 \tag{2}$$

Additionally, Totok [6] has enhanced originally introduced CBMG model by adding a finite number of finite-domain attributes for each state (Fig. 3). These attributes can be used to represent session state, i.e. session events like signing-in and signing-out of an e-Commerce Web site, or the number of items put into the shopping cart. The set of possible transitions and their corresponding probabilities can, in turn, depend on the values of these attributes. Since the set of attributes and their values is finite, each extended CBMG may be reduced to an equivalent CBMG, by duplicating states for each possible combination of attribute values [6].

Several useful performance metrics can be derived from a CBMG, such as *average number of visits (sessions)*, *average session length*, *throughput*, etc.

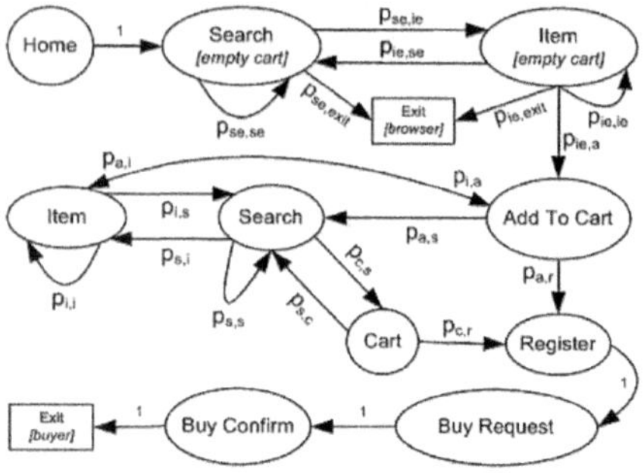

Source: Totok [6]

Fig. 3. Enhanced CBMG model of the e-shopping process

3.3 CSID Diagram

Another useful tool for modeling user behavior is the Client/Server Interaction Diagram (CSID), which was initially introduced by Menascé & Almeida [5]. The underlying idea is the fact that each e-Business function is, in fact, implemented through client/server interaction. CSIDs are a way of describing the flow of e-Business functions, i.e. it is a notation that describes all possible interactions between a client (e-Customer) and the servers (e-Commerce Web site) along the path, for each specific business function identified in the CBMG graph. More specifically, users interact with a client/server system by requesting the execution of a specific service or function. A client/server interaction starts when a client process makes a request to a server process, called primary server, and ends when the client process receives a reply from the primary server. The primary servers may need assistance from other servers called secondary servers. The basic graphical segment for building CSID is shown on Fig. 4.

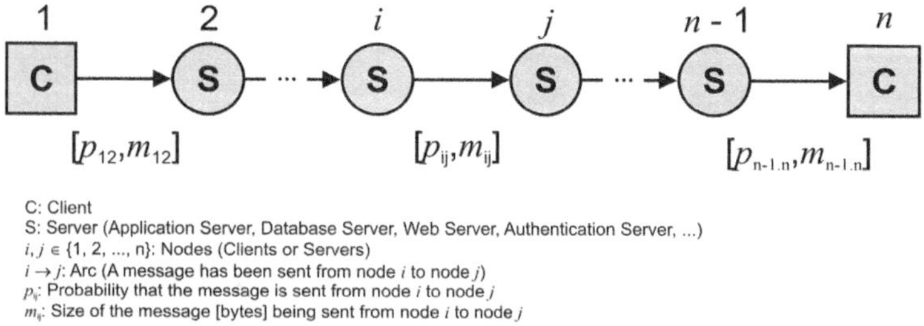

Source: Adapted from Menascé & Almeida [5]

Fig. 4. A schematic representation of the basic building segment of CSIDs

Several metrics can be derived from a CSID, such as *probability of execution of a client/server interaction*, *probability of execution associated with a node*, *number of bytes generated by the execution of a client/server interaction*, *service demand for a resource at a given server*, *communication delays*, etc.

4 Modeling e-Consumer Online Behavior with Petri Nets

Predictive modeling is critical for capacity planning. As stated previously, a starting point for capacity planning will be a performance analysis of a predictive model based on e-Consumer online behavior. Based on our previous research [3], [4], we propose a novel approach to modeling online behavior, based on usage of Deterministic and Stochastic Petri Nets (DSPNs). In computer science, Petri Nets are widely recognized and accepted as a useful mathematical modeling tool for performance and reliability analysis and simulations of concurrent systems, allowing formal specification of a system's dynamics. Moreover, the proposed framework is suitable for building a predictive model based on e-Consumer behavior. The proposed DSPN model is depicted on Fig. 5, and its underlying logic (flowchart) is given on Fig. 6.

The class of DSPN allows transitions with zero firing times, exponentially distributed, or deterministic firing times. As a result, the underlying stochastic process of a DSPN is neither a Markov, nor a semi-Markov, but rather a *Markov regenerative process*. However, DSPNs can be solved analytically with a restriction that at most one timed transition with deterministic firing time is enabled concurrently with exponentially distributed timed transitions. As a result, *the average time spent by an e-Customer*, as well as *the average number of e-Customers in the system* can be calculated by means of time and space efficient algorithms for computing steady-state solution of the DSPN [7], while the usage of a transient (time-dependent) analysis method [8] allows *general service time* to be evaluated.

The basic idea behind computing *steady-state solution of DSPN* is to study the evolution of the DSPN in a *continuous-time Markov chain* (CTMC) to be solved at the transient time τ, at which the deterministic transition $T_{TIMEOUT}$ must fire unless it has been resampled in a meantime (Fig. 5) [3]. An *Embedded Markov Chain* (EMC) is associated with each marking where the remaining firing time of the deterministic transition can be resampled, and different CTMCs, referred to as *Subordinated Markov Chains* (SMC), are employed for each marking in which the deterministic transition can begin its firing time. *The average time spent by an e-Customer in the system* is equal to the total time spent in all tangible transient markings of the DSPN. Since the number of e-Customers entering the system is equal to those completing service, the Little's law holds: *the average number of e-Customers in the system* is given by the product of *the average arrival rate of e-Customers admitted to the system*, and *the average time spent by an e-Customer in the system.*

The *transient analysis of a DSPN* can be carried out using the theory of Markov regenerative processes. The transition probability matrix **V***(t)* satisfies the generalized *Markov renewal equation* (Equation 3):

$$\mathbf{V}(t) = \mathbf{E}(t) + \mathbf{K} * \mathbf{V}(t) \tag{3}$$

where:

- **V***(t)*: Transition probability matrix;
- **E***(t)*: Local kernel; a matrix describing the behavior of the marking process between two regeneration instants (two transition epochs of the EMC);
- **K***(t)*: Global kernel; a matrix describing the behavior of the marking process at the regeneration instants themselves.

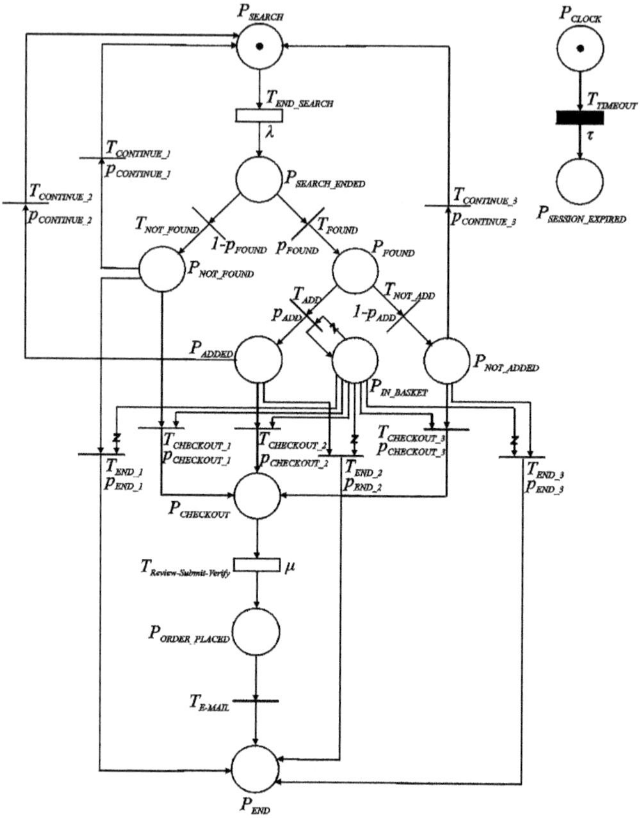

Fig. 5. The e-Customer's behavior DSPN model

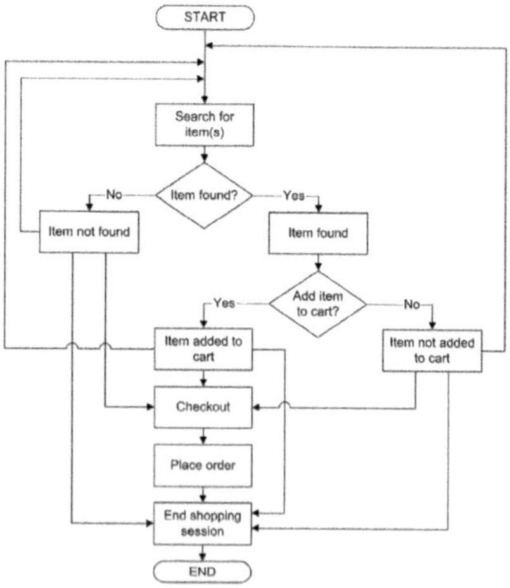

Fig. 6. The flowchart explaining the logic sequence of the e-Customer's behavior DSPN model

Given the state transition probability matrix and the initial probability distribution, the state probability at time t can be computed. Consequently, the general service time distribution is given by the probability that the marking process is in one of the absorbing states (token in place P_{END} or token in place $P_{SESSION\_EXPIRED}$) at time t. The system as a whole may then be regarded as an M/G/k queue with Poisson input, general service time distribution and k serving facilities. Nevertheless, the queue can be analyzed as a piecewise-deterministic Markov process [9].

5 Conclusion

Several models presenting e-Consumer's online behavior have been proposed so far, each of them employing rather different approach, depicting different aspect and offering different level of predicting capability regarding the e-Commerce performance metrics. Among them, the proposed DSPN-based framework of e-Consumer's online behavior offers considerable potential for carrying out a performance analysis of e-Business applications. The DSPN model captures well the e-Consumer's online behavior in a typical e-Business application, while the analysis of the stochastic process underlying the Petri Net, either steady-state or transient, allows to estimate a range of performance measures.

References

1. Menascé, D.A., Almeida, V.A.F.: Capacity Planning for Web Services: Metrics, Models, and Methods. Prentice Hall PTR, Upper Saddle River (2002)
2. Markellou, P., Rigou, M., Sirmakessis, S.: A Closer Look to the Online Consumer Behavior. In: Khosrow-Pour, M. (ed.) Encyclopedia of E-Commerce, E-Government and Mobile Commerce, pp. 106–111. Idea Group Reference, USA (2006)
3. Mitrevski, P., Manceski, G., Gusev, M.: A Framework for Performance Analysis of e-Business Applications. In: Proceedings of the 3rd CiiT Conference on Informatics and Information Technology, Bitola, Macedonia, pp. 107–114 (2002)
4. Mitrevski, P., Hristoski, I.: Customer Behavior Modeling in e-Commerce. In: Proceedings of the KEFP2007 International Conference "Business and Globalization", Ohrid, Macedonia, vol. 1, pp. 395–401 (2007)
5. Menascé, D.A., Almeida, V.A.F.: Scaling for E-Business: Technologies, Models, Performance and Capacity Planning. Prentice Hall PTR, Upper Saddle River (2000)
6. Totok, A.: Modern Internet Services: Exploiting Service Usage Information for Optimizing Service Management. VDM Verlag Dr. Müller Aktiengesellschaft & Co. KG, Saarbrücken (2009)
7. Ciardo, G., Lindemann, C.: Analysis of Deterministic and Stochastic Petri Nets. In: 5th International Workshop on Petri Nets and Performance Models, Toulouse, pp. 160–169 (1993)
8. Choi, H., Kulkarni, V., Trivedi, K.: Transient Analysis of Deterministic and Stochastic Petri Nets. In: Ajmone Marsan, M. (ed.) ICATPN 1993. LNCS, vol. 691, pp. 166–185. Springer, Heidelberg (1993)
9. Breuer, L.: Operator-Geometric Solutions for the M/G/k Queue and its Variants. Forschungsbericht 00-11, Mathematik/Informatik, Universität Trier (2000)

e-Government and e-Business in Western Balkans 2010

P. Sonntagbauer[1], M. Gusev[2], S. Tomic Rotim[3], N. Stefanovic[4], K. Kiroski[2], and M. Kostoska[2]

[1] Vienna, Austria
[2] Skopje, Macedonia
[3] Zagreb, Croatia
[4] Novi Sad, Serbia

peter.sonntagbauer@technikum-wien.at, marjangusev@gmail.com, stomic@zih.hr, nenad@empiry.com, {kiril,magi}@ii.edu.mk

Abstract. This study analyses results of the e-Government and e-Business reports for Western Balkan Countries in 2010 and also results from EBIZ4ALL project led by Austrian Agency for research promotion (FFG) within the COIN (Cooperation and Innovation) program. The results are evaluated according to well known methodologies and compared with EU average results. Results of conveyed surveys for use of e-Services by companies are provided, and their use of electronic means for exchange of invoices and orders. Conclusions also include evaluation of current situation of Western Balkan countries in development of efficient government and infrastructure for Information Society capable to be interoperable in networked world and global market.

Keywords: e-Government, e-Business, e-Invoicing, e-Ordering, benchmark.

1 Introduction

The process of globalization enforces companies not only to modernize their approach to the production process, but also to implement modern technologies, and to compete on a wider scale if they want to be successful. This implementation of modern technology implies use of information technology, not only in manufacturing of the end product, but also the way that product is to be distributed to their clients, especially the means to anticipate future client demands, how clients can order their products from the company, and how the company deals with those orders, deliver the desired products and issue invoices. To be able to compete outside of its country, company needs to comply with international standards and laws, so efforts are made to unify these rules. Today, the predominant EU government driven effort in this field is the PEPPOL (Pan-European Public eProcurement On-Line) [1], project intended to provide companies with means to compete and cooperate outside their countries. A private sector driven initiative is the Hub Alliance [16],

Governments help their domestic companies by providing infrastructure on a national level, and then by unification of this infrastructure for Europe, so every company working by these standards can equally compete on international level. These efforts result in common e-Government services, which provide IT guided interaction between

M. Gusev and P. Mitrevski (Eds.): ICT Innovations 2010, CCIS 83, pp. 152–165, 2011.

government and companies, and e-Business, using of information technology between companies themselves.

Governments can also act as a catalyst to promote e-Business through mandatory e-procurement processes with government entities. A successful example was Denmark, which made e-invoicing mandatory for all suppliers of the government. By doing this they have drastically improved the overall adoption of e-invoicing in Denmark. [17].

In this paper we present some results provided by the ongoing eBiz4All (e-Business for all) [2]. This project also involves participants from Macedonia, Croatia and Serbia, which conducted surveys in their countries.

Section 2 gives an overview of definitions used in this article, and section 3 the current evaluation of Western Balkan Countries about e-government development index. Section 4 is dedicated to e-Readiness and in Section 5, we provide insight into benchmarking of e-Government services and particularly e-Procurement. In Section 6 we discuss the results of e-Business surveys and we give our conclusions in Section 7.

2 Definitions

In this section we provide definitions about terms used in this paper.

Def 1: (e-Government) according to [3][4][5]
E-Government should include: use of ICTs, and particularly the Internet, as a tool to achieve better government, use of information and communication technologies in all facets of the operations of a government organization, and continuous optimization of service delivery, constituency participation and governance by transforming internal and external relationships through technology, the Internet and new media. ■

Def 2: (e-Readiness) according to [6]
E-Government readiness (e-Readiness) is a function of a country's state of networked readiness, its technological and telecommunication infrastructure, the level of citizen's access to electronic services and the existence of governmental policy and security mechanisms. ■

Def3: (e-Business) according to [7]
E-Business may be defined as the application of information and communication technologies (ICT) in support of all the activities of business. Commerce constitutes the exchange of products and services between businesses, groups and individuals and can be seen as one of the essential activities of any business. Electronic commerce focuses on the use of ICT to enable the external activities and relationships of the business with individuals, groups and other businesses. ■

3 E-Government and E-Readiness on World Level

E-Readiness is the degree to which a country/state is prepared to participate in the networked world. It would demand the adoption of important applications of ICTs in offering interconnectedness between government, businesses and citizens [8]. This interconnectedness is conditioned by the penetration of Internet access for the general population, and especially companies and government bodies. As much as this indicator is important, the biggest impact on development of e-government services is achieved through national authorities (governments).

Table 1. E-Government development index and word ranking for Western Balkan countries

Country	E-Gov development index	World e-Gov ranking
Croatia	0.5858	35
Macedonia	0.5261	52
Montenegro	0.5101	60
Bosnia	0.4698	74
Serbia	0.4585	81
Albania	0.4519	85

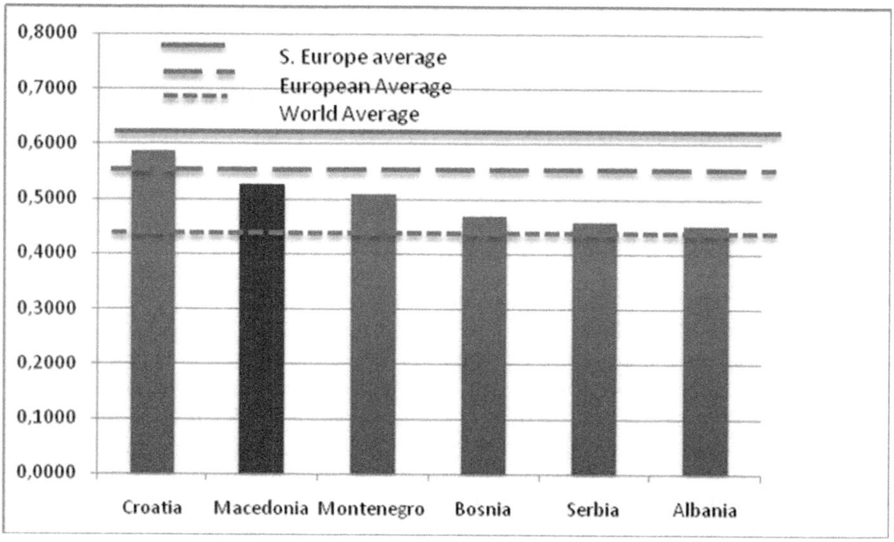

Fig. 1. E-government development index for Western Balkan countries 2010

Therefore, United Nations [9] proposed methodology for measuring e-government development index (EGDI) as a comprehensive scoring of the willingness and capacity of the national administrations to use online technology in the realization of government functions. This index is intended to present results for the national governments relative to one another, and it consists of three crucial dimensions of e-government: scope and quality of online services, telecommunication connectivity, and human capacity. Results for Western Balkan countries, Europe and World average are given in Table 1 and Figure 1.

4 E-Readiness

In the following paragraphs we used data provided by official statistical offices to present Internet usage, how companies use IT and e-Services, and how they keep and interchange data. Most of data that statistical offices collected data is by filling in a questionnaire, distributed to the companies.

ICT (Information and Communication Technology) usage in enterprises is shown on Table 2 and Figure 2, regardless of their size. We can see that these figures are fairly similar with difference not bigger than ±5% from the average. [14] and [15] give overview of EU 27 results.

Table 2. Information and communication technologies in the enterprises

Country	Macedonia	Croatia	Serbia	EU 27
Internet	86.30%	95.00%	94.50%	97.00%
LAN	71.80%	68.00%	68.90%	75.00%
Wireless	31.90%	34.00%	37.40%	27.00%
Intranet	33.40%	29.00%	43.70%	31.00%
Extranet	20.60%	13.00%	12.20%	17.00%

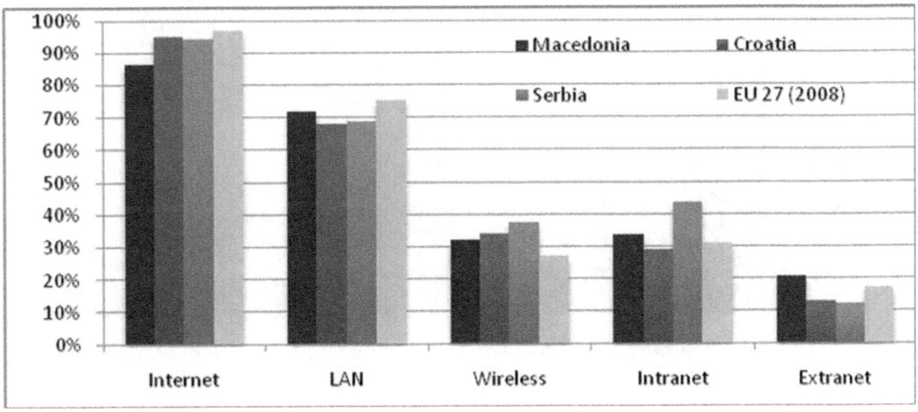

Fig. 2. Information and communication technologies in the enterprises

86.3% of companies in Macedonia, and 95% of companies in Serbia and Croatia have Internet access. The percentage of companies with wired LAN is 71.8% for Macedonia, 68% in Croatia and 68.9% in Serbia. Wireless LAN is present in 31.9% of Macedonian, 34% of Croatian, and 37.4% of Serbian companies. 33.4% of Macedonian, 29% of Croatian, and 43.7% of Serbian companies have Intranet, compared to 20.6% of Macedonian, 13% of Croatian and 12.2% of Serbian companies with Extranet.

Statistical data for Internet usage (Table 3 and Figure 3) shows that companies use Internet mostly for banking and finance (70.8% in Macedonia, 84% in Croatia and 78.1% in Serbia) and e-Government services (75.8% in Macedonia, 61% in Croatia and 69.1% in Serbia). For training and education purposes, Internet is used in 38.2% of Macedonian, 29% of Croatian, and 22.2% of Serbian companies. For e-Purchases and e-Sales, we can see that Macedonia has lowest results, where only 8.2% of companies use Internet for purchases, and 5% for sales. In comparison 22.4% of Serbian and as far as 50% of Croatian companies use Internet for e-Purchases, and e-Sale is used by 19% of Croatian and 19.9% of Serbian companies.

Table 3. Internet usage in enterprises

Country	Macedonia	Croatia	Serbia	EU 27
Banking & finance	70.80%	84.00%	78.10%	78.00%
Training & education	38.20%	29.00%	22.20%	24.00%
Using e-Gov services	75.80%	61.00%	69.10%	68.00%
E-purchases	8.20%	50.00%	22.40%	28.00%
E-sale	5.00%	19.00%	19.90%	16.00%

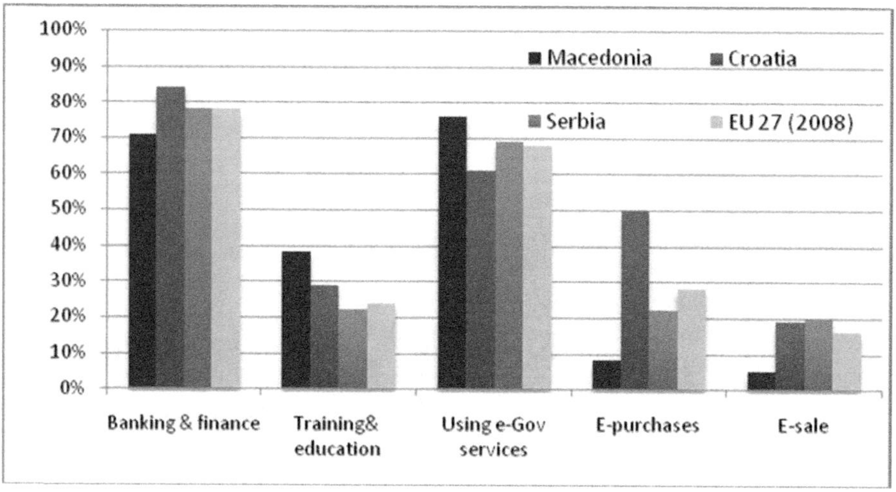

Fig. 3. Internet usage in enterprises

The next analysis concerns e-Government services usage by enterprises. Companies used e-Government services only to obtain information in 72.8 of Macedonian, 56% of Croatian, and 95.7% of Serbian companies. Forms download was used by 65.1% of Macedonian, 56% of Croatian and 86.6% of Serbian companies. Submitting of Forms was used by 32.1% of Macedonian, 37% of Croatian, and 47.4% of Serbian companies. Completion of e-Administration procedures was performed by 24.8% of Macedonian, 36% of Croatian, and 20% of Serbian companies. Public procurement (tenders) by electronic means was used by 14.5 of Macedonian, 13% of Croatian and only 7.80% of Serbian companies. These figures give us ground to conclude that the level of sophistication for e-Government services can and should be further developed, especially in providing of paperless procedure for conducting government business services and public procurement. Using results provided by [10], we can conclude that the take-up of these services should be also improved, to close the gap between facilities provided by governments and the actual use of e-Government services by companies.

For the purposes of e-Business, one of the most important prerequisites is keeping data in electronic form and ability to use and exchange this data by electronic means. These results are very interesting (Table 4 and Figure 4).

Table 4. Companies that use automatic data exchange

Country	Macedonia	Serbia	EU 27 (2008)
Automatic data exchange	29.10%	20.80%	40.00%
sending orders	21.00%	73.00%	20.00%
receiving e-invoices	13.00%	68.00%	18.00%
receiving orders	19.20%	67.40%	19.00%
sending e-invoices	9.10%	60.20%	10.00%
CRM	25.40%	23.00%	26.00%
ERP	19.60%	11.30%	16.00%

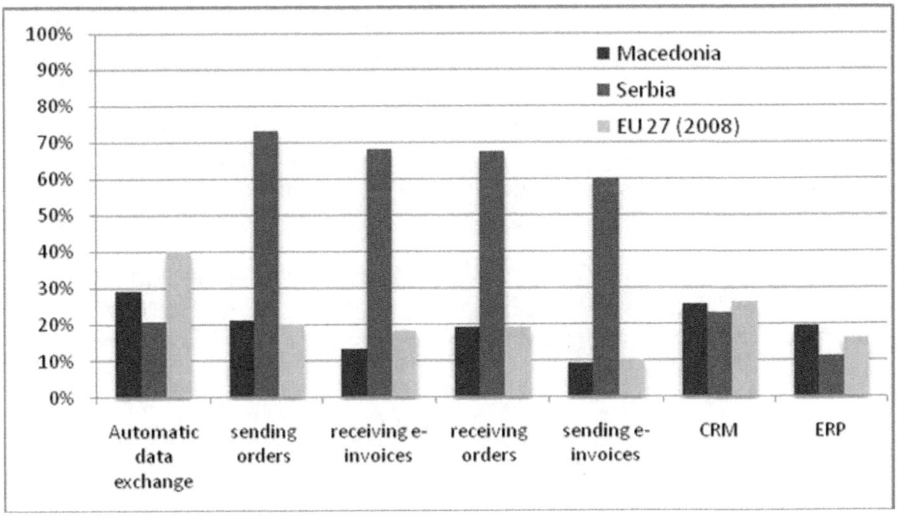

Fig. 4. Companies that use automatic data exchange

There are fairly big discrepancies in use of automatic data exchange, ERP and CRM software on one side, and electronic orders and invoices on the other. From Table 4 and Figure 4, we can see that automatic data exchange is used in 29.1% of Macedonian and 20.8% of Serbian companies, ERP is used in 19.6% of Macedonian and 11.3% of Serbian companies, and that 25.4% of Macedonian, and 23% of Serbian companies use some kind of CRM software. These numbers show slightly bigger take-up by these technologies in Macedonian, than in Serbian companies. In contrast, 73% of Serbian companies send electronic orders, compared to 21% of Macedonian, and 68% Serbian and only 13% Macedonian companies received electronic invoices. The situation with receiving orders and sending electronic invoices is quite similar – 67.4% of Serbian and 19.2% of Macedonian companies received electronic orders, and 60.2% of Serbian and only 9.1% of Macedonian companies was sending electronic invoices. This great difference in automatic data exchange used and working with electronic documents is most likely due to inappropriately data gathering methods, sample size and understanding of what is e-Purchase or e-Invoice.

5 E-Government Services

In the last ten years, there were a great number of projects and activities involved in the development of the E-government concept, which all led to the stadium in which Macedonia is today compared to other European countries, as pointed by M. Gusev et al. [8], and in the CapGemini report [18].

From this study, we excerpt the situation on online sophistication of twenty basic services, which describe the level of e-government development, and the services available for business and citizens alike. The current situation of online sophistication is shown on Figure 5, and as we can see, Macedonia has scored 53% on this benchmark, or 73% for business services and 39% for citizen services.

The situation with full availability of the 20 basic services is not so good, as we can see on Figure 6. Today Macedonia is far behind all EU27+ countries, with only 20% full availability, which equals to four out of twenty basic services reaching the best possible level of sophistication measured by this benchmark, all achieved with business services, or 50% score, while citizen services score 0%.

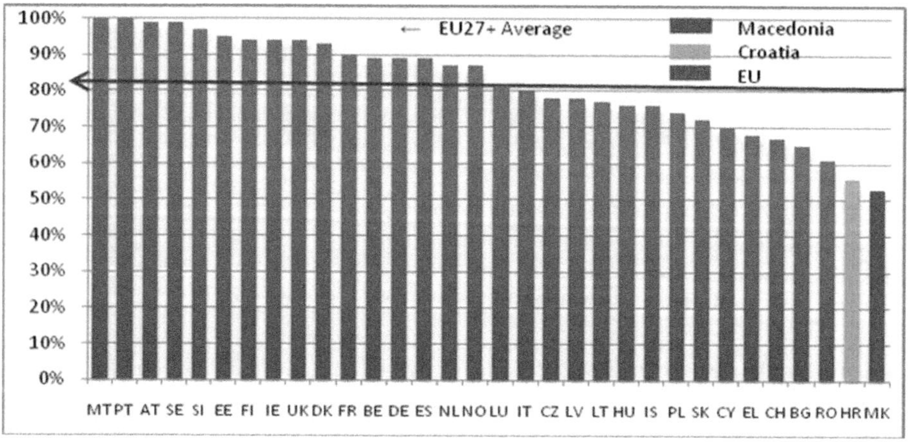

Fig. 5. Online sophistication scores for Macedonia and Croatia plus EU27+ countries

Croatia has participated in the European Commission's benchmark for the first time this year. In terms of full online availability, Croatia obtains 35% (see Figure 6). Business services are by far more mature: they obtain a score of 63% on full online availability as compared to the citizen services' score of 17% for this metric.

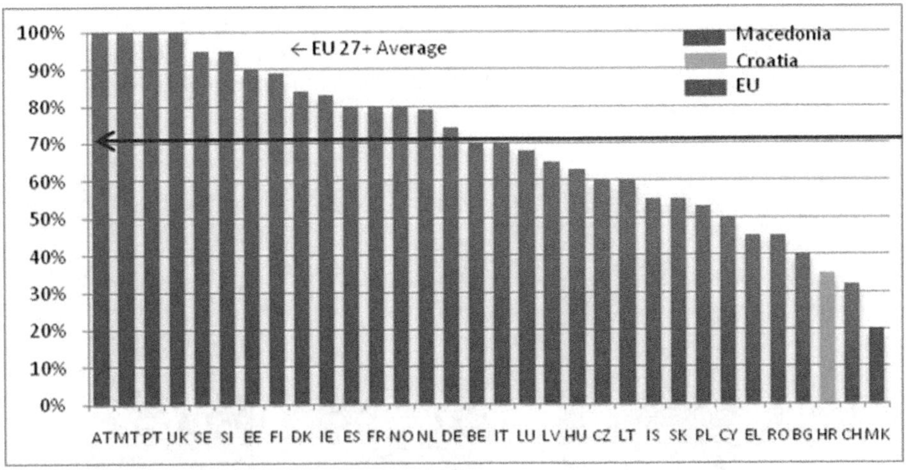

Fig. 6. Full availability scores for Macedonia and Croatia plus EU27+ countries

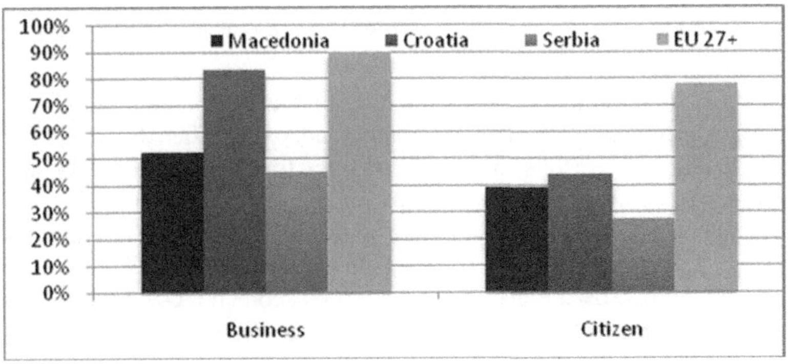

Fig. 7. Online sophistication scores for Western Balkan countries

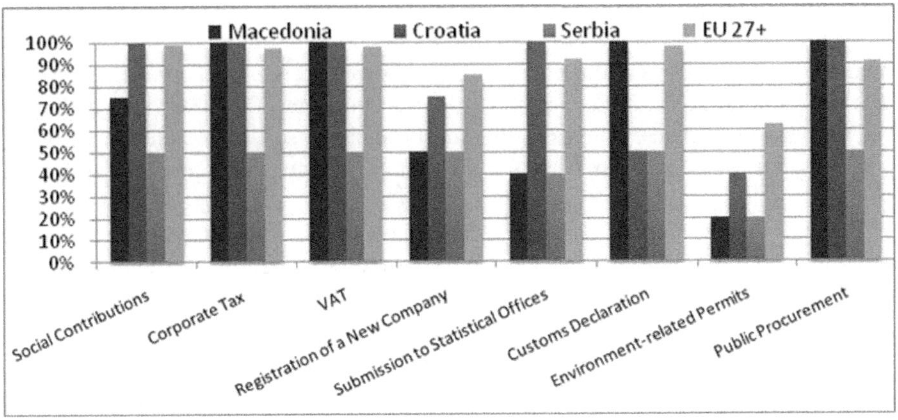

Fig. 8. Business services for Western Balkan countries

In terms of online sophistication, Croatia marks 56% (see Figure 5). This score can be split into an online sophistication score of 44% for citizen services and 74% for business services, with again a marked gap between the quality of supply for businesses and citizens.

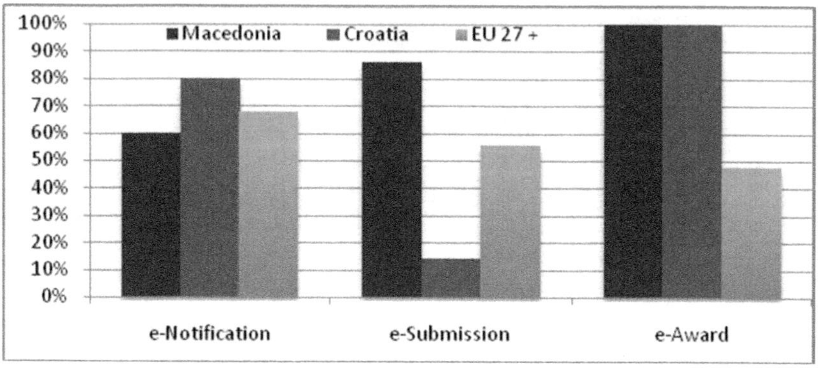

Fig. 9. E-Procurement results for Western Balkan countries

Regarding E-Procurement sophistication, both Macedonia and Croatia have made significant advancement in the last few years, and score better than EU average. For this year's benchmark, results are provided only for pre-Award phase, while post-Award phase will be included in the future. Since post-Award phase mostly comprises of e-Ordering and e-Ordering, we will give approximated insight into this phase in the next Section. As we can see on Figure 9, Macedonia scores 60% on e-Notification, while Croatia scores 80%. Macedonia has better score for e-Submission sub-phase (84%), while Croatia has only 14%. Both Macedonia and Croatia have achieved perfect score in e-Award sub-phase.

6 E-Business Survey

The e-Business survey was conducted according to the eBiz4ALL project, and in this paper we summarize results of individual research in Macedonia, Croatia and Serbia. [2] There are some discrepancies in the questionnaires used, so we include only those questions that were used in two or more countries, so as to present comparative picture.

On Figure 10 we can see that the complete awareness of e-Business benefits is entirely clear to 35% of Macedonian, 26% Croatian and 42.86% Serbian companies. Partial insight into benefits of e-Business is present in 55% of Macedonian, 74% of Croatian and 42.86% of Serbian companies. We can notice that all Croatian companies are at least partially informed about e-Business benefits, and that only 10% of Macedonian and 14.29% of Serbian companies are not aware of it. In average,

34.62% of the companies in all three countries are completely aware of e-Business benefits, 57.29% partially, and 8.1% have no information about e-Business benefits (Figure 10).

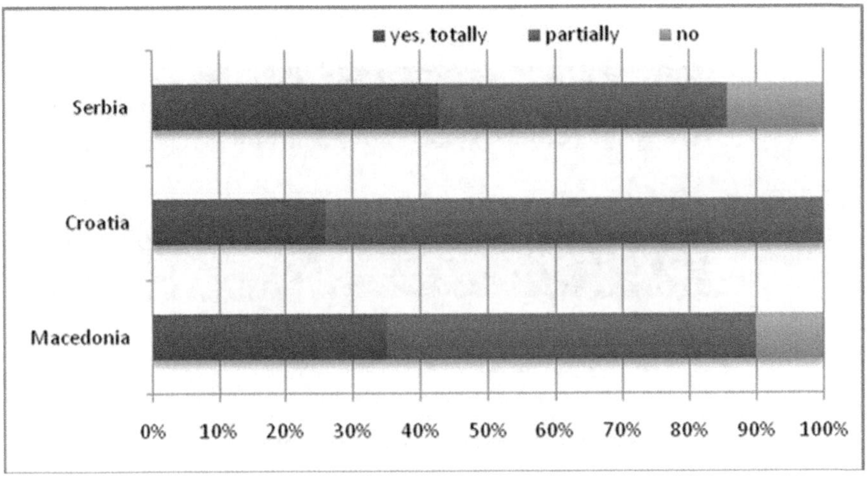

Fig. 10. Awareness about benefits of e-Business

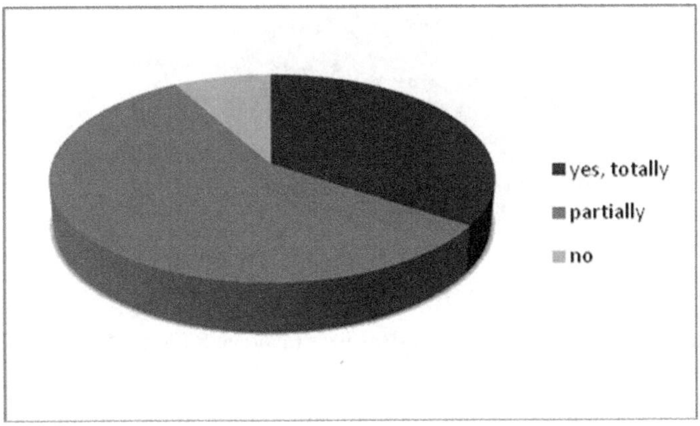

Fig. 11. Average awareness about benefits of e-Business

On the question about their timeframe to introduce e-Business into their companies, we have results on Macedonian and Croatian companies, as we can see on Figure 12. 45% of Macedonian and 66% of Croatian companies have answered that they will introduce e-Business at the latest in the first half of 2010, 17% of Macedonian and 11% of Croatian companies will introduce it in the second half of

2010, and 38% of Macedonian and 23% of Croatian companies set a later date. In average, 55.5% of companies should already use e-Business solutions, and 14% will start introducing e-Business till the end of this year.

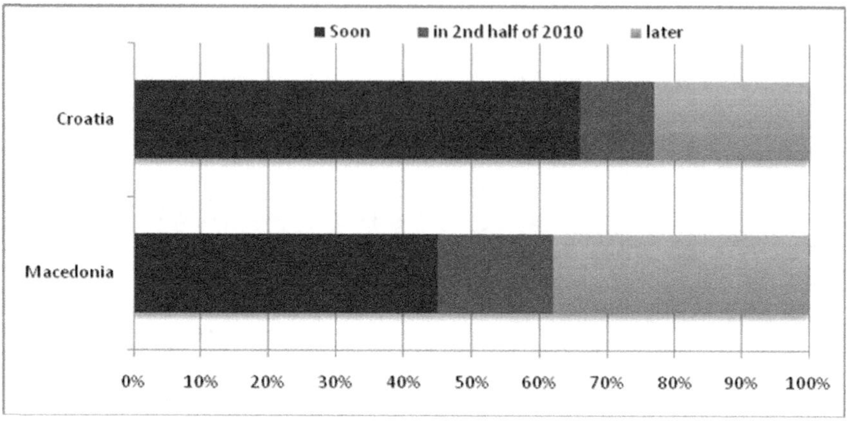

Fig. 12. Timeframe to introduce e-Business

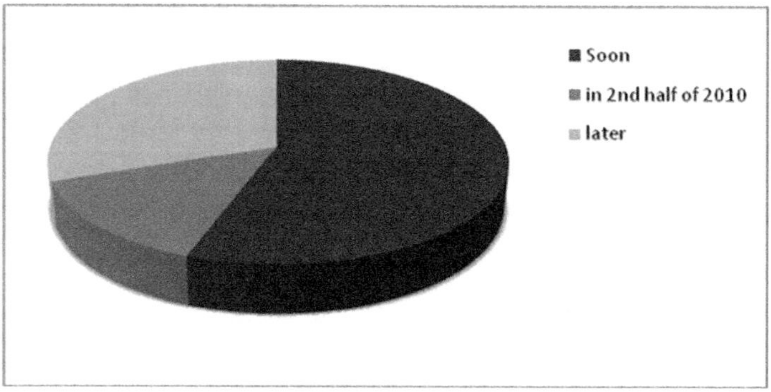

Fig. 13. Timeframe to introduce e-Business (average for Macedonia and Croatia)

Last question was about standards used when using automatic data exchange. Our survey has shown that Statistical Office of the Republic of Macedonia has made survey for e-orders and e-invoices according to their e-mail exchange of scanned version (mostly pdf, jpg), not by exchange of information as defined by the definition of e-Ordering or e-Invoicing. This means that the companies will print their invoices and orders, then make scanned version, and then exchange with other companies by e-mail (sometimes even they exchange word docs). Therefore, we here present results for Croatia and Serbia.

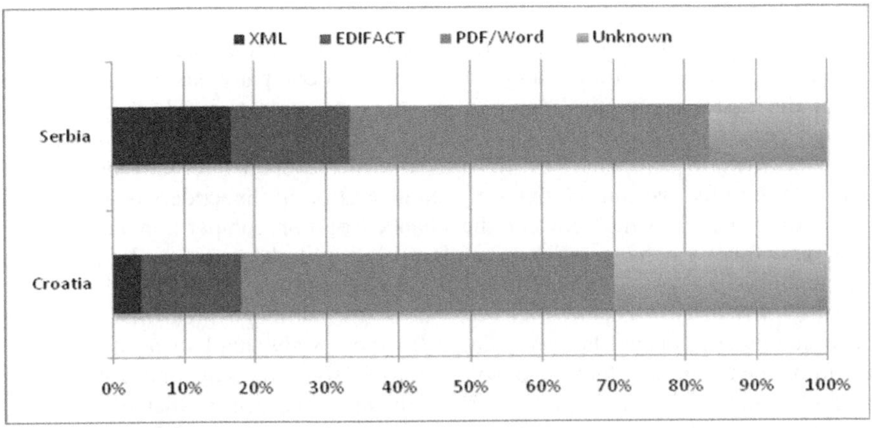

Fig. 14. Standards used for data exchange between companies

As we can see from Figure 14, 33.4% of Serbian companies use proper type of documents for exchange of information (16.7% use EDIFACT and 16.7% use XML), and only 18% of Croatian (14% EDIFACT and 4% XML). 50% of Serbian and 52% of Croatian companies use and exchange standard document types (doc, pdf or even pictures). On average, these figures are 10.35% XML, 15.35% EDIFACT, and 51% standard document types, as is shown on Figure 15.

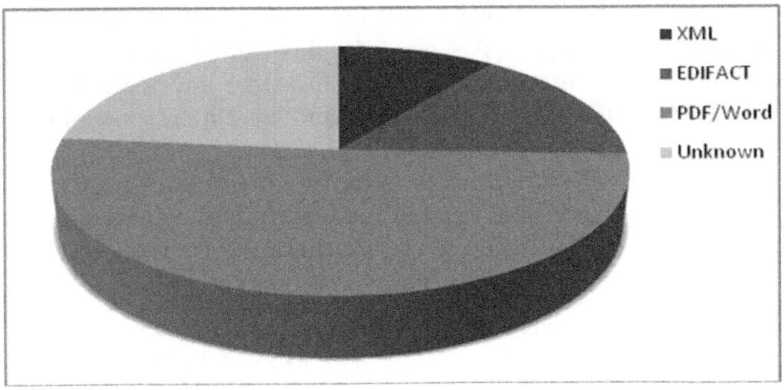

Fig. 15. Average use of standards for Croatia and Serbia

7 Conclusion

In the ever-changing world of business today, usage of ICT is essential for survival and development of small and medium enterprises. Results provided by surveys conducted as part of the eBiz4ALL project, and data from Statistical Offices give us insight into adoption of IT and e-Business by companies in Macedonia, Croatia and Serbia.

From the results shown, it is clear that although great deal of companies have Internet access, only a part of them has developed network infrastructure, and that only one third of them have intranet, and that every sixth company has extranet. This fact severely decimates companies' capabilities to exchange data inside the company or with their partners. Furthermore, we can see that Internet usage for purchasing and selling is too low, so companies exploit benefits of the open Internet market only on small scale. Finally, we can see that only small portion of the tenders is accomplished by electronic means, which lowers the chances of fair competition between companies. This fact will change with the obligatory use of electronic tender platforms in these countries.

Results provided by business surveys show that although great number of companies acknowledges benefits from using e-Business, only small share of them has already implemented it, and that the others plan to do so in the near future. What worries the most is the fairly small part of the companies recognizes that e-ordering and e-selling must implement use of sanctioned standards, such as EDIFACT and XML, and that still a great number of companies use software to produce documents, which are to be printed and distributed in paper form. We find this a key point where companies should be educated by the benefits of using electronic means of signing, distributing and keeping documents, as essential part of e-Purchasing and e-Business. A very big problem arises in legislation, changes and adoption of legal docs in Western Balkan countries due to the transition process in last 20 years.

We can conclude that these countries are not yet ready to accept the challenges of new ICT technologies and therefore can't exploit their benefits. The delay in adoption of these technologies shows that Western Balkan countries have delay between 5 and 10 years in adoption and usage of ICT for business and government usage, meaning that after 5 or 10 years these countries will be capable to have adaptation and usage levels the developed countries have now. In this period these EU countries will advance even more. The only way out to catch up the development tempo is huge investment in sophisticated ICT technologies (and have high scores like those for e-Award).

The governments in Western Balkan countries could play a significant role by adopting laws, which make e-procurement mandatory in the government sector. This would act as catalyst to the private sector to introduce e-business and e-procurement quickly.

References

1. PEPPOL, E-ordering objectives (27.01.2010), `http://www.peppol.eu/work_in_progress/wp4-eordering/objectives`
2. EBIZ4ALL: Requirements document, project sponsored by Austrian government - COIN (Cooperation and Innovation) program
3. OECD: The e-government imperative: main findings, Policy Brief, Public Affairs Division, Public Affairs and Communications Directorate, OECD (2003)
4. Koh, C.E., Prybutok, V.R.: The three-ring model and development of an instrument for measuring dimensions of e-government functions. Journal of Computer Information Systems 33(3), 34–39 (2003)

5. Gartner Group, Key Issues in E-Government Strategy and Management, Research Notes, Key Issues (May 23, 2000)
6. Zarimpas, V., Grouztidou, M., Anastasiadou, D.: Assessing e-Readiness in SEE countries: Perceptions towards e-Government Public Services, http://www.inatelecom.org/Portals/0/papers/BCI%202009%20Full%20final.pdf
7. Beynon-Davies, P.: E-Business. Palgrave, Basingstoke (2004); ISBN 1-4039-1348-X
8. Codagnone, C.: Benchmarking on-line Public Services: To develop and improve the eGovernment indicators (2008), http://www.epractice.eu/en/library/281817
9. United Nations E-Government Survey 2010: Leveraging e-government at a time of financial and economic crisis, United Nations (2010) ISBN: 978-92-1-123183-0
10. Gusev, M., Kostoska, M., Kiroski, K.: Growth of eGovernment services in Macedonia (Online sophistication of eGovernment services), Technical report, UKIM, Skopje, Macedonia
11. Communication from the commission to the council, the european parliament, the european economic and social committee and the committee of the regions, "i2010 – A European Information Society for growth and employment", Brussels (1.6.2005), http://eur-lex.europa.eu/LexUriServ/LexUriServ.do?uri=COM:2005:0229:FIN:EN:PDF
12. Europe's Digital Competitiveness Report, Vol. 1: i2010 — Annual Information Society Report (2009), Benchmarking i2010: Trends and main achievements, http://ec.europa.eu/information_society/eeurope/i2010/docs/annual_report/2009/sec_2009_1103.pdf
13. e-Invoicing and e-Archiving taking the next step, A European Survey by Pricewaterhouse Coopers (2005)
14. Gusev, M., Markoski, R.: Comparison of the e-Business Readiness Index (2008), http://ict-act.org/ICT-Innovations-10/papers09/ictinnovations2009_submission_126.pdf
15. Krizman, I., et al.: eBusiness in Enterprises in Slovenia and EU-27, http://www.stat.si/doc/pub/IKT2009-ANG.pdf
16. Hubballiance, http://www.huballiance.org/
17. Cimander, R., Hippe Brun, M.: National IT and Telecom Agency, Denmark, Good Practice Case, eInvoicing in Denmark (2007)
18. Capgemini, Rand Europe, IDC, Sogeti and DTI, Smarter, Faster, Better eGovernment: 8th Benchmark Measurement (November 2009), http://ec.europa.eu/information_society/eeurope/i2010/docs/benchmarking/egov_benchmark_2009.pdf

Information Brokering with Social Networks Analysis

Jorge Marx Gómez and Peter Cissek

Carl von Ossietzky Universität Oldenburg
Department für Informatik, Abt. Wirtschaftsinformatik I
26129 Oldenburg, Germany
jorge.marx.gomez@uni-oldenburg.de, cissek@wi-ol.de

Abstract. Social network services like Facebook are still very popular on the internet. They are also becoming useful in companies for business tasks, where their structure is examined with social network analysis. This approach makes it possible to determine, who in the social network is connected with whom and what interests these people share without regarding the formal organizational structure. In large organizations people often need information, but they do not even know that it exists in the company. So they either suffer a lack of information in business processes or keep turning to people in key positions, who get the information for them. In order to take work off the people in key positions it would be necessary to offer information to employees even before they ask for it. This paper discusses the potential of social network analysis to be used for information brokering goals.

Keywords: social network analysis, information broker, information demand, enterprise 2.0.

1 Introduction

Last year the human resources (HR) department of a big company with more than 20.000 employees introduced a BI solution for HR-reporting and HR-planning to improve the quality of decision making processes in HR to earn a higher value from the available workforce. The BI project was lead by the HR controlling team and consisted of four main phases. The first one was the conceptual phase, where an information demand analysis was performed. The findings of this analysis were used for the concept. In the next project phase the data model and the ETL-processes for the data warehouse were implemented. After that phase the planning application was created. The final phase dealt with reporting in BI.

During the implementation it all seemed going well and the project has been successfully finished almost in time and budget. Despite the success and though at first sight all the people who were important also had participated in all decisions and project team meetings from the beginning, most people of the target group were dissatisfied with the result. Even the department chief and the other team leaders in the HR department were involved. But people claimed that their needs were not met. As a result the BI system failed in being accepted by most of the users. Only the HR controlling team took a great advantage from the new software.

M. Gusev and P. Mitrevski (Eds.): ICT Innovations 2010, CCIS 83, pp. 166–175, 2011.

After the project had been finished, the failure was investigated by the internal auditing. They revealed that mistakes have already been made in the first phase of the project when the reporting and the requirements on the BI solution were analyzed. Only members of the HR controlling team and the IT consultants were involved in the information demand analysis. That was too little people. In addition to the restricted number of project members internal communication problems were also a reason for the bad results of the information demand analysis. Although the team leader of HR controlling did invite the department chief and the other team leaders to participate in the project, none of them did really understand the benefit of BI. Neither did the other team leaders ask their teams to contribute to the information demand analysis nor did the department chief talk to the top management.

In order to draw conclusions internal auditing tried to identify the people who should have contributed to the information demand analysis and to point out the difference between what has been done and how a sustainable information demand analysis should have been performed ideally. For this task internal auditing used social network analysis. In the following the basic ideas will be introduced, followed by a summary of the objectives internal auditing achieved.

2 Information Brokering

During the last forty years modern societies developed from the industrial to the information society. Information has become one of the most important goods and has also been identified as a crucial success factor for modern companies, because information is used in almost all business processes. This trend has been even amplified with the use of information technology in the value added chain [1]. Nowadays decision makers and people who deal with information in operative business processes must have access to the information they need, so that they can turn it into value for the company [2, 3]. Hence providing the right information to those who need it is highly critical for a company's success.

Making the information exchange inside and outside the organization working properly is the main task of the information management. Anyhow supplying the right information to the right people appears to be quite difficult in practice [4, 5]. The situation for the people concerned ranges from getting no information to being confronted with an information overload [6]. There are manifold reasons why people who demand information are not supplied with it in the way they need to be, like cultural aspects, individual attitudes and unclear demands. Other reasons for problems in information sharing are the difficult handling of information systems, heterogeneous master data or an incomplete map of information sources in the information system landscape, to name but a view [6].

To cope with problems in information sharing, departments who need information usually begin with performing an information demand analysis. Information demand means all information that is needed in the organization to fulfil specific tasks [7]. Usually it is triggered in the planning and controlling process by the people who need the information. In this process it appears to be very time consuming to determine, what information is really needed, because people often claim to need more than they actually do or are not completely sure about what is actually important to them. The point is to make a difference between the real information demand and the information that is considered as useful or interesting to know. The information demand analysis specifies only the information that is needed in operational business processes or in the decision making process.

In order to estimate the information demand various techniques have been proposed, among them the analysis of reports and information systems, expert interviews or context driven analysis [8, 9]. In general only if the information that is needed has been clearly defined, it can be searched for and it can be supplied. The reverse way may lead to success as well. The supply-oriented approach is used to determine what information could potentially be provided by a source, instead of waiting for the consumers to ask for information [9]. If some part of the available information has been offered in the first place, the need for more information may arise later. In both, the demand- and the supply-oriented demand analysis, finally the target group determines what information is needed.

3 Social Network Analysis

Social network systems have a great potential to be deployed in a company for business tasks. Companies already use social network systems like Facebook for marketing purpose. Coca-Cola, for instance, publishes its company profile and news on Facebook. As a result almost ten million members of Facebook like the Coca-Cola page [10]. Social network systems offer a framework for modelling the connections between people; they support the creation of groups and profile pages, where people can maintain information about themselves [11]. Companies like IBM and SAP already use individually created social network systems for knowledge management purpose [11]. Employees who need information can search for a contact person who may help them and will provide a knowledge transfer.

Social network analysis deals with the connections between the members of a social network [12]. It has even been used to analyze the performance of the football teams which played in the fifa football world cup 2010 [13]. As a result it was possible to determine who in the games was an important player because of being involved in most of the passes. But social network analysis means far more than estimating who in a social network is the one with the most connections, or in other words, is a "hub". It is also interesting to get to know who connects two groups with each other. Such a person is called "broker" or "boundary spanner" and enables the sharing of information between two groups. Also the friend-of-a-friend analysis is possible in social network. With this people can be identified, who have a close distance to all others in the social network, though they do not know all of them personally. Instead they know the persons who stay in contact with many others [12].

Various approaches have been already proposed to characterize the relationship between nodes in a social network, which also can be referred to as a graph with nodes and edges. One of them is estimating the centrality of a node in order to characterize its relevance for the whole structure. There are three basic types of centrality: the degree, the betweenness and the closeness. The degree of a node is the number of nodes it is connected to through only one single edge, what means it is adjacent to. In order to be independent from the network size, this value is divided by the maximum possible number of nodes it could be connected to. The quotient is called the relative degree. Nodes with a high relative degree are a "hub", what implicates that they communicate a lot. The betweenness on the other hand is based upon the frequency a node appears on the shortest way between two other nodes. This makes a node becoming an "information broker" or "boundary spanner". The betweenness is a measure to determine if a node is in control of the communication in a network. As there can be more than one way to connect two nodes, the betweenness for a node must be divided through the number of possible ways between two nodes and thus expressed as a probability. To become independent from the network size, a relative centrality measure has been proposed, too. As the maximum value of betweenness appears only in a star schema, the value for a node is expressed in relation to that. The approach for measuring centrality called closeness has been founded on the idea of determining how independent a node's communication ability is from other nodes in the network. The higher the centrality value for a node is the less relay-nodes are on its way to others nodes [14].

Furthermore social network analysis does not only deal with individual nodes, it also considers the network as a whole. A centralized network, for example, is dominated by a few central nodes. These nodes are vital for the network because if they fail the network will stop working as it did before. In addition it has been proved that individuals have contact to a rather small group of people who are within 2 edges [12]. What is more the centrality approach has been extended in order to analyze, what groups the individuals belong to, in other terms what affiliation they have [15]. This means, it is possible to take into consideration what business topics their experience or interests cover and to identify those people in the company, who are in a key position of a particular subnet of the social network.

A popular software for social network analysis and the visualization of social networks is UCINET [16]. This software allows computing the values of centrality using social network data. The result is a social network analysis which helps to understand the characteristics of a particular social network and what the connections between the nodes in this structure are like.

4 Social Network Analysis for Information Brokering

The reason why social network analysis should be used for information brokering is that it minimizes the duration of the whole process, which starts with the information demand analysis and ends with the sharing of information. In order to create a concept about what data is needed in a business process people from different departments are to be involved. First, there is the department, which needs the information. Next, the departments, which supply the information, are involved. Last to be mentioned is the IT department. It implements the technical data flow.

Because of the huge amount of people and the time-consuming methodology used in the information demand analysis, information brokering can last quite a long time. To remedy the problem about the mass of people who participate in the analysis process, only people who may contribute valuably to the information demand analysis must be selected. The main challenge is to identify exactly those people, who know best what information is needed and what information can be supplied not only for themselves and their tasks, but also for the group they stay in contact to. To identify these people the informal structure in the company has to be examined. In practice, a social network analysis has to be performed in order to achieve the following goals.

- A faster and more practically oriented information demand analysis
- A faster supply with information to the people who need it
- A more precise description of the information demand
- Direct access to the target groups and the people in key positions who know what information is truly needed

What is more social network analysis makes it possible to meet the needs of the people in the company before they define it precisely themselves. A social network analysis considers groups of people. Thus also people who were not involved in the information demand analysis will get access to information. This shortens the time period until the information, that has been requested, is used in a business process.

The database tables that are used by Facebook will suite as an example for what data can be expected from a simple social network service [17]. All the tables that are listed in Table 1 can be joined on the data field "user".

Table 1. Selection of tables offered by Facebook

Title	Description
friend	information about whether two users are linked together as friends
friendlist	friend lists owned by the specified user
friendlist_member	information which users are members of a friend list
group	detailed information about a group
group_member	information about the members of a group
user	detailed information from a user's profile

The tables "friendlist_member" and "group_member" are most important for social network analysis, since the connection between two users and the connection between users and groups is saved in there. The tables "friend" and "friendlist" make a join of the entire friend*-tables possible for a more detailed analysis. The other tables "group" and "user" contain useful information to enhance the social network analysis with additional data. A query on the table "group", for example, supplies information about the groups that have been created and thus is important to select those, which are significant for a specific business task. Table no. 2, 3, 4, 5, 6 and 7 correspond to the data model of the database tables used in Facebook.

Table 2. Facebook table "friend"

Field name	Description
uid1	The user ID of the first user in the pair being queried
uid2	The user ID of the second user in the pair being queried

Table 3. Facebook table "friendlis"

Field name	Description
flid	The ID of the friend list
name	The name of the friend list
owner	The user ID of the user who created the friend list

Table 4. Facebook table "friendlist_member"

Field name	Description
flid	The ID of the friend list
uid	The user ID of the friend list member

Table 5. Facebook table "group"

Field name	Description
gid	the group ID of the group being queried
name	the name of the group being queried
nid	the network ID for the network to which the group belongs
description	The description of the group being queried
group_type	The category of the group being queried
group_subtype	The group type for the group being queried

Table 6. Facebook table "group_member"

Field name	Description
uid	the user ID of the member of the group being queried
gid	the ID of the group being queried

Table 7. Facebook table "user"

Field name	Description
uid	the user ID of the user being queried
first_name	the first name of the user being queried
last_name	the last name of the user being queried
affiliations	the networks to which the user being queried belongs

Unfortunately the findings that result from a social network analysis are not sufficient enough for a reliable information brokering. A social network usually develops through the action of the users without any influence from outside. Therefore the results may not be feasible for a business oriented analysis, because a group or affiliation in the social network may not correspond to any business topic. Hence a social network service which is implemented in a company for business tasks must have certain structures, which can be expanded by the users, but will keep a connection to the business topic. Of course not all groups and affiliations will deal with business tasks, but most of them should. To make sure that a social network analysis concentrates on business structures, thus the groups and affiliations can be filtered for analysis purpose.

Furthermore the focus should be amplified on people, who are business experts or belong to the lower and middle management level. This can be only achieved, if user-data from the social network is combined with master data from the HR information system. Not before a user's job description and organizational allocation are considered in the analysis, a reliable prediction of people in true key positions can be made. And only then the result of the analysis can be used for information brokering, because thereby those people are identified, who can provide valuable suggestions about the information demand of the people they stay in contact to.

The analysis of such a social network will result in a set of people, who need to be consulted in an information demand analysis or informed, that new information is available for being used in business processes which they are involved in. Now the information demand analysis can be performed with only a few people, who indeed know, what kind of information is needed in the group. This makes the whole information brokering process less complex and time consuming. Also the changes that have to be made to the concept later on are minimized because the right people have been involved in the discussion from the beginning. In the practical scenario members of HR department have to determine what kind of data they need for their job. Without the social network analysis a classic information demand analysis would be necessary. Most of the employees and their supervisors would have to be interviewed. However because of the findings from the social network analysis it would be possible to interview the "hubs" or "information brokers" first. They are less people than all the employees and supervisors together, but can give a good view about what information will be needed. If the HR master data of the people is considered, too, then the optimal participants can be selected even more precisely. For example, one of the people might not be in the position to claim knowing what kind of information the controllers need, because he is neither a supervisor nor has to do with HR at all. He may just be interested in controlling.

5 Experiment Results

According to the social network analysis approach internal auditing decided to implement a customized social network service and to use a data model which was very like the one Facebook implemented. As there was no social network service in the company, the data had to be generated from business process models and service quality surveys. In these surveys the employees had to name who in the company they have frequently a business oriented contact to and if they were satisfied with the quality of the collaboration. Thus the tables "user", "friendlist" and "friendlist_member" could be filled. The tables "group", "group_member" and "user" could not be derived from the survey information. As only a small group of people had to be analyzed, internal auditing decided to create groups along the lines of the business processes the people are working in and to allocate them manually with the help of the team leaders. In this manner the data base for the social network analysis was fully created. In addition HR master data has been added to the datasets, so that the information content was improved. Subsequently internal auditing performed a social network analysis and drew conclusions.

The results from the social network analysis have been used by internal auditing in order to suggest people, who should have been members of the information demand analysis instead of the former project team. Table 8 compares the former project members and the suggested people, including the normalized degree of centrality that has been estimated by the social network analysis. It is defined as the degree of centralisation divided by the maximum possible value in the network in the way like it has been described before. For a given binary network with vertices ($v_1;v_n$) and a maximum degree centrality c_{max}, UCINET measures the network degree centralization as $\sum(c_{max} - c(v_i))$ divided by the maximum value possible, where $c(v_i)$ is the degree centrality of vertex v_i [16].

Table 8. Result of the social network analysis (based on centrality measures)

Former information demand analysis members	Recommended people by internal auditing
HR controlling team leader (project leader)	HR controlling team leader (project leader) (norm. degree: 5.34 %)
Senior controller (strategic HR fte-planning)	HR head office clerks responsible for head offices (norm. degree: 18.32 %)
Senior controller (strategic HR cost-planning	HR branch office clerks responsible for branch offices (norm. degree: 15.27 %)
Controller	Organization department analyst (norm. degree: 9.16 %)
	HR branch office senior clerk (norm. degree: 6.87 %)
	Senior controller (strategic HR fte-planning) (norm. degree: 3.82 %)
	Senior controller (strategic HR cost-planning (norm. degree: 3.82 %)

The comparison indicates that there are people in the target group of the BI system, who were important for the information demand analysis, but did not take place in the project. People with a high relative centrality value $c(v_i)$ are in true key positions as far as information sharing in HR-reporting and HR-planning are concerned. Neither the HR department chief nor the team leaders were in true key positions of the social network. Because of the strict distinction between the tasks of clerks and executives the team leaders were not deeply involved in operative tasks. The department chief only gave instructions to the team leaders, but did not care about details in operative business processes. Just the same did the team leaders in relation to the clerks. As a consequence not the team leaders but some of the clerks should have participated in the information demand analysis instead. They have the highest relative centrality degree in the whole social network (18.32% and 15.27%). What is more, the importance of the organization department has been severely underestimated in the project. In the social network analysis it has been ranked on third position after the clerks. Still important are members of the HR controlling team, although their centrality values are not the highest ones. Fig. 1 shows the generated structure of the social network for HR-reporting and HR-planning according to the computed centrality values by UCINET.

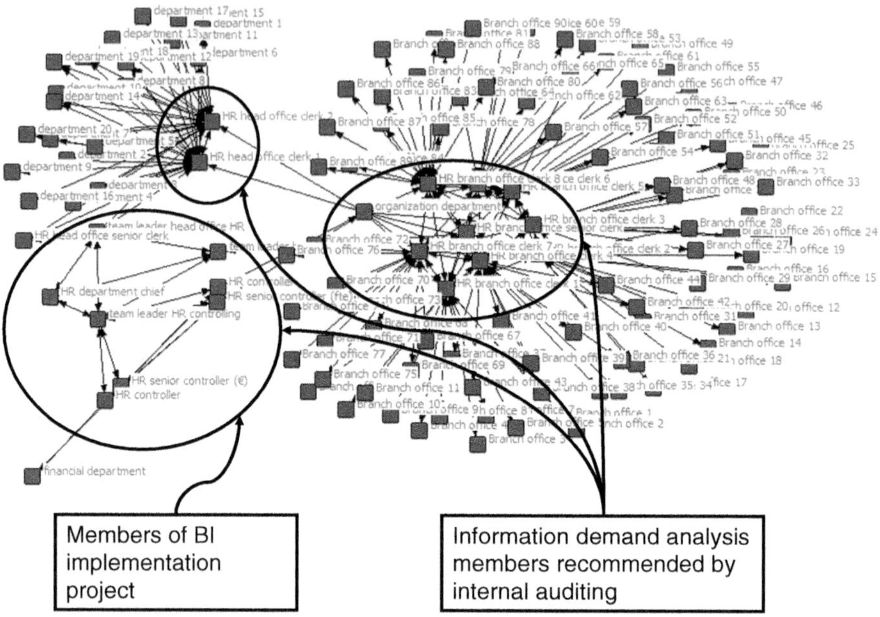

Fig. 1. Visualized result of a social network analysis (created with UCINET)

6 Conclusions

The analysis of social networks should become a part of the information demand analysis methodology. If it had been used prior to the mentioned BI project, the information demand analysis probably would have been more useful and the project may have been a success for many others instead of HR controlling team only. With social network analysis the information demand analysis becomes much faster and more accurate, because people who know very well about the information needs in their social network are pointed out. Without them, the information demand analysis is imitated to the persons that are on certain positions in the company and thus it may fail or will become far more complex due to a large group of people being involved.

Adding master data as node attributes in the social network analysis allows the analysts to limit the result to a group of people, who are not only connected to many others, but are also business experts. If the social network service inside a company has been structured, so that groups and affiliations can be referred to as a part of a business process or even a main task in the company like controlling, data mining or accounting, the social network data becomes worth to be considered, too. But also without considering the affiliations the social network analysis still is useful. In this case the HR master data becomes even more important to identify business experts or members of certain organizational units.

If social network services are used in a company or the implementation of such software is planned, the opportunities for social network analysis must be also considered in order to take advantage of the information the employees will share on the network. A survey published by Gartner claims, that still many companies do not take advantage from social network services for their business [18]. The goal must be to create a social network service that can be used for business tasks, too. This includes easy to use interfaces to the data tables and a master data management for HR data integration to make a comprehensive social network analysis possible.

References

1. Drucker, P.: The Age of Social Transformation. The Atlantic Monthly (November edition, 1994)
2. Bauer, A., Günzel, H.: Data-Warehouse-Systeme, Architektur, Entwicklung, Anwendung. Dpunkt, Heidelberg (2004)
3. Porter, M., Millar, V.E.: How Information Gives You Competitive Advantage (1985)
4. Manhart, K.: Business Intelligence: Informationsverteilung und Wissensmanagement (2008), http://www.tecchannel.de/server/sql/1742647/business_intelligence_teil_6_informationsverteilung_und_wissensmanagement/
5. Dippold, R., Meier, A., Ringgenberg, A., Schnider, W., Schwinn, K.: Unternehmensweites Datenmanagement: Von der Datenbankadministration bis zum Informationsmanagement. Vieweg, Wiesbaden (2001)
6. Krcmar, H.: Informationsmanagement. Springer, Berlin (2000)
7. Müller, J., Wildau, N.: Basis Kompendium für Controller. Josef Eul. Köln (2009)
8. Lundqvist, M., Sandkuhl, K., Levashova, T., Smirnov, A.: Context-Driven Information Demand Analysis in Information Logistics and Decision Support Practices (2005), http://www.aaai.org/Papers/Workshops/2005/WS-05-01/WS05-01-022.pdf
9. Schulze, C.: Hybride Modellierung operativer und analytischer Daten, dargestellt am Beispiel des Precision Dairy Farming, Martin-Luther-Universität Halle-Wittenberg (2008)
10. Coca-Cola (2010), http://www.Facebook.com/home.php?#!/cocacola?ref=ts&a=8&ajaxpipe=1
11. Koch, M., Richter, A., Schlosser, A.: Produkte zum IT-gestützten Social Networking in Unternehmen. Wirtschaftsinformatik 49(6), 448–455 (2007)
12. Carrington, P.J., Scott, J., Wasserman, S.: Models and Methods in Social Network Analysis. Cambridge Press, Cambridge (2005)
13. WordPress: Blogs about Social Network Analysis (2010), http://scientometrics.wordpress.com/2010/07/11/preview-netherlands-vs-spain/
14. Freeman, L.: Centrality in social networks. Conceptual clarification. Social Networks 1(3), 215–239 (1979)
15. Borgatti, S.P., Halgin, D.S.: Analyzing Affiliation Networks. LINKS Center for Social Network Analysis. Gatton College of Business and Economics. University of Kentucky. Lexington (2010), http://www.steveborgatti.com/papers/bhaffiliations.pdf
16. UCINET, http://www.analytictech.com/ucinet/
17. Facebook, http://www.facebook.com/developers
18. Gartner: Gartner Says Business Potential of Social Networking Web Sites Remains Largely Untapped (2008), http://www.gartner.com/it/page.jsp?id=718107

A Distributed Catalog for Digitized Cultural Heritage

Bojan Marinković[1], Luigi Liquori[2], Vincenzo Ciancaglini[2], and Zoran Ognjanović[1]

[1] Mathematical Institute of the Serbian Academy of Sciences and Arts, Serbia
{bojanm,zorano}@mi.sanu.ac.rs
[2] Institut National de Recherche en Informatique et Automatique, France
{luigi.liquori,vincenzo.ciancaglini}@sophia.inria.fr

Abstract. Peer-to-peer networks have emerged recently as a flexible decentralized solution to handle large amount of data without the use of high-end servers. In this paper we present a distributed catalog built up on an overlay network called "Synapse". The Synapse protocol allows interconnection of different overlay networks each of them being an abstraction of a "community" of virtual providers. Data storage and data retrieval from different kind of content providers (*i.e.* libraries, archives, museums, universities, research centers, etc.) can be stored inside one catalog. We illustrate the concept based on the Synapse protocol: a catalog for digitized cultural heritage of Serbia.

Keywords: Peer-to-peer, Distributed databases, DHT-based Overlay networks, Information retrieval, Digitized cultural heritage.

1 Introduction

1.1 Context

Digitization is an important step towards preservation and promotion of heritage. It safeguards cultural diversity in the global environment and offers a rich treasure to the world-wide public of the Web. Usually, digitization can be seen as a collection of activities, including digital capture, transformation from analogue to digital form, description and representation of heritage objects and documentation about them, processing, presentation and long-term preservation of digitized content, etc.

The document [13] states that current digitization practice in SEE is still not matching the priorities communicated on the EU-level and that the rich cultural content of the region is still underrepresented in the electronic space. One of the main principles accepted by the participants states that "It is recognized that knowledge of the cultural and scientific heritage is essential for taking decisions concerning its digitization and for interpreting the digitized resources. For this reason, inventorying and cataloging should precede or accompany the digitization of cultural and scientific assets."

At the moment, there is no widespread meta-data standard for describing digitized heritage in Serbia. Actually, although most of the institutions caring about national heritage have started the digitization process, there is no meta-data standard formally accepted at the state level. Because of that we are faced with something that can be called *the meta-data problem*. Different providers of heritage resources (libraries, museums, archives, some research institutions) use international standards appropriate for

M. Gusev and P. Mitrevski (Eds.): ICT Innovations 2010, CCIS 83, pp. 176–186, 2011.

their specific fields, or ad-hoc methods, or old procedures for describing cultural assets in classical format (formulated in 1980s or early 1990s). In fact, some providers are still waiting for some solution of the meta-data problem and do not do anything related to digital cataloging. This means that digital catalogs in Serbia, if they exist at all, cannot help in communication between different kinds of providers and users.

On the other hand, at the international level, there are plenty of meta-data standards for describing heritage resources, for example: Dublin Core [9], EAD [10], MARC [12], TEL AP [15], FRBR [14, 11], etc.

Given all of the aforementioned, the Committee for digitization of the UNESCO commission of Serbia has recognized the meta-data problem as the most sophisticated one in the cataloging phase of digitization. During the past years, some efforts were made in the field of standardization, which resulted in the development of the recommendation for the meta-data format described in [7], but this recommendation has not, still, been accepted as a formal national standard.

There were also some efforts directed towards developing technology for storing these meta-data documents, but there is still no widespread application. Recent attempts to create digital repositories, such as, for example, Europeana [16], are mostly based on centralized architectures. Here we consider an alternative, decentralized approach, based on overlay networks.

Overlay networks have recently been identified as a promising model to cope with the Internet issues of today, such as scalability, resource discovery, failure recovery, routing efficiency, and, in particular in the context of information retrieval. Many disparate overlay networks may not only simultaneously co-exist in the Internet, but can also compete for the same resources on shared nodes and underlying network links. This can provide an opportunity to collect data on various kind of digitized documents which are, by their nature, highly distributed resources, while keeping backward compatibility, efficient searching, failure resistance, etc. One of the problems of the overlay networking area is how different overlay networks may *interact* and *cooperate* with each other. Overlay networks are heterogeneous, and basically unable to cooperate with each other in an effortless way, without merging, an operation which is very costly since it is not scalable and not suitable in many cases for security reasons. However, in many situations, distinct overlay networks can take advantage of cooperating for many purposes: collective performance enhancement, larger shared information, better resistance to loss of connectivity (network partitions), improved routing performance in terms of delay, throughput and packets loss, by, for instance, cooperative forwarding of flows.

In the context of large scale information retrieval, several overlays may want to offer an aggregation of their resources to their potential common users without losing control of them. Imagine two companies wishing to share or aggregate information contained in their distributed databases, obviously while keeping their proprietary routing and their exclusive right to update it. In terms of fault-tolerance, cooperation can increase the availability of the system – if one overlay becomes unavailable the global network will only undergo partial failure as other distinct resources will be usable. The solution could be found in using a meta-protocol which allows a request to be routed through multiple overlays, where one overlay contains one kind of institutions, even using different routing algorithms, thus increasing the success rate of every request.

The ready-to-market DHT(Distributed Hash Tables)-based technology of structured overlay networks is enriched with the new capability of crossing different overlays through *co-located nodes*, *i.e.* by peers who are, by user's choice, member of several overlays [8]. Such nodes are themselves able not only to query multiple overlays in order to find a match, but also to replicate requests passing through them from one network to another and to collect the multiple results.

1.2 Problem Overview

In the digitization of catalog services, using an Information System (IS) has been shown to be essential in matching the offers, the requests, and the resources. The IS is, in most cases, a front-end web site connected to a back-end database. A classical client-server architecture is usually sufficient to manage those services. In presence of multiple services, for technical and/or commercial reasons, it is not possible to share contents across different providers, despite the evident advantage. In most cases, ISs are not suitable to communicate in any of their features (lookup, search, etc.). Although, in general, this does not affect the correct behavior of an IS, it is clear that interoperability would increase the overall quality of the service. Moreover, the classical shortcomings of client-server architectures make both services unavailable in case both servers are down. Any attempt to make different and disconnected institutional, client-server based architectures, does not foresee any form of service interconnection, with the unpleasant consequence of losing potential matches between offers and requests between users of different communities on the same subject.

As a basic example, let us consider two cultural institutions which contain digital documents inside their databases. One node of the first database stores one volume which is searched for by a node of the second one. Without "inter-network" co-operation, these two databases would never communicate together. But, if these ISs do co-operate with each other, the results can be far more precise and accurate.

As we said above, the digitized documents are, by their nature, highly distributed resources. Because of this, we decided to develop a catalog based on Synapse protocol as a real-life proof-of-concept. Here we analyze how the Synapse protocol [8] can be used as a tool to connect a huge number of content providers.

1.3 Outline

The rest of paper is organized as follows: In Section 2 we summarize some mechanisms proposed in the literature related to distributed systems and describes briefly the interconnection of different distributed catalogs by means of our Synapse protocol. In Section 3 we introduce an idea of a distributed catalog service and show how it is mapped onto a DHT. In Section 4 we show a running example with a proof-of-concept which we have implemented on the base of a real case of study. Section 5 describes the results of the deployment of a client prototype tested over a distributed platform at Mathematical Insitute. In Section 6 we present our conclusions and ideas for further work. [1]

[1] The developed software and all of the results of the tests are available at the web-page `http://www.mi.sanu.ac.rs/~bojanm/synapse`.

2 Related Work and Contributions

2.1 Related Work

The classical viewpoint on distributed databases, as it is described in [1], defines desirable properties for distributed database management systems (DBMS). These properties are: *distributed data independence*, an opportunity to send queries without specifying where the referenced relations are located, and *distributed transaction atomicity*, an opportunity to access and update data at several sites just as they would write transactions over purely local data. Depending on whether the data is distributed over the same DBMS software or not, we distinguish homogeneous and heterogeneous distributed database systems. In situations where these systems are heterogeneous, we have to establish gateway protocols.

In these systems, data is usually distributed by *fragmentation*, when fragments of data are divided over several sites. This fragmentation can be *horizontal*, when each fragment consists of a subset of rows of original relation, and *vertical*, when each fragment consists of a subset of columns of the original relation. Fragmentation is followed with replication of data and several copies of one fragment are stored in the system. We must keep track of how the relations are fragmented and replicated, which can be be complicated. The catalog of this track-keeping can be centralized, in which case the entire system would be vulnerable to failure of the site which contains the catalog, or also distributed, in which case the biggest issue is maintaining data consistency.

In [3], the authors have developed a multi-ring model based on Chord, in which each shared resource is described by one or more keywords. Nodes are organized in multiple keyword rings, and each node in a keyword ring contains the list of nodes that host resources matching a certain keyword/value pair. A new keyword ring is created only when the number of queries or registered resources for the keyword rises above a certain threshold. To enable keyword rings to be found, a Super Ring is used to host a ring of nodes which contain pointers to other rings. One major drawback of the model is that it heavily depends on the bootstrap node.

ML-Chord, presented in [6], is a multi-layered P2P resource sharing model which introduces overlay layers of categories. The number of these categories depends on the number of categories for a specific domain or ontology. Also, two types of nodes are introduced : *normal peers*, which can be associated with one or several layers and *bridge peers*, which are peers with better capabilities, linked to all categories and themselves form a category as well. The problem with this approach is that it is not possible to simply encapsulate a new system into an existing one because all of the Chord layers share the same hash function. Although this system is scalable and efficient, it is not possible to easly introduce a new category during the system lifetime. The developers suggest that one node should be linked to only one layer for better performance. So, if a node with good capabilities has not become a bridge peer at the start of the lifecycle of the system, it will remain a normal node, and its beneficial capabilities will be lost.

2.2 Interconnecting Different Overlay Networks

As said in the introduction, co-operation of different ISs implemented via overlay networks is a challenging problem which make pragmatical benefit in the context of this paper, namely catalog digitization. In the context of large scale information retrieval, several overlays may want to offer an aggregation of their information/data to their potential common users without losing control of it. One may perceive that having a single global overlay has many obvious advantages and is the *de facto* most natural solution: unfortunately it appears unrealistic in many real cases. In some optimistic case, different overlays are suitable for co-operation by opening their proprietary protocols in order to build an open standard; in many other pessimistic cases, this opening is simply unrealistic for many different reasons (backward compatibility, security, commercial, practical, etc.).

The catalog we present in this paper is based on *Synapse* [8], a scalable protocol for information retrieval over the inter-connection of heterogeneous overlay networks. The protocol is based on co-located nodes, also called *synapses*, serving as low-cost natural candidates for inter-overlay bridges. In the simplest case, where overlays to be interconnected are ready to adapt their protocols to the requirements of interconnection, every message received by a co-located node can be forwarded to other overlays that node belongs to. In other words, upon receipt of a search query, in addition to its forwarding to the next hop in the current overlay, according to their routing policy, the node can possibly start a new search, according to some given strategy, in some or all other overlay networks it belongs to. This obviously implies that a Time-To-Live value has to be provided and detection of already processed queries implemented, so as to avoid infinite looping in the networks, as it is the case in unstructured peer-to-peer systems. Applications of top of Synapse see those inter-overlays as a unique overlay.

Experiments and simulations, we run, showed that a small number of well-connected synapses is sufficient in order to achieve almost exhaustive searches in a "synapsed" network of structured overlay networks. We believe that Synapse can give an answer to circumventing network partitions; the key points being that:

- several logical links for one node lead to many alternative physical routes through these overlay, and
- a synapse can retrieve keys from overlays that it does not even know, simply by forwarding the query to another synapse that, in turn, is better connected.

For more details on the Synapse protocol, see [8].

2.3 Contribution

Our intention is not to give a final solution for a new concept of DBMS, but to show an idea that it is possible to establish a DBMS with desirable properties, which can connect heterogenous DHTs in a homogenous way and which can be easily expanded, without real fragmentation of data, while keeping the property of load balance and good performance of a whole system. Also, we will show that this system is applicable to real-life situations.

3 Application Principles

One of the main features of a distributed catalog is to assist researchers and members of the wider community in retrieving information concerning some fact of interest, information which can be provided from different kinds of sources. As mentioned before, digitized documents, by their nature, are highly distributed resources. By connecting different kinds of data providers into one system, the quality of the resulting information can be increased.

In this paper, we consider a distributed catalog which contains only meta-data on digital documents which follows a part of the Recommendation for the meta-data format for describing digitized heritage, described in [7]. One of the main reasons for this is the intellectual property rights issue. Simply, some institutions do not wish to outsource control over their digital repositories, and, instead, choose only to publish the information that they are in possession of a certain document. The digital documents themselves can be retrieved with one of the meta-data fields which contains information on their actual remote location.

A user can connect to one or more communities which he is member of (i. e. he has been invited to or his request has been accepted). Two operations are then available, namely: (i) storing a new record and (ii) finding a record which contains some information.

Suppose we wish to store the following information on a digital object:

```
<digitalObject>
  <title>Title</title>
  <creator>Name</creator>
  <location>link</location>
  <relatedAsset>
     Realife object</relatedAsset>
  <note>
    <src lang ="
     language of the value">value</src>
  </note>
  <archivalDate>date</archivalDate>
  <mimeFormat>mime type</mimeFormat>
  <digitalObjectOwner>
     Owner</digitalObjectOwner>
</digitalObject>
```

XML metadata record

Table 1. Different data structures stored in the distributed catalog DHT for each entry

No.	Key	Value
1	$title\sharp Title$	$hash$(✠)
2	$creator\sharp Name$	$hash$(✠)
3	$relatedAsset\sharp realifeObject$	$hash$(✠)
4	$mimeFormat\sharp mimeType$	$hash$(✠)
5	$digitalObjectOwner\sharp Owner$	$hash$(✠)
6	$hash$(✠)	✠

where ✠ represents the full meta-data record on one digital document

If we were to decide to make the catalog searchable for the values in the fields: *title*, *creator*, *relatedAsset*, *mimeFormat* and *digitalObjectOwner*, then we would store segments in accordance with Table 1.

More precisely:

1. For every field of a meta-data record which we choose to be searchable, the hashed value for the current overlay of the entire meta-data record as value with the key which contains information about the field and its value is stored (rows 1 to 5 in table 1).
2. The entire meta-data record as a value with the corresponding key that contains its hashed value for the current overlay is stored (row 6 in table 1).

Note that all of the keys are stored with their hashed values. With this in place, the search mechanism has two phases. During the first phase, we attempt to find the hashed value

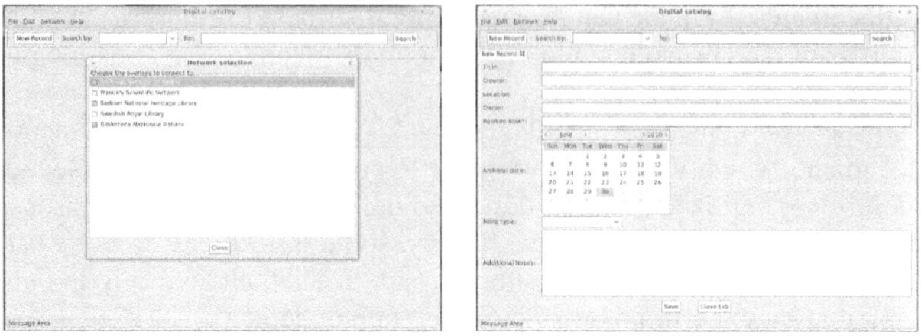

(a) Connecting to an overlay (b) Record insertion form

Fig. 1. Connecting and Inserting

of the meta-data record (the first kind of entries) and then, during the second phase, to find the entire meta-data record (the second kind of entries) only in the overlays which contain the first kind of entries. Although we have multiple copies of data, so as to accomplish failure resistance of the system, the storage space is of the same complexity as for a standard DBMS with indices. If N and M are the number of overlays and the number of nodes per overlay, respectively, then the time complexity of a search, in the worst case, is $O((N+1) * (\textit{time to search an overlay with M nodes}))$.

4 Case Study

Institutions which are interested in sharing meta-data information on their digital documents can be connected in different overlays by their nature. So, all archives may be a part of one overlay, all libraries of the other, and similarly with museums, research centers, universities, etc. These overlays can be connected by institutions which contain various kind of content, like research centers with important libraries or research centers which are part of the universities, etc. All of these institutions would run the same application.

The following proof-of-concept is a simple application to store and retrieve records from one or multiple overlays. It offers the following three functionalities, arranged in a Graphical User Interface developed in Java, for cross-platform compatibility:

- **Joining** of a new network,
- **Storing** of a new record,
- **Searching** for records.

The application is designed using a tabbed organization of different forms. This is to allow the user to easily perform multiple operations at the same time (*e.g.* doing multiple queries and comparing the results). Furthermore, it constitutes a familiar usage environment, resembling, in the approach, most of modern Internet browsers (multiple tabs, address/search on a top bar). Basic editing features, like saving and loading a record to and from an XML file, copying/pasting and printing the XML raw data, are provided.

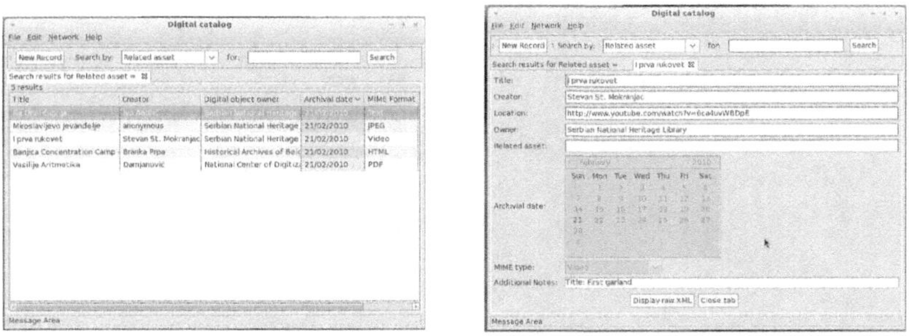

(a) Search results for a query (b) Details of a retrieved record

Fig. 2. Searching and Retrieving

Network join. As shown in Figure 1a, upon starting, the program will propose to the user a list of known DHTs to connect to. These represent existing overlays put in place using the same system, which are, therefore, compatible with our software. It is important to notice that, after having connected to a first overlay, a user can choose to further join other available networks. This can be done via the menu entry Network → Join, which will propose the same dialog box as in Figure 1a.

Once being a member of multiple overlays, not only it becomes possible to query all of the overlays simultaneously, but, thanks to the capabilities of the synapse protocol described in Section 2.2, it will also be possible to act as a relay, replicating requests from one overlay to another.

Storing a new record. Figure 1b shows the insertion form for a new record in the DHT.

In this catalog we store the records which follow a part of the mentioned recommendation of the meta-data format:

- **Title** of the digital document (*i.e.* electronic book)
- **Name of the author** who made electronic version
- **Link** of the remote location of the digital document
- **Related object** (*i.e.* hard copy book)
- **Note** or a short description
- **Date** when electronic copy was made
- **Mime type** (*i.e.* pdf)
- **Owner** of the digital object

While some of the fields may be optional, the ones used as search criteria have to be filled before the record can be saved. Therefore, the "Save" button remains disabled until all of the appropriate text boxes are filled.

Record searching. Looking for a record takes place in a way resembling the behavior of most modern Internet browsers: as one can see in Figure 2a, the search type and field are in the upper toolbar. Here the user can choose the type of search to perform (title, author, owner, related object, mime type) and fill the search key. By pressing the "Search" button, a query for the corresponding key is performed in the overlay (or overlays, if synapses are present or the software is connected to multiple networks). A

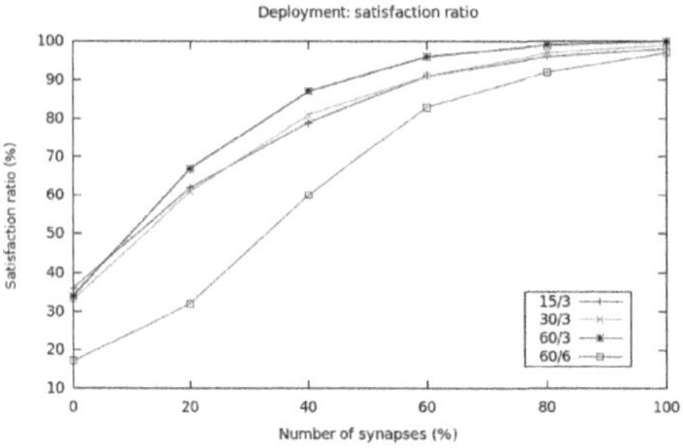

(a) Exhaustiveness

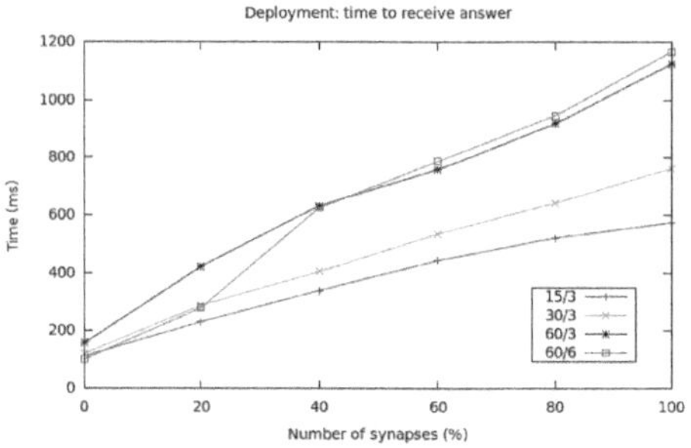

(b) Latency

Fig. 3. Deploying Synapse

result summary is displayed in a new tab once the query is over, containing the number of records found and a table with all the records.

To display the details of a record the user can double-click on the corresponding row in the table. This (showed in Figure 2b) will open a new tab containing record details.

The details tab is similar to the new record form, except that the text fields cannot be edited (although it is still possible to select and copy the text inside).

The button "Display raw XML" will open a new dialog showing the actual XML data.

5 Experiments

In order to test our inter-overlay protocol, as a ground base of our catalog, we have developed open-synapse software. It is based on the open-chord v. 1.0.5 implementation, developed by Distributed and Mobile Systems Group Lehrstuhl fuer Praktische Informatik Universitaet Bamberg, which is, essentialy, a Java implementation of the Chord protocol. This platform fully implements a Chord-based inter-overlay network, but to achieve the goal of connecting heterogenous overlay networks, we have decided that in our implementation every Chord ring has its own hash function. The experiments were realized on an IBM Beowulf Cluster 1350. During the tests we have started 5 logical nodes at each of up to 12 working nodes. The nodes have been uniformly dispatched over 3 or 6 overlays, and during deployment, the overlays were progressively bridged by synapses (the degree of each logical node was never greater than 2). So, we did tests with 15, 30 and 60 nodes uniformly dispatched over 3 overlays and 60 nodes uniformly dispatched over 6 overlays.

Figure (3a) shows the satisfaction ratio when increasing the number of synapses. By the satisfaction ratio we mean the percentige of the succesfull answers for the vaules that are, already, inserted into the system. It can be seen that a quasi-exhaustiveness has been achieved when the synapses are members of only 2 overlays. Note that the satisfaction ratio confirms the simulation results, which are available in [8].

Figure (3b) shows the average elapsed time from the moment a query is sent to some node in the system until the moment when the answer is received. This time was not so short, but this is due to the configuration of the cluster. We suppose that these results could be illustration of the performance in a real-life situation, in which the nodes would not be members of networks which are within the same infrastructure.

6 Conclusion

In this paper we have shown that the Synapse protocol has good potential as a new concept of DBMS. With this concept, it is possible to connect heterogenous DHTs in a homogenous way. We have proven the scalability of this protocol and its applicability to a real-life situation.

Since we cannot guarantee full exhaustiveness of information retrieval, we have decided that the procedure of removing/updating items should currently be out of scope of our research. The reason for this is that the only one who may remove or update items inside the catalog should be the one who inserted them in the first place, thus guaranteeing the highest probability of data consistency. For this, we would first need to implement a User Management System, for instance, by implementing cryptographic technics into our system, as described in [4].

As mentioned before, within this system we can also store the digital documents themselves. We have also decided that in the current phase, this should be out of scope of this paper, but we consider this to be a possible continuation of our research.

As a positive side-effect, we believe that our catalog can lay promising groundwork for a low-cost solution to cultural interconnection of the institutions inside the region.

Acknowledgment. The authors warmly thank Petar Maksimović and Cédric Tedeschi for their precious suggestions during the writing of this paper.

References

1. Ramakrishnan, R., Gehrke, J.: Database Management Systems. McGraw Hill, New York (2000); ISBN: 0-07-246535-2
2. Stoica, I., Morris, R., Karger, D., Kaashoek, M., Balakrishnan, H.: Chord: A Scalable Peer-to-Peer Lookup service for Internet Applications. In: ACM SIGCOMM, pp. 149–160 (2001)
3. Antonopoulos, N., Salter, J., Peel, R.: A multi-ring method for efficient multi- dimensional data lookup in p2p networks. In: Proceedings of the 1st International Conference on Scalable Information Systems (2006)
4. Avramidis, A., Kotzanikolaou, P., Douligeris, C.: Chord-PKI: Embedding a Public Key Infrastructure into the Chord Overlay Network Public Key Infrastructure. Springer, Heidelberg (2007); ISBN: 978-3-540-73407-9
5. Liquori, L., Tedeschi, C., Bongiovanni, F.: BabelChord: a Social Tower of DHT-Based Overlay Networks. In: 14th Symposium on Computers and Communications (ISCC 2009). IEEE, Los Alamitos (2009) (short paper)
6. Lu, E.J.-L., Huang, Y.-F., Lu, S.-C.: ML-Chord: A multi-layered P2P resource sharing model. Journal of Network and Computer Applications 32, 578–588 (2009)
7. Ognjanović, Z., Butigan-Vučaj, T., Marinković, B.: NCD Recommendation for the National Standard for Describing Digitized Heritage in Serbia. In: Metadata and Semantics, p. 978. Springer, Heidelberg (2009); ISBN: 978-0-387-77744-3

8. Liquori, L., Tedeschi, C., Vanni, L., Bongiovanni, F., Ciancaglini, V., Marinković, B.: Synapse: A Scalable Protocol for Interconnecting Heterogeneous Overlay Networks. Networking (2010)
9. The Dublin Core Metadata Initiative, http://dublincore.org/
10. Encoded Archival Description, http://www.loc.gov/ead/
11. IFLA Study Group, Functional Requirements for Bibliographic Records (1998), http://www.ifla.org/VII/s13/frbr/frbr.pdf
12. MARC Standards, http://www.loc.gov/marc/
13. Recommendations for coordination of digitization of cultural heritage in South-Eastern Europe, Conclusions of the Regional Meeting on Digitization of Cultural Heritage, Ohrid, Macedonia, March 17-20 (2005); Review of the National Center for Digitization, 2-7 (2005), http://elib.mi.sanu.ac.rs/files/journals/ncd/7/ncd07002.pdf
14. A weblog about FRBR: Functional Requirements for Bibliographic Records (2007), http://www.frbr.org/
15. The European Library, http://www.theeuropeanlibrary.org/
16. Europeana, http://europeana.eu/portal/

Toward an Integration Technology Selection Model for Information Systems Integration in Supply Chains

Dania Pérez Armayor[1], José Antonio Díaz Batista[1], and Jorge Marx Gómez[2]

[1] Polytechnic University of Havana (CUJAE), Cuba
dania@ind.cujae.edu.cu
diaztony@tesla.cujae.edu.cu
[2] Carl von Ossietzky University Oldenburg, Germany
jorge.marx.gomez@uni-oldenburg.de

Abstract. The need to satisfy a more demanding customer in a scenery where deadlines and costs must be ever smaller to maintain competitiveness, together with increased uncertainty about demand, has been leading organizations to collaborate to such a level that now the competition is not between isolated enterprises, but between supply chains. The integration of information systems in such environment is a recognized problem, aggravated by the selection complexity of a combination of technologies to support, to the greatest possible extent, the supply chain performance. This paper proposes an approach for a decision support model based on compensatory fuzzy logic, to facilitate the selection of technologies to be used for integrating the information systems in a supply chain.

Keywords: Decision Support, Integration Technology Selection, Supply Chain, Compensatory Fuzzy Logic.

1 Introduction

The growing need to continually reduce delivery times and decrease overall costs in order to satisfy the needs of an increasingly more exigent customer before the competition does, plus the increasing uncertainty in the demand, has paved the way for inter-organizational collaboration. This has led businesses to group them self into supply chains, replacing competition among enterprises by competition among supply chains [1, 2]. In these scenario *supply chain management* (SCM) emerged as an inter-organizational collaboration challenge that requires a decision making process based on the latest and best information from every component of the chain in order to archive a better total system performance rather than optimization of single members [1, 3].

Such inter-organizational collaboration is based on the intensive use of *information systems* (IS) supported by *information and communication technologies* (ICT). Yet, many of these existing IS were not designed to exchange information among them, or to use that exchanged information [2, 4], increasing the difficulties to reach an integrated supply network. As a solution the *enterprise application integration* (EAI) is being increasingly used, allowing the use of existing technologies in the inter-organizational environment, incorporating functionalities from disparate applications

M. Gusev and P. Mitrevski (Eds.): ICT Innovations 2010, CCIS 83, pp. 187–194, 2011.

and leading to cheaper, more functional and manageable ICT infrastructures, as well as making easier the investment returns, the cost reductions and the collaboration among the involved entities [2, 4, 5].

However, the complexity regarding the permutations of integration technologies that can be used to piece together IS remains as an important barrier to achieve the benefits expected from SCM, due to the inexistence of a unique solution able to solve all the integration problems [2, 5].

This paper proposes an approach for a decision support model based on *compensatory fuzzy logic* (CFL), to facilitate the selection of technologies to use for integrating the information systems in a supply chain.

2 Technology Selection Problem

The evolution of the information systems has been conditioned to the satisfaction of departmental functions, resulting in a surplus of different applications, each one responding to particular subsystem objectives that has proven to be dissimilar, and even contradictories [1], generating isolated information systems with a very negative impact on the global business efficiency and their effectiveness [6].

The need to give coordinate answers, in continuously decreasing time frames, to an ever more exigent customer leads to an information exchange necessity between the existing areas of work, and later on, between different enterprises in the supply chain frame [1, 7]. Integration of IS becomes a necessity to guarantee continuous and harmonic information flow across the system [4, 8]. Yet the existing autonomous, unrelated systems were not made to collaborate among them, which means that they are unable to exchange information, or use such information, holding related data without the proper global administration [4, 9].

There are many technologies to connect information systems, but none of them have claim to beat all the integration problems and, therefore, it is necessary the use of combinations [2] that must be different according to the integration requirements of the supply chains [1, 10]. So, the problem is which combination fits better a given integration necessity, but the lack of tools that support these processes [5] affects the supply chain managers as much as the technology developers.

The variety of integration technologies, the various functionalities that are partially or completely repeated in many technologies or the quality with which these technologies perform their functions are a known barrier in the selecting process of the combination in which supply chain members should invest to obtain certain benefits [2, 5].

Related with the evaluation of technologies to use in integrating information in a supply chain several investigations [2, 9, 11, 12] can be mentioned, among them the framework proposed by Themistocleous, Irani and Love [2] can be used as reference for determining desirables permutations of EAI technologies for supply chains. However, these recommendations of technological combinations are performed only focusing on the characteristics of the technologies, without strong attention to supply chain features, limiting the results to the formation of certain combinations of technologies rather than an assessment of the relevance of possible combinations of technologies for supply chain in question.

The definition of the supply chain features and requirements that may be relevant to the selection of integrations technologies usually depends on senior managers that represent to different organizations in the supply chain, are quite versed in supply chain needs, and even in the functionalities that a supply chain IS require for their supply chain or particular organization, nevertheless, they can be in the darkness when comes to integration technologies to connect the IS they used. With technology developers is the other way around, they may lack of the business perspective.

There is evidence of supply chains topologies relevant for decision-making in the selection of some IS [13], however, such approach ends in particular descriptions of some features on each particular case, preventing the establishment of general supply chain types that provide a standard point of view for further analysis.

In the case of integration requirements, they can determine the kind of technology required by the different organizations included in a supply chain, however, they definition highly depends of the subjective criteria of the people in charge, and they are usually are derived from the entity objectives [15] increasing the uncertainty related to them [12]. In consequence, integration solutions sometimes scope very specific requirements, or become mass-customized solutions that lose the approach toward particularities of business or industry sectors [14].

3 Decision Support Model

The fundamental question of the given problem is in determining how good a combination of technologies for the integration of certain supply chain is. The hypothesis is that a combination of technologies is good for a supply chain if it satisfies the requirements of integration in this type of chain, applying the rule that the characteristics of an integration requirement determine which technologies, or combination of technologies, can be "suitable" for the chain. This last issue introduces vagueness in the analysis because it depends on the criterion of more or less experienced people.

In this scenario several aspects should be considered: first, the procedure for validation of the hypothesis involves the participation of those interested in the decision (decision makers), whether supply networks managers interested in acquiring the technologies or providers of integration solutions.

Secondly, the way in which technologies meet integration requirements is a fuzzy variable, given the terms "good" and "important" that can be used to quantify the veracity of the hypothesis. These terms allow a scale in natural language that captures the decision makers' perceptions regarding the veracity of the hypothesis. This scale of subjective values (such as very good, good, fair or bad) can be turned into numerical values between 0 and 1, seeking to reach an objective sort of the priority with which technologies should be considered for application in certain types of chain, despite the subjectivity of the scale used to obtain the criteria for decision-makers.

Thirdly, the supply chain types (i=1,...,M), the integration requirements (j=1,...,N) and technologies or technology combinations (k=1,...,L) used in the model must be previously defined. These three aspects constitute the theoretical basis of the model; therefore, the more objective and explicit is the definition made of them, the better the outcome. At present the number and diversity of technologies, the highly specific and vaguely spelled out integration requirements, and the many dimensions that can be applied to classify supply chains are significant barriers to integration technology choice.

Once the theoretical bases have been designed there a three steps procedure is conceive in an initial approach. The first step focuses on determining the extent in which the integration requirement (j) is necessary for the performance of the given supply chain type (i), expressing such a result in the so-called coefficient of necessity (CN_{ij}), as represented in the first matrix in Figure 1. The second step is focused on obtaining the coefficient of satisfaction (CS_{kj}), expressing the extent in which the technology (k) satisfies the requirement (j), as shown in the second matrix of Figure 1. The third step aims to obtain a sub-matrix from the matrix built in step 2, represented as the third matrix in Figure 1, which would achieve an ordering of the technologies considered for a specific supply chain type, as shown in Figure 2.

1

Supply Chain Types	Integration Requirements				
	R_1	R_2	R_3	...	R_N
C_1	CN_{11}	CN_{12}	CN_{13}	...	CN_{1N}
C_2	CN_{21}	CN_{22}	CN_{23}	...	CN_{2N}
C_3	CN_{31}	CN_{32}	CN_{33}	...	CN_{3N}
...	...	...	...	...	...
C_M	CN_{M1}	CN_{M2}	CN_{M3}	...	CN_{MN}

2

Technologies	Integration Requirements				
	R_1	R_2	R_3	...	R_N
T_1	CS_{11}	CS_{12}	CS_{13}	...	CS_{1N}
T_2	CS_{21}	CS_{22}	CS_{23}	...	CS_{2N}
T_3	CS_{31}	CS_{32}	CS_{33}	...	CS_{3N}
...	...	...	...	...	...
T_L	CS_{L1}	CS_{L2}	CS_{L3}	...	CS_{LN}

3 **For Supply Chain Type 1**

T \ R	R_1	R_3	...	R_N
T_1	$CN_{11}*CS_{11}$	$CN_{13}*CS_{13}$	...	$CN_{1N}*CS_{1N}$
T_2	$CN_{11}*CS_{21}$	$CN_{13}*CS_{23}$	...	$CN_{1N}*CS_{2N}$
T_3	$CN_{11}*CS_{31}$	$CN_{13}*CS_{33}$	...	$CN_{1N}*CS_{3N}$
...	...	...	...	...
T_L	$CN_{11}*CS_{L1}$	$CN_{13}*CS_{L3}$	...	$CN_{1N}*CS_{LN}$

CS_{kj}: Coefficient of satisfaction of the technological combination k for the requirement j
CN_{ij}: Coefficient of necessity of the requirement j in the supply chain type i

T_1, ..., T_L: technological combinations from 1 to L
R_1, ..., R_N: requirements from 1 to N
C_1, ..., C_M: supply chain types from 1 to M

Fig. 1. Relation matrices (Source: Authors)

The sub-matrix of step 3 takes into account only the significant requirements (columns of matrix in step 2) for the i-th desired supply chain, considered as significant those requirements in the matrix in step 1 with, for example, $CN_{ij} \geq 0.6$, as shown in Figure 2. Then the ordering of the technologies is obtained by summing of the coefficients of satisfaction (CS_{kj}) weighted up by the coefficients of necessity (CN_{ij}).

The example focuses on determining the priority with which three different combinations of technologies (T_1, T_2 and T_3) should be considered for the chain C_1. From the first step significant requirements are obtain, which exclude R_2 due $CN_{12} < 0.6$, therefore the matrix in the step 3 does not consider it, resulting T_3 the "better" technological combination for that supply chain.

1	R_1	R_2	R_3
C_1	0.7	~~0.2~~	0.8
C_2	0.3	0.5	0.6
C_3	0.9	0.8	0.6

2	R_1	R_2	R_3
T_1	0.3	~~0.8~~	0.6
T_2	0.3	~~0.5~~	0.4
T_3	0.6	~~0.7~~	0.9

3	R_1	R_3	Order
T_1	0.3*0.7	0.6*0.8	0.69
T_2	0.3*0.7	0.4*0.8	0.53
T_3	0.6*0.7	0.9*0.8	1.14

Fig. 2. Example of the procedure (Source: Authors)

The technological combination ranking shown in the example is obtained through the ordering of the suitability coefficient as shown in expression 1 were CI_{ik} is the suitability coefficient that correspond to the technological combination k for the supply chain type i.

$$CI_{ik} = \sum (CS_{kj}\ CN_{ij}) \tag{1}$$

Once the array of technologies is obtained it provides a basis for finding which technological variant may be "more satisfactory", taking into account other factors such as the cost of using the technology in question.

3.1 Several Decision Makers

In order to quantify the satisfaction of a technological combination to the requirements of a supply chain (CS_{kj}), and the how much a requirement is necessary for the performance of a supply chain (CN_{ij}), as shown in the matrices obtained in the steps 1 and 2 (see Figure 1 or 2), it is necessary to consult several decision makers (p). Each person can give different values of CS_{kj} and CN_{ij}, that's why it could be as many matrices 1 and 2 as people involved in the decision process.

The setting of CS_{kj} and CN_{ij} can be done through a qualitative evaluation in common language that reflects the ambiguity of such evaluation. For example the scale to use for the CS_{kj} could be: very bad, bad, regular, good and very good. This evaluation could then be quantified in agreement to the decision makers' criteria, and then set up a signification threshold.

The common language terms that can be used for the CN_{ij} hold a greater subjectivity due the different perceptions that the decision makers could have about the performance of different supply chain types. For example: in the selection of a supply chain information system, a desirable feature can be "make to order" or "make to stock". These requirements have been considered as a typical behavior of agile and lean supply chain respectively [16], and vice versa [17].

Once that the decision makers' criteria are known, it is necessary to unify them into a single quantitative expression that reasonably represents the behavior of these opinions, even when the extreme values in the scale are included. Applying the *geometric mean* a sensitive value to all elements in the scale is obtained, without giving so much meaning to the extreme values like the *arithmetic mean*, which assign the same weight to all involved data, generating a less representative value for this case. The geometric mean also fulfill the compensation, symmetry, growing and strict veto axioms [18]. It was used as shown in the expressions 2 and 3.

$$CN_{ij} = \sqrt[p]{CN_{ij1}\, CN_{ij2} \ldots CN_{ijp}} \tag{2}$$

$$CS_{kj} = \sqrt[p]{CS_{kj1}\, CS_{kj2} \ldots CS_{kjp}} \tag{3}$$

Where:

- CN_{ijp} is the coefficient of necessity of the requirement j for chain type i given by the person p (p=1,…,P).
- CS_{kjp} is the coefficient of satisfaction of the requirement j for the technological combination k given by the person p.

CN_{ijp} and CS_{kjp} are subjective values that quantify each decision maker perception, while CN_{ij} and CS_{kj} represent a sort of consensus for a group of decision makers, that's why step 3 will result in a unique ordering of importance for a given set of technological combinations, considering a specific type of supply chain previously defined.

3.2 Future Work

The "ability" of a technological combination for enhance supply chain performance is associated to the (non-strict) fulfillment of the supply chain integration requirements. The selection process of such combination requires the integration of the different supply chain partners points of view in an environment were generally the IS keep more attention from the decision makers, eclipsing the integration technologies that must be used to communicate these systems. Additionally integration requirements are not explicitly defined and they are as diverse as the several decision makers' priorities are.

Problems with similar features can be solved by means of a decision support model with a fuzzy approach. These models usually combine simultaneously all criteria of a given alternative through a specific expression [19], which in this case correspond to the one used in the step 3 of the proposed procedure, as previously shown in expression 1. This expression in common language terms expresses that the suitability of a technological combination of integration technologies for a given supply chain depends on the measure in which this combination can fulfill the integration requirements forced by the performance of the supply chain in question. Using these measures of fulfillment an available technological combination ranking can be established.

However, the ranking is not enough to determine the aptitude of a combination of technologies for a supply chain without an analysis of cost, benefits and other important factors in the adoption of technologies. It is necessary to compensate the fulfillment of integration requirements that these technologies can provide with their cost, benefits and so on.

Fuzzy logic is not able to assume this new need to compensate conflicting criteria, therefore, a more involving approach is required.

Compensatory fuzzy logic (CFL) is a new approach with some advantages over classical systems, precisely because it is a non-associative multivalent system that incorporates the benefits of fuzzy logic and also facilitates the compensation of the truth values of some basic predicates with others, in a vision that unites the modeling of the decision and the reasoning, as explained in several investigations [18, 20].

The need to develop the previews ideas leads to future lines of work, among them: to prove the suitability of the CFL as a tool to solve such problematic, and its advantages in comparison to traditional approaches. Another important subject is to clarify (and quantify) to the greater possible extend the criteria that can compensate the ranking of technological combination suitability for a supply chain, that is propose as a selection element for further inclusion in the proposed model, based on previews researches results [5].

In addition, a detailed analysis of the relationships among the supply chain integration requirements and the information systems integration technologies is required. It is estimated that this relation should be established through a information systems types classification as used by Themistocleous [2], due to the fact that this systems constitute the link between these integration technologies and the decision makers' need of greater interest to them.

4 Conclusions

The decision support model takes into account the subjectivity and vagueness present in a decision that involves several people, even from different organizations in the supply chain, for the selection of technologies for integration.

The model considers the potential compensations that may occur due to different measures in which combinations of technologies are able to meet certain supply chain requirements for non-dominant cases.

The fact that decision makers select the coefficients of the matrices in steps 1 and 2 from scales formed in a natural language makes easier the process.

Critical to have a good model is to properly define the supply chain types and the integration requirements.

The conflicting criteria that may be necessary compensate against the ranking of technological combinations so far proposed and its modeling is a future guideline of this research.

References

1. Christopher, M.: Logistics & Supply Chain Management: creating value-adding networks, 3rd edn. Financial Times Series, p. 320. Prentice Hall, Harlow (2005)
2. Themistocleous, M., Irani, Z., Love, P.E.D.: Evaluating the integration of supply chain information systems: a case study. European Journal of Operational Research 159(2), 393–405 (2004)
3. Davenport, T.H., Brooks, J.D.: Enterprise systems and the supply chain. Journal of Enterprise Information Management 17(1), 8–19 (2004)

4. Weske, M.: Business Process Management. Concepts, Languages, Architectures. Springer, Heidelberg (2007)
5. Khoumbati, K., Themistocleous, M.: Application of fuzzy simulation for the evalua-tion of enterprise application integration in healthcare organisations. Transforming Government: People, Process and Policy 1(3), 230–241 (2007)
6. Woznica, J., Healy, K.: The level of information systems integration in SMEs in Irish manufacturing sector. Journal of Small Business and Enterprise Development 16(1), 115–130 (2009)
7. Rushton, A., Croucher, P., Baker, P.: The Handbook of Logistics and Distribution Management, 3rd edn., Kogan, p. 612 (2006)
8. Ptak, C.A., Schragenheim, E.: ERP: Tools, Techniques, and Applications for Integrating the Supply Chain, 2nd edn. Series on Resource Management, p. 464. CRC, Boca Raton (2003)
9. Kitsiou, S., Manthou, V., Vlachopoulou, M.: A Framework for the Evaluation of Integration Technology Approaches in Healthcare. In: Proceedings of the International Special Topic Conference on Information Technology in Biomedicine, Ioannina - Epirus, Greece, October 26-28, Epiru, Greece (2006)
10. Helo, P., Xiao, Y., Jiao, J.R.: A web-based logistics management system for agile supply demand network design. Journal of Manufacturing Technology Management 17(8), 1058–1077 (2006)
11. Modesto, C., Peidro, D., Poler, R.: Sistemas de Información para el soporte a la Gestión de la Cadena de Suministro: Un estudio comparativo de herramientas comerciales. In: Congreso de Ingeniería de Organización Valencia, Valencia, España, Septiembre 7-8 (2006)
12. Irani, Z., Love, P.E.D.: Evaluating Information Systems: Public and Private Sector, p. 384. Butterworth-Heinemann, Amsterdan (2008)
13. Stadtler, H., Kilger, C. (eds.): Supply chain management and advanced planning: concepts, models, software, and case studies, 4th edn. Springer, Germany (2005)
14. Helo, P., Szekely, B.: Logistics information systems: An analysis of software solutions for supply chain co-ordination. Industrial Management & Data Systems 105(1), 5–18 (2005)
15. Young, R.R.: The Requirements Engineering Handbook, ed., A.H.T.M.a.P.D. Library. Artech House, Boston (2004)
16. Emmett, S., Crocker, B.: The Relationship-Driven Supply Chain: Creating a Culture of Collaboration Throughout the Chain, p. 187. Gower Technical Press (2006)
17. Dekkers, R. (ed.): Dispersed Manufacturing Networks: Challenges for Research and Practice, p. 257. Springer, London (2009)
18. Ceruto Cordovés, T., Rosete Suárez, A., Espín Andrade, R.A.: Descubrimiento de Predicados a través de la Búsqueda Metaheurística, Ciudad de la Habana, Cuba (2009)
19. Niu, L., Lu, J., Zhang, G.: Cognition-Driven Decision Support for Business Intelligence. In: Kacprzyk, J. (ed.) Models, Techniques, Systems and Applications. Studies in Computational Intelligence, Springer, Berlin (2009)
20. Alonso, M., Rosete Suárez, M. A., Espín Andrade, R. A., Acosta Sanchéz, R.: Experiencias en el descubrimiento de conocimientos a partir de la obtención de predicados en lógica difusa compensatoria, in Segundo Taller de Descubrimiento de Conocimiento, Gestión del Conocimiento y Toma de Decisiones: Ciudad de Panamá, Panamá (2009)

Development of an English-Macedonian Machine Readable Dictionary by Using Parallel Corpora

Martin Saveski[1] and Igor Trajkovski[2]

[1] Staffordshire University, Faculty of Computing, Engineering and Technology, College Road, Stoke-on-Trent, Staffordshire, UK
saveski.martin@gmail.com
[2] Ss. Cyril and Methodius University, Faculty of Electrical Engineering and Information Technologies, Rugjer Boshkovik bb, P.O. Box 574, Skopje, Macedonia
itrajkovski@feit.ukim.edu.mk

Abstract. The dictionaries are one of the most useful lexical resources. However, most of the dictionaries today are not in digital form. This makes them cumbersome for usage by humans and impossible for integration in computer programs. The process of digitalizing an existing traditional dictionary is expensive and labor intensive task. In this paper, we present a method for development of Machine Readable Dictionaries by using the already available resources. Machine readable dictionary consists of simple word-to-word mappings, where word from the source language can be mapped into several optional words in the target language. We present a series of experiments where by using the parallel corpora and open source Statistical Machine Translation tools at our disposal, we managed to develop an English-Macedonian Machine Readable Dictionary containing 23,296 translation pairs (17,708 English and 18,343 Macedonian terms). A subset of the produced dictionary has been manually evaluated and showed accuracy of 79.8%.

Keywords: machine readable dictionary, parallel corpora, word alignment, filtering word alignments.

1 Introduction

The dictionaries are one of the most powerful reference tools that we use in our everyday lives. They are beneficial both in the process of learning a language and its everyday use. In the past all dictionaries had been in printed form. However, with the rapid growth of the technology, the need for dictionaries in digital form has tremendously increased. The process of digitalizing the existing traditional dictionaries is long, cumbersome, and requires a lot of resources. Moreover, the problem of usage of the traditional electronic dictionaries is that translations of some words are not given in explicit format (word-to-word or word-to-phrase) but with direct translation of sentences containing the word to sentences in the target language. In this case, it is hard to automatically find the translation of the word. Machine readable dictionaries, on the other hand, have exact translation, or mapping, of given a word (phrase) to a word (phrase).

M. Gusev and P. Mitrevski (Eds.): ICT Innovations 2010, CCIS 83, pp. 195–204, 2011.

The Natural Language Processing community has greatly benefited from the presence of large amount of text provided in different languages in the form of parallel and comparable corpora. These kind of textual collections have been extensively used to automatically extract bilingual lexicons for a wide variety of applications. This potential has been most recognized by the researchers in the field of Machine Translation where the statistical approaches have dominated the grammatical, rule-based techniques. Due to this trend a large number of free and open source tools for processing parallel corpora have been developed.

The main objective of this study is by making use of the available parallel corpora and the open source Statistical Machine Translation tools to develop an English-Macedonian Machine Readable Dictionary (EN-MK MRD).

The remainder of this paper is organized as follows. In the next section we provide a short overview of the related work after which we explain our methodology and the experiments conducted. In sections 4 and 5, we evaluate the results of the experiments, and discuss the pros and cons of our approach and ideas for future work.

2 Related Work

The idea of using existing resources (parallel corpora) to produce a bilingual Machine Readable Dictionaries (MRD) is not new. As mentioned in the introductory section, it origins from the studies which introduced the techniques of using parallel corpora and statistical methods for the purpose of Machine Translation. We are aware of many studies which have successfully applied this technique and resulted with satisfactory outcomes. In the remainder of this section, we outline some of the attempts found in the literature and considered as most interesting.

Due to the low processing and storage capabilities the early attempts relied on smaller corpora and consequently resulted with small size MRDs. Most notable is the early work of Tiedemann J. in [2], where Swedish-English and Swedish-German dictionaries have been extracted. Similar study was conducted by Velupillai S. and Dalianis H. [3] who created 10 pairs of parallel corpora of Nordic Languages (Swedish, Danish, Norwegian, Icelandic and Finnish) which contained on average less than 80,000 words per language pair. The results reported for some of the language pairs have been very successful and reached accuracy of 93.1%.

However, studies which adopted methodology most similar to ours are the attempts to develop Greek-English and Chinese-English dictionaries. Charitakis K. in [1] developed a Greek-English MRD of 1,276 entries and achieved accuracy of 61.7%. On the other hand, the experiments conducted by Hao-chun Xing and Xin Zhang in [4] resulted in Chinese-English dictionary of 2,118 entries with accuracy of 74.1%. Our study differs from these two mainly in the size of the parallel corpus and the MRD extracted.

Although, we are aware of studies which collected and sentence aligned English-Macedonian parallel corpora [5], we do not know of any attempts for building a large bilingual EN-MK dictionary by using the already available resources.

3 Methodology

By presenting the experiments conducted, in the remainder of this section we discuss our methodology and explain each of the stages included. The main tool used in the experiments is the *Uplug* system. Namely, Uplug provides collection of tools for linguistic corpus processing, word alignment, and term extraction from parallel corpora. The system has been designed by Tiedemann J. in order to develop, evaluate, and apply approaches to generation of translation data from bilingual text [10]. Most importantly, the system is a modular-based platform and therefore each component can be extended or modified without affecting the system pipeline as a whole.

3.1 Small Scale Experiment

In order to test whether the statistical methods are applicable for producing EN-MK MRD a small scale experiment was conducted. For the purpose of the experiment the *KDE4* parallel corpus has been used. This corpus is part of *OPUS (Open Source Parallel Corpus)* [6] collected from the localization files of KDE, which is an open source software package containing a wide variety of applications for communication, education, and entertainment. The whole corpus contains *399,597* EN-MK tokens i.e. *71,046* sentences, where all localization files were tokenized, sentence aligned, and stored in xml files in a format suitable for word alignment with Uplug. After the execution of the advanced word alignment module of Uplug a list of *62,565* EN-MK word alignments was produced. However, many entries contained noise and incorrect translations. Since, manual evaluation of the results was not possible, radical filtering was applied to retain only the meaningful translations. Thus, all word alignments which occurred less than three times or contained punctuation or numbers were removed, resulting in a MRD with *5,228* entries and accuracy of *~70%*. These results were satisfying and encouraged further experiments with larger corpus to be done.

3.2 Large Scale Experiment

For the purpose of the second experiment the data produced by South European Times (SETimes - `http://www.setimes.com/`) news website was used. This website publishes daily news for all countries in south-eastern Europe and Turkey. Most importantly, the content of the website is available in ten languages including English and Macedonian. However, unlike KDE4 this corpus was not available in any preprocessed form so a lot of preprocessing had to be done to transform it in a form suitable for applying the Uplug modules. The whole process is depicted in figure 1 and further explained in the remainder of this section.

3.2.1 Crawling and Parsing

Since the only source was the official website of SETimes, the first step was to develop a simple crawler and parser. The purpose of the crawler was to collect the URLs of each article and to download the article in both languages. Afterwards, the parser was used to extract the article's text from the HTML code and to remove all unnecessary characters. Finally, the articles were stored in two text files, one for each

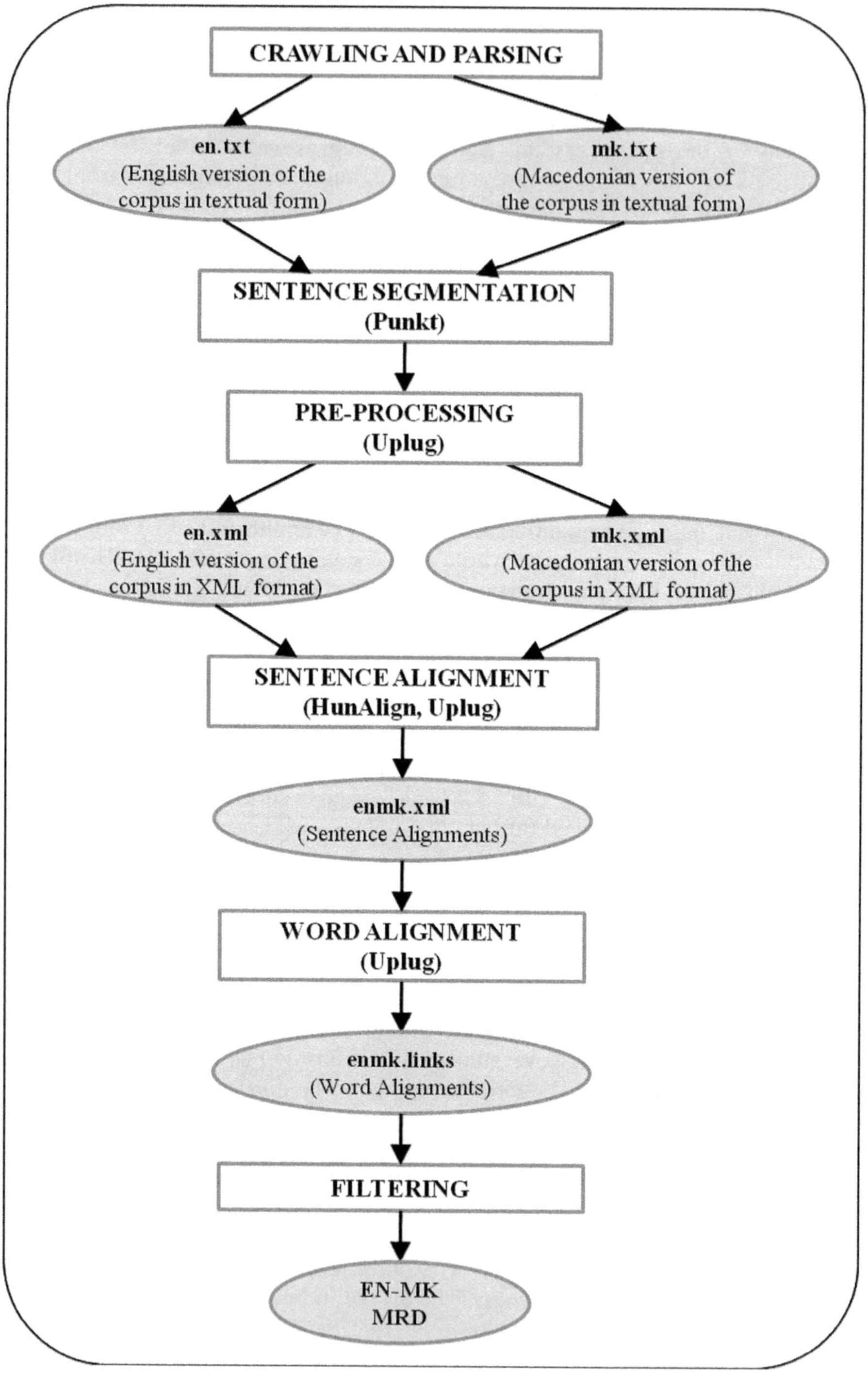

Fig. 1. The process of producing MRD from parallel corpora

language, where one line represented one article. The content of these files was manually verified to ensure that the article in the nth line in the first file corresponds to the translated article in the second. The articles which were missing in one language were removed from both files.

3.2.2 Sentence Segmentation

The next step was to segment each article in sentences. Although, Uplug includes module for sentence segmentation, this module relies on simple rules and did not produce satisfactory results. Instead, *Punkt* was considered [7]. Punkt is a computer program which implements a language-independent unsupervised algorithm for sentence boundary detection. Understood intuitively, it is based on the assumption that a large number of ambiguities in the determination of sentence boundaries can be eliminated once abbreviations have been identified [7]. Punkt is open source, available through the Python *NLTK* (Natural Language Toolkit) [8] and could be easily applied to the collected corpora. To further facilitate the process of sentence segmentation, all articles that included paragraph HTML tags were first segmented on paragraphs and then sentence segmented. After this step it could be concluded that the whole corpus contains *28,980* articles i.e. *294,693* sentences per language.

3.2.3 Pre-Processing

Once the corpus was sentence segmented the Uplug pre-processing module was applied to allow the corpus to be further processed with other Uplug modules. The pre-processing module tokenizes the text and converts the text files in XML format by using basic markup for each paragraph, sentence, and word.

3.2.4 Sentence Alignment

Next, the sentence alignment module was applied. The purpose of this module is to link all sentences in one file to the corresponding translation sentences in the other. Uplug contains several sentence alignment modules. After experimenting with each, it was concluded that the module which uses *HunAlign* [9] showed most satisfying results. HunAlign is a language independent module which aligns sentences in bilingual texts by combining the so-called length-based and dictionary-based approaches. In the first pass of the corpus, HunAlign uses the sentence-length information to make a rough alignment of the sentences and to build a dictionary based on this alignment. In the second pass, it uses the produced dictionary to realign

```
...
<linkGrp targType="s" toDoc="setimes/mk.xml"
   fromDoc="setimes/en.xml">
 <link certainty="3.64407" xtargets="s1.1;s1.1" id="SL2" />
 <link certainty="3.374068" xtargets="s1.2;s1.2" id="SL3" />
 <link certainty="1.819944" xtargets="s1.3;s1.3" id="SL4" />
 <link certainty="4.003576" xtargets="s1.4;s1.4" id="SL5" />
 <link certainty="11.63679" xtargets="s1.5;s1.5" id="SL6" />
...
```

Fig. 2. Sample output of the Uplug (HunAlign) sentence alignment module the sentences. Furthermore, HunAlign includes one-to-many and many-to-one alignments, which allows the errors made in the sentence segmentation stage to be corrected with proper sentence alignment. The result of this step is an XML file containing the sentence links and the alignment certainty of each link. Sample output is shown in figure 2.

3.2.5 Word Alignment

Once the sentences were aligned the word alignment module was applied to the corpus. Word alignment refers to the process of linking corresponding words and phrases in the aligned sentences. For this purpose Uplug has three different modules: basic, tagged, and advanced. Since, part-of-speech tagger for the Macedonian language was not available at our disposal to achieve best results we used the advanced word alignment module. This module includes several sub-modules which run in the following order:

1. **Basic Clues:** computes basic alignment clues using association measures,
2. **Giza-word-refined:** runs GIZA++ in both alignment directions and converts the lexical probabilities to the clue aligner format,
3. **Dynamic Clues:** learns clues from the "refined" combination of both Viterbi alignments,
4. **Gizaclue-word-prefix:** takes only the three initial characters of each token and runs GIZA++ in both directions and converts probabilities to clues,
5. **Link:** clue alignment using basic clues, GIZA++ clues, and learned clues,
6. **Dynamic Clues:** learns clues from previously aligned data,
7. **Link:** clue alignment using all clues (basic, giza, learned),
8. The last three steps are repeated 3 times. [10]

Clue alignment refers to incorporating several knowledge resources (clues) in the process of word alignment. This module is the result of extensive research and experiments conducted in [10].

The output of this step is an *XCES* XML file [11] which includes the word links and the certainty of each alignment. Figure 3, shows sample output of this file, where each word link element has a certainty, lexical pair, and xtragets (link word ids) attributes.

```
...
<linkGrp targType="s" toDoc="setimes/mk.xml"
  fromDoc="setimes/en.xml">
  <link certainty="3.64407" xtargets="s1.1;s1.1"id="SL2">
    <wordLink certainty="0.04366786" lexPair="week;недела"
      xtargets="w1.1.9;w1.1.13" />
    <wordLink certainty="0.02486187" lexPair="prize;награда"
      xtargets="w1.1.7;w1.1.9" />
    <wordLink certainty="0. 03209486"
      lexPair="mayor;градоначалникот" xtargets="w1.1.2;w1.1.2" />
...
```

Fig. 3. Sample output of the Uplug advanced word alignment module

To produce more readable output the *xces-to-text* Uplug module was applied. As figure 4 shows, the result is a text file containing all word alignments and their frequency of occurrence. As expected, the conjunctions occur most frequently.

44352	and	и	12950	in	во
24692	the	на	12605	serbia	србија
24538	in	во	11708	bih	бих
22182	with	со	11401	also	исто така
21006	eu	еу	11209	that	дека
14615	is	е	10430	kosovo	косово
13927	will	ќе	9378	turkey	турција
13091	on	ти	9352	the	на
12984	he	тој	8833	as	како

Fig. 4. Sample output of the xces-to-text Uplug module

3.2.6 Filtering

Due to the errors made in the previous stages of processing the corpus, the word alignments contain a lot of noisy and incorrect translations which need to be excluded. The process of filtering the word alignments consists of two stages, where each stage includes several rules. All alignments which occurred less than 3 times were considered as a noise produced by the word alignment module and were excluded prior to applying the filtering rules.

The first stage considers each of the terms in the word alignments pairs as one string. The following rules apply:

- If one of the terms in the pair is an empty string, than the word alignment is considered invalid and is excluded.
- If the English term contains an alphabetical character and the Macedonian term does not contain a Cyrillic character, or vice verse, the word alignment is excluded as well.
- If both terms do not contain letters, then the pair is considered as numeric pair and is removed.
- If one term contains digit, while the other does not, the pair is also excluded.

The second stage checks the single tokens in both terms. Prior to applying the rules the strings are tokenized and processed with a method which removes the leading and trailing non-alphabetic/non-Cyrillic characters.

- If the number of tokens in one of the terms is greater than 3, the pair is excluded. Phrases in the word alignments are unusual output of the word alignment module and therefore are considered as an erroneous behavior.
- If one of the terms contains stop word token, than the pair is considered invalid.
- Finally, the one-to-one word alignments were lemmatized. The English words were lemmatized by using the Princeton WordNet [16], while for the purpose of lemmatizing the Macedonian words the lexicon developed in [12] was used.

After applying the filtering rules the list of *46,875* word alignments was shortlisted to *23,296* translation pairs. This is the size of the extracted dictionary which includes *17,708* English and *18,343* Macedonian unique terms.

4 Results and Evaluation

Several methods for evaluating the quality of the automatically extracted dictionaries have been proposed in the literature. Dagan I. and Church W. in [13] and Fung P. and McKeown K. in [14], measure the accuracy of the extracted dictionary by measuring the increase in efficiency that can be observed when translators are using the dictionary. A similar scenario of practically evaluating the automatically extracted dictionary is when lexicographers use the extracted dictionary to extend the existing dictionaries. In this case, the quality of the extracted dictionary is measured by the number of entries added to the existing dictionary.

However, two most common techniques for evaluating the automatically extracted dictionaries are: (1) automatic comparison with existing MRD and (2) manual evaluation of a subset of the dictionary entries. However, the use of the first technique may result in inaccurate evaluation of the extracted dictionary. Non-standard translations, translations of collocations, technical terminology, etc. are often not found in standard dictionaries and as a consequence may produce misleading evaluation [15]. Therefore, we have decided to use the second technique for the purpose of evaluating the EN-MK dictionary extracted during the course of this study.

Namely, we selected a subset of 2000 entries of the extracted dictionary, which is 8.5% of the dictionaries entries, to be manually evaluated. The entries were uniformly selected form the dictionary, i.e. every ~14th entry was taken, so that alignments which occurred most and less frequently are equally included. We believe that in this way we will get the most accurate and objective evaluation of the extracted dictionary. Each entry in the subset was given one of the following three scores:

- ***C – Correct***: The translation is correct and the both the English and Macedonian terms are in the same case and gender (e.g. *army – армија*).
- ***S – Somewhat Correct***: The translation captures the meaning of the English word – some will understand the original term, but quality of the translation is low, or the case and genre are incorrect (e.g. *vote – гласање, sell – продаде*).
- ***W – Wrong***: The translation fails to capture the meaning of the English word (e.g. *back – поддржи, news – друг, wing – левичарски*, etc.).

The evaluation was performed by volunteers who are fluent speakers in both languages. Figure 5, shows the results of the evaluation.

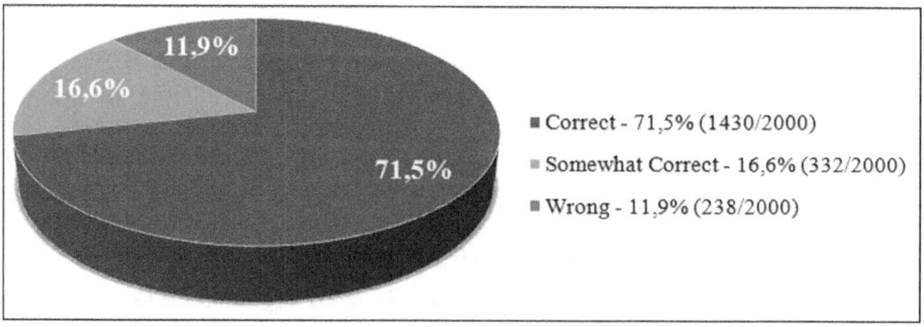

Fig. 5. Results of the manual evaluation of the extracted dictionary

In order to give a single measure of the accuracy of the dictionary we have combined the results by using the following formula [1]:

$$Accuracy = \frac{Correct\ Translations + 0.5 * Somewhat\ Correct\ Translations}{Number\ of\ Translations\ Evalvuated}$$

For example, if there are three translations, one is accurate, one is somewhat correct, and the last one is wrong, then the accuracy will be (1+0.5*1)/3=50%. By using this formula, we concluded that the accuracy of the extracted dictionary is ***79.8%***.

5 Conclusion and Future Work

The series of experiments reported in this paper, to our knowledge, are the first attempt to develop a large bilingual English-Macedonian dictionary by using purely statistical methods. We have conducted two experiments. The first, small scale, experiment proved that the technique of using parallel corpora to develop bilingual dictionaries is applicable and yields satisfactory results. This has encouraged us to conduct a second experiment with much larger corpus. By making use of the Statistical Machine Translation tools available at our disposal, we have processed the corpus in order to acquire a list of word alignments. This list has been further filtered to remove incorrect and noisy alignments and to acquire the final result of the experiment – the bilingual dictionary. The manual evaluation of a subset of the extracted dictionary resulted in an accuracy of *79.8%*. The extracted dictionary has been made available for public use on the Web through the following URL: `http://www.time.mk/trajkovski/tools/dict/`.

In the future, we plan to further study the process of filtering the word alignments. Namely, we believe that modeling the problem of filtering the word alignments as a supervised learning problem will allow us to detect more incorrect translations. The frequency of the word alignments and the word and sentence alignment probabilities are good indicators of the accuracy of the word alignment and therefore can be used as features. On the other hand, the manually verified translations or the entries of exiting dictionaries found in the alignments can be used as a training data. We believe that by using this, more sophisticated, technique we will be able to improve the filtering of the word alignments and thus significantly increase the accuracy of the resulting dictionary.

References

1. Charitakis, K.: Using parallel corpora to create a Greek-English dictionary with Uplug. In: Nodalida (2007)
2. Tiedemann, J.: Automatical Lexicon Extraction from Aligned Bilingual Corpora. Master Thesis at University of Magdeburg (1997)
3. Velupillai, S., Dalianis, H.: Automatic Construction of Domain-specific Dictionaries on Sparse Parallel Corpora in the Nordic Languages. In: Coling (ed.) Workshop on Multi-source Multilingual Information Extraction and Summarization, Manchester (2008)

4. Hao-chun, X., Xin, Z.: Using parallel corpora and Uplug to create a Chinese-English dictionary. Master Thesis at Stockholm University, Royal Institute of Technology (2008)
5. Stolic, M., Zdravkova, K.: Resources for Machine Translation of the Macedonian Language. In: ICT Innovations Conference, Ohrid, Macedonia (2009)
6. Tiedemann, J.: News from OPUS - A Collection of Multilingual Parallel Corpora with Tools and Interfaces. In: Nicolov, N., Bontcheva, K., Angelova, G., Mitkov, R. (eds.) Recent Advances in Natural Language Processing, vol. 5, pp. 237–248. Amsterdam (2009)
7. Tibor, K., Strunk, J.: Unsupervised Multilingual Sentence Boundary Detection. Computational Linguistics 32(4) (2006)
8. NLTK - Natural Language Toolkit, http://www.nltk.org/
9. Varga, D., et al.: Parallel corpora for medium density languages. In: Recent Advances in Natural Language Processing, pp. 590–596 (2005)
10. Tiedemann, J.: Recycling Translations - Extraction of Lexical Data from Parallel Corpora and their Application in Natural Language Processing. Doctoral Thesis at Uppsala University (2003)
11. XCES - Corpus Encoding Standard for XML, http://www.xces.org/
12. Petrovski, A.: Морфолошки компјутерски речник - придонес кон македонските јазични ресурси. Doctoral Thesis, Cyril and Methodius University. In Macedonian (2008)
13. Dagan, I., Church, W.: Termight: Identifying and Translating Technical Terminology. In: Conference on Applied Natural Language Processing, pp. 34–40 (1994)
14. Fung, P., McKeown, K.: A Technical Word and Term Translation Aid using Noisy Parallel Corpora Across Language Groups. In: The Machine Translation Journal, Special Issue on New Tools for Human Translators, pp. 53–87 (1996)
15. Merkel, M., Ahrenberg, L.: Evaluating Word Alignment Systems. In: Second International Conference on Language Resources and Evaluation (LREC), pp. 1255–1261 (2000)
16. WordNet, http://wordnet.princeton.edu/

Information Retrieval Using a Macedonian Test Collection for Question Answering

Jasmina Armenska[1], Aleksandar Tomovski[2], Katerina Zdravkova[2], and Jovan Pehcevski[1]

[1] European University, Faculty of Informatics, Republic of Macedonia
{jasmina.armenska,jovan.pehcevski}@eurm.edu.mk
[2] Ss. Cyril and Methodius University, Faculty of Natural Sciences and Mathematics, Republic of Macedonia
aleksandar.tomovski@gmail.com, keti@ii.edu.mk

Abstract. Question answering systems solve many of the problems that users encounter when searching for focused information on the web and elsewhere. However, these systems cannot always adequately understand the user's question posed in a natural language, primarily because any particular language has its own specifics that have to be taken into account in the search process. When designing a system for answering questions posed in a natural language, there is a need of creating an appropriate test collection that will be used for testing the system's performance, as well as using an information retrieval method that will effectively answer questions for that collection. In this paper, we present a test collection we developed for answering questions in Macedonian language. We use this collection to test the performance of the vector space model with pivoted document length normalization. Preliminary experimental results show that our test collection can be effectively used to answer multiple-choice questions in Macedonian language.

Keywords: Information retrieval, Question answering, Macedonian test collection.

1 Introduction

The World Wide Web is an attractive resource for searching for valuable information. People increasingly rely on it to satisfy their daily information needs. However, despite the huge success of information retrieval systems in recent years, finding an answer to a particular question is not a simple task. First, it is quite difficult for the system to extract the query semantics and that of the underlying natural-language texts. Second, the amount of information on the Web increases every day, making the retrieval process even more difficult. Last, most of the users would not spend more time than necessary in finding the exact answer for their question. Indeed, even for a simple question users usually have to spend a lot of time, because the answer is rarely given in an explicit form. Therefore, they need to inspect every document retrieved by the system in order to find the required information.

M. Gusev and P. Mitrevski (Eds.): ICT Innovations 2010, CCIS 83, pp. 205–214, 2011.

As a result, more sophisticated retrieval tools for providing the correct answer to a user question are needed. This has led to the development of the so-called *question answering* systems (QA). QA systems provide the users with the answer for their question using certain information sources, such as the Web or a local document collection [10]. Two basic types of QA systems are distinguished: systems that try to answer the question by accessing structured information contained in a database; and systems that analyze unstructured information, such as plain text [4]. According to Belkin and Vickery [1], the systems of the first type are limited to a specific domain unlike the systems of the second type, which can cover different domains. A significant impact on question answering as a research area has been made by the Text REtrieval Conference (TREC), which has promoted a textual question answering track since 1999 [3]. Mulder was developed as a result, which is the first general-purpose, fully-automated question answering system available on the Web [4].

Currently, there are several textual question answering systems that include different techniques and architectures. Most of them have a number of components in common, and these are: question analysis, retrieval of relevant documents, document analysis and answer selection [5]. The question analysis component includes morpho-syntactic analysis of the given user question posed in a natural language text, as well as determining its type and consequently the type of the answer that is expected. Depending on the performed morpho-syntactic analysis, a retrieval query is formulated in order to identify relevant documents that are likely to contain the answer of the original question. Document analysis component extracts a number of candidate answers that are then ranked by the answer selection module according to their estimated likelihood of relevance.

Test collections are usually used for measuring the performances of information retrieval systems. A certain test collection consists of three parts: *a document collection* that comprises documents written in a particular language (in our case in Macedonian language), a set of *user queries* required for information retrieval from the document collection (in our case questions), and a set of *relevant documents* that correspond to the user queries (in our case relevant answers). Well-known forums for creating test collections for the most popular world languages are: Text REtrieval Conference (TREC)[1], INitiative for the Evaluation of XML retrieval (INEX)[2], NII Test Collection for IR Systems (NTCIR)[3] and Cross-Language Evaluation Forum (CLEF)[4]. They are primarily maintained for testing the well-established (or new) models for information retrieval on different test collections and for exchange of useful information and knowledge from the gained experiences. To the best of our knowledge, there is no existing Macedonian test collection that can be used for empirical testing of various question answering retrieval methods.

In this paper, we describe a test collection that consists of documents and questions posed in Macedonian language, as well as their relevant answers. We use this test collection to investigate the effectiveness of one of the best performing information retrieval methods, the pivoted cosine document length normalization [8].

---

[1] http://trec.nist.gov/
[2] http://www.inex.otago.ac.nz/
[3] http://research.nii.ac.jp/ntcir/index-en.html
[4] http://www.clef-campaign.org/

2 A Macedonian Test Collection for Question Answering

We have created our own test collection that can be used for developing and testing systems for answering questions posed in Macedonian language. The collection consists of four documents and 163 multiple-choice questions taken from the courses History of Informatics and Computer Applications that are part of the curriculum of the Institute of Informatics at the Faculty of Natural Sciences and Mathematics at the Ss. Cyril and Methodius University in Skopje. The document names are: "A brief history of computers", "Introductory concepts", "Hardware" and "Software". Fig. 1 shows a snippet taken from the document "Hardware".

Двата најзастапени влезни уреда на сметачите се тастатурата (keyboard) и глувчето (mouse). Тие се најчесто поврзани со кутијата на сметачот со помош на кабел, но можат да бидат на далечинско управување (remote control) или безжични (wireless).

Fig. 1. A snippet from the document "Hardware"

All the questions are extracted from these four documents, and every question belongs to only one of the existing question types: Who, When, Why, What, What (description), What (size), How, How Many, Where and Other (for uncategorized questions). Four answers for every question are given and only one of them is correct.

Below is an example of a question whose answer can be found in the document "Hardware", which belongs to the Who question type. There are four answers given for the question, and only the first one is correct.

Кои се најважните влезни уреди?

1. глувчето и тастатурата (correct)
2. екранот и тастатурата
3. глувчето и екранот
4. екранот и мониторот

Our test collection consists of a set of 163 questions, divided into two subsets: a training set (containing 83 questions) and a testing set (containing the remaining 80 questions). The training set is used to determine the optimal values of the tuning parameters in our retrieval system. That is, we set optimal values for those parameters that maximize the retrieval performance on the training set, and then use these optimal parameter values on the testing set with the assumption that for these values our system will produce the best results. The testing set is therefore used to confirm the retrieval performance previously achieved on the training set.

2.1 Training Set

Table 1 shows the overall breakdown of questions comprising the training set, i.e. their distribution over documents (columns) and over question types (rows). We observe that most of the questions belong to the document "Hardware" (42%), followed by "A brief history of the computers" (29%), "Introductory concepts" (17%)

and "Software" (12%). On the other hand, the two mostly used question types are What (43%) and Who (28%), with the rest of the question types almost uniformly distributed.

Table 1. A breakdown of questions comprising the training set

Question Type/Document	A brief history of computers	Introductory concepts	Hardware	Software	Total
Who	11	2	7	3	**23**
What	7	6	18	5	**36**
When	3	/	/	/	**3**
Why	1	/	1	/	**2**
What (desc)	1	1	2	/	**4**
What (size)	1	/	/	/	**1**
How	/	1	2	1	**4**
How Many	/	1	2	/	**3**
Where	/	/	3	1	**4**
Other	/	3	/	/	**3**
Total	**24**	**14**	**35**	**10**	**83**

2.2 Testing Set

Table 2 shows the overall breakdown of questions comprising the testing set, i.e. their distribution over documents (columns) and over question types (rows). It can be noticed that very similar distribution of questions is observed for the testing set as it was previously observed for the training set.

Table 2. A breakdown of questions comprising the testing set

Question Type/Document	A brief history of computers	Introductory concepts	Hardware	Software	Total
Who	11	/	3	2	**16**
What	8	6	21	7	**42**
When	3	/	/	/	**3**
Why	/	/	/	/	**0**
What (desc)	1	/	1	/	**2**
What (size)	/	/	1	/	**1**
How	/	2	3	1	**6**
How Many	/	1	2	/	**3**
Where	/	/	2	/	**2**
Other	/	5	/	/	**5**
Total	**23**	**14**	**33**	**10**	**80**

3 Information Retrieval Methods

In order for the information retrieval (IR) system to understand the user's need, it has to be represented by a query request comprising a set of terms. Most of the existing IR systems index terms, phrases or other document content identification units [6]. Usually the indexing is based on a structure called *inverted index*, which is considered as one of the most efficient ways to process vast amounts of text [11].

3.1 Collection Statistics

The similarity of a document to a given query indicates how *closely* the content of the document matches the content of the query. In order to measure this similarity, statistical information about the distribution of the query terms in the document as well as in the whole collection is needed. Many similarity measures have been proposed, and most of them implement one of the three major IR models: the vector space model [7], the probabilistic model [9], and the language model [12].

We define the following statistics for a given document collection and a query:

- q - a query
- t - a query term
- d - a document
- N - number of documents in the collection
- $tf_{t,d}$ - the frequency of t in document d
- df_t - number of documents containing the term t (document frequency)
- $tf_{t,q}$ - the frequency of t in query q
- V - number of unique terms from the document collection

3.2 Vector Space Model

In the statistically based vector space model, each document is represented by a vector, whose components are the unique terms derived from the documents in the collection, with associated weights representing the importance of the terms in the document as well as in the whole document collection. The set of documents in the collection may thus be viewed as a set of vectors in a vector space. On the other hand, each query can also be treated as a short document so that it too can be represented by a vector in the same vector space as that used for the documents in the collection.

Three important components that affect the term weight in a given collection are the term frequency (tf), the inverse document frequency (idf) and the document length. The weight of a term in a document vector can be determined in many ways. A common approach uses the so-called $tf \times idf$ method, in which the weight of a term is determined by using only these two factors [7].

More formally, one representation of the weight of the term t in a document d is:

$$w_{t,d} = tf_{t,d} \times idf_t = tf_{t,d} \times log \frac{N}{df_t} \qquad (1)$$

The standard way of measuring the similarity between a document d and a query q is the cosine measure, which determines the angle between their vector representations $\vec{V}_d$ and $\vec{V}_q$ in the V - dimensional Euclidean space:

$$sim(q,d) = \frac{\vec{V}_d \cdot \vec{V}_q}{V_d \cdot V_q} = \frac{\sum_{t \in V} w_{t,d} \times w_{t,q}}{\sqrt{\sum_{t \in V} w_{t,d}^2} \times \sqrt{\sum_{t \in V} w_{t,q}^2}} \tag{2}$$

The denominator in this equation is a product of the Euclidean lengths of the vectors $\vec{V}_d$ and $\vec{V}_q$ which represent their *cosine document length normalizations*.

The document length normalization is a way to penalize the term weights for a document in accordance with its length. Empirical results obtained from TREC documents and queries show that more effective are those techniques which implement normalization strategies that retrieve documents with similar chances to their probability of relevance [8]. Cosine normalization has a tendency to retrieve short documents with higher probability than their probability of relevance. On the other hand, the probability to retrieve longer documents is lower than their probability of relevance. In order to promote retrieval of longer documents and at the same time to retrieve less short documents, *pivoted document length normalization* is used.

3.3 Pivoted Document Length Normalization

The main idea is that the probability of document retrieval is inversely related to the normalization factor. It means that increasing the chances of retrieval of longer documents can be achieved by lowering the value of the normalization factor for those documents, and vice-versa. If the curves of probability of retrieval and probability of relevance are plotted against the document length, they intersect in a point called *pivot*. Usually, the documents on one side of the pivot are retrieved with probability higher than their probability of relevance and the documents on the other side of the pivot are retrieved with probability lower than their probability of relevance. The idea of the pivot normalization is to rotate the curve of probability of retrieval counter-clockwise around the pivot so that it more closely matches the curve of probability of relevance [8].

The simplest implementation of the pivoted cosine normalization is achieved by using a normalization factor that is linear in vector length:

$$u = (1 - S) + S \cdot \frac{V_d}{V_{avg}} \tag{3}$$

Here, S is a *slope* that receives values in the interval [0, 1], and V_{avg} represents an average length of the documents in the collection. This normalization factor shows that the most appropriate length has a document with average length, which means that the weights of its terms should remain unchanged. It should be emphasized that the cosine normalization is a specific case of the pivoted normalization (S=1).

Initial tests show that the deviation of the retrieval probability from the probability of relevance is systematic across different query sets and different documents collections, where an optimal slope value S=0.2 is identified [8]. This suggests that the slope trained on one collection can effectively be used on another one. However, recent research shows that the slope should be carefully calibrated according to the document collection [2]. In our experimental results, we will also experiment with different values for the slope parameter S on the training set in order to determine its optimal value that can be achieved on our Macedonian test collection.

4 Experiments and Results

In this section we present results from the practical implementation of the vector space model with pivoted document length normalization, applied to our Macedonian test collection for question answering. The implemented retrieval system is developed in C# (.Net Framework 3.5). Matrices and vectors are used as basic data structures that are manipulated in many ways in order to get the results.

4.1 Retrieval Strategies

Two phases are used to find answers for questions posed in Macedonian language.

1) Phase 1: Document selection

In this phase, one of the four documents that is most likely to contain the correct answer to a question is first selected. Two types of queries are used by our system to select the right document: the first query contains only the question, while the second query contains the question combined with all of the provided answers. Regardless of the query type, the highest ranked document is considered to contain the correct answer to the question, and is further processed in phase two.

2) Phase 2: Answering the question

Based on the selected document in phase one, our retrieval system utilizes one of the following two strategies to select the correct answer for the question: (1) using the whole document, or (2) using document passages. The passages are identified by the way MS Word defines paragraphs – namely, each section that ends with pressed Enter (new line) is treated as a retrieval passage.

When using the whole document as a retrieval strategy, the system uses four queries, each containing the initial question *combined* with only one of the four provided answers. In this case, a correct answer is considered to be the answer for which the corresponding query returns the highest ranking score for the document.

When using document passages as a retrieval strategy, the system again uses the same four queries, only this time for each query the score of the highest ranking passage is first noted. The four scores (obtained for each of the four queries) are then sorted in a descending order, and a correct answer is considered to be the answer for which the corresponding query returns the highest score for the top ranked passage.

In both cases, the score for a given document or passage is obtained by using the vector space model with pivoted document length normalization.

4.2 Training Set

We now present experimental results obtained on the training set of our test collection, when using the vector space model with pivoted normalization. The idea is to determine the values for the parameters that maximize the retrieval performance.

1) Phase 1: Selecting the right document

In this phase, we want to determine which of the two query types is better for selecting the right document that contains the answer for a given question. For this experiment we use the vector space model with cosine normalization (S=1). We have found that using the question combined with all of the answers as a query produces 87% accuracy (across all the 83 questions in the training set), as opposed to when using the question alone that produces 72%. In the further analysis we therefore use the question combined with all of the answers as a query to our system.

In order to determine the optimal value for the slope parameter S when selecting the document that contains the answer to a particular question, we analyzed twenty values for the slope S, in the range between 0 and 1, with a step of 0.05. We found that there are two values for S (0.25 and 0.30) for which an accuracy of 92% is obtained (percent of questions with correctly selected documents). This is a 5% relative performance improvement against the previous value obtained by using the vector space model with cosine normalization.

2) Phase 2: Finding the correct answer

In this phase, we want to determine which of the two retrieval strategies works better for selecting the correct answer for a given question. We have found that, when using the whole document (previously selected in phase one), there is a 35% accuracy obtained by our system (which represents the percent of correctly answered questions by the system). Since only one document is used for answering the questions, any value of S in this case produces the same result.

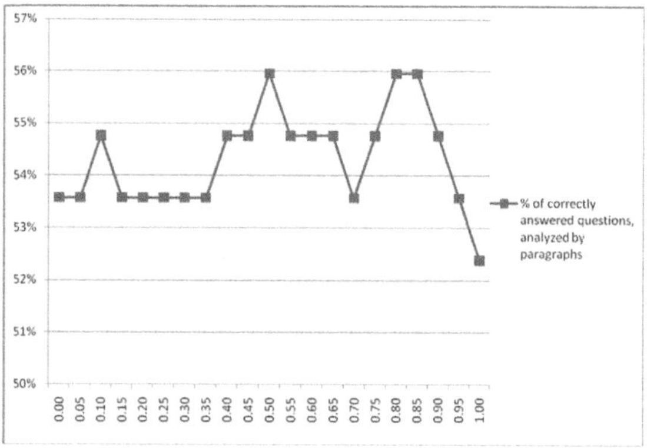

Fig. 2. Percent of correctly answered questions when using passages from previously selected document on the training set, as the slope parameter S varies between 0 and 1

Fig. 2 shows the accuracy obtained by our system when using document passages as a retrieval strategy, as the slope parameter S varies between 0 and 1. We observe that there are three values for S (0.50, 0.80, and 0.85) for which an accuracy of 56% is obtained. This is a 62% relative performance improvement against the previous value obtained when using the whole document as a retrieval strategy.

4.3 Testing Set

We now present experimental results obtained on the testing set of our test collection, when using the vector space model with pivoted normalization. The idea is to confirm the performances for the optimal values of retrieval parameters, obtained previously on the training set.

1) Phase 1: Selecting the right document

In this phase, we compared two retrieval methods for selecting the right document on the testing set: one that uses the vector space model with cosine normalization (S=1) as a baseline, and another using the optimal value for the slope parameter S, previously determined on the training set (S=0.3). With the optimal S value we have achieved 95% accuracy in selecting the right document, against the baseline where we achieved 87% accuracy (which is around 8% relative performance improvement).

2) Phase 2: Finding the correct answer

When using the whole document as a retrieval strategy on the testing set, our system obtained an accuracy of 34%, which is almost identical to the accuracy obtained on the training set (35%).

When using document passages as a retrieval strategy, we compared two retrieval methods for finding the correct answer on the testing set: one that uses the vector space model with cosine normalization (S=1) as a baseline, for which we obtained 51% accuracy; and another using the optimal value for the slope parameter S, previously determined on the training set (S=0.85), for which we obtained 55% accuracy (a 7% relative performance improvement).

5 Conclusion and Future Work

The technology for answering questions is very important part of (focused) information retrieval, because the precise question answering is the key in handling the information explosion. The main goal with the research presented in this paper was creating a test collection for question answering in Macedonian language, in order to implement and test the well-established IR methods for question answering purposes. Our experiments with the vector space model using pivoted document length normalization show that the document (or passage) lengths, as well as the choice of a retrieval strategy from the document itself are key factors in determining the correct answer to a particular question.

In the future, we intend to enrich the Macedonian test collection with additional documents and questions, as well as to share this collection with existing forums for research purposes, in order to improve the performances on other existing re trieval methods. We also plan to compare the performances of other well-established (or novel) IR methods on the Macedonian test collection.

References

1. Belkin, N.J., Vickery, A.: Interaction in information systems. The British Library (1985)
2. Chowdhury, A., Catherine McCabe, M., Grossman, D., Frieder, O.: Document normalization revisited. In: Proceedings of the ACM-SIGIR International Conference on Research and Development in Information Retrieval, Tampere, Finland, pp. 381–382 (2002)
3. Dang, H.T., Kelly, D., Lin, J.: Overview of the TREC 2007 Question Answering Track. In: NIST Special Publication 500-274: The Sixteenth Text REtrieval Conference Proceedings (TREC 2007), Gaithersburg, Maryland (2007)
4. Kwok, C., Etzioni, O., Weld, D.: Scaling Question Answering to the Web. ACM Transactions on Information Systems 19(3), 242–262 (2001)
5. Magnini, B., Negri, M., Prevete, R., Tanev, H.: Mining the Web to validate answers to natural language questions. In: Proceedings of Data Mining 2002, Bologna, Italy (2002)
6. Manning, C., Raghavan, P., Schutze, H.: Introduction to Information Retrieval. Cambridge University Press, Cambridge (2008)
7. Salton, G., Wong, A., Yang, C.S.: A vector space model for automatic indexing. Communications of the ACM 18(11), 613–620 (1975)
8. Singhal, A., Buckley, C., Mitra, M.: Pivoted document length normalization. In: Proceedings of the ACM-SIGIR International Conference on Research and Development in Information Retrieval, Zurich, Switzerland, pp. 21–29 (1996)
9. Sparck Jones, K., Walker, S., Robertson, S.E.: A probabilistic model of information retrieval: Development and comparative experiments. Parts 1 and 2. Information Processing and Management 36(6), 779–840 (2000)
10. Sultan, M.: Multiple Choice Question Answering, MSc thesis, University of Sheffield (2006)
11. Witten, I.H., Moffat, A., Bell, T.C.: Managing Gigabytes: Compressing and Indexing Documents and Images, 2nd edn. Morgan Kaufmann Publishers, San Francisco (1999)
12. Zhai, C., Lafferty, J.: A study of smoothing methods for language models applied to information retrieval. ACM Transactions on Information Systems 22(2), 179–214 (2004)

A Modeling Framework for Performance Analysis of P2P Live Video Streaming Systems

Zoran Kotevski and Pece Mitrevski

University of St. Kliment Ohridski, Faculty of Technical Sciences, Ivo Lola Ribar bb, 7000 Bitola, Macedonia
{Zoran.Kotevski,Pece.Mitrevski}@uklo.edu.mk

Abstract. Client/server media streaming systems exhibit streaming limitations when number of clients rises and the server can no longer sustain the upload load. At first, IP Multicast was proposed as an alternative solution to this problem but its deployment brought many practical issues in scalability and deployment that prevented it from wider use. Recently, a new promising technique emerged which is cost effective, easy to deploy and can support thousands of simultaneous users. It's a peer to peer network of logically connected clients which form an application level overlay network on top of the physical network. This new paradigm brings numerous advantages, but also a lot of open issues that need to be resolved. This paper exposes the fundamental characteristics of p2p live video streaming systems, gives a survey of p2p video streaming applications and presents a novel modeling framework for performance analysis of such systems as our main goal in future research.

Keywords: Petri nets, p2p networks, IP video broadcast, performance analysis.

1 Introduction

Today, the use of Internet video streaming services is spreading rapidly. Web locations for live video broadcast attract more visitors every day. In the classical client/server system architecture the increase in number of clients requires more resources in manner of high bandwidth transmission channels with large upload rates. Since they are extremely expensive it results in a limited number of unicast connections that a server can support at a given time.

In the early '90s it was expected that IP Multicast will be the natural technology to satisfy the requirements of large number of users with lower cost. However, lack of support for functionality of higher level, scalability issues and requirements for hardware Internet technology changes have prevented its wider deployment. In the last decade, the limited deployment of IP Multicast has motivated the science community to work in the field of new approach for Internet video streaming by use of Peer to Peer networking technologies. In this paradigm every user (peer, node) maintains connections with other peers and forms an application level logical network on top of the physical network. Video stream originates at a source and every peer acts as a client as well as a server forwarding the received video packets to the next peer.

M. Gusev and P. Mitrevski (Eds.): ICT Innovations 2010, CCIS 83, pp. 215–225, 2011.

P2P logical network is used to deliver video without the need of broadband server connections. This class of "One to Many" video streaming is easy to deploy because p2p technology does not require network infrastructure support and offers scalability of resources having peers act as clients or servers, leading to small bandwidth server being able to transmit video to hundreds of thousands of users. P2P networks have huge economical benefit in deploying and managing IP video streaming, but brings a lot of open issues and research challenges that need to be tackled. Besides the existing numerous applications, p2p video streaming systems are still in the early stages.

This paper is organized in 5 sections. Section 2 gives detailed overview of P2P streaming system's characteristics, technical challenges and issues that need to be addressed when modeling and designing p2p video streaming system for live video broadcast. Section 3 presents overview of existing p2p video streaming solutions. In section 4 our idea for new modeling framework for performance analysis of p2p video streaming systems is presented and the paper is summed up with concluding remarks.

2 Technical Characteristics of P2P Live Video Streaming Systems

Two types of data are used in these logical p2p networks. First type of data is control data that is used to organize participating peers into a logical topology on top of the underlying physical network, and manages connections between parent and child peers (*Control Scheme*). Second type of data is the data that needs to be disseminated through the network which in this case is the video data (*Data Scheme*).

Control scheme. Control scheme forms three different types of logical topologies used in such systems: Tree, Mesh or Hybrid. The tree topology can be formed as a single spanning multicast tree [10], [13], [14], [17], [35], [36], or multiple multicast trees [1], [3], [5], [6], [7], [8], [11], [15], [16], [18], [23], [24], [27], [30], [45], [46], [47], [53] where the root of the tree is the video source. Mesh topology, also called Unstructured, does not form any firm logical construction, but organizes peers in swarming or gossiping like environment [2], [4], [9], [19], [20], [21], [22], [25], [26], [29], [31], [32], [34], [38], [39], [40], [42], [48], [49], [50], [51], [52]. In hybrid systems combination of tree and mesh constructions is used [28], [37], [43].

Data scheme. In combination with control scheme, data scheme forms several different approaches for video data dissemination in p2p networks. *Source driven* approach means that data scheme is built as a tree on top of the control scheme, where data is pushed down the tree from the root (source) to the leaves (peers). This approach is also called Push based approach. Typically source driven approach forms tree data scheme on top of tree control scheme [14], [17], [18], [49], but some p2p protocols build tree data scheme on top of mesh control scheme such as Narada [2]. *Data driven* approach is data oriented and doesn't form data distribution trees. Instead peers periodically exchange information about pieces of video data they possess, and every piece of data is explicitly requested. This approach is also called Pull based approach [19], [51]. There are many efforts that combine these two approaches (Push/Pull) and present substantial results [21], [28], [29], [31], [40], [43]. At

Receiver driven approach, the data scheme is a tree rooted at the receiver [1], [8], [9], [31], [39]. Beside the formation of logical network the receivers also organize resources. This approach is usually related to scalable video coding techniques where different descriptions or layers are distributed through different branches.

Peer churn. In p2p video streaming systems members are free to join or leave the system at will. The result of this user driven dynamics is constant disruption of the streaming data delivery. Hence, p2p network formation is dynamic stochastic process that highly influences the quality of offered service, especially for p2p live video broadcast. Solving this problem is complex combinatorial problem, especially for mesh based systems. To prevent the interruptions originating from this peer churn, robust and adaptive mechanism for managing this peer dynamics is needed.

Member's bandwidth heterogeneity. P2P network members are heterogeneous in their network capabilities in the way that all peers show diversity in capacities of download/upload links as well as variability in time of a single peer download/upload link capacity.

Video data latency (Delay). Efficient construction of p2p live video streaming network requires data scheme latency reduction as much as possible, in order to disseminate the content in live manner. This latency is firstly introduced by network infrastructure latency presented as a sum of serialization latency, propagation delay, router processing delay and router queuing delay. The second type of delay is introduced by peer churn and bandwidth heterogeneity. Concerning the structure it is only natural that p2p live streaming systems introduce larger data scheme delay compared to client/server systems, but it's possible and also required to keep this delay to a minimal level. However, any user that is served with live video content is more concerned about retaining Quality of Experience after starting the initial session. Resolving this latency requires careful buffer modeling and management.

Buffer management. The buffer is used for short term storage of video packets (chunks) that often arrive out of sequence in manner of order and/or time. Buffer is needed to reorder the sequence and compensate for packet latency. Buffer size requires precise dimensioning because even though larger buffer offers better sequence order or latency compensation, introduces larger video playback delay. Contrary, small buffer offers smaller playback delay but the system becomes more error prone. Also, the buffer content (buffer map) is usually exchanged between peers and used to locate missing video chunks and request data scheme connections.

Video coding Scheme. To distribute the video data, at first (at the source) the video stream is split into small pieces called chunks. Every chunk is marked with sequence order number which is used to reorder chunks at receiver before play out time deadline. To compensate for negative network impacts in packet loss or out of time delay, many systems implement different types of video coding that belong in the group of Scalable Video Coding. Two different concepts are increasingly implemented in p2p live video streaming systems: Layered Video Coding (LVC) and Multiple Description Coding (MDC) [54]. In both this paradigms video stream is split and coded in several different streams and sent through different paths in the p2p network. Each sub-stream contributes to one or more characteristics of video content in terms of temporal, spatial and SNR/quality scalability. In layered coding these separate streams are called layers, sequentially ordered, where the first layer is base layer and all remaining layers are enhancement layers. These layers are not independently decodable meaning that a member receiving video stream coded with LVC must have the Base layer to be able to decode it, and every other layer requires previous layer to be downloaded and decoded first. If its bandwidth allows, a member can require more or all other layers and receive full video signal.

Oppositely to LVC, MDC splits the video stream in several descriptions (sub-streams) which are independently decodable. Any description is sufficient to play the video, and additional received descriptions contribute to video quality enhancement. Many p2p video streaming models use LVC [1], [8], [42], [44] or MDC [31], [45], [48] and report promising results.

Chunk Scheduling. As we mentioned before, at the source, video data is partitioned in small pieces called chunks and distributed the p2p network. Tree push based systems don't require complex packet forwarding algorithm, but mesh, data driven approaches need carefully designed chunk scheduling algorithm, usually based on the available content and bandwidth of its neighbors. At first sight this technique may appear similar to BitTorrent [61], but the key differences are the realtime constraints which imply that video chunks need to be obtained in a timely manner. There are lots of research activities strictly focused on designing better chunk scheduling algorithms [38], [39], [40], [41], [44] that present the great importance of carefully composed scheduling algorithm that can significantly compensate for churn or bandwidth/latency disruptions.

There are also other issues to be addressed in this manner as whether TCP or UDP is better choice for use as transport protocol [55], defining most suitable chunk size, network conditions monitoring, incentives for peer that contribute the most resources to the system, congestion control mechanism, data protection, security issues, billing issues, digital rights management etc. but, this second group of characteristics can be considered as an enhancement to the existing p2p live streaming system.

3 Brief Review of P2P Video Streaming Applications

S. McCanne et al. [1] proposed a model that represents the beginnings of p2p media streaming. It's a receiver driven model with multicast tree network structure and layered video coding, where each video layer contributes to the quality of received signal. This way the distributed algorithm running at each peer compensates for network resource fluctuations in heterogeneous networks.

Y. Chu et al. [2] modeled Narada, distributed p2p protocol that at first organizes peers in a mesh and in the second step forms spanning trees for data dissemination. Narada uses a variant of standard distance vector routing algorithm over mesh control scheme and uses well known algorithms for construction of shortest path spanning trees for construction of data scheme. Narada implements strategies similar to the BGP routing protocol strategies and each member keeps routing cost to any other member and maintains information about the routes.

J. Jannotti et al. [3] presented Overcast, a protocol that constructs multiple distribution trees with one source. Members at start communicate with the source and self organize in distribution tree. Data is moved between parent and child members using TCP transport protocol. Overcast works with VoD as well as Live Broadcast systems and manifests service delay of about 10 to 15 seconds.

R. Rejaie et al. [8] introduced PALS, p2p adaptive layered streaming with receiver driven approach for quality adaptive playback of layer encoded media streaming. Control scheme is multiple trees where receiver manages adaptable layered stream delivery from group of congestion controlled senders to single receiver. In PALS the receiver orchestrates coordinated delivery among active senders by adaptively determining: a subset of senders that maximize overall throughput, overall quality (number of layers) that can be delivered and most importantly, required packets to be delivered by each active sender in order to effectively cope with any sudden change in throughput from individual senders.

E. Setton et al. [18] proposed Rate-Distortion optimized streaming model with multiple tree control scheme structure. It is a distributed algorithm where each member reports its own bandwidth and it is assumed that bandwidth doesn't change in time. Control and data scheme are implemented over UDP/IP protocol stack and all NAT servers and Firewalls are ignored. All members are synchronized and have heterogeneous but constant upload bandwidths. It is source driven approach that uses push method to forward packets after connection is established in a six way handshake. Entire model is video rate and distortion oriented that is calculated as a sum of distortion in the coder and packet loss through the network.

V. Pai et al. [19] created pull based system with mesh control scheme called Chainsaw. These lists of available chunks are constantly exchanged between peers so they can request missing chunks. It is assumed that the source generates chunks with constant rate (stream rate) and peers slide forward their list of chunks at the same rate as stream rate. If the chunk isn't requested by the time to play, it is dropped. Simulations demonstrated system's capability of high rate data dissemination to a large number of peers with no packet loss and extremely low duplicate data rates. Its low playback delay of about fraction of a second after joining the network, makes it highly suitable for applications like live p2p video broadcast.

X. Zhang et al. [20] presented CoolStreaming/DONet, data driven overlay network with mesh control scheme construction. Similar as in the previous system, every node periodically exchanges data availability information with group of partners and requests missing chunks from one or more partners or supplies available data to partners. Analytical results showed that DONet can scale to large network with limited delay. Large scale tests revealed quality enhancement of delivered stream as the overlay network increases in size.

M. Zhang et al. [21] introduced GridMedia, push pull model for media streaming over gossip control scheme structure. Pure pull model is similar to DONet, but uses one UDP packet as a data unit instead of segment consisting of one second video data. Because it adopts RTP protocol at application level, the sequence number field in RTP packet is used for buffer management, while the time stamp field is used for synchronization between nodes. Even though pure pull method works well in high churn rate and dynamic network conditions, it can't meet the demands of delay sensitive applications due to high latency accumulated hop by hop. In push pull method each node uses the pull method at startup and after that switches to push mode which contributes to better performance to the overall p2p streaming system.

N. Magharei et al. [31] constructed PRIME, receiver driven p2p streaming system with mesh control scheme structure that effectively incorporates swarming content delivery. In this model, two performance bottlenecks are identified: bandwidth bottleneck and content bottleneck. Proper peer connectivity is derived to minimize bandwidth bottleneck and also efficient pattern of delivery is constructed to minimize content bottleneck. It's also shown that pattern of delivery can be divided into diffusion and swarming phases and then proper packet scheduling algorithm is identified at individual peers. Each participating peer in the overlay has multiple parent and multiple child peers. All connections are congestion controlled and are always initiated by the corresponding child peer.

F. Covino et al. [50] presented StreamComplete, a new architecture and prototype system for mesh based p2p live video streaming. It realizes new concept of overlay network management and merges the best practices of tree and mesh based approaches. It also provides two new important distributed algorithms: Fast Top procedure that improves general performance in building network topology and Loop Check procedure that checks for existence of bounding loops in the mesh. StreamComplete uses RTP protocol at application level. It also uses UDP as transport protocol for data traffic and the TCP protocol for control traffic.

J. Chakareski et al. [51] created delay based overlay construction for p2p live video broadcast. The system's control scheme is mesh and uses pull mechanism for data exchange. The key idea of this data driven system is to organize peers in neighborhoods with similar delays from the origin media server. Peers in the neighborhood periodically exchange buffer maps while missing packets are requested by the receiver.

4 Modeling Framework for p2p Live Video Streaming Systems

Prior to creating p2p live streaming application it is necessary to analyze system's behavior via representative model which can provide insight in system's performance. Modeling and performance analysis of p2p live video streaming systems is challenging task which requires addressing many properties and issues of p2p systems that create complex combinatorial problem. Several related articles inspired us to research the possibilities for model development and performance analysis of such systems. D. Qiu, et al. [56] modeled file sharing p2p system, developing simple deterministic fluid model that provides good insights in the system's performance. Then, simple stochastic fluid model is developed and performance, efficiency and scalability of the model are studied. S. Tewari et al. [57] proposed analytical model for BitTorrent based live video streaming. In this paper, importance of well designed p2p system is pointed out, with a conclusion that peer group size has no influence on system efficiency when group size exceeds 7-8 peers. This paper proposes analytical model that concentrates on: the fraction of the total peer upload capacity that can be utilized, the number of fragments available for sharing, fragment size and video playback latency. Inspired by [56], they use the equation describing the fragment exchange efficiency (η),

$$\eta = 1 - \sum_{n_i=0}^{N-1} \frac{1}{N} \left(\frac{N - n_i}{N(n_i + 1)} \right)^k, \tag{1}$$

that after expanding it and eliminating negligible values, η is given as:

$$\eta = 1 - \frac{1}{N}, \tag{2}$$

where N is the number of fragments available for exchange, infering that the efficiency of fragment exchange heavily depends on the number of available fragments (except for large size fragments). After summarizing the relations between playback delay, fragment size, streaming rate and peer upload capacity, expression of this analytical model is given as:

$$\eta = 1 - \frac{S}{\tau R}, \tag{3}$$

where, η is a fraction of utilizable peer upload capacity, S is fragment size, τ is playback delay and R is streaming rate. In this paper, fragment size influence to the playback delay is emphasized. R. Kumar et al. [58] developed stochastic fluid theory for p2p streaming systems. Their simple model exposes the fundamental characteristics of such systems as well as its limitations. It represents general base for modeling such systems while interpreting peer churn as multiple levels Poison processes and adopting fluid flow model for video streaming. The analysis include modeling a system with streaming without buffering and churn, bufferless system with churn and p2p model with peer churn and buffering, while its analytical expressions bring insights in service degradation in all this cases. Many other similar research papers use fluid models, stochastic or otherwise, as [59], [60] for performance analysis of p2p live streaming systems, but they lack deeper performance assessment of certain p2p live streaming systems in terms of: most suitable number of video descriptions, data loss rate, playback time lag etc.

To the best of our knowledge there is no prior work on using Petri nets for modeling and performance analysis of such systems. Knowing that p2p streaming systems and their behavior can be described as processes with alternately changing states, it is only natural that such systems can be described with Petri nets. As a graphical tool Petri nets provide visual and communicational assistance for representing certain network and network flow. As a mathematical tool there are many possibilities of setting up equations for analyzing the behavior of the systems. Petri nets represent universal tool for theoreticians and practitioners bringing the gap closer between them, providing practitioners a tool to make their models more methodical and giving theoreticians a way to do more realistic models.

Inspired by these ideas, our future work we'll be concentrated on developing fluid stochastic Petri net model for performance analysis of p2p live video streaming systems. We believe that the model can address many of the fundamental properties of p2p streaming systems and thus deliver accurate performance assessment providing information that is necessary for development of actual p2p live streaming system.

5 Conclusion

In this paper we reviewed the state of the art of p2p live video streaming technology. We presented the fundamental characteristics of p2p live video streaming systems that need to be addressed while modeling. A short review of p2p live streaming applications including their main characteristics is also given, concluding that modeling and performance analysis is crucial research activity that should be performed prior creating such complex system. Inspired by several research papers developing fluid model (deterministic or stochastic), we propose strong idea of using Petri nets for fluid model development and performance analysis. We believe that in this manner lot of questions about the behavior of p2p streaming systems can be answered. Based on all aspects of this article we present our future work that will be concentrated on creating a fluid stochastic Petri net model for p2p live video streaming system.

References

1. McCanne, S., Jacobson, V.: Receiver Driven Layered Multicast. In: ACM SIGCOMM, Stanford, California (1996)
2. Chu, Y., Rao, S.G., Seshan, S., Zhang, H.: A Case for End System Multicast. In: ACM SIGMETRICS, Santa Clara (2000)
3. Jannotti, J., Gilford, D.K., Johnson, K.L., Kaashoek, M.F., O'Toole, Jr., J.W.: Overcast: Reliable Multicasting with an Overlay Network. In: Proceedings of OSDI, San Diego (2000)
4. Rowstron, A., Druschel, P.: Pastry: Scalable, Decentralized Object Location and Routing for Large Scale Peer to Peer Systems. In: 18th IFIP/ACM International Conference on Distributed Systems Platforms, Heidelberg (2001)
5. Castro, M., Druschel, P., Kermarrec, A.M., Nandi, A., Rowstron, A., Singh, A.: SplitStream: High Bandwidth Content Distribution In Cooperative Environments. In: 19th ACM Symposium on Operating Systems Principles, New York (2003)
6. Tran, D.A., Hua, K.A., Do, T.T.: ZIGZAG: An Efficient Peer to Peer Scheme for Media Steaming. In: IEEE INFOCOM 2003, San Francisco (2003)
7. Nicolosi, A., Annapureddy, S.: P2Pcast: A Peer to Peer Multicast Scheme for Streaming Data. Technical report, University of New York, New York (2003)
8. Rejaie, R., Ortega, A.: PALS: Peer to Peer Adaptive Layered Streaming. In: Int. Workshop on Network and Operating Systems Support for Digital Audio and Video, Monterey (2003)
9. Jiang, X., Dong, Y., Xu, D., Bhargava, B.: GnuStream: A P2P Media Streaming System Prototype. In: IEEE International Conference on Multimedia and Expo, Baltimore (2003)
10. Kostic, D., Rodriguez, A., Albrecht, J., Vahdat, A.: Bullet: High Bandwidth Data Dissemination Using an Overlay Mesh. In: ACM Symposium on Operating Systems Principles, New York (2003)

11. Hefeeda, M., Habib, A., Botev, B., Xu, D., Bhargava, B.: PROMISE: Peer-to-Peer Media Streaming Using CollectCast. In: ACM Multimedia, Berkeley, California (2003)
12. Tran, D. A., Hua, K. A., Do, T. T.: A Peer to Peer Architecture for Media Streaming. In: Journal of Selected Areas in Communication (2004)
13. Dobuzhskaya, M., Liu, R., Roewe, J., Sharma, N.: Zebra: Peer to Peer Multicast for Live Streaming Video. Technical report, Massachusetts Institute of Technology (2004)
14. Jin, H., Zhang, C., Deng, D., Yang, S., Yuan, Q., Yin, Z.: Anysee: Multicast based P2P Media Streaming Service System. In: Asia-Pacific Conf. on Communications, Perth (2005)
15. Wan, K.H., Loeser, C.: An Overlay Network Architecture for Data Placement Strategies in a P2P Streaming Network. In: 18th IEEE International Conference on Advanced Information Networking and Application, Fukuoka (2004)
16. Vuong, S., Liu, X., Upadhyaya, A., Wang, J.: CHIPS: An End-System Multicast Framework for P2P Media Streaming. In: 10th International Conference on Distributed Multimedia Systems, Sab Francisco (2004)
17. Tan, X., Datta, S.: Building Multicast Trees for Multimedia Streaming in Heterogeneous P2P Networks. In: IEEE Systems Communications, ICW 2005 (2005)
18. Setton, E., Noh, J., Girod, B.: Rate-Distortion Optimized Video Peer-to-Peer Multicast Streaming. In: ACM P2PMMS, Singapore (2005)
19. Pai, V., Kumar, K., Tamilmani, K., Sambamurthy, V., Mohr, A.E.: Chainsaw: Eliminating Trees from Overlay Multicast. In: 4th Int. Workshop on P2P Systems, New York (2005)
20. Zhang, X., Liu, J., Li, B., Yum, T.-S.P.: CoolStreaming/DONet: A Data Driven Overlay Network for Efficient Live Media Streaming. In: IEEE INFOCOM, Miami (2005)
21. Zhang, M., Zhao, L., Tang, Y., Luo, J.-G., Yang, S.-Q.: Large Scale Live Media Streaming over Peer to Peer Networks Through Global Internet. In: ACM Workshop on Advances in Peer to Peer Multimedia Streaming, New York (2005)
22. Tang, Y., Sun, L., Zhang, M., Yang, S., Zhong, Y.: A Novel Distributed and Practical Incentive Mechanism for Peer to Peer Live Video Streaming. In: IEEE International Conference on Multimedia and Expo, Toronto (2006)
23. Mol, J.J.D., Epema, D.H.J., Sips, H.J.: The Orchard Algorithm: P2P Multicasting without Free-riding. In: 6th IEEE International Conference on P2P Computing, Cambridge (2006)
24. Kalapriya, K., Nandy, S.K.: On the Implementation of a Streaming Video over Peer to Peer network using Middleware Components. In: IEEE, ICN, ICS and ICMCLT, Morne (2006)
25. Pianese, F., Keller, J., Biersack, E.W.: PULSE, a Flexible P2P Live Streaming System. In: 25th IEEE International Conference on Computer Communications, Barcelona (2006)
26. Nguyen, T., Kolazhi, K., Kamath, R.: Efficient Video Dissemination in Structured Hybrid P2P Networks. In: IEEE International Conference on Multimedia and Expo, Toronto (2006)
27. Setton, E., Noh, J., Girod, B.: Low Latency Video Streaming Over Peer to Peer Networks. In: IEEE International Conference on Multimedia and Expo, Toronto (2006)
28. Wang, F., Xiong, Y., Liu, J.: mTreebone: A Hybrid Tree/Mesh Overlay for Application Layer Live Video Multicast. In: International Conference on Distributed Computer Systems, Toronto (2007)
29. Agarwal, S., Dube, S.: Gossip Based Streaming with Incentives for Peer Collaboration. In: 8th IEEE International Symposium on Multimedia, San Diego (2006)
30. Venkataraman, V., Yoshida, K., Francis, P.: Chunkyspread: Heterogeneous Unstructured End System Multicast. In: 14th Int. Conf. on Network Protocols, Santa Barbara (2006)
31. Magharei, N., Rejaie, R.: PRIME: Peer to Peer Receiver Driven Mesh Based Streaming. In: IEEE INFOCOM, Anchorage (2007)

32. Liang, J., Nahrstedt, K.: Dagstream: Locality aware and Failure Resilient P2P Streaming. In: S&T/SPIE Conference on Multimedia Computing and Networking, San Jose (2006)
33. Jinfeng, Z., Jianwei, N., Rui, H., Jian, M.: Adaptive Video Streaming over P2P Multi-Hop Path. In: 21th IEEE International Conference on Advanced Information Networking and Applications Workshops, Niagara Falls (2007)
34. Lan, X., Zheng, N., Xue, J., Wu, X., Gao, B.: A p2p Architecture for Efficient Live Scalable Media Streaming on Internet. In: ACM Multimedia, Augsburg (2007)
35. Li, J., Yeo, C.K., Lee, B.S.: Fast Scheduling on P2P Streaming Overlay. In: 2nd Int. Conference on Ubiquitous Information Management and Communication, Suwon (2008)
36. Tu, X., Jin, H., Liao, X.: Nearcast: A Locality-Aware P2P Live Streaming Approach for Distance Education. ACM Transactions on Internet Technology (2008)
37. Lu, Z., Li, Y., Wu, J., Zhang, S.Y., Zhong, Y.P.: MultiPeerCast: A Tree-mesh-hybrid P2P Live Streaming Scheme Design and Implementation based on PeerCast. In: 10th IEEE Int. Conference on High Performance Computing and Communications, Dalian (2008)
38. Da Silva, P.C., Leonardi, E., Mellia, M., Meo, M.: A Bandwidth-Aware Scheduling Strategy for P2P-TV Systems. In: 8th IEEE Int. Conference on P2P Computing, Aachen (2008)
39. Tu, X., Jin, H., Liao, X., Wang, W., Yang, S., Huang, Q.: Collaboratively Scheduling to Decrease Inter-AS Traffic in P2P Live Streaming. In: 22nd IEEE International Conference on Advanced Information Networking and Applications Workshops, Okinawa (2008)
40. Guo, Y., Liang, C., Liu, Y.: Adaptive Queue Based Chunk Scheduling for P2P Live Streaming. LNCS. Springer, Heidelberg (2008)
41. Xue, Z.C.K, Hong, P.: A Study on Reducing Chunk Scheduling Delay for Mesh-Based P2P Live Streaming. In: 7th IEEE International Conference on Grid and Cooperative Computing, Shenzhen (2008)
42. Guo, H., Lo, K. T., Qian, Y., Li, J.: Peer-to-Peer Live Video Distribution under Heterogeneous Bandwidth Constraints. IEEE Transactions on Parallel and Distributed Systems (2009)
43. Li, Z., Yu, Y., Hei, X., Tsang, D.H.K.: Towards Low-Redundancy Push-Pull P2P Live Streaming. In: ICST QShine, Hong Kong (2008)
44. Xiao, X., Shi, Y., Gao, Y.: On Optimal Scheduling for Layered Video Streaming in Heterogeneous Peer-to-Peer Networks. In: ACM Multimedia, Vancouver (2008)
45. Mushtaq, M., Ahmed, T.: Adaptive Packet Video Streaming Over P2P Networks Using Active Measurements. In: 11th IEEE Symposium on Computers and Communications, Paula-Cagliari (2006)
46. Mushtaq, M., Ahmed, T.: P2P-based Collaborative Media Streaming for Heterogeneous Network Terminals. In: IEEE International Conference on Automation, Quality and Testing, Robotics, Cluj-Napoca (2008)
47. Liu, X., Yin, H., Lin, C., Liu, Y., Chen, Z., Xiao, X.: Performance Analysis and Industrial Practice of Peer-Assisted Content Distribution Network for Large-Scale Live Video Streaming. In: 22nd IEEE International Conference on Advanced Information Networking and Applications, Okinawa (2008)
48. Guo, H., Lo, K.T.: Cooperative Media Data Streaming with Scalable Video Coding. IEEE Transactions on Knowledge and Data Engineering (2008)
49. Feng, C., Li, B.: On Large-Scale Peer-to-Peer Streaming Systems with Network Coding. In: ACM Multimedia, Vancouver (2008)
50. Covino, F., Mecella, M.: Design and Evaluation of a System for Mesh-based P2P Live Video Streaming. In: ACM MOMM, Linz (2008)

51. Chakaereski, J., Frossard, P.: Dellay-Based Overlay Construction in P2P video Broadcast. In: IEEE ICASSP, Taipei (2009)
52. Bertinat, M.E., De Vera, D., Padula, D., Amoza, F.R., Rodriguez-Bocca, P., Romero, P., Rubino, G.: GoalBit: The First Free and Open Source Peer to Peer Streaming Network. In: 5th ACM Latin America Networking Conference, Pelotas (2009)
53. Zezza, S., Magli, E., Olmo, G., Grangetto, M.: Seacast: A Protocol for Peer to Peer Video Streaming Supporting Multiple Description Coding. In: IEEE International Conference on Multimedia and Expo, New York (2009)
54. Chakareski, J., Han, S., Girod, B.: Layered Coding vs. Multiple Descriptions for Video Streaming Over Multiple Paths. In: 11th ACM Int. Conf. on Multimedia, Berkeley (2003)
55. Chang, J.-Y., Su, X.: An Evaluation of Transport protocols in Peer to Peer Media Streaming. In: IEEE Int. Conference on Networking Architecture and Storage, Chongqing (2008)
56. Qiu, D., Srikant, R.: Modeling and Performance Analysis of BitTorrent-Like Peer to Peer Networks. In: ACM SIGCOMM, Portland (2004)
57. Tewari, S., Kleinrock, L.: Analytical Model for BitTorrent Based Live Video Streaming. In: 4rd IEEE Conference on Consumer Communications and Networking, Las Vegas (2007)
58. Kumar, R., Liu, Y., Ross, K.: Stochastic Fluid Theory for P2P Streaming Systems. In: IEEE INFOCOM, Anchorage (2007)
59. Zhou, Y., Chiu, D.M., Lui, J.C.S.: A Simple Model for Analyzing P2P Streaming Protocols. In: IEEE International Conference on Network Protocols, Beijing (2007)
60. Wu, J., Tao, J., Zou, Z.: Maximizing Universal Streaming Rate in Peer-to-Peer Streaming Networks. In: 7th IEEE Int. Conf. on Grid and Cooperative Computing, Shenzen (2008)
61. `http://www.BitTorrent.com/`

Correlation between Object-Oriented Metrics and Refactoring

Daniela Boshnakoska[1] and Anastas Mišev[2]

[1] Innovaworks, Skopje, Macedonia
[2] University Sts Cyril and Methodius, Faculty of Natural Sciences and Mathematics, Institute of Informatics, Skopje, Macedonia
daniela.bosnakoska@gmail.com, anastas@ii.edu.mk

Abstract. Repeated code modification lowers code quality and impacts object-oriented system design. Object-oriented metrics have proven as indicators of problems in system design. They have been grouped in minimal sets, known as quality models, to assess object-oriented system quality. Improvement can be gained by establishing relationships between quality characteristics and metrics computed from object-oriented diagrams. Quality models include metrics that can produce better code in object-oriented systems. Code quality can also be gained with refactoring. Refactoring is used to reduce complexity and eliminate redundant code. It is important to identify when and where to use refactoring. There are many different approaches. This work presents early stage analysis and focuses on exploring whether object-oriented metrics can be used as indicators where in the code refactoring can be used. Through multiple iterations of successive measurement and refactoring, relation between metric values and need of refactoring can be concluded.

Keywords: Object-oriented metrics, object-oriented quality models, refactoring, automated metric collection, metric based refactoring.

1 Introduction

Object-oriented technology introduced new aspects of development and software maintenance. Object-oriented development require different approach from traditional functional decomposition, data flow and quality assessment. To enhance quality in such environment, object-oriented metrics were established. They measure characteristics of object-oriented systems in a way to improve them. Many aspects have been proposed to improve code quality using these metrics, including the attempts to combine them with software refactoring. Refactoring is known as "a change made to the internal structure of software to make it easier to understand and cheaper to modify without changing its observable behavior" [4]. Refactoring is one of the best techniques used to improve code quality and reduce code complexity. Aside from its benefits, refactoring is an expensive process. To reduce barriers where and when to apply refactoring, many approaches are considered [24], [25], [26], [27].

M. Gusev and P. Mitrevski (Eds.): ICT Innovations 2010, CCIS 83, pp. 226–235, 2011.

This paper investigates correlation between object-oriented metrics, the refactoring process and the possibility to use these metrics as valid indicators for code regions that need special attention. Iterative process of measuring, refactoring and analysis is made on three projects. We are trying to formulate dependence between changes of metric values within refactoring activities. Unique approach is taken and instead of open source code, it uses well known and documented projects to verify the correlation, where problematic classes and "code smells" are known in advance.

2 Related Work

In order to improve system design, in their case study [16], Crespo, L´opez, Manso and Marticorena use metrics as indicators of bed smells. This method is accomplished using UML and metamodels that represent any object-oriented language. Using metrics as indications of "bad smells", they suggest suitable refactoring action.

Zhao and Hayes [15] compared refactoring decision tool against programmer's code inspection on finding design problems. They used class-based approach to find refactoring candidate. Tool was designed to prioritize classes that require refactoring, based on static set of metrics and weighted method. Results indicated that such designed tool can be of significant help in the development process.

Simon, Steinbrückner and Lewerentz [17] showed that special kind of metrics can help to indentify class irregularities and ease the decision where to apply refactoring. They presented a generic approach using source code analysis, to generate tool based visualizations that can help developers to identify problematic code.

3 Object-Oriented Metrics and Quality Models

All industry branches use measurements in order to validate their improvements. Measurement in software industry is used to give guidelines to managers and practitioners to make informed decisions and intelligent choices, plan and schedule activities or allocate resources. Software metric is a measurement scale and method to determine values of some indicators of a certain software product. Software metric has been defined as a measure of some property of a piece of software or its specification.

Object-oriented metrics are category of software metrics introduced as a way to measure quality of object-oriented systems. These metrics are focused on measurements applied to class and design characteristics. They help designers to make changes early in the development phase in a way to reduce further code complexity. There are at least three ways in which object oriented metrics can be used: quality estimation, risk management and estimation of system testability. Quality estimation means to build estimation model from gathered historical data. In practice, quality estimation is gained either by estimating reliability (number of defects) or maintainability (change effort). Risk management is concerned with finding potentially problematic classes as early as possible. Process and product metrics can help managing activities (scheduling, costing, staffing and controlling) and engineering activities (analyzing, designing, coding, documenting and testing).

Object-oriented metrics are grouped in meaningful sets to estimate system design, known as quality models. They provide a relationship between desired design attributes and grant estimation for code quality. The aim is to improve quality attributes in a quantitative way, connecting quality characteristics and metrics calculated from object-oriented diagrams. A significant number of quality models have been proposed from different authors: Brito e Abreu [7], Bucci, Chidamber-Kemerer [14], Fioravanti [3], Henderson-Sellers [3], Kim, Li [11], and Thomas [3].

C.K. metric suite [14], known also as MOOSE metrics, is the deepest research regarding object-oriented metrics. MOOSE indicates whether developers are following object-oriented principals in their design. C.K. suite has developed significant interest and is currently is the most well-known and used suite for object-oriented software measurement.

Li and Henry metrics [11] are an extension from MOOSE suite, introduced to express maintainability in object oriented systems.

Lorenz and Kidd metrics [6] are focused on object orientation in systems.

MOOD suite [6] defined from Brito e Abreu and Rogerio Capurca, is one of the newest sets and has been empirically validated. Together with its extension known as MOOD 2 are used to measure class diagrams.

QMOOD [6] variation uses predefined formulas built from quality attributes. It is a measure for class diagrams, which can be applied on UML diagrams and can provide important information in early phases of the software lifecycle.

4 Refactoring through Object-Oriented Metrics

Refactoring is one of the most important software transformations used to improve code complexity and mitigate maintainability. Refactoring process was introduced by William Opdyke and practical implementation was established by Martin Fowler [4]. They suggested list of code problems known as "bad smells" to decide where to apply refactoring. Code becomes complex and non usable because of its size, logic, constant modification or interactions. Difficulty emerges where to apply refactoring technique. Aside from programmer's intuition, additional aspects are necessary to assist in identifying segments that need refactoring. There are efforts to mitigate this recognition process with variety of approaches. This paper shows that object-oriented metrics can be used to point out classes that require immediate attention. Extended set of C.K. suite will be used as quality model because of its ability to measure bad code agents such as complexity, cohesion and couplings. C.K values can be automatically assembled by evident number of tools.

5 Practical Implementation

The goal is to find correlation between object-oriented metrics and the refactoring process. Moreover, we have to investigate if object-oriented metrics can be used to identify classes that are preferential to refactor. Analyzing distributions of metric values can be concluded that C.K. metrics are connected with class internal structure and the intense of its optimization. Unlike previous research, where open source projects were analyzed, we apply the methodology on well-known projects where "smelly" classes are known in advance. Without further inspections, testing, and doubts that previous studies suffered from, early estimation can be done with well defined filters to identify potential classes. Results will be compared against problematic classes quoted in projects documentation.

5.1 Projects Specification

Inspected solution is a platform composed of multiple projects, using N-tier architecture. This multiuse system can be easily configured from the outermost presentation projects to behave as an event management system, complex marketing system or content management system. Multiple client-presentation projects share the same business, data and administrative core. Since the number of presentation project rises, administrative and business layers became larger, heavier and more complex.

Projects are developed using .NET technology, MSSQL database, LINQ extension and variation of MVC pattern for client-projects. The practice to frequently include new presentation projects with intense speed made common classes to enlarge in size and they became complex to extend and modify. To proceed with rapid development, refactoring was needed.

Business layer, administrative project and data layer were common among all presentation projects which made them our subject of interest.

Modified MVC patter in the administrative web application caused certain classes to grow in size. Code was not spread among pages and classes, but was collected in specified containers known as "controllers". Modules that have similar logic shared "controllers" and these files grow in size and complexity. Common "controller" classes from administrative project become bottleneck and needed immediate refactoring. Business and data project are shared between administrative project and all client projects. The goal was to develop a framework that can be used by all presentation projects. To get framework capabilities, data and business objects were abstracted and funneled with logic. Commonly used objects in these layers are candidates for deeper consideration and refactoring.

Object-oriented metrics were collected using automated tools Understand [20] and NDepend [21]. Initial graphic report produced from NDepend on the overall solution, can provide approximate review on complex classes in short time. This report displays projects as separate sections where problematic classes are emphasized:

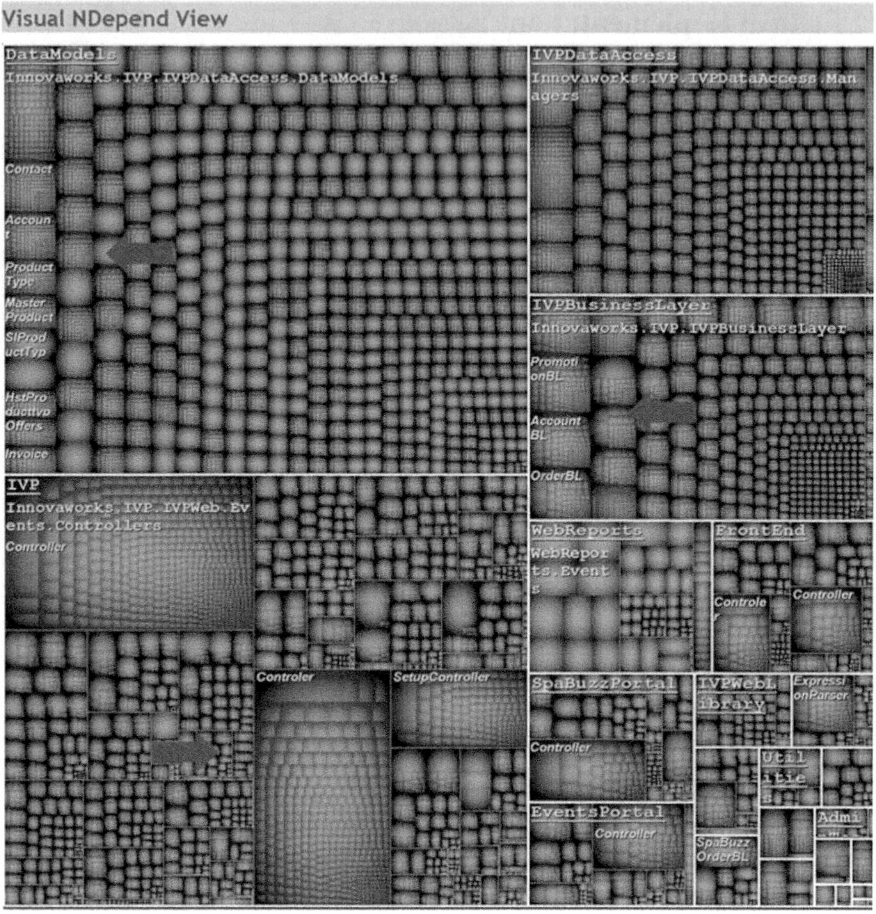

Fig. 1. NDepend graphic solution representation

Once these metrics are analyzed to point candidates, refactoring process was made using Resharper [23], Refactor Pro [22] and the refactoring capabilities of Visual Studio.

5.2 Iterations

The very first step is to select area of inspection. From the selected project, class, module or library metrics are calculated using Understand tool. This tool integrates many reports, including extended C.K. metrics as "Class OO metrics" report, listed below:

Table 1. Object-oriented metrics rrepresentation in Understand [20]

Metric	Description
LCOM (% Lack of Cohesion)	100 % minus the average cohesion for class data members. (A method is cohesive when it performs a single task)
DIT (Max Inheritance Tree)	Maximum depth of the class in the inheritance tree.
IFANIN (Count of Base Classes)	Number of immediate base classes.
CBO (Count of Coupled Classes)	Number of other classes coupled to this class.
NOC (Count of Derived Classes)	Number of immediate subclasses this class has.
RFC (Count of All Methods)	Number of methods this class has, including inherited methods.
NIM (Count of Instance Methods)	Number of instance methods this class has.
NIV (Count of Instance Variables)	Number of instance variable this class has.
WMC (Count of Methods)	Number of local methods this class has.

Gathered object-oriented metrics are analyzed to point out candidate classes. These classes are then refactored using automated tools and code inspection. Metric collection and refactoring process are repeated in two iterations, after which global elaboration is done, based on the difference between calculated metrics among iteration activities. To select efficient filters for iteration processes, general guidelines are followed:

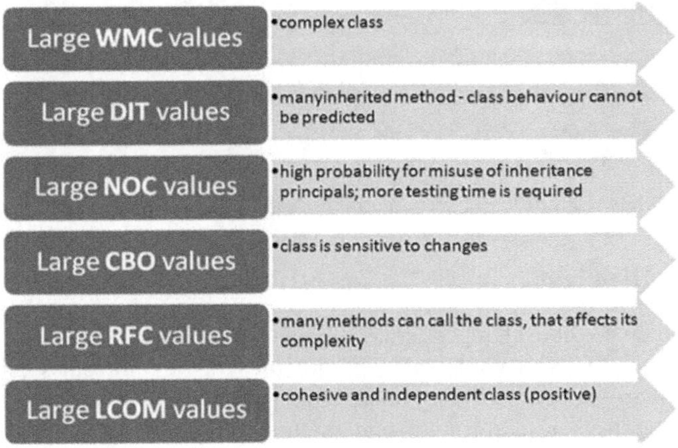

Fig. 2. Value interpretation for metrics defined in C.K. (MOOSE) metric suite

After collecting metrics in first iteration, classes that need refactoring process are selected based on two filters applied consequently: high values for MOOSE metrics; high values for class size and overall complexity. Refactoring process in this phase is simple and no inner class code violation is done. Changes are method oriented, including aesthetic modification, lambda expressions, removal of code duplicates, reduction of temporal variables, lazy classes [4] etc. Once these adjustments are done, metrics are recalculated and used as input parameters for the second iteration.

Second iteration sort classes that require refactoring based on metric values using simple filter – maximum class complexity. Refactoring actions in this stage are more aggressive, resulting with global code changes inside classes. With automated tools and manual code inspection unused - methods, variables and declarations are removed. Fowler's Long Methods, Long Parameter Lists, Switch Statements, Lazy Methods, Duplicated Code, Inappropriate Intimacy, Primitive Obsessions [4] are reduced. Second iteration phase is finalized with additional metric recalculation.

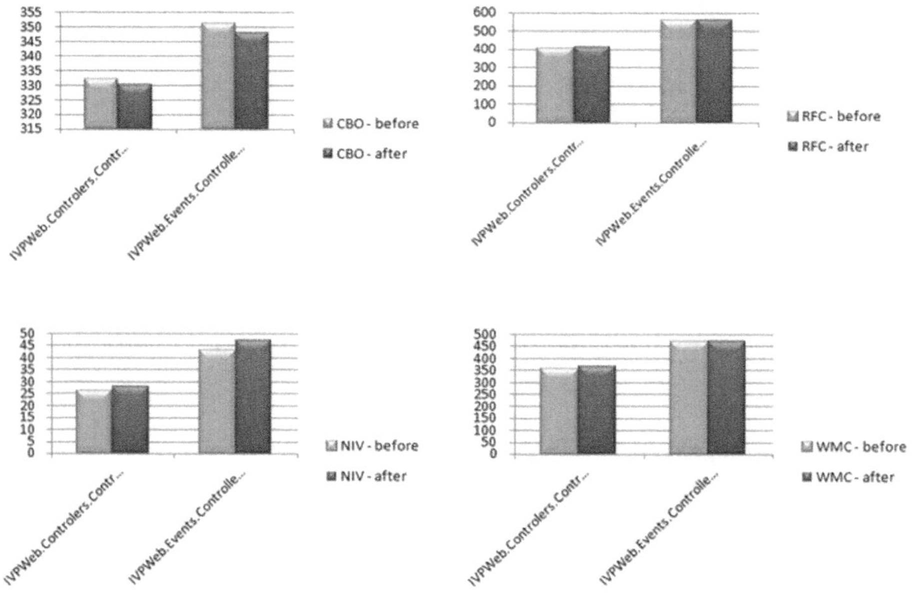

Fig. 3. Value changes for OO metrics in administration project before and after refactoring

5.3 Iteration Highlights

Because of inner method changes, class object–oriented metrics in the first iteration are slightly changed. Noticeable changes are present only in class and file metric values, which are concerned with class size and overall complexity. First stage pointed out that light refactoring inside methods couldn't be tracked with object-oriented metrics, but rater with file metrics.

Coarse inner class refactoring from second iteration resulted with noticeable changes in object-oriented metrics. This type of refactoring does not affect metrics gathered from class diagrams such as inheritance metrics. NIM, NIV, RFC, WMC and CBO values are modified, but there is no general conclusion for their value distributions. This is because when "bad smells" like Long Method, Long Class and Feature Envy [4] are refactored, they increase the number of methods in the inspected class and lower its coupling. On the other hand, Duplicated Code, Lazy Methods, Lazy Classes are changed in a way that lowers the number of methods and increase coupling. Since basic calculation for given metrics is dependent upon the number of methods, generalization change formula cannot be derived. This is opposite from previous studies [17] where specific "bad smells" are associated with static set of metrics. Ground reason for the difference is that inspected classes from our three projects are large in size, containing many methods and cannot be classified as purely Data Classes, Lazy Classes or Parallel Inheritance Hierarchies [4]. Instead their code is sublimation of different smells. Second iteration showed that object-oriented metrics could point out problematic classes that need special attention. It can be concluded that these metrics cannot be taken as valid indicator for good inner class code and its quality, but instead they are tied with the overall design.

Object-oriented metric values that were used as indicators and filters in both iterations proposed exactly the same classes and problematic areas already recognized in project documentation. Controller-classes in administration project, commonly used object classes from business and data layers deviate in reports taken with Understand. This proves our hypothesis that object-oriented metrics can mark potential problems and report troublesome classes.

5.4 System Based Analysis

In order to explore how C.K. metrics behave and their value distribution in larger environment, metric analysis can be run on the overall solution. Comparison has been made between metrics gathered from business application examined in solution environment, and metrics for the same isolated project. Metrics such as DIT, RFC and CBO are increased when project is inspected as part of broader scope. DIT values are enlarged because as the system grows, the inheritance tree expands. This expansion affects RFC metrics as in its calculation RFC includes inherited metrics. When number of method increases, more method to method connections raise, resulting with increased values for CBO metric. Generally, as the system enlarges, its complexity grows, and so values for these metrics. It is noticeable that WMC, NIV, NIM and LCOM values remain same although the project was inspected in larger environment. Dependence is not upon system complexity, but rely on inner class complexity.

It can be concluded that extended C.K. suite is complete for refactoring demands and can be successfully applied on solutions and single classes to point out potential problems.

6 Conclusions

Object-oriented metrics indicate good system design. Particularly inheritance metrics are tightly coupled with system architecture. On the other hand, there is a correlation between object-oriented metrics and the refactoring process. Metrics can indicate problematic code that needs refactoring. Important are complexity metrics, which can point out frequently changed sections and size metrics that show where immediate optimization is needed.

Analysis connection between extended MOOSE metric suite and class refactoring, shows that value changes are noticeable among metrics depended from the number of methods. There is no linear dependence between refactoring and MOOSE metrics value changes, because refactoring actions have different impact on the class/method structure. Small value changes are present with large classes, or when loose refactoring actions are taken. Combination of "Class Metrics" and "Class Object-oriented Metrics" applied on three different projects successfully reported classes that should be redesigned, refactored and needed special attention.

Software companies should constantly include metrics. Object-oriented metrics can be used from the very beginning, when system architecture is set. Moreover, design metrics, complexity metrics and reusability metrics will give insight in system size, testability time and possibility for reuse, maintenance or extension during early phases. In planning and management process, product metrics are important and can give meaningful results. Object-oriented metrics is a must in coding phase since they can prompt potential code problems and refactoring need will be minimized. Particularly important are these metrics to point where to use refactoring on purely documented projects, open source projects or projects developed from outsourcing companies.

7 Future Work

Current research, done on small number of projects can be extended and generalize if applied on broad set of applications, including different types of systems, developed using different object-oriented languages. MOOSE suite used in this research should be extended and completed with useful and valid metrics from other quality models. Further research can be also focused on the relations between refactoring, metric sets and specific code smells. This will give complete metric model that can categorize class problems and produce logic refactoring actions. After validating this process, it can be used to build composite intelligent tools for measurement, code inspection and refactoring. Continuous use of such tool will result with compact, better code, easy for manipulation, extension, maintenance and modification. This will lead to code and software standardization and improved software quality.

References

1. Laird, L.M., Brennan, C.M.: Software Measurement and Estimation: A Practical Approach. Wiley-IEEE Computer Society Press (2006)
2. Kan, S.H.: Metrics and Models in Software Quality Engineering, 2nd edn. Addison-Wesley Professional, Reading (2002)
3. Fioravanti, F.: Skills for Managing Rapidly Changing IT Projects. IRM Press (2006)
4. Fowler, M., Beck, K., Brant, J., Opdyke, W., Roberts, D.: Refactoring: Improving the Design of Existing Code. Addison-Wesley Professional, Reading (1999)
5. Emam, K.: A Primer on Object-Oriented Measurement. In: Metrics, Seventh International Software Metrics Symposium (METRICS 2001), London, UK (2001)
6. El-Wakil, M., El-Batawisi, A., Boshra, M., Fahmy, A.: Object-Oriented Design Quality Models. In: A Survey and Comparison, International Conference on Informatics and Systems (2004)
7. Brito e Abreu, F., Melo, W.L.: Evaluating the Impact of Object-Oriented Design on Software Quality. In: 3rd International Software Metrics Symposium (METRICS 1996). IEEE, Berlin (1996)

8. Jamali, S.M.: Object Oriented Metrics. Survey paper, Sharif University of Technology, Tehran Iran (2006)
9. Rosenberg, L.H.: Applying and Interpreting Object Oriented Metrics. In: Proc. Software Technology Conf., NASA (1998)
10. Basili, V.R., Briand, L., Melo, W.L.: A Validation of Object-Oriented Design Metrics as Quality Indicators. IEEE Transactions on Software Engineering 22(10) (1996)
11. Li, W., Henry, S.: Object-Oriented Metrics Which Predict Maintainability. Technical report (1993)
12. Kaner, C., Bond, W.P.: Software Engineering Metrics: What Do They Measure and How Do We Know? In: 10th International Software Metrics Symposium, Chicago (2004)
13. Demeyer, S., Ducasse, S.: Metrics, Do They Really Help? In: Proceedings of Languages et Modèles à Objets (LMO 1999). HERMES Science Publications, Paris (1999)
14. Chidamber, S.R., Darcy, D.P., Kemerer, C.F.: Managerial Use of Metrics for Object-Oriented Software: An Exploratory Analysis. IEEE Transactions on Software Engineering (2005)
15. Zhao, L., Hayes, J.H.: Predicting Classes in Need of Refactoring: An Application of Static Metrics. In: Proceedings of the Workshop on Predictive Models of Software Engineering (PROMISE), associated with ICSM (2006)
16. Crespo, Y., López, C., Manso, E., Marticorena, R.: Language Independent Metric Support towards Refactoring Inference. In: 9th Workshop on Quantitative Approaches in Object-Oriented Software Engineering, QAOOSE, Glasgow, UK (2005)
17. Simon, F., Steinbrückner, F., Lewerentz, C.: Metrics based refactoring. In: Fifth European Conference on Software Maintenance and Reengineering, 2001 (2001)
18. Moser, R., Sillitti, A., Abrahamsson, P., Succi, G.: Does refactoring improve reusability? In: Morisio, M. (ed.) ICSR 2006. LNCS, vol. 4039, pp. 287–297. Springer, Heidelberg (2006)
19. Iyer, S.S., Tech, B.: An Analytical Study of Metrics and Refactoring. Master's Thesis, The University of Texas at Austin (2009)
20. Understand, `http://www.scitools.com/index.php`
21. NDepend, `http://www.ndepend.com`
22. Code Rush Refactor!, `http://www.devexpress.com/coderush`
23. Resharer, `http://www.jetbrains.com/resharper`
24. Refactoring support, `http://patterninsight.com/solutions/refactoring.php`
25. Roberts, D., Brant, J., Johnson, R., Opdyke, W.: An Automated Refactoring Tool. In: Proceedings of ICAST 1995: International Conference on Advanced Science and Technology, Chicago, Illinois (1995)
26. Melton, H., Tempero, E.: Identifying Refactoring Opportunities by Identifying Dependency Cycles. In: Proceedings of the Twenty-Ninth Australasian Computer Science Conference, Hobart, Australia (2006)
27. Murphy-Hill, E., Andrew, P., Black, A.P.: Breaking the Barriers to Successful Refactoring. In: Proceedings of the 30th International Conference on Software Engineering (ICSE 2008), Leipzig, Germany (2008)

Mobile Robot Environment Learning and Localization Using Active Perception

Petre Lameski[1,2] and Andrea Kulakov[2]

[1] NI TEKNA – Intelligent Technologies, Negotino, Macedonia
petre.lameski@ni-tekna.com
[2] University of Sts. Cyril and Methodius,
Faculty of Electrical Engineering and Information Technologies, Skopje, Macedonia
{lameski,kulak}@feit.ukim.edu.mk

Abstract. The human brain does not remember the images seen through the eyes just by the light influx into the retina, but by the sensory-motor interaction between the human movement (including eye movement) and the environment. We propose a system for autonomous mobile robot localization in the environment that uses the behavioral aspects of the human brain, especially the saccadic movement of the eyes. The hypothesis for the robot location in the environment is built not by the image itself, but as a collection of saccadic sensory-motor pairs of the image observations that create the mental representation of all perceived objects in the environment. This approach is implemented and tested on a dataset of images taken from a real environment. The obtained results from the localization show that the comparison of the saccadic sequences of the descriptors outperforms the naïve descriptor matching of the images.

Keywords: Active Perception, Mobile Robot Localization, Saccades, Behaviorism.

1 Introduction

The problem of localization of mobile robots is resolved by using different localization algorithms that use probabilistic theory to maximize the likelihood of guessing the robot position based on the information obtained from the environment [1]. The information obtained from the environment is the data that the robot gets from the sensors it possesses. Mostly laser range finders, ultrasound sensors, and other types of distance sensors are used for obtaining data about the environment. Good results are obtained by using distance sensors for the problems of both localization and simultaneous localization and mapping. Integration of these sensors with other types shows good results especially when combined with the GPS sensors for outdoors localization. In recent years due to the increased processor power and the advances of image processing and computer vision, the camera becomes more and more used sensor in robotics. Promising results are shown when using the camera as a sensor for mobile robot localization and mapping [2]. One of the widely used approaches is to obtain rotation, translation and scale invariant descriptors from the

M. Gusev and P. Mitrevski (Eds.): ICT Innovations 2010, CCIS 83, pp. 236–244, 2011.

image in order to represent the information it contains. Such descriptor is the SURF (Speeded Up Robust Features) descriptor [3]. These descriptors, however, are also limited in their invariance. The use of these types of descriptors for the problem of robotic localization is also known [4]. Other approaches for indoor localization that don't use cameras, but demand a fixed indoor infrastructure are shown in [11,12,13]. The strength of fixed sources of radio signals are used for indoor localization in these approaches.

A good approach exists in the literature for solving the problem of room localization [9]. It is based on training data using SIFT (Scale Invariant Feature Transformation) descriptors taken from omnidirectional and perspective images from the environment and SVM (Support Vector Machine) classifiers. This approach gives good results, but uses offline learning of the environment. Other authors address the problem of room classification using visual data from the environment [8].

Bearing in mind that the mobile robot is an active agent in the environment, actions executed by the robot can also be used for improving the localization precision of the robot. This allows the robot to plan the next move in order to maximize the information it gains from the environment. This concept is called active perception or active vision [6]. The robot actively observes the environment by deciding where to "look" next. Similar approaches are already used for object recognition [5].

The active vision used in that manner, allows the robot or the agent to actively observe the environment by moving or rotating the camera in order to obtain the image from the environment from more than one location. It, however, does not observe the image in an active manner. The taken image is considered as a static sensory input. The manner in which the human eye observes the environment is not static [6]. The human eye is able to see only a small portion of the area. The illusion that one sees a whole image is created by the constant movement of the eyes. When one looks at an object, one doesn't see the whole object at once. Pieces of the object are in the viewers' fixation point at different times, and this focus is moved around the object by a brain mechanism that moves the attention from one piece to another. As the viewer observes the object, it remembers not only the image characteristics of the fixation point, but the movements that were made in order to view the whole object [7]. These movements of the eyes are called saccadic movements.

In this paper we propose an active vision system for mobile robots' localization that combines the active observation of images by using saccadic movements' viewing of the images with the invariant image descriptors in order to maximize the probability of positive localization of the mobile robot. The system uses semi-supervised learning based only on the saccadic sequences that it obtains from the percepts of the environment.

2 System Architecture

The system we suggest is consisted of two subsystems. The first subsystem is the learning subsystem that learns the environment and builds the internal representation of the states that the robot has learned or visited.

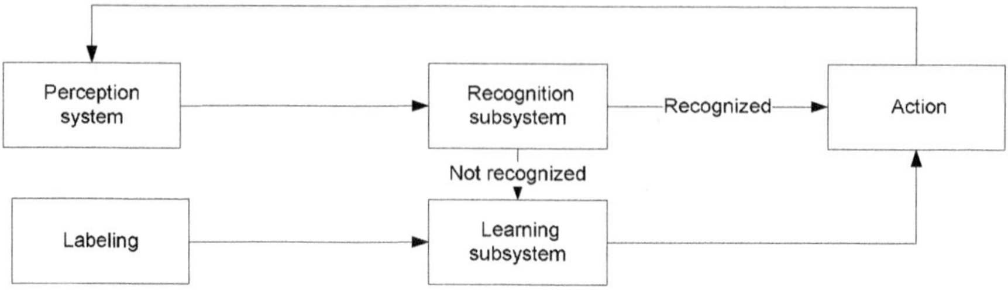

Fig. 1. System architecture

The second subsystem is used for recognition of the states thus enabling the robot to recognize the location it is in. The global system architecture is given in Fig 1. The robot roams the environment and obtains images from the environment. The images are taken in a sequence. The nearer images of the sequence correspond to images taken from locations that are closer to each other. For each image taken, the robot tries to recognize the location by trying to remember whether it visited that state previously.

If the state has been visited, the robot continues executing another action and then obtains another percept of the environment. Otherwise the robot remembers the state with its recognition subsystem. This system allows the robot to learn the environment in a semi-supervised manner. For each new state that the robot is in, the operator can give a label of the state or the robot can generate a label by itself.

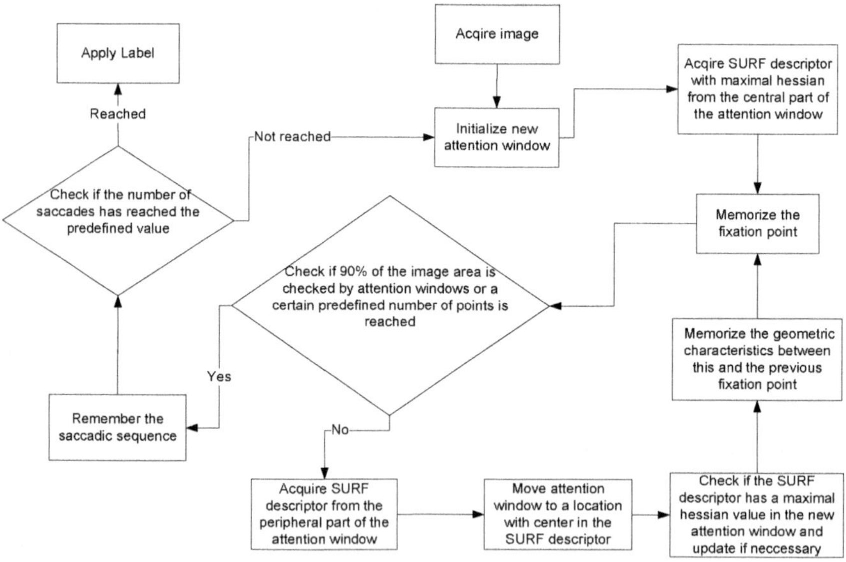

Fig. 2. UML Activity diagram of the Learning subsystem

The image is represented in the memory of the robot by a saccadic sequence. The environment is learned by the robot through the learning subsystem (Fig 2). For each taken image, a random attention window is selected. The attention window is the area around the saccadic location where the fixation point is located. The attention window is separated in two parts: the central part and the periphery. From the central part of this window, the SURF descriptor with the largest value of the hessian determinant is extracted. This is done because the higher the hessian value, the more stable the descriptor is for that part of the image. The highest hessian-valued SURF descriptor gives the fixation point for the attention window from the image. After the central feature is extracted, a new attention window is selected by moving to the periphery of the current attention window. From the periphery, again, the highest hessian valued SURF descriptor is selected, and the new attention window is created so that the peripheral SURF descriptor becomes its center.

In this way the attention of the view is moved from one fixation point (A SURF descriptor with highest hessian value), to another fixation point, thus simulating the saccadic movement of the eye. If the window comes to a region from the image, in which no SURF descriptor could be extracted, then a new random window is selected from areas that were not seen previously. Information about visited areas are kept in order to avoid visiting already seen locations in the image. This allows the attention window to move to locations that would give larger information gain and make the system more curious. For each descriptor, the descriptor value and its direction are kept. For two consecutive descriptors, the distance between them and the angle between the first descriptor direction and the direction of the connecting line segment are remembered. Descriptors hold the information about their angle directions, thus allowing the use of this approach with some rotation invariance of the input images. In this way a saccadic sequence is generated for each image. The saccadic sequence may have variable number of fixation points and saccadic movements. Each set of saccadic sequences for the image is memorized and they represent the image in the robot's memory. The saccadic sequence for each consecutive image begins with an attention window that is in the same location as the attention window of the previous image.

The localization of the robot is performed by comparing the obtained image from the robot camera to the saccadic sequences that the robot has in its memory. For the recognition of the image (Fig 3), the process of obtaining the saccadic sequence is done in a similar manner as in the learning subsystem, but with few differences. The robot takes an image from the environment and a random attention window is generated for this image. A hypothesis for the location is generated and initialized to equal probability for the full set of memorized saccades. From the attention window, initialized from a remembered saccade, the SURF descriptors are extracted and are compared to the corresponding memorized fixation point. If a similar SURF descriptor is found, then the saccadic sequence from the memory is followed. For each similar descriptor found in the image, that also belongs to the memorized saccadic sequence, the probability that the robot is in the state that is represented by that saccadic sequence in the memory increases. If enough similar descriptors are found in the image, compared to the descriptors retrieved from the memorized saccadic sequences of images in the memory, a decision is made that the robot is in the position that corresponds to the sequence in the memory.

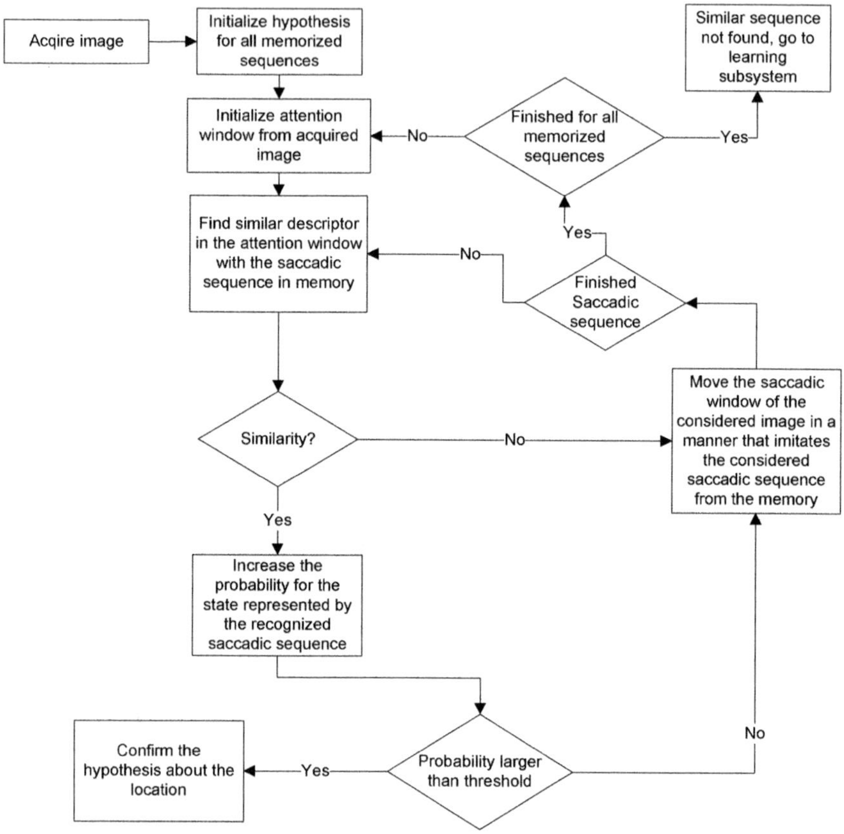

Fig. 3. UML Activity diagram of the recognition subsystem

If a similar SURF descriptor is not found, the next fixation point from the saccadic sequences in the memory is taken into consideration, the attention window of the current image is moved in the same way. The process is repeated until one hypothesis is confirmed or all hypotheses are disproved. If a hypothesis is confirmed, then the robot successfully localized itself. Otherwise, the robot is in a new state that is labeled by the robot itself or by the robot operator. The hypothesis is confirmed if enough fixation points are recognized on the input image. Example of the saccadic sequence extraction is given on Fig 4.

a. b. c.

Fig 4. a. Image from the environment b. Single extracted saccadic sequence, c. Multiple saccadic sequences for the same image

3 Experimental Results

The proposed architecture was implemented and tested for its ability to recognize the distinct rooms in an indoor environment dataset. The dataset [10] is consisted of an image sequence from an indoor environment. It is consisted of 7 distinct rooms and contains 1793 images taken consecutively during the movement of the robot. The images were taken with frequency of 2-3 images per second each with resolution of 320x240 pixels. Part of these images (1408) was taken for the learning and the rest of the images (taken in continuity of the previous images, but repeating the places that the robot has visited before) were used for testing of the recognition subsystem. From the second part of the images, a random subset of images was taken for testing the system. Since the images were taken consecutively during the movement of the robot, each image was represented by only one saccadic sequence, but the series of the images taken in a single room were represented by a consecutive saccadic sequence. (The ending attention window of a previous image is a starting attention window for the next image).

The system was tested first by naively comparing the remembered SURF descriptors from the training images with the extracted SURF descriptors from the test images. The system checks the similarity of the images. If images have larger number of similar descriptors than a given threshold value, then the similarity is confirmed. If, however, none of the memorized images achieves the desired threshold, then the image is considered unknown, and the system doesn't give a response. In such case, the learning subsystem should be executed since the robot is probably in a previously not visited state. The obtained results are shown in Table 1.

Table 1. Results from direct descriptor matching without saccadic sequences

Percentage of matched descriptors	Percentage of guessed rooms	Responsiveness
80%	56,25%	40%
60%	48,6%	60%

The results show relatively low percentage of guessed rooms. This is due to the ambiguity of the dataset and because of the information loss due to the smaller number of SURF descriptors remembered in the memory of the robot. The responsiveness result in the table shows on what percentage of the images the system was able to give judgment about the location.

The second test was done by using the system proposed in this paper. The obtained results are shown in Table 2.

Table 2. Results from tests on the implemented system

Percentage of guessed rooms	Responsiveness
54%	70%
70%	25%

The results show better precision of the proposed system in comparison to the naïve matching of the descriptors in the previous test. This is a result of the remembered saccadic sequences for the image. The system was tested for its ability to recognize a room from a single image. Since the system tries to mimic the way that humans observe objects and scenes, the same sequence of training images was given to human volunteers and their performance was tested. The test group was shown the image sequence used for learning by the robot only once. The image sequence was taken by the robot during its movement (the learning image sequence from the dataset). Each image had a number indicating the room. The sequence simulates walking around the rooms in a laboratory. During the observation, candidates could take notes in order to remember certain features that could be used to characterize a room.

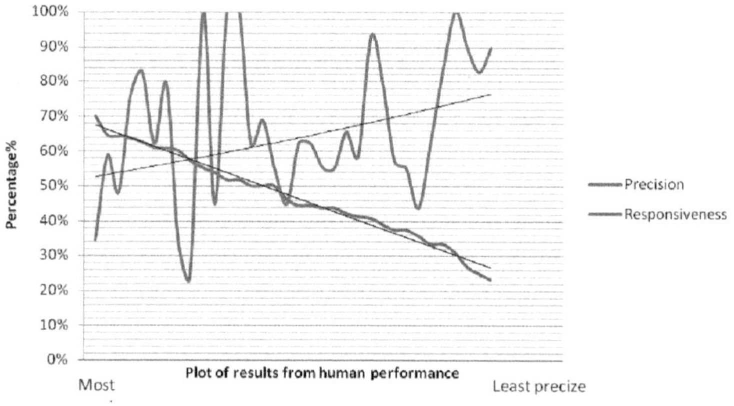

Fig. 5. Precision and responsiveness of humans on the same test as the proposed system

After the sequence finished, the candidates were then given time of 3 seconds for observation and 2 seconds for response on a random subset of the images used in the test set of the robot. For each image, candidates had the task to guess the room that the image is taken from. The results are shown on Fig 5. As it can be seen from the results, the tested candidates have similar percentage of guesses and responses to the tests as the system. Roughly, the average precision of humans was around 45% and the responsiveness was around 67%. The reason is that the localization or the room guessing is done on the bases of only one image. The same experiment, repeated on a different group of humans that were given more time to response (5 seconds for observation and 3 seconds to response), resulted in a slight increase of precision but in a large increase of responsiveness (Precision of 50% and responsiveness of around 85%). The graph on Fig 5 shows similar conduct of the proposed system with the human results: larger responsiveness - smaller precision.

4 Conclusion

As it can be seen from the results, the proposed system nearly equals the performance of the participants under similar conditions (Only one saccadic sequence and only one image per room for guessing) and outperforms the naïve descriptor matching. This shows that the local invariant descriptors, combined with the relative geometric positions, improve the precision of the localization on the given dataset image sequence. The smaller number of SURF descriptors remembered during the learning phase also contributes towards increased performance. Instead of matching large number of descriptors, the number of matches needed to be done is much smaller. The number of remembered saccadic sequences by image can be tuned in the system. For our experiment only one saccadic sequence was taken for each image. Further saccadic sequences would result in larger information gain but would slow down the response time of the system since more saccadic sequences would need to be learnt in the learning phase and checked in the recognition (localization) phase.

On the downside, the system is less accurate than the proposed system in [9]. The system proposed in [9], however, uses images with higher resolutions and an offline training phase that takes much more time than the learning phase of our approach, which can be done on the fly. Further, the SURF descriptor does not take advantage of the colors and unlike humans, describes only local invariant features from the image. It doesn't describe objects from the rooms. Having a system that recognizes objects in the rooms and gives correspondence between the objects and the rooms, would improve the precision. Additional sensory data might improve the precision of the system too. Even the proposed semantic classification of the rooms and using the semantic labeling [8], could improve the precision of the system significantly. The system would then integrate the knowledge not only from the room, but from the abstraction of the type of the room (is the room a kitchen, a classroom etc.).

The proposed system can be used with combination of other systems as a support unit in the mobile robot localization and learning of indoor environments. If possible, the local SURF descriptors might be replaced by objects and their geometrical relations. Further usage of the system, that might be considered, is the usage of a sequence of images for the purpose of room recognition and not just one image. The usage of consecutive images would be possible with the use of some of the known localization algorithms based on Bayesian filters. For this purpose, the perception phase of the system would be integrated with the actions in order to plan the next action of the robot so that the information gain from the room could be maximized. In other words, the robot would chose where to look next in order to increase the time it needs to conclude the localization.

References

1. Thrun, S., Burgard, W., Fox, D.: Probabalistic Robotics, 1st edn. The MIT Press, Cambridge (September 2005)
2. Karlsson, N., Bernardo, E., Ostrowski, J., Goncalves, L., Pirjanian, P., Munich, M.E.: The vSLAM Algorithm for Robust Localization and Mapping. In: Proc. of Int. Conf. on Robotics and Automation (ICRA) (2005)
3. Bay, H., Ess, A., Tuytelaars, T., Vangool, L.: Speeded-up robust features (surf). Computer Vision and Image Understanding 110(3), 346–359 (2008)
4. Davison, A.J., Reid, I.D., Molton, N.D., Stasse, O.: Monoslam: Real-time single camera slam. IEEE Transactions on Pattern Analysis and Machine Intelligence 29(6), 1052–1067 (2007)
5. Dutta Roy, S., Chaudhury, S., Banerjee, S.: Active recognition through next view planning: a survey. Pattern Recognition 37(3), 429–446 (2004)
6. Noe, A.: Action in Perception (Representation and Mind). MIT Press, Cambridge (March 2006)
7. Rybak, I., Gusakova, V., Golovan, A., Podladchikova, L., Shevtsova, N.: A model of attention-guided visual perception and recognition. Vision Research 38(15-16), 2387–2400 (1998)
8. Rottmann, A., Mozos, M., Stachniss, C., Burgard, W.: Semantic place classification of indoor environments with mobile robots using boosting. In: AAAI Conference on Artificial Intelligence, pp. 1306–1311 (2005)
9. Ullah, M.M., Pronobis, A., Caputo, B., Luo, J., Jensfelt, P., Christensen, H.I.: Towards robust place recognition for robot localization. In: Proc. IEEE Int'l Conf. Robotics and Automation, pp. 530–537 (2008)
10. Stachniss, C.: Dataset: Freiburg Indoor Building 079 (January 18, 2006), `http://cres.usc.edu/radishrepository/view-one.php?name=albert-b-laser-vision` (accessed, November 20, 2009)
11. Ferris, B., Hahnel, D., Fox, D.: Gaussian processes for signal strength-based location estimation. In: Robotics: Science and Systems II (2006)
12. Pan, S.J., Kwok, J.T., Yang, Q., Pan, J.J.: Adaptive localization in a dynamic WiFi environment through multi-view learning. In: Proceedings of the 22nd AAAI Conference on Artificial Intelligence, pp. 1108–1113 (2007)
13. Ferris, B., Fox, D., Lawrence, N.: WiFi-SLAM using gaussian process latent variable models. In: Proceedings of the 20th International Joint Conference on Artificial Intelligence, pp. 2480–2485 (2007)

Diatom Classification with Novel Bell Based Classification Algorithm

Andreja Naumoski and Kosta Mitreski

University Ss. Cyril and Methodius, Faculty of Electrical Engineering and Information Technologies, Skopje, Karpos 2 bb, Skopje, Macedonia
{andrejna,komit}@feit.ukim.edu.mk

Abstract. Diatoms are ideal indicators of certain physical-chemical parameters and in the relevant literature they are classified into one of the water quality classes (WQCs). Using information technologies methods, we can classify old and new diatoms directly from measured data. In this direction, a novel method for diatom classification is proposed in this paper. The classification models are induced by using modified bell fuzzy membership functions (MFs) in order to make more accurate models. An intensive comparison study of the fuzzy MFs distribution with the proposed method and the classical classification algorithms on the classification accuracy is studied. Based on this evaluation results, three models are presented and discussed. The experimental results have shown that the proposed algorithm remains interpretable, robust on data change and achieve highest classification accuracy. The obtain results from the classification models are verified with existing diatom ecological preference and for some diatoms new knowledge is added.

Keywords: Aggregation Trees, Bell distribution, Diatom classification, Lake Prespa.

1 Introduction

In this research, we use the property of the diatoms relationship with the physical-chemical parameters to classify the appropriate indicator for newly discovered diatom. Diatoms as bio-indicators serve as early indicators of the water quality. With their property as indicators they can indicate the health state of the ecosystem. But, not for all diatoms, the property of indicating specific water quality class is known. In this direction, the information technology helps to find the correct diatom-indicator relationship directly from measure data. Following this directives, the WQCs defined in the traditional way can be interpreted as a classification problem in terms of data mining point of view. In this research, we deal with a typical classification problem, when we build a classification model that classifies the diatom into one of the WQ classes as indicator.

In this domain, classical statistical approach, such as canonical correspondence analysis (CCA), detrended correspondence analysis (DCA) and principal component

M. Gusev and P. Mitrevski (Eds.): ICT Innovations 2010, CCIS 83, pp. 245–254, 2011.

analysis (PCA), are most widely used as a modelling techniques [18]. Although these techniques provide useful insights into data, they are limited in terms of interpretability. Obvious progress in this research area in a direction of interpretability, have been made using data mining techniques, especially decision trees. These methods have improved the interpretability and increased the prediction power of the models. The first attempt to model diatom-environment relationship for Lake Prespa, have been made by [4]. Several of the models produced unknown knowledge about the newly discovered diatoms for the first time [4]. Multi-target decision trees later were used, in order to reveal entire set of influencing factors on the diatoms in this lake ecosystem [15]. However, these methods were not robust on data change. This is an important property, because the environmental condition inside of the lake changes rapidly. Also these methods were not used for classification, only for regression analysis.

The robustness of data change and resistant to over-fitting of the fuzzy inducted trees concept as a classification tool is the main reason of extensive research on fuzzy set based machine learning. Wang and Mendel [12] have presented an algorithm for generating fuzzy rules by learning from examples. Inspired by the classic decision tree induction by Quinlan [10], there are substantial works on fuzzy decision trees. Janikow [11], Olaru and Wehenkel [8] have presented different fuzzy decision tree inductions. Suárez and Lutsko [14], and Wang and Chen, et al. [13] have presented optimizations of fuzzy decision trees. Most of the existing fuzzy rule induction methods including fuzzy decision trees [9] focus on searching for rules, which only use t-norm operators [7] such as the MIN and algebraic MIN. Research has been conducted to resolve this problem. Kóczy, Vámos and Biró [3] have proposed fuzzy signatures to model the complex structures of data points using different aggregation operators including MIN, MAX, average, and etc. Nikravesh [5] has presented evolutionary computation (EC) based multiple aggregator fuzzy decision trees. The method that is used for classification is based on fuzzy theory approach, so that the problem with data change robust has been overcome.

The main question is: why to use fuzzy aggregation trees (ATs) in the process of diatom classification? There are several reasons for this. First of all, the proposed method is robust to over-fitting because it uses fuzzy induction method, which is not the case with the classical methods and decision trees. Second, they obtain a compact structure, which is essential in the process of knowledge obtained from the biological data. And third, these models can achieve high classification accuracy. One of the reasons, why this method is better compared with the previous one, is the use of different fuzzy MFs. In this paper work, we propose a novel MF; modified bell MF, which was not used in the process of fuzzy induced trees [11, 20]. Aggregation trees follows the induction process proposed in [20], but with novel bell MF. Later in the paper the proposed function is tested with the previous used MF for diatom dataset.

The rest of the paper is organized as follows: Section 2 provides definitions for similarity metrics and fuzzy aggregation operators. In Section 3 the proposed evenly distributed bell MF is presented. Section 4 presents the diatoms abundance water quality datasets as well as the experimental setup. In section 5, model for each WQ class is discussed together with the verification of the model results. Finally, Section 6 concludes the paper and gives some future research directions.

2 Similarity Metrics and Fuzzy Aggregation Operators

The aggregation tree induction method is made by using similarity metrics and fuzzy aggregation operators, which are presented in this section.

Let A and B be two fuzzy sets [10] defined on the universe of discourse U. The RMSE based fuzzy set similarity (*Sim_RMSE*) of fuzzy sets A and B is computed as:

$$Sim\_RMSE(A;B)=1-\sqrt{\frac{\sum_{i=1}^{n}(\mu_A(x_i)-\mu_B(x_i))^2}{n}}, \tag{1}$$

where x_i, $i = 1, \ldots, n$, are the crisp values discretized in the variable domain, and $\mu_A(x_i)$ and $\mu_B(x_i)$ are the fuzzy membership values of x_i for A and B. The larger the value of *Sim_RMSE*(A,B) is, the more similar A and B are. The $\mu_A(x_i)$, $\mu_B(x_i) \in [0, 1]$, $0 \leq Sim\_RMSE(A;B) \leq 1$ holds according to (1). Note that the proposed classification method follows the same principle, if an alternative fuzzy set similarity definition such as Jaccard is used.

According to the fuzzy logic theory, the fuzzy aggregation operators are logic operators applied to fuzzy membership values or fuzzy sets. They have three sub-categories, namely t-norm, t-conorms, and averaging operators such as weighted averaging (WA) and ordered weighted averaging (OWA) [8]. In our experimental setup, we use the basic operators (*Algebaric AND/OR*) which operate on two fuzzy membership values a and b, where a, $b \in [0, 1]$. No influence of the averaging operators on the classification models are studied in this research.

3 Proposed Bell Membership Function

The straight line MFs (triangular and trapezoidal) has the advantage of simplicity. They are simple, and in some case in the process of building aggregation trees obtained relatively good classification accuracy. However, many of the datasets have smoothed values and nonzero points, which apply to use different MFs.

In this paper section, the modified bell MF is defined, which in general is specified by three parameters, shown with equation (2). In this equation, the parameters a and b are usually positive, while the c parameter is located at the centre of the curve.

$$f(x;a;b;c)=\frac{1}{1+\left|\frac{x-c}{a}\right|^{2b}}. \tag{2}$$

We modify the equation 2, by taking into account the mean (μ) and standard deviation (σ). This is due to the specific nature of the diatom dataset, meaning that the distribution of the diatoms versus environmental parameters can be described with bell MF. To take this property into account we preserve this information with the μ and σ into the algorithm. To achieve complete evenness, or intersection between the two MF is 0.5, the value for the σ, is calculated according equation 3.

$$\sigma = \sqrt{\frac{Log[a]}{2 * Log[0.5 * r]}}, \ a = 10 . \tag{3}$$

Now, when all this changes are taken into account, replacing the c parameter with μ, b-constant with the standard deviation σ, calculated according 3, the equation (4) mathematically represents the modified bell MF used with the proposed method for diatom classification:

$$f(x;\mu;\sigma) = \frac{1}{1 + \left| \frac{x - \mu}{10} \right|^{2\sigma}} . \tag{4}$$

4 Data Description and Experimental Setup

The dataset used in the experiments consist from 13 input parameters representing the TOP10 diatoms species (diatom species that exist in Lake Prespa [2]) with their abundance per sample, plus the three WQ classes for conductivity, pH and Saturated Oxygen. The one dataset is created for each WQC class as output class.

Table 1. Water quality classes for the physical-chemical parameters [16, 17]

Physical-chemical parameters	Name of the WQC	Parameter range	Name of the WQC	Parameter range
Saturated Oxygen	oligosaprobous	SatO > 85	α-mesosaprobous	25-70
	β-mesosaprobous	70-85	α-meso / polysaprobous	10-25
pH	acidobiontic	pH < 5.5	alkaliphilous	pH > 7.5
	acidophilous	pH > 5.5	alkalibiontic	pH > 8
	circumneutral	pH > 6.5	Indifferent	pH > 9
Conductivity	fresh	Conduc < 20	brackish fresh	90 – 180
	fresh brackish	Conduc < 90	brackish	180 - 900

These measurements were made as a part of the TRABOREMA project [6]. The WQ classes were defined according to the three physical-chemical parameters: Saturated Oxygen [16], Conductivity [17] and pH [16, 17] and they are given in Table 1. We conducted three types of experiments, which are set up as follows:

1) **Train:** A fuzzification method based on the modified bell MF, presented in this paper, for each input variable are used to transform the crisp values into fuzzy values. The same dataset is used as a train and test set;

2) **Exp2, Exp3:** The whole data are divided into two parts, namely the odd labeled data and the even labeled data. Two experiments are carried out, with the first (Exp2) using odd labeled data as training set and even labeled data as test set, and the second (Exp3) using even labeled data as training set and odd labeled data as test set. This

experimental setup is actually 2-fold cross validation. We will examine the influence of the number of MFs per attribute in more details.

3) **xVal:** Standard 10-fold cross validation is used for evaluation of the classification accuracy of the algorithm against some classical classification algorithms (C4.5, kNN, SVM, FT and, etc.).

For classification model interpretation purpose, we induce a general aggregation tree which consists from 2 candidate trees, 3 low level trees and have depth equal to 3. Later, comparison with other crisp classifiers is done with simple (SAT) and general aggregation trees (AT) with two different depths named (AT5 and AT10). Furthermore, the effect of the MF number per attribute is studied for different number of membership functions per attribute (3, 4, 5, 10, 20, 30, 50 and 100). The average value of these experiments for the bell MF is given in Table 2. Bolded and underlined values are the highest scores for classification accuracy.

Table 2. Average classification accuracy per WQC, (in %)

Conductivity WQC – Average Classification Accuracy				
	Triangular	Trapezoidal	Gaussian	Bell
Train	73.80	**74.66**	74.03	73.57
Exp2	69.15	**71.22**	68.12	67.89
Exp3	**69.61**	69.50	69.27	69.38
pH WQC – Average Classification Accuracy				
	Triangular	Trapezoidal	Gaussian	Bell
Train	59.40	60.95	58.66	**61.98**
Exp2	46.30	41.90	47.92	**54.86**
Exp3	46.53	45.83	48.61	**51.85**
Saturated Oxygen WQC – Average Classification Accuracy				
	Triangular	Trapezoidal	Gaussian	Bell
Train	**62.13**	61.13	62.00	62.00
Exp2	52.75	56.00	50.50	**56.13**
Exp3	50.37	52.35	51.36	**52.48**

5 Experimental Results

Based on the performance results, in this section we give an interpretation of several classification models and the rules derived from them. One model for each pH WQ class is discussed and later the classification results are verified with the known diatom ecological references. The experiments are conducted with the modified bell MF with number of MF per attribute equal to 5. For similarity definition, we use *Sim_RMSE* and only *Algebraic AND/OR* as a fuzzy aggregation operator.

5.1 Performance Evaluation

The Table 2 presents the highest prediction accuracy of aggregation trees over different combinations of training-test sets, especially in the Exp2 and Exp3. Due to paper constrains we present only the average accuracy for MF per attribute. Concerning the performance evaluation of the proposed bell MF, this distribution outperformed 2 of the 3 diatom WQ classes compared with other MFs used previously. Both trapezoidal and the bell MF achieved highest classification accuracy than the triangular and the Gaussian MF in Exp2 and Exp3.

Regarding the water quality classes for Conductivity, according to Table 2 the trapezoidal MF outperformed other MFs. For the pH WQCs, the proposed method with the bell MF achieved highest classification accuracy among all the compared MFs. The proposed method obtained better classification accuracy for the Saturated Oxygen WQ class for the bell MF in Exp2 and Exp3 compared with triangular, trapezoidal and Gaussian MF.

5.2 Classification Models for the Water Quality Classes

We have built many classification models for each WQC, but due to paper constrains, we present the only the models for the pH WQC. The output of the aggregation tree for each leaf is a Fuzzy Term. To make the models easy for interpretation, each Fuzzy Term is labelled according the two values μ and σ {Bad Indicator, Low Indicator, Good Indicator, Very Good Indicator and Excellent Indicator}.

The pH water quality class consists from 5 output classes as it is shown with Table 1. The proposed method has generated a separate model tree for each class, which classifies the diatom into one or several classes. The aggregation tree shown in Fig. 1 (left) can be converted into a rule which is stated below.

Rule1: If pH class is ***circumneutral*** **THEN** (*Navicula subrotundata* (NSROT) is **Excellent Indicator** OR *Cyclotella ocellata* (COCE) is **Very Good Indicator**) OR *Cyclotella juriljii* (CJUR) is **Low Indicator** OR *Cavinula scutelloides* (CSCU) is **Bad Indicator**. The rule has confidence of 69.70%.

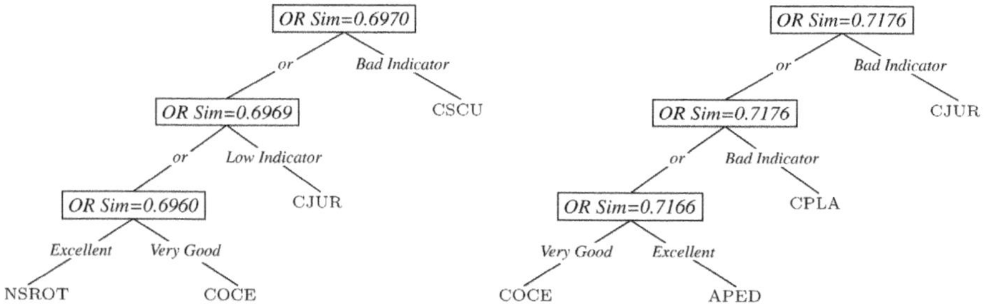

Fig. 1. Classification model generated using proposed bell MF for the circumneutral pH WQC (left) and alkaliphilous pH WQC (right)

According to the classification model, NPRE diatom is an excellent indicator of *circumneutral* waters, followed by the COCE diatom which is very good indicator. The model identifies the CSCU diatom as a bad indicator of such waters. Regarding the CJUR diatom, the model identified him as low indicator of *circumneutral* waters.

Furthermore, two more classification models are presented, one for the pH WQC – *alkaliphilous* and other one for pH WQC – *alkalibiontic*. The rule induced from the tree shown in Fig. 1 – right, states:

Rule2: If pH class is ***alkaliphilous*** **THEN** (COCE is **Very Good Indicator** OR *Amphora pediculus* (APED) is **Excellent Indicator**) OR *Cocconeis placentula* (CPLA) is **Bad Indicator** OR CJUR is **Bad Indicator**. The rule has confidence of 71.76%.

Concerning the indicator of the *alkaliphilous* water, the classification model have identify two diatoms APED and COCE that are closely related to this WQC and they can be used to indicate *alkaliphilous* waters. The other two diatoms; CJUR and CPLA cannot be used as bio - indicators of such water.

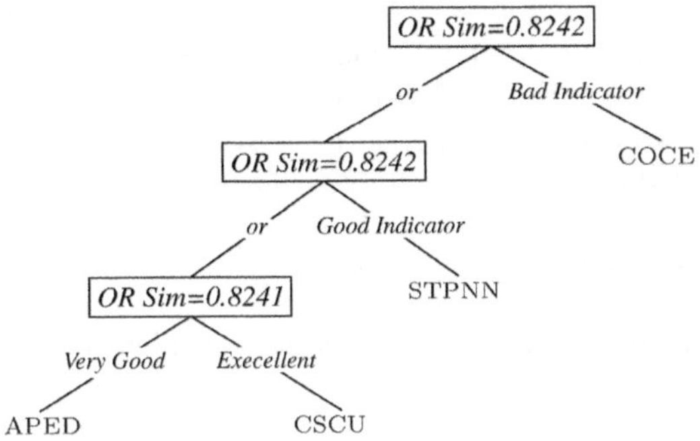

Fig. 2. Classification model generated using proposed bell MF for the *alkalibiontic* pH WQC

Using the proposed method, the induced classification model presented with Fig. 2 shows the indicating properties of the four diatoms (APED, STPNN, COCE and CSCU) for the pH WQC - *alkalibiontic*.

Rule3: If pH class is ***alkalibiontic*** **THEN** (APED is **Very Good Indicator** OR CSCU is **Excellent Indicator**) OR *Staurosirella pinnata* (STPNN) is **Good Indicator** OR COCE is **Bad Indicator**. The rule has confidence of 82.42%.

From the Rule3, it is easy seen that the CSCU is an excellent indicator of such waters followed by the APED diatom according to the model. The modern affinity to this pH WQC has STPNN, followed by bad indicator properties of the COCE diatom.

5.3 Verification of the Results from the Models

Ecological references for the TOP10 diatoms are taken from the latest diatom ecology publications (Van Dam *et. al.*, 1994) and the European Diatom Database (http://craticula.ncl.ac.uk/Eddi/jsp/index.jsp). Other publications where these references are used for comparison with previous models are given in [1, 2, 4, 15]. Concerning the ecological preferences of the TOP10 dominant diatoms in the Lake Prespa, CJUR and NPRE are newly described taxa (diatoms) with no records for their ecological references in the literature. Some of the results from the classification models are the first known ecological references for certain WQC classes.

In the relevant literature the APED diatom is known to as *alkaliphilous*, fresh-brackish, nitrogen-autotrophic (tolerates elevated concentrations of organically bound nitrogen), high oxygen saturation (>75%), *β-mesosaprobic* and *eutrophic* (because of Organic N tolerance) diatom indicator [19]. The classification models have successfully found the indicating properties of the APED diatoms as *alkaliphilous* and added the property of indicator for *alkalibiontic*. In the relevant literature that CSCU is known as *alkalibiontic*, *freshwater* to *brakish* water taxon, being *oligosaprobic* indicators with eutrophic preferences [19]. According the classification models CSCU diatom is *alkalibiontic*. COCE is known as meso-eutro taxon [19], while concerning the pH properties there is no known ecological preference. According the models, the COCE diatom is very good indicator for *alkaliphilous* and *circumneutral* waters, but further investigation is needed before to any conclusion is made. Regarding the STPNN diatom, in the literature is known as *hyper-eutrophic* (*oligo-eutrophic*; indifferent) taxon frequently found on moist habitats, while the models have found that this diatom is good indicator of *alkalibiontic* waters. The NSROT diatom has no ecological references in the literature, so the results of the model are the first to be known. The NSROT diatom can be used for indicating *circumneutral* waters.

5.4 Comparison with Classical Classifiers

Most of the classic decision trees - classification algorithms produce very strict interpretable decisions of the acquired knowledge from the environmental data. But these algorithms are not robust on data change which is not case with the proposed method. In order to improve the classification accuracy and maintaining the robustness of the data change which comes by fuzzification of the input data, we will use the proposed method, which perform better according to the results (see Table 3).

Table 3. 10-fold cross validation classification accuracy of crisp classifiers algorithms against variants of the method with bell MF (in %)

Conductivity WQC – Average Prediction Accuracy (in %)				
	C 4.5	kNN	Bagging C4.5	Boosted C4.5
xVal	65.60	66.51	63.30	63.76
	SAT5	SAT10	AT5	AT10
xVal	**75.13**	**74.67**	**73.74**	**74.20**
pH WQC – Average Prediction Accuracy (in %)				
	C 4.5	kNN	Bagging C4.5	Boosted C4.5
xVal	54.73	47.26	53.23	56.22
	SAT5	SAT10	AT5	AT10
xVal	**59.02**	**58.57**	**59.02**	**59.02**
Saturated Oxygen – Average Prediction Accuracy (in %)				
	C 4.5	kNN	Bagging C4.5	Boosted C4.5
xVal	**62.13**	**61.13**	**62.00**	**62.00**
	SAT5	SAT10	AT5	AT10
xVal	57.00	56.50	56.50	57.50

For the evaluation purpose, the classification models were obtained with the number of MF per attribute equal to 8. This comparison was made between variants of ATs and classical classification algorithms. Most of the cases obtained from 2% to 5% increase of classification power. Increased classification accuracy of the proposed method has been achieved for the conductivity WQC and pH WQC, for some cases up to 8%. The Saturated Oxygen WQC obtained low classification results, because the number of MF and the shape of MF are unsuitable for this WQC.

6 Conclusion

Classification of diatoms from measured data can be significantly improved with the proposed method. Because the diatoms are not influence by the geographical location, but rather the physico-chemical parameters of the environment [21], the proposed method could be used for diatom classification for any ecosystem, not just for Lake Prespa. The experimental results from the proposed method have shown that the models can be easily compared with the known ecological reference of the diatoms.. To best of our knowledge, this is the first time the prosed method to be applied for diatom classification of any ecosystem.

The experiments with the diatom WQC dataset shown that the modified bell MF outperformed previously used MFs in terms of classification accuracy. 10-fold cross validation used to compare the performance of the proposed method with the classical classification algorithms, proof that the bell MF outperformed classical classification algorithms in terms of classification accuracy and maintained the interpretability of the obtain models. The proposed method which is based on fuzzy logic theory reduces uncertainty in the environmental data and thus maintains the resistance to data change of the algorithm. This is very important in environmental domain data.

More important is the interpretation of the classification models, which outperformed the classical statistical methods such as: PCA, CCA, DCA and other methods [10]. For example, we can note that the classification model for pH WQC *alkalibiontic* unmistakeably show that the CSCU diatom can be used to indicate *alkalibiontic* waters. The experimental results showed that this machine learning method can extract valuable knowledge in a relatively comprehensible form, even when the application area is so extremely complex for humans and the data is far from being perfect.

From ecological point of view, it is very important that the proposed method have acknowledged ecological references for some of the known diatoms and thus it can be used for learning a new knowledge for the recently discovered diatoms. Verification of the obtained models have successfully classified the known diatoms, and added new ecological knowledge for the unknown diatoms for pH WQ classes. We believe that studies like ours that combines the ecological, hydro-biological and the information technologies, especially in the area of eco-informatics, are necessary to provide understanding of the physical, chemical and biological processes and their relationship to aquatic biota for predicting a certain effect.

Further research needs to be focus on developing more membership function in the process of building classification models. More similarity metrics may be more suitable for diatom dataset and can therefore, lead to higher accuracy of the classification model. The classification of the diatoms can be made not just for WQ classes, but also for trophic state index and metal parameters classes.

References

1. Krstič, S.: Description of sampling sites. FP6-project TRABOREMA: Deliverable 2.2 (2005)
2. Levkov, Z., Krstič, S., Metzeltin, D., Nakov, T.: Diatoms of Lakes Prespa and Ohrid (Macedonia). Iconographia Diatomologica 16, 603 (2006)
3. Kóczy, L.T., Vámos, T., Biró, G.: Fuzzy signatures. In: EUROFUSE-SIC, pp. 210–217 (1999)
4. Naumoski, A., Kocev, D., Atanasova, N., Mitreski, K., Krtić, S., Džeroski, S.: Predicting chemical parameters of water quality form diatoms abundance in Lake Prespa and its tributaries. In: 4th International ICSC Symposium on Information Technologies in Environmental Engineering - ITEE 2009, Thessaloniki, Greece, pp. 264–277. Springer, Heidelberg (2009)
5. Nikravesh, M.: Soft computing for perception-based decision processing and analysis: web-based BISC-DSS. Studies in Fuzziness and Soft Computing, vol. 164, pp. 93–188. Springer, Heidelberg (2005)
6. TRABOREMA Project WP3.: EC FP6-INCO project no. INCO-CT-2004-509177 (2005-2007)
7. Schweizer, B., Sklar, A.: Associative functions and abstract semigroups. Publ. Math. Debrecen 10, 69–81 (1963)
8. Olaru, C., Wehenkel, L.: A complete fuzzy decision tree technique. Fuzzy Sets and Systems 138, 221–254 (2003)
9. Yuan, Y., Shaw, M.J.: Induction of fuzzy decision trees. Fuzzy Sets and Systems 69(2), 125–139 (1995)
10. Quinlan, R.J.: Decision trees and decision making. IEEE Transactions on Systems, Man, and Cybernetics 20(2), 339–346 (1990)
11. Janikow, C.Z.: Fuzzy decision trees: issues and methods. IEEE Transactions on Systems, Man, and Cybernetics 28(1), 1–14 (1998)
12. Wang, L.X., Mendel, J.M.: Generating fuzzy rules by learning from examples. IEEE Transactions on Systems, Man, and Cybernetics 22(6), 1414–1427 (1992)
13. Wang, X., Chen, B., Olan, G., Ye, F.: On the optimization of fuzzy decision trees. Fuzzy Sets and Systems 112, 117–125 (2000)
14. Suárez, A., Lutsko, J.F.: Globally optimal fuzzy decision trees for classification and regression. IEEE Transactions on Pattern Analysis and Machine Intelligence 21(12), 1297–1311 (1999)
15. Kocev, D., Naumoski, A., Mitreski, K., Krstić, S., Džeroski, S.: Learning habitat models for the diatom community in Lake Prespa. Journal of Ecological Modelling 221(2), 330–337 (2009)
16. Krammer, K., Lange-Bertalot, H.: Die Ssswasserflora von Mitteleuropa 2: Bacillariophyceae. 1 Teil, p. 876. Gustav Fischer-Verlag, Stuttgart (1986)
17. Van Der Werff, A., Huls, H.: Diatomeanflora van Nederland. Abcoude - De Hoef (1957, 1974)
18. Stroemer, E.F., Smol, J.P.: The diatoms: Applications for the Environmental and Earth Sciences. Cambridge University Press, Cambridge (2004)
19. Van Dam, H., Martens, A., Sinkeldam, J.: A coded checklist and ecological indicator values of freshwater diatoms from the Netherlands. Netherlands Journal of Aquatic Ecology 28(1), 117–133 (1994)
20. Huang, Z.H., Gedeon, T.D., Nikravesh, M.: Pattern Trees Induction: A New Machine Learning Method. IEEE Transaction on Fuzzy Systems 16(3), 958–970 (2008)
21. Gold, C., Feurtet-Mazel, A., Coste, M., Boudou, A.: Field transfer of periphytic diatom communities to assess shortterm structural effects of metals (Cd Zn) in rivers. Water Research 36, 3654–3664 (2002)

Organizations Analysis with Complex Network Theory

Todorka Banova[1], Igor Mishkovski[2], Dimitar Trajanov[3], and Ljupco Kocarev[3,4]

[1] FON University, Skopje, Macedonia
todorka.banova@fon.edu.mk
[2] Politecnico di Torino, Turin, Italy
igor.mishkovski@polito.it
[3] University Ss. Cyril and Methodius, Faculty of electrical engineering and information technologies, Skopje, Macedonia
mite@feit.ukim.edu.mk, lkocarev@feit.ukim.edu.mk
[4] Macedonian Academy of Sciences and Arts, Skopje, Macedonia
lkocarev@manu.edu.mk

Abstract. In this paper, we propose network measures and analytical procedures for modeling the structure and the behavior of the basic types of organizations, such as: line, functional, line-and-staff, project and matrix organization. In order to obtain some tangible information about the connectivity between employees and structural properties of organizations, we develop network generators for all five types of organizations. We review various roles and groups of employees within the organizational network, and we assess social position and impact of a particular employee. Except, assessed locations of actors within an organizational network, we analyze the structure of network to find specific employees who have similar roles in the organization and have a tendency to be equivalent in terms of their potential to act in the organization. We estimate what is the confidentiality of the organizational network depending on the removal of a certain communication between employees and what is the percentage of communications that disconnect the organization in unconnected parts.

Keywords: Organization, complex networks, organizational network models, measurements, organizational network analysis.

1 Introduction

Management is a multidisciplinary activity that plays a crucial role for development of organizations. It is characterized by universality, but its implementation requires respect on the particularities for each organizational type, separately. In fact, globalization as a social phenomenon imposes new standards in management of organizations. In that way, connections and flows between employees in organizations are often unplanned and unpredictable. Also, organization's growth must be sporadic and self organizing [1]. Therefore, the main goal of this work is to analyze the basic types of organizations using the concepts of complex systems. Complex systems are an inevitable part of infrastructure of the modern world, and they can be represented as networks with a certain number of nodes joined together by edges [2,3,4]. People with its functioning establish mutual links and create social networks for exchanging

M. Gusev and P. Mitrevski (Eds.): ICT Innovations 2010, CCIS 83, pp. 255–265, 2011.

information, views and ideas. As an example of such networks can be listed networks of friends, networks of people with specific training and organizational networks [5]. Organizational networks [5] play a key role in hiring, business success, and in job performance [6]. Nodes in organizational networks (which are generally individuals of organizations) are tied by one or more specific types of interdependency, such as values, visions, ideas, financial exchange, friendship, kinship, dislike, conflict or trade. Network communications between employees are unevenly distributed, so some areas of organizational network have high density of links, while other areas are poorly connected. Thus, organizational networks correspond to small-world networks of Watts and Strogatz [7,8,9,10]. The main goal of this work is to analyze basic types of organizations and evaluate functionality and location of employees using the model [11,12] developed by David Krackhardt. Similarly, individuals can exercise influence or act as brokers within their organizations by bridging two parts of organizations that are not directly linked (called filling structural holes) [13]. Thus, discovering mapping of relationships and flows between employees and also exploring the structure of organizations or nodes that are most suitable to achieve the desired goals of organizations is of great importance for every organization. This analysis provides ways for companies to gather information, deter competition, collude in setting prices or policies and pick up which type of organizational structure is most suitable for the company.

The rest of the paper is organized as follows. In Section 2 we present a short overview for basic types of organizations, line, functional, line-and-staff, project and matrix organization. Afterwards, in Section 3 we give a description of the various network metrics for modeling organizations, and we give simulation results and analysis. Section 4 concludes this paper.

2 Types of Organizational Structures

Organizations can be structured in many different ways and styles, depending on their objectives and ambience. Structure of an organization determines modes in which it operates and performs. The most common types of organizational structures are: line, functional, line-and-staff, project and matrix organizational structure [14].

2.1 Line Organizational Structure – LO

Line organizational structure is the oldest and simplest type of organization. It is characterized by direct transfer of authority from top, through various managers to workers and following the command chain tends to simplify and clarify the responsibility and authority in the organization. This organization has no positions of staff or advisers, so is less expensive in terms of costs. In addition, simplicity and comprehensiveness make a clear separation of authority and accountability among managers, easier, faster and more stable decisions. Line organizational structure promotes fast decision making, which enables faster change of direction, because several people will be consulted on issues as they arise. Also, there is greater feeling of closeness between managers and employees. This structure may depend on few key people who carried out a number of things and furthermore may appear insufficient efficiency if the organization grows.

2.2 Functional Organizational Structure – FO

Functional organizational structure was introduced by Frederick W. Taylor, who was trying to establish specialization in management. In functional structure people are grouped according to their ability to perform similar tasks, such as: marketing, manufacturing, finance, personnel, investment, research and development. Functional authority has direct line authority of a special function or activity. Main advantages of functional structure are: efficient utilization of resources, technical high-level solving problems and clear opportunities for promotion within the function. Each function is operated by a specialist and an assembly of experts is always available to employees. Finally, functional organization overcomes the lack of line organization, which is inefficient control of one employee. However, high degree of specialization, involve series of specialists who operate not as a system, but as independent entities. As a result, organization often has a lack of good governance.

2.3 Line-and-Staff Organizational Structure – LSO

Line-and-staff structure is developed to take advantages of line and functional organizational structures. In fact, line part of the line-and-staff organizational structure is used for emphasis on stability and discipline, while staff part serves to bring expert knowledge for solving problems. However, authority and responsibility of staff may cause confusion if is not clearly set. Introducing of staff personnel may cause line managers to feel that have lost authority over a particular specialized function or that depend from staff, so they lose the ability for original thoughts, initiatives and actions [15].

2.4 Project Organizational Structure – PO

Project organizational structure provides high efficiency. It is a temporary organization established to achieve concrete results by using a team of specialists from different functional areas within the organization. Team is focused on the project. When the project is completed, project team is disbanded and its members are returning to their regular positions in the organization. Project organizational structure is possible when the job is [16]: defined in specific goals, tasks and terms to complete; unique and unusual for an existing organization; complex, respecting the interdependence of activities and specialized skills necessary to achieve; critical in terms of income or loss, and temporary, with respect to the duration of needs.

2.5 Matrix Organizational Structure – MO

Concept of matrix organization gets in importance in recent decades and represents an extension of concept of project organization. Matrix organization is based on application of two types of organizations, functional and project way of departmentalization. It is also called dual or hybrid organization. Matrix organizational structure does not apply in all companies. It is a complex structure and its application must meet certain conditions. This structure has a high degree of flexibility in utilization of human resources, rapid adaptation to changes, strong manufacturing and project coordination. Furthermore, it enhances and develops skills, increases motivation and commitment and assists in planning in top management [17]. Besides this, matrix organization manifested certain weaknesses, such as: violation of principle of unity of command, creates confusion with double authority, requires time and generates high costs for execution because requires a high level of interpersonal interaction.

3 Simulation and Results

In this section, we give a short description of the various network metrics for modeling organizations, and we interpret them in the context of organizational network analysis using the measured results. For our simulations, we are using a network generator. The generator generates samples of the 5 various types of organizations, preserving their basic characteristics. Each sample has a different number of nodes (N) ranging from 35 to 1900 employees. In Figure 1 is given a simple toy organization with 35 employees in order to illustrate the structure of the line organization.

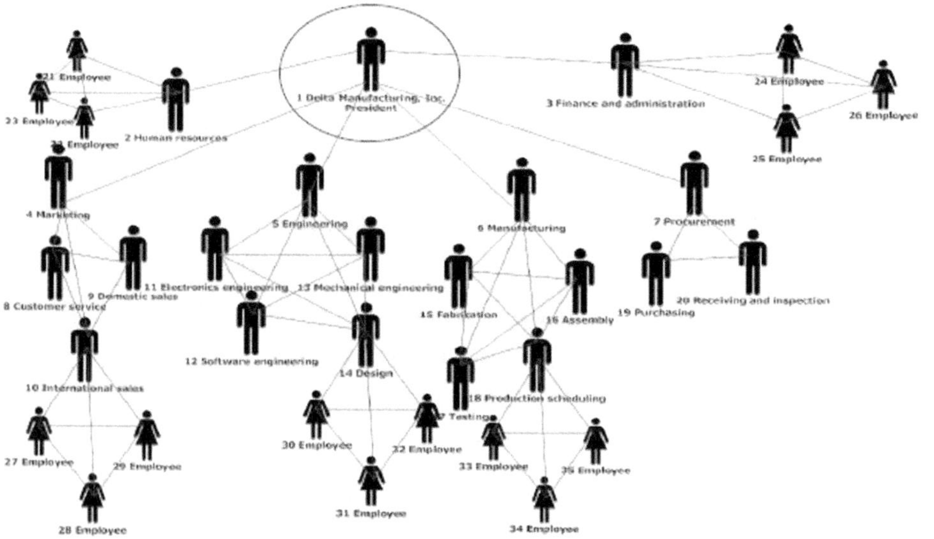

Fig. 1. Line organization with departments for Human resources, Finance and administration, Marketing, Engineering, Manufacturing and Procurement. Delta Manufacturing, Inc. President (in the red circle) is the top manager of this toy organization.

3.1 Structural Equivalence

First network metric that can be applied in a social context is a clique. The clique consists of people who mutually communicate with one another. The clique within organizations can be based on attributes that are present within employees in organization [18, 19, 20], e.g. race, age, mobility, educational achievements and location. Thus, employees who belong to same clique have similar job responsibilities and as a consequence those employees should be physically close or in same offices.

Through analysis of structural equivalence, we revealed social position or set of employees with similar ties to others. Analysis uses Euclidian distance for structural equivalence. Euclidean distance between nodes i and j is calculated by their vectors of links to and from the other *N-2* employees in the network, excluding loops and common links:

$$d_{ij} = \sqrt{\sum_{k=1}^{N-2} \left[(x_{ik} - x_{jk})^2 + (x_{ki} - x_{kj})^2 \right]}, (k \neq i \neq j) \quad (1)$$

Figure 2 presents dendrogram for hierarchical clustering using the concept of structural equivalence for the toy organization in Figure 1. This line organization has 9 clusters of employees, which are similar in their social relations. Employees with ordinal number 33, 34 and 35 belong to same cluster and are structurally equivalent, so if any of them is absent from work for a longer period or there is another work with higher priority, manager can find his replacement from the same because everyone of that cluster has same connections to other employees in the organization.

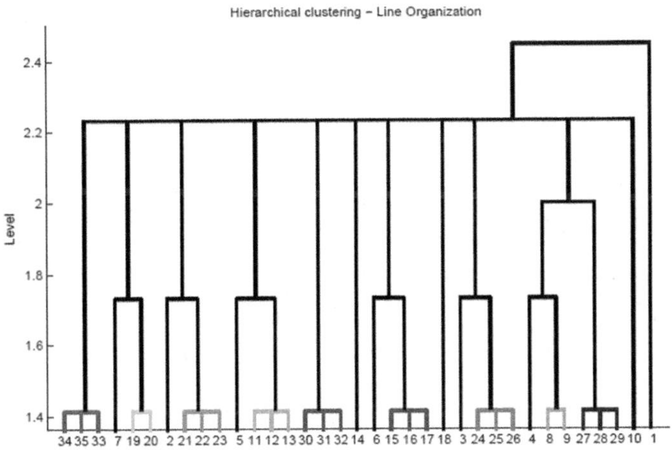

Fig. 2. Hierarchical clustering for line organization with 9 clusters of employees that have the same position in the organization with similar relationships to others and same potential to act in the organization

3.2 Average Path Lengths for Organizations

A small average path length for organizational network indicates that anyone can reach someone else simply and quickly, without going through intermediate colleagues. In other words, shorter paths mean a faster arrival of information, which is less distorted and employees have better visibility and awareness of what is happening in other parts of organization. Mainly, shorter paths are important for better learning within the group and for effective reconfiguration after topological changes. From the analysis shown in Figure 3 (left), the functional organization has the larger average path length. This is consequence from the fact that employees from one functional department do not communicate with employees in another department, because they are appointed for a single specialized function. In functional organization the main lack is communication between functional managers and between employees who are specialized for different functions within the same or different department. To be more precise, the average path length is around 5 form small organizations (with no more than 100 employees), then it starts to increase and for bigger organizations (with 1500 employees) it is around 7. In the case of project organization the average path length is smaller than that for functional organization because there is communication within a given project (Figure 3, left). In the case of the average path length from the top manager to the rest of the employees the results differ, i.e., both, the functional and the project organization have the same value (see Figure 3, right). This result coincides with the real work of project organization, because project organization is the highest form of organization with a very small span of management, with mostly hierarchical levels, more channels of communication and difficult coordination.

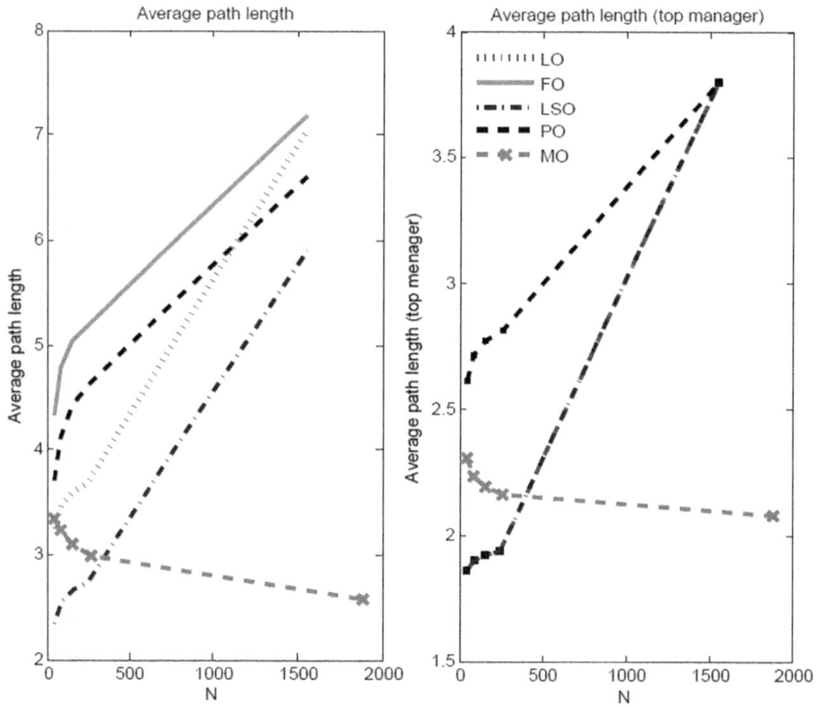

Fig. 3. Average path length for entire network (left) and from the top manager (right) for growing line, functional, line-and-staff, project and matrix organizations

From the analysis made, (shown in Figure 3) we can conclude that the line organization is good for small number employees (up to 50). In the line organization, employees that are in given department communicate with each other because they are not specialized for a particular job and must exchange information, knowledge, and often change their positions within the department in order to accomplish their tasks. The average path length for the line organization has the steepest growth, making it not suitable for lager organizations.

Results of Figure 3 shows that line-and-staff organization has better results than functional, line and the project organization. This is because line-and-staff organization belongs to flat organization where there are less hierarchical levels, immediate communication, easier and more efficient coordination. Finally, the matrix organization is a winner-winner for large organizations, because the average path length of the whole network (Figure 3, left) and the average path length from the top manager (Figure 3, right) decreases by increasing the number of employees. The result for lowest average path length for the average path length from the top manager in larger organizations, with more than 1000 employees, confirms the fact that this type of organization helps in planning for top management and has more time for long-term planning, given the fact that the matrix structure allows daily operational decisions to be delegated to the project and functional managers. In our simulations, the average path length for matrix organization with 1500 employees is more than 2.5 times smaller than the other types of organization. The average path length from the top manager is around 1.5 times smaller.

3.3 Labeled Average Path Lengths for Organizations

Figure 4 presents average path lengths between managers and employees in all types of organizations. Within this research we label every node of network as employee or manager. According to results for average path length between managers and employees of all organizations in Figure 4 and characteristics of different types of organizations in Section 2, it can be seen that these basic characteristics of each organization are confirmed and they meet similar form as in Figure 3. For organizations with 250 employees, the biggest average path length has the functional organization,

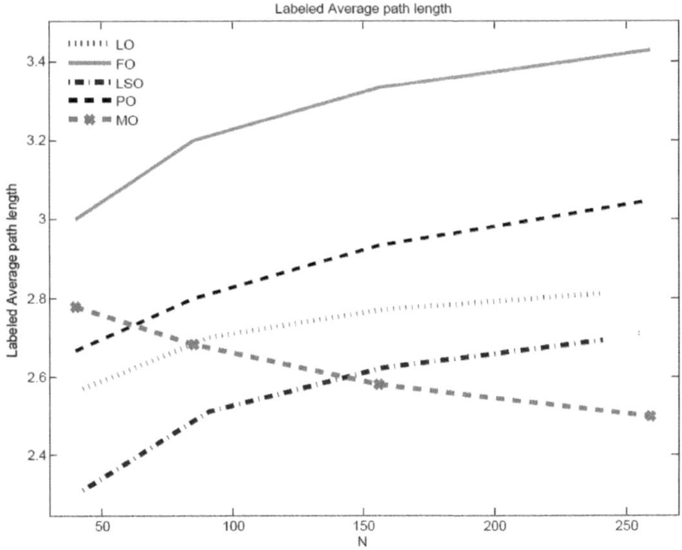

Fig. 4. Labeled average path length between managers and employees for entire network, for growing line, functional, line-and-staff, project and matrix organizations

around 3.4, the project organization has around 3, the line organization has around 2.7, the line-and-staff organization has around 2.6 and the lowest average path length has the matrix organization, around 2.5. It is obvious that the average path length will increase as new employees are employed in the organization for all type of organizations, except for the matrix organization.

3.4 Hierarchy for Organizations

Hierarchy answers questions like: how to find nodes constituting the highest part of the hierarchical structure of network or how to measure strength of the hierarchical structure. We measure strength of hierarchy as defined in [21]. Functional organization has biggest hierarchy (Figure 5), which coincides with definition of this type of organization because functional managers are specialists in those areas that work, and the line of authority is functional or diagonal, meaning that functional manager has precise authority over the functions carried out. Then follow project and line organization, and the remaining two organizations have lowest value for hierarchy, because they introduce additional personnel and management staff who can communicate with employees and weak hierarchy. It is important to note that increasing the number of employees in line and line-and-staff organization introduces new hierarchical levels and these two organizations are more hierarchical compared with project organization. Matrix organization with a larger number of employees is at least hierarchical, which is consistent with its definition.

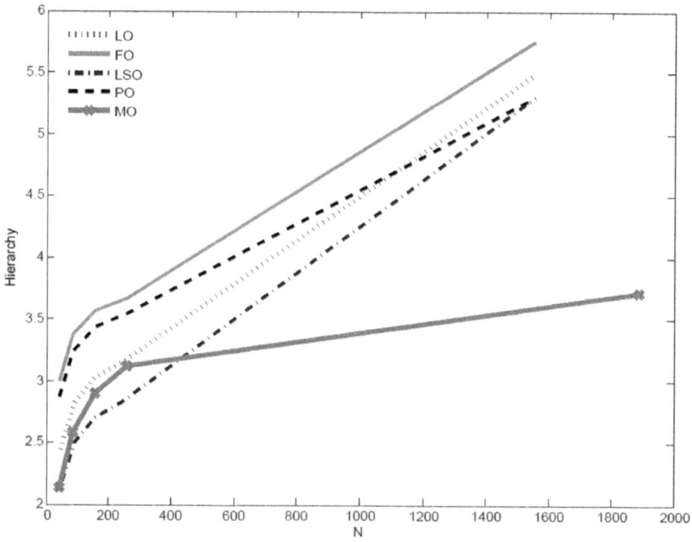

Fig. 5. Strength of hierarchy for growing line, functional, line-and-staff, project and matrix organizations

3.5 Redundant Paths

Path redundancy is a key measure for organizations when employee leaves organization or is absent for a certain period. For such cases it is necessary to have insight on path redundancy, i.e. what is the number of paths that connect any two nodes in organizational network. By increasing this number, organization is more stable and can withstand removal of an employee from organization. According to previous analysis of organizations we expect path redundancy to be greater in more expensive organizations, which introduces additional personnel through which communication is increased. These include line-and-staff, project and matrix organization. In research of redundant paths we also include how removal of a link between two nodes, or interruption of communication between two employees, will affect the average path length for whole network or time to transfer information between any two employees. The results for the dependence between the removals of links and the average path length for the line organization are given in Figure 6 (left). We can see that elimination of a random link can sometimes mean more than 5% more expensive communication or 5% more time for communication between any two employees in line organization. Also, removal of some links can cause disconnecting the entire network in unconnected clusters, so we find the percentage of links that disconnect the network. We also assess betweenness of those links in correlation with maximum edge betweenness for the network and we found that connections that disconnect network are influential links in entire organizational network (Figure 6 - right). Such connections is important to maintain because their removal would cause disruption of normal functioning of the organization and these are links that do not has redundant paths. In line organization, removal of 9.23% of communications between employees can cause disconnected organization, and 83.33% of these links have betweenness greater than 50% compare to the largest betweenness for edge for the whole network (Figure 6 - right).

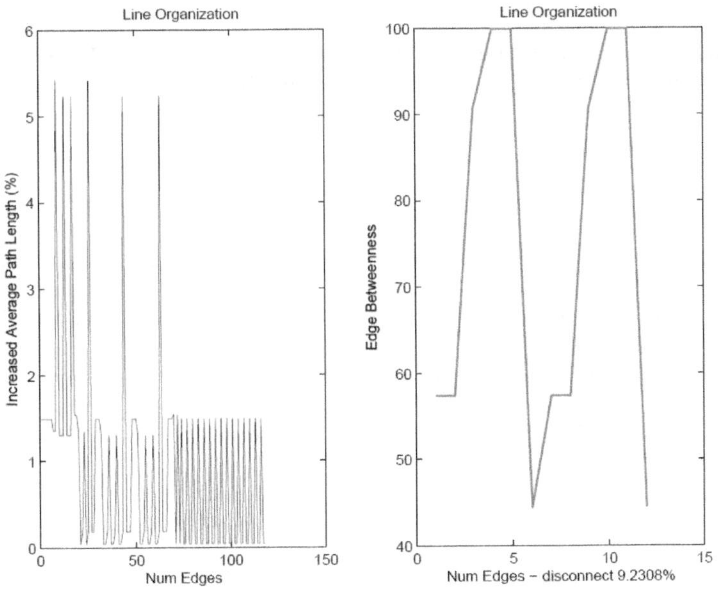

Fig. 6. Dependence of the average path length for the whole organization after interruption of communication between two employees (left). Percentage of links that disconnect the network and betweenness of those links in correlation with maximum edge betweenness for the network (right).

4 Conclusion

This brief has studied structure and relationships between employees in line, functional, line-and-staff, project and matrix organizations. We give short overview of what are different types of organizations and their characteristics. Afterwards, we give proposal of network measures and analytical procedures for modeling each type of organization. These network measures provide tangible image of organizations, because they quantitatively define connection between nodes and structural properties of organizations, and results obtained from network measures are reflected on real functioning of organizations. Obtained results confirmed proposed models and network measures, algorithms and properties of complex networks, which are applied over models to be able to depict real work of organizations. According to results and characteristics of different types of organizations may be noted that basic characteristics of each organization are confirmed, meaning that the design of various organizations is successfully done.

Future work should include improving or expanding of existing models. Because of specific interaction between employees in organizations, in many of networks is not just enough information for connectivity with other nodes, but also is needed a quantitative measure of interaction. For that purpose in future will be proposed several algorithms to provide weights of connections that are based on properties of organizational networks. Future work also will include analysis of dynamic properties of organizations and how they change when structure of organizations is changing.

Acknowledgment

LK thanks ONR Global (Grant number N62909-10-1-7074) and Macedonian Ministry of Education and Science (grant 'Annotated graphs in system biology') for partial support.

References

1. Krebs, V.: Visualizing Human Networks. Release 1.0, Esther Dyson's Monthly Report (February 1996)
2. Asavathiratham, C., Roy, S., Lesieutre, B., Verghese, G.: The Influence Model. IEEE Control Systems (December 2001)
3. Hofstad, R.: Random Graphs and Complex Networks, Kaleidoscoopdag, Leiden, May 16 (2007)
4. Newman, M.E.J.: The structure and function of complex networks. SIAM Rev. 45, 167–256 (2003)
5. Krebs, V.: Social Network Analysis, A Brief Introduction (2006)
6. Wasserman, S., Faust, K.: Social Network Analysis: Methods and Applications. Cambridge University Press, Cambridge (1994)
7. Milgram, S.: The small world problem. Psychology Today 2, 60–67 (1967)
8. Watts, D.J., Strogatz, S.H.: Collective dynamics of small-world networks. Nature 393(6684), 440–442 (1998)

9. Watts, D.J.: Six Degrees: The Science of a Connected Age. W.W. Norton & Company, New York (2003)
10. Watts, D.J.: Small Worlds: The Dynamics of Networks between Order and Randomness. Princeton University Press, Princeton (2003)
11. Burt, R.S.: Structural Holes—The Social Structure of Competition. Harvard University Press, Cambridge (1992), ISBN 0674843711
12. Retana, A., Slice, D., White, R.: Advanced IP Network Design. Cisco Press (1999) ISBN 1578700973
13. Scott, J.: Social Network Analysis. Sage, London (1991)
14. Stanford, N.: Economist Guide to Organization Design - Creating high-performing and adaptable Enterprises, Profile Books Ltd 3a Exmouth House, London (2007)
15. George Jr., C.S.: Management for business and industry, pp. 93–94. Prentice Hall, Inc., Englewood Cliffs (1970)
16. Mondy, W.R., Holmes, R.E., Flippo, E.B.: Management: concepts and practices, p. 174. Allyn & Bacon, Inc., Boston (1980)
17. Aldag, R.J., Stearns, T.M.: Management, pp. 306–309. South – Western Publishing Co., Cincinnati (1987)
18. Mehra, A., Kilduff, M., Brass, D.J.: At the margins: A distinctiveness approach to the social identity and social networks of under-represented groups. Academy of Management Journal 41, 441–452 (1998)
19. Krackhardt, D., Kilduff, M.: Whether close or far: Social distance effects on perceived balance in friendship networks. Journal of Personality and Social Psychology 76, 770–782 (1999)
20. Kilduff, M.: The friendship network as a decision-making resource: Dispositional moderators of social influences on organizational choice. Journal of Personality and Social Psychology 62, 168–180 (1992)
21. Eum, S., Arakawa, S., Murata, M.: A new approach for discovering and quantifying hierarchical structure of complex networks, 1-5 Yamadaoka, Suita, Osaka, 565-0871 Japan

An Agglomerative Clustering Technique Based on a Global Similarity Metric

Angel Stanoev[1], Igor Trpevski[1], and Ljupco Kocarev[1,2]

[1] Research Center for Energy, Informatics and Materials,
Macedonian Academy of Sciences and Arts, Skopje, Macedonia
{astanoev,itrpevski}@manu.edu.mk
[2] BioCircuits Institute,
University of California San Diego, La Jolla, CA, USA
lkocarev@ucsd.edu

Abstract. In this paper we address the problem of detecting communities or clusters in networks. An efficient hierarchical clustering algorithm based on a global similarity metric is introduced. The technique exploits several characteristic average values of the similarity function. Also an analytical result is provided for the average similarity of vertices on an Erdos-Renyi graph in the asymptotic limit of the graph size. Finaly the performance of the algorithm is evaluated over a set of computer-generated graphs. Our analysis shows that newly proposed algorithm is superior when compared to the popular algorithm of Girvan and Newman and has equal or lower running time.

Keywords: Similarity metrics, Clustering Algorithms, Community Detection, Complex Networks.

1 Introduction

Complex networks are graph represenations of physical, biological, technological and social systems [1–3]. Examples include power plants and distribution lines, metabolic and gene regulatory networks, food webs, the Internet and the World Wide Web, and socioeconomic relations between humans, to name but a few. With the availability of large datasets and the increase in computing power it has become possible to perform large-scale statistical analysis on these networked systems. One of their properties that has received much attention lately is *community structure.* This feature relates to the organization of network nodes into groups within which the network connections are dense but which are otherwise sparsely connected between each other [4]. Communities have been empirically observed to exist in various kinds of networks ranging from social and economic networks [5, 6], to molecular [7, 8] and artificial networks such as the web [9]. Furthermore, it is widely believed that the modular structure of complex networks is closely connected with their functionality [10] and revealing it can help elucidate the organization of the systems. Indeed, it has been shown that communities correspond to functional units such as cycles or pathways in metabolic

M. Gusev and P. Mitrevski (Eds.): ICT Innovations 2010, CCIS 83, pp. 266–275, 2011.

networks [7, 11] and clusters found on the Web were actually a collection of web pages on a single topic [9].

Because of these and other reasons it is hardly surprising that there has been enormous effort in recent years to develop new algorithms that can detect and quantify community structure in networks. Various techniques have been developed based on modularity optimization [7, 12, 13], spectral algorithms [14], spin models [15] and random walks [16] and many other approaches. For a detailed review on these and other techniques see [17].

Our approach to solving this problem is by combining a traditional hierarchical clustering algorithm i.e. clustering technique that reveal the multilevel structure of the graph with a novel global similarity metric. These type of clustering algorithms have been extensively used in social network analysis, machine learning, bioinformatics etc., and are generally divided into two broad classes, agglomerative and divisive, depending on whether they merge or split clusters in the network. We use an agglomerative-like technique where clusters are merged when they satisfy a certain similarity criterion. As we shall see our algorithm can effectively reveal the community structure on computer generated graphs as well as on several real networks.

The paper proceeds as follows. We begin by defining the similarity metric in Sec. 2 Then we present its properties in Sec. 3. In Sec. 4 we elaborate the workings of our algorithm and discuss the results of the algorithm's performance. Finally, in Sec. 5 we conclude this paper and discuss some problems which are left open.

2 Definition of the Similarity Metric

The starting point of every hierarchical clustering algorithm is the calculation of the similarity between all pairs of vertices in the graph. The usual way to obtain the similarity between two vertices a and b is to take the information contained in the adjacency matrix A of a graph i.e. the connectivity vectors for the vertices and apply a similarity function like the cosine similarity or the Pearson coefficient:

$$cos(a,b) = \frac{\sum_{i=1}^{N} A_{ai} * A_{bi}}{\sqrt{\sum_{i=1}^{N} A_{ai}^2} * \sqrt{\sum_{i=1}^{N} A_{bi}^2}}, \tag{1}$$

$$P(a,b) = \frac{\sum_{i=1}^{N}(A_{ai} - \mu_a)(A_{bi} - \mu_b)}{\sqrt{\sum_{i=1}^{N}(A_{ai} - \mu_a)^2} * \sqrt{\sum_{i=1}^{N}(A_{bi} - \mu_b)^2}}, \tag{2}$$

where μ_a and μ_b are the averages $\sum_{i=1}^{N} A_{ai}/N$ and $\sum_{i=1}^{N} A_{bi}/N$ respectively. Calculating similarity using the elements of the adjacency matrix is local in the sense that one uses only the information about the connectivity of two nodes to their neighbors. In the following we present our concept of similarity on graphs.

Let $G = (V, E)$ represent an undirected graph where V is the set of vertices and E is the set of edges. We take the size of the graph to be the cardinality of the vertex set $N = |V|$. Then, for each node v in the graph we can define N-dimensional vector of shortest paths $(v_1, v_2, \ldots, v_N)$ where the coordinates v_i represent the shortest paths to the vertices in the graph. Note that this vector also contains the distance to the node itself which is set to 0. This ensures that no two vertices have the same shortest path vector. If a shortest path between two vertices does not exist, as in the case of a disconnected graph, then the distance is said to be infinite.

Now, we define the similarity $S_r(a, b)$ between two nodes a and b with shortest path vectors $(a_1, a_2, \ldots, a_N)$ and $(b_1, b_2, \ldots, b_N)$ as

$$S_r(a,b) = \frac{\sum_{i=1}^{N} M_r\left(a_i, b_i\right)}{\sum_{i=1}^{N} \max\left(\frac{1}{k^{a_i}}, \frac{1}{k^{b_i}}\right)}, \tag{3}$$

where

$$M_r(a_i, b_i) = \left(\frac{1}{2} * \left(\frac{1}{k^{a_i * r}} + \frac{1}{k^{b_i * r}}\right)\right)^{\frac{1}{r}}, \tag{4}$$

is actually the generalized mean with exponent r and k is a positive integer larger than one. It is known that M_r is a monotonically non-decreasing function of r. i.e. $M_{r-1}(a_i, b_i) \leq M_r(a_i, b_i)$ with equality holding when $a_i = b_i$ for $i = 1, \ldots, N$. This property is naturally transferred to S_r as well. For different values of r the function M_r takes the form of several already known means

$$\begin{aligned}
\lim_{r \to -\infty} M_r(x_1, x_2, \ldots, x_n) &= \min\left(x_1, x_2, ..., x_n\right), \\
M_{-1}(x_1, x_2, \ldots, x_n) &= \frac{n}{\frac{1}{x_1} + \frac{1}{x_2} + \cdots + \frac{1}{x_n}}, \\
\lim_{r \to 0} M_r(x_1, x_2, \ldots, x_n) &= \sqrt[n]{x_1 * x_2 * ... * x_n}, \\
M_1(x_1, x_2, \ldots, x_n) &= \frac{x_1 + x_2 + \cdots + x_n}{n}, \\
\lim_{r \to +\infty} M_r(x_1, x_2, \ldots, x_n) &= \max\left(x_1, x_2, ..., x_n\right).
\end{aligned}$$

It can also be easily verified that S_r is a decreasing function of k and its values range in the interval from 0 to 1. Later, we discuss the choice of the values for parameters k and r.

What makes our approach different is not primarily the form of the similarity function, but rather the set of points on which the function operates, namely the shortest path vectors. Calculating similarity over the shortest paths between all pairs of vertices is by all means different since it uses the information about the global connectivity of the graph. The similarity space of the vertices now reflects the relative positioning of the vertices not just in the local neighborhood but in the whole graph as well. Note that it is possible to modify the equations (1) and (2) for the cosine similarity and the Pearson coefficient so they can work with shortest path vectors. We now proceed with what we believe are the most relevant properties of this novel method for calculating similarity between vertices.

3 On the Average Similarity for Erdos-Renyi Graphs

It is widely known that random graphs have no community structure. Indeed this fact is exploited by a whole class of community detection algorithms which optimize a so called modularity function. The definition of the modularity involves a comparison of the number of within-group edges in a real network and in some equivalent randomized model network in which edges are placed without regard to community structure. We ourselves follow similar reasoning, namely that some characteristic values of the similarity function such as the average value show different properties when the graph has random structure from one with communities.

Our first important finding is that the average value of the similarity function $S_r(a, b)$ can be calculated analytically for the Erdos-Renyi (ER) random graph [18]. In brief, an ER random graph is a graph with N vertices where each of the $N(N-1)/2$ possible edges is present with independent probability p.

We consider an ER graph with N vertices and probability p. With probability $P_0 = 1/N$ we randomly choose one particular vertex v_1. We denote the probabilities that another randomly chosen vertex v_2 is at distance $1, 2, 3, \ldots, N-1$ from vertex v_1 as $P_1, P_2, \ldots, P_{N-1}$. The probability that the two are not connected is $P_\infty = 1 - \sum_{i=0}^{N-1} P_i$. From these probabilities one can easily obtain the expected values for the number of vertices at distance $0, 1, 2, 3, \ldots, N-1$ as $E_0 = P_0 * N$, $E_1 = P_1 * N$, $E_2 = P_2 * N$, ..., $E_{N-1} = P_{N-1} * N$, $E_\infty = P_\infty * N$ where E_∞ is the expected number of vertices which are segregated from the vertex v_1. In the asymptotic limit of large N the sum $E_0 + E_1 + E_2 + \cdots + E_{N-1} + E_\infty$ closes to N as the expected values close to the exact number of such vertices. In practice this actually works for N over 100. The set of probabilities can now be calculated from the following set of equations:

$$
\begin{aligned}
P_0 &= \frac{1}{N}, \\
P_1 &= (1 - P_0) * p, \\
P_2 &= (1 - P_0) * (1 - q^{E_1}) * q^{E_0}, \\
&\ldots, \\
P_k &= (1 - P_0) * (1 - q^{E_{k-1}}) * q^{\sum_{i=0}^{k-2} E_i}, \\
&\ldots, \\
P_{N-1} &= (1 - P_0) * (1 - q^{E_{N-2}}) * q^{N - E_\infty}, \\
P_\infty &= 1 - \sum_{i=0}^{N-1} P_i.
\end{aligned}
$$

Further, consider the following scenario. We pick two nodes v_1 and v_2 at random with probabilities $1/N$ and $1/(N-1)$ respectively. Then the joint probability that a third randomly chosen vertex v_3 is at distance i from node v_1 and at distance j from node v_2 is denoted as P_{ij} and in the asymptotic limit of $N \to \infty$ it becomes the product of the two independent probabilities P_i and P_j.

Finally, one can calculate analytically the average value of the similarity metric S_r for a random graph by weighting the functions $M_r(i,j)$ and $max(i,j)$ with the corresponding probabilities over all possible combinations of distances between the third vertex v_3 and the other two fixed vertices:

$$avg(S_r^{ER}) = \frac{\sum_{i=0}^{N-1}\sum_{j=0}^{N-1} P_i * P_j * M_r(i,j) + +2 * \sum_{i=0}^{N-1} P_\infty * P_i * M_r(\infty, i)}{\sum_{i=0}^{N-1}\sum_{j=0}^{N-1} P_i * P_j * \max(i,j) + +2 * \sum_{i=0}^{N-1} P_\infty * P_i * \max(\infty, i)} \quad (5)$$

The validity of this result was confirmed with numerical simulations for 2 random graphs of different size. In Fig. 1 we show the results for the average value of the similarity function according to eq. (5) as a function of the probability of connecting two nodes. On the same plot we also show the average value calculated using numerical simulations and it can be seen that there is a clear agreement between both results.

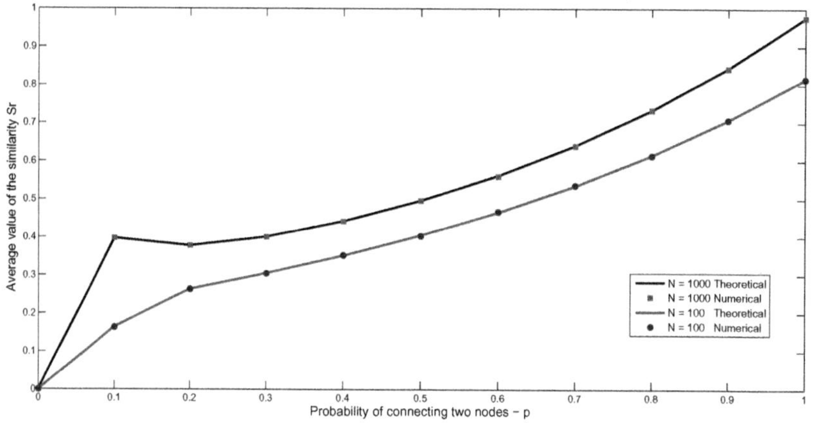

Fig. 1. The average value of the similarity metric as a function of the probability of connecting two vertices. The solid lines represent the analytical results. The markers are the results of numerical simulation on graphs with $N = 100$ and $N = 1000$ vertices with parameter values $r = 0$ and $k = 16$ for equations (3), (4), (5). Each marker on the plot is an average of 10 graph realizations.

The second important observation regarding the similarity function comes from its behavior when the graph structure changes from random into one with communities. In order to describe it we generate artificial graphs with community structure according to the *planted l-parition model* [19]. The N vertices of a graph are placed in N_c communities with N_s vertices each. Then edges are generated at random between vertex pairs with probability p_{in} for an edge to fall between vertices in the same community and probability p_{out} to fall between vertices in different communities. The expected internal degree of a vertex is $z_{in} = p_{in} * (N_s - 1)$, and the expected external degree is $z_{out} = p_{out} * N_s * (N_c - 1)$. Thus the total average degree of the vertices is $\langle z \rangle = p_{in} * (N_s - 1) + p_{out} * N_s * (N_c - 1)$.One then fixes the total average degree to a certain value, so that p_{in} and p_{out} are no longer independent. In the following we consider the case for $\langle z \rangle$ set to 16 so that the relationshuip between the within-cluster and between-cluster probability is $p_{in} + 3 * p_{out} \approx 1/2$. For the threshold $p_{in} = p_{out} = 1/8$ the graph is Erdos-Renyi and for values of p_{in} larger than 1/8 the graph structure starts to organize itself into one with communities. For these graphs the average value of the similarity function is calculated for all vertices which belong in the same cluster and for all vertex pairs belonging to different clusters. These two quantities are denoted as S_r^{in} and S_r^{out} respectively. In the absence of community structure the two values are very close to the average similarity for an ER graph. On the other hand, when the graph has communities ($p_{in} > 1/8$) the two values show completely opposite behavior. As it is shown in Fig. 2, the value of S_r^{in} starts to rise showing the increasing similarity between vertices of the same cluster, while S_r^{out} decreases. It is this property of the similarity metric that can be used for determining whether there is community structure in the graph.

We further calculate these same quantities for a local similarity metric ω_{ab} which is actually the ratio between the intersection and the union of the neighborhoods $\Gamma(a)$ and $\Gamma(b)$ of two vertices a and b i.e.

$$\omega_{ab} = \frac{\Gamma(a) \cap \Gamma(b)}{\Gamma(a) \cup \Gamma(b)}. \tag{6}$$

From Fig. 2 it can be seen that the average within cluster similarity S_ω^{in} is slightly larger than the average value $avg(\omega^{ER})$ when p_{in} is close 0. Note that the values of S_ω^{in} and S_ω^{out} for $p_{in} \sim 0.3$ are no different those for p_{in} near zero. In this case, we cannot make the same conclusion as before that the graph has community structure when S_ω^{in} and S_ω^{out} move away from the average similarity $avg(\omega^{ER})$. This is due to the fact that vertices in the same original groups of 32 vertices will be more similar even though they are not connected to each other but rather to the same vertices in other groups. Such local similarity metrics are unsuitable for community detection as they can make an algorithm produce clusters even when the structure of the graph is completely random.

4 The Algorithm and Its Performance

We use an agglomerative technique for clustering which means that it starts with each vertex being a cluster and it continues by merging clusters based on a certain similarity criterion. The algorithm steps are as follows:

1. Calculate the shortest paths between all pairs of vertices and then use them to calculate the similarity between all pairs of vertices. Also calculate the average similarity $avg(S_r^{ER})$ for the corresponding ER graph.

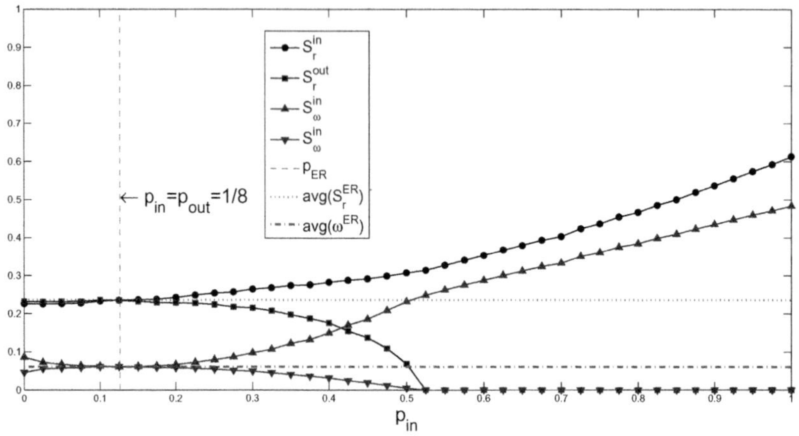

Fig. 2. Within and between cluster average similarities for the metrics S_r and ω, along with the average values of these functions for an ER graph (horizontal lines) are shown for 40 different values of p_{in} on the interval from 0 to 1. The parameters of the S_r metrics are $r = 0$ and $k = 16$. Each point is an average of 10 graph realizations.

2. Find the vertex with highest average similarity to all other vertices and use it as starting vertex of a new cluster.
3. For each of the vertices that are not clustered yet calculate the average similarity to the vertices in the new cluster $avg(S_{in})$ and to the rest of the vertices in the graph $avg(S_{out})$.
4. For the vertex with the highest value $avg(S_{in})$ check whether the following two conditions are satisfied: $avg(S_{in}) > avg(S_r^{ER})$ and $avg(S_{in}) \geq 2 * avg(S_{out})$. If the conditions are met, include the vertex in the cluster and go back to step 3 for the remaining vertices. If they aren't, then go back to step 2 with the remainder of the unclustered vertices or if there are no such vertices proceed to the next step meaning that the clusters are obtained.
5. Starting from the last cluster created in steps 1-4, calculate the intercluster average similarity (the average similarity for all pairs of nodes in two clusters) between that cluster and each of the other clusters. For the most similar one check if the average intercluster similarity is larger than $avg(S_r^{ER})$ and if it is then proceed by merging them. Repeat this step for the new set of clusters until no merging is possible.

The conditions for including a vertex into a cluster in step 4 are quite intuitive. We have already seen in the previous section that the average intracluster similarity needs to be larger than the average similarity obtained by eq. (5), a fact which explains the use of the first condition. The second condition is stringent enough so that it does not include vertices which are obviously not similar enough to the cluser that is being constructed at that point. The consequence of using a strict condition like this is that the procedure can create a larger set of clusters which are otherwise very similar and should be merged. The last step of the algorithm ensures that this happens. The condition for merging two clusters in the last step of the algorithm is again readily explained by the fact that the average intracluster similarity should always be larger than $avg(S_r^{ER})$, if we are to have a good partitioning of the graph.

We compared our algorithm to that of Girvan and Newman on a set of artificial graphs generated according to the planted l-partiotion model. The size of the graphs was set to $N = 128$ with four communities ($N_c = 4$) each contating 32 nodes ($N_s = 32$). The total average degree of the nodes was set to $\langle z \rangle = 31$ in order to obtain a more dense graph. For evaluating the performance of both algorithms we adopted the measure called *fraction of correctly classified nodes* first introduced in [4]. A vertex is correctly classified if it is in the same cluster with at least half of its orginial 31 "partners" that are specified at the beginning of the graph generating procedure. If some of the clusters obtained by the algorithm are given by merging of two or more "original" groups, all vertices of the cluster are considered as incorrectly classified. The results in Fig. 3 show that our algorithm clearly outperforms the algorithm of Girvan and Newman all the way up to the point where there is meaningful community structure in the graph i.e. where the ratio of the average intercluster degree of the vertices to the overall average degree of the vertices is 0.6 as can be seen in the figure. Only when there is hardly any community structure does the algorithm of Girvan and Newman seems to perform better i.e. for values of the $z_{out}/\langle z \rangle$ larger than 0.6.

Calculation of all shortest paths using Johnson's algorithm has a worst-case time of $O(N * log(N) + N * E)$ where E is the number of edges in the graph. For a sparse graph the number of edges scales with the number of vertices i.e. $E \sim V$ so that the total time of Johnson's algorithm is actually $O(N^2)$. Then for each

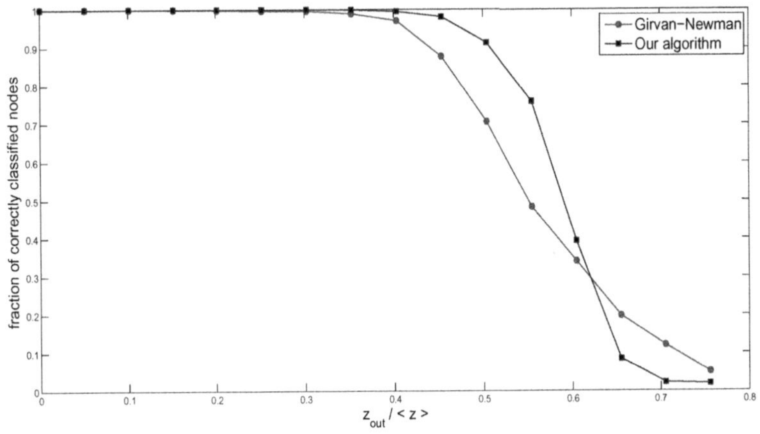

Fig. 3. Fraction of correctly classified nodes as a function of the average intercluster degree z_{out} for our algorithm and that of Girvan and Newman. Each point in the plot is an average of 100 graph realizations. The Parameters in the similarity metric were set to 0 and 16 for r and k respectively.

pair the cost of calculating the similarity is $O(N)$ because of the sums in eq. 3. Since there are N^2 vertex pairs the total cost for calculating the similarity matrix is $O(N^3)$. Further steps 2-5 require a total time which scales with $O(N^2)$, so the total worst case running time the algorithm is $O(N^3)$. The popular algorithm of Girvan and Newman [4] has a running time of $O(N * E^2)$ and in the case of a sparse graph $O(N^3)$. So our algorithm is at least as fast as that of Girvan and Newman.

5 Conclusion

In this paper, we have described a new agglomerative algorithm for performing network clustering, the task of extracting the natural community structure from networks of vertices. Our method is simple, intuitive and is characterized by two crucial features. The first is the use of a global similarity metric and the second is the clustering criterion derived from the behavior of this metric when the structure of the graph changes from random to one with communities. The algorithm can reliably and sensitively extract community structure from artificially generated networks with known network communities and clearly outperforms that of Girvan and Newman [4].

The primary remaining difficulty of our of our algorithm is the relatively high computational demands it makes. The calculation of the similarity matrix is performed in $O(n^3)$ time, which makes it usable for networks of up to about 10 000 vertices. Another disadvantage is the use of a multiplicative constant in Step. 4 because there is no optimal choice for the its value. A more complete algorithm would be free of such parameters. Also it is worth mentioning that the selection of the parameter values $r = 0$ and $k = 16$ for the similarity metric is rather arbitrary and different values can produce different partitioning of the graph. The impact of these values will be examined in another paper. There is certainly still room for improvement however in both the speed and sensitivity, and we would be delighted to see our method applied as a solution to a variety of problems.

Acknowledgments. L. K. thanks ONR Global (Grant number N62909-10-1-7074) and Macedonian Ministry of Education and Science (grant 'Annotated graphs in system biology') for partial support.

References

1. Bornholdt, S., Schuster, H.G. (eds.): Handbook of graphs and networks: from the Genome to the Internet. Wiley VCH, Weinheim (2003)
2. Newman, M.E.J.: The structure and function of complex networks. SIAM Review 45, 167–256 (2003)
3. Barrat, A., Barthelemy, M., Vespignani, A.: Dynamical processes on complex networks. Cambridge University Press, Cambridge (2008)

4. Girvan, M., Newman, M.E.J.: Community structure in social and biological networks. Proceedings of the National Academy of Sciences 99, 7821–7826 (2002)
5. Newman, M.E.J., Girvan, M.: Finding and evaluating community structure in networks. Phys. Rev. E 69, 026113 (2004)
6. Boss, M., Elsinger, H., Summer, M., Thurner, S.: The network topology of the Interbank market, `http://arxiv.org/abs/cond-mat/0309582`
7. Guimera, R., Amaral, L.A.N.: Functional cartography of complex metabolic networks. Nature 433, 895–900 (2005)
8. Holme, P., Huss, M., Jeong, H.: Subnetwork hierarchies of biochemical pathways. Bioinformatics 19, 532–538 (2003)
9. Flake, G.W., Lawrence, S.R., Giles, C.L., Coetzee, F.M.: Self-organization and identification of Web communities. IEEE Computer 35, 66–71 (2002)
10. Ravasz, E., Somera, A.L., Mongru, D.A., Oltavi, Z.N., Barabasi, A.-L.: Hierarchical organization of modularity in metabolic networks. Science 297, 1551–1555 (2002)
11. Palla, G., Derenyi, I., Farkas, I., Viscek, T.: Uncovering the overlapping community structure in complex networks in nature and society. Nature 435, 814–818 (2005)
12. Duch, J., Arenas, A.: Community detection in complex networks using extremal optimization. Phys. Rev. E 72, 027104 (2005)
13. Newman, M.E.J.: Modularity and community structure in networks. Proceedings of the National Academy of Sciences 103, 8577–8582 (2006)
14. Donetti, L., Munoz, M.: Detecting network communities: a new systematic and efficient algorithm. J. Stat. Mech., P10012 (2004)
15. Reichardt, J., Bornholdt, S.: Detecting fuzzy community structures in complex networks with a Potts model. Phys. Rev. Lett. 93, 218701 (2004)
16. Zhou, H.: Distance, dissimilarity index, and network community structure. Phys. Rev. E 67, 061901 (2003)
17. Fortunato, S.: Community detection in Graphs. Physics Reports 486, 75–174 (2010)
18. Erdos, P., Renyi, A.: On random graphs I. Publicationes Mathematicae 6, 290–297 (1959)
19. Condon, A., Karp, R.: Algorithms for graph partitioning on the planted partition model. Rand. Struc. Algor. 18, 116–140 (2001)

Accelerating Clustering Coefficient Calculations on a GPU Using OPENCL

Leonid Djinevski, Igor Mishkovski, and Dimitar Trajanov

Ss Cyril and Methodius University, Faculty of Electrical Engineering and Information Technologies, ul. Rugjer Boshkovikj bb, P.O. Box 574, 1000 Skopje, Macedonia
{leonid.dzinevski,igorm,mite}@feit.ukim.edu.mk

Abstract. The growth in multicore CPUs and the emergence of powerful manycore GPUs has led to proliferation of parallel applications. Many applications are not straight forward to be parallelized. This paper examines the performance of a parallelized implementation for calculating measurements of Complex Networks. We present an algorithm for calculating complex networks topological feature clustering coefficient, and conducted an execution of the serial, parallel and parallel GPU implementations. A hash-table based structure was used for encoding the complex network's data, which is different than the standard representation, and also speedups the parallel GPU implementations. Our results demonstrate that the parallelization of the sequential implementations on a multicore CPU, using OpenMP produces a significant speedup. Using OpenCL on a GPU produces even larger speedup depending of the volume of data being processed.

Keywords: Complex Networks, Parallel, CPU, GPU, speedup, OpenMP, OpenCL.

1 Introduction

Traditionally, the majority of the current software is written as sequential programs. As new generations of processors are coming, historically is expected the same sequential programs to run much faster. These expectations have slowed down since 2003 onwards, due to energy consumption, limited increase of clock frequencies and level of productive activities that can be performed in each clock period within a single CPU [1], therefore almost all microprocessor manufactures have switched to multicore processors. Today a sequential program will not run much faster on a new generation processor, because it will be using only one core from the multicore processor.

In order to keep the software expectations of performance improvements with each new generation of microprocessors, the software applications have to turn to parallel programming.

The GPUs since their emergence as peripheral units have become probably the most powerful computational processor for the cost at which are being sold. Their architecture is making them much more superior than the CPUs regarding the execution throughput. Much of the CPU resources are dedicated for non-computational

M. Gusev and P. Mitrevski (Eds.): ICT Innovations 2010, CCIS 83, pp. 276–285, 2011.

tasks like branch prediction and caching and their focus is more into maintaining the execution speed of sequential programs, while increasing the cores in the meanwhile. This architectural difference allows the GPUs to have much bigger growth than the CPUs.

A recent survey on graphic hardware computation performance [2] gives an overview of the execution throughput of GPUs in comparison to CPUs. The overview states that the GPUs have a huge advantage over the CPUs, which is a very justifiable reason for the software developers to move their applications on GPUs.

A science discipline of our interest is the area of Complex Networks. Complex Networks by their nature are an interdisciplinary area of graph theory and natural and social sciences. One of the main features regarding complex networks is the computationally intense calculations of their measurements, which require lots of resources. This is why we decided to harvest the power of the GPUs in this science discipline.

The model of complex networks permeates our everyday life, due to its simplicity (a certain number of nodes representing individual sites and edges representing connections) and its ability to grasp the essence of many different systems. Commonly cited examples include social networks, technological networks, information networks, biological networks, communication networks, neural networks, ecological networks and other natural and man-made networks. Abundant study of their topology and models is presented in [3] [4] [5].

Each complex network has specific topological features, which characterize its connectivity and highly influence the dynamics of processes executed on the network. The analysis of complex networks, therefore, relies on the use of measurements capable of expressing the most relevant topological features. However, in order to find the topological features of a given real complex networks the researchers are using programs and packages, such as Pajek [6], Ucinet [7], matlab_bgl [8] etc. From our own experience the code for these measurements it is not so complex, but as the real networks become more and more complicated (enormous number of nodes and edges) we often encountered memory or computation related problems. More specifically, the simulations could not be done (or some tricks had to be used) because of memory constraints and sometimes the simulations took too much time. Thus, in this work we address and overcome these two problems, by representing the network via hash-table based structure instead of traditional adjacency matrices (see Section 3), and we speed up the simulations via parallel programming algorithms for CPU and GPU execution in OpenCL (see Section 4). The main contribution of this work is to make possible or easier to analyze large-scale networks mapped over real world examples, by harvesting the tremendous power of the GPU performance.

At the end of this paper, a comparison of the results is presented. The results are obtained by running the sequential, OpenMP and OpenCL implementations of the calculation of the clustering coefficient. Conclusions about the maximum accelerations are specified, according to the parallelization of portions of the sequential code.

2 Related Work

Pawan Harish and P. J. Narayanan presented fast implementations of a few fundamental graph algorithms for large graphs on the GPU hardware [9]. Their implementations present fast solutions of BFS (breadth-first search), SSSP (single-source shortest path), and APSP (all-pairs shortest path) on large graphs at high speeds using a GPU instead of expensive supercomputers.

Joerkki Hyvoenen, Jari Saramaeki and Kimmo Kaski presented an article about a cache efficient data structure, a variant of a linear probing hash table, for representing edge sets of large sparse complex networks [10]. Their performance benchmarks show that the data structure is superior to its commonly used counterparts in programming applications.

Eigenvalues are a very important feature of Complex Networks. NVIDIA CUDA 1.1 SDK contains a parallel implementation of a bisection algorithm for the computation of all eigenvalues of a traditional symmetric matrix of arbitrary size with CUDA that is optimized for NVIDIA's GPUs [11]. V. Volkov and J. W. Demmel in [12] have improved the algorithm from the CUDA SDK.

Another useful feature is finding the shortest path between nodes. Gary J. Katz and Joseph T. Kider Jr in [13] describe a GPU implementation that solves shortest-path problems on directed graphs for large data sets.

3 Complex Networks

There are many relevant measurements that describe the complex networks like: measurements related with distance; clustering; degree distribution and correlation; entropy; centrality measurements; spectral measurements; and many others. These measures are important to capture the topological properties of real complex networks, which will further give insights of the robustness, efficiency, vulnerability, synchronization, virus propagation, etc. For this paper the clustering coefficient measure is chosen, because it is a property that is quite computationally intense and is also similar to other measures.

Clustering represents a local feature for a given node which is a measurement of how much its neighbours are grouped. The effect of clustering is measured by the clustering coefficient C which represents the mean value of the probability that two neighbouring nodes of a given node are also neighbours between each other. The equations for obtaining the clustering coefficient C_i for a given node, i and the clustering of the network $\langle C \rangle$ are the following:

$$C_i = \frac{2E_i}{k_i(k_i-1)} . \tag{1}$$

$$\langle C \rangle = \frac{1}{N}\sum_{i=1}^{N} C_i . \tag{2}$$

In the equation (1), E_i stands for the number of links between the neighbours of the node i, k_i is number of neighbor nodes of the node i, and N is the total number of nodes in the network.

4 Implementation

Real complex networks are typically very sparse and large structures. Mainly, in the literature the complex networks are represented mathematically with an adjacency matrix A. The elements a_{ij} are equal to 1 if the nodes i and j are neighbours, or 0 if they are not, involves a lot of redundancy in the adjacency matrix. Having in mind the memory capacity that is needed for encoding the complex networks, the adjacency matrix is difficult or cannot be directly used as data structure.

From a hardware perspective, the problem lies in the latency of the memory chip. By the time the data from the main memory arrives to the processor registers, several hundreds of clock cycles would have been finished. The modern processors solve this problem in 2 ways. As mentioned in the introduction, the CPUs introduce cache memory between them and the main memory. The cache memory, which is quite faster [14] and more expensive then the main memory, keeps the recently accessed data. Another way to reduce the main memory latency is to increase the bandwidth by using per-fetching where adjacent locations are loaded simultaneously, which increases the cache hits.

As mentioned in the introduction, the GPUs advantage over the CPUs is the execution throughput, which hides the main memory latency, but only by ensuring that the processor is always busy with computations, while other computations are waiting on memory access. This latency hiding is useful when encountered with larger complex network load data, which results with higher number of calculation. For smaller complex network load data, the calculations number is lower, which makes the GPU's execution throughput not useful because just the time spent for transferring the data from host memory to the processor registers of the GPU is quite big compared to the time for execution on the CPU.

Nevertheless, for large complex networks, the cache does not improve the latency much. The data cannot be stored into memory such that the adjacent memory elements are neighbouring nodes in the networks and the cache misses being bound to happen. Introducing an efficient data structure based on hash-tables [10] for encoding the complex network data is a way to solve the problem in larger networks.

0	-1	-1	-1	-1	...	-1
1	2	-1	-1	-1	...	-1
2	3	10	12	-1	...	-1
3	7	15	-1	-1	...	-1
4	-1	-1	-1	-1	...	-1
5	6	6	17	-1	...	-1
6	-1	-1	-1	-1	...	-1
7	11	-1	-1	-1	...	-1
			...			
N	124	-1	-1	-1	...	-1

N x max_links

Fig. 1. Representation of a complex network using a hash-table based data structure

As it can be seen from Figure 1, the data is represented by a hash-table based structure, where the index of each row represents the index of the appropriate node i, and N stands for the number of nodes and *max_links* for the maximum number of neighbours. Each row contains the neighbouring nodes of the node *i*, which are marked with a grey background. The width of the rows is fixed and the value of the width is determined by the maximum number of neighbours (*max_links*) that a node from the complex network can have. For the many cases where the number of neighbours is less than the maximum, the rest of the data elements are filled with a negative number, so there is a difference between nodes and empty data. The reduction of the redundancy of the adjacency matrix has a big contribution towards optimizing the parallel implementations in regards to memory bandwidth, resulting in less data being copied from host memory to the processor register. Also, with this structure the GPU eliminates few memory accesses to the main memory. The penalty for the exclusion is paid by transferring the extra padding of empty data to the shared memory, which in the end proves to be more efficient (See 4.1).

Currently there are 3 major GPU parallel programming languages DirectCompute [15][16], CUDA [17] and OpenCL [18]. For the GPU parallel programming OpenCL is used. OpenCL is a standardized programming language, formed by the major industry leaders Apple, Intel, AMD/ATI, NVIDIA, and others [19]. OpenCL is an open standard, parallel programming language of modern processors found in PCs, servers and embedded devices. It is very much similar to CUDA, but unlike CUDA it is agnostic and manufactures independent. Also an open standard, the source code is portable across implementations.

The OpenCL standard is designed to take advantage of all of the system resources available. Unlike GPU programming languages in the pass which were just specifically multimedia, the standard supports general purpose parallel computing. It is based on ANSI-C99 with additional qualifier, data types and build-in functions. When working with GPUs, the focus in OpenCL goes into data parallelisation.

4.1 Clustering Coefficient

The sequential implementation of the clustering coefficient is quite straight forward. From equation (1), the implementation needs to find the number of links E_i between the neighbours, and the number of all neighbours k_i for each node *i* form the hash table structure. In order to calculate the clustering coefficient C_i for every node in the complex network, few nested loops are needed. The first level loop is iterated *N* times, where *N* is the number of nodes that the network contains. The second level nested loop iterates the vector for each node *i*, in order to obtain the values for k_i, which is the degree of each node *i*. Another second level nested loop, and a third level nested loop inside it, are iterated in order to find the value E_i. This is done by comparing if every pair of the neighboring nodes is connected. So because of the hash table structure, the third level nested loop iterates through other vectors according to the values in the data elements for the neighbors of the node *i*. Having the values for E_i and k_i, the final calculation describe in equation (1) is performed.

Developing the parallel OpenMP implementation is based on the sequential implementation and is performed quite easy because there are no data dependencies. All nested loops are under one OpenMP pragma *parallel for* directive [20], which defines the private, shared, and reduction properties, which can be seen in the Listing 1.

Listing 1. OpenMP implementation of Clustering Coefficient

```
#pragma omp parallel for default(none)  \
shared(max_links, node_size, net_data, h_C, Ei, ki, \
search_index, search_row_size) \
private(i,j,k,z)
for(i = 0; i < node_size; i++){
  Ei = 0;
  ki = net_data[i*max_links + 0];
  for(j = 1; j <= ki; j++){
    for(k = j + 1; k < ki; k++){
      search_index = net_data[i*max_links + k]  *
                                              max_links;
      search_row_size = net_data[search_index + 0];
      for (z = 1; z < search_row_size; z++)
        if(net_data[i*max_links + j] ==
                        net_data[search_index + z]) Ei++;
    }
  }
  h_C[i] = (float)(2*Ei)/(ki*(ki-1));
}
```

For each nested loop the compiler creates a separate team of threads only if the nested parallelism is enables, otherwise only the outer loop is parallelized, and the other loop are serialized. The nested parallelism is supported in OpenMP 3.0 [21] by adding the collapse clause in the pragma *parallel for* directive. For earlier versions [22], only the outer loop is parallelized, while the other nested loops are performed by each of the 1/p threads, where p is number of core that the CPU has. We recommend using the early version for nested parallelism because the version 3.0 may introduce some overhead.

The parallel OpenCL implementation harvests the power of the GPU by using the shared memory. Before executing on the GPU, the host CPU takes care of the compiling and building of the OpenCL kernels (Just In Time – compiler), and initializes other OpenCL necessary objects. The complex network data, before is loaded from the host to global memory using OpenCL input buffer, an additional padding is introduced while allocation, so the number of nodes are a multiple of the number of assigned workgroup size [23]. A unit of work in OpenCL is called a work-item, which can be conceptualized as a thread, because each instance of a kernel execution is done by a single thread. A group of work-items form a work-group, which is the local size, and the minimal value is limited to 32 because of the hardware limitation of a warp. In our case the maximum number of local workgroup size 512 proved most efficient. The number of workitems is initialized with the number of nodes N in the complex network, which is our global size, thus N threads are executed. A fragment of the kernel is presented in the Listing 2.

Listing 2. OpenCL implementation of Clustering Coefficient

```
for(j = 1; j <= ki; j++){
  first = input[gid*max_links + j];
  for(k = j + 1; k <= ki; k++){
    search_index = input[gid*max_links + k]*max_links;
    for (z = 1; z < max_links; z += lsize){
      if((z + lsize)>max_links) lsize = max_links - z;
      if((z + lid) < max_links)
        sh_tmp[lid] = input[(search_index + z + lid)];
      barrier(CLK_LOCAL_MEM_FENCE);


      for(i = 0; i < lsize; i++)
        Ei += (sh_tmp[i] == first);
        barrier(CLK_LOCAL_MEM_FENCE);
    }
  }
}
if (gid < node_size) output[gid] = (float)(2*Ei)/
                                    (ki*(ki-1));.
```

For obtaining the degree k_i of each node, in the kernel code, a simple parallel reduction is performed. In order to calculate the value for E_i, a first level nested loop iterates through the neighbors for each node *i*. A second level nested loop iterates through the rows, which are the values neighbors of the node *i*, with a step iteration *lsize*, where *lsize* is the size of the local memory. This is done in order to take advantage of the local memory, so when the synchronization barrier is passed, the local memory is loaded by all the free threads with the *lsize* elements. This allows for the third level nested loop to efficiently access the local memory and compare if the neighbors are connected, which is much faster than accessing the global memory. The number of connected neighbors is contained in E_i, which is a local integer register. The output, which is the calculation described in equation (1) is read into main memory using OpenCL output buffer.

5 Results

The results from the sequential and parallel implementation are system dependent. Therefore, this is a case-study to determine how much the performance of parallel implementations using both OpenMP and OpenCL are improving the sequential implementation. The implementations were executed on the computer which specification is presented on table 1:

Table 1. System specifications

Devices	Specs
CPU	Intel(R) Core(TM) i7 CPU 920 @ 2.67GHz 4 cores 8 thread Hyper-Threading Technology
RAM	12GB DIMM 1333 MHz (0.8ns) 64bit
GPU	NVIDIA GeForce GTX 285 1GB 240 CUDA cores @ 1476MHz

All executions were run on Ubuntu 10.04. The CPU implementations were written in C using standard and OpenMP libraries. Nvidia Graphics driver version 3.1 was used for OpenCL compatibility.

There are seven datasets that are generated for each of the three main network models. Each data set is generated with different number of nodes and links, thus obtaining different sizes of the networks. The sizes are noted as scaling factors 1, 2, 5, 10, 20, 50 and 100. For the scaling factor 1, 500 nodes are generated, which results in an adjacency matrix of 250000 elements. The other nodes are chosen by doubling the elements of the adjacency matrix, so for scaling factor 2 the adjacency matrix has 499749 elements, for scaling factor 5 it has 1249924 elements, and so forth until scaling factor 100 when the matrix has 25000000 elements.

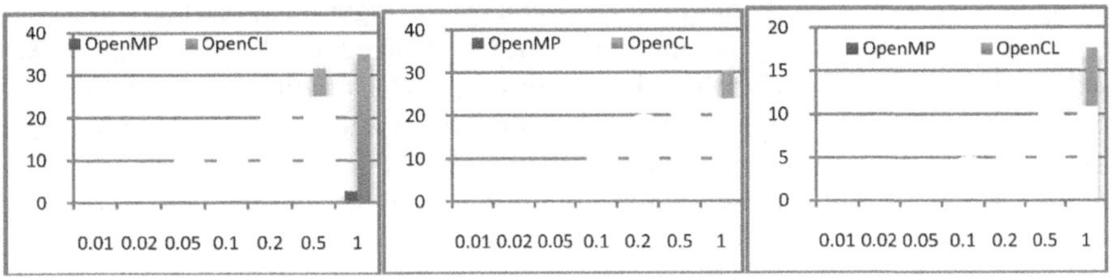

Fig. 2. The speedup of executions for the clustering coefficient calculations on CPU and GPU including the transfer time of the load data for random, small-world, and scale-free complex networks

The obtained results for each of the implementations are summarized on figure 2 for each of the main complex network models: random, small-world and scale free model respectively. Each of the implementations is executed 10 times, and average execution times are obtained. Looking at the results for the times of the OpenCL implementation, for all scaling factors, a conclusion can be made that for small volumes of data, executing the implementation on a GPU is not a smart way to go. For example in the executions for a scaling factor 1, the time spent for initializing OpenCL objects, building of kernels and programs, and allocating memory, is close or sometimes even bigger to the time spent for the CPU implementations. This proves that only by working with larger volumes of data, using the GPU is justifiable.

From figure 2, it can be seen that for different complex network models with the same number of nodes and appropriate number of links, the speedups are different. In average we obtained speedups of x3 for OpenMP, while for OpenCL we achieved x20. A conclusion can be made that for the random model of complex networks, the acceleration of calculations using the GPU is the greatest, while for the scale-free model the accelerations are smallest. The problem why we get worse speedups for the scale-free complex networks that the neighbours are concentrated around few nodes, because they have power law degree distribution, while in the other complex networks the distribution of neighbours is spread more equally. This makes us believe that another algorithm should be chosen for more efficient calculating of clustering coefficient for scale-free complex networks.

6 Conclusion

In this paper, we presented an implementation of an algorithm for calculation of the clustering coefficient measure of complex networks, for the three main complex network models. By utilizing hash-table base structure, we organized the complex network graph, which resulted of less data copied from host memory to the GPU processor registers. Also, because of the padding introduced of the hash-table base structure, more efficient use of the GPU's shared memory was achieved. We demonstrated the power of using the GPUs, providing a further evidence of effectiveness for accelerating complex networks calculations. The size of the GPU memory limits the size of the graphs handled on a single GPU. However, OpenCL provides for multiple devices to be interfaced, such that the work is distributed to each of them, thus expanding the capacity for calculating measurement for larger complex networks.

We have also performed comparisons with optimized implementations of CPU-based sequential and OpenMP parallel algorithms. The obtained acceleration of the measure calculation of complex networks is another example of the tremendous parallel power of the modern programmable GPU devices. These results of acceleration on the GPU provide a big interest. Seeing the GPU as high performance co-processing unit for any application eligible for data parallelization and having in mind the low cost of the GPU hardware, compared to the expensive CPUs of similar calculation power, points to GPUs as interesting area for future research and commercial development.

References

1. Kirk, D.B., Hwu, W.W.: Programming Massively Parallel Processors: A Hands-on Approach, Published February 5 (2010)
2. Owens, J.D., Luebke, D., Govindaraju, N., Harris, M., Krüger, J., Lefohn, A.E., Purcell, T.J.: A Survey of General-Purpose Computation on Graphics Hardware. In: Eurographics 2005, State of the Art Reports, August 2005, pp. 21–51 (2005)
3. Strogatz, S.H.: Exploring complex networks. Nature 410(6825), 268–276 (2001)
4. Albert, R., Barabasi, A.L.: Statistical mechanics of complex networks. Reviews of Modern Physics 74(1), 47–97 (2002)
5. Newman, M.E.J.: The structure and function of complex networks. SIAM Review 45(2), 167–256 (2003)
6. Batagelj, V., Mrvar, A.: Pajek – Analysis and Visualization of Large Networks. In: Junger, M., Mutzel, P. (eds.) Graph Drawing Software. Series Mathematics and Visualization, pp. 77–103. Springer, Berlin (2003)
7. Borgatti, S.P., Everett, M.G., Freeman, L.C.: Ucinet 6 for Windows: Software for Social Network Analysis, H.A. Technologies, Editor (2002)
8. Gleich, D.: Matlab BGL v1.0, April 27 (2006), `http://www.stanford.edu/dgleich/programs/matlab_bgl/` (retrieved April 2010)
9. Harish, P., Narayanan, P.J.: Accelerating Large Graph Algorithms on the GPU Using CUDA. In: Aluru, S., Parashar, M., Badrinath, R., Prasanna, V.K. (eds.) HiPC 2007. LNCS, vol. 4873, pp. 197–208. Springer, Heidelberg (2007)
10. Hyvoenen, J., Saramaeki, J., Kaski, K.: Efficient data structures for sparse network representation. International Journal of Computer Mathematics 85(8), 1219–1233 (2008)

11. Lessig, C.: Eigenvalue Computation with CUDA, NVIDIA CUDA SDK 1.1 (2007)
12. Volkov, V., Demmel, J.W.: LAPACK working note 197: Using GPUs to accelerate the bisection algorithm for finding eigenvalues of symmetric tridiagonal matrices. Technical Report UCB/EECS-2007-179, EECS Department, University of California, Berkeley (2007)
13. Katz, G.J., Kider, Jr. J.T.: All-Pairs Shortest-Paths for Large Graphs on the GPU. In: Proceedings of the 23rd ACM SIGGRAPH/EUROGRAPHICS Symposium on Graphics Hardware (2008)
14. Cantin, J., Hill, M.: Cache performance for selected SPEC CPU2000 benchmarks. ACM SIGARCH Computer Architecture News 29, 13–18 (2001)
15. Direct Compute Support on NVIDIA's CUDA Architecture GPUs, `http://developer.nvidia.com/object/directcompute_home.html/`
16. Nigel, D.: Senior VP and CMO at AMD about DirectCompute, `http://developer.nvidia.com/object/directcompute_home.html/`
17. OpenCL Programming for the CUDA Architecture, Version 2.3 (8/31/2009)
18. The OpenCL Specification, Version 1.0, document Revision 43 (2009), `http://www.khronos.org/opencl/` (retrieved February 2010)
19. The Khronos Group, Open Standard for Media Authoring and Acceleration, `http://www.khronos.org/`
20. Chapman, B., Jost, G., van der Pas, R.: Using OpenMP, Portable Shared Memory Parallel Programming. The MIT Press, Cambridge
21. OpenMP Application Program Interface, OpenMP Architecture Review Board, Version 3.0 (May 2008)
22. OpenMP Application Program Interface, OpenMP Architecture Review Board, Version 2.5 (May 2005)
23. NVIDIA OpenCL, Best Practices Guide, Version 1.0, August 10 (2009)

Selective Attack in Virus Propagation Processes

Miroslav Mirchev[1], Igor Mishkovski[1], and Ljupco Kocarev[1,2,3]

[1] Faculty of Electrical Engineering and Information Technologies, Skopje, Macedonia
[2] Macedonian Academy of Sciences and Arts, Skopje, Macedonia
[3] University of California, San Diego, CA, USA
{miroslavm,igorm,lkocarev}@feit.ukim.edu.mk

Abstract. Computer viruses are still one of the main security threats in the Internet. For virus outbreaks prevention, we need to fully understand their spreading dynamics and how it can be affected. Many viruses include inter-human contacts in their spreading and observations have shown that these inter-contact times are often heavy-tail distributed. The contacts between humans form a logical network over which viruses spread and the topology of this network plays important role in the spreading dynamics. The rapidity of spreading also depends on the location of initially infected nodes in the network. By selectively infecting the most influential nodes in the network the virus outbreak can grow faster. We analyze this effect for networks with different topologies, by using nodes selection based on several node centrality measures and the k-medoids graph clustering algorithm.

Keywords: Computer viruses, Complex networks, Selective attack.

1 Introduction

The concept of a computer virus is relatively old in the field of information security. It was first developed by Cohen in [1, 2] and it is still an active research area. Computer viruses still accounts for a significant share of the financial losses that large organizations suffer for computer security problems. According to The WildList Organization International [3] there were 70 widespread computer viruses in July 1993. That number has increased up to 1067 in October 2009, but it has dropped to 587 in May 2010. With the proliferation of broadband connections, file downloads, instant messaging, Bluetooth-enabled mobile devices, and all the other communications technologies, the mechanisms used by viruses to spread have evolved as well [4, 5]. Still, many viruses continue to spread by using inter-human contacts such as email communication, instant messaging and MMS. Indeed, according to the Virus Bulletin [6], these viruses still account for large share of the virus prevalence today.

Viruses which abuse inter-human contacts spread by sending infected messages. When a virus infects a user, it sends an infected message to all of the user's contacts. This self-broadcast mechanism allows the virus to spread rapidly, explaining why these viruses continue to be one of the main security threats. While some viruses use only infected messages to propagate, many of them can also use other infection mechanisms in order to increase their spreading rate. Although virus spreading through messages is an old technique, it is still effective and is widely used by current viruses.

M. Gusev and P. Mitrevski (Eds.): ICT Innovations 2010, CCIS 83, pp. 286–295, 2011.

It is attractive to virus writers, because it doesn't require any security holes in computer operating systems or software, almost everyone uses email, instant messaging, etc., and many users have little knowledge of these viruses and trust most messages they receive (especially when they are received from friends).

In order to control and limit the impact of an outbreak, we need to have a detailed and quantitative understanding of the spreading dynamics and the spreading environment. Most virus propagation models have assumed that the contact process between individuals follows Poisson statistics, but recent studies of email and instant messages exchange records have shown that the probability density function of the time interval between two consecutive messages sent by a single user is well approximated by a heavy-tailed distribution [7, 8, 9], which increases the virus prevalence time in 2-3 orders of magnitude. In [10] the authors prove that this deviation from the Poisson process has a strong impact on the email virus's spread, offering a coherent explanation of the anomalously long prevalence times observed for email viruses. In [11] we confirmed these claims and we proposed an email virus propagation model which considers both heavy-tailed inter-contact time distribution and heavy-tailed topology of email networks and we revealed a new form of the epidemic threshold condition.

The topology of the network defined by users' contacts plays important role in the spreading dynamics. Studies have showed that node degrees in email networks are heavy-tail distributed [12, 13], so they can be modeled as scale-free networks. Another study [14] has revealed that networks created by instant messaging communication also have scale-free topology. The problem of virus spreading in scale-free networks has been studied in [12, 15]. Many social networks also have the small-world property [16], which means that the average distance between any pair of nodes is small. In [17] it is shown that email networks also have this property.

The spreading dynamics also depends on the location where the virus spreading starts. If the initially infected nodes are more influential the virus outbreak can happen faster. In [12] it is shown that if nodes with higher degree are initially infected the spreading rate is faster, with a model which doesn't consider the communication dynamics. In [18] the authors argue that the Eigen-vector centrality of a node is a good indicator of that node's overall spreading power.

In this paper we analyze the effect of selective attack in virus propagation processes for networks with different topologies, by using several node centrality measures. We also consider the k-medoids graph clustering algorithm to determine if the distance between initially infected nodes affects the spreading rate.

The rest of the paper is organized as follows. In Section 2, we define the network model. After that in Section 3, we define the virus propagation model which considers both network topology and communication dynamics. Several methods which can be used for selective attack are given in Section 4. Simulation results and analyses are given in Section 5 and Section 6 concludes the paper.

2 Network Model

We will represent the users and their interactions by a connected, undirected graph $G = (V, E)$. There are N nodes in the set V, which represent the users, and there are m edges in the set E, which represent the contacts between the users. Every user contacts only with some subset of the set of all users V. These subsets are represented with the adjacency matrix **A** of the graph G, i.e., $a_{ij} = 1$ if $(i, j) \in E$ (user i contacts with user j) and $a_{ij} = 0$ otherwise.

The network topology is determined by the adjacency matrix **A**. The size of the subset of users with which one user communicates is the degree of the corresponding node in the network graph. Based on the characteristics of the adjacency matrix there are many different networks models which capture different features such as the degree distribution of the nodes, the average path length between nodes and the clustering coefficient of the network. We will consider the Erdős-Rényi model of random networks, the Barabási-Albert model of scale-free networks and the Watts-Strogatz model of small-world networks.

The *Erdős-Rényi model* [19] of random networks can be considered as the most basic model. A random network is obtained by starting with a set of n nodes and randomly adding edges between them. The model is denoted as $G(n, p)$, in which every possible edge between the n nodes occurs independently with probability p. The degree distribution p_k has a Poisson distribution.

Many real world networks exhibit what is called the small world property, i.e. most nodes can be reached from the others through a small number of edges. This property is found in many social networks, where everyone in the world can be reached through a short chain of social acquaintances. Another property of many networks is the presence of a large number of loops of size three, i.e. if node i is connected to nodes j and k, there is a high probability of nodes j and k being connected. Networks with abundance of these short loops are said to have clustering effect. The most popular network model which captures both small world property and clustering effect is the *Watts-Strogatz small-world model* [20]. The degree distribution for small-world networks is similar to random networks.

After Watts-Strogatz's model, *Barabási-Albert* showed that the degree distribution of many real systems is characterized by an uneven distribution [21]. Instead of the nodes of these networks having a random pattern of connections with a characteristic degree, as with the ER and WS models, some nodes are highly connected while others have few connections, with absence of a characteristic degree.

More specifically, the degree distribution has been found to follow a power law for large k, $P(k) \sim k^{\gamma}$, where γ is a constant whose value is typically in the range $2<\gamma<3$, although occasionally it may lay outside these bounds. Networks with these characteristics are called *scale-free* networks. In these networks typically there are only several nodes called hubs, which are highly connected, and many others with only few connections mainly towards some of the hubs. Despite some social networks many other real networks appear to be scale-free, including the Internet, the World Wide Web, protein networks, and citation networks [22].

3 Virus Propagation Model

We need to represent how a virus spreads in a network over time. Let first assume that at time k, each node i can be in one of two possible states: **S** (susceptible) or **I** (infected). The state of the node i is indicated by a status vector $\mathbf{s}_i(k)$ which contains a single "1" at the position corresponding to the present status, and "0" at the other position:

$$\mathbf{s}_i(k) = [s_i^S(k) \;\; s_i^I(k)]^T \tag{1}$$

and let

$$\mathbf{p}_i(k) = [p_i^S(k) \;\; p_i^I(k)]^T \tag{2}$$

be the probability mass function of node i at time k. For every node i it states the probability of being in each of the possible states at time k.

When a user receives infected message by some of his contacts, he may discard the message or open it. When the infected message is opened, the virus immediately infects the user and sends infected messages to all of his contacts. We assume that the probability that a user opens an infected message, after he has received it, is constant and denote it with β. The infected user will not send out infected message again unless the user receives another infected message and opens it again.

It takes time before a recipient receives an infected message sent out by an infected user, but the message transmission time is usually much smaller comparing to user's checking time. Thus in our model we neglect the transmission times. In most cases received messages are responded to in the next activity burst [8], and viruses act when messages are read, approximately the same time when the next bunch of messages is written. According to this we can represent users' activity as follows. Let $b_j(k)$ represent user's j activity at time k. If user j is active at time k $b_j(k) = 1$, otherwise $b_j(k) = 0$. We assume that a user reads all his messages at the moment he is active.

For users' activity modeling we use chaotic-maps. This method is used in [23, 24] for modeling packet traffic and for our purposes the following map is convenient:

$$x_j(k+1) = \begin{cases} \dfrac{x_j(k)}{(1 - c_1 x_j(k)^{m_1 - 1})^{\frac{1}{m_1 - 1}}}, & \text{if } x_j(k) < d \\ 1 - \dfrac{1 - x_j(k)}{(1 - c_2(1 - x_j(k))^{m_2 - 1})^{\frac{1}{m_2 - 1}}}, & \text{if } x_j(k) \geq d \end{cases} \tag{3}$$

where $c_1 = \dfrac{1 - d^{m_1 - 1}}{d^{m_1 - 1}}$, $c_2 = \dfrac{1 - (1-d)^{m_2 - 1}}{(1-d)^{m_2 - 1}}$, and $d \in [0, 1]$. At each time k, the value of $x_j(k)$ is evaluated for each user j, and then $b_j(k) = 0$ if $x_j(k) < d$ and $b_j(k) = 1$ if $x_j(k) \geq d$.

We choose this chaotic map, because for values of m_1 and/or m_2 in the range (3/2, 2) the map generates inter-event times that have heavy-tailed distribution. More precisely for d=0.7, $m_1 = 1.53$ and $m_2 = 1.96$ the distribution approximately follows a power law with exponent $\alpha \approx 2.4$ and a cut-off at large τ values, very similar to the true inter-event time distribution (this can be achieved with other values as well).

Let represent users' unread messages, regardless of the communication type, with an infected inbox matrix $V(k)$. So, $v_{ij}(k) = 1$ if user j have unread infected message from user i at time k, otherwise $v_{ij}(k) = 0$. At the beginning ($k = 0$) there is a small number of initially infected users, and $v_{ij}(0) = 1$ if user j contacts with the initially infected user i, otherwise $v_{ij}(0) = 0$. At each time k:

$$v_{ij}(k+1) = (a_{ij} h_i(k) + v_{ij}(k)(1 - h_i(k)))(1 - b_j(k)) \tag{4}$$

where $h_i(k) = 1$ if user i opens an infected message at time k, otherwise $h_i(k) = 0$.

Previously we assumed that a user reads all his messages at the moment he is active. So if user j is active at time k ($b_j(k) = 1$), all his messages from the infected inbox matrix V should be removed, $v_{ij}(k+1) = 0$ for all i.

We introduce another parameter δ, which represents the curing probability, i.e. the probability that a virus is removed. As with β we assume constant curing probability. Eventually, we can define the equations describing the evolution of the virus propagation model as:

$$\begin{aligned} p_i^S(k+1) &= b_i s_i^S(k)(1-f_i(k)) + (1-b_i)s_i^S(k) + s_i^I \delta \\ p_i^I(k+1) &= b_i s_i^S(k) f_i(k) + s_i^I(k)(1-\delta) \\ s_i^T(k+1) &= Multirealize[\mathbf{p}_i^T(k+1)] \end{aligned} \tag{5}$$

$$f_i(k) = 1 - \prod_{j=1}^{N} (1 - \beta v_{ji}(k))$$

where *Multirealize*[.] performs a random realization of the probability distribution.

4 Methods for Selective Attack

The rate of the virus spreading depends on the location from where the virus has started to spread. We can find the nodes whose initial infection would cause fastest virus propagation. For this we need to determine the initial influence of the nodes and then start the virus spread from the most influential nodes. There are various measures for determination of node centrality in a network, which in different ways assess the influence of the node in the network processes [25]. We will consider the most popular measures such as degree, betweeness, closeness and Eigen-vector centrality.

If the virus spread starts from multiple locations, and if these locations are positioned in such a way that they are not very close to each other, the virus spreading rate might be even bigger. For this we will consider using network clustering by using the k-medoids algorithm and then start the spreading from the cluster medoids.

Degree centrality is the simplest measure of node centrality and it is defined with the number of links a node is connected with. It can be interpreted as a direct risk of infection. For a graph $G=(V,E)$ which has N nodes, the degree centrality $C_D(v)$ for node v is defined as:

$$C_D(v) = \frac{\deg(v)}{N-1}. \tag{6}$$

Betweeness centrality is determined by the fraction of shortest paths which goes through the node and it is defined as:

$$C_B(v) = \sum_{\substack{s \neq v \neq t \in V \\ s \neq t}} \frac{\sigma_{st}(v)}{\sigma_{st}} \tag{7}$$

where σ_{st} is the number of shortest path from s to t, and $\sigma_{st}(v)$ is the number of shortest paths from s to t which goes through node v. It can be normalized with division by the number of pairs of nodes which doesn't include node v, which is $(N\text{-}1)(N\text{-}2)/2$ for undirected graph.

Closeness centrality is another measure of node centrality in which nodes which are closer to other nodes are considered as most central. It is defined as:

$$C_C(v) = \frac{\sum_{t \epsilon V \setminus v} d_{G(v,t)}}{n-1}, \tag{8}$$

where $n \geq 2$ is the size of the network connected component V reachable from v.

Eigen-vector centrality assigns nodes importance based on the principle that links to more important nodes influence more on the nodes importance. Let $C_E(v)$ denotes nodes v importance and let $\mathbf{A}_{i,j}$ be the adjacency matrix of the network. The Eigen-vector centrality of node v would then be proportional to the sum of the centralities of his neighbors:

$$C_E(v) = \frac{1}{\lambda} \sum_{i \epsilon S(v)} C_E(i) = \frac{1}{\lambda} \sum_{i=1}^{N} A_{v,i} C_E(i) \tag{9}$$

where $S(v)$ is the set of nodes connected to node v and λ is a constant.

The *k-medoids* clustering algorithm [26] is a simple algorithm which is a discrete version of the well known *k*-means clustering algorithm [27]. The algorithm requires that the value of *k* is known in advance. It uses some measure to represent the distance between a pair of instances. The procedure is as follows: (1) randomly select *k* instances to serve as "seeds" for the *k* clusters; (2) assign the remaining instances to the cluster of the nearest seed; (3) calculate the medoid of each cluster; and 4) repeat steps 2 and 3 using the medoids as seeds until the clusters stabilize. The algorithm can be extended to network domain [28] where for the distance measure we have the geodesic distance, or number of hops between nodes. The clusters are initialized by randomly selecting k nodes in the graph as seeds and assigning all nodes to the cluster of the nearest seed node. The medoids are chosen by computing the local closeness centrality among nodes in each cluster and selecting the node with the greatest closeness score. This process terminates when the cluster medoids stabilize.

5 Simulations and Analyses

For our simulations, we use networks with 1000 nodes representing the human users and 3000 links representing the users' contacts. We observe the number of infected nodes N_I over time in virus propagation for the different network topologies described previously. The parameter values we use are $\beta = 0.5$, $d = 0.9$, $\delta = 0$ (because we are only interested in the spreading rate) and we use three initially infected nodes. For each topology we use all the different nodes centrality measures described previously for selection of the initially infected nodes. For each measure we consider both the most central and the least central nodes as initially infected in order to see how well the measures estimate node's impact on the spreading rate if it is initially infected. So we are interested not just in finding the nodes which cause most rapid spread, but we like to measure the impact of the different nodes on the spreading rate. For each topology we also consider using the k-medoids clustering algorithm for selection of the initially infected nodes.

The results for networks generated with the Erdős-Rényi model are shown on Fig.1. The different node centrality measures find the nodes which cause most rapid spread with equal success. The *k*-medoids algorithm gives slightly worse results than the node centrality measures, but still finds nodes that cause more rapid spread better than if they are arbitrarily chosen. On the other hand the node centrality measures differ in finding the nodes which cause slowest spread. Namely, the closeness centrality is most successful, next come degree centrality and betweeness centrality, while Eigen-vector centrality is least successful. But still, they all give better results than random selection.

On Fig.2 are the results for the Barabási-Albert model. Again, all the centrality measures successfully find the nodes which cause fastest spread, but in this case the *k*-medoids algorithm is almost as successful as them. This happens because in these networks there are hub nodes, which have huge number of links, and it is most likely that they will also become cluster medoids, so the initially infected nodes would be the same. The success of centrality measures in finding the nodes which cause slowest spread are different than in random networks. Closeness centrality finds these nodes successfully and then comes betweeness centrality. Degree centrality is not successful in this case and gives same results as random selection, while Eigen-vector centrality is even worse. This means that although degree and Eigen-vector centrality find the initial nodes which cause most rapid spread, they are not always good in estimating node's impact on spreading rate if initially infected.

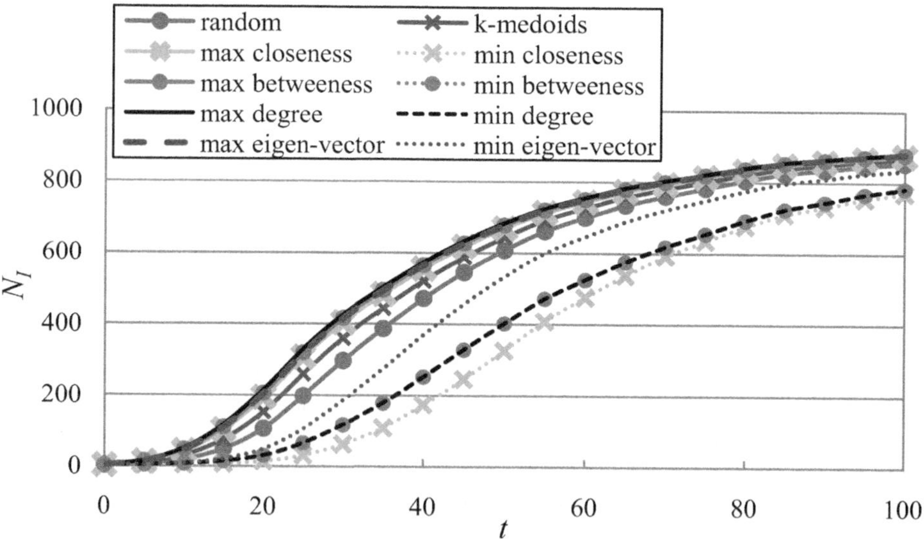

Fig. 1. Number of infected nodes N_I in a virus propagation process for different selection methods of initially infected nodes. Networks are generated with the Erdős–Rényi model.

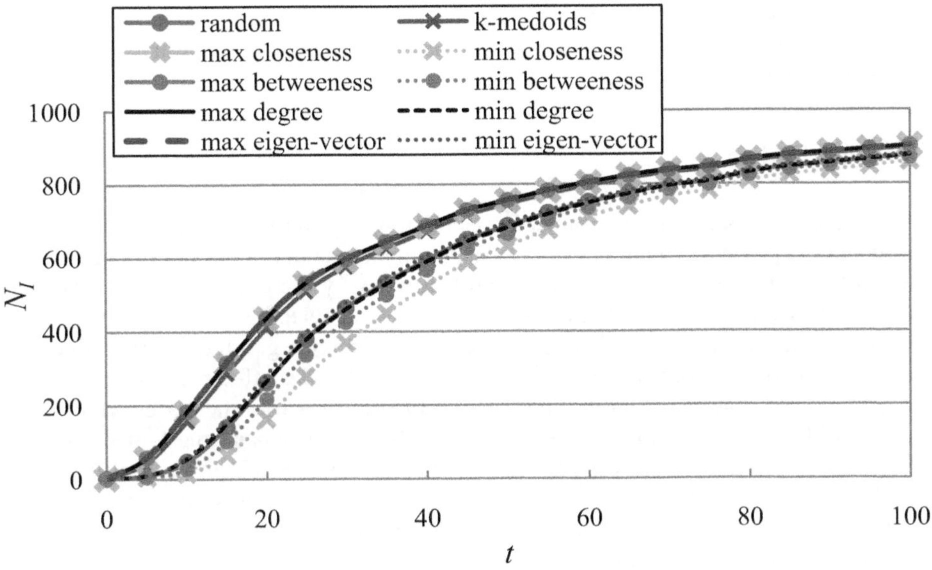

Fig. 2. Number of infected nodes N_I in a virus propagation process for different selection methods of initially infected nodes. Networks are generated with the Barabási-Albert model.

On Fig. 3 we can see the results for the Watts-Strogatz small-world model. Here the centrality measures slightly differ in finding the nodes which cause fastest spread, but the differences are minor. The *k*-medoids algorithm is not successful at all and is

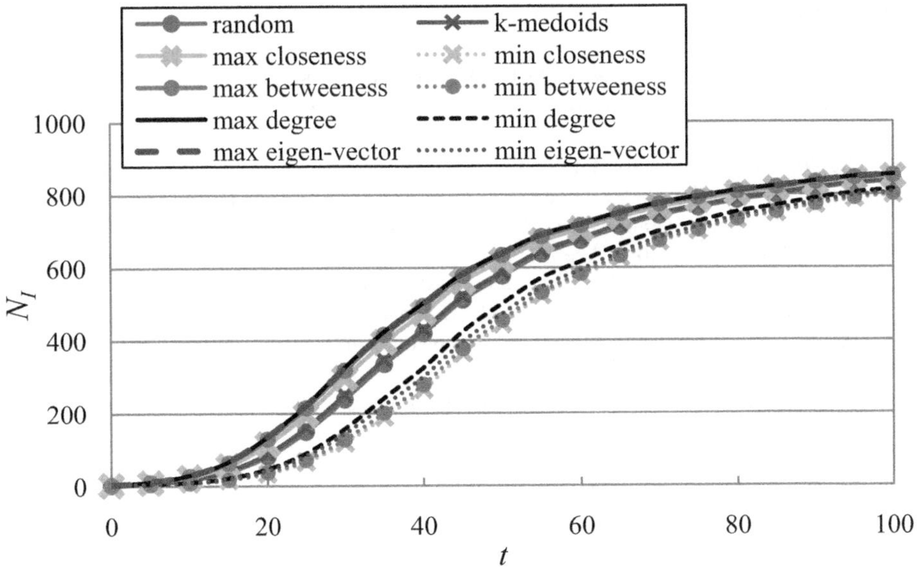

Fig. 3. Number of infected nodes N_I in virus propagation for different selection methods of initially infected nodes. Networks are generated with the Watts-Strogatz small-world model.

almost as good as random selection. The success for all centrality measures in finding the nodes which cause slowest spread is similar, but closeness centrality once again is most successful.

6 Conclusion

In this paper we analyzed the impact of selection of initially infected nodes on virus propagation processes which include inter-human contacts. We considered several network topologies for the logical network formed by the contacts and showed that the effect differs in the different networks. For node selection we used several node centrality measures and we also considered the k-medoids graph clustering algorithm to determine if the distance between initially infected nodes affects the spreading rate.

We showed that the different node centrality measures find the nodes which cause most rapid spread with almost equal success. On the other hand the k-medoids algorithm find these nodes well only for scale-free networks, which means that increasing the distance between initially infected nodes doesn't increases the spreading rate. Centrality measures differ in finding the nodes which cause slowest spread and closeness centrality is clearly most successful in that. So, we can conclude that closeness centrality is best in estimating the impact of the selection of initially infected nodes on virus spreading rate.

Acknowledgments. LK thanks ONR Global (Grant number N62909-10-1-7074) and Macedonian Ministry of Education and Science (grant 'Annotated graphs in system biology') for partial support.

References

1. Cohen, F.: Computer Viruses. PhD Thesis, University of Southern California (1985)
2. Cohen, F.: Computer viruses: theory and experiments. Computers&Security 6, 22–35 (1987)
3. The WildList Organization International, `http://www.wildlist.org`
4. Wang, P., González, M.C., Hidalgo, C.A., Barabási, A.-L.: Understanding the Spreading Patterns of Mobile Phone Viruses. Science 324, 1071–1076 (2009)
5. Hu, H., Myers, S., Colizza, V., Vespignani, A.: WiFi networks and malware epidemiology. Proc. of the National Academy of Sciences 106, 1318–1323 (2009)
6. Virus Bulletin, `http://www.virusbtn.com`
7. Barabasi, A.L.: Modeling bursts and heavy tails in human dynamics. Phys. Rev. E 73 (2006)
8. Vazquez, A.: Impact of memory on human dynamics. Physica A: Statistical and Theoretical Physics 373, 747–752 (2007)
9. Dewes, C., Wichmann, A., Feldmann, A.: An analysis of Internet chat systems. In: Proc. of the 2003 ACM/SIGCOMM Internet Measurement Conference, pp. 51–64 (2003)
10. Vazquez, A., Racz, B., Lukacs, A., Barabasi, A.L.: Impact of Non-Poissonian Activity Patterns on Spreading Processes. Physical Review Letters 98 (2007)
11. Mirchev, M., Kocarev, L.: Non-Poisson Processes of Email Virus Propagation. In: ICT Innovations 2009, pp. 187–196. Springer, Heidelberg (2009)

12. Zou, C., Towsley, D., Gong, W.: Email Virus Propagation Modeling and Analysis. Technical Report TR-CSE-03-04. Univ. of Massachusetts. Amherst (2003)
13. Ebel, H., Mielsch, L.-I., Bornholdt, S.: Scale-free topology of e-mail networks. Physical Review E 66 (2002)
14. Smith, R.D.: Instant Messaging as a Scale-Free Network. cond-mat/0206378v2 (2002)
15. Pastor-Satorras, R., Vespignani, A.: Epidemic Spreading in Scale-Free Networks. Physical Review Letters 86(14), 3200–3203 (2001)
16. Albert, R., Barabasi, A.-L.: Statistical mechanics of complex networks. Rev. Mod. Phys. 74, 47–97 (2002)
17. Dodds, P.S., Muhamad, R., Watts, D.J.: An Experimental Study of Search in Global Social. Science 301, 827–829 (2003)
18. Canright, G.S., Engø-Monsen, K.: Spreading on Networks: A Topographic View. Complexus 3, 131–146 (2006)
19. Erdos, P., Renyi, A.: On random graphs. Publicationes Mathematicae 6, 290–297 (1959)
20. Watts, D.J., Strogatz, S.H.: Collective dynamics of small-world networks. Nature 393 (1998)
21. Barabási, A.-L., Albert, R.: Emergence of scaling in random networks. Science 286, 509–512 (1999)
22. Newman, M.E.J.: The structure and function of complex networks. SIAM Review 45(2), 167–256 (2003)
23. Erramilli, A., Roughan, M., Veitch, D., Willinger, W.: Self-Similar Traffic and Network Dynamics. Proc. of the IEEE 90(5), 800–819 (2002)
24. Erramilli, A., Singh, R.P., Pruthi, P.: An application of deterministic chaotic maps to model packet traffic. Queueing Systems 20, 171–206 (1995)
25. Freeman, L.: Centrality in Social Networks. Social Networks 1, 215–239 (1979)
26. Kaufman, L., Rousseeuw, P.: Finding groups in data: An introduction to cluster analysis. In: Applied Probability and Statistics. Wiley, New York (1990)
27. MacQueen, J.: Some methods for classification and analysis of multivariate observations. In: Proc. of the 5th Berkeley Symposium on Mathematical Statistics and Probability, vol. 1, pp. 281–297 (1967)
28. Rattigan, M.J., Maier, M., Jensen, D.: Graph Clustering with Network Structure Indices. In: Proceedings of the 24th International Conference on Machine Learning, vol. 277, pp. 783–790 (2007)

Object Recognition Based on Local Features Using Camera – Equipped Mobile Phone

Saso Koceski, Natasa Koceska, and Aleksandar Krstev

University "Goce Delcev", Faculty of Computer Sciences, Stip, Macedonia
{saso.koceski,natasa.koceska,aleksandar.krstev}@ugd.edu.mk

Abstract. The work presented in this paper analyses the viability of using a cell-phone as students' guidance for literature selection. The integrated cell-phone camera is used to recognize the book covers in the bookstores and libraries. The chosen solution is based on client-server architecture and the object recognition is based on local features. Detecting, identifying, and recognizing salient regions or feature points in images is a very important and fundamental problem to the artificial intelligence and computer vision community. This paper mainly focuses on the comparison, in terms of time and performance, of two promising new approaches for markerless object recognition algorithms: the Scale-Invariant Feature Transform (SIFT) and the Speeded Up Robust Features (SURF). The study was performed using a smart cell-phone with Symbian OS and the results are reported.

Keywords: Artificial intelligence, object recognition, image analysis, Mobile Phone technologies.

1 Introduction

Mobile devices equipped with camera are a ubiquitous part of our daily life. There is an increasing interest in extending the interaction between the users and their phones to an interaction between the user, the phone and real world objects, offering that way a numberless use-cases and applications. Enhancing mobile phones in this way is promising, because they are in constant reach of their users and are thus available in many everyday situations. They also provide continuous wireless connectivity.

Mobile phones come with integrated digital cameras, enables users to retrieve, use, and share digital information and services connected to physical objects. Recognizing physical objects is thus a fundamental precondition for such applications. The ability to detect objects in the user's vicinity strengthens the role of mobile phones in m-commerce, education, and gaming scenarios. It offers a natural way of interaction and makes data entry more convenient. The mobile phone becomes a kind of "bridge" between entities in the real world and associated counterparts in the virtual world.

Approaches to sense real world objects are usually based on visual markers (e.g. QR-Codes or other 2D barcodes [1]) or digital markers (e.g. RFID tags [2]). Several studies which are reporting a markerless approach are published in the last years. Scene recognition by distinguishing local discriminative patches described by color and edge information is presented in [3]. Recently developed methods perform the

M. Gusev and P. Mitrevski (Eds.): ICT Innovations 2010, CCIS 83, pp. 296–305, 2011.

identification of the images directly on mobile phones by applying object recognition algorithms based on local features [4]. Algorithm for extraction of image features directly on mobile device is also presented in [5]. However, all these solutions suffer from high demands on the available processing power, with a delay of up to several seconds.

The prototype presented in this paper enables a camera phone to act as a student guide in book selection: the user points with his camera phone to the book cover of interest and takes a picture. Image processing technology recognizes the input picture and provides context-sensitive information regarding the identified book. The prototype is integrated with our University eLearning system and provides details such as book information, information whether the book is recommended as an obligatory or supplemental literature for some university subject, chapters recommended by the professor, information about the availability of the book in the university library, prices of the book in the nearest bookstores and on world services such as Amazon.com, as well as information about the best price for the book.

Object recognition is still an open problem in artificial intelligence and computer vision, and the reasons for this are numerous. Images may be subject to variations in point of view, illumination and sharpness; different camera characteristics can also be an issue. On the other hand, camera phones still tend to have cheap lenses that produce noisy photographs of poor quality. As cell phones are not primarily designed for taking pictures they are more difficult to hold steady which in turn increases the likelihood of camera shake. In a library or bookstore books might be partly occluded by other persons or even cropped. Also, more than one book may appear on the image if the books have been arranged close together. Both the shape and shadows of the frame complicate a possible segmentation of the book incredibly. In order to successfully recognize an object with a cell phone four steps have to be performed. First an image containing the objet has to be acquired. We used a camera cell phone (Nokia E52) with Symbian OS. Since images cannot be compared as they are, in a second step, a signature has to be extracted. Third, a matching process is run against a database containing the signatures of the books. Finally useful information about the book is returned. We have implemented two promising new approaches for markerless object recognition algorithms: the Scale-Invariant Feature Transform (SIFT) [6] and the Speeded Up Robust Features (SURF) [7]. We have evaluated performances of both algorithms on different influencing factors. The results of this evaluation study are reported and important conclusions are derived.

2 Overview of the Methods

Scale Invariant Feature Transform (SIFT) consists of four major stages: scale-space extrema detection, keypoint localization, orientation assignment and keypoint descriptor. Key-point detection is done by building a scalespace representation of the original image. This is achieved by repeatedly convolving the image with a Gaussian function. A Difference of Gaussian (DoG) approach combined with interpolation over the scale-space leads to the locations of stable key-points in that scale-space representation of the image.

$$D(x, y, \sigma) = (G(x, y, k\sigma) \quad G(x, y, \sigma)) * I(x, y) = L(x, y, k\sigma) \quad L(x, y, \sigma) \tag{1}$$

After that localization, each key-point is assigned an orientation, which leads to the desired rotation invariancy. The key-point descriptors are calculated from the local gradient orientation and magnitudes in a certain neighborhood around the identified key-point. The gradient orientations and magnitudes are combined in a histogram representation, from which the descriptor is formed as a normalized vector of 128 elements. Descriptors and their positions are illustrated in the Figure 1 with arrows. To check for a match, the thereby received key-point descriptors are compared with those of a reference image. This way one can find the best matching picture within a database.

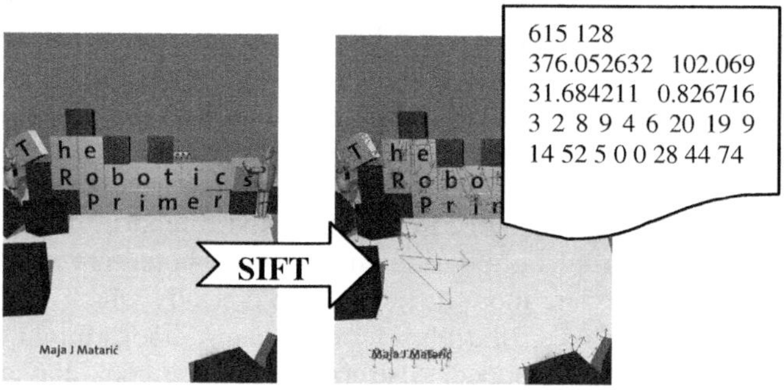

Fig. 1. Transformation from an image into feature vectors

Speeded Up Robust Features (SURF). Like SIFT, the SURF approach describes a key-point detector and descriptor (Fig.2). Key-points are found by using a so called Fast-Hessian Detector that bases on an approximation of the Hessian matrix for a given image point. The responses to Haar wavelets are used for orientation assignment, before the key-point descriptor is formed from the wavelet responses in a certain surrounding of the key-point. The descriptor vector has a length of 64 floating point numbers but can be extended to a length of 128. As this did not significantly improve the results in our experiments but rather increased the computational costs, all results refer to the standard descriptor length of 64.

Fig. 2. SURF descriptors with their orientation and size

3 System Architecture

A mobile phone with integrated camera was enabled to act as a student guiding device for book selection in bookstores and libraries.

Speed is an important issue on a mobile phone in this kind of application. Some preliminary experiments to test the performances of the CPU of mobile client were performed. Both algorithms were implemented on Symbian OS and tested on different images and different image resolutions. Depending on the image resolution SIFT algorithm takes from 32 seconds to extract the descriptors of an image with resolution 512x384 pixels, up to 9 seconds for images with resolution 128x96 pixels. Of course the number of descriptors decreases with smaller image size, but the result is still applicable. These tests showed that the CPU of mobile clients is generally very slow and running the feature extraction on the mobile client results in unbearably long waiting times for the user. Thus, client - server architecture was chosen: the client only acts as periphery, which acquires and sends sample data and receives the results. System architecture is given in Figure 3.

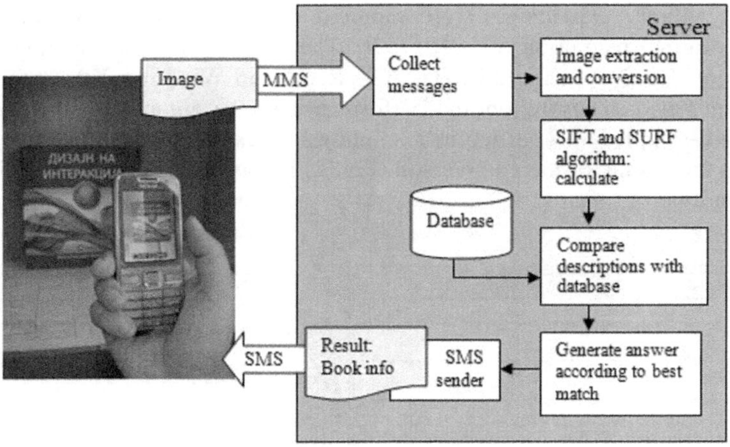

Fig. 3. System architecture

3.1 Communication with the Server

In this architecture, where the image is sent from the mobile phone to the server, a method for file transmission is needed. Bluetooth is - due to the easy handling and because it is free - an option. But the limited connection range would be a significant disadvantage for the system. A user would be bound to a bluetooth sender and therefore no real mobility would be possible. For the same reasons infrared and other ways of near distance communication are also discarded here. There are only a few far distance data transfer possibilities on a mobile phone. All of them are not free of costs. One of them is SMS, which is due to the text limitation, not usable for images. Another approach is the Internet access (either through WAP, GPRS, UMTS or similar services). But here the applications differ with device, manufacturer, and provider.

Limited connection range is also considered as a problem in the case of internet access. Therefore Internet communication was discarded for this project.

So, MMS was chosen as an alternative, because it gives an easy and widely used messaging possibility. So the user does not have to install anything before the service can be used. Most of the mobile phones which are able to photograph have a built-in option to send a picture right after it was taken. MMS consists (like emails) of several parts which can be either multimedia or a text elements. Mobile phones and system providers offer the possibility to send an MMS to an email address instead of a phone number. On the target mailbox just a normal email will arrive which contains the image. The server can easily load the images from an IMAP service of the mailbox. Therefore, in this work MMS was chosen as the transport medium from the mobile phone to the server. For the return path MMS could also be considered. But for this project, SMS was chosen to reduce costs.

Since in this configuration images have to be sent over the phone connection, we are interested in transmitting scaled down images representing smaller data size. In the other hand, smaller resolution may imply a decrease in recognition performance. In the following we study the corresponding trade-off on set of experiments.

The test sample data consists of photo series of 50 covers of books taken in the University library. All images were captured with a Nokia E52 mobile phone and have an original resolution of 2048x1536. The server part was implemented on Intel(R) Core™ 2 DUO CPU 2.0GHz, 2GB RAM and Windows XP. To evaluate the correlation between resolution and performance of the algorithms, the images have been down-sampled to 4 different resolutions: 512x384, 256x192, 128x96, 64x48. Based on the results of the comparison (Fig. 4) it was decided to work with 512x384 resolution images.

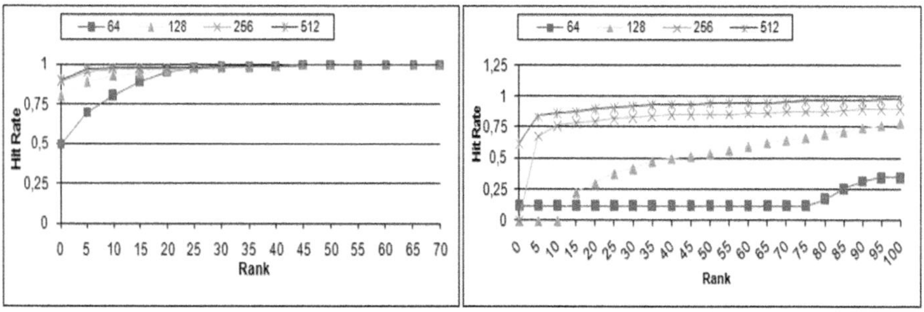

Fig. 4. CMC curves comparing (on the left) SIFT based NNS matching and (on the right) SURF based NNS matching for four different image resolutions

3.2 Server Processing

Given the communication methods, an appropriate server side implementation can be established. The following steps have to be done (according to Fig. 3):

1. **Collect messages:** The first step is to take the emails out of the mailbox and read it. Here the image is separated from the text and also the sender has to be stored for to send a response later. The image is also converted into a suitable format.

2. **SIFT algorithm or SURF algorithm:** Calculation of the descriptors.
3. **Matching:** The query descriptors are compared with those of reference images from a database. The result is the reference image which matches best to the input.
4. **Generate answer:** According to the result an answer is generated for the user.
5. **SMS sender:** Eventually the answer is sent back to the mobile phone by SMS.

Server database contains collection of books with all necessary textual information, reference images together with their descriptors.

4 Experimental Results

Comparative evaluation of the above algorithms with a dataset of images has been performed, in order to confirm and evaluate their invariance against

- scale change
- image blur
- rotation
- change in lighting conditions

Starting from an initial image, the images were altered according to the performed test, i.e. they were rotated or the camera zoomed closer to the object etc. Feature points and their descriptors were determined in the initial and the secondary images.

The first thing that became obvious during the tests was that the total number of key-points is generally higher for SIFT than it is for SURF. However, the quality of the matches is almost equal for the both implementations (SIFT and SURF), with small advantages for the SIFT algorithm.

The stability of detectors is evaluated using the repeatability criteria introduced in [8]. The repeatability score is computed as a ratio between the number of point-to-point correspondences that can be established for detected points and the mean number of points detected in two images:

$$r_{1,2} = \frac{C(I_1, I_2)}{mean(m_1, m_2)} \tag{2}$$

where $C(I_1, I_2)$ denotes the number of corresponding couples and m_1, m_2 the numbers of detected points in the images. Two points correspond if the error in relative location does not exceed 1,5 pixel in the coarse resolution image and the ratio of detected scales for these points does not differ from the real scale ratio by more than 20%.

Scale change. Scale changes hardly influence the matching quality of both algorithms. The images used for the scale invariancy test are derived from the original one and are scaled in 4 different levels (scale factors 0.8, 0.6, 0.4, 0.2). The original image was chosen as the initial image, i.e. the key-points found in all other images were matched with the initial one. Figure 5 presents the repeatability score for the compared methods. As expected, the total number of matches decreases with increasing scale change.

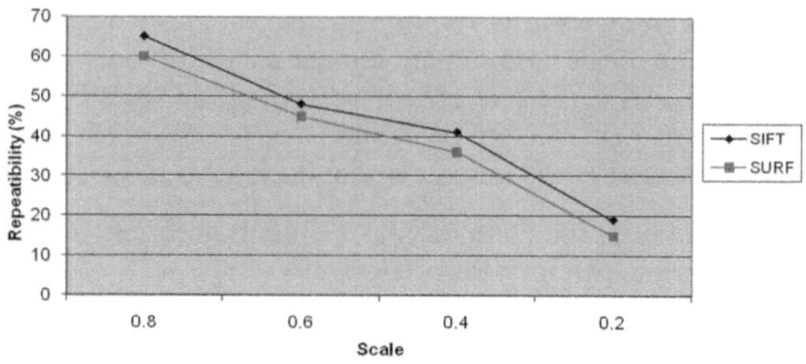

Fig. 5. Repeatability of interest point detectors with respect to scale changes

Image blur. This second experiment uses the image series like those presented in Figure 6, affected by Gaussian blur. The radius of the blur changes from 0.5 to 8.0. As shown in Figure 7, SIFT shows better performance when the blur radius gets larger. Image blurring does hardly influence the high quality of key-point matching, and increasing blur significantly reduces the total number of matched key-points by both algorithms.

Fig. 6. A subset of the series of images used for the blur invariancy test

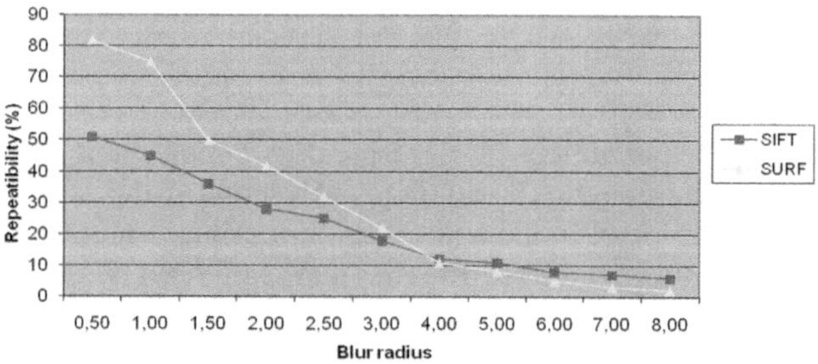

Fig. 7. Repeatability under image blurring

Image rotation. The third experiment shows the influence of rotation on the two methods. Figure 8 represents the matching of the key-points done by the SIFT and SURF algorithm when the comparing image is rotated for 45º in respect to the initial one. The overall comparison results for the repeatability are presented in Figure 9. It can be observed that SIFT outperforms the SURF algorithm.

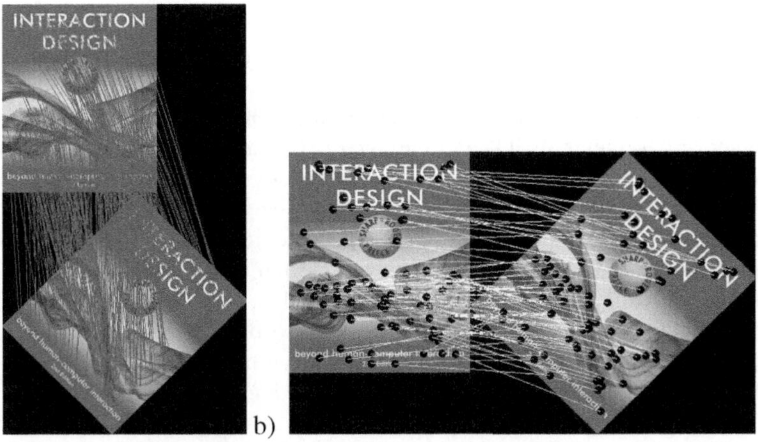

Fig. 8. Key-point matching done by the a) SIFT and b) SURF algorithm

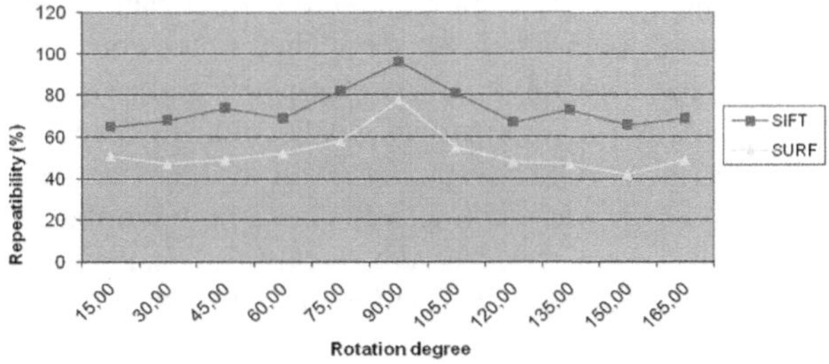

Fig. 9. Repeatability under image rotation

Illumination change. The fourth experiment evaluates the methods' stability on brightness decreasing, and the results are shown in Fig. 10. Both algorithms can cope with changing illumination conditions up to certain extend where simply not enough key-points are generated. Level 0 is the original image. It can be observed that in these conditions SIFT algorithm also outperforms the SURF algorithm.

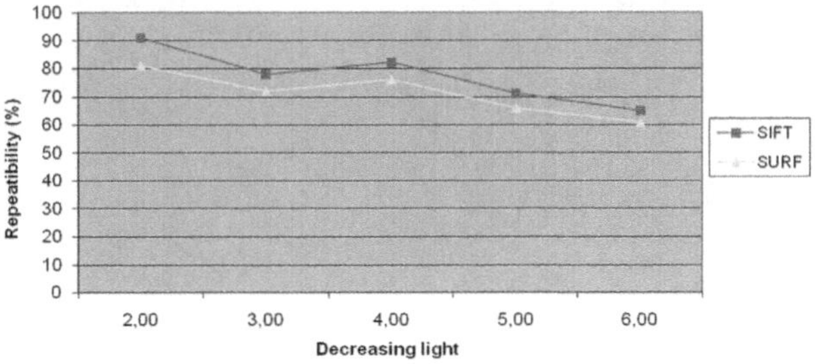

Fig. 10. Repeatability under decreasing image brightness

Processing Time. Time evaluation is a relative result, which only shows the tendency of the three methods' time cost. There are factors that influenced on the results such as the size and quality of the image, image types (e.g. scenery or texture), and the parameters of the algorithm (e.g. the distance ratio). Both algorithms were tested with the same set of parameters [6][7] and they were compared on 50 images dataset. Time is counted for the complete processing which includes feature detecting and matching. Results show that SURF in average is the fastest one, SIFT is the slowest but it finds most matches. For example for the image pair presented in Fig. 11a (both of them are with resolution 384x512) SIFT has detected 286 matching points for 5.234s, and SURF has successfully matched 190 points for 4.945s.

Because of the above analysis, it was decided to use the SIFT algorithm. For test purposes the reference pictures have been made with a 5 megapixel digital camera from which a small test database of 200 different pictures of books prepared on the server. The total number of descriptors in our database is 157832. The system was started and several test images were taken in real environment with the mobile phone and sent by MMS to the server. On average 400 descriptors could be extracted per received MMS picture. This resulted in a very high matching quality. An example is given in Figure 11a, where 286 descriptors have been matched. If the object is photographed without occlusions, then it is always matched to the correct reference image of the test database. Also the viewpoint can be changed a little bit, with still correct results. In Figure 11b you can see an example with occlusion. Even though parts of the book are covered by an object (CD cover), the result of the matching are still 168 similar descriptors. Since these are very distinctive, such a high number is enough to match the image correctly with its reference image in the test database. Object recognition rate is about 87% for the SURF algorithm and about 89% for the SIFT algorithm.

Fig. 11. a. An example for the server side matching images with SIFT b. An example for the server side matching with occlusion where still 168 key-points match

5 Conclusion

The results presented in this article demonstrate the feasibility of a market-ready mobile pattern recognition system in the form of a student book selection guide.

Prototype clients and the server software were fully implemented and have been subject to thorough evaluation under realistic conditions.

Our tests showed the advantages of an architecture where the feature extraction part is done on the server. Such a setup requires uploading images and favors low resolutions, as this decreases the response time. Although the SURF algorithm is faster than the SIFT one, for low-resolution images SURF's performance is unacceptable.

Finally, based on this study, we conclude that a combination of client-server architecture, the use of a SIFT algorithm on images with a resolution of 512x384, is most appropriate for deployment.

References

1. Junaini, S.N., Abdullah, J.: MyMobiHalal 2.0: Malaysian Mobile Halal Product Verification using Camera Phone Barcode Scanning and MMS. In: IEEE Proceedings of the International Conference on Computer and Communication Engineering 2008 (ICCCE 2008), Kuala Lumpur, Malaysia, May 13-15 (2008)
2. Bruns, E., Brombach, B., Zeidler, T., Bimber, O.: Enabling mobile phones to support large-scale museum guidance. Journal of MultiMedia 14(2), 16–25 (2007)
3. Lim, J.H., Li, Y., You, Y., Chevallet, J.P.: Scene recognition with camera phones for tourist information access. In: Proceedings of the IEEE International Conference on Multimedia and Expo, pp. 100–103 (2007)
4. Chen, W., Xiong, Y., Gao, J., Gelfand, N., Grzeszczuk, R.: Efficient Extraction of Robust Image Features on Mobile Devices. In: Proceedings of the 2007 6th IEEE and ACM international Symposium on Mixed and Augmented Reality, November 13-16 (2007)
5. Takacs, G., Chandrasekhar, V., Gelfand, N., Xiong, Y., Chen, W.-C., Bismpigiannis, T., Grzeszczuk, R., Pulli, K., Girod, B.: Outdoor augmented reality on mobile phone using loxel-based visual feature organization. In: Multimedia Information Retrieval (2008)
6. Lowe, D.: Distinctive Image Features from Scale-Invariant Keypoints. International Journal of Computer Vision 60(2), 91–110 (2004)
7. Bay, H., Ess, A., Tuytelaars, T., Van Gool, L.: SURF: Speeded Up Robust Features. Computer Vision and Image Understanding (CVIU) 110(3), 346–359 (2008)
8. Schmid, C., Mohr, R., Bauckhage, C.: Evaluation of interest point detectors. International Journal of Computer Vision 37(2), 151–172 (2000)

HDL IP Cores Search Engine Based on Semantic Web Technologies

Vladimir Zdraveski, Milos Jovanovik, Riste Stojanov, and Dimitar Trajanov

University Ss Cyril and Methodius, Faculty of Electrical Engineering and Information Technologies – Skopje, Rugjer Boskovic bb, 1000 Skopje, Republic of Macedonia
{vladimir.zdraveski,milos,ristes}@feit.ukim.edu.mk,
dimitar.trajanov@feit.ukim.edu.mk

Abstract. A few years ago, the System on Chip idea grew largely and 'flooded' the market of embedded systems. Many System on Chip designers started to write their own HDL components and made them available on the Internet. The idea of searching for a couple of pre-written cores and building your own System on Chip only by connecting them seemed time saving. We've developed a system that enables a semantic description of VHDL IP components, allows search of specific components based on the unambiguous semantic description and works with prebuilt VHDL IP cores. We present an application built around the system and focus on the benefits the application user gains during the process of System on Chip design.

Keywords: HDL, Semantic Web, VHDL, System on Chip, Components, Search, Composition.

1 Introduction

Embedded systems give intelligence to many devices that we use in everyday life – they are found in everything from mobile phones and MP3 players, cars and home appliances, to complex controllers. The continuous progress of semiconductor technology has made it possible to implement complex systems on a single chip, which has led to new challenges in design methodologies. System on Chip (SoC) is a complex integrated circuit, or integrated chipset, which combines the major functional elements or subsystems of a complete end product into a single entity.

The design of SoC would not be possible if every design started from scratch. In fact, the design of SoC depends heavily on the reuse of Intellectual Property blocks - which are called "IP Cores." IP reuse has emerged as a strong trend over the last years and has been one key element in closing what the International Technology Roadmap for Semiconductors calls the "design productivity gap" - the difference between the rate of increase of complexity offered by advancing semiconductor process technology, and the rate of increase in designer productivity offered by advances in design tools and methodologies [1], important to offer ways of enhancing designer productivity - although it has dramatic impacts on that. It also provides a mechanism for design teams

M. Gusev and P. Mitrevski (Eds.): ICT Innovations 2010, CCIS 83, pp. 306–315, 2011.

to create SoC products that span multiple design disciplines and domains. The availability of both hard (laid-out and characterized) and soft (synthesizable) IP cores from a number of IP vendors allows design teams to drop them into their designs and thus add required functionality to an integrated SoC. In this sense, the advantages of IP reuse go beyond productivity—it offers both a large reduction in design risk, and also a way for SoC designs to be done that would otherwise be infeasible owing to the length of time it would take to acquire expertise and design IP from scratch.

Soft IP cores are usually written in some Hardware Description Language (HDL) like VHDL [2], Verilog or SystemC and System Verilog. Following the trend for open source development, there are a large number of available open source HDL components. In order to design a complete system-on-chip, one should interconnect many single VHDL components, spending a lot of time on the compatibility analysis. Today's HDL search tools are generally statistic-based, so the process of searching a specific component is quite difficult. For instance, it is not a trivial task to search for an 8–bit counter with 1 clock pin and 1 chip-enable pin. Instead, one should download, open and analyze many HDL projects, before deciding whether the IP core matches or not. In order to solve this problem, there is a need to have a more meaningful description of attributes and the function of the HDL component. One of the ways to accomplish this is to add semantic description to the HDL component. The use of semantic annotation of HDL files gives way to many new and different opportunities for improvement to the storage and search process of HDL search engines.

Semantic information gives the machine the ability to know and decide and do much more of the work than it was doing previously. Instead of storing HDL information simply as a text file, with the use of semantic web technologies the machine can understand more about the kind and interface of a HDL component. That knowledge enables automated search by I/O interfaces, component type, and further composition of an entire System on Chip by the use of HDL IP cores.

In order to test the idea in practice, we developed a semantic extension of VHDL and designed a system for it. The system has module for automatic VHDL annotation, module for manual semantic annotation, annotated semantic data storage, search and composition of HDL IP cores.

2 Related Work

2.1 HDL Repository Web Portals

There are numerous open source HDL code projects and a few web portals (groups, environments) that enable storage and search of HDL projects. One of them is "Open Cores" [3], where existing IP cores can be found and downloaded. The search process requires the user to search only by name or by the type of the IP core needed. Although there are thousands of projects in this repository, it is quite difficult to find a specific IP component that contains specific ports (e.g. an 8-bit buffer).

Another example is the Java optimized processor's group [4], where a project for building a processor from scratch and optimizing it to execute Java instructions is shown. But, here the user faces the same problem: despite the fact that this project contains many IP cores, e.g. 8-bit buffers, finding a specific one is not so straightforward. To find a specific core, one should search through all the folders and analyze files one at a time, which takes a lot of time and sometimes ends unsuccessfully. There are also many other similar examples, [5][6][7][8][9].

Also, there are some plug-ins for programming environments that enable inserting of pre-made IP cores, such as standard types of memories, buffers, counters, etc. For instance, Xilinx ISE [10] has its own library, which makes it quite user-friendly. But, the same problem of finding a specific component exists.

2.2 Semantic Search Systems

On the other hand, the technologies of the Semantic Web allowed development of novel approaches to data storage and retrieval. A semantic search system is essentially an information retrieval system which employs semantic technologies in order to enhance different parts of the information retrieval process. This is achieved by semantic indexing and annotation of content, query expansion, filtering and ranking the retrieved information [11]. The semantic search also introduces additional possibilities, such as search for online ontology [12], search for online (distributed) knowledgebase, retrieval of facts from the ontology and knowledgebase and question answering.

A recent survey showed that there is a diversity of approaches in semantic search systems, based on the following categories: search goals, scope, ontology encoding, knowledge richness, user input, architecture, and search phrase support [11].

From the viewpoint of search goals, semantic search can be classified into information retrieval, data retrieval [13], question answering [14] or ontology retrieval [12]. The scope of a semantic search can be the Web [15][16][17][18], desktop search [19][20] or domain repositories [21]. The encoding format of the ontologies used can be a proprietary format [22], OWL or RDFS as open standards [13][20], or even some other format [23][24][25]. In order to enhance the semantic search over the traditional, statistical and syntactical search, the researchers used to focus on the use of thesaurus and taxonomy [26][27]. But in recent year, with the development of the semantic web technologies, it is possible to use richer and more complex knowledge structures, such as classes, instances, object properties, relations, axioms, etc. [14]. Based on the user interactions required by the system, the different approaches fall into one of the following categories [11]: simple keyword based entry into text field [18], natural language sentences [14], graphical taxonomy/ontology browsing [23][28], multi-optional specification of search parameters [27], use of a formal ontology query language [29][30], and interactive with explicit user feedback [31].

From the perspective of the architecture of semantic search systems, most of the developed applications are domain-specific intranet or desktop applications, built over semantically annotated data from a certain domain [20][24]. The main reason for this is the most common problem the semantic web researchers face: the lack of semantically annotated data on the Web. Still, there are other types of applications which use different semantic techniques on top of existing standard search engines [18].

3 Overview of HDL IP Cores Search Engine

Our approach is to use information retrieval for desktop search over a local, domain ontology-based knowledgebase. We use an OWL domain ontology and an RDF [33] knowledgebase. The documents needed for the application (HDL IP cores) are semantically annotated with concepts from the domain ontology. The architecture of the application puts it in the category of stand-alone web applications and uses its own data repository.

3.1 HDL Ontology

For the purpose of the system, we designed the HDL ontology. Although we would present this ontology from a VHDL perspective, it can be used for classification of any kind of hardware units, chips, etc.

There are specifications about VHDL components and many classes that enable quite original and intuitive classification of different commonly used VHDL components, written by different authors. Furthermore, there are some predicates and relations that could be used to specify the hierarchy in the RDF description.

The HDL ontology was designed using the Protégé editor [32], shown in Fig. 1. The ontology is used to classify and annotate all of the VHDL components in order to store the details of the users' source code into the system.

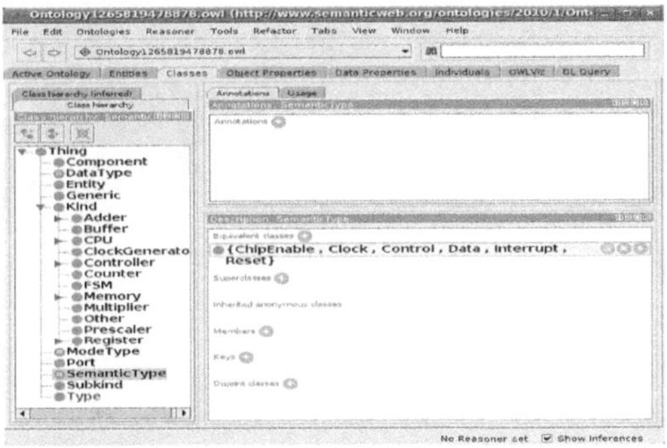

Fig. 1. VHDL ontology in Protégé. A component could be classified as *Counter*, *Register*, *CPU*, etc. There is information about mode type, data type and semantic type of all the ports. The semantic type describes whether the pin/port is *data*, *control*, *enable*, etc.

The ontology covers relations and classes inside the VHDL code. It allows description of the entity, its ports, their data type, length and mode. A generic section is also considered. In most of the classes the "*Other*" class was nested in order to classify all uncovered hardware components.

Besides VHDL mapping, the ontology also includes additional metadata. There is a semantic kind of the component (to specify whether it is an Adder, a Buffer, a CPU, etc.), author info and frequency specification. Ports are described with *SemanticType* property, which allows us to assign semantic meaning to a port. Thus, we could define the port as *data*, *control*, *enable*, *clock*, etc. These additional information gives novelty to the storage and search engines for HDL components, and adds benefit for the end users. By semantically annotating the different components of a VHDL solution, the user can search for a component that matches some specific pattern, at the level of ports and pins interface, kind and working frequency.

4 Solution Description

As shown in Fig. 2, the HDL IP cores search system consists of a presentation layer (developed using JSP technology), a business layer (developed in Java) and Jena-based data storage [34][35].

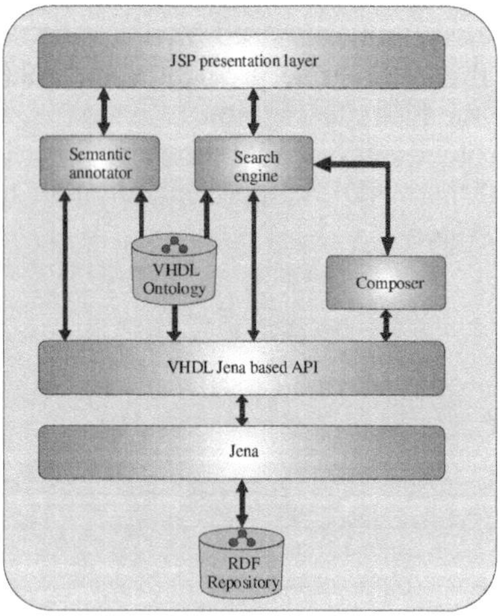

Fig. 2. System architecture

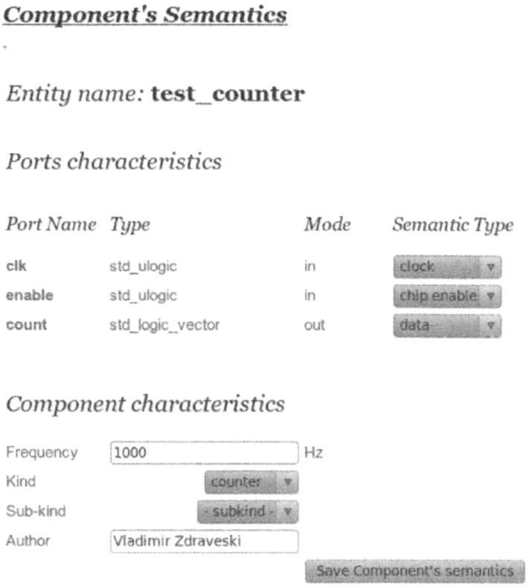

Fig. 3. Ports semantics

The business tier includes the semantic annotator, the search engine and the composition engine. The core of the system is the Jena Framework, a Java framework which allows the use of the technologies of the Semantic Web. We also use the Jena repository, which serves for data storage.

4.1 Semantic Annotator

This module is used for uploading VHDL files on the server. The server parses the files, extracts the needed HDL information of the component and allows adding an additional semantic description (Fig. 3). We modified the Hardware-Vhdl-Parser [36] in order that it converts the VHDL entity into its appropriate RDF representation.

```
--* * * * * * * * * * * * * * * * * * * * * * * * * * * * * * * * * * * * * * *
--* * * * * * * * * * * * * * * * * VHDL Source Code * * * * * * * * * * * * *
--* * * * * * * * * * * * * * * * * * * * * * * * * * * * * * * * * * * * * * *
--<rdf:RDF
--      xmlns:rdf="http://www.w3.org/1999/02/22-rdf-syntax-ns#"
--      xmlns:vhdl="http://localhost:8080/WebSite/vhdl.owl#"
--      xmlns:rdfs="http://www.w3.org/2000/01/rdf-schema#">
--    <vhdl:Component>
--      <vhdl:rdfFileURL>files/rdf/1276176487342.txt</vhdl:rdfFileURL>
--      <vhdl:ofKind>http://localhost:8080/WebSite/vhdl.owl#Other</vhdl:ofKind>
--      <vhdl:author>student</vhdl:author>
--      <vhdl:hasEntity>
--        <vhdl:Entity>
--          <vhdl:hasPort rdf:parseType="Collection">
--            <vhdl:Port>
--              <vhdl:semanticType>vhdl:Data</vhdl:semanticType>
--              <vhdl:ofType>
--                <vhdl:Type>
--                  <vhdl:ofDataType> vhdl:std_ulogic</vhdl:ofDataType>
--                </vhdl:Type>
--              </vhdl:ofType>
--              <vhdl:ofMode>vhdl:in</vhdl:ofMode>
--              <vhdl:name>A</vhdl:name>
--            </vhdl:Port>
--            <vhdl:Port>
--              <vhdl:ofType>
--                <vhdl:Type>
--                 <vhdl:ofDataType> vhdl:std_ulogic</vhdl:ofDataType>
--                </vhdl:Type>
--              </vhdl:ofType>
--              <vhdl:ofMode>vhdl:out</vhdl:ofMode>
--              <vhdl:name>X</vhdl:name>
--              <vhdl:semanticType>vhdl:Data</vhdl:semanticType>
--            </vhdl:Port>
--          </vhdl:hasPort>
--        </vhdl:Entity>
--      </vhdl:hasEntity>
--      <vhdl:name>Test_Gates</vhdl:name>
--      <vhdl:frequency>1000000</vhdl:frequency>
--      <vhdl:vhdlFileURL>files/vhdl/1276176487342.txt</vhdl:vhdlFileURL>
--    </vhdl:Component>
--</rdf:RDF>

library ieee;
use ieee.std_logic_1164.all;

entity Test_Gates is

  port (A : in  std_ulogic;   -- Simple inputs
        X : out std_ulogic);  -- Simple outputs

end Test_Gates;
```

Fig. 4. Nested RDF description

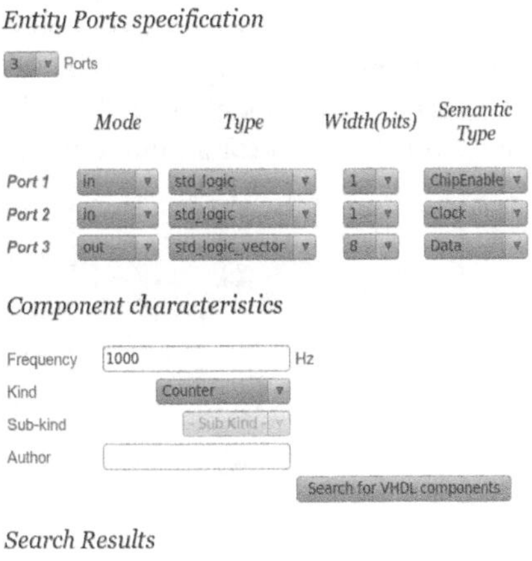

Fig. 5. Search for a VHDL component

In order to create self contained, semantically described VHDL documents, this module allows embedding of RDF code directly into the VHDL file, as a VHDL comment. If such a comment exists in the loaded VHDL file, the application reads it directly and doesn't show the form, shown in Fig. 3. An example of a nested RDF description within a standard VHDL file is shown in Fig. 4.

4.2 Repository

The data is stored with the use of the Jena Framework libraries. The Jena Framework stores the data in a graph-like structure, instead of the common database approach which uses strictly formed tables. This graph-like structure is commonly known as an RDF Repository. On top of the Jena Framework we wrote our own API, that provides the functionality according to the VHDL structure. The API provides ontology and data access and is used by the upper layers of the system.

4.3 Search Engine

The search engine is a Java application that uses the Jena API for querying the RDF repository. It is at this point where the semantic annotations of the VHDL components are used to increase the effectiveness over the classic ways of search and retrieval, from the aspect of precision. The search is made by matching the semantic concepts specified in the user request and the semantic annotations of the available components from the RDF repository of the system. We use a semantic based comparison algorithm, which checks for port, frequency and component's class matching. We assigned different weighs for different properties, and the final matching score is sum of all matching weighs (the numbers below the component names in Fig. 6 represent the matching score).

The search form is shown in Fig. 5, where a user needs to simply specify the type, frequency and port interface of the needed VHDL component. The results are listed as shown in Fig. 6. An AJAX add-on gives a review of the located component (Fig. 7). The buttons on the right side allow further search for similar components, based on the current component. The "Find Similar" button puts the current component on top and starts a search for similar components.

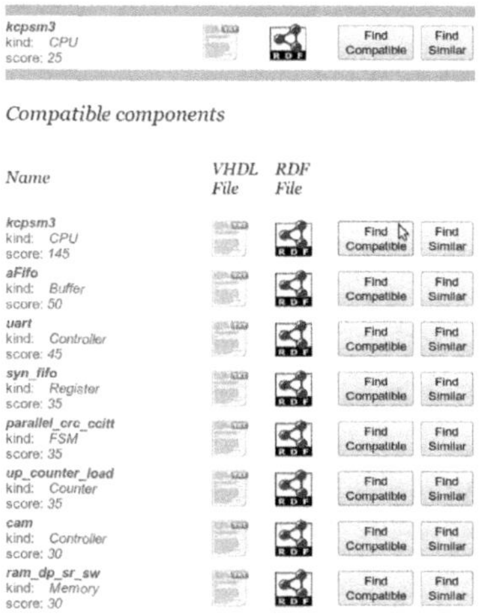

Fig. 6. Compatible components

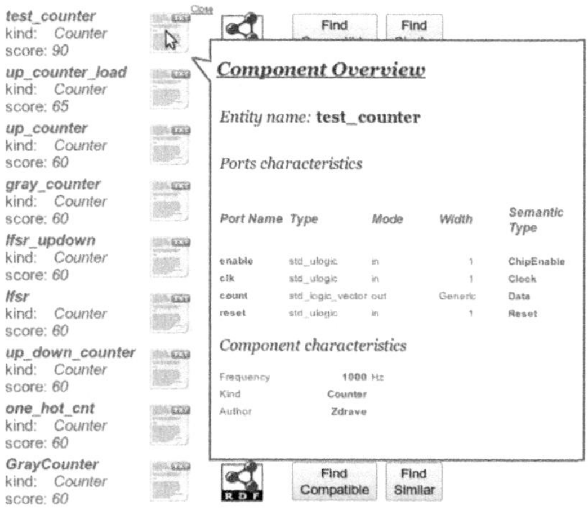

Fig. 7. AJAX component preview

4.4 Composer

This module is a base for making a composition of IP cores. The composer module API contains functions for compatibility check, which means that compatible components can be located. Finding a compatible component ("Find Compatible" button in Fig. 6) means finding components that can be connected to a chosen one, for instance, 8-bit output port is compatible with 8-bit input port. An example of usage is shown in Fig. 6, where compatible components for the PicoBlaze CPU-kcpsm3 are listed (e.g. ram_dp_sr_sw RAM component at the bottom). This is the first step of creating an entire SoC composition by the use of IP cores.

4.5 Advantages and System Usability

When searching through existing HDL portals (aforementioned in the related work section) the result is a folder with the full HDL project, containing many files. In contrast, our HDL IP cores search engine gives a single HDL file that represents a specific component as a result. However, despite this difference, these two approaches (file-based and project-based) are applicable to different problems, so they would and should exist concurrently.

Another advantage of the proposed system is that the component classification is based on an OWL ontology, which enables knowledge sharing and easy resolution of ambiguity. There are common methods for merging semantic data from different ontologies, which makes the HDL IP cores system really scalable and easy to maintain and improve.

Unique features of the HDL IP cores system that is a direct result of usage semantic technologies are effortless retrieval of similar components and ability to search for compatible components. As shown in Fig. 5, Fig. 6 and Fig. 7, the HDL IP cores system enables search "by port" and reliable ranking of the similar and compatible components available in the repository. An IP core compatibility feature is an approach that allows SoC design via browse through search results.

5 Conclusion and Future Work

The system and the application we designed and developed are intended to demonstrate the ability of the semantic web technologies for building a more precise search engine for VHDL components. The same principle can be used for describing and searching specific chip-products, too. Such a system can be easily implemented within the hardware producer's web sites or a web market engine.

In general, the improvements which our system offers are quite a large step to a faster and smarter way of storing and searching data. It is described as VHDL tool here, but it easily applies to any hardware or software, class-based programming code or product specification.

Our future plans include an extension of the current semantic description of the port, with provision of information about whether the port is buffered or not. This feature will introduce the ability to build a complete system automatically. The application itself would be able to decide whether a buffer component is needed or not and find some of the available from the repository.

With this feature, we will be able to develop a system that automatically composes a logical block of components solely from the user specifications. The user will be required to define the needed inputs and outputs of the circuit, and the system will be able to compose a logical block which consists of semantically annotated VHDL components from the repository, components which can be connected together in a way that satisfies the user's specifications. This is a problem similar to the problem of automatic composition of semantic web services, and our intention is to apply these concepts to composition of IP cores.

References

1. International technology roadmap for semiconductors, Design, 2007 edition (2007), http://www.itrs.net/Links/2007ITRS/2007_Chapters/2007_Design.pdf

2. VHDL – Very High Speed IC Hardware Description Language, `http://www.vhdl.org/`
3. Open Cores – web portal, `http://opencores.org/`
4. Java optimized processor - group, `http://tech.groups.yahoo.com/group/java-processor/`
5. IP supermarket – web portal, `http://www.ipsupermarket.com/index.php`
6. Infineon – web portal, `http://www.ipsupermarket.com/index.php`
7. Lattice – web portal, `http://www.latticesemi.com/`
8. Chip Estimate – web portal, `http://www.chipestimate.com/`
9. Design & Reuse – web portal, `http://www.design-reuse.com/`
10. Xilinx ISE – HDL programming environment, `http://www.xilinx.com/`
11. Strasunskas, D., Tomassen, S.L.: On Variety of Semantic Search Systems and Their Evaluation Methods. In: Proceedings of International Conference on Information Management and Evaluation, University of Cape Town, South Africa, March 25-26, pp. 380–387. Academic Conferences Publishing (2010)
12. Pan, J.Z., Thomas, E., Sleeman, D.: Ontosearch2: Searching and querying web ontologies. In: Proc. of the IADIS International Conference, pp. 211–218 (2006)
13. Guha, R., McCool, R., Miller, E.: Semantic search. In: Proc. of WWW 2003, pp. 700–709 (2003)
14. Lopez, V., Uren, V., Motta, E., Pasin, M.: AquaLog: An ontology-driven question answering system for organizational semantic intranets. Web Semantics 5(2), 72–105 (2007)
15. Stojanovic, N., Studer, R., Stojanovic, L.: An approach for the ranking of query results in the Semantic Web. In: Fensel, D., Sycara, K., Mylopoulos, J. (eds.) ISWC 2003. LNCS, vol. 2870, pp. 500–516. Springer, Heidelberg (2003)
16. Rocha, C., Schwabe, D., de Aragao, M.: A hybrid approach for searching in the semantic web. In: Proc. of WWW 2004, pp. 374–383. ACM Press, New York (2004)
17. Corby, O., Dieng-Kuntz, R., Faron-Zucker, C., Gandon, F.L.: Searching the Semantic Web: Approximate Query Processing Based on Ontologies. IEEE Intelligent Systems 21(1), 20–27 (2006)
18. Tomassen, S.L., Strasunskas, D.: A semiotics-driven approach to Web search: analysis of its sensitivity to ontology quality and search tasks. In: Proc. of iiWAS 2009, ACM, New York (2009)
19. Kiryakov, A., Popov, B., Terziev, I., Manov, D., Ognyanoff, D.: Semantic annotation, indexing, and retrieval. Journal of Web Semantics 2(1), 49–79 (2004)
20. Chirita, P.-A., Costache, S., Nejdl, W., Paiu, R.: Beagle ++ : Semantically enhanced searching and ranking on the desktop. In: Sure, Y., Domingue, J. (eds.) ESWC 2006. LNCS, vol. 4011, pp. 348-362. Springer, Heidelberg (2006)
21. Castells, P., Fernandez, M., Vallet, D.: An Adaptation of the Vector-Space Model for Ontology-Based Information Retrieval. IEEE TKDE 19(2), 261–272 (2007)
22. Amaral, C., Laurent, D., Martins, A., Mendes, A., Pinto, C.: Design and Implementa-tion of a Semantic Search Engine for Portuguese. In: Proc. LREC 2004, vol. 1, pp. 247–250 (2004)
23. Brasethvik, T.: Conceptual modelling for domain specific document description and retrieval- An approach to semantic document modelling. PhD thesis, NTNU, Trondheim, Nor-way (2004)
24. Zhang, L., Yu, Y., Zhou, J., Lin, C., Yang, Y.: An enhanced model for searching in semantic portals. In: WWW 2005, pp. 453–462 (2005)

25. Burton-Jones, A., Storey, V.C., Sugumaran, V., Purao, S.: A heuristic-based methodology for semantic augmentation of user queries on the web. In: Song, I.-Y., Liddle, S.W., Ling, T.-W., Scheuermann, P. (eds.) ER 2003. LNCS, vol. 2813, pp. 476–489. Springer, Heidelberg (2003)
26. Ciorascu, C., Ciorascu, I., Stoffel, K.: knOWLer - ontological support for information retrieval systems. In: Proc. of SIGIR 2003 Conference, Workshop on Semantic Web (2003)
27. Aitken, S., Reid, S.: Evaluation of an ontology-based information retrieval tool. In: Proc. of Workshop on the Applications of Ontologies and Problem-Solving Methods, ECAI 2000, Berlin (2000)
28. Suomela, S., Kekäläinen, J.: Ontology as a search-tool: A study of real users' query formulation with and without conceptual support. In: Losada, D.E., Fernández-Luna, J.M. (eds.) ECIR 2005. LNCS, vol. 3408, pp. 315–329. Springer, Heidelberg (2005)
29. Blacoe, I., Palmisano, I., Tamma, V., Iannone, L.: QuestSemantics - Intelligent Search and Retrieval of Business Knowledge. Frontiers in Artificial Intelligence and Applications 178, 648–652 (2008)
30. Wang, H., Zhang, K., Liu, Q., Tran, T., Yu, Y.: Q2Semantic: A Lightweight Keyword Interface to Semantic Search. In: Bechhofer, S., Hauswirth, M., Hoffmann, J., Koubarakis, M. (eds.) ESWC 2008. LNCS, vol. 5021, pp. 584–598. Springer, Heidelberg (2008)
31. Nagypal, G.: Possibly imperfect ontologies for effective information retrieval. PhD thesis, University of Karlsruhe (2007)
32. Protégé – semantic data editor, RDF, OWL., Stanford Center for Biomedical Informatics Research (2010), http://protege.stanford.edu/
33. RDF: Resource Description Framework (2010), http://www.w3.org/RDF/
34. Jena – A semantic web, java framework, Official API documentation and examples for Jena libraries (2010), http://jena.sourceforge.net/
35. Jena TDB storage (2010), http://openjena.org/wiki/TDB
36. Vhdl-Parser (2000), http://search.cpan.org/~gslondon/Hardware-Vhdl-Parser-0.12/Parser.pm

Monitoring Wireless Sensor Network System Based on Classification of Adopted Supervised Growing Neural Gas Algorithm

Stojanco Gancev and Danco Davcev

University Ss Cyril and Methodius, Faculty of Electrical Engineering and IT, Skopje, Macedonia
gancevstojan@yahoo.com, etfdav@feit.ukim.edu.mk

Abstract. Wireless sensor network system for monitoring predefined events with adaptation of one popular model of neural networks algorithm - Supervised Growing Neural Gas will be presented. Data reduction, energy savings, detection of dead nodes and event notification over internet are implemented. Architecture of the system allows investigating and comparing proposed algorithm results with Fuzzy ART model of neural network. Real-time measurements of physical data when vehicle is present in the sensed area are used to investigate advantages and disadvantages of neural networks adaptation in WSN based system.

Keywords: wireless sensors network, classification; supervised growing neural gas, monitoring, Fuzzy ART, comparison.

1 Introduction

Wireless sensor networks (WSN) are taking important part in different real-time systems and environments. Possibility for easy deployment and mobility are key assets of wireless sensor networks; In addition as a result of rapid technological progress more advanced and cheaper sensor are produced allowing integration with online accessible systems. Still in the field of data classification and categorization and energy efficiency lot of improvements can be made and the paper is offering a solution with improvements in these areas.

We have built a WSN monitoring system based on Supervised Growing Neural Gas (SGNG) network [1] that is data redundant, energy efficient, capable to alarm on predefined events (like detecting vehicle presence) and overcoming the problem of dead sensors nodes in the system. Use of SGNG is wide and performing better compared to other supervised clustering algorithms for both cluster impurities and total running times given in [2]. Robustness for classification of large datasets of Growing Neural Gas when combined with support vector machines is given in [3].

System clearly points advantages/disadvantages of proposed algorithm with Fuzzy ART neural network [4] allowing raw sensor data to be processed from both of the algorithms in the same time. Output results of both networks will be presented and analyzed when neural networks are sensing presence of vehicle in the system.

Paper is organized as follows. In section 2 the system architecture is given, while section 3 gives detail explanation of SGNG and his adaptation. In section 4 a brief

M. Gusev and P. Mitrevski (Eds.): ICT Innovations 2010, CCIS 83, pp. 316–324, 2011.

comparison with Fuzzy ART network is presented, where outputs of both approaches are presented.

2 System Architecture

The system we develop is mainly based for experimental needs to monitor predefined events and compare the algorithms capabilities on the same event occurrence.

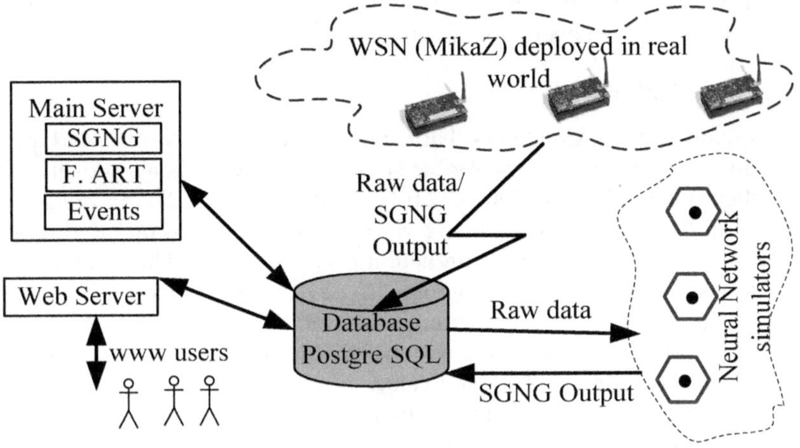

Fig. 1. Components of our WSN System

Physical variables that we measure and process in order to detect events from the real world are: temperature, magnet fields, light, acceleration over x and y axis and sound density. Build in capability of control, monitor and alarm from anywhere within the internet connection is setting a prototype model for a commercial use.

System components are following:

- **Wireless MicaZ sensor network** for collecting data from physical world. MicaZ is a 2.4GHz, IEEE802.15.4 compliant, Mote module used for enabling low power, wireless sensor networks. In this version of the system, we used the sensors just for raw data processing and simulated the output of equipped with trained SGNG and Fuzzy ART neural network sensors with PC simulator.
- **Postgre Sql database** for storing data from sensors and processed data from Mica Server.
- **Main Server -** implements the main logic for signaling events when certain state detected from the sensors and mechanism for detection of dead motes. The server has an integrated module that can send e-mail messages when previously trained outputs of the sensor will be received on sensor side. The server has also integrated SGNG and Fuzzy Art neural network for classification of raw sensor data and data from the categorized outputs of the sensors.
- **Web Access** – Web interface that allows current sensed states or raw measurement to be seen from internet.

2.1 Hardware Platform

Hardware platform is based on wireless sensors hardware and personal computers where we hosted the main server and database. Wireless MicaZ motes (see Fig. 1) are 8-bit microcontrollers running at 16 MHz and have only 4 Kbytes of RAM.

We have used 7 such motes, 4 of them equipped with MTS310 sensor boards having a light sensor, 2 accelerometers, 2 magnetic sensors, a thermometer and a microphone, while 3 of them were equipped with MTS300 sensor boards having only a light sensor, a thermometer and a microphone. The operating system that runs on the motes is Tiny OS (see: http://en.wikipedia.org/wiki/TinyOS) which is a free and open source component-based operating system and platform targeting WSNs.

2.2 Software Platform

System is using sensors simulators that we developed for SGNG network processing developed in native C++. Version for the sensors of SGNG was also developed in Nes C. In further connotation simulators will be used as sensors. The Fuzzy ART model (developed in Nes C and in C++ for server side) was deployed on the sensors that in parallel send raw measured data with neural network output. This configuration provides us to test the neural network outputs in the real-time on the same events and on the same measured data. Data reduction 7-to-1 ratio when used with MTS310 sensor boards and 3-to-1 ration when used with MTS300 sensor boards was achieved when sensors were sending only categorized value.

Sensed real-time measurements from the wireless sensors are stored in PostgreSQL database; then the values are processed from the neural networks in main server and sensors simulators. Outputs from neural networks processing are stored in the database for further analyze.

2.2.1 Web Interface

The web application demonstrates remote monitoring and control of the systems equipped with wireless sensors. Capabilities of the web interface are given below:

- Monitor the life status of the sensors and values they measure. Neural networks (SGNG and FuzzyART) outputs from each sensor and the main server processing are also available online.
- Remotely configure the main server parameters for sending events to predefined system states.

Monitor interface presents updated snapshot of the system every 4 seconds. Sensor state can be alive or not working (death sensor node). Not working status is when sensor is not sending new values in certain time period. In order to reduce communication the sensors are not reporting data for 10 minutes if they measure the same value. If not working sensor occurs the main server is configured to send alarm email so the sensor can be replaced quickly which is crucial part of system reliability.

3 The SGNG Algorithm

Supervised Growing Neural Gas is defined by Bernd Fritzke [1] as an RBF network with a slightly modified version of the GNG ([5], [6] [7] and [8]) algorithm as the method for constructing and managing the hidden layer.

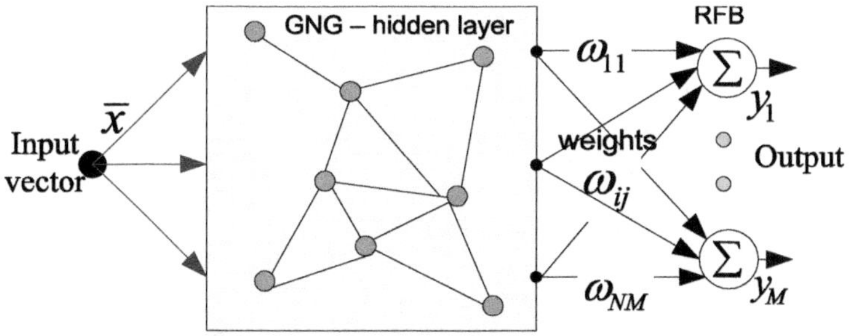

Fig. 2. SGNG-network composed from regular RBF network with a modified version of the GNG algorithm as the clustering algorithm for the hidden layer

The equation (1) is defining the output of our RFB network where the hidden layer is interpreted with Gaussian function see Fig.3.

$$\overline{x} \in R^n \quad \overline{\mu}_k \in R^n, \text{ k=1..N}$$

$$y_j(\overline{x}) = \sum_{i=1}^{N} \omega_{ij} \exp(-\frac{\|\overline{x} - \overline{\mu}_i\|^2}{2\delta_i^2}) \tag{1}$$

Each node k in the hidden layer has a vector $\overline{\mu}_k$ that determines the position of the node in input space and a standard deviation δ_k that defines the width of the local receptive field of node *k*. Hidden layer nodes are connected to all other nodes in the output layer with a connection weight ω_{ij}, which is a real value. In our model as activation function of the hidden nodes, denoted $f_i(\overline{x})$ in Fig. 3 the Gaussian function that is positive radial symmetric function with a unique maximum at its centre $\overline{\mu}_k$.The output of the nodes are consisted from linear function presented as a sum of the hidden layer output with ω_{ij} weight per connection, trained with the delta rule in equation:

$$\omega_{ij} \leftarrow \omega_{ij} + \eta(d_i - y_i)z_i \tag{2}$$

Where d_i is the desired response, y_i is the actual response, η is the step-size and z_j is the output from hidden node *j*.

4 Adopted SGNG Algorithm

We propose an adapted SGNG algorithm to classify the sensed values of temperature, magnet fields, acceleration over x y axel, light and sound density. We took the max and min value of each type of sensed data and adapted to a decimal values from 0 until 1. Without the data normalization we were not able correctly to train the SGNG neural network and the results we get were not as we expected. In figure 4, two series of data sets that define the sets that we train the network are shown. Marked lines with 1 and 2 are show the area that distingue between the sets.

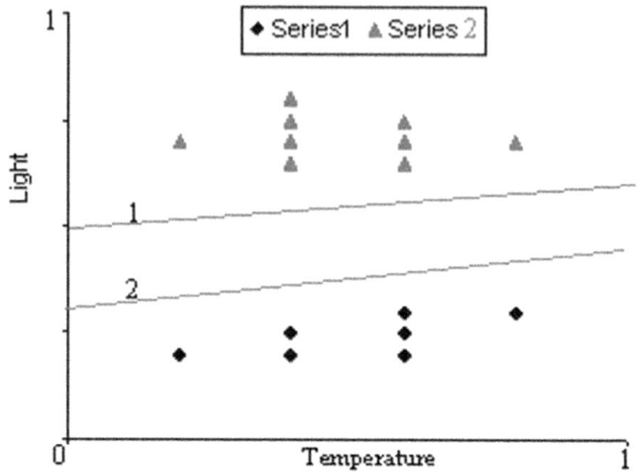

Fig. 3. Light/Temperature scale of 25 measurements taken from one sensor. Series 1 show when no vehicle is present; Series 2 when present. Axes x and y representing normalized sensor data. (Some of dots overlap).

In each of the sensors we deployed trained SGNG; On the Main server we have two SGNG networks first for processing raw data, second network to process SGNG sensor outputs. Defining the training sets is very important for relevance of results that system will produce and requires monitoring for a longer period of time. The trained dataset of neural network for the experiment also included night condition where we additionally sensed the light from the vehicles. To deploy a system that operates in various outdoor conditions when composing the training dataset a lot of factors should be taken like day nigh changes, weather changes, season changes etc.

One of the limitations of the SGNG neural networks we had to be overcome during the adaptation was the fixed number of inputs. For example, in the main server the inputs of the SGNG neural network, obtained from certain sensor nodes, may become unavailable due to a power failure as the result of node's batteries. (The fixed number of inputs is not a problem in each of the nodes in the wireless sensor network since the physical sensors are supposed to function continuously and their malfunction is rare). We solve this scenario training the network on the main server side with values set to zero for the malfunctioning sensors.

In order to make system data redundant sensors made processing with SGNG only if new values are sensed; in the real sensors this will increase lifetime as result of reduced processing operations (low battery usage). In order to reduce transmission of data we send measured data each 10 minutes when no new values are sensed. With this model we have data transfer reduction sending only certain sensors classified states for further processing on the main server side.

Also the option for multiple outputs of the SGNG networks expands the possibility for defining separate sets of data from the input vector. With proper training data definition one of the outputs can show when death sensors are present in the system.

5 Comparison of SGNG Neural Network and FuzzyART

5.1 Overview of FuzzyART Algorithm

Adaptive Resonance Theory (ART) has been developed by Grossberg and Carpenter for pattern recognition primarily. Models of unsupervised learning include ART1 [9] for binary input patterns and FuzzyART for analog input patterns. Detail explanation of FuzzyART algorithm can be found in [4] and there use in different systems in [10] and [11].

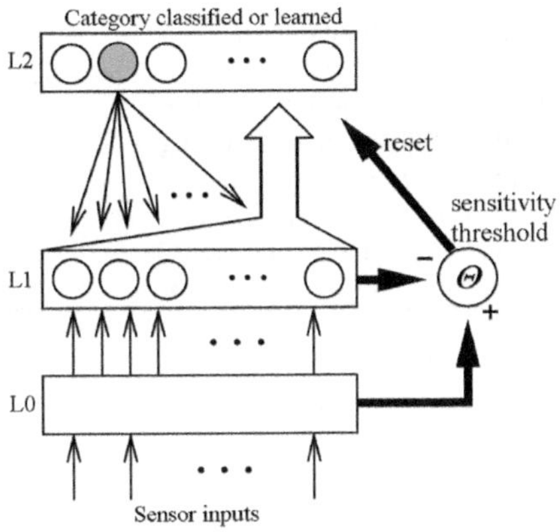

Fig. 4. ART neural network architecture

We chose ART network to compare SGNG model due to robustness to variations in intensity, detection of signals mixed with noise, and model both short- and long-term memory to accommodate variable rates of change in the environment.

In Fig. 5, a typical representation of an ART Artificial Neural Network is given. Winning L2 category nodes are selected by subsystem. Category search is controlled by the orienting subsystem. If the degree of category match at the L1 layer is lower than the sensitivity threshold Θ, originally called vigilance level, a reset signal will be triggered, which will deactivate the current winning L2 node for the period of presentation of the current input. Numbers of inputs in the network are fixed and the number of categories of the output can be limited with vigilance level calibration. The network can readjust output categories depending on the input data.

Due to stability-plasticity property, the ART neural networks are capable of learning "on-line", refining their learned categories in response to a stream of new input patterns, as opposed to being trained "off-line" on a finite pre-chosen training set. Our Fuzzy ART was modified so the network is not necessary to load a certain set of input patterns on which the learning will take place, but rather it is done after each new signal pattern has been given to the inputs.

5.2 System Setup for Vehicle Detection and Experimental Results

We made real-time experiments and measurements when vehicle is present in the sensed area and our goal was to detect it.

In order to train the SGNG network we used data gathered for 24 hours and used to mark the states of the crossing vehicle with SGNG output 5 and 0 when no detection is made. Configuration of the neural network is given in Table 1.

Table 1. System SGNG Configuration

Neural Network Property	Value
n - Input vector size	28
M - Output nodes	1
N- Nodes	50
Learning step of winner cell	0.1
Learning step of neighbour	0.002
Learning step of neural weights	0.1
Squared deviation during learning	0.01
Threshold for edge - removal	0,01
Maximum connections per cell	20
Cell insertion after learning steps	200
Edge removal after learning steps	100

The network standard deviation training error was δ = 0.2 and the epoch of training were with 10000 samples.

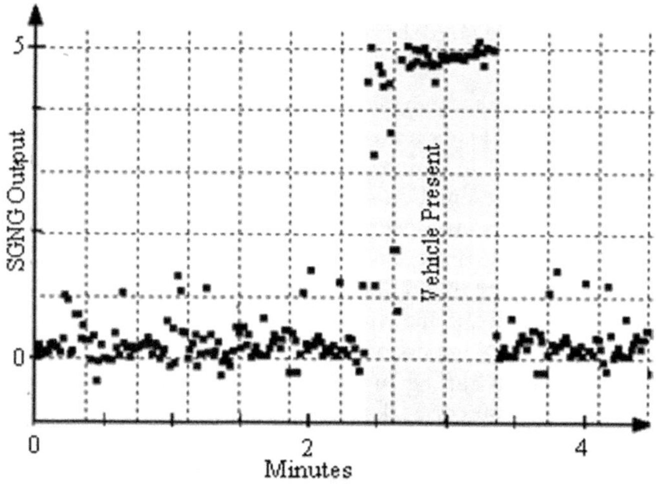

Fig. 5. SGNG classification of the data obtained at the cluster head node in the environmental setup. Marked grey background is time when the vehicle in the sensed area.

Fig 6 is giving the SGNG output in 4.5 minutes of time when vehicle is present in sensed area. During the testing vehicle stayed in the sensed area for 1 minute. When entering in the area the speed was very slow (5-10 km/h) and stayed in the area on without movement round 50 seconds.

From Fig. 6 can be seen some undefined states in the beginning when vehicle is entering the area and in first 10 seconds of the event we have 40% of SGNG as undefined. After that time when the vehicle was in the area from 40 processed values (1 per 4 seconds) we had one undefined state which is 97.5 % correct output. Trained SGNG give the expected results in the range of 5+/-2 δ where $\delta = 0.4$.

In order to make comparison of the SGNG model in parallel we integrated FuzzyART neural and use it in the real-time experiments for data classification and categorization. The architecture of the system and the measured data was the same so we can easy compare and point the advantages and disadvantages of both networks.

Fuzzy art output on the same raw sensor data processed in fig. 6 is given in Fig. 7.

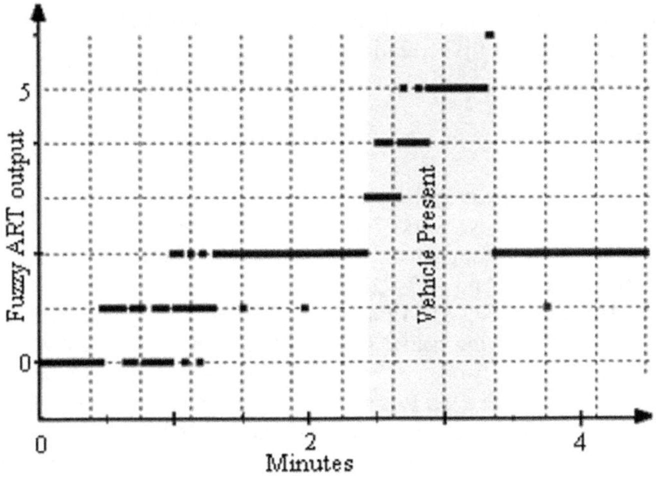

Fig. 6. Fuzzy ART classification of the data obtained at the cluster head node in the environmental setup. Marked grey background is time when the vehicle in the sensed area.

The Vigil value for FuzzyART was set on 0.93 and the network during measurement in Fig. 7 sensed 6 categorized outputs. The vehicle presence was defined with 4 tagged categories 3, 4, 5 and 6.

Outputs of both neural networks when sensing the same event are presented in the fig. 6 and 7. One advantage of the SGNG is supervised learning where we define output values during training, despite Fuzzy ART model where categories are generated in relation with timeline of sensed values, meaning different sensors will give different output for same data; Process of tagging the categories for marking the event is simple on server side but doing on WSN with many sensors requires huge effort.

Another advantage are SGNG multiple outputs that can be easy used to give report on multiple events (for example one output can be trained to inform for malfunctioning sensors while the second to detect vehicle presence).

Benchmark where unsupervised version of GNG is compared to Fuzzy ART is presented in detail in [12] where GNG advantage on classification error, number of training epochs and sensitivity toward variation are statistically presented.

6 Conclusion

We have built a data efficient WSN system for monitoring based on SGNG neural network and detection vehicle in the sensed area by overcoming the issues of the integration and nonworking sensor nodes (due to battery fault). Provided web interface made the system accessible from internet capable of alarming on vehicle presence and death sensor.

Our conclusion is that SGNG algorithm is applicable in WSN system and can be widely used, taking into account that definition of training data sets are very important for system effectiveness. SGNG model showed better results than Fuzzy ART in our WSN system when we compare network outputs and capabilities. Both models are memory efficient and easy applicable in WSN based systems.

Our future work will be based of integrating and combining in system additional neural networks for further investigation.

References

1. Fritzke, B.: Growing cell structures—A self-organizing network for unsupervised and supervised learning. Neural Networks 7(9), 1441–1460 (1994)
2. Jirayusakul, A., Auwatanamongkol, S.: A supervised growing neural gas algorithm for cluster analysis, vol. 4(4), pp. 217–229 (2007)
3. Linda, O., Manic, M.: GNG-SVM framework: classifying large datasets with support vector machines using growing neural gas. In: Proceedings of the 2009 International Joint Conference on Neural Networks, Atlanta, Georgia, USA, June 14-19, pp. 927–933 (2009)
4. Carpenter, G.A., Grossberg, S., Rosen, D.B.: Fuzzy ART: Fast stable learning and categ. of analog patterns by an adaptive resonance system. Neural Networks 4, 759–771 (1991)
5. Fritzke, B.: A Growing Neural Gas Network Learns Topologies. In: Tesauro, G., Touretzky, D.S., Leen, T.K. (eds.) Advances in Neural Information Processing Systems 7. MIT Press, Cambridge (1995)
6. Fritzke, B.: A self-organizing network that can follow non-stationary distributions. In: Gerstner, W., Hasler, M., Germond, A., Nicoud, J.-D. (eds.) ICANN 1997. LNCS, vol. 1327, pp. 613–618. Springer, Heidelberg (1997)
7. Costa, J.A.F., Oliveira, R.S.: Cluster Analysis using Growing Neural Gas and Graph Partitioning Neural Networks. In: International Joint Conference, pp. 3051–3056 (August 2007)
8. Holmström, J.: Growing neural gas experiments with gng, gng with utility and supervised gng, Master's thesis, Uppsala University (August 2002)
9. Grossberg, S.: Adaptive Resonance Theory. In: Encyclopedia of Cognitive Science. Macmillan Reference Ltd, Basingstoke (2000)
10. Carpenter, G.A., Grossberg, S.: A massively parallel architecture for a self-organizing neural pattern recognition machine. Computer Vision, Graphics, and Image Proc. 37, 54–115 (1987)
11. Sapojnikova, E.: ART-based Fuzzy Classifiers: ART Fuzzy Networks for Classification, PhD Thesis, Department of Computer and Cognitive Science at the University of Tübingen, Germany (2003)
12. Heinke, D., Hamker, F.H.: Comparing neural networks: a benchmark on growing neural gas, growing cell structures, and fuzzy ARTMAP. IEEE Transactions on Neural Networks 9, 1279–1291 (1998)

Assessing the Performance of Assembly Tools on Simulated Sequencing Data and Their Sensitivity to GC Content

Aleksandra Bogojeska, Mihaela Angelova, Slobodan Kalajdziski, and Ljupco Kocarev

University Ss Cyril and Methodius, Faculty of Electrical Engineering and Information Technologies, Ruger Boskovic, bb, P.O. Box 574 1000 Skopje, R.Macedonia
aleksandra.bogojeska@feit.ukim.edu.mk,
mihaelaangelova@yahoo.com,
{skalaj,lkocarev}@feit.ukim.edu.mk

Abstract. De novo assembly remains an ongoing challenge for the bioinformatics community. Many strategies have been developed; however there is no perfect *de novo* assembler. This publication evaluates four assemblers run on simulated data, comparing their outputs and testing their performance on two bacterial strains with different GC content (guanine – cytosine content). The results suggest assemblers' sensitivity on GC content and highlight their advantages and disadvantages.

Keywords: next-generation sequencing, simulation, Roche/454, assembly, Newbler, Mira, CLC Genomics Workbench, GC content.

1 Introduction

Recent advent in new technologies resulted with a revolution in genome sequencing. The next-generation sequencing platforms enabled performing experiments on large scales, opening new fields of research and interest [1]. *De novo* assembly, metagenomics, SNP's detection, and ChIP sequencing are just a few of the many fields that use the advantages of these technologies. The new sequencing techniques have different characteristics compared to the old Sanger method [2], used since the '70s. The bioinformatics tools used for the Sanger data manipulation are not applicable to the new data volumes. The data analysis processes, alignment, assembly, and viewing are affected by the new data format introduced with NGS (Next Generation Sequencing) platforms. Therefore, the new bioinformatics community is responding with development of new tools adapted for the NGS data analysis.

The breakthrough in sequencing technologies resulted in prolific production of sequencing data. The sequenced DNA is scattered into hundreds of thousands of small pieces. The reconstruction of the sequenced data is inevitable in order to analyze the genome. The process of combining the reads based on similarity is called assembly.

One of the basic approaches for assembly is *de novo* assembly. A *de novo* assembler searches for overlapping sequences and attempts to join them and create bigger **contig**uous sequences called contigs. A perfect de novo assembler detects all the

M. Gusev and P. Mitrevski (Eds.): ICT Innovations 2010, CCIS 83, pp. 325–332, 2011.

repeats and correctly resolves them, identifies all the true overlaps, corrects all errors by examining the mismatches, and outputs the whole genomic sequence, without human intervention. However, the *de novo* assembly problem is NP-hard and there is no perfect assembler.

The process of assembly represents the biggest remaining issue concerning data analysis. The large diversity of assembly tools available represents difficulty when determining the appropriate tool to use. One researcher has no other choice than to trust the algorithms and its accuracy by all means. In order to investigate these methods and their results, a simulation of sequencing data was performed. The main reason for simulating the data is the lack of NGS platforms in some medical and research institutions e.g. in Macedonia. Solving the unavailability of real NGS sequencing data with simulations also has the advantage of saving money when testing and evaluating algorithms.

2 Roche/454 Technology

Our work concentrates on simulating sequencing data from GS FLX Roche/454 sequencer and subsequent evaluation of genome assemblers on the simulated data.

The Roche/454 sequencer is the first next generation sequencer, introduced comercially. It is based on a combination of pyrosequencing and PCR (Polymerase Chain Reaction) emulsion [3]. The pyrosequencing techniques yield relatively long reads. Compared to the data produced by other next-generation sequencing technologies, Roche/454 sequencing data are characterized with highest average read length, which makes them suitable for assembly of new genomes.

The pyrosequencing technique starts with application of more than one million beads on a picotiter plate, achieving one bead per well. By means of PCR emulsion, approximately one million copies of each fragment are produced on a single bead. The next step consists of inserting the four nucleotides, one at a time in a determined order. The nucleotides are synthesized and attached to their complementary strands. The following cascade of enzyme reactions results in light signals from each of the beads where synthesis occurred. The intensity of the light signal is proportional to the number of bases synthesized on one bead. The more nucleotides added to the strand, the more intensive the light signal is.

The light signals are captured by a special camera. Therefore, the process of locating the bead on which synthesis has occurred is based on image processing i.e. translation of the pixels into flow signals. A series of translated signals is called a flowgram.

Some flow signals do not indicate precisely the number of synthesized nucleotides. This implies that there is a high probability that the base call will be false. In order to mark the possibility of mistake, a lower quality value is assigned to the base call. However, when the number of synthesized nucleotides is bigger than 6, the Roche/454 sequencer cannot accurately interpret the flow signal. Consequently, the homopolymer regions larger than 6 bases are prone to deletions and insertions. Substitution is exceedingly rare.

Recent improvements in Roche/454 technology led to longer reads, achieving a leap from 250 to 400 average read length.

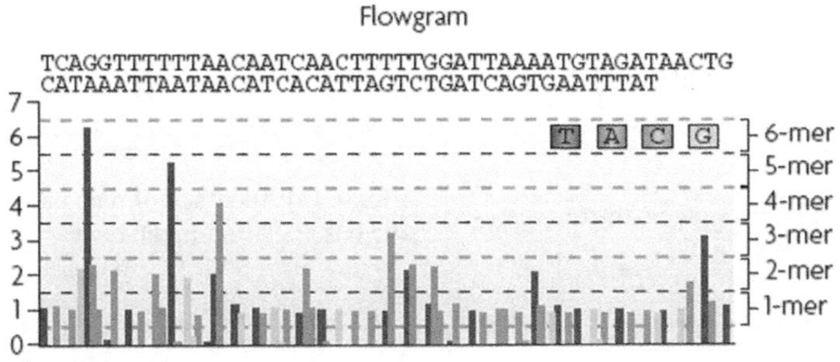

Fig. 1. Flowgram [4]. Time series of the flow signals, derived from the light intensity of one selected well. The fifth signal, for example, has a value between 6 and 7.

3 Generating Simulated Sequencing Data

When independent and anonymous testing of bioinformatics tools is performed, then an *in silico* method is used for data generation. [6][7][8] In order to produce simulated data, its characteristics should be known. Hence, the first step is to assess the features and the error model of the GS FLX Roche/454 platform. In order to obtain this information, a few different methods are employed. Perl scripts and modules were developed to generate the simulated reads.

3.1 Characteristics and Features of Data

The main and common characteristics such as average read length and coverage are reported at the Roche platform features sections at their web site [9]. There are a few publications that share information for the platform characteristics such as error model, read length distribution and rate of indels and SNPs occurring during the sequencing process. These statistical features were later utilized in the *in silico* method for generation.

The average read length is 250bp and the coverage is 25, as it is reported by Roche[9]. Quilian *et al* [5] reports 0,12% error of the GS FLX Roche/454 platform where 72% are insertions, 24% are deletions and 4% are substitutions. The quality per base decreases in the end of the read. Figure 3 depicts the quality as a function of the length of homopolymers. The experience on real data from Roche in many scientific publications [10,12] shows that the reads characteristics differ from those reported by Roche.

The average read length is estimated on 230 base pairs, having standard deviation of 20. On Figure 5 it can be noticed that the read lengths can be approximated with a normal distribution, whose mean is the average read length, plus uniform distribution in the interval from 50 to 230.

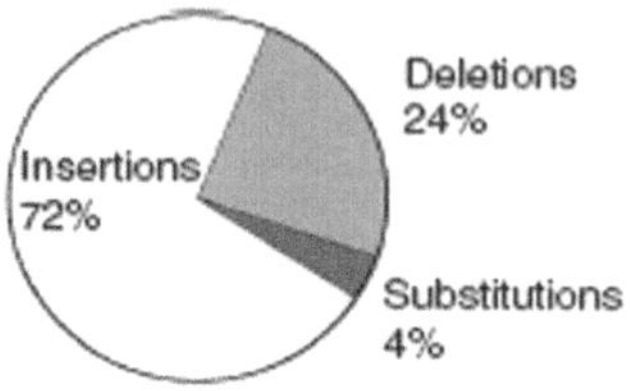

Fig. 2. [5] Percentage of error types

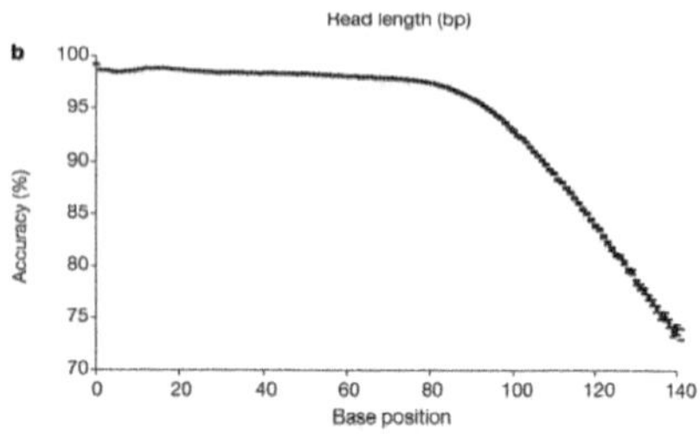

Fig. 4. [3] Accuracy of read base according to the base position in the read

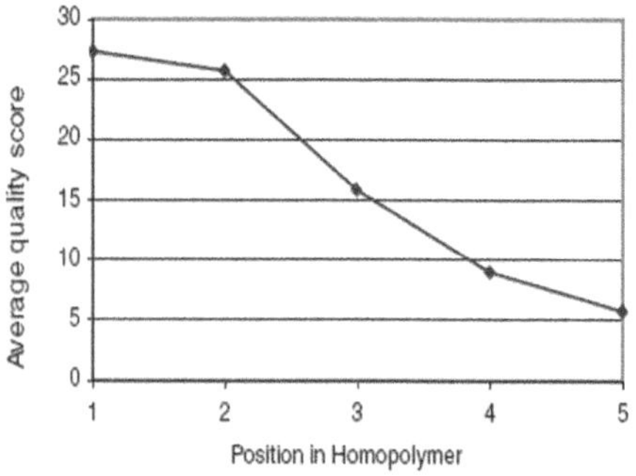

Fig. 3. [11] Value score per homopolymer position

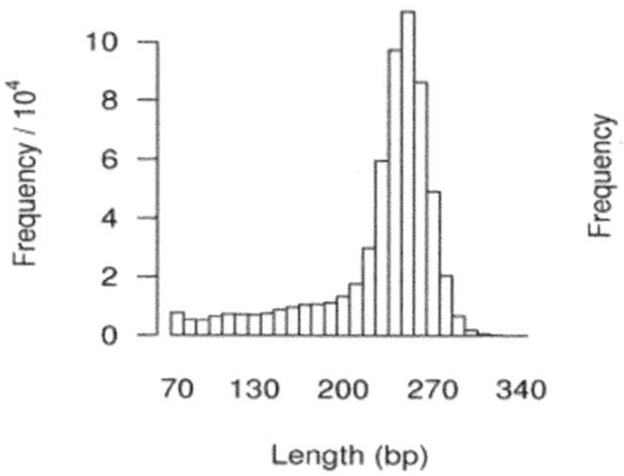

Fig. 5. [12] Real data reads length distribution

3.2 Performing Data Simulation

The data is simulated using Perl scripts and modules for text file manipulation. In the first step of the simulation, a genome reference is used as input. This genome can be any genome of interest. Here, the selected input genomes are the complete genome sequences of *Pseudomonas aeruginosa* LESB58 and *Dyadobacter fermentans* DSM 18053, which have approximately equal lengths, but different percentage of GC content. The number of the reads generated is determined by the required coverage. The coverage is calculated by counting the number of occurrences of a specific base at a determined position. In this way, minimal coverage is guaranteed for each base, which results in higher average coverage of all the reads. Parameters such as mean value for the read length, standard deviation and coverage can be modified and adapted. Additionally, as shown in Figure 5, some of the generated reads have uniform distribution and shorter length. After the generation of the reads, quality values are assigned to each base. The quality value for each base is generated randomly following normal distribution with mean 27 and standard deviation of 10. Lower quality values are inserted when homopolymers longer than four occur and the base position in the read is longer than 200. Again, the information for the quality value statistics is based on the previously presented Figure 3 and Figure 4. Figure 5 represents the read length distribution of the generated reads. Statistical analysis on the simulated data was performed and the following results were yielded:

Table 1. Simulated reads characteristics

Average read length	Platform error	Reported overall coverage	Coverage	Number of reads generated	Simulated reads avg length	Simulated reads stand. dev.
250	0,12%	25	20	613580	230	20

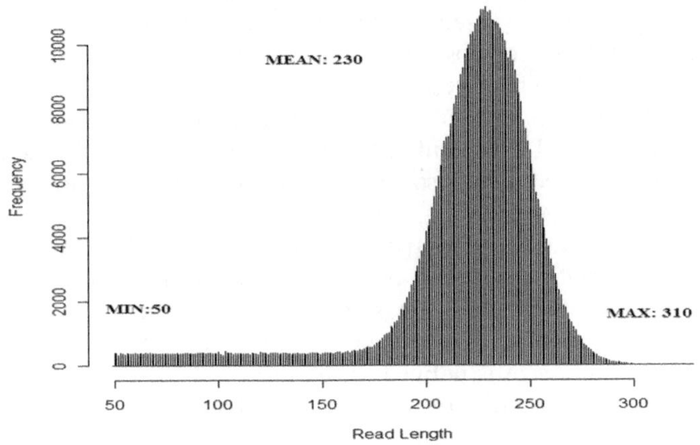

Fig. 6. Read length distribution of the simulated reads

At the end, the output files are in FASTA format for the reads and QUAL format for the quality values. Additionally, files with inserted errors are output. In the header of each read, information for the length and the start and end position in the reference genome is stored.

4 *De novo* Assembly

Many tools have been developed for automatic de novo assembly of NGS reads. Different computational methods yield different output. Using the simulated data, we perform *de novo* assembly in order to recreate the genomic sequence of Pseudomonas *aeruginosa* LESB58. For this purpose, the following de novo assemblers were tested: Velvet [13], Newbler, MIRA [14], and CLC Genomics workbench.

Velvet uses the Eulerian path strategy to generate contigs. It breaks the set of reads into a set of oligomers with a determined length k. The next step is creating a de-Bruijn graph by linking the reads that have an overlap with length k-2 bases. The last step is finding the Eulerian path, which visits every edge exactly once. The disadvantages of Velvet are:

- Sensitivity to sequencing errors
- Loss of connectivity information implied by the read

These features make Velvet more appropriate for very short reads with equal length, which are produced by the next generation sequencers Illumina and Solid.

The GS De Novo assembler aka *Newbler* is distributed together with the 454 Life Sciences instruments. Based on Overlap-Layout-Consensus (OLC) approach, it first searches overlapping sequences, performs multiple sequence alignment and resolves the mismatches using the flow values of the mismatches.

The biggest advantage of Newbler is that it is Roche/454 proprietary, which means it is well adapted to the features of the data sequenced by Roche/454 sequencers, considers the error model in order to alleviate the sequencing errors and additional information from the flowgrams, when performing the assembly.

The *MIRA* algorithm also resembles the OLC strategy. MIRA gives the high priority to the high confidence regions. The main goal of MIRA is to reduce the assembly errors and to resolve the repetitive sequences.

The *CLC genomics workbench* is a commercial product and little is known about the way it works. The CLC algorithm for *de novo* assembly at first aligns the reads and creates contigs. In the second stage, it uses the contigs as a reference to assemble the reads.

Because the described tools handle the sequencing data in a different way, they were tested on simulated data; their outputs were compared and analyzed. The performance of the assembly tools is measured with the number of contigs, the average contig length, the N50 contig size, number of non-assembled reads and average coverage. The N50 contig size is defined as the length of the last contig which covers half of the genome together with the contigs larger than it.

5 Results

This section observes the reconstruction of the simulated sequencing data by the four assemblers: Newbler, MIRA, Velvet, CLC Genomics Workbench and Velvet.

Table 2. Testing the Assembly Tools on *Pseudomonas aeruginosa* LESB58

Assembler	Total # Contigs	# Large Contigs (> 500)	Contig Length Min/Avg/Max			Avg Cov	N50 Contig Size	NAR	GC Content
Newbler 2.0.01	128	87	108	74883	647647	25,23	245456	5159	66,35%
MIRA 3.0.0	220	166	225	29981	281969	29,76	93015	1167	66,33%
CLC 4.0	51	47	297	128090	665232	24,27	408167	27	N/A
Velvet 0.7.55	8433	4031	41	785,49	10976	26,96	1545	-	66,42%

The Newbler assembler was expected to yield the best results, because it is Roche/454 proprietary. However, the simulated data are already translated flow signals into bases in FASTA format; therefore the assembler could not make use of the flow signals and the additional information packed in SFF (Standard Flowgram Format) file formats. One more reason for aggravated performance of Newbler is its approach to repetitive sequences. Newbler ignores repeats, which are more numerous in GC-rich organisms.

The *de novo* algorithm of CLC Genomics workbench produced the least number of contigs with the largest average contigs size, leaving the least number of non-assembled reads. The N50 contig size has the highest value, meaning that 50% of the genome is small number of large contigs. However, the low average coverage of CLC might be the reason for the good results. CLC is more tolerant when it comes to the threshold coverage for making contigs.

The bad performance of Velvet is one more proof that Velvet is preferable for short reads. It produced a huge number of short contigs.

MIRA's sensitivity to quality values and coverage prevented it from achieving the best contigs statistics.

Table 3. Testing the Assembly Tools on *Dyadobacter fermentans* DSM 18053

Assembler	Total # Contigs	# Large Contigs (> 500)	Contig Length Min/Avg/Max			Avg Cov	N50 Contig Size	NAR	GC Content
Newbler 2.0.01	49	41	124	169033	1111321	29,76	536812	5778	51,56%
MIRA 3.0.0	116	99	241	60033	594815	19,59	185135	1228	51,54%
CLC 4.0	43	38	81	161217	1171246	29,98	536852	399	N/A
Velvet 0.7.55	4470	2801	41	1557	17881	41,49	3179	-	51,54%

The *de novo* assemblers were also run on reads generated from a genomic sequence from an organism with normal GC content and approximately the same genome size, the bacterial strain *Dyadobacter fermentans* DSM 18053. MIRA, Newbler and Velvet exhibited apparent improvement in the results. Changes in the performance of CLC are negligible. Newbler showed the biggest improvement, which proved its high sensitivity to GC content. In GC-rich organisms, the repeats are more numerous, as a result of the higher frequencies of Gs (guanine) and Cs (cytosine). The inability of Newbler to resolve the repeats affects its performance on data with high GC content.

In spite of the results, all the assemblers have their own advantages and disadvantages. The Newbler algorithm ignored a lot of reads for the reason it finds them too short. Just like MIRA, its output depends on the additional information in the SFF files inserted by the Roche/454 sequencer. The Velvet algorithm cannot reconstruct well the fragmented reads. With the newest version of CLC, the output of the algorithms can be manipulated only by the CLC workbench. No further processing outside the workbench is allowed, because of the algorithm – specific file format that is not compatible with other tools for genome analysis.

6 Conclusion

In order to test assembly tools on different organisms, without the possibility to generate real data from different organisms and/or save money in the same time, the genomes from two different bacterial strains were used to generate simulated data form Roche/454 sequencer and input in the most widespread assembly tools.

All assembles have their own strengths and weaknesses. The CLC algorithm outperforms the Roche/454 proprietary tool, Newbler on translated flow signals (into bases).

Moreover, the results show that Newbler's performance depends on the GC-content of the organism. On the opposite side, the results show that the GC-content does not influence the results from CLC, which means that CLC copes well with the repetitive sequences.

Acknowledgment

Ljupco Kocarev thanks ONR Global (Grant number N62909-10-1-7074) and Macedonian Ministry of Education and Science (grant 'Annotated graphs in system biology') for partial support.

References

1. Kahvejian, A., Quackenbush, J., Thompson, J.F.: What would you do if you could sequence everything? Nat. Biotechnol. 26, 1125–1133 (2008)
2. Sanger, F., Nicklen, S., Coulson, A.R.: Dna Sequencing with Chain-Terminating Inhibitors. Proceedings of the National Academy of Sciences of the United States of America 74, 5463–5467 (1977)
3. Margulies, M., Egholm, M., Altman, E.W., et al.: Genome sequencing in open Microfabricated High Density Picoliter Reactors. Nature 437(7057), 376–380 (2005)
4. Metzker, M.L.: Applications of Next-Generation Sequencing Sequencing Technologies - the Next Generation. Nature Reviews Genetics 11, 31–46 (2010)
5. Quilian, A.R., Stewart, A.D., Stromberg, M.P., Marth, T.G.: Pyrobyes: An improved base caller for SNO discovery in pyrosequences. N. Meth. 5(2), 179–181 (2008)
6. Myers, G.: A dataset generator for whole genome shotgun sequencing. In: Proceedings of ISMB 1999 (1999)
7. Richter, C.D., Ott, F., et al.: Metasim-A sequencing Simulator for Genomics and Metagenomics. PLoS ONE 3(10), e3373
8. Mavromatis, K., Ivanova, N., Barry, K., et al.: Use of simulated data sets to evaluate the fidelity of metagenomics processing methods. Nat. Met. 4(6), 495–500 (2007)
9. Roche 454 Live Sciences, `http://454.com/products-solutions/system-features.asp`
10. Gerlach, W., Jünemann, S., Tille, F., et al.: WebCARMA: a web application for the functional and taxonomic classification of unassembled metagenomic reads. BMC Bioinformatics 10, 430 (2009)
11. Huse, M.S., Huber, A.J., et al.: Accuracy and quality of massively parallel DNA pyrosequencing. Gen. Biol. 8, R143 (2007)
12. Meyer, E., Aglyamova, G., Wang, S., et al.: Sequencing and de novo analysis of a coral larval transcriptome using 454 GS-FLX. BMC Genomics 10, 219 (2009)
13. Zerbino, D.R., Birney, E.: Velvet: Algorithms for de novo short read assembly using de Bruijn graphs. Genome Research 18, 821–829 (2008)
14. Chevreux, B., Wetter, T., Suhai, S.: Genome Sequence Assembly Using Trace Signals and Additional Sequence Information. Com. Sci. and Biol.: Proceedings of the German Conference on Bioinformatics (GCB) 1999, 45–56 (1999)

Durkin's Propagation Model Based on Triangular Irregular Network Terrain

Marija Vuckovik, Dimitar Trajanov, and Sonja Filiposka

University Ss Cyril and Methodius, Faculty of Electrical Engineering and Information Technology, Karpos 2 bb, Skopje, Macedonia
{marija.vuckovic,mite,filipos}@feit.ukim.edu.mk

Abstract. Propagation models that are commonly used in assessing the performances of ad hoc networks, take into account the mechanisms of reflection, diffraction and scattering on the ground. However, it must not be forgotten that the communication between devices is usually carried out in irregular terrain, so it's necessary to use the terrain profile in order to determine the signal coverage. In this paper we layout the extension of the Durkin's propagation model using Triangular Irregular Network (TIN) based terrain. The verification of the proposed propagation model is done by comparing the results with the ones obtained with a SRTM map used in the Radio Mobile software.

Keywords: TIN Terrain, Durkin's propagation model, wireless networks.

1 Introduction

The dynamics of life imposes the need for mobile communication, while the technical development allows permanent connection between people in different environments. In the last decade in order to achieve a greater degree of freedom and maximized use of the capabilities of wireless networks there is increased interest in ad hoc networks research [1]. The main characteristic of the ad hoc networks is that they can be established anywhere, which means that they do not rely on any infrastructure. The wireless mobile nodes which are part of the network are the main creators of communication in the network, because of their capability of self-organization, which leads to a decentralized network [2]. The network is called ad hoc because each node transmits data to another node, and the decision for forwarding is made dynamically depending on the connectivity of the network. In order to establish communication, ad hoc networks allow for multihop transmission of data between nodes outside of their direct radio range. This kind of communication is controlled by a special ad hoc routing protocol that is concerned with discovery, maintenance and proper use of the multihop paths [3].

The main problem when determining the performance of networks is that usually the irregularities of the terrain that exist in real environments are left out. This leads to poor performance evaluation of the networks. Most of the simulators provide modeling and evaluation of performance of the networks on a two-dimensional terrain on which the network is set, not taking into account the elevation of the terrain which

M. Gusev and P. Mitrevski (Eds.): ICT Innovations 2010, CCIS 83, pp. 333–341, 2011.

has a major role in enabling communication between nodes in the network. Hence, there is obvious need for using three-dimensional terrain modeled in space in order to provide realistic and accurate measurement of networks performance.

In order to make our performance observations more realistic, we decided to use a propagation model that incorporates the nature of propagation over irregular terrain and losses caused by obstacles in the radio path. In our previous work, we made an implementation of the Durkin's model as an extension for the NS-2 simulator [4], thus allowing us to conduct more realistic simulation scenarios and analyze the way the terrain profile affects the ad hoc network performances. This implementation was based on a Digital Elevation Model (DEM) terrain which is a type of representation for irregular terrain included in the original Durkin's model [12].

The DEM files store elevation information (integer values) for a number of positions on Earth's surface at regular spatial intervals (divided by geographic latitude or longitude) [5][6]. However, this model includes a huge number of data that need to be stored in one file. However, the Triangulated Irregular Network (TIN) file can be used as replacement for the DEM file. It also stores digital data structures which are used in terrain files for the representation of surfaces. TIN is a vector-based representation of the surface, which is obtained by improperly allocated points and lines in three-dimensional system (x, y, z), organized into a network of triangles that do not overlap [7]. This model is derived from the elevation data stored in raster-based models, such as DEM. In this paper, we present the implementation of the Durkin's model based on terrain data that is read from a TIN file. The model implementation is made so that it takes advantage of the way the data is stored in the TIN model eliminating the need to asses every point along the line of sight.

2 TIN Terrain

The model of a network of irregular triangles represents an alternative to the regular raster DEM files used in a range of geographic information systems [7] [8]. This model is developed in the early 70s of the last century as a simple way to create an area of irregular points in space. However, its commercial use began in the 80s of last century.

The network of irregular triangles (Triangular Irregular Network - TIN) is a digital data structure used in geographic information systems for representation of surfaces. The advantage of the TIN model compared to the DEM alternative is in the mapping and analysis of the TIN model points that are randomly distributed with an algorithm that determines which points are the most necessary to obtain more accurate possible representation of the ground. Therefore, the input data is flexible and the number of points that should be saved is less than the raster DEM.

The TIN model is composed of a triangular network of points which are called concentrators with three-dimensional coordinates, connected with links to form a mosaic of triangles. In areas with small variation of the height of the surface the points are widely installed, while in areas where we find more intense variation of the height of the surface the density of points is greater.

2.1 Creation of TIN Terrain

TIN is created from point-concentrators, which are actually points with heights collected from various sources. Usually TIN is created from digitized contours, raster with z values, collections of data structures or other operations on the TIN. The triangulation to obtain triangles known as surfaces is performed on these entry points, called nodes and lines known as edges. Each area is part of the plane in three-dimensional space and there is no intersection between the defined areas. In this paper, the TIN terrain file is obtained using a DEM data file.

We use the LandSerf software [9] in order to generate the TIN terrain data. LandSerf is a software that enables visualization and analysis of spatial data. It was firstly designed to be used with surfaces and elevation models, but now it works with many types of terrain data. Currently supports raster DEM, vector TIN and contours.

The process of triangulation is carried out by adding triangles in the network until some condition such as mean or maximum error, or maximum number of triangles is met. The created TIN is exported in a VRML TIN format which is supported by LandSerf. VRML (Virtual Reality Modeling Language) is a standardized text file format for presenting three-dimensional vector graphics [10]. It is accepted as an international standard (ISO / IEC 14772-1:1997) by International Organization for Standardization ISO. An example obtained TIN terrain is shown on Fig. 1.

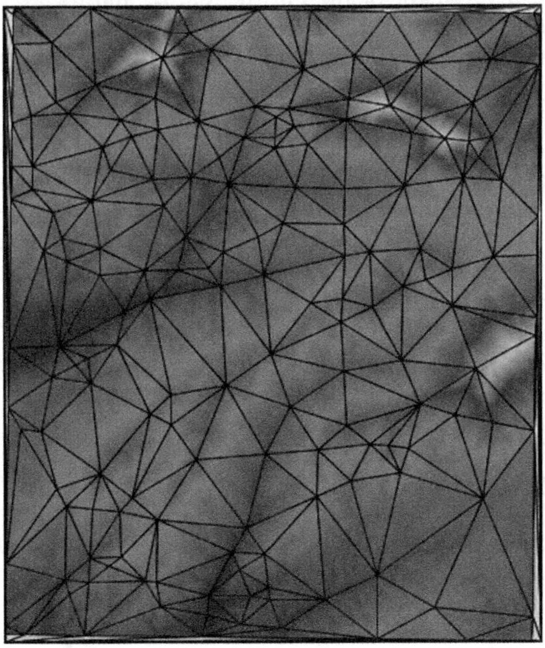

Fig. 1. TIN terrain

3 Durkin's Model

The main goal of the Durkin's model is to predict the median transmission loss using the path geometry of the terrain profile [11]. The original execution of the path loss estimation consists of two parts. The first part consists of loading a topographic DEM file which is turned into a topographical database and reconstruction of the ground profile information along the path between the transmitter and the receiver (T-R). The second part of the algorithm calculates the expected path loss along that path.

The first step of the algorithm is to decide whether a line-of-sight (LOS) path exists between T-R. This can be done by computing the difference between the height of the line joining T-R antennas and the height of the ground profile in 3D space. If any difference is found to be positive, it is concluded that a LOS path does not exists, otherwise, a LOS path exists. Assuming the path has a clear LOS, the next step is to see whether first Fresnel zone clearance is achieved. If the Fresnel zone of the radio path is unobstructed, then the resulting loss mechanism is approximately that of free space. But, if there is any kind of obstruction, then the Fresnel- Kirchoff diffraction parameter v must be calculated as in [11].

$$v = h\sqrt{\frac{2(d_1 + d_2)}{\lambda d_1 d_2}} \tag{1}$$

where h is the relative height of the obstruction, d_1 and d_2 are distanced from the obstacle to the transmitter and the receiver, respectively, and λ is the radio signal wavelength. In practice, graphical or numerical solutions are relied upon to compute the diffraction gain.

If the terrain profile failed the first Fresnel zone test then there are two possibilities: Non-LOS and LOS, but with inadequate first Fresnel zone clearance.

For both of these cases, the program calculates the free space loss and the received power using the plane earth propagation equation known as two ray ground model. The algorithm then selects the smaller value as the appropriate received power for the terrain profile. If the profile is LOS with inadequate first Fresnel zone clearance there is additional diffraction loss that is added (in dB) to the appropriate received power according to the approximate solution given by Lee as in [11].

After implementing the original Durkin's model we decided to make a new implementation of the Durkin's model which will be based on the original properties and calculations, but it will work with a TIN based terrain.

3.1 Durkin's Model for TIN Terrain

The algorithm for Durkin's model for TIN terrain was created based on knowledge of geometry and solid geometry and uses only simple geometric calculations corresponding to three-dimensional space. Instead of checking every point along and around the LOS, we now work with the LOS and the triangle planes defined in the TIN file. In order to avoid the complexity of the calculations within the algorithm instead of trying to calculate the intersection between the Fresnel ellipsoid and a triangle from the terrain, the test for checking the clearance of the Fresnel zones is based solely on the calculation of the radius of the first Fresnel zone at a given point in the ellipsoid.

This algorithm consists of several steps:

- Check whether there is a point of intersection of LOS with a given triangle
- If there is an intersection then find the maximum normal distance from the point of intersection to each side of the triangle
- If there is no intersection then calculate the shortest distance from the normal line of the transmitter and receiver to each side of the triangle
- Calculate the diffraction parameter v.

First, the algorithm checks if there is an intersection between the line of the transmitter and receiver with a given triangle. If there is a point of intersection, that means that there is no line of sight, and the next step of the algorithm is calculation of the diffraction parameter v. In order to calculate the diffraction parameter for the knife-edge diffraction, it is necessary to determine the maximum distance from the point of intersection to the sides of a triangle and the radius of the first Fresnel zone at the point of intersection. If there is no point of intersection, then there is a LOS between T-R. But that does not imply that there is a clear first Fresnel zone. At this stage the minimum distance between the line which connects the transmitter and receiver, and each side of the triangle should be calculated in order to find the worst case of penetration into the zone. Then the radius of the first Fresnel zone at the point of the segment from the transmitter to the receiver that is closest to the side of a triangle is calculated. If the difference between distance and radius of first Fresnel zone is negative, it means that there is an obstacle in the first Fresnel zone and the obtained difference is used for the calculation of the diffraction parameter v. If this is not the case, then we have a clear first Fresnel zone.

The calculation of the power of the received signal is carried out according to standard procedure described in Durkin's model.

4 Model Verification

Radio Mobile is a free and powerful tool for drawing RF patterns and predicting the performance of radio systems [13]. By using freely available data it can create gray, X-Ray and virtual maps painted in the colors of the rainbow. In this paper, we use it as a tool for verification of our implementation of the Durkin's model based on the TIN file format by performing a comparison of the results obtained from our model and the results obtained with Radio Mobile for the same real terrain. Radio Mobile uses SRTM map for examination. SRTM (Shuttle Radar Topography Mission) produces the fullest, elevation digital model of Earth with the highest resolution.

We used the 802.11b network with 2,4 GHz. We observed a single polar coverage, where the transmitter was positioned in one point, and all other nodes were distributed over the terrain. We used two real terrain areas derived from SRTM map which are shown on Fig. 2. The transmitter was being placed at various locations. The TIN terrains that comply to the area bordered with SRTM map were generated with LandSerf software, from the appropriate DEM terrains set as a base.

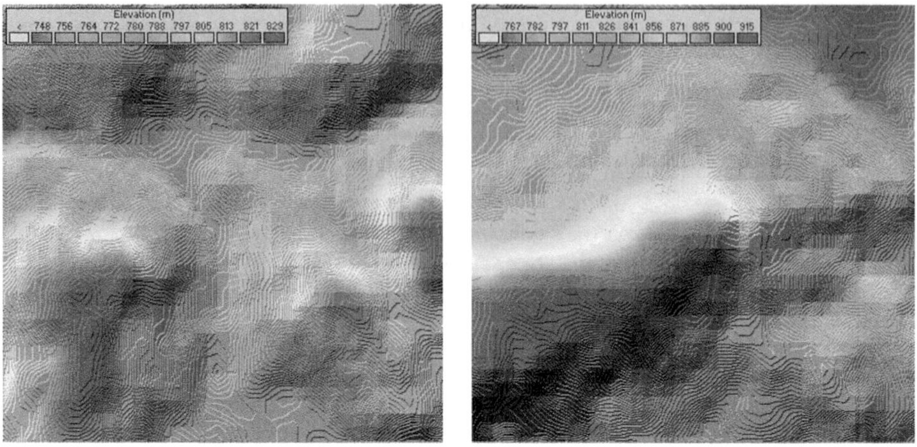

a) Terrain 1 b) Terrain 2

Fig. 2. Terrain view in SRTM format in Radio Mobile

We observed the terrain radio coverage given with Radio Mobile and with our implementation of the Durkin's model. We were especially interested in the points were the two overlap and differ (whether this area is radio covered by Radio Mobile, but not with Durkin's and vice versa).

We present the results obtained when the transmitter was positioned in coordinates (x,y)=(100,100) for the first terrain, and (x,y)=(800,800) for the second terrain.

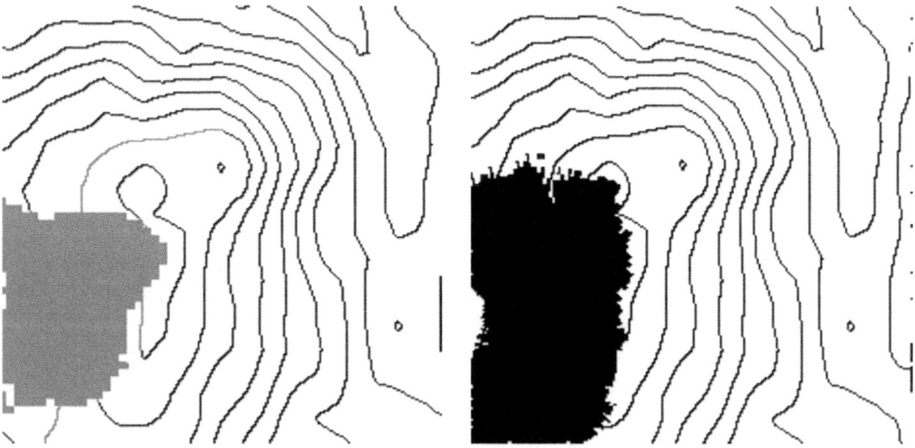

a) TIN terrain 1 b) SRTM terrain 1

Fig. 3. Signal Coverage on Terrain 1; T in (100,100)

On Fig. 3 the radio coverage over TIN terrain 1 (Fig. 3a) and SRTM terrain 1(Fig. 3b) are presented.

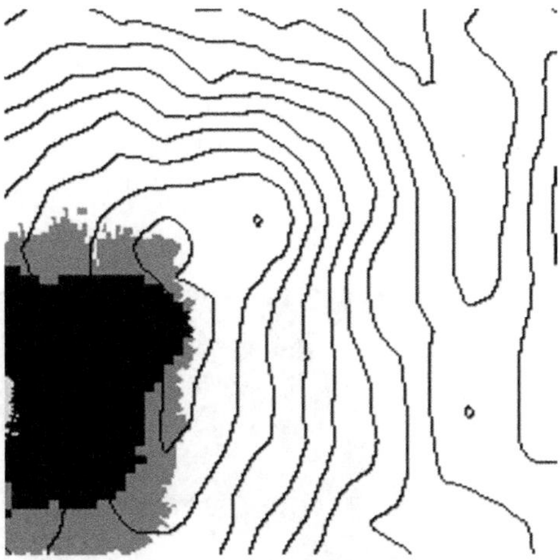

Fig. 4. Comparison of TIN and SRTM Terrain 1 radio coverage when the T is placed in (100,100)

On Fig. 4 the overlapping of signal coverage on SRTM and TIN terrain with black color, the deviation of the TIN model in terms of total coverage with light grey and the deviation of the SRTM model with dark grey color are presented. Statistically, when comparing the TIN model radio coverage with the SRTM Radio Mobile radio coverage, the area of signal coverage overlap is 61%, while the deviation of the TIN is 3% and of SRTM is 36%. This is a good result when taking into account the high resolution of SRTM terrain and the difference in the radio coverage calculations.

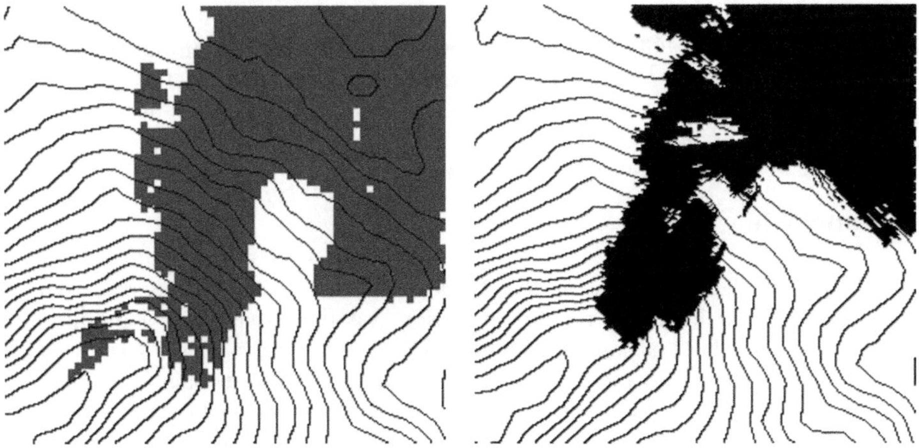

a) TIN terrain 2 b) SRTM terrain 2

Fig. 5. Signal Coverage on Terrain 2; T in (800,800)

On Fig. 5 the radio coverage over TIN terrain 2 (Fig. 5a) and SRTM terrain 2(Fig. 5b) are presented.

On Fig. 6, the overlapping of signal coverage on SRTM and TIN terrain is represented with black color, the deviation of the TIN model in terms of total coverage with light grey and the deviation of the SRTM model with dark grey color. The comparison of the TIN model with the SRTM radio coverage model shows that the area of signal coverage overlap is 70,5%, while the deviation of the TIN is 21% and of SRTM is 8,5%.

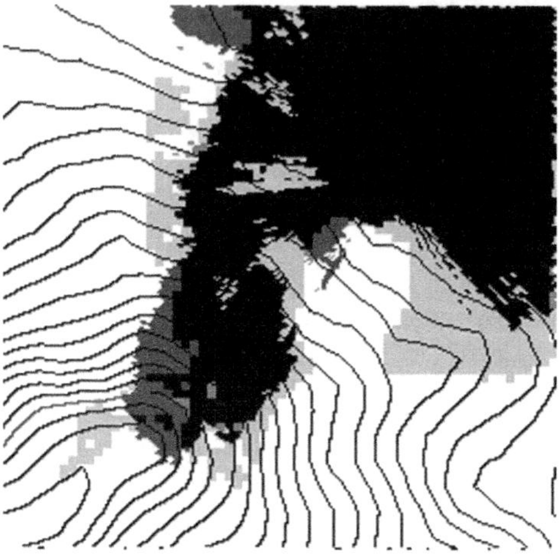

Fig. 6. Comparison of TIN and SRTM Terrain 2 radio coverage when the T is placed in (800,800)

From the results shown above, it is obvious that the irregularity of the terrain on which the network is established has impact on the performances of the network. The main conclusion in this stage of the research is that Durkin's model for TIN terrain gives satisfactory results for signal coverage over an irregular terrain and thus can be used for creation of more realistic MANET scenarios.

5 Conclusion

In this paper, the extension of the Durkin's model using TIN terrain data is introduced. The main reason for this extension was the possibility for definition of more realistic MANET scenarios using the TIN representation of the terrain and an appropriate terrain aware radio propagation model. The TIN terrain gives accurate representation of the terrain by placing a few points in the areas where there is a small variation of the elevation of the terrain, and a huge number of points in areas with more intense variation of the elevation of the terrain.

The Durkin's model for TIN terrain is based on simple geometry and solid geometry, which does not need a large number of calculations or memory resources. The advantage of this model based on TIN terrain over the original one for DEM terrain is in the mapping and analysis in the TIN model points that are randomly distributed on the basis of the algorithm that determines which points are necessary to obtain more accurate possible representation of the terrain. Therefore, input data is flexible and the number of points that should be saved is less than the raster DEM.

In order to verify the accuracy of the results obtained by the Durkin's model for TIN terrain, a comparison with the SRTM terrain in Radio Mobile was performed. The results show that the Durkin's model for TIN terrain gives satisfactory signal coverage compared to the SRTM terrain in Radio Mobile. If we take into consideration that the SRTM terrain has higher resolution than the TIN terrain, than the results obtained by the TIN terrain are more than satisfactory especially because it works with a small amount of terrain data. Also, we must bare in mind that the Durkin's propagation model itself is more pessimistic compared to Radio Mobile, especially in case of narrow canyons.

As future work, we intend to implement the new model in the NS2 simulator in order to measure the performances of ad hoc networks with different clustering capabilities.

References

1. Hekmat, R.: Ad-hoc Networks: Fundamental Properties and Network Topologies. Springer, Heidelberg (2006)
2. Ozan, K., Tonguz, G., Ferrari, G.: Ad Hoc Wireless Networks: A Communication Theoretic Perspective. John Wiley & Sons, Chichester (2006)
3. Royer, E., Toh, C.: A Review of Current Routing Protocols for Ad Hoc Mobile Wireless Networks. IEEE Personal Communications 6(2), 46–552 (1999)
4. NS-2 network simulator, `http://nsnam.isi.edu/nsnam/index.php`
5. U.S. Geological Survey National Mapping Division: Part 1 General, Standards for Digital Elevation Models
6. U.S. Geological Survey National Mapping Division: Part 2 Specifications, Standards for Digital Elevation Models
7. Zeiler, M.: Modeling Our World, Environmental Systems Research Institute, Inc. (1999)
8. Rognant, L., Goze, S., Planes, J.G., Chassery, J.M.: Triangulated Digital Elevation Model: Definition of a New Representation
9. Wood, J.: The LandSerf Manual (December 2009)
10. The Virtual Reality Modeling Language, International Standard ISO/IEC 14772-1 (1997)
11. Rappaport, T.S.: Wireless Communications, 2nd edn. Prentice-Hall, Englewood Cliffs (2002)
12. Filiposka, S., Trajanov, D., Vuckovik, M.: Performances of Clustered Ad Hoc Networks on 3D Terrains, Simutools, Rome, Italy (2009)
13. Radio Mobile, `http://www.cplus.org/rmw/english1.html`

An Enhanced Visualization Ontology for a Better Representation of the Visualization Process

Alberto Morell Pérez[1], Carlos Pérez Risquet[1], and Jorge Marx Gómez[2]

[1] Central University of Las Villas,
Faculty of Mathematics, Physics and Computing, Department of Computing Science
Carr. a Camajuaní, Km. 5, Santa Clara, Cuba
{amorellp,cperez}@uclv.edu.cu
[2] Carl von Ossietzky University Oldenburg,
Department of Computing Science, Business Information Systems I/VLBA
Ammerländer Heerstrasse 114-118, 26129 Oldenburg, Germany
jorge.marx.gomez@wi-ol.de

Abstract. One purpose of the Top Level Visualization Ontology is to provide a common vocabulary to describe visualization data, processes, and products. However, there are two aspect where its expressiveness is poor: the models of the visualization process and the data used on it. The aim of this paper is to describe some modifications of this ontology which lead to a better representation of the visualization process and data models, and facilitate the accommodation of new models. A detailed description of the new ontology's components is given.

1 Introduction

The maturity of the visualization field and the developments in other areas, especially the semantic web, have motivated the creation of a visualization ontology. An initial step in this direction was the sketch of a Top Level Visualization Ontology (TLVO) during a workshop held at the UK's National e-Science Center in April 2004 [1]. As the report says, the ontology is going to provide a common vocabulary for describing visualization data, processes, and products. Furthermore, it is intended to support the description and discovery of web services, the interchange of process models (pipelines) between visualization developers and users curation and provenance management of visualization processes as well as data collaboration and interaction across distributed sites.

However, its authors consider the TLVO as tentative and incomplete, because the ontology creation is an iterative activity, that requires consensus within the visualization community itself. For this reason, they made a call to collaborate in this effort, in order to promote the debate and feedback. We consider that two aspects which need more consideration are the accommodation of the visualization process and data models.

Regarding the models of the visualization process, the TLVO is not very expressive: only the visualization pipeline – which is associated with the dataflow model [2,3] – is represented (by the Pipeline class); other important models,

M. Gusev and P. Mitrevski (Eds.): ICT Innovations 2010, CCIS 83, pp. 342–347, 2011.

as the data-state [4] and spreadsheet [5] models, are missing. Even worst, a general way to accommodate new models is not offered, because it is not always conceptually appropriate to represent these models as subclasses of Method, as the Workflow class suggest was the intention of the TLVO creators. Moreover, no matter the chosen model, this arrangement limits the possibility to express a visualization at the three levels of abstraction, i.e., Conceptual, Logical and Physical, and the mapping between them.

Regarding the data models, there is no a clear separation between the model and the concrete data it describes. In fact, there is only one data branch in the TLVO, which makes impossible to commute between different interpretation of the same data at different times.

In this paper, we propose some modifications of the TLVO (Section 3), which better represent the visualization process and data models. For doing this, we made an analysis of the most important visualization taxonomies of the last 30 years, as well as the recent work in visualization ontologies. Conclusions and issues for future research are given in Section 4.

2 Visualization Ontologies

Maybe the first effort to build a visualization ontology was a workshop held at the UK's National e-Science Center on April 2004 [1]. The meeting gathered together 18 delegates, representing a range of visualization communities, to investigate the structure for such an ontology. As a result, they identified an initial set of concepts and relationships, and sketched the top-level hierarchy, shown in Figure 1. The TLVO is divided into four groups of concepts: the world of users (Task sub-tree), the world of data (Data sub-tree), the world of representation (Representation sub-tree) and the world of techniques (Transformation sub-tree). Three levels of abstraction were also depicted: Conceptual (C), Logical (L) and Physical (P). Duke et al. [6] modified the TLVO, interchanging the Task and Representation concepts.

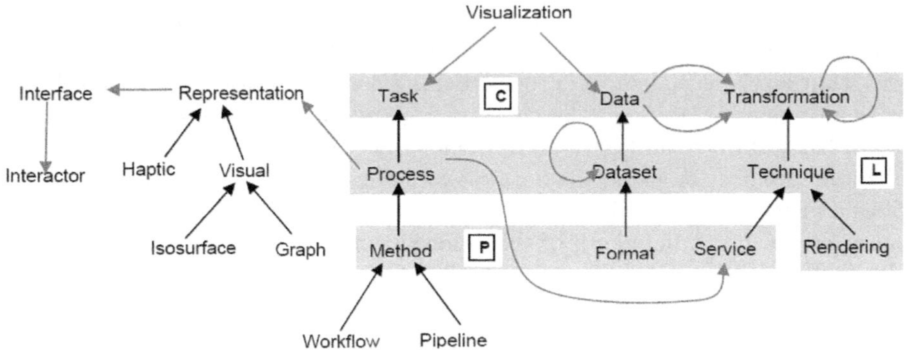

Fig. 1. Top Level Visualization Ontology

Shu et al. [7] takes a step further, and define a visualization ontology in OWL using the tool Protege. Three of the groups identified in [1] are used: Representation, Data and Technique. They also illustrate how to use the ontology in a portal for discovery visualization services.

Existing visualization taxonomies were used as a starting point for the development of the TLVO. The visualization community have been fruitful in taxonomies. Since 1996, nearly every year at least one relevant taxonomy have been published. If we also consider the interaction taxonomies from the interface design field, the number rise much more. Even though many of them share common units, the taxonomies have significantly different levels of granularity [8]. Some categorize low-level interaction techniques, and other high-level user tasks. Some are oriented toward a specific application area (e.g., decision support environments [9] and graph visualization [10]) or research field (e.g., Scientific Visualization and Information Visualization) and others use a more holistic approach. There are also many taxonomy reviews, some of them very detailed [11,8].

3 The Enhanced Top Level Visualization Ontology (E-TLVO)

We believe that the TLVO needs a general way to accommodate any model of the visualization process, besides the data-flow model, similar to how the OWL-S Web Service Ontology [12] allows the description of a service by different service models. This can be done representing each model with a class, and abstracting its common characteristic in a super-class each class will be descendant of. These ideas led us to suggest some modifications to the TLVO, showed in Figure 2, which are going to be discussed below.

The VisualizationApplication class provides a reference point for identifying a visualization application. One instance of this class will exist for every particular visualization application: one that transforms certain data using some resources (like a specific visualization system) to obtain a final image. A visualization application may be seen as a ready-to-use program that, once instantiated, can be used by a user to solve a specific task. Each instance of VisualizationApplication will be "describedBy" a descendant of the class VisualizationModel.

The VisualizationModel class describes how the visualization application works, that is, the visualization process behind a visualization application. VisualizationModel is an abstract class and its descendants are used to define specific models, like data-flow and data-state model. The DataFlow class describes a visualization application using the data-flow model. Each instance of this class describes a visualization application as a set of transformations. The visualization pipeline can be constructed out of this information, using the transformations as nodes and extracting the links from the "input" and "output" properties relating Transformation and Data classes: if the output data of one transformation is used as input by another transformation, there is a link between them. The DataState class describes a visualization application using the data-state model. In this case, each instance of this class describes a visualization application as a

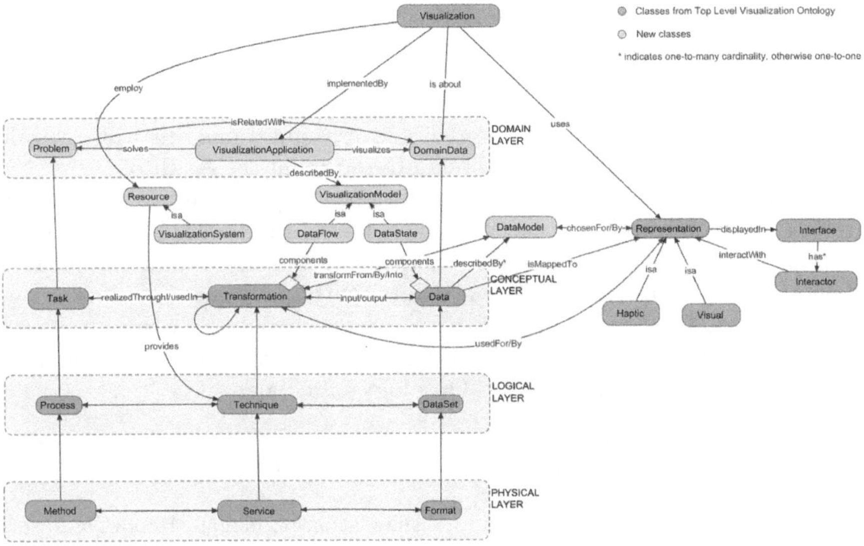

Fig. 2. Modified Top Level Visualization Ontology

set of data states. The sequence of the states can also be constructed from the "input" and "output" properties but in the opposite way.

Each instance of the VisualizationApplication class is used to solve a specific problem by means of the visualization of the correspondent data, respectively these entities are represented by the Problem and DomainData classes. As the instances of these classes are more related with the application domain, they are at a higher level of abstraction than the Conceptual layer. For this reason, we add the Domain layer to group them together.

The Resource class specifies the means through which a visualization application is carried out. Surely this class needs a more thorough decomposition, but in this case we only include the VisualizationSystem class as a descendant of it, to represent software resources like visualization systems. The property "provides" of the Resource class allows to describe the available transformations in a specific resource, that may be used to select which resource shall be employed in a certain case.

The DataModel class tells how to interpret the data. As Tory and Ller pointed [13], "a single data set may be interpreted quite differently by different people, or by the same person at different times, greatly affecting the type of visualization". They also distinguish the user model from the design model, in which the algorithm developer incorporates specific choices such as interpolation method. Then, an instance of Data is "describedBy" an instance of DataModel, or preferably, of DataModel's descendants. In the same way, an instance of Transformation transforms From/Into a data model. This representation is consistent with the work of Shu et al. [14].

4 Conclusions and Future Work

In this paper we propose some modifications to the TLVO, which result in a better representation of existing visualization process and data models, and facilitate the accommodation of new models. Several questions are still open, for example: is the Data class hierarchy enough to represent the result of every stage of the pipeline (raw data, analytical abstraction, visualization abstraction, image), taking into consideration that they have different semantic levels? How are represented the high level analytical tasks, as overview, zoom and comparison? How could the Chi's classification of operators (within-stage and stage-to-stage) [4] be represented? For future research, we propose to validate the expressiveness of the ontology integrating on it the most important visualization taxonomies, as well as to represent it using a Web Ontology Language.

References

1. Brodlie, K.W., Duce, D.A., Duke, D.J.: Visualization ontologies: Report of a workshop held at the national e-science centre. Report e-Science Institute (April 2004)
2. Upson, C., Thomas Faulhaber, J., Kamins, D., Laidlaw, D.H., Schlegel, D., Vroom, J., Gurwitz, R., van Dam, A.: The application visualization system: A computational environment for scientific visualization. IEEE Comput. Graph. Appl. 9(4), 30–42 (1989)
3. Haber, R.B., McNabb, D.A.: Visualization idioms: A conceptual model for scientific visualization systems. In: Visualization in Scientific Computing (1990)
4. Chi, E.H.h., Riedl, J.T.: An operator interaction framework for visualization systems. In: INFOVIS 1998: Proceedings of the 1998 IEEE Symposium on Information Visualization, Washington, DC, USA, pp. 63–70. IEEE Computer Society, Los Alamitos (1998)
5. Chi, E.H.h.: A Framework for Information Visualization Spreadsheets. PhD thesis, University Of Minnesota (1999)
6. Duke, D.J., Brodlie, K.W., Duce, D.A.: Building an ontology of visualization. In: VIS 2004: Proceedings of the Conference on Visualization, Washington, DC, USA, p. 598.7. IEEE Computer Society, Los Alamitos (2004)
7. Shu, G., Avis, N.J., Rana, O.F.: Bringing semantics to visualization services. Adv. Eng. Softw. 39(6), 514–520 (2008)
8. Yi, J.S., Kang, Y.a., Stasko, J., Jacko, J.: Toward a deeper understanding of the role of interaction in information visualization. IEEE Transactions on Visualization and Computer Graphics 13(6), 1224–1231 (2007)
9. Adnan, W.A.W., Daud, N.G.N., Noor, N.L.M.: Expressive information visualization taxonomy for decision support environment. In: ICCIT 2008: Proceedings of the Third International Conference on Convergence and Hybrid Information Technology, Washington, DC, USA, pp. 88–93. IEEE Computer Society, Los Alamitos (2008)
10. Herman, I., Melançon, G., Marshall, M.S.: Graph visualization and navigation in information visualization: A survey. IEEE Transactions on Visualization and Computer Graphics 6(1), 24–43 (2000)
11. Qin, C., Zhou, C., Pei, T.: Taxonomy of visualization techniques and systems - concerns between users and developers are different. In: Asia GIS Conference 2003 (2003)

12. Burstein, M., Hobbs, J., Lassila, O., Mcdermott, D., Mcilraith, S., Narayanan, S., Paolucci, M., Parsia, B., Payne, T., Sirin, E., Srinivasan, N., Sycara, K.: Owl-s: Semantic markup for web services. Website (November 2004)
13. Tory, M., Ller, T.: A model-based visualization taxonomy. Technical Report SFU-CMPT-TR2002-06, Computing Science Dept., Simon Fraser University (2002)
14. Shu, G., Avis, N.J., Rana, O.F.: Investigating visualization ontologies. In: Proceedings of the UK e-Science All Hands Meeting 2006 (2006)

Framework to Design a Business Intelligence Solution

Pablo Marin Ortega[1], Lourdes García Ávila[1], and Jorge Marx Gómez[2]

[1] Central University of Las Villas, Santa Clara, Cuba
Department of Industrial Engineering
[2] Carl von Ossietzky University Oldenburg, Oldenburg, Germany
Department of Computing Science, Business Information Systems I / VLBA
{pablomo,Lourdes}@uclv.edu.cu, jorge.marx.gomez@wi-ol.de

Abstract. In the present research we propose a framework to design a business intelligence solution based on the integration of business and technological domains. The main contributions of the framework are: 1) enterprise architecture that combines the approach of the Zachman Framework and the Balanced Scorecard, 2) mapping the System Model layer with the tools of the Pentaho BI Suite and 3) an indicator for the control management that facilitates to measure the performance of the strategy from the compensation of the indicators defined in a Balanced Scorecard, based on compensatory fuzzy logic.

Keywords: Business Intelligence, Enterprise Architecture, Compensatory Fuzzy Logic, Balanced Scorecard.

1 Introduction

The business intelligence (BI) have the capability to take the information flow, that the organization gathers every day and transforms it into active information that allows to improve the decision making process in order to assure the success of an enterprise. Today the companies invest a lot of money to buy the best applications that allow them to develop BI solutions. Nevertheless, these applications do not guarantee, that all the necessary information for the decision making process is available. Most of the existing solutions are concentrated on the technological capabilities, and designed to answer the question of, how to achieve the solution. They are not answering what would be the necessary information that the solution must support, in accordance with the real needs. This problem occurs because of the lack of alignment between business and technological domains.

A survey of 385 finance and IT executives, by CFO Research Services (Fig. 1), asked them to identify the drivers for poor information quality (IQ). Nearly half of them pointed (45 percent) the non-integration of IT systems and the variability of business processes as an acute problem that constrains management's ability to work effectively and focus on high-value activities. Approximately the same number agrees that finance and business units alike spend too much time developing supplemental reports and analysis. Other disappointing and productivity sapping by products of poor information quality include that "multiple versions of the truth," misguides incentive programs, and leads to unrealistic plans and budgets.

M. Gusev and P. Mitrevski (Eds.): ICT Innovations 2010, CCIS 83, pp. 348–357, 2011.

In fact, 61 percent of respondents say they could still do a better job of just making sure the financial information they generate accurately reflects the performance of their businesses.

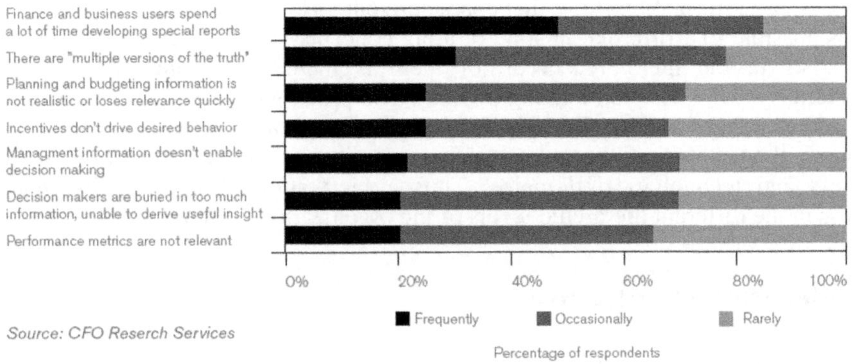

Fig. 1. Implications of Poor Information Quality To what extent do you believe your management suffers from the following decision-making problems?

The business impact of this poor IQ, say respondents, includes widespread decision-making problems that are often tied to inaccurate, untimely, and irrelevant information [1].

The main goal of this paper was to develop a framework that facilitates the design of BI solutions based on the integration of the both: business and technology domains, as a tool that contributes to the improvement of the availability of necessary information in the decision making process.

2 Business Intelligence

The BI term is not used uniformly by all authors. From its creation in the 90s by Gartner Group, the persons have interpreted it from very narrow up to very wide perspectives, due to the fact that there does not exist any strict scientific definition of the term.

Microsoft Corporation raises that it is the "Aptitude to take the flow of information that every organization gathers every day and to transform it into active information that allows obtaining the success"[2].

On the other hand Gartner Group rises that it is "An interactive process for exploring and analyzing structured, domain-specific information (often stored in data warehouses) to discern business trends or patterns, thereby deriving insights and drawing conclusions. The BI process includes communicating, discovering and effecting change. Domains include customers, suppliers, products, services and competitors"[3].

Marrero Atunez brings up that it is "A set of systems, strategies and informatics tools, whose functionalities are oriented to the support to the decision making process in an organization. Its enhance the availability and timely analysis of key data for the performance of the organization and its proper implementation and use requires a comprehensive vision and strategic operation of the entity, as well as mastering processes and information flows that characterize it”[4].

It is possible to affirm that in spite of a big concepts variety related to the BI term, that exists in the literature, in all of them is included the aptitude to extract information for the decision making process. The principal differences are focused in that, some authors see the BI only from a technological perspective, while others including the authors of the present paper; see it from as an integration of both: business and technological domains. Thus a facilitation of the decision making process in the different hierarchic levels of the organizations is to be made.

3 Enterprise Architecture

Enterprise Architecture (EA) is a framework or “blueprint” for how the organization achieves the current and future business objectives. It examines the key business, information, application, and technology strategies and their impact on business functions. Each of these strategies is a separate architectural discipline and Enterprise Architecture is the glue that integrates each of these disciplines into a cohesive framework [5].

Table 1. The purpose/function of enterprise architecture

The purpose/function of enterprise architecture is	Responses		Mean	Std. Deviation
	Valid	Missing		
To provide blueprint of data, application, & technology	373	4	4,40	0,68
A tool for a planning	373	4	4,25	0,68
A tool for decision-making	374	3	4,13	0,71
A tool for alignment of business & IT	372	5	4,08	0,86
To facilitate systematic change	374	3	4,02	0,74
A tool for communicating objectives	372	5	3,67	0,90
To provide a snapshot in time of an organization	374	3	2,87	1,10

A study realized in the year 2007 led by the Society for Information Management's (SIM) Enterprise Architecture Working Group (EAWG) was aiming to understand better the state of the practices of the AE in the organizations and to evaluate the state of the capacities of IT of the organizations in means to develop an AE, had the following principal results (Table 1) [6].

In a general way, we can summarize that because of the changes of the environment, the manager tries to discover the data, which supports having the general perspective of the business, and he has to be enabled to understand how the parts of the organization are interrelated with each other’s.

4 Design of BI Solutions

In accordance with the expressed previously, a BI solution is a finished platform that helps to compile automatically the flow of information, generated in a company, provided, there is a computer network, which has to be capable to transform this data into information to improve the decision making process.

On the other hand, it is important to understand that the BI tools alone facilitate "how" it is possible to achieve a solution from the computer point of view, but they do not assure, "what" is the information that is really needed. Often occurs that only a part of the whole the information needed to make decisions is missing. The reason for that is either lack of knowledge of the person requesting it, or because the information is not supported from the organization's database (Fig. 2)[7].

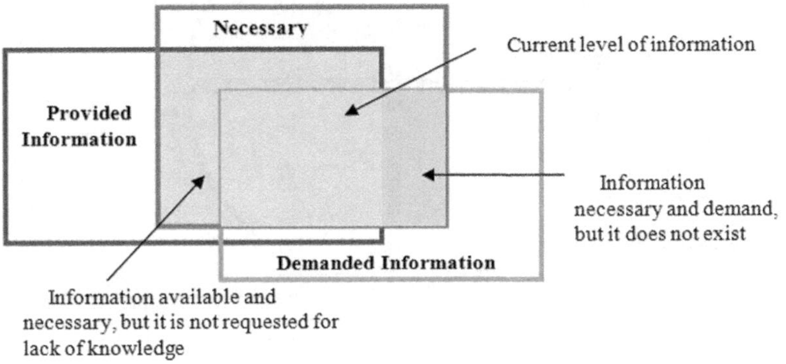

Fig. 2. Current situation of the information in the enterprise

A management system based on the strategy is a tool that helps the manager discovering what is really important in order to achieve the company's goals. The knowledge in which moment the right amount and quality of information is achieved in order to provide the right focus enabling the success of the enterprise.

Finally it is important to know that the enterprise architecture is not a simple description of a collection of documents and plans; it is a model of how the different parts of an organization are related. Without a model of enterprise architecture, the executives, the agents and the technologists are essentially "blind runners", making decisions based on their personal perception of the company. It is often the case, that this picture is not shared by the staff rest of the organization. An enterprise architecture model is a tool which helps the executives to think about the organization as a homogeneous system. The architecture captures a wide information variety, establishes relations between the technological domains and the business domains, and stores all the information joined on a single repository. This is a good starting point for the design of any business intelligence solutions. Thus the manager can make decisions, identify problems and analyze information of the business by means of the efficient integration of the technological domain and business domain.

5 Proposed Framework

The definition of the framework to facilitate the design of a BI solution is based on the elements expressed previously, as well as on the integration of Zachman Framework, the Balanced Scorecard, and the Pentaho BI Suite.

The proposed framework is based on four phases, which associate different procedures, rules and tools facilitating the framework's fulfillment (Fig.3).

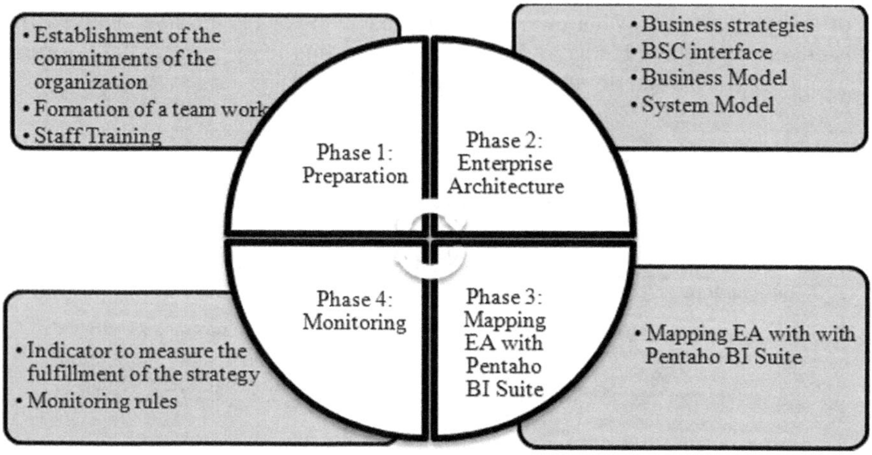

Fig. 3. Proposed Framework

5.1 Phase 1: Preparation

The main goal of this phase is the preparation of the necessary conditions for the change, which the company must confront to assume a project of design and development of a BI solution.

5.2 Phase 2: Enterprise Architecture

The aim of this phase is to define an EA for designing the BI solution. The methods and the tools to be used for its fulfillment are defined here too. The proposed framework is based structurally on the matrix proposed by the Zachman Framework [8], considering their first three layers, which are defined as: the strategy model, business model and system model. We considered the necessity of including an interface with the Balanced Scorecard (BSC) between the strategy model and the business model, targeting the translation to operative terms of the strategy of the company, since in Zachman Framework it is not contemplated. The general idea will be to construct a pyramid (architecture), which is incorporating in each of its layers the necessary specifications, to support the top level.

From this structure and according to the development of a BI solution, was deployed how to reach the elements that appear in each of the cells, specifying inputs, outputs and tools to use it (Table 2).

Table 2. Structure of the proposed enterprise architecture

	Data (what)	Functions (How)	Network (where)	People (who)	Time (when)	Motivation (why)
Objectives Scope	List of things important to the Business	List of Processes the Business	List of Locations in which the Business Operates	List of Organizations and people important to the Business	List of Events Significant to the Business	List of Business Goals / Strategies
BSC Interface	Translation and/or transformati on of the mission, vision and the strategy	Choice of indicators for perspectives the BSC	Architecture and indicators landscape	List of owner for each action variables for goal	List of measuring frequency	BSC design
Business Model	Semantic Model	The Business Process Model	The Business Logistics System	Work Flow Model	Master Schedule	Business Plan
System Model	Logical Data Model	Application Architecture	The Distributed Systems Architecture	Human Interface Architecture	Processing Structure	Business Rules

5.2.1 Fulfillment Rules

Based on the structure defined in the architecture above, which must be firstly completed by layers, provide that each layer represents a top level, with regard to the one that follows it. Nevertheless a big dependency among the elements in the columns is sometimes is strongly sized. In Table 3 are represented the dependencies among each cell and the order to be completed it.

Table 3. Fulfillment rules

	Data (what)	Functions (How)	Network (where)	People (who)	Time (when)	Motivation (why)
Objectives Scope	A1	B1	C1	D1	E1	F1
BSC Interface	A2 ← (F1)	B2 ← (F1 + A2)	C2 ← (B2)	D2 ← (B2 + D1)	E2 ← (F1 + A2)	F2 ← (A2 + B2 + C2 + D2 + E2)
Business Model	A3 ← (A1 + F2)	B3 ← (B1 + A3)	C3 ← (C1 + B3)	D3 ← (D1 + B1)	E3 ← (E1 + B3 + C3)	F3 ← (F2 + A3 + B3)
System Model	A4 ← (A3 + B3 + F2 + F3)	B4 ← (F2 + F3 + B3)	C4 ← (B4)	D4 ← (D3 + F2 + B4)	E4 ← (E3 + B4 + C4)	F4 ← (F3 +B4)

5.3 Phase 3: Mapping the Enterprise Architecture with Pentaho BI Suite

The purpose of this phase is to map the results of enterprise architecture, specifically in the layer of the system model, with the tools of Pentaho BI Suite.

For the development of the application, the analysts of the system must be based fundamentally on the System Model layer. In Table 4. we present the mapping between the System Model layer with the tools in Pentaho BI Suite. It provides the necessary information for the implementation of a solution, that truly meets the information needs of the managers, required for the decision making process. The main responsible for this phase is the technological staff.

Table 4. Mapping EA with Pentaho BI Suite

	Data (what)	Functions (How)	Network (where)	People (who)	Time (when)	Motivation (why)
System Model	Logical Data Model	Application Architecture	The Distributed Systems Architecture	Human Interface Architecture	Processing Structure	Business Rules
Out || In	Data Warehouse Model	System model with each of the system's functionality OLAP cubes	Matrix of relation: Logical data model vs. Logical data model of the architecture of the computer systems of the institution ETL definition	Matrix between: system's functionality vs. owner Role model User story	Template with the function's trigger that respond it to the defined restrictions in the master schedule and BSC design	Functionality and capabilities of the system Technical documentation User guide
Tools in Pentaho BI suite	Managmnt system database: MySql Postgree Hibernate	Mondrian Scheme Workbench Design Studio	Kettle ETL	Pentaho administration console	Pentaho administrat ion console Design Studio	Pentaho Reporting Pentaho Analysis Dashboards Data Mining

5.4 Phase 4: Monitoring

This phase has as a goal to design an indicator of management control that allows making a measurement, according the behavior of the indicators of the BSC. This phase facilitates the continuous process in the organization and gives the latter the possibility to adapt itself rapidly to the changes of the environment.

5.4.1 Indicator to Measure the Performance of the Strategic Plan

One of the points of major importance in the development of any strategic control tool is the development of strategic plans, through feedbacks, where the indicators capable of monitoring the management control, play an important role. Being it, one of the principal difficulties found in the literature used for this research.

In this sense, we proposed an indicator to measure of management control using compensatory fuzzy logic; it is capable to evaluate based on the behavior of the indicators defined in the BSC.

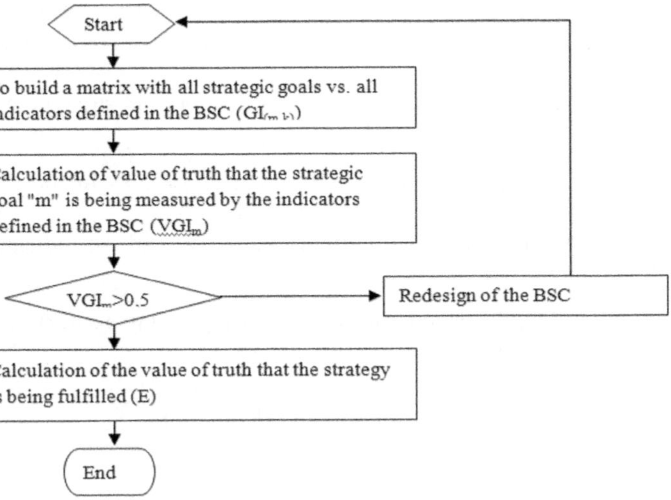

Fig. 4. Specific method for calculating the truth value of the strategic plan implementation

Step 1: Built the matrix $GI_{m,k}$.
To prepare a matrix where all the indicators and the strategic goals appear defined for the organization. The prepared matrix, must be presented to a group of chosen experts who have to answer the question: How true is it, that the indicator "k" is an important element in the measurement of the fulfillment of the strategic goal "m"? The scale to be used would be a continuous scale between 0 and 1; where 0 would be the most false value and 1 the most truthful one.

Step 2: Calculation of value of truth, that the strategic goal "m" is being measured by the indicators defined in the BSC (VGI_m).

With the previous information we can answer the question: How true it is, that the strategic goal "m" is being measured by the indicators defined in the BSC?

- A strategic goal is being measured if and only if exist indicators that measure it.

This can be expressed using compensatory fuzzy logic as:

$$VGI_m = \exists_k\left(VGI_{(m,k)}\right) \tag{1}$$

Where:

VGI_m: Value of truth that the strategic goal "m" is being measured by the indicators defined in the BSC.

$VGI_{(m,k)}$: Matrix with the truth value of the expert consensus that the presence of the strategic goal “m” is measuring by the indicator “k”.

The people in charge of designing the BSC should be ensuring that the value obtained in VGI_m for each goal, has a value greater than 0.5.The ideal value would be given by: maximizing VGI_m and minimize the number of indicators defined in the BSC.

Step 3: Calculation of the value of truth that the strategy is being fulfilled (E).

As a premise, must be ensured that the VGI_m value was more true than false for all strategic goals.

A strategy is being fulfilled if and only if all the important strategic goals are being met.

- A strategic goal is important if there are critical success factors that justify its approach.
- An important strategic goal is being met if and only if all the indicators defined in the BSC for its measurement are being met.

Based on the principles stated above and using compensatory fuzzy logic to compensate the indicator defined in the BSC, given as:

$$E = \forall_m \left(VG_m \rightarrow \left(\forall_k (VGI_m \rightarrow VI_k) \right) \right) \quad (2)$$

Where:

E: Value of truth that the strategy is being fulfilled.

VG_m: Value of truth that the element "j" is a key success factor and in turn advises the strategic goal "m".

VGI_m: Value of truth that the strategic goal "m" is being measured by the indicators defined in the BSC.

VI_k: Value of truth of the criterion of measurement of indicator "k“.

To calculate VI_k we propose to use the sigmoidal membership function.

Where:

$S = VI_k$: Value of truth of the criterion of measurement of indicator "k".

$X = I_k$: Calculated value of the indicator "k" according to the company.

Gamma (γ): Value acceptable. It would be equal to the value at which the indicator is considered acceptable.

Beta (β): Value almost unacceptable: It would be equal to the pre-image of a symmetric sigmoidal function for the optimal value defined for the indicator, or it would be the same β = (Value at which the indicator is acceptable - Value from which the indicator is optimal).

Alfa (α): Sigmoidal function parameter.

6 Conclusion

The proposed framework, as well as all the tools that conform it, help to improve the availability of the necessary information for the decision making process, based on the integration of the business and technological domains. Beside as complement to the tools which compose the framework, we included an indicator useful for the measurement of the strategy performance based on the indicators behavior defined in a

BSC. It gives a solution to the problem found in the literature according to the absence of management control indicators, capable of integrating in a single value the different results of the BSC and to formulate strategic plans based on the received feedback.

7 Outlooks

In order to facilitate the application of the specific procedures defined into the framework for the final users is necessary to design and to integrate a graphical interface software package. Beside with the enterprise architecture and the proposed fulfillment rules in the framework, it is possible to define an ontological model to support the improvement of the mapping process between the enterprise architecture and BI tools. Finally we want to design an indicator based on compensatory fuzzy logic to measure the degree of alignment between business and technological domains.

References

1. Myers, R.: IT Executives Seek to Boost Information Quality, CFO Research Services (2005), `http://www.cfo.com/article.cfm/5545859/c_2984335/?f=archives`
2. Microsoft Corporation, Guía de Estrategia de Business Intelligence (2004)
3. Gartner, G.: The Gartner Glossary of Information Technology Acronyms and Terms (2004)
4. Marrero Antunez, I.: La inteligencia de negocios desde la perspectiva cubana: retos y tendencias, Ciudad de la Habana, Cuba (2008)
5. Minoli, D.: Enterprise Architecture A to Z. Frameworks, Business Process Modeling, SOA, and Infrastructure Technology. Editor T.F. Group. Auerbach Publications, Broken Sound Parkway NW, Suite 300, Boca Raton, FL 33487-2742 (2008)
6. Kappelman, L. (ed.) The SIM Guide to Enterprise Architecture ed. C.P.T.F. Group. Taylor & Francis Gruop, an informabusiness, 6000 Broken Sound Parkway NW, Suite 300. Boca Raton, FL 3487-2742 (2010)
7. Marx Gómez, J.: Business Intelligence – Data Warehousing, in Business Intelligence – Data Warehousing. In: Wirtschaftsinformatik I, Very Large Business Applications. Carl von Ossietzky Universität Oldenburg, Oldenburg (2009)
8. Zachman, J.: Enterprise Architecture: The Issue of the Century, Zachman Institute for Framework Advanced, ZIFA (2010), `http://www.cioindex.com/nm/articlefiles/63503-EAIssueForTheCenturyZachman.pdf` [cited 20 de enero del 2010]

A New Methodology to Benchmark Sophistication of e-Invoicing and e-Ordering

Kiril Kiroski, Marjan Gusev, and Magdalena Kostoska

University Ss Cyril and Methodius, Faculty of Natural Sciences and Mathematics, Institute of Informatics, Arhimedova b.b. Skopje, Macedonia
{kiril,magi}@ii.edu.mk, marjangusev@gmail.com

Abstract. This paper introduces new, innovative means for benchmarking on line sophistication of e-Ordering and e-Invoicing solutions. Today, electronic means to conduct purchases and sales are essential activities for companies operations, and they need to decide how to implement e-Ordering and e-Invoicing, what software solutions to use, and how to integrate them successfully with their current software. Due to non-existence of such methodology, our primary goal is to present methods and indicators which constitute new benchmark for this type of software. We also give detailed description of the introduced indicators, and means to assess relative importance of different indicators. This methodology will be used to evaluate current solutions assessable by Internet in form of web service solutions (SAAS, plug in service, etc.). In this paper we have compared results and confirmed the validity of the new methodology.

Keywords: e-Government, e-Business, e-Invoicing, e-Ordering, benchmark.

1 Introduction

Business deals of each company always concern a sort of purchase or selling. Computer applications and Internet introduce automation of processes including invoices and purchase orders. The first step in this automation process is using some sort of template (written with help of Some Office tool). Afterwards the process includes management of these documents in a much better and faster way. There are a lot of applications supporting these tasks, and although they have common characteristics, they have a lot of differences, mostly in solving interoperability issues and possibility to integrate, or work as part of cloud computing paradigm [1].

During our research, we noticed the lack of a benchmarking tool, which can provide means to asses various software solutions. ICT surveys of countries' Statistical Offices implement only Eurostat's methodology and recommendations for statistical measurements of information society in EU-countries according to [2]. This means that they concentrate only on e-Impact phase, mainly about quantitative values of usage of e-Invoices and e-Orders, while our methodology evaluates sophistication of e-Invoicing and e-Ordering services by qualitative indicators.

Therefore, our first goal became focusing our attention on providing a methodology and indicators for evaluating software solutions that treat these problems, and through

M. Gusev and P. Mitrevski (Eds.): ICT Innovations 2010, CCIS 83, pp. 358–368, 2011.

analysis, propose the basics which should be followed when creating software for e-Ordering and e-Invoicing. These two services can be approached as separate issues, but can also be viewed as a part of e-Business and a bigger, integrated solution which provides all steps for completing procurement through electronic means, also known as e-Procurement or e-Supply.

EU has realized numerous projects with given e-Procurement development guidelines, but has introduced no complete set of indicators. In [3], we find only few indicators, which are also included in our methodology. What we have found during our research is that only business aspects are addressed, and the issues of security and legal obligations, as given in [4] and [5]. We also used e-Purchase indicators included in e-Government Services Benchmark [6]. There are also other initiatives related to the subject, but there is none which gives comprehensive and compact methodology to help benchmark e-Ordering and e-Invoicing solutions, so we introduce our methodology as a contribution in this field.

2 A New Methodology

2.1 e-Ordering and e-Invoicing System Description

E-Government should include: use of ICTs, and particularly the Internet, as a tool to achieve better government, use of information and communication technologies in all facets of the operations of a government organization, and continuous optimization of service delivery, constituency participation and governance by transforming internal and external relationships through technology, the Internet and new media (according to [7], [8] and [9]). According to [10], **e-Business** is defined as the application of information and communication technologies (ICT) in support of all the activities of business. **E-Procurement** is the business-to-business or business-to-consumer or Business-to-government purchase and sale of supplies, Work and services through the Internet as well as other information and networking systems, such as Electronic Data Interchange and Enterprise Resource Planning [11].

E-Ordering deals with the electronic transmissions of documents during the e-Procurement phase that starts with the issuing of orders by the buyer and ends with the receipt of an order response and the transmission of the delivery instructions of the ordered goods or services from the supplier [11].

According to [12], **e-Invoicing** is the process of sending invoices "by electronic means", i.e. transmission or making available to the recipient and storage using electronic equipment for processing (including digital compression) and storage of data, and employing wires, radio transmission, optical technologies or other electromagnetic means.

The desired e-Ordering and e-Invoicing system should implement following features:

E-Invoicing system should provide **search and report facilities**, which can give prompt look into needed report (chart, quarterly or annual report, etc.) or search criteria (by client, paid or stored, etc.). E-Ordering system should provide search by client, shipment status, and payment status.

Level of customization for given application, such as templates, time and date, company details, document details and shipment details. Impression is important for the system, since the amount of features that can be adjusted usually describes the personal **identity and appearance** the solution can offer to different companies.

Since almost every other country has different tax rates, every e-Invoicing application that should be internationally used requires **customizability** in this field. Giving the fact that there are countries with more than one tax rate, the ability to implement more than one tax rate on an invoice is also a "must-have".

E-Invoicing or e-Ordering application should be able to give different sorts of **view** for issued invoices (or orders), as well as their status (late, paid, stored), etc. Views on invoices or orders give good insight into their overall state (number or value of orders/ invoices for a given client, their payment status, purchase trends, etc.).

Keeping and delivering of invoices and orders is another requirement which must be implemented for dependable use of these applications, therefore, they are referred as **dependability**. The invoices must be preserved for future reference and legal matters. Invoices should be delivered in a **form** acceptable for the client [3].

One key requirement for a good system which includes working with documents is the backup facility. Database must be backed up regularly, and the system should provide easy-to-use tools for performing backup or restore of the database, all of which contributes to the **availability** of the software.

Ordering application should provide item details, which helps when making orders. Those details can vary from using nothing more than text description, to different photographs or graphics for a given product or even datasheets for items to be purchased. Additional information for products can be given in a form of **e-Catalogue**, which can be used not only as a help for the ordering application, but also as a powerful marketing tool. E-Catalogue should be implemented with **configuration** according to the nature of procurement.

Set-up of **order placing automated online procedures** is also an important part of this system, as it provides means for completing ordering and invoicing procedure without human interaction on behalf of the service provider [13].

Application should provide **document flow**, which can give to the user help in what is expected from him next. There should be some waypoint to indicate the progress of document creation [13].

The objective of this methodology is benchmarking of e-Invoicing and e-Ordering, and both of them are rarely found as bundle software at one place. For the purpose of integrating e-Ordering and e-Invoicing as sub-phases of e-Procurement, we will evaluate only solutions which provide them both. Indicators will be grouped in three major categories: technical, functionality and usability indicators.

2.2 Technical Indicators

Technical indicators (also described as non-functional requirements) for this kind of software, in general, are mostly described by type of software, its requirements (both hardware and software), how they are distributed or installed, data protection they are using and their capabilities to adapt to most popular software suites used today. These indicators are given as follows:

1 Type of software: 0=not realized as web application, 1=includes authentication and authorization, form submission and checking status, 2=includes full transactions and delivery, 3=includes possibility for accounting, reporting and user management,

4=realized as a web service, 5=realized as a web service with initiation of customized features and add ons.

2 Installation: 0=requires full installation as special application, 1=special application with upload feature, 2=thick client installation, 3=web browser, needs additional application installation, 4=thin client, 5= just web browser.

3 Customization: 0=no customization is possible, 1=rudimentary customization, 2=customization templates, 3=upload of graphics and schemes, 4=options can be set in details, 5=open code.

4 Integration: 0=no integration possible, 1=integration through export/import data, 2=integration using database connectors, 3=application suite, 4=application using web service, 5=plug in web service.

5 Browser support: 0=no browser support possible, 1=desktop application with upload capability, 2=works with specified browsers, 3=does not work with older browsers, 4=plug ins required, 5=works with all browsers.

6 Interface to ERP products: 0=no data interchange possible, 1=requires manual adaptation, 2=has custom made ERP, 3=plug in convertor required, 4=need technical assistance for integration with specified web services, 5=easy integration with specified web services.

7 Interface to CRM: 0=no data interchange possible, 1=requires manual adaptation, 2=has custom made CRM, 3=plug in convertor required, 4=need technical assistance for integration with specified web services, 5=web service integration.

8 Backup facility: 0=no backup possible, 1=can be saved as document locally, 2=database backup facility, used locally, 3=backup provided by server, 4=backup made by server, can be downloaded locally 5=easy-to-use customized backup facility.

2.3 Functional Indicators

Under functional indicators we understand features implemented in the software, which are roughly divided into functionalities regarding users and user administration, document handling, additional facilities and application flexibility. We specified these eight functional indicators:

1 User administration: 0=no user data interchange possible, 1=special importer application required, 2=semi-automatic import through type-specific document, 3=plug in importer required, 4=requires technical help in integration with LDAP, 5=easy integration with LDAP web services.

2 Export capability: 0=no export capability, 1=mail only, 2=limited export types, 3=support most common types (doc, pdf, xls), 4=requires additional plug-ins, 5=fully customizable export.

3 Search facility: 0=no search facility, 1=basic search facility, 2=search by one or more field, 3=search with advanced choice criteria, 4=search with customizable fields, 5=full search facility.

4 Report facility: 0=no report facility, 1=basic report facility, 2=report by one or more field, 3=report with advanced choice criteria, 4=report with customizable fields, 5=report facility with graphics.

5 Tax: 0=no tax included, 1=fixed tax, 2=choice from predefined tax rates, 3=predefined tax rates, more than one per invoice, 4=customizable tax rate, 5=fully customizable tax rates, can include more than one per invoice.

6 Status and View: 0=no status and view facility, 1=basic status/view facility, 2=status and view by one or more field, 3=status and view with advanced choice criteria, 4=status and view with customizable fields, 5=full status and view facility with graphics.

7 Document types and delivery options: 0=can only be printed, 1=application specific type, 2=e-mail, can only be printed, 3=common document type (doc, pdf, xls), 4=implemented delivery mechanism, 5=full support using custom made add-ons.

8 Item details: 0=no item details, 1 – only item code, 2=short description, 3=description and graphic, 4=item detailed specification, 5=full specification, datasheets, links to product page.

2.4 Usability Indicators

Software is often judged by the appeal it has to the users. These indicators may be the crucial difference that can decide between two solutions with equal quality. Users should feel comfortable in everyday use of the software; they should be able to have where to go and who to ask if they find themselves in odd position. Additional features that can help them to do their work more easily and which can tell them what to do next are also important. So we introduced next few indicators as most important for this category:

1 Personalization: 0=no personalization possible, 1=limited personalization, 2=common application elements can be personalized, 3=user can personalize the application according to his preferences, 4=fully customizable application, including skins, adding or removing fields, 5=user can personalize application behavior.

2 Support: 0=no help and technical documentation, 1=frequently asked questions, 2=only help or technical support, 3=video presentation, forums, 4 full support of help and technical documentation with video and other sophisticated tools, 5=live support.

3 Ease of use: 0=new application with unique interface, 1=application with familiar interface, 2=application with help and hints, 3=web-form-like interface, 4=web form with customizable fields, 5=WYSIWYG interface.

4 Language support: 0=no language support possible, 1=more than one language, 2= limited language support implemented, 3=multilingual support implemented – according to EU, 4= Native language support, 5=full language support implemented.

5 E catalogue: 0=no catalogue, 1=item classification by type, 2=downloadable catalogue, 3=online catalogue, 4=catalogue connected with order, 5=fully customizable.

6 Established workflow: 0=no workflow, 1=simple menu, 2=interactive menu, 3=simple workflow, 4=step by step document creation, 5=workflow with proving.

7 Process automation procedures: 0=no automation, 1=requires user attention on each step, 2=limited human interaction, 3=requires higher approval, 4=full automation without human interaction, 5=customizable automation level.

2.5 Overall Evaluation

Although we established over twenty indicators we will be using to evaluate software solutions, not every one of them has the same impact on decision which of them is (are) the best, which features must be implemented, or what can be regarded as an optional feature. According to [11], "... every software solution must structure should be sufficiently flexible and rich so as to support integration with other elements of the supply chain. In order to achieve this, the invoice has to be created in a structure, which is unambiguously intelligible... and able to work for all parties." We will refer to these indicators as **"core"**. The most important indicators for this kind of software, beside **core** indicators, include type of software and installation, integration capabilities and data integrity. We will refer to them also as the **"essence"** of the solution. Most of the functional features, as well as usability feature such as workflow, will be the **"quality"** of the software. Most of the usability features and customization options will be referred as the **"appeal"**. These factors together with corresponding indicators are given in the next table:

Table 1. Classification of indicators, according to the type of indicator and weight category

	core	essence	quality	appeal
Technical	6	1, 2, 4, 7, 8	3, 5	
Functionality	1, 2, 5, 7		3, 4, 6	8
Usability	7		6	1, 2, 3, 4, 5

The comparison will be given separately for each solution using their average scores per group, to determine which software performs best for given indicator group. Software that scores "0" in at least one indicator will not be considered when evaluating given group.

$$\text{Technical}_{\text{average}} = \frac{1}{n} \times \sum_{i=1}^{n} \text{technical}_i \tag{1}$$

$$\text{Functionality}_{\text{average}} = \frac{1}{n} \times \sum_{i=1}^{n} \text{functionality}_i \tag{2}$$

$$\text{Usability}_{\text{average}} = \frac{1}{n} \times \sum_{i=1}^{n} \text{usability}_i \tag{3}$$

Then we will use our categorization to see how applications perform regarding each category, and regarding combinations of most important categories. First we will give scores by each category (fields with N/A will be regarded as 0):

$$\text{Core}_{\text{average}} = \frac{1}{n} \times \sum_{i=1}^{n} \text{core}_i \tag{4}$$

$$\text{Essence}_{\text{average}} = \frac{1}{n} \times \sum_{i=1}^{n} \text{essence}_i \tag{5}$$

$$\text{Quality}_{\text{average}} = \frac{1}{n} \times \sum_{i=1}^{n} \text{quality}_i \tag{6}$$

$$\text{Appeal}_{\text{average}} = \frac{1}{n} \times \sum_{i=1}^{n} \text{appeal}_i \tag{7}$$

At the end we will give overall view on all evaluation put together, with applied weight factors, using different weights for each category, in the order to note relative importance of categories regarding the overall score:

$$\text{overall} = \frac{w_1 \times \text{core}_{\text{score}} + w_2 \times \text{essence}_{\text{score}} + w_3 \times \text{quality}_{\text{score}} + w_4 \times \text{appeal}_{\text{score}}}{w_1 + w_2 + w_3 + w_4} \tag{8}$$

3 Benchmarking

We will evaluate the sophistication of e-Ordering and e-Invoicing software using indicators specified in part 2 of this paper. The best way to compare software and try to find common ground and differences will be by putting them in one table. Indicators will be given by their category and item number and put into rows, while columns will represent different applications. By this approach we will find out what is "must have" for invoicing (ordering) software, and what can be regarded as an additional feature. In choosing contextual indicators for invoicing and ordering software, we used some of the guidelines and resources found at [3], [4], [5], [8], [11] and [13].

3.1 Analyzed Solutions

Most of the solutions we analyzed during our research represent part of a much bigger solution, usually an e-Procurement platform. We have analyzed a lot of web resources, then the sourceforge library, other internet places, and expert interviews and analysis. The overview of existing applications is listed in alphabetic order, and not listed in any other order (best to worst, or most popular to least popular). Our goal was to analyze working solutions, not experimental ones or platforms. The elimination criteria was probably the web based solutions with described features and characteristics and also to provide solutions which apply both e-Orders and e-Invoices, and to be used worldwide. Information we include is gathered through practical demonstration of the software, first-hand experience, as well as using documentation provided by software developers.

Table 2. Evaluated e-Invoicing and e-Ordering solutions

Name	*Short description*
Coupa	e-Procurement system based on a cloud platform http://www.coupa.com/solutions/e-Procurement/
ePMX	Bellwether's e-Series is a complete web-based and SaaS Purchasing SW http://www.bellwethercorp.com/web-based-series/
eRequester	eRequester is a robust and highly scalable Web-based requisition and authorization routing platform http://www.erequester.com/index.php
Pakom Shop	A web application for company's partners https://shop.pakom.com.mk
Peppol	Pan-European Public eProcurement On-Line project with goal to set up a pan-European pilot solution http://www.peppol.eu/About_PEPPOL
SpendMap	SaaS e-Procurement software capable of automating and streamlining any or all stages of a purchase-to-pay process http://www.spendmap.com
Verian Solutions	ProcureIt is SaaS suite of purchase-to-pay solutions http://www.verian.com/purchase-to-pay-suite

Table 3. Score for e-Ordering and e-Invoicing solutions by group

	Technical	Functional	Usability
Coupa	87.50%	90.00%	82.86%
Verian Solutions	75.00%	70.00%	80.00%
SpendMap	72.50%	67.50%	80.00%
ePMX	75.00%	65.00%	80.00%
eRequester	65.00%	62.50%	77.14%
Pakom	52.50%	57.50%	74.29%
PEPPOL	52.50%	40.00%	54.29%

Table 4. Score for all indicators for e-Invoicing and e-Ordering solutions

	Core	Essence	Quality	Appeal	Core & essence	All but appeal	All but quality	All
No of indicators	6	5	6	6	11	17	17	23
Coupa	96.00%	80.00%	90.00%	80.00%	88.00%	88.67%	85.33%	86.50%
Verian Solutions	76.00%	76.00%	73.33%	70.00%	76.00%	75.11%	74.00%	73.83%
ePMX	68.00%	80.00%	76.67%	70.00%	74.00%	74.89%	72.67%	73.67%
SpendMap	66.00%	76.00%	76.67%	73.33%	71.00%	72.89%	71.78%	73.00%
eRequester	74.00%	68.00%	66.67%	63.33%	71.00%	69.56%	68.44%	68.00%
Pakom	56.00%	60.00%	43.33%	83.33%	58.00%	53.11%	66.44%	60.67%
PEPPOL	68.00%	60.00%	23.33%	46.67%	64.00%	50.44%	58.22%	49.50%

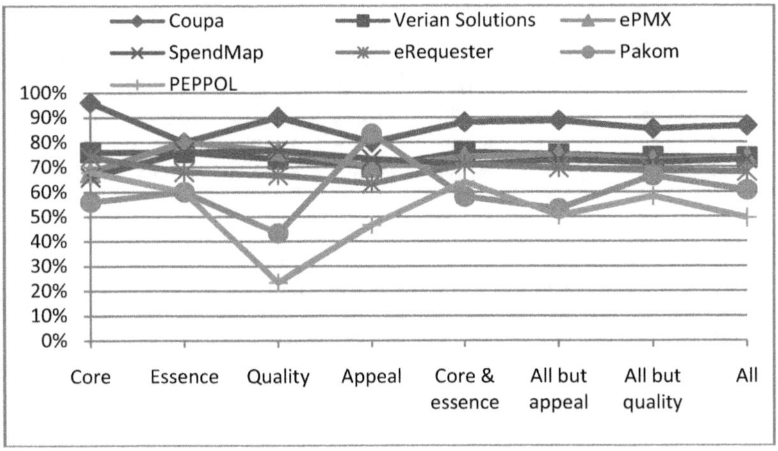

Fig. 1. Score for e-Invoicing and e-Ordering solutions

Score achieved for solutions are shown in Table 4 and Figure 1. When we put all software solutions back to back and drew our average score, we see that clear winner is Coupa software, mostly thanks to the score it achieved in Technical and Functional indicators, followed by a group of products which achieved also good scores (Verian Solutions, SpendMap and ePMX), and the group of products which should improve in the future to be able to compete with best solutions (eRequester, Pakom WebShop and PEPPOL). What is interesting is the fact that various category combinations have great impact on score for PEPPOL and Pakom, while other software has achieved almost constant scores, with Coupa outstanding between them.

In our work, we concluded that not all of the indicators have same importance for this software class, so we divided all indicators into four categories, described earlier, and we will evaluate our solutions with included weight factors. In our benchmarking, we used various combinations of weight factors, so as to notice the degree of impact of various categories on the final evaluation.

As we can see from Table 5 and Figure 2, the overall winner is Coupa software, which is not surprising, then we have a group of four solutions, Verian Solutions, ePMX, SpendMap and eRequester, which have similar scores, varying only 3-6%, and at the end, we have PEPPOL and Pakom, which lag additional 6-10% behind. From these figures, we can conclude that almost all solutions (with exception of Pakom), have turned much more attention to indicators we pointed out as most important, than on the overall look and appeal of the solution.

Table 5. Benchmarking for e-Invoicing and e-Ordering solutions with various weight factors

	B1	B2	B3	B4	B5	B6	B7	B8
Weights	$w_1=1$ $w_2=1$ $w_3=1$ $w_4=1$	$w_1=2$ $w_2=2$ $w_3=1.5$ $w_4=1$	$w_1=2$ $w_2=1$ $w_3=1$ $w_4=1$	$w_1=5$ $w_2=3$ $w_3=2$ $w_4=1$	$w_1=8$ $w_2=4$ $w_3=2$ $w_4=1$	$w_1=10$ $w_2=5$ $w_3=2$ $w_4=1$	$w_1=15$ $w_2=6$ $w_3=3$ $w_4=1$	$w_1=30$ $w_2=10$ $w_3=3$ $w_4=1$
Coupa	86.50%	87.23%	88.40%	89.09%	89.87%	90.00%	90.80%	91.59%
Verian Solutions	73.83%	74.46%	74.27%	74.97%	75.24%	75.37%	75.44%	75.68%
ePMX	73.67%	74.00%	72.53%	73.03%	72.49%	72.41%	72.00%	71.36%
SpendMap	73.00%	72.67%	71.60%	71.33%	70.58%	70.37%	69.97%	69.17%
eRequester	68.00%	68.82%	69.20%	70.06%	70.71%	70.93%	71.25%	71.89%
Pakom	60.67%	58.51%	59.73%	57.27%	57.20%	57.22%	56.53%	56.67%
PEPPOL	49.50%	51.95%	53.20%	55.76%	58.49%	59.63%	59.87%	62.65%

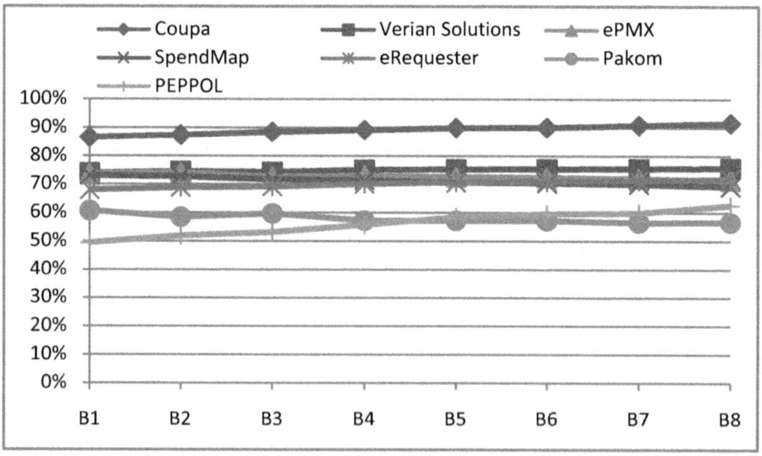

Fig. 2. Benchmarking for e-Invoicing and e-Ordering solutions with various weight factors

4 Conclusion

Today, e-Business is becoming the most prevalent way to conduct business. Solutions which introduce electronic purchasing and selling are quite numerous, but there is no benchmark methodology present which can help distinguish them, and decide which to use. This study presents new means for evaluation of these solutions, and divides them by their relative importance regarding to principles of e-Business. We acknowledge that the three categories in which we split all the indicators should be further updated, to give best insight into the most important characteristics for this type of software and following future trends. The proposed categorization and evaluation methodology can give meaningful directions for the developers of this kind of software, and help them develop better solutions, or help them compete with the best in this field.

What has became clear during this analysis is that all solutions, in order to be regarded as viable, must comply with conclusions drawn in [3] and [12], and in order with EU member and candidate countries laws. They also must be compliant to the SAAS idea, to implement interoperability to enable it for wide use, and provide means to interface with CRM and ERP products.

In this paper, we have shown that existence of a methodology which measures the quality of solutions and services for e-Ordering and e-Invoicing can be only beneficial, both to developers and customers. The existent methodologies which measure only business use and security issues are not complete without newly introduced indicators. We present a new methodology, and divided all indicators into three distinguished groups, give detailed description of these indicators, we applied our methodology to produce results, and we evaluated a number of existent solutions. As a part of our future work, we plan using mathematical means, such as factor analysis, for more precise defining of the weight scores for different indicators.

We also want to stress that most of the software solutions included in this analysis support not only functionalities we found interesting for our work, but also features like benchmark KPIs, Business analysis, expend and asset tools, which also makes them much expensive solution for companies or organizations who need nothing more than sophisticated e-Ordering and e-Invoicing software, and we believe that a smaller, much compact solution can be designed to use this difference in target field.

References

1. Kiroski, K., Gusev, M.: e-Invoicing and e-Ordering: Analysis and Comparison. In: Proceedings of The 7th International Conference for Informatics and Information Technology, CIIT 2010 (2010)
2. Regulation (EC) No 808/2004 of the European Parliament and of the Council, concerning Community statistics on the information society, April 21 (2004), `http://eur-lex.europa.eu/smartapi/cgi/sga_doc?smartapicelexapiprodCELEXnumdoc&lg=EN&numdoc=32004R0808&model=guicheti`
3. E-Invoicing compliance guidelines, CEN Workshop Agreement 16047 (December 2009)

4. Benchmarking of existing national legal e-business practices, from the point of view of enterprises (e-signature, e-invoicing and e-contracts), European Commission Directorate-General for Enterprise and Industry (November 2006)
5. The E-Payables Benchmark Report, Aberdeen Group (March 2007), http://www.ob10.com/Docs/Aberdeen_The_E-Payables_Benchmar_%20Report_March%202007.pdf
6. Capgemini, Rand Europe, IDC, Sogeti and DTI. Smarter, Faster, Better eGovernment: 8th Benchmark Measurement (November 2009), http://ec.europa.eu/information_society/eeurope/i2010/docs/benchmarking/egov_benchmark_2009.pdf
7. OECD: The e-government imperative: main findings, Policy Brief, Public Affairs Division, Public Affairs and Communications Directorate, OECD (2003)
8. Koh, C.E., Prybutok, V.R.: The three-ring model and development of an instrument for measuring dimensions of e-government functions. Journal of Computer Information Systems 33(3), 34–39 (2003)
9. Deloitte Research – Public Sector Institute, At the Dawn of e-Government: The Citizen as Customer (2000)
10. Beynon-Davies, P.: E-Business. Palgrave, Basingstoke (2004) ISBN 1-4039-1348-X
11. Baily, P.J.H.: Procurement principles and management, p. 394. Prentice Hall Financial Times, Harlow (2008)
12. Directive 2001/115/EC, Official Journal L 015, 0024–0028, January 17 (2002)
13. Final Report of the Expert Group on e-Invoicing, DG Internal Market and Services (November 2009), http://www.ob10.com/Docs/eInvoicingExpertGroup_final_report_e-invoicing_EN_1.pdf

ASGRT – Automated Report Generation System

Dejan Gjorgjevikj, Gjorgji Madjarov, Ivan Chorbev, Martin Angelovski, Marjan Georgiev, and Bojan Dikovski

University Ss Cyril and Methodius, Faculty of electrical engineering and information technology, P.O. BOX 574, Skopje, R. of Macedonia
{dejan,madzarovg,ivan}@feit.ukim.edu.mk, {mangelovski,marjan.georgiev}@gmail.com, b.dikovski@yahoo.com

Abstract. We have come to a point in time when there is an abundance of database usage in almost all aspects of our lives. However, most of the end users have neither the knowledge nor the need to manage the databases. Even more important, they are unable to generate the ever changing reports they need, based on the data in their databases. Our Applicative Solution for Generating Reports from Templates (ASGRT) tries to deal efficiently with this issue. It has a simple yet effective architectural design aimed to give power to the more experienced administrators and simplicity to common end users, to generate reports with their own criteria and design, from their databases. The presented software enables creation of templates containing text and tags that are recognized and substituted by values retrieved from the database, therefore enabling creation of customized reports with varying ease of use and flexibility.

Keywords: Template, Reports, Generator, Database Management.

1 Introduction

The advancement of technology and information society is evident in our everyday life. Seeing from the end user perspective, the various IT services that we use daily seem simple and easy functional. However, in the background, there are complex databases, data warehouses and service based technologies that become more and more widespread. Databases are used to store various types of information in hospitals, schools, universities, municipalities, government agencies and almost in all businesses services. In these complex systems, the management and presentation of the information stored in the databases are strictly defined within the software applications and information systems. Only a small room for customization is left to the people who actually use the information.

The document and report templates that are an essential parts of any software application or information system are most often predefined, and the user can only choose from the predefined templates to generate documents or reports. With this concept, the template generating process is limited to the programmers and database administrators. The common software user can use only the previously defined document and report templates. In this paper we propose an applicative solution for generating documents and reports from user defined templates - ASGRT.

M. Gusev and P. Mitrevski (Eds.): ICT Innovations 2010, CCIS 83, pp. 369–376, 2011.

The applicative solutions that we propose enable the common user to create his own templates and gather the info he needs from the database. Following an easy step by step wizard allows users to gather new types of information from the database without knowing any query languages or database design issues whatsoever.

The proposed applicative solution can be used by two types of users. The first type of users is the one lacking sufficient knowledge of database architectures, database management or database query language. The majority of users fall into this category. Therefore it is crucial for this application to be user friendly so that the users do not find the application too complex to use. The second type of users are more experienced database administrators, users with higher application access permissions and people with better knowledge of this system. For this type users it is essential to provide a way for faster creation of document and report templates without the redundancy of the user friendly GUI.

One of the advantages of ASGRT is its interoperability. With minor changes it can be made to work well with all kinds of SQL databases and thereby be used in different institutions, organizations and even in some types of software.

This paper is organized as follows. The next section presents a short overview of similar software products. In section 3 the overall program architecture is presented, while more details about the Database Architecture and ways of interoperability are given in section 4. Section 5 explains the concept of Tags and Templates, their structure and use. Section 6 explains the way the system is used, and the conclusion is given in section 7.

2 Overview of Similar Products

Automated generation of reports from databases and other data sources like XML files has been a task set to software developers ever since information systems were first introduced. There are various ways of achieving this goal, with varying simplicity of use or flexibility of the results, usually two opposed demands.

One of the most powerfull database platforms - Oracle [1] includes a tool named Oracle Reports. The layout models included allow the creation of reports for both paginated output, such as printing, as well as Web-oriented output. Oracle Reports consists of two components - Reports Builder and Reports Services. Various data sources can be used - relational databases, text files, XML or OLAP. The tool contains a WYSIWYG reports editor and templates to design the report. There is also the flexibility to define a report layout by placing the fields anywhere in a page.

Microsoft also includes a less versatile reporting tools in their database platform – MS SQL Server. MSSQL Reporting services [2] and SQL Server Business Intelligence development studio include features like support for multiple data sources, dynamic end-user sorting, cascading, and multivalue parameters. Thre is also the tool named Report Builder, which is an ad-hoc reporting tool that allows business users to create their own reports and explore corporate data. Its query model supposedly lets end users build reports without a deep technical understanding of the underlying data sources.

An additional powerfull tool provided by SAQP is Crystal reports [7]. Crystal Reports is a business intelligence application used to design and generate reports from a wide range of data sources. Its version is integrated in software development tools from Microsoft. Crystal Reports allows users to graphically design data connections and report layout. Same as all other previously described tools, software development experience is necessary for using Crystal reports. Also, knowledge of the database in question is needed.

Various other tools and aproaches to automated reporting have been described in literature [3], [4], [5], [6]. They all use templates and have various levels of complexity vs ease of use. The more flexibility is added to the final result, the work in the tool becomes more complicated and more knowledge of the database in question is needed.

When analyzing similar products we must not forget the MS Word mail merge feature readily available in MS Office. However, its shortcomings, among other things being a desktop application, opposed to a more flexible contemporary web based approach, limit its usefulness. Also, this approach suffers from inefficient joins, is limited to a single source, there are versioning issues and most important, complicated documents are hard to process.

There are three main factors when selecting a tool for automated generation of reports from databases. Firstly obviously the cost of the tool is of essence, and then the opposing demands for simplicity of use and abstraction from the database design versus the flexibility of the generated reports and the features available. The aforementioned tools score differently in all criteria, focusing on separate goals.

3 Program Architecture

The architecture solution that we propose for solving this problem is composed of 3 main modules: document parser, tag engine and tag generator. The first two modules, the document parser and tag engine, are the core of our application. The last module, the document parser, is an optional module intended to make the interface for creating tags more friendly and easy to understand. If the client does not need this kind of redundancy, the application can be used without the last module and tags can be created in a more direct way.

The document parser module is designed to import a report template - a document containing tags (more about tags in the following sections), go through its content and identify the tags. The parser can be customized to parse through various kinds of documents containing text (txt, xml, pdf, word, excel, html, etc.), depending on the user's needs.

A part of the document is identified as a tag if it has the following structure:

```
<#tag_name attribute1_name = "attribute1_value"
attribute2_name = "attribute2_value" #>
```

The symbols "<#" and "#>" mark the beginning and the end of the tag respectively. The tag name along with its attributes uniquely identifies the tag. One tag can have an arbitrary number of attributes including no attributes. Two tags with the same name can exist, as long as they have different attributes.

The parser can recognize the expected result from the tag location and the surrounding contents. For instance, if the tag is placed in a table cell, the resulting records will be placed in consecutive rows, vertically. Otherwise, if the tag is placed alone, the resulting records will be presented concatenated one after the other, horizontally.

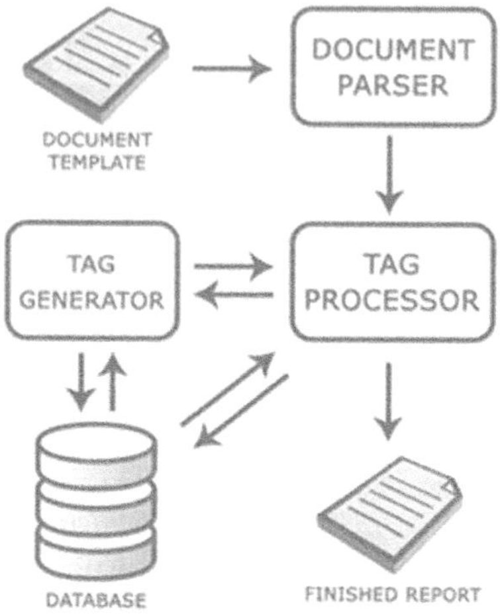

Fig. 1. Data flow in the ASGRT application

The processor goes through each of the tags that the document parser finds. It then checks whether the particular tag exists in the database. If it does, the program executes the tag's predefined SQL query stored in the database, formats the result and returns it as the value that will replace the tag in the document. The SQL query can incorporate the tag's attributes as variables, and use their stated values. If the tag does not exist, it transfers control to the tag generator, where the user can define the SQL query for the tag, then executes it and returns the result. The tag is then saved in the database for future use. The attributes can be interoperable in various tags. For example, an attribute can be defined in one tag, and then the same attribute can be used in other tags that tend to use the same value from the database. The visual presentation of the data flow is shown on figure 1.

After the whole document is processed and all identified tags are replaced with retrieved data from the database, the document is saved and offered to the user for download.

4 Database Architecture

The program works with 2 databases. The first one is for its internal use: for storing the user data and tags. The second database is the one that contains the actual data the program uses to generate the reports. This can be any kind of database which the program can connect to and run queries over. The type and quantity of the data in this database is not important for the application, as it is made to work with any kind of database using minor configurations.

The SQL_query attribute of the tag contains an SQL query that should be executed over the part of the database containing the data used in the document. This design allows the program to be connected to any database and start working right away. There is no extra set-up, and the user can start creating tags, provided he is familiar with the database structure.

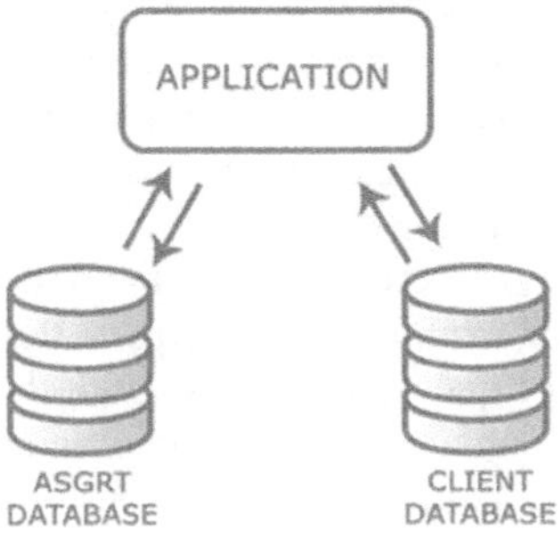

Fig. 2. Databases used by the ASGRT application

The first database shown on figure 2 is the ASGRT application database. This database is used to store information about the users and tags. The general information about each user, his user group, and the permissions and access rights that the user has when using the application are all stored in this database. For each tag, the name of the tag is stored as well as the database query that the tag will execute during report generation. Some notes and explanations about the tag can also be stored. Some of the data stored are shown on figure 3. The ASGRT application database contains all the documents and reports that the users previously developed, that can be used again. Also, there is a log of events and errors that might have happened during the application execution.

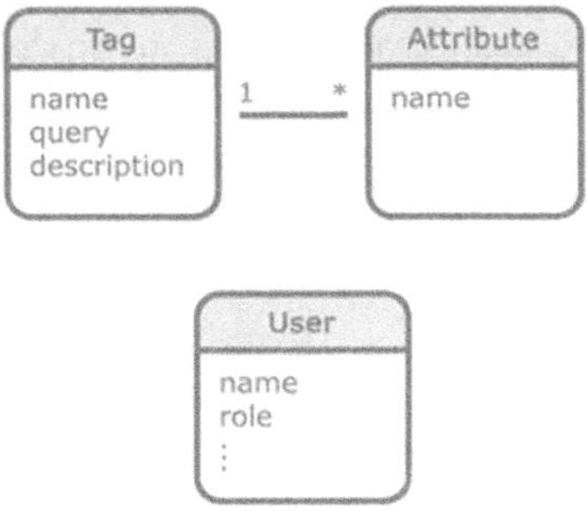

Fig. 3. Types of data stored in the ASGRT database

5 Tags

Tags define the columns and contents of the reports to be generated. Tags are the fields that a client inserts into a text document before using that document for report generation. These fields contain information about what clients want to be put into a report. When a document with tag fields is passed to the application, the parser goes through the whole text and reads all the tags. In order for the parser to be able to set aside tags from what is otherwise ordinary text, every tag needs to have the standard construction defined by the application. A tag effectively consists of two parts. The first part is the field that is inserted into a document (the name of the tag), and optionally some values for the tag's attributes (there can be more than one field in the same document referencing the same tag). The second, and main part, is the information stored for each tag in the database.

There are two different ways to create tags in the database. The first one is through a user friendly wizard which explains each step of the process. The user needs to insert a tag name, tag database query, and notes about the tag which are optional. It is important to state that a tag cannot have the same name as another tag that already exists in the ASGRT database. In the first step of the tag creation, the SELECT part of the query is created. The wizard shows the user each table name and attribute that he can select, so only minor knowledge about the client database is needed. Next comes the FROM part of the query where in a similar way the user selects his options. Other parts of the query follow, such as WHERE, GROUP BY and HAVING, but they are optional and do not have to be included in the query. The second way to generate a tag is to directly type or insert the query into a text box, and just add the name and notes for the tag. This is intended for users that are familiar with the client database and are experienced with database usage, or already have obtained the database query in another way and they just need to insert it into the text box.

The attributes that are part of the database query can have static or dynamic values. If a dynamic value is used, the value is specified in the tag written in the text file used to generate a report. If a static value is used, it needs to be specified in the query during the tag creation. Dynamic values are stated simply by adding '@' in front of the attribute name. The dynamic values are then used as attribute values (ex. Name=@Name, Date=@Date, etc.).

As noted in the Architecture part, attributes can be taken from various sources. Attributes are hierarchical meaning that after their first definition within a tag they can be used in new tags without redefinition. Every newly defined tag can use previously defined attributes within previous tags.

6 Reports Generating

A report is the final product of this application. For a report to be generated, a text file template is imported in the application. After the file is imported and selected for report generating, the application parses the whole text in the file. When a part of the text is recognized as a tag, it is identified by its name and looked up into the ASGRT database. If the tag name doesn't exist in the database, its name is added in a special table used to collect all unknown tags. If the tag exists in the database, the tag database query is executed, and the tag in the text file is replaced by the value returned by its database query.

After the whole file is parsed and there are no unknown tags found, the process of report generation is finished, and the user is allowed to download his finished report from the application. If any unknown tags were found, the user is informed about these tags and asked to create them into the ASGRT database. After all of the unknown tags are created, the file is parsed again and all of the previously unknown tags are replaced with the values which the execution of their database queries returned. Once all steps have finished, the user can download the completed report.

7 Conclusion

The main goal of the presented program is to simplify the work of clerks that do not have any knowledge in database management - they could still use this application to easily get vast amounts of different reports generated from data stored in databases. They can retrieve reports as an automated process where little or no human influence is needed whatsoever. The ASGRT can be implemented in numerous places where databases are used for storage, where various unpredictable reports need to be generated and where database data gathering needs to be automated. It can be used in public administration, in hospitals for patient's medical record generating, at schools to easily generate student reports when needed, in warehouses and accounting firms for various tasks.

ASGRT main advantage is that it is not limited to desktop applications and can be easily incorporated in applications that use reach web interface. Using this application it is very easy to make a template for a new report that should be generated from a given database without change in the application logic. Only very limited knowledge of the database is needed for the process of tags generation that can be reused to gather information in different templates. We had in mind the reusability of the application so it can be implemented with only minor configuration changes on any kind of database, thus making it interoperable and widely available.

The users of ASGRT interact only with its interface, a web-based GUI (Graphical User Interface). It is made of several web pages allowing the user to login to the application, list all the available tags, their notes and explanations, create new tags, browse and select files for the application to process and download a finalized report.

References

1. Oracle Reports (June 29, 2010), `http://www.oracle.com/technetwork/middleware/reports/overview/index.html`
2. Microsoft SQL Server Reporting Services (June 29, 2010), `http://www.microsoft.com/Sqlserver/2005/en/us/reporting-services.aspx`
3. Chan, D.K.C.: A Document-driven Approach to Database Report Generation. In: Proceedings of the 9th International Workshop on Database and Expert Systems Applications (DEXA 1998), pp. 925. IEEE Computer Society, Los Alamitos (1998)

4. Mario Guillén, R., Victor, J., Sosa, S., Mario Guillén, Ma., del Rosario Vázquez, A., Humberto Hernández, G.: GARP: A Tool for Creating Dynamic Web Reports Using XSL and XML Technologies. In: Proceedings of the Fourth Mexican International Conference on Computer Science (ENC 2003), Tlaxcala, Mexico, September 08-12, p. 54 (2003)
5. Chen, W.-K., Chung, K.-H.: A Table Presentation System for Database and Web Applications. In: 2004 IEEE International Conference on e-Technology, e-Commerce and e-Service (EEE 2004), pp. 492–498 (March 2004)
6. Zhou, C.-S., Lin, L.: Research and Design of Task Driven Based Web Report Model. In: 2009 Ninth International Conference on Hybrid Intelligent Systems, pp. 359–362 (August 2009)
7. SAP Crystal Reports (June 29, 2010), `http://www.crystalreports.com/`

Author Index

GPSR Compliance

The European Union's (EU) General Product Safety Regulation (GPSR) is a set of rules that requires consumer products to be safe and our obligations to ensure this.

If you have any concerns about our products, you can contact us on ProductSafety@springernature.com

In case Publisher is established outside the EU, the EU authorized representative is:

Springer Nature Customer Service Center GmbH
Europaplatz 3
69115 Heidelberg, Germany

Batch number: 10844619

Printed by Printforce, the Netherlands